Managerial Finance: Concepts, Applications, and Practices

Volume II

Claud Pitts III
George K. Sharghi
Larry Gonzales

University of Phoenix

SIMON & SCHUSTER
CUSTOM PUBLISHING

Cover Design by Caldera Design, Phoenix, AZ
Cover Illustration by Dave Cutler/Spots on the Spot!

Excerpts taken from:

Fundamentals of Financial Management, Ninth Edition,
by James C. Van Horne and John M. Wachowicz

Simon & Schuster Company/A Viacom Company
Upper Saddle River, New Jersey 07458

Basic Financial Management, Seventh Edition,
by Arthur J. Keown, David F. Scott, Jr., John D. Martin, and J. William Petty

Essentials of Finance: An Integrated Approach,
by George W. Gallinger and Jerry B. Poe

Foundations of Finance: The Logic and Practice of Financial Management,
by Arthur J. Keown, David F. Scott, Jr., John D. Martin, and J. William Petty

Principles of Managerial Finance, Seventh Edition,
by Lawrence J. Gitman

This special edition published in cooperation with
Simon & Schuster Custom Publishing

Printed in the United States of America

10 9 8 7 6 5 4 3 2 1

ISBN 0-536-59902-5
BA 96410

SIMON & SCHUSTER CUSTOM PUBLISHING
160 Gould Street/Needham Heights, MA 02194
Simon & Schuster Education Group

To the Student:

This is Volume II of *Managerial Finance: Concepts, Applications, and Practices.*
It contains pages 405 through 840.
Volume I, a separate volume, contains pages 1 through 404.

Contents

VOLUME I

SECTION I
FINANCIAL MANAGEMENT ENVIRONMENT

SECTION VII
COST OF CAPITAL, FINANCING MIX AND DIVIDEND POLICY

SECTION VIII
FUNDAMENTALS OF CAPITAL BUDGETING

CHAPTER 23
Capital Budgeting and Risk Analysis 697

SECTION IX
CONVERTIBLE SECURITIES, WARRANTS, OPTIONS, AND RESTRUCTURING AND REORGANIZATION

CHAPTER 24
Convertibles, Exchangeables, and Warrants 735

CHAPTER 25
Corporate Restructuring: Combinations and Divestitures 763

CHAPTER 26
Business Failure and Reorganization 795

SECTION X
INTERNATIONAL FINANCE

CHAPTER 27
International Finance: Concepts and Applications 811

SECTION VI

Capital Markets and Long-Term Financing

FINANCIAL MARKETS

LONG-TERM DEBT, PREFERRED STOCK, AND COMMON STOCK

THE VALUATION OF LONG-TERM SECURITIES

CHAPTER 14

Financial Markets

On any day, *The Wall Street Journal* carries announcements of new security issues of corporations and governments totaling billions of dollars. On the same day, thousands of businesses and individuals contact their local banks about new loans. These events have one feature in common—they are attempts to raise funds for expenditures. Retailers need funds for inventories before they receive the cash from sales and receivables. Governments spend funds for social programs and to build infrastructure before receiving full tax payments from businesses and individuals. Farmers need funds for fertilizer and seed before they get cash for their crops. Financial institutions make it possible for some businesses, governments, and consumers to spend their expected income before they receive it and for others to earn money on funds that they want to hold for future expenditures. These transactions link the real world of goods and services with the financial world of money and credit, commonly called the financial markets.

There is no central market for economic capital, that is, the plant and equipment and inventory produced. But there is a group of financial markets for the monetary instruments that represent either title to or claims to economic capital and to the other resources owned by government, business, and individuals. We divide these markets into *money markets* and *capital markets,* and further divide money and capital markets into *primary markets* and *secondary markets.* The *money market* provides for quick and dependable transfer of claims with maturities of less than one year. Longer-term claims are transferred in *capital markets.* If the claims are newly created, they exchange in *primary markets.* Already outstanding claims trade from old to new owners in *secondary markets* without generating new funds or creating new obligations.

Important participants in the financial system are financial intermediaries (financial institutions) responsible for moving funds from savings pools into the primary markets. These intermediaries provide centralized markets for users and

TABLE 14-1 Major Types of Financial Intermediaries

Commercial banks
Businesses chartered by either the Comptroller of the Currency or a state agency. These banks receive deposits and make loans. *Example:* Chemical Bank.

Saving and loan associations (S&L)
Businesses chartered by federal and state agencies that receive savings deposits and checkable deposits. They use the funds primarily to make mortgage loans. *Example:* Home Savings of America.

Mutual savings banks
Similar to savings and loan associations, but only chartered by a state agency. They accept deposits and make mortgage loans. *Example:* Green Point Savings Bank.

Credit unions
Small cooperative institutions often organized in a place of work or by a labor union. They take deposits and make consumer loans. *Example:* Arizona State Employees Credit Union.

Mutual funds
Businesses that obtain funds by selling shares and using the proceeds to buy a portfolio of securities. In the case of money-market mutual funds, shareholders can write checks against the value of their shares. *Example:* Fidelity Investment Trust.

Life insurance companies
Businesses that insure people against the financial result of death, receiving their funds in the form of periodic payments (premiums). The companies invest most of their funds in long-term corporate bonds and commercial mortgages. *Example:* The Travelers Insurance Company.

Property and casualty insurance companies
Businesses that receive premiums from individuals and companies to insure them against burglary, fire, negligence lawsuits, auto collision, and other losses. They invest primarily in low-risk debt and equity securities. *Example:* State Farm Insurance Company.

Pension plans
Plans whose inflow of money comes from working people building monetary reserves for their retirement years. Investment of most funds is in long-term corporate bonds and stocks. *Example:* CalPERS.

Real estate investment trusts (REITs)
Investment organizations that hold properties, cash, and sometimes mortgages. REITs issue equity securities that trade on major stock exchanges. *Example:* DeBartolo Realty Corporation.

savers of funds. Relying on portfolio diversification strategies, intermediaries make borrowing, selling stock, and investing easier and less costly.

After you have studied this chapter, you should have a better understanding of:

- The major types of financial intermediaries and how they function in the financial market.
- The role of investment bankers.
- The use of shelf registrations, rights offerings, and private placements to raise funds.
- The distinction between the various secondary markets.

FINANCIAL INTERMEDIATION

Financial intermediaries responsible for transferring funds from savers to users are mentioned in the financial columns of the newspapers and are briefly described in Table 14-1. Essentially, these intermediaries buy and sell rights to future payments.

TABLE 14-2 World's Largest Banks and Insurance Companies

Rank 1992	Rank 1991	Name (Country)	Assets (U.S. $Million)
Banks:			
1	1	Dai-Ichi Kangyo Bank (Japan)	$473,276
2	3	Sumitomo Bank (Japan)	453,274
3	2	Sakura Bank (Japan)	446,448
4	5	Fuji Bank (Japan)	443,833
5	4	Sanwa Bank (Japan)	437,294
6	6	Mitsubishi Bank (Japan)	425,019
7	9	Credit Lyonnais (France)	350,870
8	11	Norinchukin Bank (Japan)	326,899
9	7	Industrial Bank of Japan (Japan)	321,188
10	10	Deutsche Bank (Germany)	305,002
Insurance Companies:			
1	1	Nippon Life (Japan)	$236,380
2	2	Prudential Insurance (U.S.)	199,625
3	3	Zenkyoren (Japan)	167,555
4	4	Dai-Ichi Mutual (Japan)	164,856
5	5	Sumitomo Life (Japan)	144,398
6	6	Allianz Group (Germany)	128,114
7	8	Union des Assurances de Paris (France)	123,736
8	-	AXA (France)	120,068
9	7	Metropolitan Life (U.S.)	118,178
10	10	Meiji Mutual Life (Japan)	99,386

Note the relative absence of U.S. companies. The six largest banks are Japanese companies and not one U.S. bank is listed. Two U.S. companies made the insurance list, which is also dominated by Japanese companies.

Source: The Wall Street Journal, September 24, 1993, p. R26–27.

For instance, if you open a savings account at Home Savings of America, you give it a current payment in exchange for its promise to make a payment to you in the future. Home Savings then turns around and uses your payment to make a loan to someone. Thus, financial intermediaries obtain funds by issuing their own financial securities to investors and then invest the cash received in securities issued by borrowers.

The largest intermediaries are banks and insurance companies. Table 14-2 lists the world's ten largest banks and insurance companies as of 1992. Many of the firms listed operate internationally. These intermediaries established foreign offices to serve their homeland clients who were aggressively acquiring companies and building production facilities around the world. The international integration of financial intermediaries is apparent by the ease by which funds of corporations and large investors in one country are transferred to borrowers in other countries. Dollars, Deutsche marks, yen, sterling, or other currencies deposited in a bank almost anywhere in the world are usually transferred via a computerized system called CHIPS (Clearing House Interbank Payments System) to a bank in London and then on from London to a bank in some other country for lending to customers in that country.

The process of *financial intermediation,* which means receiving money from savers and transferring it to borrowers and sellers of equity, results in two important benefits for the financial system. First, consider the difficulty and expense individual borrowers and lenders have matching each other's needs. Financial institutions reduce transaction and monitoring costs by providing centralized markets for borrowers and lenders of all types. Because a financial intermediary specializes in "buying and selling" money, it is able to realize economies of scale not available to most borrowers or individual investors. These economies result from the volume of money the intermediary buys and sells.

Financial intermediaries lower monitoring costs because they can develop information on organizations needing funds more efficiently than individual investors can. If several investors who lent money to one borrower each had to incur their own costs watching the borrower directly, it would be far more costly than if an intermediary performed this service for multiple clients. The intermediary can also reduce the problem of unreliable information by using specialized resources, such as computerized databases.

A second benefit of intermediation is that the process overcomes any barriers arising from the incompatibility of the financial needs and objectives of borrowers and lenders. The lender is looking for *liquidity,* that is, safety and an ability to redeem the investment quickly and at low cost. Often the borrower cannot promise liquidity. Financial institutions reconcile these different needs by offering suppliers of funds safety and liquidity, and by turning around and using the funds for loans and investments with varying degrees of risk and liquidity. Intermediaries can give their cash suppliers long-term contracts and lend to borrowers on short-term contracts, or vice versa. For example, Home Savings of America buys a security that promises to pay $100 for each of the next three years. Based on these expected cash flows, Home Savings can issue three securities with maturities of one year, two years, and three years.[1] The ability of intermediaries to change the maturities on securities makes financial markets more attractive to both borrowers and investors than if a loan were between the borrower and the investor directly, bypassing the intermediation process.

The secret in being able to match different types of contracts lies in the structure of financial intermediaries. These institutions consist of two large diversified portfolios of financial contracts—their sources of funds (that is, their liabilities) and their assets. The intermediary's success depends upon the overall performance of these portfolios, which are shaped by individual contracts. However, the performance of the portfolios is much more dependable and predictable than that of individual contracts.

The portfolios have the statistical advantage of large numbers. This means that the average loss rates and the average liquidity requirements can be predicted with considerable accuracy even when the prospects for individual contracts are uncertain. For example, a bank's asset portfolio may consist of mortgages, car loans, and government-guaranteed loans to a broad cross section of borrowers. Such a portfolio is better diversified than most individuals could easily achieve by their own efforts. The risks to each investor are much lower than they would be if he or she had to lend directly to individual borrowers. As a result, the security issued by the

[1]The process is actually complex. Mathematicians and statisticians determine the default risk associated with the security bought by the intermediary. The securities issued by the intermediary promise lower payoffs than the payments the intermediary receives.

intermediary provides a higher degree of liquidity to the investor than does a similar commitment to a single security of a corporate borrower.

COMPREHENSION CHECK

1. *Define each of the following financial intermediaries and include in your definition the primary sources and uses of funds for each: commercial banks, savings and loan associations, mutual savings banks, credit unions, mutual funds, life insurance companies, property and casualty insurance companies, private pension funds, and real estate investment trusts.*
2. *Define financial intermediation.*
3. *Discuss the benefits provided by financial intermediaries.*

THE MONEY AND CAPITAL MARKETS

We noted how financial intermediaries assist in the process of bringing savers and borrowers together to reallocate funds. There cannot, however, be a single pool of funds up for competitive bids. There must be separate markets for short-term funds and long-term funds. Some borrowers can only obtain short-term loans until they establish their credit worthiness; other borrowers are well known and can borrow long term. The subject of finance broadly classifies these submarkets into either the money market or the capital market, respectively. These two markets are closely linked with the money market acting as the central mechanism of the financial system. The money market provides a major link between monetary authorities, such as the U.S. Federal Reserve Bank and the German Bundesbank, and the financial system. The money market absorbs the day-to-day pressures of monetary adjustments that cannot be handled by the normal financing channels.

The Money Market

The money market is not easy to identify. It consists of the set of markets for financial instruments that is normally used by financial institutions, businesses, and individuals to adjust their cash positions. The instruments used may vary from time to time, and the nature and structure of the markets may change. In the United States and other countries with highly developed secondary markets, many types of government or private securities may be traded as money-market instruments. In less well-developed countries, money-market transactions may be confined to trades among banks and with the central bank or monetary authorities.

The most active money market outside of the United States is the *Eurodollar market*. The *Eurodollar market* is a network of financial centers around the world that provides much of the innovation in international banking and finance. The prefix *Euro*-indicates that the markets exist principally in Europe; however, the markets do cover transactions in other parts of the world. London is the largest Eurodollar market with Paris a distant second. The Cayman Islands and the Bahamas have become major Eurodollar markets primarily because of tax advantages.

A major difference between the Eurodollar market and domestic money markets is that the Eurodollar market operates free from government regulations and

TABLE 14-3 Principal Money-market Instruments

Instrument	Borrower	Term to Maturity and Denominations	Interest Payment
Treasury bills (T-bills)	Federal government	91- and 182-day bills sold weekly; 52-week bills sold monthly; denominations of $10,000 to $1 million or more	Discounted; interest exempt from state income taxes
Federal funds	Commercial banks temporarily short of reserves borrow from banks with excess reserves	Overnight to 3 days; denominations of $1 million or more	Interest paid at maturity
Federal agency notes	Various agencies	6 months to 10 years; denominations of $10,000 and up	Usually discounted
Commercial paper (unsecured note)	Large companies with high credit ratings	Up to 270 days; denominations of $25,000 to $1 million or more	Discounted or interest bearing
Negotiable certificates of deposit (receipts for time deposits)	Commercial banks	14 days and over; denominations of $100,000 or more	Usually interest bearing; paid at maturity
Eurodollar deposits (dollar time deposits at overseas banks)	London and other non-U.S. branches of banks	Overnight to 1 year; denominations for $1 million or more	Interest bearing; paid at maturity
Bankers' acceptances (negotiable bills accepted by banks and sold to investors)	Commercial banks	Up to 6 months; denominations of $25,000 to $1 million	Discounted
Repurchase agreements or repos (sale of government securities with an agreement to repurchase them)	U.S. government securities dealers	Overnight to 180 days; denominations of $100,000 and up	Interest paid at maturity in the form of a higher repurchase price
Money-market mutual funds (invested in the money-market securities)	Investment companies such as Merrill Lynch	No maturity date; minimum deposits as low as $500	Interest earned daily by the fund

control. It has the tacit approval of all major governments of the world. The absence of government controls allows the Eurodollar market to provide special services to businesses, such as:

- Lower costs on loans and deposits
- Immediate and complimentary response to liquidity needs
- Reduction in political risk due to future changes in existing regulations.

However, the lack of government controls means that more default risk exists in the Eurodollar market than in the domestic market. More risk means higher expected returns to investors.

Money-market instruments must meet all the requirements for easy secondary trading and, in addition, must carry very little market and default risks. Compared to capital-market securities, money-market securities offer lower return, lower risk, and shorter maturities. Marketability and liquidity of money-market securities are comparable to capital-market securities. Table 14-3 summarizes the major money-market instruments. Each of the securities is a relatively safe investment. A U.S. Treasury bill is the safest; commercial paper is the least safe.

The Money Market As a Source Of Funds. Access to the money market as a source of new funds is limited to a relatively small number of large, well-established borrowers, such as the U.S. Treasury, government agencies, and many large well-known financial and business organizations such as First Chicago Corporation and Union Carbide Company. These borrowers use money-market securities as an alternative to other sources of funds when flexibility is needed or when they reduce borrowing costs. Money-market securities are most attractive to borrowers when they are less expensive than longer-term funds or when the issuer does not want to get locked into high long-term interest rates.

The Money Market As An Investment. An investor's access to the market is limited only by the large denominations involved. Anyone with enough money can buy money-market securities. However, we can classify potential buyers into two types. The first group includes anyone who holds or manages cash. They are willing and happy to invest their cash balances if their conditions can be met: assurance of access to the funds when they need them, and rates that are high enough to cover transactions costs. These buyers are important because they control a source of funds that would otherwise not be available.

Money-market mutual funds (MMMFs), such as Merrill Lynch Ready Cash Fund, provide a concrete illustration of the role of the money market in activating idle money balances of this first group. MMMFs appeared on the scene when the cost of money became high enough to justify the expense of trying to reach holders of small amounts of idle balances. By serving as intermediaries between the money market and cash managers of businesses and individuals who would not otherwise have access to the market, MMMFs add to the effectiveness of the money market in mobilizing idle balances.

The second group of investors of money-market instruments includes banks, financial institutions, governments, corporations, and anyone else who uses money-market instruments as part of an investment portfolio to achieve the desired mix of liquidity and yield. These investors provide the regular demand for money-market instruments and absorb the newly issued instruments as part of the turnover of their portfolios as their money-market investments mature.

The Capital Market

Capital markets are for the issuing and trading of securities with maturities in excess of one year; generally, the securities issued by governments and businesses. The bulk of capital-market activity occurs in secondary markets, with the most active and best known being the New York Stock Exchange (NYSE) located in New York City. Later in this chapter, we will describe how the NYSE functions. Figure 14-1

Together, the American and Japanese capital markets represent about $13.7 trillion, or 64 percent, of world value. The graphs show that for investors from any particular country, the investment opportunities outside the home country are greater than those within the home country.

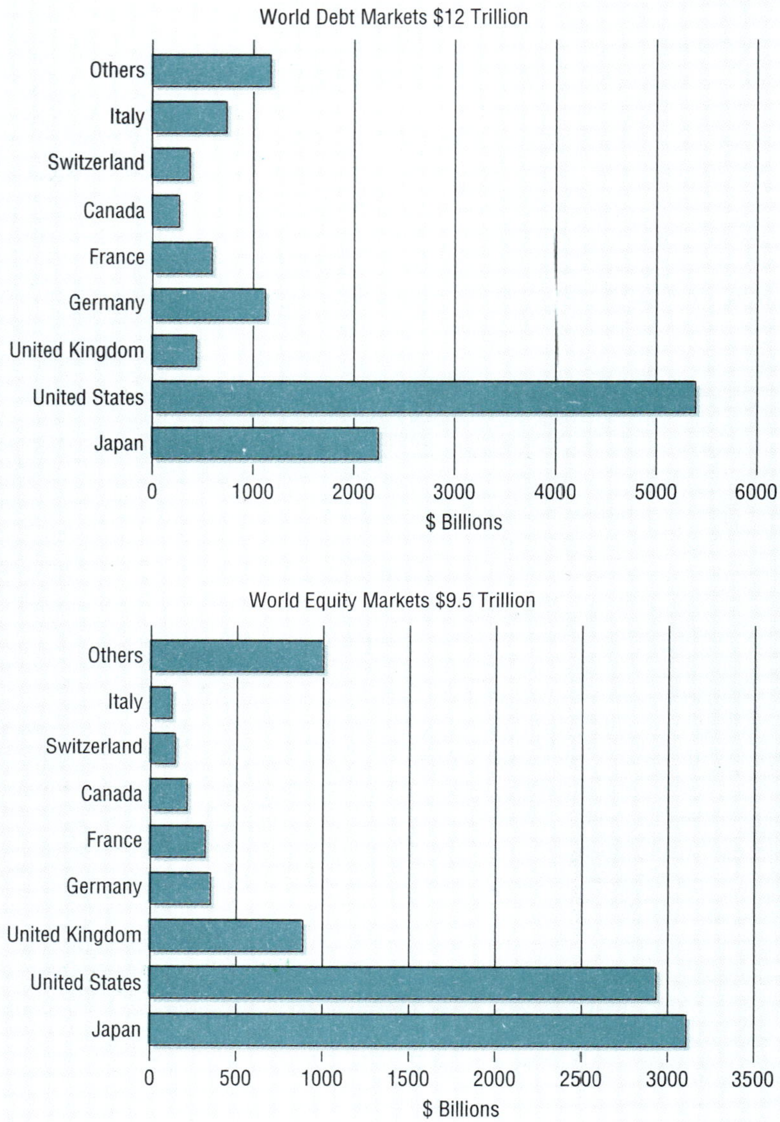

FIGURE 14-1
Size of world debt and equity markets as of June 1991

summarizes the allocation of the world's secondary capital markets as of June 1991 between debt and equity, and by country. The equity market was about $9.5 trillion and the debt market was approximately $12 trillion.

A less well-known capital market to most people is the *Eurocapital market*. It consists of three distinct submarkets of *Eurocurrency loans*, *Eurobonds*, and *Euroequity*. *Eurocurrency loans* from commercial banks are loans denominated in a currency other than that of the country in which the bank is located. (For example, U.S. Sprint borrows Italian lira from a Swiss bank.) *Eurobonds* are bonds offered for sale in a country or countries other than the one in whose currency the bonds are denominated. (For example, the Spanish firm Telephona España sells bonds denominated in peseta to investors in Germany.) *Euroequity* is an equity interest of a company that is sold in a country or countries other than the one in whose currency the equity shares are denominated. (For example, the British firm BAT Industries sells equity denominated in sterling to investors in France.) Eurocapital securities with long maturities, such as bonds or stocks, typically sell in more than one country simultaneously.

COMPREHENSION CHECK

1. *Distinguish between money markets and capital markets.*
2. *Define the following money-market securities: Treasury bills, federal funds, federal agencies' debt instruments, commercial paper, negotiable certificates of deposit, Eurodollars, banker's acceptance, repurchase agreement, money-market mutual funds.*
3. *Describe the Eurocapital market. Define its three submarkets.*

THE PRIMARY MARKETS

When corporations, governments, or individuals short of funds raise capital by issuing new securities, these securities initially sell in primary markets. Examples of primary market transactions include a sale of U.S. Treasury bonds by the federal government to investors, a new mortgage loan from Countrywide Mortgage Company issued on a home, and new stock sold by Lotus Development Corporation to financial institutions and the public. In developed primary markets, the borrower does not have to find a lender or investor directly; there are many kinds of go-betweens to bring primary issuers and investors together. Typically, corporations in need of funds use *investment bankers* as the go-between to help them raise new capital in primary markets. Other alternatives to raise new capital are *shelf registrations*, *rights offerings*, and *private placements*.

Transactions Through Investment Bankers

A business usually requires large amounts of funds to support growth opportunities. Often the fund requirements are beyond the business's capacity to save in any reasonable period. The financial market permits the firm to raise needed funds by selling securities in primary markets. However, many financial managers undertake an offering of securities only once in their lifetime, if ever. To help sell securities to investors, the firm hires the services of investment bankers, who are financial ser-

TABLE 14-4 The World's Leading Investment Bankers

Rank 1993	Name	Volume ($ Billions)	Number Of Issues	Rank 1992
1	Merrill Lynch	$ 155.4	908	1
2	Goldman Sachs	123.2	626	2
3	Lehman Brothers	99.7	612	3
4	First Boston	94.3	470	4
5	Kidder Peabody	83.6	288	5
6	Salomon Brothers	79.3	439	6
7	Morgan Stanley	66.2	379	7
8	Bear Stearns	40.3	192	8
9	Numura Securities	28.7	89	11
10	Donaldson, Lufkin & Jenrette	27.5	162	13
	Industry totals	$1153.1	7275	

These rankings are based on underwriting activity of worldwide debt and equity offerings for the first nine months of 1992 and 1993. Full credit for the issue is given to the originating house, or lead manager. The lead manager is the investment bank with primary responsibility for the issue.

Source: Investment Dealers Digest, October 11, 1993, p. 32.

vices companies familiar with the financial markets (see Table 14-4). Functions performed by investment bankers include *investigative, risk bearing,* and *selling.*

Investigative Function. The investment banker is the *originating house.* It serves as an informational link between the capital markets, the company issuing securities, and other investment bankers who may join to form an *underwriting group* or *syndicate.* Important responsibilities of the investment banker include drawing up mandatory provisions (known as *covenants*) of the security issue and ensuring the securities to be issued comply with state and federal regulations.[2] The covenants are to protect investors but they must not be so restrictive that the firm issuing the securities has too little flexibility.

The investment banker and the firm must agree on a price for the securities. The pricing decision begins with the investment banker's expert estimate of what the primary market will pay for the securities, given the proposed features of the offering. The investment banker considers the current market prices of *seasoned* (that is, existing) securities of similar quality and similar features trading in the secondary market. Since seasoned securities have some market history, the investment banker usually wants to price the new issue a little lower to help it sell. However, the firm wants to get as much for the securities as possible. If the price is set too high, the securities are difficult to sell.

Risk-Bearing Function. The investment banker can either leave the risk associated with the security offering with the firm issuing the securities or assume the risk and relieve the issuer of the uncertainty. By assuming the risk, the investment banker

[2]Securities market regulation, under the Securities and Exchange Commission, had the laudable objective of assuring full disclosure of material information concerning the condition and operations of corporations whose securities are offered to the public. However, the rules and regulations, particularly those applying to new issues of securities, add significantly to the costs of financing in public markets in the United States. These costs have helped to divert a large volume of financing of both U.S. and foreign corporations away from U.S. capital markets and into the Euromarkets, where regulatory constraints are less stringent.

Information contained herein is subject to completion or amendment. A registration statement relating to these securities has been filed with the Securities and Exchange Commission. These securities may not be sold nor may offers to buy be accepted prior to the time the registration statement becomes effective. This prospectus shall not constitute an offer to sell or the solicitation of an offer to buy nor shall there be any sale of these securities in any State in which such offer, solicitation or sale would be unlawful prior to registration or qualification under the securities laws of any such State.

SUBJECT TO COMPLETION, DATED JUNE 4,1993

PROSPECTUS
, 1993

7,200,000 Shares

PETsMART

Common Stock

Of the 7,200,000 shares of Common Stock offered, 5,748,494 shares are being offered by the Company and 1,451,506 shares are being offered by the Selling Stockholders. See "Principal and Selling Stockholders." The Company will not receive any proceeds from the sale of shares by the Selling Stockholders.

Of such 7,200,000 shares, 5,760,000 shares are being offered hereby in the United States and Canada by the U.S. Underwriters and 1,440,000 shares are being offered in a concurrent offering outside of the United States and Canada by the International Managers, subject to transfers between the U.S. Underwriters and the International Managers. The initial public offering price and the aggregate underwriting discount per share are identical for both offerings.

Prior to this offering, there has been no public market for the Common Stock. It is currently estimated that the initial public offering price will be between $15.50 and $17.50 per share. See "Underwriting" for a discussion of the factors considered in determining the initial public offering price. The Common Stock has been approved for quotation on the NASDAQ National Market System under the symbol "PETM," subject to official notice of issuance.

See "Certain Investment Considerations" for information that should be considered by prospective investors.

THESE SECURITIES HAVE NOT BEEN APPROVED OR DISAPPROVED BY THE SECURITIES AND EXCHANGE COMMISSION OR ANY STATE SECURITIES COMMISSION NOR HAS THE SECURITIES AND EXCHANGE COMMISSION OR ANY STATE SECURITIES COMMISSION PASSED UPON THE ACCURACY OR ADEQUACY OF THIS PROSPECTUS. ANY REPRESENTATION TO THE CONTRARY IS A CRIMINAL OFFENSE.

	Price to the Public	Underwriting Discounts and Commissions(1)	Proceeds to the Company(2)	Proceeds to Selling Stockholders
Per Share	$	$	$	$
Total (3)	$	$	$	$

(1) The Company and the Selling Stockholders have agreed to indemnify the U.S. Underwriters and the International Managers against certain liabilities, including liabilities under the Securities Act of 1933, as amended. See "Underwriting."

(2) Before deducting expenses estimated at $810,000, payable by the Company.

(3) The Company has granted the Underwriters a 30-day option to purchase up to 1,080,000 additional shares of Common Stock, on the same terms and conditions as set forth above, solely to cover over-allotments, if any. If such option is exercised in full, the total Price to the Public, Underwriting Discounts and Commissions and Proceeds to the Company will be $, $ and $, respectively. See "Underwriting."

The shares of Common Stock are being offered by the several Underwriters when, as and if delivered to and accepted by the Underwriters and subject to various prior conditions, including their right to reject orders in whole or in part. It is expected that delivery of the shares will by made in New York, New York, on or about July ,1993.

Donaldson,Lufkin & Jenrette
Securities Corporation

Alex. Brown & Sons
Incorporated

Montgomery Securities

FIGURE 14-2
PETsMART's red herring

Financial Reality

STUDY THAT RED HERRING

A prospectus is a legal document that must be issued by a firm making a public offering of securities. Ignore this document at your own peril!

Consider the red herring of Lezak Group. It discloses many interesting items. It was prepared by an investment banker who is a market maker in the securities of six of the companies that Mr. Lezak, the CEO of Lezak Group, is associated. Mr. Lezak is also a significant brokerage customer of the underwriter. Legal counsel to the company in this offering is counsel to the underwriter (but not for this offering). The prospectus further informs you:

> *. . . the funds to be raised are not all allocated; the company does not know what business it will engage in; has no plan of operations; owns no assets; and investors will entrust their funds to management on whose judgment they must depend with no information whatsoever about management's intentions.*

The prospectus lists 19 "extremely high risk factors" that an investor should note. An important risk listed is that the stock issue is a blind-pool offering. This means the prospective investors are told nothing, promised nothing, and assured only that management doesn't have any idea of what it will do with the money from the offering.

Another risk factor states that the firm is totally dependent on the CEO. However, the very next risk factor informs you that the firm has "no employment agreement with the chief executive officer." While many investors balked at taking a plunge into the blind-pool offering, many others thought nothing of the risk. Adventuresome investors contributed $440,000 for 9.7 million shares. That works out to 4.5 cents a share, on average. Mr. Lezak got 5 million shares for just $5010. The cash from that sale was the only asset owned by the Lezak Group. Four years later the stock traded over the counter for between 3 and 6 cents.

A prospectus like this may seem like a joke, but it isn't. The Securities and Exchange Commission can order the seller to send a prospectus to a buyer. However, it can't force the buyer to read it.

Adapted from Alan Abelson, "Up & Down Wall Street," *Barron's*, June 13, 1983, p. 41. Used with permission of Dow Jones, 1983.

acts as a *principal* and agrees to *underwrite* the issue. *Underwriting* is the process whereby the investment banker buys all the securities for resale at a preestablished price. Such an arrangement is a *firm-commitment offering*. An alternative arrangement is a *best-efforts offering*. In this latter case, the investment banker acts as an *agent* and the risk associated with the sale of the security issue remains with the issuer. There is a fixed selling price, but the amount of the securities that will sell at that price is uncertain.

When the investment banker or syndicate agrees to underwrite the issue, each agrees to deliver a check to the issuer for the price paid by the public investors less an amount called the *spread*. The *spread* is the fee paid to the investment banker for selling the issue. It must cover all costs of investigating, risk bearing, and selling the issue if the investment banker is to realize a profit.

Selling Function. The securities sell through the sales divisions of the underwriting syndicate and selected retail brokerage houses. The selling effort begins before the offering date. An announcement of the forthcoming offering alerts prospective investors. The formal announcement is via a *prospectus*, which is filed with the Securities and Exchange Commission (SEC) and made available to interested investors. The *prospectus* sets forth the basic facts about the company and states the use of the funds; it is the only means of legal solicitation. Initially, the prospectus is a *red herring* because it is not known when the SEC will permit the sale of the securities. Figure 14-2 shows the front page of a red herring issued by PETsMART Company, a warehouse retailer of pet foods and supplies. Notice that the red herring has warnings across the top and down the left margin, and excludes information about the price of the securities and specific dates. The above Financial Reality reading suggests that prospective investors should carefully read the red herring.

Only a few days, or even a few hours, before the sale of the initial public offering (IPO) is there final agreement on the price and the spread. The late signing of the agreement permits the investment banker to consider any last-minute changes in capital-market conditions. The firm receives the check for the sale of the securities on the *settlement date*. This date is within a specified number of days after the public offering date.

As shown on the front page of the official prospectus for PETsMART Company, in Figure 14-3A, the spread is the "underwriting discount" of $8.64 million—the fee earned by the investment bankers.[3] However, as the above Financial Reality article reveals, not all costs are of a monetary nature. The back page of the prospectus, shown in Figure 14-3B, provides an index of the information contained in the document. It indicates that a fairly complete history of the firm is revealed in the prospectus.[4]

The corporation issuing the securities pays all underwriting costs of the issue, which allows investors to buy the stock free of any commissions or other charges. In general, the initial offering of stock is the only time a fixed price exists for the stock. The investment bankers support the price temporarily. Shortly after an issue's initial public sale, any price stabilization by the underwriter ceases. Share price is then set according to supply and demand in the secondary market.

The public becomes aware of the sale of securities after the fact in an announcement called a *tombstone* (see Figure 14-4). It shows the company name, the underwriters, and some information about the issue. This nonsales-oriented announcement must contain no exaggeration, elaboration, or solicitation.

Alternatives to Investment Bankers

If a firm is making an initial issue of securities to the public, it uses an investment banker because of its specialized knowledge. However, once firms mature they may

[3]Costs associated with issuing securities vary significantly. The costs are a function of size of the issue and whether it is a firm-commitment offer or a best-efforts offer. Best-efforts offers are more expensive for two reasons. They are more often associated with speculative firms and, therefore, the success of the offering is riskier. And best-efforts offers usually involve a smaller issure size than firm-commitment offers. Larger issues realize monetary cost economies of scale.

[4]This information is also revealed in the red herring.

PROSPECTUS
July 22, 1993

7,200,000 Shares

PETsMART

Common Stock

Of the 7,200,000 shares of Common Stock offered, 6,445,688 shares are being offered by the Company and 754,312 shares are being offered by the Selling Stockholders. See "Principal and Selling Stockholders." The Company will not receive any proceeds from the sale of shares by the Selling Stockholders.

Of such 7,200,000 shares, 5,760,000 shares are being offered hereby in the United States and Canada by the U.S. Underwriters and 1,440,000 shares are being offered in a concurrent offering outside of the United States and Canada by the International Managers, subject to transfers between the U.S. Underwriters and the International Managers. The initial public offering price and the aggregate underwriting discount per share are identical for both offerings.

Prior to this offering, there has been no public market for the Common Stock. See "Underwriting" for a discussion of the factors considered in determining the initial public offering price. The Common Stock has been approved for quotation on the NASDAQ National Market System under the symbol "PETM."

See "Certain Investment Considerations" for information that should be considered by prospective investors.

THESE SECURITIES HAVE NOT BEEN APPROVED OR DISAPPROVED BY THE SECURITIES AND EXCHANGE COMMISSION OR ANY STATE SECURITIES COMMISSION NOR HAS THE SECURITIES AND EXCHANGE COMMISSION OR ANY STATE SECURITIES COMMISSION PASSED UPON THE ACCURACY OR ADEQUACY OF THIS PROSPECTUS. ANY REPRESENTATION TO THE CONTRARY IS A CRIMINAL OFFENSE.

	Price to the Public	Underwriting Discounts and Commissions(1)	Proceeds to the Company(2)	Proceeds to Selling Stockholders
Per Share	$18.00	$1.20	$16.80	$16.80
Total (3)	$129,600,000	$8,640,000	$108,287,558	$12,672,442

(1) The Company and the Selling Stockholders have agreed to indemnify the U.S. Underwriters and the International Managers against certain liabilities, including liabilities under the Securities Act of 1933, as amended. See "Underwriting."

(2) Before deducting expenses estimated at $810,000, payable by the Company.

(3) The Company has granted the Underwriters a 30-day option to purchase up to 1,080,000 additional shares of Common Stock, on the same terms and conditions as set forth above, solely to cover over-allotments, if any. If such option is exercised in full, the total Price to the Public, Underwriting Discounts and Commissions and Proceeds to the Company will be $149,040,000, $9,936,000 and $126,431,558, respectively. See "Underwriting."

The shares of Common Stock are being offered by the several Underwriters when, as and if delivered to and accepted by the Underwriters and subject to various prior conditions, including their right to reject orders in whole or in part. It is expected that delivery of the shares will by made in New York, New York, on or about July 29,1993.

Donaldson,Lufkin & Jenrette
Securities Coporation

Alex. Brown & Sons
Incorporated

Montgomery Securities

FIGURE 14-3A
PETsMART's prospectus

No dealer, salesperson or other person has been authorized to give any information or to make any representations not contained in this Prospectus, and, if given or made, such information or presentations must not be relied upon as having been authorized by the Company, any Selling Stockholder or the U.S. Underwriters. This Prospectus does not constitute an offer to sell or a solicitation of an offer to buy to any person or by anyone in any jurisdiction in which such offer or solicitation would be unlawful or to any person to whom it is unlawful. Neither the delivery of this Prospectus nor any sale made hereunder shall, under any circumstances, create any implication that there has been no change in the affairs of the Company or that the information contained herein is correct as of any time subsequent to the date hereof.

TABLE OF CONTENTS

Until August 16, 1993 (25 days after the date hereof), all dealers effecting transactions in the Common Stock, whether or not participating in this distribution, may be required to deliver a Prospectus. This delivery requirement is in addition to the obligation of dealers to deliver a Prospectus when acting as Underwriters and with respect to their unsold allotments or subscriptions.

7,200,000 Shares

PETsMART

Common Stock

PROSPECTUS

Donaldson, Lufkin & Jenrette
Securities Corporation

Alex. Brown & Sons
Incorporated

Montgomery Securities

July 22, 1993

FIGURE 14-3B
PETsMART's prospectus (*Continued*)

Financial Reality

NONFINANCIAL COSTS OF AN IPO

Going public is attractive to closely held firms because it provides nonrefundable funds that can be used for expansion, research and development, or some other pressing need facing the company. But it also presents problems that are frequently overlooked.

Going public brought tiny Dynatrend, Inc. $1.9 million for product development. Ronald Massa, the founder and chief executive officer, could have raised the money from a venture capitalist. But this meant giving up control of the company, something he didn't want to do.

Massa had mixed feelings about going public. It meant he had to change his management style with the result that he became less friendly with his employees. Public companies are judged by Wall Street standards that he disagrees with, but which he is forced to try and meet.

A New York investment banker says that going public puts owners "through an emotional wringer." Information that used to be just his business now must be disclosed to the public.

Being public costs Dynatrend about $100,000 a year. There are costs for a transfer agent, legal, auditing, investment banking, financial public relations, printing, and mailing costs. And time is spent talking to brokers, analysts, and investors looking for information.

Massa says that investors like to see earnings rise each quarter. Everyone judges the company by the stock price, which can change for reasons having nothing to do with the company's performance. That influences his decisions. He says a quarter-to-quarter emphasis results in him manipulating the company and not managing it.

Adapted from "Small Bus iness," *The Wall Street Journal*, November 15, 1982, p. 31. Reprinted by permission of *The Wall Street Journal*,

find that they can raise funds through *shelf registrations*, *rights offerings*, and *private placements*. Let's now discuss these methods.

Shelf Registrations. In 1982, the SEC changed the practice of negotiated agreements between firms and investment bankers. SEC Rule 415 allows large firms to register securities with the SEC and sell them piecemeal during a two-year period. Securities sold this way are called *shelf registrations* because in effect they are "on the shelf" and can be taken down and sold on short notice (as short as one day) whenever it suits the issuing firm. In early December 1993, Commonwealth Edison Company registered $1 billion of debt securities as a shelf offering. Typically, firms use shelf registrations for the sale of debt rather than equity securities.

At the original shelf registration filing with the SEC, the firm does not designate an investment banker as the official underwriter. The firm hires an underwriter when the shares are taken down from the shelf. Some people worry that the speed with which the firm wants the shares to be issued from the shelf may prevent underwriters from providing adequate *due diligence*, that is, adequate analysis of risk associated with the securities and ensuring the completeness of the registration statement.

This announcement is under no circumstances to be construed as an offer to sell or as a solicitation of an offer to buy any of these securities. The offering is made only by the Prospectus.

March 10, 1994

7,446,250

Gaylord Entertainment Company

Class A Common Stock

Price $26 Per Share

Copies of the Prospectus may be obtained in any State or jurisdiction in which this announcement is circulated from only such of the undersigned or other dealers or brokers as may lawfully offer these securities in such State or jurisdiction.

5,957,000

The above shares were underwritted by the following group of U.S. Underwriters.

Merrill Lynch & Co.

CS First Boston **Morgan Stanley & Co.** Incorporated **PaineWebber Incorporated**

Prudential Securities Incorporated **UBS Securities Inc.** **S.G. Warburg & Co. Inc.**

J. C. Bradford & Co. **Equitable Securities Corporation** **Gerard Klauer Mattison & Co., Inc.**

J. J. B. Hilliard, W.L. Lyons, Inc. **Josephthal Lyon & Ross** Incorporated **Legg Mason Wood Walker** Incorporated

Morgan Keegan & Company, Inc. **The Seidler Companies** Incorporated **Wheat First Butcher & Singer** CAPITAL MARKETS

1,489,250 Shares

The above shares were underwritten by the following group of International Underwriters.

Merrill Lynch International Limited

CS First Boston **Daewoo Securities (Europe) Limited** **Dresdner Bank** Aktiengeselischaft

Nomura International **UBS Limited** **S.G. Warbury Securities**

FIGURE 14.4
A tombstone and its interpretation

Executive Commentary

PRIVATE PLACEMENTS FOR THE SMALL FIRM

by David G. Bonagura, Partner-in-Charge of Entrepreneurial Services of the Long Island Office of Ernst & Young

A new product or service may exist only in an entrepreneur's mind or on blueprints. A private placement offers an avenue to financing when bankers prove reluctant to lend without a record of profitability. The entrepreneur should not be concerned whether the financing is in the form of debt or equity. Assuring an infusion of cash for facilities, equipment, payroll, and working capital is of paramount importance. Successful rounds of private financing may help grow a business to a point at which the entrepreneur can successfully offer stock to the general public, an event that may handsomely reward early investors if the company has done well and the public is eager to snap up shares.

Private financing is highly customized; many aspects of a deal can be negotiated after an investor has expressed interest. Entrepreneurs and investors may seem fairly far apart at first, but deals are limited only by the creativity of the parties involved. For example, a Washington, DC-area high-tech startup, stymied by bankers' loan turndowns, teamed up with a real estate developer that had space to spare in a new project. In exchange for locating in the building and an option to purchase stock, the developer provided financial backing.

Private placements can be completed in a matter of days, but the entrepreneur must be prepared to devote considerable time and energy to the search for financing. Prior to the search, the entrepreneur and his or her advisers should prepare a document known as a private placement memorandum for circulation to potential investors. There is no legal requirement for this document, but similar to a detailed business plan, it presents the company's case to those who do not personally know the entrepreneur. The memorandum should contain information on how the capital will be used, include business forecasts, and disclose risks to potential investors. Preparation of a memorandum is a valuable exercise in its own right; it helps entrepreneurs take stock of their business and consider the future in some detail. At a later date, the document may serve as the centerpiece of the registration statement for an initial public stock offering.

Attorneys and accountants can often introduce the entrepreneur to potential investors. Professional business brokers can locate investors and arrange deals for a fee. Even the commercial banker who holds the mortgage on an entrepreneur's house can be a source of leads. However, the relationship between the entrepreneur and investor must click on the personal level. The entrepreneur must be sure there is a commonality of interest and goals and a shared vision of the future. Entrepreneurs should take their time to get to know potential investors—away from the office.

The Securities and Exchange Commission and the securities departments of the individual states recognize that a minimum of regulations helps smaller companies quickly raise the capital they need. Private equity placements are "exempt" financing because the entrepreneur does not have to file registration documents that would precede a public stock sale. The entrepreneur simply completes a form, which provides general information about the company and the stock the company plans to issue, the costs associated with the financing, and the uses planned for the proceeds. Entrepreneurs should be aware that federal antifraud and civil liability statutes remain in force.

Executive Commentary

With knowledge and persistence, entrepreneurs can strategically use private capital to add value to their company and make it more attractive to future investors. Entrepreneurs should constantly build their network of potential investors. It does not hurt to get to know potential investors long before they are needed.

A chief advantage of shelf registration is that the fixed cost of registration is distributed over a series of issuances, which results in lower overall transaction cost. Another advantage is that competitive bidding between investment bankers is aggressive, which in turn results in lower fees paid by the issuer to the investment banker. For instance, Morgan Stanley, an investment banking company, netted about $400,000 on one deal that would have netted about $3 million before Rule 415. The Financial Reality article on page 209 discusses how Time Warner Inc. threatened to take its business to more accommodating investment bankers if the bankers did not waive their contractual rights.

Rights Offering. A company can bypass investment bankers and issue new equity securities directly to existing shareholders through a *preemptive rights offering. Preemptive rights* are certificates issued by the corporation to the existing shareholders that specify the conditions under which the shareholders may purchase shares of the new equity issue. The rights grant current shareholders an option, not an obligation, to buy some proportion of new shares issued at a *price below market value* before the general public has a chance to buy them. One right is distributed for each share the shareholder owns. The company may stipulate the number of rights necessary for the purchase of one or more shares of the new stock. For example, four rights may enable a shareholder to buy one share. By exercising the rights, shareholders can maintain their respective ownership percentages of the company's common stock. Figure 14-5 outlines the key dates associated with a rights offering.

The *ex-rights date* is the day when the old stock begins trading in the market without the subscription privilege, or rights. Buyers are no longer entitled to receive rights to subscribe for shares. The share price decreases by the value of the right to which it is no longer entitled. Rights are exercisable before a final expiration date. The length of the subscription period during which rights are exercisable is typically from two to four weeks. Figure 14-5 identifies this period as the*stock trades ex-rights period.* Shareholders can sell the rights in secondary markets if they do not want to exercise them.[5]

[5]The theoretical value of a right is:

$$\frac{\text{Price of old stock with rights} - \text{price of new stock}}{\text{Number of rights for one share} + 1}$$

For example, a company permits its stockholders to subscribe to one new share of stock at $45 for each four shares of that stock currently owned. The stock is trading at $55 per share. The theoretical value of a right is $2: ($55 − $45) ÷ (4 + 1). The actual value may deviate from the theoretical value because of transactions costs and speculation.

Financial Reality

TIME WARNER MUSCLES ITS UNDERWRITERS

Wall Street investment bankers don't usually let themselves get pushed around by the corporate clients. But that's exactly what Time Warner did to Salomon Inc. and Lazard Freres & Co.

Salomon and Lazard Freres were left with millions of dollars in paper losses on Time Warner notes after they bowed to the demands of Time Warner.

The bankers got hurt when Time Warner, eager to take advantage of plunging interest rates, unloaded its latest batch of $1 billion in 30-year bonds authorized by a shelf registration. The problem: Wall Street underwriters led by Salomon were still trying to find buyers for Time Warner's last $1 billion offering of a week earlier.

The new bonds hammered the price of Time Warner notes held by Salomon, Lazard, and their customers. What made matters worse is that Salomon, as lead manager, had the legal right to delay the Time Warner bond sale by three days. Time Warner made it clear that if Salomon didn't waive its legal right, Salomon's entire relationship with Time Warner could be in jeopardy. And that could deprive Salomon of its chance for big fees on future sales of securities and corporate assets for Time Warner. Bond market watchers say the episode shows the ability of corporate giants such as Time Warner to play big Wall Street firms off against each other.

Before the advent of shelf registrations, big corporations would plan their entire program of bond sales in advance with a small circle of underwriters. Now the companies can fire off bond sales at a moment's notice, moving quickly to take advantage of market conditions and letting big Wall Street firms bid for the bonds.

Wall Street firms don't want to alienate big issuers because the bond sales carry sizable fees. On the $1 billion Time Warner bonds, the fee was $10 million.

Adapted from Randall Smith and Thomas T. Vogel, Jr., "Time Warner Muscles Its Underwriters," *The Wall Street Journal*, January 28, 1993, pp. C1, C12. Reprinted by permission of *The Wall Street Journal*,

The issuing firm may engage an investment banker to stand by to purchase shares not subscribed on an underwritten basis. The investment banker would then sell the unsubscribed shares to other investors. The *standby agreement* calls for the issuing firm to pay a standby fee to the investment banker.

From the perspective of the corporation and management, there are benefits to using a rights offering to raise new financing. By offering the stock to existing shareholders, who are presumably happy with the present firm management, the likelihood of successfully raising the amount of new funds is increased. Furthermore, the underwriting costs of a rights offering, compared to a public offering of new stock, are substantially lower. Hence, it is normally in the firm's best interest to issue stock to a friendly, receptive audience while at the same time save the underwriting costs. However, companies in the United States tend to rely on rights offerings to raise additional equity capital to a lesser extent than foreign companies.[6]

[6]A review of *The Wall Street Journal* for December 14, 1993 indicated that rights for only two firms traded on the previous day: Latin American Discovery Fund and D&N Financial.

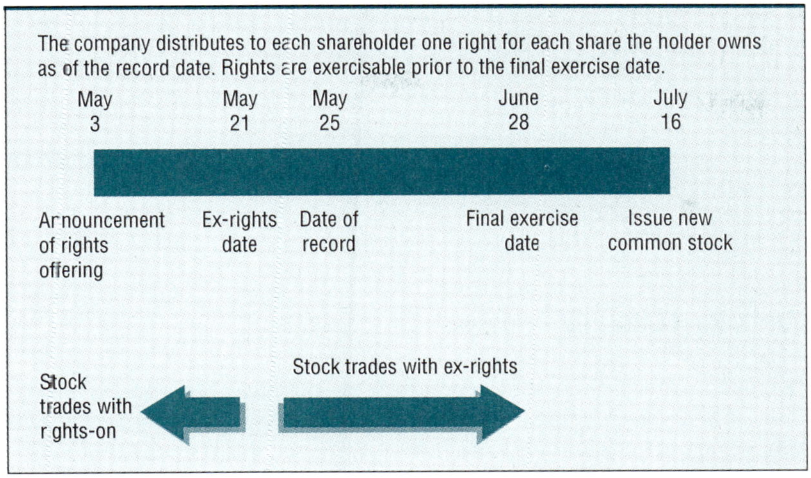

FIGURE 14-5
Key rights offering dates

Private Placement. An organization issuing securities can also bypass investment bankers by placing an entire issue of new securities directly with investors.[7] This process is called *private placement*.[8] The Prudential Corporation Finance Group has a portfolio of about $20 billion of loans privately placed with it.[9] As a rule of thumb, private placements are about 25 to 50 percent less costly than using an investment banker. The savings may result from two sources. First, if investment bankers are not used, the investment banking fee is saved. Second, privately placed securities are exempt from the costly SEC registration requirement of issuing a prospectus.

Private placements allow the issuer and investor to negotiate specialized contract terms. The terms may be either less or more restrictive to the firm than a public offering. For example, the issuer of debt securities may be able to convince investors to allow the firm to forgo any repayments of the loan for several years. Such a deferral is difficult to achieve with a public offering. On the other hand, an investor may require a higher rate of return for a private placement of securities.

COMPREHENSION CHECK

1. *Define: investment banker, underwriter, spread.*
2. *What does the term syndicate mean when applied to investment banking?*
3. *Describe the three essential functions performed by investment bankers in issuing new securities in the primary market.*

[7]Sometimes companies use an investment banker to locate investors to purchase the securities from the company. The banker receives a fee for this service.

[8]Private placements are prevalent in most countries. However, Japan had virtually no private placement activity of foreign stocks. Moreover, for a company listed on the Tokyo Stock Exchange, no private placement of shares is allowed unless the value of the placement is less than 1 million yen and the number of investors the securities are placed with is less than 50.

[9]The source of this information is *The Corporate Finance Sourcebook, 1993* (New Providence, NJ: National Register Publishing), p. 388.

4. *Discuss the dilemma faced by the investment banker in pricing an issue of new securities.*
5. *What is the difference for a corporation which is selling its common stock to the public for the first time if the investment banker underwrites the issue or sells the stock on a best-efforts basis?*
6. *Define shelf registration (SEC Rule 415). What are the advantages and disadvantages of shelf registrations?*
7. *Describe the rights offering process.*
8. *What is a private placement and why would a firm choose this type of financing?*

THE SECONDARY MARKETS

Earlier discussion mentioned that secondary market transactions have no effect on the original issuers of securities: Issuers do not receive additional cash from trades in secondary markets. However, well-functioning secondary markets make it possible for investors to convert claims issued by primary borrowers into cash or other securities on a moment's notice. This feature frees investors from the need to wait for financial contracts to mature before they can recover their funds, thereby increasing their willingness to invest in financial assets. Secondary markets also serve as sensitive indicators for borrowing and lending decisions in primary markets and for pricing new loans and securities.

Secondary markets range from informal groups of traders who deal with each other by telephone, making verbal agreements that are later confirmed in writing, to highly organized markets where brokers meet each other face to face. In either case, an investor places an order to buy or sell a specific security, say, Long Island Power and Lighting Company, with a broker or a dealer. A broker acts as the investor's agent but does not take title to the security. Brokers execute trades with other brokers for a commission. A dealer buys a security from one investor and resells it to another investor or another dealer. The dealer's profit (or loss) is the difference between the price he or she pays and the price at which he or she sells. The dealer bears the risk of price changes while owning the security. The primary service of both brokers and dealers is to bring buyers and sellers together.

In the secondary markets the migration of securities brokers and dealers to other countries from their home markets has been stimulated by the rapid growth of crossborder investing by individuals and institutions such as mutual funds, insurance companies, and pension funds. In Japan, for example, governmental authorities attempted until the late 1970s to control the direction and volume of financial flows into and out of Japan. The relaxation of Japanese capital controls on international transactions in the late 1970s was followed by an outpouring of Japanese investment funds into the securities of other countries. Japanese securities dealers established large operations in New York and London and other major capital markets to buy and sell foreign securities for their Japanese clients. As another step in the liberalization of its financial system, Japan granted European and North American banks and securities firms greater access to the Tokyo market, to buy Japanese securities for foreign investors and to sell foreign securities to Japanese investors.

We can think of secondary markets as consisting of four submarkets: *organize stock exchanges, over-the-counter (OTC) markets, third market,* and *fourth market.* Figure 14-6 shows the relationship between these markets.

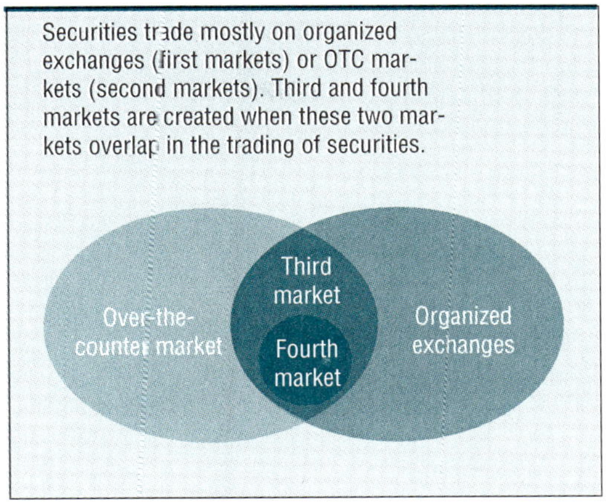

FIGURE 14-6
The secondary markets

Organized Stock Exchanges

Corporations like Blockbuster Entertainment Corporation and Xerox Corporation list their equity securities for trading on a *stock exchange (first market).* The two national U.S. stock exchanges are the New York Stock Exchange (NYSE) and the American Stock Exchange. There are five regional U.S. exchanges: Boston Stock Exchange, Cincinnati Stock Exchange, Midwest Stock Exchange, Pacific Stock Exchange, and Philadelphia Stock Exchange. The operation of stock exchanges in other parts of the world is similar in nature to U.S. exchanges.

The *stock exchange* centralizes trading in one location, the floor of the exchange (see Figure 14-7). Public buy and sell orders for stocks of companies are conducted on the floor at *trading posts* by participants yelling out prices. A *trading post* is the location at which various stocks or groups of stocks are traded on the floor of the exchange. Each company's stock trades at only one post so that trading can be tracked and kept orderly. At each trading post is a *specialist.* A *specialist* is a dealer assigned to the stocks trading at the post; he or she has the responsibility of ensuring that each listed stock experiences an "orderly succession of prices."[10] If the demand for Xerox stock equals the supply of Xerox stock at a given price, the shares trade. If there is more stock for sale than buyers are willing to buy, the specialist can buy the excess stock using her or his own capital. The specialist will mark up the price of the stock and, hopefully, later sell it for a profit. If prices move down, the specialist may have to sell the stock at a loss.

However, not all trades at the post go through the specialist. Many trades occur between two floor brokers who show up at a post at the same time. When floor brokers are unable to execute a trade, the trade goes through the specialist. In 1993, specialists participated in about 20 percent of all trades on the NYSE.[11]

[10]Tokyo's stock exchange operates without specialists. Thes *aitori* who keep the records of the bid and asked prices for the stocks traded at their posts work for stock exchange member firms. But they do not in fact buy and sell, and they have no obligations to maintain a market—indeed, quite the contrary. If the best bid they have is 10 percent below the closing price of the day before, they are required not to open the stock at all.

[11]*New York Stock Exchange Fact Book, 1993.*

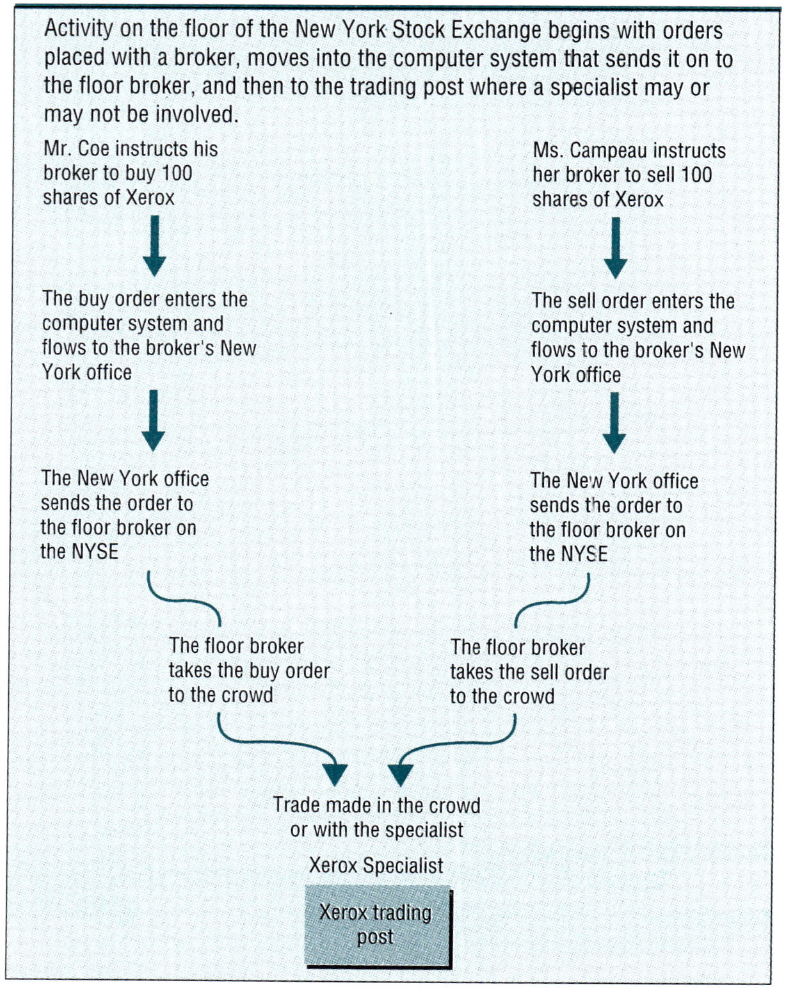

FIGURE 14-7
Order flow for a NYSE listed security

Firms that list their securities on an exchange receive a number of benefits. Their shares are more marketable due to greater awareness of the firm by investors and public confidence in standards for trading enforced by the stock exchange. The increased marketability makes it easier for the firm to raise equity funds from both individuals and institutions. However, public listing incurs significant reporting costs for issuing 10-Ks, annual reports, and other documents required by regulatory agencies.

Table 14-5 summarizes the criteria for both listing and possible delisting of a security on the NYSE.[12] Requirements for listing on other stock exchanges, both in the United States and abroad, are less rigorous. Generally, the NYSE requires all the

[12]An alternative set of listing standards exists for companies organized outside the United States that meet the normal size and earnings yardsticks for NYSE listing.

TABLE 14-5 NYSE Listing and Delisting Requirements

Initial Listing Requirements:

1. Either (a) the pretax income for the most recent year must be at least $2.5 million and the pretax income over each of the preceding two years must be at least $2 million, or (b) the pretax income over the most recent three years must be at least $6.5 million in total with a minimum of $4.5 million in the most recent year. All three years must be profitable.
2. Net tangible assets must be worth at least $18 million.
3. There must be at least 1.1 million shares outstanding that are publicly held, and these shares must have an aggregrate market value of at least $18 million. (This amount is subject to periodic adjustment based on market conditions.)
4. There must be either (a) at least 2000 stockholders who each own a minimum of 100 shares, or (b) at least 2200 stockholders with the monthly trading volume averaging at least 100,000 shares over the most recent six months.

Conditions For Possible Delisting:

1. The number of stockholders with each owning at least 100 shares falls below 1200.
2. The number of shares that are publicly held falls below 600,000.
3. The aggregate market value of publicly held shares falls below $5 million. (This amount is subject to periodic adjustment based on market conditions.)

Adapted from the New York Stock Exchange Fact Book, 1993.

criteria to be met for an initial listing. Any subsequent violation of a requirement risks possible expulsion from the exchange.

One of the most significant developments in equity markets that began in the 1980s was the growing trend toward the trading of common stocks across political borders. For instance, the common stock of Texas Instruments Corp. trades on the London and Tokyo exchanges and in Switzerland on the Zurich, Geneva, and Basel stock exchanges. London's International Stock Exchange displays prices for over 600 overseas securities.

It is clear that one reason companies seek a foreign listing relates to lowering the cost of financing. Corporations confined to a single financial market may feel constrained in various ways. For example, a company such as Philip Morris, Inc., which has global operations, may have such substantial demands for capital that it must tap several financial markets simultaneously. A presence in a number of markets can increase the size of any given issue and enhance the flexibility for raising funds. As another example, issuing stock in other markets can help raise the name recognition of a company with potentially beneficial effects on sales and profits. Also, having a presence in various world stock markets may serve strategic interests. By broadening the shareholder base, the company may be better able to resist takeover pressure from another company and, in turn, may be able to undertake foreign mergers and acquisitions more easily.

Of course, there are disadvantages to overseas listings, not the least of which are disclosure requirements and investor relations. Differences in the quantity of information, the frequency of disclosure, and accounting procedures all pose burdens in both financial and managerial terms. When a company decides to seek a foreign listing, investor relations can be a delicate issue because of cultural differences and may demand particular attention. A variety of other barriers such as foreign exchange controls, limitations on domestic ownership of foreign securities and different tax rules can present problems.

Financial Reality

THIRD-MARKET TRADING CROWDS EXCHANGES

The third market is coming on strong in competition with stock exchanges for trading business. And one big third-market player is speeding the growth by paying brokers to funnel their customers' orders through his system.

The third market is off-exchange trading in stocks that are listed on exchanges. The growth in trade and share volume in the third market is a serious concern for executives at the New York Stock Exchange, which still dominates the activity in its own listings but lately has lost business to others, including regional exchanges.

In 1989, the third market became the third-largest trading arena for New York Stock Exchange listed stocks, behind the Big Board itself and the Midwest Stock Exchange in Chicago.

What's especially frustrating, regional exchange executives say, is that the third market plays by different rules. "We are being forced to play full-contact football in tennis whites," says Caroline B. Austin, president of the Midwest specialist firm Dempsey & Co. "We must abide by the rules of the exchangele competing in a relatively deregulated environment."

Nothing can be more deregulated than paying brokers for their business. That's what Bernard L. Madoff Investment Securities, a New York firm, is doing. Mr. Madoff gives brokers a rebate of one cent a share on orders of 3000 shares or less.

A 500-share order would cost a broker about 80 cents to trade on the Midwest exchange. That order can earn the broker $5 when traded with Mr. Madoff.

Mr. Madoff can make money even with rebates by rapidly turning over those transactions at slightly better prices elsewhere, often on the very exchanges he competes with. "We have more efficient, faster execution than any exchange, and absolutely at a competitive price," says Mr. Madoff.

Mr. Madoff won't talk about his customers. But people close to the situation say they include many brokers that specialize in small investor orders: Alex. Brown & Sons Inc.; A.G. Edwards & Sons Inc. and Charles Schwab & Co., among others.

Mr. Madoff says the exchanges feel threatened by automated trading systems, which are proving to be faster and cheaper than the specialists who handle trading on the exchange floor.

Adapted from Craig Torres, "Third-Market" Trading Crowds Stock Exchanges," *The Wall Street Journal*, March 8, 1990, pp. C1, C9. Reprinted by permission of *The Wall Street Journal*,

The Over-the-Counter Market

The *over-the-counter (OTC) market* (second market) comprises thousands of security dealers linked by a computerized network. The OTC market is a *negotiated market* in contrast to the auction markets of the organized exchanges. Individual dealers, actually the brokerage firms they work for, declare themselves "market makers" in an OTC-listed stock. These brokerages buy the stock directly from the seller, mark it up, and sell it to someone else. OTC dealers do not have an obligation to make a fair and orderly market. And unlike exchanges, which operate within fixed trading hours, OTC market hours are not fixed. Securities continue to trade in the OTC market even if an exchange halts trading.

The OTC market consists of two classes of securities. One class is for relatively inactive securities that normally trade in regional brokerage offices. The second class is for actively traded OTC securities. These securities trade on the National Association of Securities Dealers' Automated Quotation System (NASDAQ) or on the National Market System (NMS). NASDAQ and NMS are computer-based quotation systems.

NASDAQ is the largest market in the world as measured by the number of companies listed, the second largest based on dollar volume of equity trading, and the third largest in terms of number of shares traded.[13] NASDAQ International is a U.K.-based version of the U.S. NASDAQ system. Its purpose is to provide transatlantic securities markets for U.S. stocks.

The Third Market

The *third market* refers to the trading of any *exchange-listed* security in the over-the-counter (OTC) market by firms that are not members of an exchange. The transaction bypasses an organized exchange, such as the NYSE. Weeden and Co., for example, is a large brokerage firm that operates in the third market. It maintains inventories of about 300 securities and competes with the specialists on the floor of the exchange who deal in these issues. The company finances its inventory of securities with loans payable on demand from commercial banks. Since Weeden's inventories average four to five times its equity capital, an unexpected change in the market price of the securities it holds could cause a decline in the value of its inventory that would substantially lower or even destroy the value of Weeden's stockholders' equity. The Financial Reality article on the previous page discusses the emerging prominence of the third market and how it is affecting securities trading on organized exchanges.

The Fourth Market

The *fourth market* is an electronic trading system for securities. Buyers and sellers in this market deal directly with each other to trade securities without the aid of brokers. Several NYSE member firms, such as Morgan Stanley, Salomon Brothers, and Bear, Stearns and Company, and institutional investors, such as pension funds and mutual funds, are participants.

Much of the trading in the fourth market is done through computerized systems called *Instinet Crossing Network, Portfolio System for Institutional Investors,* and *Single Price Auction Network.* For instance, Morgan Stanley may enter the price per share that it is willing to pay for Microsoft Corporation stock. TIAA-CREF, a large pension fund, may enter the price per share it is willing to accept to sell Microsoft stock. These systems automatically record any transaction and set up the paperwork for

[13] *1993 NASDAQ Fact Book & Company Directory,* p. 4.

its completion without revealing the identity of the transacting parties to each other. Electronic trading systems represent an important step in the continuing development of secondary markets for trading securities without an exchange floor.

COMPREHENSION CHECK

1. *Why is a secondary market an important part of the financial system?*
2. *Describe how the first, second, third, and fourth secondary markets differ from each other.*
3. *Why would a U.S. company's management apply to have its common stock listed on a major exchange such as the NYSE? Why would management want to list the company's stock on a foreign exchange?*

SUMMARY

- Markets are differentiated as to money markets and capital markets. Securities with maturities of one year or less trade in money markets. Securities with maturities of more than one year trade in capital markets.
- Primary markets are markets for the sale of new securities.
- Secondary markets are markets for the sale of securities subsequent to their initial sale.
- Financial intermediaries are specialists in bringing together investors and net fund users without direct contact between these parties. These intermediaries lower transaction costs associated with securities, lower monitoring costs of lenders who oversee the borrowers, vary the maturities of securities, allow securities to be divided, and lower the risk of investing.
- Financial intermediaries issue their own securities to investors and then use the funds obtained to buy securities of other issuers.
- Money markets are referred to as near-money markets since money and close substitutes are exchanged in this market. These securities offer lower return, lower risk, and shorter maturities than capital-market securities.
- The capital market consists of long-term debt and equity securities. These markets are both national and international in scope.
- The Eurodollar market is a network of world financial centers to transfer funds from surplus units to deficit units. The Eurodollar market is less regulated than domestic money markets.
- The Eurocapital market has three submarkets: Eurocurrency loans, Eurobonds, and Euroequity. The distinctive feature of these markets is that the securities are denominated in a currency other than that of the country in which the issuer of the security is located.
- Investment bankers play an important role in issuing new securities in primary markets. These bankers are financial services organizations specializing in

transferring funds from those who wish to invest to those who need the funds. Their role in issuing securities includes three functions: investigative, risk bearing, and selling.

- Investment bankers can either assume the risk of selling the securities by underwriting the sale of the securities (firm-commitment offering) or leave the risk with the issuer (best-efforts offering).
- Alternate means of issuing new securities are shelf registrations, rights offerings, and private placements.
- Secondary markets consist of organized stock exchanges (first markets), over-the-counter market (second markets), third market, and fourth market.
- First markets are auction markets. The other markets are negotiated markets. The third market is the trading of exchange listed securities in the OTC (or second) market. The fourth market is an electronic trading system in which participants deal directly with each other without the aid of brokers.

SELF-CORRECTION PROBLEMS

1. Distinguish between financial intermediation and financial intermediaries.
2. What is the difference between money-market mutual funds (MMMFs) and other money-market instruments? How have investors been benefited by the development of MMMFs?
3. Since trading on the New York Stock Exchange (NYSE) and the over-the-counter (OTC) markets do not provide new capital to business corporations and governments, how can the NYSE and the OTC markets be justified as part of the system of financial markets?

QUESTIONS

1. When are the services of a financial intermediary required? Who uses financial intermediaries? Why?
2. There are many different types of financial intermediaries. How do they differ and what do they have in common?
3. Financial intermediaries provide useful roles in financial markets. What are they?
4. Financial intermediaries are often quite profitable businesses. Can you provide an argument that justifies high profits?
5. Distinguish between the money market and the capital market.
6. What ties the money market to the capital market? Why can capital markets be considered more important than money markets?
7. What are Eurodollars? Why do Eurodollar deposits typically pay higher returns than deposits in the United States?
8. Defend the stock market as a financial institution of real social and economic value.
9. What role do investment bankers play in the capital markets? Are investment bankers brokers, dealers, both brokers and dealers, or neither of these?
10. a. Why might a corporation decide to use the services of an investment banker to sell an issue of its common stock on an underwritten basis?

b. Why might a corporation decide to have an investment banker sell an issue of its common stock on a best-efforts basis?

11. Figure 14-3 in the chapter indicates that the investment bankers Donaldson Lufkin & Jenrette Securities Corporation were hired by PETsMART, Inc. to sell common stock of the firm to the public. Within the prospectus there is mention that the initial offering price of $18 "has been determined by negotiations between the Company, the Selling Stockholders and the Representative of the Underwriters."
    a. Who are the "Selling Stockholders"?
    b. What factors do you think were considered in determining the $18 price?
12. Why should an investor interested in buying a new security issue pay close attention to the red herring?
13. Describe the difference between shelf registrations, rights offerings, and private placements.
14. Why should stockholders sell their rights to a new security issue if they do not wish to exercise the rights and make an additional investment in the corporation?
15. Indicate if the following transactions taking place in financial markets are examples of primary or secondary market transactions. If the transaction is in the secondary market, indicate whether it occurs in the first, second, third, or fourth market.
    a. Ms. Jewell instructs her broker to buy U.S. government bonds issued seven years ago with a remaining maturity of three years. (The bonds had an original maturity of ten years.) The broker executes the order in the OTC market.
    b. Mr. Ifflander buys through his broker some newly issued Apple Computer common stock.
    c. An insurance company buys a new issue of bonds sold by the State of Arizona through Merrill Lynch brokerage.
    d. Mr. Griggs withdraws $10,000 from his passbook savings account and uses the money to purchase General Motors stock, which is listed on the New York Stock Exchange. The broker fulfilled the transaction by buying the stock in the OTC market.
    e. Wesley Mutual Fund sells 100,000 shares of Apple Computer common stock to another mutual fund using the Instinet Crossing Network.
    f. Ms. Bender instructs her broker to trade 100 shares of General Motors stock (listed on the New York Stock Exchange). The broker transacts through the Pacific Stock Exchange.
16. Write a one-page report comparing the amount of new equity securities issued in two foreign markets of your choice. Your report should include both private placements and initial public offerings.

INTEGRATIVE PROBLEM

As a registered sales representative for a New York Stock Exchange firm, you have been asked to address a group of undergraduate students about the financial markets. In background preparation for your remarks, you outline the answers to the following questions.

a. What is the role of financial intermediaries?

b. What are the main types of financial intermediaries?
c. What benefits for the financial system do financial intermediaries provide?
d. What is the distinction between the money and capital markets?
e. What is the distinction between primary and secondary securities markets?
f. How do investment bankers facilitate the operation of the primary security market?
g. What alternatives to the use of an investment banker does a firm have in selling its securities?
h. How do the secondary securities markets work to the advantage of both users and savers of funds?
i. What submarkets make up the secondary securities markets?

SOLUTIONS TO SELF-CORRECTION PROBLEMS

1. Financial intermediation is the process of receiving money from savers and transferring it to users through the creation of debt and equity contracts. Financial intermediaries are the numerous classes of financial institutions such as banks, insurance companies, mutual investment funds, and pension funds that carry out the process of financial intermediation. These institutions provide two important benefits for the financial system through intermediation. First, by taking advantage of economies of scale, the financial institutions are able to reduce transaction and monitoring costs by providing central markets for savers and users of funds. Second, financial intermediaries create a variety of financial instruments to meet the saving and investment needs of various types of savers and users.
2. Money-market mutual funds (MMMFs) receive cash from small businesses or individuals who do not have sufficient money to invest in a diversified portfolio of regular money-market instruments which have minimum denominations ranging from $10,000 to $100,000 or more. MMMFs are organized by investment bankers and other money managers to pool the short-term funds of small investors for the purchase of large-denomination money-market instruments such as Treasury bills, commercial paper, negotiable certificates of deposit, and bankers' acceptances. Thus, small investors have access to a portfolio of money-market investments with a minimum of from $500 to $1000. Thus, MMMFs have benefited small investors by giving them greater access to a variety of short-term investments other than passbook savings accounts in banks and savings and loan institutions.
3. It is true that transactions on the New York Stock Exchange and other stock exchanges constitute trading in the secondary market (with sellers not being the original issuers of the securities traded). However, if no secondary securities markets existed, such as organized exchanges or over-the-counter markets, the liquidity of corporate and government securities would be greatly impaired. This would make it difficult for investors who purchased the corporate or governmental securities at the time of their original issue to find buyers at some future date. In the case of bonds, this would mean that original purchasers might be locked into holding the debt until its maturity even though the purchaser needed funds for some other purpose. Since common stocks have no maturity date, investors in common stocks would have even less liquidity

unless they undertook an expensive and tedious process of seeking out interested buyers. By providing an after market for securities, organized secondary markets such as the stock exchanges facilitate raising capital by corporations and governments.

SELECTED REFERENCES

Dougall, Herbert E., and Jack E. Gaumnitz, *Capital Markets and Institutions,* 4th ed. Englewood Cliffs, NJ: Prentice-Hall Foundations of Finance Series, 1980. The authors provide an uncomplicated study of ever-changing capital markets and institutions.

Hayes, Samuel L., III and Philip M. Hubbard, *Investment Banking: A Tale of Three Cities.* Boston, MA: Harvard Business School Press, 1990. This excellent book provides unique insight into the business of investment banking in the international arena.

O'Connor, Dennis, "For Best Underwriting, Pick Right Issues to Negotiate," *Corporate Cashflow* (February 1993), pp. 24–25. This article provides a practitioner's view of issuing stocks.

Zayachek, Jon, *Jon Z's Primer.* Upper Montclair, NJ: X-Rho Enterprises, Inc., 1988. This book provides a concise, readable guide about money markets.

CHAPTER 15

Long-Term Debt, Preferred Stock, and Common Stock

In Chapter 14, we explored the *capital market* for corporate securities—the market for relatively long-term financial instruments. In this chapter, we examine the major long-term securities issued by firms to provide for their long-term financing needs—long-term debt (bonds), preferred stock, and common stock—as well as evaluate their features. Also, in the addendum to this chapter we analyze the potential profitability of a company refunding (replacing) an existing bond issue with a new one.

BONDS AND THEIR FEATURES

A *bond* is a long-term debt instrument with a final maturity generally being 10 years or more. If the security has a final maturity shorter than 10 years, it is usually called a *note*. In order to fully understand bonds, we must be familiar with certain basic terms and common features.

Basic Terms

Par Value. *Par value* for a bond represents the amount to be paid the lender at the bond's maturity. It is also called *face value* or *principal*. Par value is usually $1,000 per bond (or some multiple of $1,000). With the major exception of a zero-coupon bond, most bonds pay interest that is calculated on the basis of the bond's par value.

Coupon Rate. The stated rate of interest on a bond is referred to as the *coupon rate*. For example, a 13 percent coupon rate indicates that the issuer will pay bondholders $130 per annum for every $1,000-par-value bond that they hold.

Maturity. Bonds almost always have a stated *maturity.* This is the time when the company is obligated to pay the bondholder the par value of the bond.

Trustee and Indenture

Trustee
A person or institution designated by a bond issuer as the official representative of the bondholders. Typically, a bank serves as trustee.

A company issuing bonds to the public designates a qualified **trustee** to represent the interests of the bondholders. The obligations of a trustee are specified in the Trust Indenture Act of 1939, administered by the Securities and Exchange Commission. The trustee's responsibilities are to authenticate the bond issue's legality at the time of issuance, to watch over the financial condition and behavior of the borrower, to make sure that all contractual obligations are carried out, and to initiate appropriate actions if the borrower does not meet any of these obligations. The trustee is compensated directly by the corporation, a compensation that adds to the effective costs of borrowing.

Indenture
The legal agreement, also called the *deed of trust,* between the corporation issuing bonds and the bondholders, establishing the terms of the bond issue and naming the trustee.

The legal agreement between the corporation issuing the bonds and the trustee, who represents the bondholders, is defined in the bond **indenture.** The indenture contains the terms of the bond issue as well as any restrictions placed on the company. These restrictions, known as *protective covenants,* are very similar to those contained in a term loan agreement. (Because we analyze protective covenants extensively in the next chapter, when we deal with term loans, we will not describe them here.) The terms contained in the indenture are established jointly by the borrower and the trustee. If the issue is a negotiated underwriting, the underwriter will also be involved. If the corporation defaults under any of the provisions of the indenture, the trustee, on the behalf of the bondholders, can take action to correct the situation. If not satisfied, the trustee can then call for the immediate repayment of all outstanding bonds.

Bond Ratings

The creditworthiness of a publicly traded debt instrument is often judged in terms of the credit ratings assigned to it by investment rating agencies. The principal rating agencies are Moody's Investors Service (Moody's) and Standard & Poor's (S&P). The issuer of a new corporate bond contracts with the agency to evaluate and rate the bond, as well as to update the rating throughout the bond's life. For this service, the issuer pays a fee. In addition, the rating agency charges subscribers to its rating publications.

Based on their evaluations of a bond issue, the agencies give their opinion in the form of letter grades, which are published for use by investors. In their ratings, the agencies attempt to rank issues according to the perceived probability of default. The highest grade issues, whose risk of default is felt to be negligible, are rated triple-A, followed by double-A, single-A, B-double-A (Moody's) or triple-B (S&P), and so forth through C and D, which are the lowest grades of Moody's and S&P, respectively. The first four grades mentioned are considered to represent investment-quality issues, whereas the other rated bonds are considered speculative. The ratings by the two agencies are widely respected as measures of default risk. In fact, many investors do not separately analyze the default risk of a company.

TYPES OF LONG-TERM DEBT INSTRUMENTS

Bonds can be issued on either an *unsecured* or *secured* (asset-backed) basis. Debentures, subordinated debentures, and income bonds form the major categories of unsecured bonds, while mortgage bonds represent the most common type of secured long-term debt instrument.

Debentures

The word **debenture** usually applies to the unsecured bonds of a corporation. Because debentures are not secured by any specific company property, the debenture holder becomes a general creditor of the firm in the event of company liquidation. Therefore, investors look to the earning power of the firm as their primary security. Although the bonds are unsecured, debenture holders are afforded some protection by the restrictions imposed in the bond indenture, particularly any *negative-pledge clause,* which precludes the corporation from pledging any of its assets (not already pledged) to other creditors. This provision safeguards the investor in that the borrower's assets will not be additionally restricted. Because debenture holders must look to the general credit of the borrower to meet principal and interest payments, typically only well-established and creditworthy companies are able to issue debentures.

Debenture A long-term, unsecured debt instrument.

Subordinated Debentures

Subordinated debentures represent unsecured debt with a claim to assets that ranks behind all debt senior to these debentures. In the event of liquidation, subordinated debenture holders usually receive settlement only if all senior creditors are paid the full amount owed them. These subordinated debenture holders would still rank ahead of preferred and common stockholders in the event of liquidation. The existence of subordinated debt may work to the advantage of senior bondholders because senior holders are able to assume the claims of the subordinated holders. To illustrate, suppose that a corporation is liquidated for $600,000. It had $400,000 in straight debentures outstanding, $400,000 in subordinated debentures outstanding, and $400,000 in obligations owed to general creditors. One might suppose that the straight debenture holders and the general creditors would have an equal and prior claim in liquidation—that each would receive $300,000. The fact (of law) is that the straight debenture holders are entitled to use the subordinated debenture holders' claims, giving them $800,000 in total claims for purposes of determining a partial repayment. As a result they are entitled to two-thirds ($800,000/$1,200,000) of the liquidating value, or $400,000, whereas the general creditors are entitled to only one-third ($400,000/$1,200,000) of the liquidating value, or $200,000.

Subordinated debenture A long-term, unsecured debt instrument with a lower claim on assets and income than other classes of debt; known as junior debt.

Because of the nature of the claim, a subordinated debenture issue has to provide a yield significantly higher than does a regular debenture issue in order to be attractive to investors. Frequently, subordinated debentures are convertible into common stock. Therefore, this added option feature may allow the convertible subordinated debenture to sell at a yield that is actually less than what the company would have to pay on an ordinary debenture.

Income Bonds

Income bond A bond where the payment of interest is contingent upon sufficient earnings of the firm.

A company is obligated to pay interest on an **income bond** only when the interest is earned. There may be a *cumulative feature* where unpaid interest in a particular year accumulates. If the company does generate earnings in the future, it will have to pay the cumulative interest to the extent that earnings permit. However, the cumulative obligation is usually limited to no more than three years. As should be evident, this type of security offers the investor a rather weak promise of a fixed return. Nevertheless, the income bond is still senior to preferred and common stock, as well as to any subordinated debt. Unlike preferred stock dividends, the interest payment is deductible for tax purposes. Because income bonds are not popular with investors, their issuance has been primarily limited to situations involving reorganizations.

Junk Bonds

Junk bond A high-risk, high-yield (often unsecured) bond rated below investment grade.

During the 1980s an active market developed for noninvestment-grade bonds. These are bonds with a rating of Ba (Moody's) or less, and they are called "junk" or "high-yield" bonds. The market for **junk bonds** was fostered by the investment banking firm of Drexel Burnham Lambert, which dominated this market until Drexel's demise in 1990. A number of companies used the market to raise billions of dollars, displacing what was previously bank and private placement financing. In addition, junk bonds were used in acquisitions and leveraged buyouts.

Principal investors in junk bonds include pension funds, high-yield bond mutual funds, and some individuals who invest directly. A secondary market of sorts exists, but in any kind of financial panic or "flight to quality" by investors in the bond markets, such liquidity dries up. In the late 1980s, bonds issued in connection with highly levered transactions (leveraged buyouts) began to experience difficulty and many issues defaulted. Investors lost confidence and there was a sharp drop in new issues. The market recovered somewhat, particularly for higher quality issues. While junk bonds are a viable means of financing for some companies, it must be recognized that there are windows of opportunity. In an unstable market, few investors are to be found.

Mortgage Bonds

Mortgage bond A bond issue secured by a mortgage on the issuer's property.

A **mortgage bond** issue is secured by a *lien* (creditor claim) on specific assets of the corporation—usually fixed assets. The specific property securing the bonds is described in detail in the *mortgage,* which is the legal document giving the bondholder a lien on a property. As with other secured lending arrangements, the market value of the collateral should exceed the amount of the bond issue by a reasonable margin of safety. If the corporation defaults on any of the provisions in the bond indenture, the trustee, on behalf of the bondholders, has the power to *foreclose.* In a foreclosure, the trustee takes over the property and sells it, using the proceeds to pay the bondholders. If the proceeds are less than the amount of the bond issue outstanding, the bondholders become general creditors for the residual amount.

A company may have more than one bond issue secured by the same property. A bond issue may be secured by a *second mortgage* on property already used to secure another bond issue under a *first mortgage*. In the event of foreclosure, the first-mortgage bondholders must be paid the full amount owed them before there can be any distribution to the second-mortgage bondholders.

Equipment Trust Certificates

Although equipment trust financing is a form of lease financing, the **equipment trust certificates** themselves represent an intermediate- to long-term investment. This method of financing is used by railroads to finance the acquisition of rolling stock. Under this method, a railroad arranges with a trustee to purchase equipment from a manufacturer. The railroad signs a contract with the manufacturer for the construction of specific equipment. When the equipment is delivered, equipment trust certificates are sold to investors. The proceeds of this sale, together with the down payment by the railroad, are used to pay the manufacturer. Title to the equipment is held by the trustee, which in turn leases the equipment to the railroad. Lease payments are used by the trustee to pay a fixed return on the certificates outstanding—actually a dividend—and to retire a specified portion of the certificates at regular intervals. Upon the final lease payment by the railroad, the last of the certificates is retired, and title to the equipment passes to the railroad.

Equipment trust certificate
An intermediate- to long-term security, usually issued by a transportation company such as a railroad or airline, that is used to finance new equipment.

The life of the lease varies according to the equipment involved, but 15 years is rather common. Because rolling stock is essential to the operation of a railroad and has a ready market value, equipment trust certificates enjoy a very high standing as fixed-income investments. As a result, railroads are able to acquire cars and locomotives on favorable financing terms. Airlines, too, use a form of equipment trust certificate to finance aircraft. Although these certificates are usually sold to institutional investors, some issues are sold to the public.

RETIREMENT OF BONDS

The *retirement* (repayment) of bonds may be accomplished in a number of different ways. For example, bonds may be retired by making a single-sum payment at final maturity, by conversion if the bonds are convertible, by calling the bonds if there is a call feature, or by periodic repayment. Periodic repayment of the debt is possible if either a sinking-fund or serial bond issue is involved. But first we turn our attention to sinking-fund and serial bonds.

Sinking Funds

The majority of corporate bond issues carry a provision for a **sinking fund** that requires the corporation to make periodic sinking-fund payments to a trustee in order to retire a specified face amount of bonds each period. The sinking-fund retirement of a bond issue can take two forms. The corporation can make a cash payment to the trustee, which in turn calls the bonds for redemption at the sinking-

Sinking fund
Fund established to periodically retire a portion of a security issue before maturity. The corporation is required to make periodic sinking-fund payments to a trustee.

fund *call price.* The bonds themselves are called on a lottery basis by their serial numbers, which are published in *The Wall Street Journal* and other newspapers. The second option available to the issuing firm is to purchase bonds in the open market and to deliver a given number of bonds to the trustee.

The corporation should purchase the bonds in the open market as long as the market price is less than the sinking-fund call price. When the market price exceeds the call price, it should make cash payments to the trustee. If interest rates increase and/or credit quality deteriorates, the bond's price will decline in relation to the sinking-fund call price. As a result, the option of the corporation to deliver either cash or bonds to the trustee can have significant value. As with any option, the option feature works to the advantage of the holder—in this case the corporation—and to the disadvantage of the bondholders. The greater the volatility of interest rates and/or the volatility of the firm's value, the more valuable the option to the corporation.

On the other hand, the sinking-fund provision may benefit the bondholder. By delivering bonds whose cost is lower than the call price, the company conserves cash, which may lower the probability of default. Because of the orderly retirement of sinking-fund debt, known as the *amortization effect,* some feel that this type of debt has less default risk than non-sinking-fund debt. In addition, steady repurchase activity adds liquidity to the market, which may be beneficial to the firm's bondholders.

Balloon payment
A payment on debt that is much larger than other payments. The ultimate balloon payment is the entire principal at maturity.

The two factors discussed work in opposite directions. The "delivery" option works to the disadvantage of bondholders, but debt amortization and other things that reduce risk and/or increase liquidity work to the bondholders' advantage. The limited empirical evidence available supports both effects but the amortization effect somewhat more so. Also, sinking-fund payments do not necessarily retire the entire bond issue. There can be a **balloon payment** at final maturity.

Serial Payments

Serial bonds
An issue of bonds with different maturities, as distinguished from an issue where all the bonds have identical maturities (term bonds).

All sinking-fund bonds in an issue mature on the same date, although specific bonds are retired before that date. **Serial bonds,** however, mature periodically until final maturity. For example, a $20 million issue of serial bonds might have $1 million of predetermined bonds maturing each year for 20 years. With a serial bond issue, the investor is able to choose the maturity that best suits his or her needs. Thus, a bond issue of this type might appeal to a wider group of investors than an issue in which all the bonds have the same maturity.

Call Provision

Call provision
A feature in an indenture that permits the issuer to repurchase securities at a fixed price (or a series of fixed prices) before maturity; also called *call feature.*

Call price
The price at which a security with a call provision can be repurchased by the issuer prior to the security's maturity.

Corporate bond issues often provide for a **call provision,** which gives the corporation the option to buy back its bonds at a stated price (or series of stated prices) before their maturity. However, not all bond issues are callable. Particularly in times of low interest rates some corporations issue noncallable bonds. When a bond is callable, the **call price** is usually above the par value of the bond and often decreases over time. A bond with 20 years to maturity might be callable at 110 ($1,100 per $1,000-face-value bond) for the next 2 years, 109 for the following 2 years, and so on until the final 2 years, when it is callable at 101.[1] Frequently, the call price in the first year is established at 1 year's interest above the face value of the bond. If the coupon rate is 14 percent, the initial call price may be 114 ($1,140 per $1,000 face value).

There are two types of call provisions, according to when they can be exercised. The security may be immediately callable, which simply means that the instrument may be bought back by the issuer at the call price at any time. Alternatively, the call provision may be deferred for a period of time. The most widely used deferred call periods are 5 years for public utility bonds and 10 years for industrial bonds. During this deferment period, the investor is protected from a call by the issuer. In recent years, virtually all issues of corporate bonds have involved a deferred call as opposed to an immediate call feature.

The call provision gives the company flexibility in its financing. If interest rates should decline significantly, it can call the bonds and refinance the issue at a lower interest cost. Thus, the company does not have to wait until the final maturity to refinance. In addition, the provision may be advantageous to the company if it finds any of the protective covenants in the bond indenture to be unduly restrictive. By calling the bonds before maturity, the company can eliminate these restrictions. Of course, if the issue is refinanced with a new bond issue, similar restrictions may be imposed.

Value of Call Privilege. Although the call privilege is beneficial to the issuing corporation, it works to the detriment of investors. If interest rates fall and the bond issue is called, the investors can invest in other bonds only at a sacrifice in yield to maturity. Consequently, the call privilege usually does not come free to the borrower. Its cost, or value, is measured at the time of bond issuance by the difference in yield on the callable bond and the yield that would be necessary if the security were noncallable. This value is determined by supply and demand forces in the market for callable securities.

One can think of the value of a callable bond as

$$\textbf{Callable-bond value} = \textbf{Noncallable-bond value} - \textbf{Call-option value} \qquad (20\text{-}1)$$

where the noncallable bond is identical to the callable bond in all respects except for the call feature. The greater the value of the call feature, the lower the value of the callable bond relative to that of the noncallable one. The level and volatility of interest rates are key factors giving value to the call feature.

If interest rates are high and expected to fall, the call feature is likely to have significant value. Because the call price limits the upside potential in price movement, bondholders do not realize the full benefit of a significant interest-rate decline. Just as the bondholders' party gets going, the bonds are called, and they can invest in other bonds only at a lower coupon rate than the rate they currently enjoy. As a result, investors demand a significantly higher yield (and lower price) on the callable bond than they do on the noncallable one. In contrast, when interest rates are low and expected to rise, the threat of a call is negligible. As a result, the yields on the two bonds (callable and noncallable) may be nearly the same. The volatility

[1]Among professionals (and in the newspaper bond quotations) bonds are always quoted as a percentage of their face value. For example, a bond callable at 105 and 5/8 would actually be callable at 105 and 5/8 percent of $1,000, or $1,056.25 per $1,000 face value.

of interest rates determines the magnitude of bond price movement. The greater the volatility, the greater the magnitude of *possible* interest-rate decline. As with any option, the greater the volatility of the associated asset, the more valuable the option.

In the addendum to this chapter, we explore how a company decides whether or not calling its bonds will be a profitable undertaking. By refunding (replacing) the bonds with a bond issue with a lower coupon, certain costs may be more than offset, and the call would be worthwhile.

PREFERRED STOCK AND ITS FEATURES

Preferred stock is a hybrid form of financing, combining features of debt and common stock. In the event of liquidation, a preferred stockholder's claim on assets comes after that of creditors but before that of common stockholders. Usually, this claim is restricted to the par value of the stock. If the par value of a share of preferred stock is $100, the investor will be entitled to a maximum of $100 in settlement of the principal amount. Although preferred stock carries a stipulated dividend, the actual payment of a dividend is a discretionary rather than a fixed obligation of the company. The omission of a dividend will not result in a default of the obligation or insolvency of the company. The board of directors has full power to omit a preferred stock dividend if it so chooses.

The maximum return to preferred stockholders is usually limited to the specified dividend, and these stockholders do not share in the residual earnings of the company. Thus, if you own 100 shares of 10 1/2 percent preferred stock, $50 par value, the maximum return you can expect in any year is $525, and this return is at the discretion of the board of directors. The corporation cannot deduct this dividend on its tax return. This fact is the principal shortcoming of preferred stock as a means of financing. In view of the fact that interest payments on debt are deductible for tax purposes, the company that treats a preferred stock dividend as a fixed obligation finds the explicit cost to be rather high.

Cumulative Dividends Feature

Cumulative dividends feature
A requirement that all cumulative unpaid dividends on the preferred stock be paid before a dividend may be paid on the common stock.

Almost all preferred stocks have a **cumulative dividends feature,** providing for unpaid dividends in any single year to be carried forward. Before the company can pay a dividend on its common stock, it must pay dividends *in arrears* on its preferred stock. Suppose that a board of directors omits the preferred stock dividend on the company's 8 percent cumulative preferred stock for three consecutive years. If the stock has a $100 par value, the company is $24 per share in arrears on its preferred stock. Before it can pay a dividend to its common stockholders, it must pay preferred stockholders $24 for each share of preferred stock held. It should be emphasized that just because preferred stock dividends are in arrears, there is no guarantee that they will ever be paid. If the corporation has no intention of paying a common stock dividend, there is no need to clear up the **arrearage** on the preferred stock. The preferred stock dividend is typically omitted for lack of earnings, but the corporation does not have to pay a dividend even if earnings are restored.

Arrearage
A late or overdue payment, which may be cumulative.

Participating Feature

A *participating feature* allows preferred stockholders to participate in the residual earnings of the corporation according to some specified formula. The preferred stockholders might be entitled to share equally with common stockholders in any common stock dividend beyond a certain amount. Suppose that a 6 percent preferred issue ($100 par value) was **participating preferred stock,** so that the holders were entitled to share equally in any common stock dividends in excess of $6 a share. If the common stock dividend is $7, the preferred stockholders will receive $1 in extra dividends for each share of stock owned. The formula for participation can vary greatly. The essential feature is that preferred stockholders have a prior claim on income and an opportunity for additional return if the dividends to common stockholders exceed a certain amount. Unfortunately for the investor, practically all preferred stock issues are nonparticipating, with the maximum return limited to the specified dividend rate.

Participating preferred stock Preferred stock where the holder is allowed to participate in increasing dividends if the common stockholders receive increasing dividends.

Voting Rights (in Special Situations)

Because of their "preferred" (prior) claim on assets and income, preferred stockholders are not normally given a voice in management unless the company is unable to pay preferred stock dividends during a specified period. Arrearages on four quarterly dividend payments might constitute such a default. Under such circumstances, preferred stockholders as a class would be entitled to elect a specific number of directors. Usually, the number of directors is rather small in relation to the total. Also, by the time the preferred stockholders obtain a voice in management, the company is probably in considerable financial difficulty. Consequently, the voting power that preferred stockholders are granted may be virtually meaningless.

Depending on the agreement between the preferred stockholders and the company, the preferred stockholders may obtain voting power under other conditions as well. The company may default under restrictions in the agreement that are similar to those found in a loan agreement or a bond indenture. One of the more frequently imposed restrictions is that dividends on common stock are prohibited if the company does not satisfy certain financial ratios. We note, however, that default under any of the provisions of the agreement between the corporation and its preferred stockholders does not result in the obligation's becoming immediately payable, as does default under a loan agreement or bond indenture. The preferred stockholders are merely given a voice in management and assurance that common stock dividends will not be paid during the period of default. Thus, preferred stockholders do not have nearly the same legal power in default as do debt holders.

Retirement of Preferred Stock

The fact that preferred stock, like common stock, has no maturity does not, however, mean that most preferred stock issues will remain outstanding forever. Provision for retirement of the preferred stock invariably is made.

Call Provision. Almost all preferred stock issues have a stated call price, which is above the original issuance price and may decrease over time. Like the call provision on bonds, the call provision on preferred stock affords the company flexibility. Long-term debt, unlike preferred stock, has a final maturity that ensures the eventual retirement of the issue. Without a call feature on preferred stock, the corporation would be able to retire the issue only by the more expensive and less efficient methods of purchasing the stock in the open market, inviting tenders of the stock from preferred stockholders at a price above the market price, or offering the preferred stockholders another security in its place.

Sinking Fund. Many preferred stock issues provide for a sinking fund, which partially ensures the orderly retirement of the stock. Like bond issues, a preferred stock sinking fund is advantageous to investors because the retirement process exerts upward pressure on the market price of the remaining shares.

Conversion. Certain preferred stock issues are convertible into common stock at the option of the holder. Upon conversion, of course, the preferred stock is retired. Because virtually all convertible securities have a call feature, the company can force conversion by calling the preferred stock if the market price of the preferred is significantly above the call price. Convertible preferred stock is used frequently in the acquisition of other companies. In part, its use in acquisitions stems from the fact that the transaction is not taxable for the company that is acquired or its stockholders at the time of the acquisition. It becomes a taxable transaction only when the preferred stock is sold.

Use in Financing

Nonconvertible preferred stock is not used extensively as a means of long-term financing. One of its drawbacks is the fact that the preferred dividend is not tax deductible by the issuer. Public utilities, however, employ it with a certain degree of regularity. Why? Public utilities are allowed to take preferred dividends into account when they set their rates. Thus, these regulated monopolies can pass through the higher cost of preferred stock to their customers.

For the corporate investor, however, preferred stock may be more attractive than debt instruments because generally 70 percent of the dividends received by the corporation is not subject to taxation.[2] It is not surprising, then, that most preferred stock is held by corporate investors.

This attraction for corporate investors has given rise to floating-rate preferred stock. In one variation, *money market preferred stock (MMP)*, the dividend rate is set by auction every 49 days. Put another way, the dividend rate is established by the forces of supply and demand in keeping with money market rates in general. A typical rate might be .75 times the commercial paper rate, and more creditworthy issuers may command an even greater discount. As long as enough investors bid at each auction, the security's effective maturity date is 49 days. As a result, there is little variation in the market price of the investment over time. For the issuer, the relevant cost comparison is with the after-tax cost of other methods of short-term financing.

[2]Corporate investors receiving dividends from less-than-20-percent-owned corporations are allowed the 70 percent deduction. Dividends from 20-percent-or-more-owned corporations are subject to an 80 percent deduction.

Apart from such short-term financing considerations, one advantage of regular (long-term) preferred stock financing is that it is a flexible financing arrangement. The dividend is not a legal obligation of the corporation issuing the securities. If earnings falter and the financial condition of the company deteriorates, the dividend can be omitted. With debt financing, interest must be paid regardless of whether earnings are good or bad. To be sure, companies that are accustomed to paying dividends on their common stock certainly regard the preferred dividend as a fixed obligation. Nevertheless, under dire circumstances, a company that omits its common stock dividend can also omit its preferred dividend.

Another advantage of a straight (nonconvertible) preferred stock issue is that it has no final maturity. In essence, it is a perpetual loan. From the standpoint of creditors, preferred stock adds to the equity base of the company and thereby strengthens its financial condition. The additional equity base enhances the ability of the company to borrow in the future. Although the explicit, after-tax cost of preferred stock is considerably higher than that of bonds, the implied benefits just discussed may offset this cost. In addition, the implicit cost of preferred stock financing, from the standpoint of penalizing the **price/earnings ratio** of the common stock, may be somewhat less than that of debt financing. To the extent that investors are apprehensive over legal bankruptcy, they would regard debt as a riskier form of leverage. Unlike creditors, preferred stockholders cannot force a company into legal bankruptcy.

Price/earnings ratio The market price per share of a firm's common stock divided by the most recent 12 months of earnings per share.

COMMON STOCK AND ITS FEATURES

The common stockholders of a company are its ultimate owners. Collectively, they own the company and assume the ultimate risk associated with ownership. Their liability, however, is restricted to the amount of their investment. In the event of liquidation, these stockholders have a residual claim on the assets of the company after the claims of all creditors and preferred stockholders are settled in full. Common stock, like preferred stock, has no maturity date. However, shareholders can still liquidate their investments by selling their stocks in the secondary market.

Authorized, Issued, and Outstanding Shares

The corporate charter of a company specifies the number of *authorized shares* of common stock, the maximum that the company can issue without amending its charter. Although amending the charter is not a difficult procedure, it does require the approval of existing shareholders, which takes time. For this reason, a company usually likes to have a certain number of shares that are authorized but unissued. These unissued shares allow flexibility in granting stock options, pursuing merger targets, and splitting the stock. When authorized shares of common stock are sold, they become *issued shares. Outstanding shares* refers to the number of shares issued and actually held by the public. The corporation can buy back part of its issued stock and hold it as **treasury stock.**

Treasury stock Common stock that has been repurchased and is held by the issuing company.

Par Value

Par value
The face value of a stock or bond.

A share of common stock can be authorized either with or without **par value.** The par value of a share of stock is merely a recorded figure in the corporate charter and is of little economic significance. A company should not, however, issue common stock at a price less than par value, because any discount from par value (amount by which the issuing price is less than the par value) is considered a contingent liability of the owners to the creditors of the company. In the event of liquidation, the shareholders would be legally liable to the creditors for any discount from par value. Consequently, the par values of most stocks (if they have any par values at all) are set at fairly low figures relative to their market values. Suppose that Fawlty Pacemakers, Inc., is ready to start business for the first time after just having sold 10,000 shares of $5-par-value common stock at $45 a share. The shareholders' equity portion of the balance sheet would be

Common stock ($5 par value; 10,000 shares issued and outstanding)	$ 50,000
Additional paid-in capital	400,000
Total shareholders' equity	$450,000

Assigned (or stated) value
A nominal value assigned to a share of no-par common stock that is usually far below the actual issuing price.

Additional paid-in capital
Funds received by a company in a sale of common stock that are in excess of the par or stated value of the stock.

Common stock that is authorized without par value (no-par stock) is carried on the books at the original market price or at some **assigned (or stated) value.** The difference between the issuing price and the par or stated value is reflected as **additional paid-in capital.**

Book Value and Liquidating Value

The *book value per share* of common stock is the shareholders' equity—total assets minus liabilities and preferred stock as listed on the balance sheet—divided by the number of shares outstanding. Suppose that Fawlty Pacemakers is now one year old, has generated $80,000 in after-tax profit, but pays no dividend. Thus, retained earnings are $80,000; the shareholders' equity is now $450,000 + $80,000 = **$530,000;** and the book value per share is $530,000/10,000 shares = **$53.**

Although one might expect the book value per share of stock to correspond to the *liquidating value (per share)* of the company, most frequently it does not. Often assets are sold for less than their book values, particularly when liquidating costs are involved. In some cases, certain assets—notably land and mineral rights—have book values that are modest in relation to their market values. For the company involved, liquidating value may be higher than book value. Thus, book value may not correspond to liquidating value, and, as we shall see, it often does not correspond to market value.

Market Value

Market value per share is the current price at which the stock is traded. For actively traded stocks, market price quotations are readily available. For the many inactive stocks that have thin markets, prices are difficult to obtain. Even when obtainable, the information may reflect only the sale of a few shares of stock and not typify the market value of the firm as a whole. For companies of this sort, care must be taken in interpreting market price information.

The market value of a share of common stock will usually differ from its book value and its liquidating value. Market value per share of common stock is a function of the current and expected future dividends of the company and the perceived risk of the stock on the part of investors. Because these factors bear only a partial relationship to the book value and liquidating value of the company, the market value per share may not be tied closely to these values.

Typically, the shares of a newer company are traded in the *over-the-counter (OTC) market*, where one or more security dealers maintain an inventory in the common stock and buy and sell it at the bid and ask prices that they quote. As a company grows in financial stature, number of shareholders, and volume of transactions, it may qualify for **listing** on a stock exchange, such as the New York Stock Exchange. However, many firms prefer to remain a part of the OTC marketplace. The National Association of Securities Dealers Automated Quotations (NASDAQ) system for many of these OTC stocks provides significant marketability to the investor.

Listing Admission of a security for trading on an organized exchange. A security so admitted is referred to as a *listed security*.

RIGHTS OF COMMON SHAREHOLDERS

Right to Income

Common shareholders are entitled to share in the earnings of the company only if cash dividends are paid. Shareholders also prosper from the market value appreciation of their shares, but they are entirely dependent on the board of directors for the declaration of dividends that give them income from the company. Thus, we see that the position of a common shareholder differs markedly from that of a creditor. If the company fails to pay contractual interest and principal payments to creditors, the creditors are able to take legal action to insure that payment is made or the company is liquidated. Common shareholders, on the other hand, have no legal recourse to a company for not distributing profits.

Voting Rights

Because the common shareholders of a company are its owners, they are entitled to elect a board of directors. In a large corporation, shareholders usually exercise only indirect control through the board of directors they elect. The board, in turn, selects the management, and management actually controls the operations of the company. In a sole proprietorship, partnership, or small corporation, the owners usually control the operation of the business directly. In a large corporation, there may be times when the goals of management differ from those of the common shareholders. The only recourse of a shareholder who wishes to affect management is through the board of directors.

Because common shareholders are often geographically widely dispersed and thus operatively disorganized, management can often exercise effective control of a large corporation if it controls only a small percentage of the outstanding common stock. By proposing a slate of directors that is favorable to its own interests, management is able to maintain control.

Proxy
A legal document giving one person the authority to act for another. In business, it generally refers to the instructions given by a shareholder with regards to voting shares of common stock.

Proxies and Proxy Contests. Voting can be done either in person at the shareholders' annual meeting or by proxy. A **proxy** is a form that a shareholder signs giving his or her right to vote to another person or persons. Because most shareholders do not attend the annual meeting, voting by proxy is the mechanism by which most votes are cast. The Securities and Exchange Commission (SEC) regulates the solicitation of proxies and also requires companies to disseminate information to their shareholders through proxy mailings. Prior to the annual meeting, management solicits proxies from shareholders to vote for the recommended slate of directors and for any other proposals requiring shareholder approval. If shareholders are satisfied with the company, they generally sign the proxy in favor of management, giving written authorization to management to vote their shares. If some shareholders do not vote their shares, the number of shares voted at the meeting and the number needed to constitute a majority are lower. Because of the proxy system and the fact that management is able to mail information to shareholders at the company's expense, management has a distinct advantage in the voting process.

But the fortress is not invulnerable. Outsiders can seize control of a company through a proxy contest. Obviously, they would not attempt a takeover if management controlled a large percentage of shares outstanding. When an outside group undertakes a proxy raid, it is required to register its proxy statement with the SEC to prevent the presentation of misleading or false information. Despite the fact that the insurgents are usually unsuccessful, the undertaking of a proxy contest is often associated with a higher share price performance than would otherwise be the case. Apparently, the challenge itself is sufficient to change investor expectations about management in the future behaving more in keeping with maximizing shareholder wealth.

Majority-rule voting
A method of electing corporate directors, where each common share held carries one vote for each director position that is open; also called *statutory voting*.

Cumulative voting
A method of electing corporate directors, where each common share held carries as many votes as there are directors to be elected and each shareholder may accumulate these votes and cast them in any fashion for one or more particular directors.

Voting Procedures. Depending on the corporate charter, the board of directors is elected under either a **majority-rule voting** system or a **cumulative voting** system. Under the majority-rule system, stockholders have one vote for each share of stock that they own, and they must vote for each director position that is open. A stockholder who owns 100 shares will be able to cast 100 votes for each director's position open. Because each person seeking a position on the board must win a majority of the total votes cast for that position, the system precludes minority interests from electing any of their own directors. If management can obtain proxies for over 50 percent of the shares voted, it can select the entire board of directors.

Under a cumulative voting system, a stockholder is able to accumulate votes and cast them for less than the total number of directors being elected. The total number of votes for each stockholder is equal to the number of shares the stockholder owns times the number of directors being elected. If you are a stockholder who owns 100 shares and 12 directors are to be elected, you may cast $100 \times 12 =$ **1,200** votes. All 1,200 of your votes may be cast for one director, or these votes may be spread over whatever other number of directors you choose.

A cumulative voting system, in contrast to a majority-rule system, allows minority interests a greater chance to elect a certain number of directors. The mini-

New Proxy Disclosures Provide Wealth of Information

As proxy statements for this spring's corporate annual meetings begin dropping in the mail, a remarkable transformation seems to have taken place. The familiar traits of impenetrable corporate legalese and mind-bending complexity have given way to a more user-friendly source of critical data for shareholders. Indeed, the proxy revamping mandated by the Securities and Exchange Commission's new executive compensation disclosure requirements is yielding an abundance of clear, concise information previously buried in a blizzard of verbiage or unavailable altogether. Here are some of the key features of the new format:

- **SUMMARY TABLE** The compensation of the five highest paid executives is displayed in a table with specific breakdowns for salary, bonus, other annual compensation, the value of restricted stock awards, the number of options granted, and other long-term cash payouts. This table includes breakouts for each of the past three years.

- **OPTION TABLES** A separate table records the number of stock options granted to each executive in the most recent fiscal year, their exercise price, date of expiration, and the estimated present value of the grant. Another details the number of options exercised by each executive in the last year, the gain realized on the exercise, and the number and value of unexercised options that the executive continues to hold.

- **PERFORMANCE GRAPH** A brand-new element of the proxy statement is a graph plotting five-year cumulative returns compared with a market-based index (S&P 500) and an index of competing companies. This will allow shareholders to determine whether their companies' performance measures up, and to compare performance to changes in executive compensation.

- **COMPENSATION COMMITTEE REPORT** The new disclosure format requires a statement by the compensation committee describing the rationale of the compensation program and specifying the performance variables that must be met to earn bonuses or other extraordinary compensation. Although this report has the potential to be used by the compensation committee to supply shareholders with platitudes about good intentions, it should still provide more information about specific goals and objectives than was previously required.

Source: *USA Advocate* (March–April 1993), pp. 2–3.

mum number of shares necessary to elect a specific number of directors is determined by the following equation[3]

$$\frac{\text{Total number of voting shares} \times \text{Specific number of directors sought}}{\text{Total number of directors to be elected} + 1} + 1 \qquad (15\text{-}2)$$

If there are 3 million voting shares, if the total number of directors to be elected is 15, and if a minority group wishes to elect 2 directors, it will need at least the following number of shares:

$$\frac{3{,}000{,}000 \times 2}{15 + 1} + 1 = 375{,}001$$

[3]This formula assumes that the minority votes are cast evenly for only the specific number of directors sought and that the majority votes are cast evenly for the majority's entire slate of directors.

In this example, 375,001/3,000,000 = **12.5%** of the voting shares has been sufficient to elect 2/15 = **13.3%** of the board of directors.

As you can see, cumulative voting gives minority interests a better opportunity to be represented on the board of directors of a corporation. Because this system is more democratic, a number of states require that companies chartered in their states elect directors in this way. Even with cumulative voting, however, management is able to take steps that may effectively preclude minority interests from obtaining a seat on the board. One method involves reducing the number of directors on the board. Suppose that the minority group actually owns the 375,001 shares mentioned earlier. With 15 directors to be elected the group can elect 2 directors. If the board is reduced to 6 members, however, the minority group can elect no directors because the minimum number of shares needed to elect a single director is

$$\mathbf{\frac{3{,}000{,}000 \times 1}{6 + 1} + 1 = 428{,}572}$$

Another method of thwarting a minority interest from obtaining representation is to stagger the terms of the directors so that only a portion of the board is elected each year. If a firm has 15 directors and the term is for 5 years, it is possible to have only 3 directors elected each year. As a result, a minority group needs considerably more shares voted in its favor—750,001 shares to be exact—to elect a director than it would if all 15 directors came up for election each year.

Right to Purchase New Shares (Maybe)

A firm's corporate charter or state statute may require that a new issue of common stock or an issue of securities convertible into common stock be offered first to existing common shareholders because of their *preemptive right.* If the preemptive right applies to a particular firm, existing common shareholders would have the right to preserve their proportionate ownership in the corporation. Thus, if the corporation issues common stock, the common shareholders must be given the right to subscribe to the new stock so that they can maintain their pro rata interest in the company.

DUAL-CLASS COMMON STOCK

To retain control for management, for company founders, or for some other group, a company may have more than one class of common stock. For example, common stock might be classified according to voting power and to the claim on income. Class A common stock of a company may have inferior voting privileges but may be entitled to a prior claim to dividends, while Class B common stock may have superior voting rights but a lower claim to dividends. Dual classes of common stock are common in new ventures where promotional common stock usually goes to the founders. Usually, the promoters of a corporation and its management hold the Class B common stock, while the Class A common stock is sold to the public.

Suppose that the Class A and Class B common shareholders of a company are entitled to one vote per share but that the Class A stock is issued at an initial price of $20 a share. If $2 million is raised in the original offering through the issuance of

80,000 shares of Class A common stock for $1.6 million and 200,000 shares of Class B common stock for $400,000, the Class B shareholders will have over twice as many votes as Class A holders have, although their original investment is only one-fourth as large. Thus, the Class B holders have effective control of the company. Indeed, this is the purpose of **dual-class common stock.**

Dual-class common stock
Two classes of common stock, usually designated Class A and Class B. Class A is usually the weaker voting or nonvoting class, and Class B is usually the stronger.

For this control, the Class B holders must be willing to give up something in order to make Class A common stock attractive to investors. Usually, they take a lower claim both to dividends and assets. An appropriate balance must be struck between voting power and the claim to dividends and assets if the company is to bargain effectively for Class A equity funds. Sometimes, the Class B common stock is simply given to the promoters of a corporation without any cash investment on their part. Perhaps the most famous example of a company with classified common stock is the Ford Motor Company. The Class B common stock is owned by members of the Ford family, and the Class A common stock is held by the general public. Regardless of the number of shares of Class A common stock issued, the Class B common stock constitutes 40 percent of the voting power of the Ford Motor Company. Thus, members of the Ford family retain substantial voting power in the company, despite the fact that they hold far fewer shares than does the general public.

SUMMARY

- A *bond* is a long-term debt instrument with a final maturity generally being 10 years or more. Basic terms related to bonds include par value, coupon rate, and maturity.
- A *trustee* is a person or institution designated by a bond issuer as the official representative of the bondholder, while an *indenture* is the legal agreement between the corporation issuing bonds and the bondholders establishing the terms of the bond issue and naming the trustee.
- Bonds can be issued on either an *unsecured* or *secured* (asset-backed) basis. *Debentures, subordinated debentures,* and *income bonds* form the major categories of unsecured bonds, while *mortgage bonds* represent the most common type of secured long-term debt instrument.
- The *retirement* (repayment) of bonds may be accomplished in a number of different ways. For example, bonds may be retired by making a single-sum payment at final maturity, by conversion if the bonds are convertible, by calling the bonds, if there is a call feature, or by periodic repayment. Periodic repayment of the debt is possible if either a *sinking-fund* or *serial bond* issue is involved.
- Preferred stock is a hybrid form of security having characteristics of both debt and common stock. The payment of dividends is not a legal but rather a discretionary obligation, although many companies regard the obligation as fixed. Preferred stockholders' claims on assets and income come after those of creditors but before those of common shareholders.
- Preferred stock, like common stock, has no maturity. However, retirement of the preferred stock can occur through the use of a *call provision,* a *sinking fund,* or *a conversion.*
- Because of the generally 70 percent exemption of dividends to the corporate investor, preferred stock typically has a lower yield than corporate bonds. Particularly popular for marketable security portfolios of corporations is *money*

market preferred stock (MMP). The principal disadvantage of preferred stock to the issuer is the nondeductibility for tax purposes of preferred dividends paid.

- The common stockholders of a company are its ultimate owners. As such they are entitled to share in the residual earnings of the company if cash dividends are paid. As owners, however, they have only a residual claim on assets in the event of liquidation.
- Common stockholders are also entitled to a voice in management through the board of directors that they elect. Many shareholders vote by means of a *proxy*. The directors are elected under either a *majority-rule voting* system or a *cumulative voting* system. The cumulative system allows minority interests a greater chance to obtain representation on the board of directors.
- The use of different classes of common stock allows the promoters and management of a corporation to retain voting control without having to make a large capital contribution.

ADDENDUM: REFUNDING A BOND ISSUE

Refunding
Replacing an old debt issue with a new one, usually to lower the interest cost.

In this Addendum, we analyze the profitability of a company's refunding a bond issue before its maturity. By **refunding,** we mean calling the issue and replacing it with a new issue of bonds. In this regard, we focus our attention on only one reason for refunding—profitability—which, in turn, is due to interest rates having declined since the bonds were issued.

A REFUNDING EXAMPLE

The refunding decision can be regarded as a form of capital budgeting. There is an initial cash outlay followed by future interest savings. These savings are represented by the difference between the annual net cash outflow required under the old bonds and the net cash outflow required on the new, or refunding, bonds. Calculating the initial cash outlay is more complex. Consequently, it is best to show an example of this method of evaluation.[4]

A company currently has a $20 million, 12 percent debenture issue outstanding, and the issue still has 20 years to final maturity. Because current interest rates are significantly lower than at the time of the original offering, the company can now sell a $20 million issue of 20-year bonds at a coupon rate of 10 percent that will net it $19,600,000 after the underwriting spread.

Call premium
The excess of the call price of a security over its par value.

For federal income tax purposes, the unamortized (not-yet-written-off) issuing expense of the old bonds, the **call premium,** and the unamortized discount of the old bonds, if they were sold at a discount, are deductible as expenses in the year of the refunding. The old bonds were sold 5 years ago at a $250,000 discount from par value, so the unamortized portion now is $200,000. Moreover, the legal fees and other issuing expenses involved with the old bonds have an unamortized balance of $100,000. The call price on the old bonds is 109 ($1,090 per $1,000-face-value bond);

[4]This section draws upon Oswald D. Bowlin, "The Refunding Decision: Another Special Case in Capital Budgeting," *Journal of Finance* 21 (March 1966), 55–68.

issuing expenses on the new bonds are $150,000; the income tax rate is 40 percent; and there is a 30-day period of overlap. The period of overlap is the lag between the time the new bonds are sold and the time the old bonds are called. This lag occurs because most companies wish to have the proceeds from the new issue in hand before they call the old issue. Otherwise, there is a certain amount of risk associated with calling the old issue and being at the "mercy" of the bond market in raising new funds. During the period of overlap, the company pays interest on both bond issues.

FRAMEWORK FOR ANALYSIS

With this rather involved background information in mind, we can calculate the initial cash outflow and the future cash benefits. The net cash outflow at the time of the refunding is as follows:

Cost of calling old bonds (call price, 109)		$21,800,000
Net proceeds of new bond issue		19,600,000
Difference		$ 2,200,000
Expenses		
Issuing expense of new bonds	$ 150,000	
Interest expense on old bonds during overlap period	200,000	350,000
Gross cash outlay		$ 2,550,000
Less: Tax savings		
Interest expense on old bonds during overlap period	$ 200,000	
Call premium	1,800,000	
Unamortized discount on old bonds	200,000	
Unamortized issuing expenses on old bonds	100,000	
Total	$2,300,000	
Tax savings (40% of $2,300,000)		920,000
Net cash outflow		**$ 1,630,000**

For ease of presentation, we ignore any interest that might be earned by investing the refunding bond proceeds in marketable securities during the 30-day period of overlap. The annual net cash benefits may be determined by calculating the difference between the net cash outflow required on the old bonds and the net cash outflow required on the new or refunding bonds. We assume for simplicity that interest is paid but once a year, at year end. The annual net cash outflow on the old bonds is

Interest expense, 12% coupon rate		$2,400,000
Less: Tax savings		
Interest expense	$2,400,000	
Amortization of bond discount ($200,000/20)	10,000	
Amortization of issuing costs ($100,000/20)	5,000	
Total	$2,415,000	
Tax savings (40% of $2,415,000)		966,000
Annual net cash outflow, old bonds		**$1,434,000**

For the new bonds, the bond discount as well as the issuing costs may be amortized for tax purposes in the same manner as were the old bonds. The annual net cash outflow on the new bonds is as follows:

Interest expense, 10% coupon rate		$ 2,000,000
Less: Tax savings		
Interest expense	$2,000,000	
Amortization of bond discount ($400,000/20)	20,000	
Amortization of issuing costs ($150,000/20)	7,500	
Total	$2,027,500	
Tax savings (40% of $2,027,500)		811,000
Annual net cash outflow, new bonds		**$1,189,000**
Difference between annual net cash outflows ($1,434,000 – $1,189,000)		$ 245,000

DISCOUNTING

Thus, for an initial net cash outflow of $1,630,000, the company can achieve annual net cash benefits of $1,434,000 – $1,189,000 = **$245,000** over the next 20 years. Because the net cash benefits occur in the future, they must be discounted back to present value. But what discount rate should be used? Certain individuals advocate the use of the cost of capital. However, a refunding operation differs from other investment proposals. Once the new bonds are sold, the net cash benefits are known with certainty. From the standpoint of the corporation, the refunding operation is essentially a riskless investment project. The only risk associated with the cash flows is that of the firm's defaulting in the payment of principal or interest. Because a premium for default risk is embodied in the market rate of interest the firm pays, a more appropriate discount might be the after-tax cost of borrowing on the refunding bonds. Using this cost, $(.10) \times (1 - .40) =$ **6%**, as our discount factor, the refunding operation would be worthwhile if the net present value were positive.[5] For our example, the net present value is $1,180,131, indicating that the refunding operation is worthwhile. The internal rate of return is 13.92 percent, indicating again that the refunding is worthwhile, because the internal rate of return exceeds the required rate of 6 percent.[6]

OTHER CONSIDERATIONS

Just because a refunding operation is found to be worthwhile, it should not necessarily be undertaken right away. If interest rates are declining and this decline is expected to continue, management may prefer to delay the refunding. At a later

[5]Net present value is the present value of net cash benefits less the initial cash outflow.

[6]An alternative method of analysis is to replicate the cash outflows of the old bond issue and then determine the present value of this stream using as the discount rate the interest rate at which new bonds could be sold in the current market. If this present value exceeds the call price of the old bonds, the refunding would be worthwhile. Among others using this approach are Jess B. Yawitz and James A. Anderson, "The Effect of Bond Refunding on Shareholder Wealth," *Journal of Finance* 32 (December 1979), 1738–46.

date, the refunding bonds can be sold at an even lower rate of interest, making the refunding operation even more worthwhile. The decision concerning timing must be based on expectations of future interest rates.

Several points should be raised with respect to the calculations in our example. First, most firms refund an existing issue with a new bond issue of a longer maturity. In our example, we assumed that the new bond issue had the same final maturity date as that of the old bond issue. Our analysis needs to be modified slightly when the maturity dates are different. The usual procedure is to consider only the net cash benefits up to the maturity of the old bonds. A second assumption in our example was that neither issue involved sinking-fund bonds or serial bonds. If either issue calls for periodic reduction of the debt, we must adjust our procedure for determining future net cash benefits. Finally, the annual cash outflows associated with the refunded bonds are usually less than those associated with the refunded bonds. As a result, there is a decrease in the degree of financial leverage of the firm. While this effect is likely to be small, on occasion it can be a significant consideration.

QUESTIONS

1. Contrast serial bonds and bonds requiring a sinking fund.
2. How does an income bond differ from a mortgage bond issue?
3. Explain why a commercial bank loan officer would be particularly concerned that debt owed by a corporate borrower to the principal stockholders or officers of the company be subordinated debt.
4. What are "junk bonds"? How might they be used in financing a corporation?
5. In issuing long-term debt, which types of debt instruments would most likely be used by (a) railroads? (b) public utilities? (c) strong industrial firms?
6. Why do callable bonds typically have a higher yield to maturity than noncallable bonds, holding all other things constant? Is the yield differential between callable and noncallable bonds likely to be constant over time? Why?
7. Because the dividend payments on preferred stock are not a tax-deductible expense, the explicit cost of this form of financing is high. What are some of the offsetting advantages to the issuing firm and to the investor that enable this type of security to be sold?
8. From the standpoint of the preferred stock issuer, why is it desirable to have a *call feature?*
9. How does a money market preferred (MMP) stock differ from regular preferred stock?
10. Why do most preferred stock issues have a cumulative feature? Would the company be better off with a noncumulative feature?
11. If not otherwise stated, what would you "typically" expect to find with respect to the following features for a preferred stock: cumulative feature, participation, voting rights, call feature, and claim on assets?
12. Why would a company ever wish to use dual-class common stock in its financing instead of straight common stock?
13. Why does most common stock have a low par value in relation to its market value?
14. The common stockholder is considered the residual owner of a corporation. What does this mean in terms of risk and return?

15. In any proxy attempt by an outside group to gain control of a company, the advantage lies with management. What are the reasons for this advantage?
16. If Congress were to eliminate the double taxation of dividends so that a company could deduct dividend payments in the same way it does interest payments for tax purposes, what would be the effect on preferred stock and common stock financing?

SELF-CORRECTION PROBLEMS

1. The Phelps Corporation has $8 million of 10 percent mortgage bonds outstanding under an open-end indenture. The indenture allows additional bonds to be issued as long as all of the following conditions are met:
   a. Pretax interest coverage [(income before taxes + bond interest)/bond interest] remains greater than 4.
   b. Net depreciated value of mortgage assets remains twice the amount of mortgage debt.
   c. Debt-to-equity ratio remains below .5.

   The Phelps Corporation has net income after taxes of $2 million and a 40 percent tax rate, $40 million in equity, and $30 million in depreciated assets, covered by the mortgage. Assuming that 50 percent of the proceeds of a new issue would be added to the base of mortgaged assets and that the company has no sinking-fund payments until next year, how much more 10 percent debt could be sold under each of the three conditions? Which protective covenant is binding?
2. Alvarez Apparel, Inc., could sell preferred stock with a dividend cost of 12 percent. If it were to sell bonds in the current market, the interest rate cost would be 14 percent. The company is in a 40 percent tax bracket.
   a. What is the after-tax cost of each of these methods of financing?
   b. Powder Milk Biscuits, Inc., holds a limited number of preferred stocks as investments. It is in a 40 percent tax bracket. If it were to invest in the preferred stock of Alvarez Apparel, what would be its after-tax return? What would be its after-tax return if it were to invest in the bonds?
3. Thousand Islands Resorts has 1,750,000 shares of authorized common stock, each having a $1 par value. Over the years, it has issued 1,532,000 shares, but presently 63,000 are held as treasury stock. The additional paid-in capital of the company is presently $5,314,000.
   a. How many shares are now outstanding?
   b. If the company were able to sell stock at $19 per share, what is the maximum amount it could raise under its existing authorization, including treasury shares?
   c. What would be its common stock and additional paid-in capital accounts after the financing?
4. Roy's Orbs & Sons, Inc., has a nine-person board and 2 million shares of common stock outstanding. It is chartered with a cumulative voting rule. Tammy Whynot, a granddaughter of the founder, directly or indirectly controls 482,000 shares. As she disagrees with present management, she wants a slate of her own directors on the board.
   a. If all directors are elected once a year, how many directors can she elect?

b. If directors' terms are staggered so that only three are elected each year, how many can she elect?

PROBLEMS

1. Gillis Manufacturing Company has in its capital structure $20 million of 13.5 percent sinking-fund debentures. The sinking-fund call price is $1,000 per bond, and sinking-fund payments of $1 million in face amount of bonds are required annually. Presently, the yield to maturity on the debentures in the market is 12.21 percent. To satisfy the sinking-fund payment, should the company deliver cash to the trustee or bonds? What if the yield to maturity were 14.60 percent?
2. Five years ago, Zapada International issued $50 million of 10 percent, 25-year debentures at a price of $990 per bond to the public. The call price was originally $1,100 per bond the first year after issuance, and this price declined by $10 each subsequent year. Zapada is now "calling" the bonds in order to refund them at a lower interest rate.
   a. Ignoring taxes, what is a bondholder's return on investment for the 5 years? (Assume that interest is paid once a year and that the investor owns one bond.)
   b. If the bondholder can now invest $1,000 in a 20-year security of equivalent risk that provides 8 percent interest, what is the overall return over the 25-year holding period? How does this compare with the return on the Zapada bonds had they not been called? (Assume again that interest is paid once a year. Both rates of return can be approximated using the present value tables at the end of the book.)
3. Crakow Machine Company wishes to borrow $10 million for 10 years. It can issue either a noncallable bond at 11.40 percent interest or a bond callable at the end of 5 years for 12 percent. For simplicity, we assume that the bond will be called only at the end of year 5. The interest rate that is likely to prevail 5 years hence for a 5-year straight bond can be described by the following probability distribution:

Interest rate	9%	10%	11%	12%	13%
Probability	.1	.2	.4	.2	.1

   Issuing and other costs involved in selling a bond issue 5 years hence will total $200,000. The call price is assumed to be par.
   a. What is the total absolute amount of interest payments for the noncallable issue over the 10 years? (Do not discount.) What is the expected value of total interest payments and other costs if the company issues callable bonds? (Assume that the company calls the bonds and issues new ones only if there is a savings in interest costs after issuing expenses.) On the basis of total costs, should the company issue noncallable or callable bonds?
   b. What would be the outcome if the probability distribution of interest rates 5 years hence were the following?

Interest rate	7%	9%	11%	13%	15%
Probability	.2	.2	.2	.2	.2

Assume that all other conditions stay the same.

4. *Research Project:* Obtain copies of several bond indentures. Pay particular attention to the restrictive covenants concerning things such as dividends, working capital, additional debt, and nature of the business. Try to relate the cost of debt to the firm to the relative restrictiveness of these provisions. How would you go about finding a measure of the degree of restriction so that trade-offs with interest cost could be made?
5. The O.K. Railroad needs to raise $9.5 million for capital improvements. One possibility is a new preferred stock issue—8 percent dividend, $100 par value—stock that would yield 9 percent to investors. Flotation costs for an issue this size amount to 5 percent of the total amount of preferred stock sold. These costs are deducted from gross proceeds in determining the net proceeds to the company. (Ignore any tax considerations.)
   a. At what price per share will the preferred stock be offered to investors? (Assume that the issue will never be called.)
   b. How many shares must be issued to raise $9.5 million for the O.K. Railroad?
6. Lost Dutchman Silver Mining Company has 200,000 shares of $7 cumulative preferred stock outstanding, $100 par value. The preferred stock has a participating feature. If dividends on the common stock exceed $1 per share, preferred stockholders receive additional dividends per share equal to one-half of the excess. In other words, if the common stock dividend were $2, preferred stockholders would receive an additional dividend of $.50. The company has 1 million shares of common stock outstanding. What would dividends per share be on the preferred stock and on the common stock if earnings available for dividends in three successive years were (a) $1,000,000, $600,000, and $3,000,000? (b) $2,000,000, $2,400,000, and $4,600,000? (c) $1,000,000, $2,500,000, and $5,700,000? (Assume that all of the available earnings are paid in dividends, but nothing more is paid.)
7. Mel Content, a disgruntled stockholder of the Penultimate Corporation, desires representation on the board. The Penultimate Corporation, which has 10 directors, has 1 million shares outstanding.
   a. How many shares would Mel have to control to be assured of 1 directorship under a majority-rule voting system?
   b. Recompute Part (a), assuming a cumulative voting system.
   c. Recompute parts a and b, assuming that the number of directors was reduced to 5.

ADDENDUM QUESTIONS

1. In the refunding decision, differential cash flows are discounted at the after-tax cost of debt. Explain why these cash flows are not discounted at the average cost of capital.

2. Are refundings by corporations likely to occur steadily over time? If not, when are waves of refundings likely to occur?

ADDENDUM PROBLEM

1. The U.S. Zither Corporation has $50 million of 14 percent debentures outstanding, which are due in 25 years. USZ could refund these bonds in the current market with new 25-year bonds, sold to the public at par ($1,000 per bond) with a 12 percent coupon rate. The spread to the underwriter is 1 percent, leaving $990 per bond in proceeds to the company. The old bonds have an unamortized discount of $1 million, unamortized legal fees and other expenses of $100,000, and a call price of $1,140 per bond. The tax rate is 40 percent. There is a one-month overlap during which both issues are outstanding, and issuing expenses are $200,000. Compute the present value of the refunding, using the after-tax rate on the new bonds as the discount rate. Is the refunding worthwhile?

SOLUTIONS TO SELF-CORRECTION PROBLEMS

1. (Dollars in millions) Let X = the number of millions of dollars of new debt that can be issued.

   a.

$$\frac{[\$2/(1-.40)] + [\$8(.10)]}{[\$8(.10)] + [(.10)X]} = 4$$

$$\frac{\$3.33 + \$.80}{\$.80 + (.10)X} = \frac{\$4.13}{\$.80 + (.10)X} = 4$$

$$4(\$.80) + (4)(.10)X = \$4.13$$
$$(.40)X = \$.93$$
$$X = \$.93/.40 = \mathbf{\$2.325}$$

   b.

$$\frac{\$30 + (.5)X}{\$8 + X} = 2$$

$$2(\$8) + 2(X) = \$30 + (.5)X$$
$$(1.5)X = \$14$$
$$X = \$14/(1.5) = \mathbf{\$9.33}$$

   c.

$$\frac{\$8 + X}{\$40} = .5$$

$$\$8 + X = (.5)(\$40)$$
$$X = \$20 - \$8 = \mathbf{\$12}$$

   Condition (a) is binding, and it limits the amount of new debt to $2.325 million.

2. a. After-tax cost:

   Preferred stock = **12%**

   Bonds = 14%(1 – .40) = **8.40%**

   b. The dividend income to a corporate investor is generally either 70 or 80 percent exempt from taxation. With a corporate tax rate of 40 percent, we have for the preferred stock either

   after-tax return = 12%(1 – [(.30)(.40)]) = **10.56% or**

   12%(1 – [(.20)(.40)]) = **11.04%**

   For the bonds,

   after-tax return = 14%(1 – .40) = **8.40%**

3. a.

Issued shares	1,532,000
Treasury shares	63,000
Outstanding shares	**1,469,000**

   b.

Authorized shares	1,750,000
Outstanding shares	1,469,000
Available shares	281,000
281,000 shares × $19 =	**$5,339,000**

   c.

Common stock ($1 par)	$ 1,750,000
Additional paid-in capital*	10,372,000

*Consists of $18 × 281,000 shares plus $5,314,000

4. a. Number of shares necessary to elect one director =

$$\frac{2{,}000{,}000 \times 1}{(9 + 1)} + 1 = 200{,}001$$

   Therefore, she can elect two directors.

   b. Number of shares necessary to elect one director =

$$\frac{2{,}000{,}000 \times 1}{(3 + 1)} + 1 = 500{,}001$$

   Therefore, she can elect no directors.

SELECTED REFERENCES

Alderson, Michael J., and K. C. Chen. "Excess Asset Reversions and Shareholder Wealth." *Journal of Finance* 41 (March 1986), 225–42.

Ang, James S. "The Two Faces of Bond Refunding." *Journal of Finance* 30 (June 1975), 869–74.

Bhagat, Sanjai. "The Effect of Pre-emptive Right Amendments on Shareholder Wealth." *Journal of Financial Economics* 12 (November 1983), 289–310.

Bowlin, Oswald D. "The Refunding Decision: Another Special Case in Capital Budgeting." *Journal of Finance* 21 (March 1966), 55–68.

DeAngelo, Harry, and Linda DeAngelo. "Managerial Ownership of Voting Rights: A Study of Public Corporations with Dual Classes of Common Stock." *Journal of Financial Economics* 14 (March 1985), 33–70.

______. "Proxy Contests and the Governance of Publicly Held Corporations." *Journal of Financial Economics* 23 (June 1989), 29–59.

Donaldson, Gordon. "In Defense of Preferred Stock." *Harvard Business Review* 40 (July–August 1962), 123–36.

______. "Financial Goals: Management vs. Stockholders." *Harvard Business Review* 41 (May–June 1963), 116–29.

Dyl, Edward A., and Michael D. Joehnk. "Sinking Funds and the Cost of Corporate Debt." *Journal of Finance* 34 (September 1979), 887–94.

Finnerty, John D. "Preferred Stock Refunding Analysis: Synthesis and Extension." *Financial Management* 13 (Autumn 1984), 22–28.

Fooladi, Iraj, and Gordon S. Roberts. "On Preferred Stock." *Journal of Financial Research* 9 (Winter 1986), 319–24.

Kalotay, Andrew J. "On the Management of Sinking Funds." *Financial Management* 10 (Summer 1981), 34–40.

Levy, Haim. "Economic Evaluation of Voting Power of Common Stock." *Journal of Finance* 38 (March 1983), 79–94.

Linn, S. C., and J. Michael Pinegar. "The Effect of Issuing Preferred Stock on Common and Preferred Stockholder Wealth." *Journal of Financial Economics* 22 (October 1988), 155–84.

Markese, John. "Shareholder Voting Rights: Differences Among Classes." *AAII Journal* 11 (February 1989), 35–37.

McConnell, John J., and Gary G. Schlarbaum. "Returns, Risks, and Pricing of Income Bonds, 1956–76." *Journal of Business* 54 (January 1981), 33–64.

McDaniel, Morey W. "Are Negative Pledge Clauses in Public Debt Issues Obsolete?" *Business Lawyer* 38 (May 1983), 867–81.

______. "Bondholders and Corporate Governance." *Business Lawyer* 41 (February 1986), 413–60.

Ofer, Aharon R., and Robert A. Taggart, Jr. "Bond Refunding: A Clarifying Analysis." *Journal of Finance* 32 (March 1977), 21–30.

Pound, John. "Proxy Contests and the Efficiency of Shareholder Oversight." *Journal of Financial Economics* 20 (January–March 1988), 237–65.

Van Horne, James C. "Implied Fixed Costs in Long-Term Debt Issues." *Journal of Financial and Quantitative Analysis* 8 (December 1973), 821–33.

______. *Financial Market Rates and Flows*, 4th ed. Englewood Cliffs, NJ: Prentice Hall, 1994, Chaps. 7 and 11.

CHAPTER 16

The Valuation of Long-Term Securities

In previous chapters we discussed the *time value of money* and explored the wonders of compound interest. We are now able to apply these concepts to determining the value of different securities. In particular, we are concerned with the valuation of the firm's long-term securities—bonds, preferred stock, and common stock (though the principles discussed apply to other securities as well). Because the major decisions of a company are all interrelated in their effect on valuation, we must understand how investors value the financial instruments of a company.

DISTINCTIONS AMONG VALUATION CONCEPTS

The term *value* can mean different things to different people. Therefore, we need to be precise in how we both use and interpret this term. Let's look briefly at the differences which exist among some of the major concepts of *value*.

Liquidation Value Versus Going-Concern Value

Liquidation value is the amount of money that could be realized if an asset or a group of assets (e.g., a firm) is sold separately from its operating organization. This value is in marked contrast to the **going-concern value** of a firm, which is the amount the firm could be sold for as a continuing operating business. These two values are rarely equal, and sometimes a company is actually worth more dead than alive.

The security valuation models that we will discuss in this chapter will generally assume that we are dealing with *going concerns*—operating firms able to generate

Liquidation value The amount of money that could be realized if an asset or a group of assets (e.g., a firm) is sold separately from its operating organization.

Going-concern value The amount a firm could be sold for as a continuing operating business.

positive cash flows to security investors. In instances where this assumption is not appropriate (for example, impending bankruptcy), the firm's liquidation value will have a major role in determining the value of the firm's financial securities.

Book Value Versus Market Value

Book value
(1) An *asset:* the accounting value of an asset—the asset's cost minus its accumulated depreciation; (2) a *firm:* total assets minus liabilities and preferred stock as listed on the balance sheet.

Market value
The market price at which an asset trades.

The **book value** of an *asset* is the accounting value of the asset—the asset's cost minus its accumulated depreciation. The book value of a *firm,* on the other hand, is equal to the dollar difference between the firm's total assets and its liabilities and preferred stock as listed on its balance sheet. Because *book value* is based on historical values, it may bear little relationship to an asset's or firm's *market value.*

In general, the **market value** of an asset is simply the market price at which the asset (or a similar asset) trades in an open marketplace. For a firm, market value is often viewed as being the higher of the firm's *liquidation* or *going-concern value.*

Market Value Versus Intrinsic Value

Based on our general definition for market value, the market value of a security is the market price of the security. For an actively traded security, it would be the last reported price at which the security was sold. For an inactively traded security, an estimated market price would be needed.

Intrinsic value
The price a security "ought to have" based on all factors bearing on valuation.

The **intrinsic value** of a security, on the other hand, is what the price of a security *should be* if properly priced based on all factors bearing on valuation—assets, earnings, future prospects, management, etc. In short, the intrinsic value of a security is its economic value. If markets are reasonably efficient and informed, the current market price of a security should fluctuate closely around its intrinsic value.

The valuation approach taken in this chapter is one of determining a security's *intrinsic value*—what the security ought to be worth based on hard facts. This value is the present value of the cash-flow stream provided to the investor, discounted at a required rate of return appropriate for the risk involved. With this general valuation concept in mind, we are now able to explore in more detail the valuation of specific types of securities.

BOND VALUATION

Bond
A long-term debt instrument issued by a corporation or government

Face value
The stated value of an asset. In the case of a bond, the face value is usually $1,000.

Coupon rate
The stated rate of interest on a bond; the annual interest payment divided by the bond's face value.

A **bond** is a security that pays a stated amount of interest to the investor, period after period, until it is finally retired by the issuing company. Before we can fully understand the valuation of such a security, certain terms must be discussed. For one thing, a bond has a **face value.**[1] This value is usually $1,000 per bond. The bond almost always has a stated *maturity,* which is the time when the company is obligated to pay the bondholder the face value of the instrument. Finally, the **coupon rate,** or nominal annual rate of interest, is stated on the bond's face.[2] If, for example,

[1]Much like criminals, many of the terms used in finance are also known under a number of different aliases. Thus, a bond's *face value* is also known as its *par value,* or *principal.* And, like a good detective, you need to become familiar with the basic terms used in finance as well as their aliases.

[2]The term *coupon rate* comes from the detachable coupons that are affixed to *bearer bond* certificates which, when presented to a paying agent or the issuer, entitle the holder to receive the interest due on that date. Nowadays, *registered bonds,* whose ownership is registered with the issuer, allow the registered owner to receive interest by check through the mail.

the coupon rate is 12 percent on a $1,000-face-value bond, the company pays the holder $120 each year until the bond matures.

In valuing a bond, or any security for that matter, we are primarily concerned with discounting, or capitalizing, the cash-flow stream that the security holder would receive over the life of the instrument. The terms of a bond establish a legally binding payment pattern at the time the bond is originally issued. This pattern consists of the payment of a stated amount of interest over a given number of years coupled with a final payment, when the bond matures, equal to the bond's face value. The discount, or capitalization, rate applied to the cash-flow stream will differ among bonds depending upon the risk structure of the bond issue. In general, however, this rate can be thought to be composed of the risk-free rate plus a premium for risk.

Perpetual Bonds

The first (and easiest) place to start determining the value of bonds is with a unique class of bonds that never matures. These are indeed rare, but they help to illustrate the valuation technique in its simplest form. Originally issued by Great Britain after the Napoleonic Wars to consolidate debt issues, the British **consol** (short for *consolidated annuities*) is one such example. This bond carries the obligation of the British government to pay a fixed interest payment in perpetuity.

Consol
A bond that never matures; a perpetuity in the form of a bond.

The present value of a perpetual bond would simply be equal to the capitalized value of an infinite stream of interest payments. If a bond promises a fixed annual payment of I forever, its present (intrinsic) value, V, at the investor's required rate of return for this debt issue, k_d, is

$$V = \frac{I}{(1+k_d)^1} + \frac{I}{(1+k_d)^2} + \cdots + \frac{I}{(1+k_d)^\infty} \qquad (16\text{-}1)$$

$$= \sum_{t=1}^{\infty} \frac{I}{(1+k_d)^t}$$

$$= I(PVIFA_{k_d,\infty}) \qquad (16\text{-}2)$$

which, from Chapter 10's discussion of perpetuities, we know should reduce to

$$V = I/k_d \qquad (16\text{-}3)$$

Thus, the present value of a perpetual bond is simply the periodic interest payment divided by the appropriate discount rate per period. Suppose you could buy a bond that paid $50 a year forever. Assuming that your required rate of return for this type of bond is 12 percent, the present value of this security would be

$$V = \$50/.12 = \$416.67$$

This is the amount that you would be willing to pay for this bond. If the market price is greater than this amount, however, you would not want to buy it.

Bonds With a Finite Maturity

Non-Zero Coupon Bonds. If a bond has a finite maturity, then we must not only consider the interest stream, but also the terminal or maturity value (face value) in valuing the bond. The valuation equation for a such a bond is

$$V = \frac{I}{(1+k_d)^1} + \frac{I}{(1+k_d)^2} + \cdots + \frac{I}{(1+k_d)^n} + \frac{MV}{(1+k_d)^n}$$

$$= \sum_{t=1}^{n} \frac{I}{(1+k_d)^t} + \frac{MV}{(1+k_d)^n} \tag{16-4}$$

$$= I(PVIFA_{k_d,n}) + MV(PVIF_{k_d,n}) \tag{16-5}$$

where n is the number of years until final maturity and MV is the maturity value of the bond.

We might wish to determine the value of a $1,000-par-value bond with a 10 percent coupon and nine years to maturity. The coupon rate corresponds to interest payments of $100 a year. If our required rate of return on the bond is 12 percent, then

$$V = \frac{\$100}{(1.12)^1} + \frac{\$100}{(1.12)^2} + \cdots + \frac{\$100}{(1.12)^9} + \frac{\$1{,}000}{(1.12)^9}$$

$$= \$100(PVIFA_{12\%,9}) + \$1{,}000(PVIF_{12\%,9})$$

Referring to Table E in the Appendix at the back of the book, we find that the present value interest factor of an annuity at 12 percent for nine periods is 5.328. Table C in the Appendix reveals under the 12 percent column that the present value interest factor for a single payment nine periods in the future is .361. Therefore, the value, V, of the bond is

$$V = \$100(5.328) + \$1{,}000(.361)$$
$$= \$532.80 + \$361.00 = \$893.80$$

The interest payments have a present value of $532.80, whereas the principal payment at maturity has a present value of $360.00. (Note: All of these figures are *approximate* because the present value tables used are rounded to the third decimal place; the true present value of the bond is $893.44).

If the appropriate discount rate is 8 percent instead of 12 percent, the valuation equation becomes

$$V = \frac{\$100}{(1.08)^1} + \frac{\$100}{(1.08)^2} + \cdots + \frac{\$100}{(1.08)^9} + \frac{\$1{,}000}{(1.08)^9}$$

$$= \$100(PVIFA_{8\%,9}) + \$1{,}000(PVIF_{8\%,9})$$

Looking up the appropriate interest factors in Tables C and E in the Appendix, we determine that

$$V = \$100(6.247) + \$1{,}000(.500)$$
$$= \$624.70 + \$500.00 = \$1{,}124.70$$

In this case, the present value of the bond is in excess of its $1,000 par value because the required rate of return is less than the coupon rate. Investors would be willing to pay a *premium* to buy the bond. In the previous case, the required rate of return was greater than the coupon rate. As a result, the bond has a present value less than its par value. Investors would be willing to buy the bond only if it sold at a *discount* from par value. Now if the required rate of return equals the coupon rate, the bond has a present value equal to its par value, $1,000. More will be said about these concepts shortly.

Zero-coupon bond A bond that pays no interest but sells at a deep discount from its face value; it provides compensation to investors in the form of price appreciation.

Zero-Coupon Bonds. A **zero-coupon bond** makes no periodic interest payments but instead is sold at a deep discount from its face value. Why buy a bond that pays no interest? The answer lies in the fact that the buyer of such a bond does receive a return. This return consists of the gradual increase (or appreciation) in the value of the security from its original, *below-face-value* purchase price until it is redeemed *at face value* on its maturity date.

The valuation equation for a zero-coupon bond is a truncated version of that used for a normal interest-paying bond. The "present value of interest payments" component is lopped off, and we are left with value being determined solely by the "present value of principal payment at maturity," or

$$V = \frac{MV}{(1 + k_d)^n} \tag{16-6}$$

$$= MV(PVIF_{k_d,n}) \tag{16-7}$$

Suppose that Pace Enterprises issues a zero-coupon bond having a 10-year maturity and a $1,000 face value. If your required return is 12 percent, then

$$V = \frac{\$1,000}{(1.12)^{10}}$$

$$= \$1,000(PVIF_{12\%,10})$$

Using Table C in the Appendix, we find that the present value interest factor for a single payment 10 periods in the future at 12 percent is .322. Therefore,

$$V = \$1,000(.322) = \$322$$

If you could purchase this bond for $322 and redeem it 10 years later for $1,000, your initial investment would thus provide you with a 12 percent compound annual rate of return.

Semiannual Compounding of Interest. While some bonds (typically those issued in European markets) make interest payments once a year, most bonds issued in the United States pay interest twice a year. As a result, it is necessary to modify our bond valuation equations to account for compounding twice a year.[3] For example, Eqs. (16-4) and (16-5) would be changed as follows

$$V = \sum_{t=1}^{2n} \frac{I/2}{(1 + k_d/2)^t} + \frac{MV}{(1 + k_d/2)^{2n}} \tag{16-8}$$

$$= (I/2)(PVIFA_{k_d/2,2n}) + MV(PVIF_{k_d/2,2n}) \tag{16-9}$$

where k_d is the nominal annual required rate of interest, $I/2$ is the semiannual coupon payment, and $2n$ is the number of semiannual periods until maturity. Notice that semiannual discounting is applied to both the semiannual interest payments *and* the lump-sum maturity value payment. While it may seem inappropriate to use semiannual discounting on the maturity value, it isn't. The assumption of semiannual discounting, once taken, applies to all inflows.

To illustrate, if the 10 percent coupon bonds of U.S. Blivet Corporation have 12 years to maturity and our nominal annual required rate of return is 14 percent, the value of one $1,000-par-value bond is

$$V = (\$50)(PVIFA_{7\%,24}) + \$1,000(PVIF_{7\%,24})$$

$$= (\$50)(11.469) + \$1,000(.197) = \$770.45$$

[3]Even with a zero-coupon bond, the pricing convention among bond professionals is to use semiannual rather than annual compounding. This provides consistent comparisons with interest-bearing bonds.

Rather than having to solve for value by hand, professional bond traders often turn to bond value tables. Given the maturity, coupon rate, and required return, one can look up the present value. Similarly, given any three of the four factors, one can look up the fourth. Also, some specialized calculators are programmed to compute bond values and yields, given the inputs mentioned. In your professional life you may very well end up using these tools when working with bonds.

PREFERRED STOCK VALUATION

Preferred stock
A type of stock that promises a (usually) fixed dividend, but at the discretion of the board of directors. It has preference over common stock in the payment of dividends and claims on assets.

Most **preferred stock** pays a fixed dividend at regular intervals. Preferred stock has no stated maturity date and, given the fixed nature of its payments, is similar to a perpetual bond. It is not surprising, then, that we use the same general approach applied to valuing a perpetual bond to the valuation of preferred stock.[4] Thus, the present value of preferred stock is

$$V = D_p/k_p \qquad \textbf{(16-10)}$$

where D_p is the stated annual dividend per share of preferred stock and k_p is the appropriate discount rate. If Margana Cipher Corporation had a 9 percent, \$100-par-value preferred stock issue outstanding and your required return was 14 percent on this investment, its value per share to you would be

$$V = \$9/.14 = \$64.29$$

COMMON STOCK VALUATION

The theory surrounding the valuation of common stock has undergone profound change during the last two decades. It is a subject of considerable controversy, and no one method for valuation is universally accepted. Still, in recent years there has emerged growing acceptance of the idea that individual common stocks should be analyzed as part of a total portfolio of common stocks that the investor might hold. In other words, investors are not as concerned with whether a particular stock goes up or down as they are with what happens to the overall value of their portfolios. This concept has important implications for determining the required rate of return on a security. Unlike bond and preferred stock cash flows which are contractually stated, much more uncertainty surrounds the future stream of returns connected with common stock.

Are Dividends the Foundation?

When valuing bonds and preferred stock, we determined the discounted value of all the cash distributions made by the firm to the investor. In a similar fashion, the

[4]Virtually all preferred stock issues have a call feature (a provision that allows the company to force retirement), and many are eventually retired. When valuing a preferred stock that is expected to be called, we can apply a modified version of the formula used for valuing a bond with a finite maturity; the periodic preferred dividends replace the periodic interest payments and the "call price" replaces the bond maturity value in Eqs. (16-4) and (16-5), and all the payments are discounted at a rate appropriate to the preferred stock in question.

value of a share of common stock can be viewed as the discounted value of all expected cash dividends provided by the issuing firm until the end of time.[5] In other words,

$$V = \frac{D_1}{(1+k_e)} + \frac{D_2}{(1+k_e)^2} + \cdots + \frac{D_\infty}{(1+k_e)^n} \tag{16-11}$$

$$= \sum_{t=1}^{\infty} \frac{D_t}{(1+k_e)^t} \tag{16-12}$$

where D_t is the cash dividend at the end of time period t and k_e is the investor's required return, or capitalization rate, for this equity investment. This seems consistent with what we have been doing so far.

But, what if we plan to own the stock for only two years? In this case, our model becomes

$$V = \frac{D_1}{(1+k_e)} + \frac{D_2}{(1+k_e)^2} + \frac{P_2}{(1+k_e)^2}$$

where P_2 is the expected sales price of our stock at the end of two years. This assumes that investors will be willing to buy our stock two years from now. In turn, these future investors will base their judgments of what the stock is worth on expectations of future dividends and a future selling price (or terminal value). And so the process goes through successive investors.

Note that it is the expectations of future dividends and a future selling price, which itself is based on expected future dividends, that gives value to the stock. Cash dividends are all that stockholders, as a whole, receive from the issuing company. Consequently, the foundation for the valuation of common stock must be dividends. These are construed broadly to mean any cash distribution to shareholders, including share repurchases.

The logical question to raise at this time is, why do the stocks of companies that pay no dividends have positive, often quite high, values? The answer is that investors expect to sell the stock in the future at a price higher than they paid for it. Instead of dividend income plus a terminal value, they rely only on the terminal value. In turn, terminal value depends on the expectations of the marketplace viewed from this terminal point. The ultimate expectation is that the firm will eventually pay dividends, either regular or liquidating, and that future investors will receive a company-provided cash return on their investment. In the interim, investors are content with the expectation that they will be able to sell their stock at a subsequent time, because there will be a market for it. In the meantime, the company is reinvesting earnings and, everyone hopes, enhancing its future earning power and ultimate dividends.

Dividend Discount Models

Dividend discount models are designed to compute the intrinsic value of a share of common stock under specific assumptions as to the expected growth pattern of

[5]This model was first developed by John B. Williams, *The Theory of Investment Value* (Cambridge, MA: Harvard University Press, 1938). And, as Williams so aptly put it in poem form, "A cow for her milk/A hen for her eggs/And a stock, by heck/For her dividends."

future dividends and the appropriate discount rate to employ. Merrill Lynch, First Boston, and a number of other investment banks routinely make such calculations based on their own particular models and estimates. What follows is an examination of such models, beginning with the simplest one.

Constant Growth. Future dividends of a company could jump all over the place; but, if dividends are expected to grow at a constant rate, what implications does this hold for our basic stock valuation approach? If this constant rate is g, then Eq. (16-11) becomes

$$V = \frac{D_0(1+g)}{(1+k_e)} + \frac{D_0(1+g)^2}{(1+k_e)^2} + \cdots + \frac{D_0(1+g)^\infty}{(1+k_e)^\infty} \quad \textbf{(16-13)}$$

where D_0 is the present dividend per share. Thus, the dividend expected at the end of period$n$is equal to the most recent dividend times the compound growth factor, $(1 + g)^n$. This may not look like much of an improvement over Eq. (16-11). However, assuming that k_e is greater than g (a reasonable assumption since a dividend growth rate which is always greater than the capitalization rate would imply an infinite stock value), Eq. (16-13) can be reduced to[6]

$$V = D_1/(k_e - g) \quad \textbf{(16-14)}$$

Rearranging, the investor's required return can be expressed as

$$k_e = (D_1/V) + g \quad \textbf{(16-15)}$$

The critical assumption in this valuation model is that dividends per share are expected to grow perpetually at a compound rate of g. For many companies this assumption may be a fair approximation of reality. To illustrate the use of Eq. (16-14), suppose that LKN, Inc.'s dividend per share at $t = 1$ is expected to be \$4, that it is expected to grow at a 6 percent rate forever, and that the appropriate discount rate is 14 percent. The value of one share of LKN stock would be

$$V = \$4/(.14 - .06) = \$50$$

For companies in the mature stage of their life cycle, the perpetual growth model is often reasonable.

Conversion to an Earnings Multiplier Approach. With the constant growth model, we can easily convert from dividend valuation, Eq. (16-14), to valuation based on an

[6]If we multiply both sides of Eq. (16-13) by $(1 + k_e)/(1 + g)$ and subtract Eq. (16-13) from the product, we get

$$\frac{V(1+k_e)}{(1+g)} - V = D_0 - \frac{D_0(1+G)^\infty}{(1+k_e)^\infty}$$

Because we assume that k_e is greater than g, the second term on the right-hand side approaches zero. Consequently,

$$V\left[\frac{(1+k_e)}{(1+g)} - 1\right] = D_0$$

$$V\left[\frac{(1+k_e)-(1+g)}{(1+g)}\right] = D_0$$

$$V(k_e - g) = D_0(1+g) = D_1$$

$$V = D_1/(k_e - g)$$

This model is sometimes called the "Gordon Dividend Valuation Model" after Myron J. Gordon, who developed it from the pioneering work done by John Williams. See Myron J. Gordon, *The Investment, Financing, and Valuation of the Corporation* (Homewood, IL: Richard D. Irwin, 1962).

A common mistake made in using Eqs. (16-14) and (16-15) is to use, incorrectly, the firm's most recent annual dividend for the variable D_1 instead of the annual dividend expected by the end of the coming year.

earnings multiplier approach. The idea is that investors often think in terms of how many dollars they are willing to pay for a dollar of future expected earnings. Assume that a company retains a constant proportion of its earnings each year; call it *b*. The dividend-payout ratio (dividends per share divided by earnings per share) would also be constant. Therefore,

$$(1 - b) = D_1/E_1 \quad (16\text{-}16)$$

and

$$(1 - b)E_1 = D_1$$

Where E_1 is expected earnings per share in period 1. Eq. (16-14) can then be expressed as

$$V = [(1 - b)E_1]/(k_e - g) \quad (16\text{-}17)$$

where value is now based on expected earnings in period 1. In our earlier example, suppose that LKN, Inc., has a retention rate of 40 percent and earnings per share for period 1 are expected to be \$6.67. Therefore,

$$V = [(.60)\$6.67]/(.14 - .06) = \$50$$

Rearranging Eq. (16-17), we get

$$\textbf{Earnings Multiplier} = V/E_1 = (1 - b)/(k_e - g) \quad (16\text{-}18)$$

Eq. (16-18) thus gives us the highest multiple of expected earnings that the investor would be willing to pay for the security. In our example,

$$\textbf{Earnings Multiplier} = (1 - .40)/(.14 - .06) = 7.5 \text{ times}$$

Thus, expected earnings of \$6.67 coupled with an earnings multiplier of 7.5 values our common stock at \$50 a share (\$6.67 × 7.5 = \$50). But remember, the foundation for this alternative approach to common stock valuation was nevertheless our constant growth dividend discount model.

No Growth. A special case of the constant growth dividend model calls for an expected dividend growth rate, *g*, of zero. Here the assumption is that dividends will be maintained at their current level forever. In this case, Eq. (16-14) reduces to

$$V = D_1/k_e \quad (16\text{-}19)$$

Not many stocks can be expected simply to maintain a constant dividend forever. However, when a stable dividend is expected to be maintained for a long period of time, Eq. (16-19) can provide a good approximation of value.[7]

[7]AT&T is one example of a firm that maintained a stable dividend for an extended period of time. For 36 years, from 1922 until December 1958, AT&T paid \$9 a year in dividends.

TABLE 16-1 Two-phase Growth and Common Stock Valuation Calculations

Phase 1: Present Value of Dividends to be Received Over First 5 Years

End of Year	Present Value Calculation (Dividend	×	$PVIF_{14\%,t}$)		Present Value of Dividend
1	$\$2(1.10)^1 = \$2.20$	×	.877	=	$1.93
2	$2(1.10)^2 = 2.42$	×	.769	=	1.86
3	$2(1.10)^3 = 2.66$	×	.675	=	1.80
4	$2(1.10)^4 = 2.93$	×	.592	=	1.73
5	$2(1.10)^5 = 3.22$	×	.519	=	1.67
		or	$\left[\sum_{t=1}^{5} \frac{\$2(1.10)^t}{(1.14)^t}\right]$	=	**$8.99**

Phase 2: Present Value of Constant Growth Component

Dividend at the end of year 6 = $3.22(1.06) = $3.41

Value of stock at the end of year 5 $= \frac{D_6}{(k_e - g)} = \frac{\$3.41}{(.14 - .06)} = \mathbf{\$42.63}$

Present value of $42.63 at end of year 5 $= (\$42.63)(PVIF_{14\%,5})$

$= (\$42.63)(.519) = \mathbf{\$22.13}$

Present Value of Stock

$V = \$8.99 + \$22.13 = \mathbf{\$31.12}$

Growth Phases. When the pattern of expected dividend growth is such that a constant growth model is not appropriate, modifications of Eq. (16-13) can be used. A number of valuation models are based on the premise that firms may exhibit above-normal growth for a number of years (g may even be larger than k_e during this phase), but eventually the growth rate will taper off. Thus, the transition might well be from a presently above-normal growth rate to one that is considered normal. If dividends per share are expected to grow at a 10 percent compound rate for five years and thereafter at a 6 percent rate, Eq. (16-13) becomes

$$V = \sum_{t=1}^{5} \frac{D_0(1.10)^t}{(1 + k_e)^t} + \sum_{t=6}^{\infty} \frac{D_5(1.06)^{t-5}}{(1 + k_e)^t} \tag{16-20}$$

Note that the growth in dividends in the second phase uses the expected dividend in period 5 as its foundation. Therefore, the growth-term exponent is $t - 5$, which means that the exponent in period 6 equals 1, in period 7 it equals 2, and so forth. This second phase is nothing more than a constant growth model following a period of above-normal growth. We can make use of that fact to rewrite Eq. (16-20) as follows:

$$V = \sum_{t=1}^{5} \frac{D_0(1.10)^t}{(1 + k_e)^t} + \left[\frac{1}{(1 + k_e)^5}\right]\left[\frac{D_6}{(k_e - .06)}\right] \tag{16-21}$$

If the current dividend, D_0, is $2 per share and the required rate of return, k_e, is 14 percent, we could solve for V. (See Table 16-1 for specifics.)

$$V = \sum_{t=1}^{5} \frac{\$2(1.10)^t}{(1.14)^t} + \left[\frac{1}{(1.14)^5}\right]\left[\frac{\$3.41}{(.14 - .06)}\right]$$
$$= \$8.99 + \$22.13 = \$31.12$$

The transition from an above-normal rate of dividend growth could be specified as more gradual than the two-phase approach just illustrated. We might expect dividends to grow at a 10 percent rate for five years, followed by an 8 percent rate for the next five years and a 6 percent growth rate thereafter. The more growth segments that are added, the more closely the growth in dividends will approach a curvilinear function. But, no firm can grow at an above-normal rate forever. Typically, companies tend to grow at a very high rate initially, after which their growth opportunities slow down to a rate that is normal for companies in general. If maturity is reached, the growth rate may stop altogether.

RATES OF RETURN (OR YIELDS)

So far, this chapter has illustrated how the valuation of any long-term financial instrument involves a capitalization of that security's income stream by a discount rate (or *required rate of return*) appropriate for that security's risk. If we replace intrinsic value (V) in our valuation equations with the market price (P_0) of the security, we can then solve for the *market required rate of return.* This rate, which sets the discounted value of the expected cash inflows equal to the security's current market price, is also referred to as the security's (market) *yield.* Depending on the security being analyzed, the expected cash inflows may be interest payments, repayment of principal, or dividend payments. It is important to recognize that only when the intrinsic value of a security to an investor equals the security's market value (price) would the investor's required rate of return equal the security's (market) yield.

Market yields serve an essential function by allowing us to compare, on a uniform basis, securities that differ in cash flows provided, maturities, and current prices.

Yield to Maturity (YTM) on Bonds

The market required rate of return on a bond (k_d) is more commonly referred to as the bond's yield to maturity. **Yield to maturity (YTM)** is the expected rate of return on a bond if bought at its current market price and held to maturity; it is also known as the bond's *internal rate of return.* Mathematically, it is the discount rate that equates the present value of all expected interest payments and the payment of principal (face value) at maturity with the bond's current market price. For an example, let's return to Eq. (16-4), the valuation equation for an interest-bearing bond with a finite maturity. Replacing intrinsic value (V) with current market price (P_0) gives us

Yield to maturity (YTM) The expected rate of return on a bond if bought at its current market price and held to maturity.

$$P_0 = \sum_{t=1}^{n} \frac{I}{(1 + k_d)^t} + \frac{MV}{(1 + k_d)^n} \quad \text{(16-22)}$$

If we now substitute actual values for I, MV, and P_0, we can solve for k_d, which in this case would be the bond's yield to maturity. However, the precise calculation for yield to maturity is rather complex and either requires bond value tables, a sophisticated hand-held calculator, or a computer.

Interpolation. If all we have to work with are present value tables, we can still determine an approximation of the yield to maturity by making use of a trial-and-error procedure. To illustrate, consider a $1,000-par-value bond with the following characteristics: a current market price of $761; 12 years until maturity; and an 8 percent coupon rate (with interest paid annually). We want to determine the discount rate that sets the present value of the bond's expected future cash-flow stream equal to the bond's current market price. Suppose that we start with a 10 percent discount rate and calculate the present value of the bond's expected future cash flows. For the appropriate present value interest factors, we make use of Appendices C & E at the end of the book.

$$\begin{aligned} V &= \$80\,(PVIFA_{10\%,12}) + \$1{,}000\,(PVIF_{10\%,12}) \\ &= \$80(6.814) + \$1{,}000(.319) = \$864.12 \end{aligned}$$

A 10 percent discount rate produces a resulting present value for the bond that is greater than the current market price of $761. Therefore, we need to try a higher discount rate in order to handicap further the future cash flows and drive their present value down to $761. Let's try a 15 percent discount rate.

$$\begin{aligned} V &= \$80(PVIFA_{15\%,12}) + \$1{,}000\,(PVIF_{15\%,12}) \\ &= \$80(5.421) + \$1{,}000(.187) = \$620.68 \end{aligned}$$

This time the chosen discount rate was too large. The resulting present value is less than the current market price of $761. The rate necessary to discount the bond's expected cash flows to $761 must fall somewhere between 10 and 15 percent.

Interpolate Estimate an unknown number that lies somewhere between two known numbers.

To approximate this discount rate, we **interpolate** between 10 and 15 percent as follows:

$$.05\left[\; X\left[\begin{array}{ll} .10 & \$864.12 \\ YTM & \$761.00 \end{array}\right]\$103.12 \atop \begin{array}{ll} .15 & \$620.68 \end{array}\right]\$243.44$$

$$\frac{X}{.05} = \frac{\$103.12}{\$243.44} \quad \text{Therefore, } X = \frac{(.05) \times (\$103.12)}{\$243.44} = .0212$$

In this example $X = YTM - .10$. Therefore, $YTM = .10 + X = .10 + .0212 = .1212$, or **12.12 percent.** The use of a computer provides a precise yield to maturity of 11.82 percent. It is important to keep in mind that interpolation gives only an approximation of the exact percentage; the relationship between the two discount rates is not linear with respect to present value. However, the tighter the range of discount rates that we use in interpolation, the closer the resulting answer will be to the mathematically correct one. For example, had we used 11 and 12 percent, we would have come even closer to the "true" yield to maturity.

Behavior of Bond Prices. On the basis of an understanding of Eq. (16-22), a number of observations can be made concerning bond prices:

1. When the market required rate of return is *more* than the stated coupon rate, the price of the bond will be *less* than its face value. Such a bond is said to be selling at a *discount* from face value. The amount by which the face value exceeds the current price is the **bond discount.**
2. When the market required rate of return is *less* than the stated coupon rate, the price of the bond will be *more* than its face value. Such a bond is said to be selling at a *premium* over face value. The amount by which the current price exceeds the face value is the **bond premium.**
3. When the market required rate of return *equals* the stated coupon rate, the price of the bond will *equal* its face value. Such a bond is said to be selling at *par.*
4. If interest rates *rise* so that the market required rate of return *increases,* the bond's price will *fall.* If interest rates *fall,* the bond's price will *increase.* In short, interest rates and bond prices move in opposite directions.

Bond discount
The amount by which the face value of a bond exceeds its current price.

Bond premium
The amount by which the current price of a bond exceeds its face value.

From the last observation, it is clear that variability in interest rates should lead to variability in bond prices. This variation in the market price of a security caused by changes in interest rates is referred to as **interest-rate (or yield) risk.** It is important to note that an investor incurs a loss due to interest-rate (or yield) risk only if a security is sold prior to maturity *and* the level of interest rates has increased since time of purchase.

Interest-rate (or yield) risk
The variation in the market price of a security caused by changes in interest rates.

A further relationship, not as apparent as the previous four observations, needs to be illustrated separately.

5. For a given change in market required return, the price of a bond will change by a greater amount, the longer its maturity.

In general, the longer the maturity, the greater the price fluctuation associated with a given change in market required return. The closer in time that you are to this relatively large maturity value being realized, the less important are interest payments in determining the market price, and the less important is a change in market required return on the market price of the security. In general, then, the longer the maturity of a bond, the greater the risk of price change to the investor when changes occur in the overall level of interest rates.

Figure 16-1 illustrates our discussion by comparing two bonds which differ only in maturity. The price sensitivities of a 5-year bond and a 15-year bond are shown relative to changes in market required rate of return. As expected, the bond with the longer term to maturity shows a greater change in price for any given change in market yield. (All points on the two curves are based on the use of pricing Eq. (16-22).)

One last relationship also needs to be addressed separately, and it is known as the *coupon effect.*

6. For a given change in market required rate of return, the price of a bond will change by proportionally more, the lower the coupon rate. In other words, bond price volatility is *inversely* related to coupon rate.

The reason for this effect is that the lower the coupon rate, the more return to the investor is reflected in the principal payment at maturity as opposed to interim interest payments. Put another way, investors realize their returns later with a low-coupon-rate bond than with a high-coupon-rate bond. In general, the further in the future the bulk of the payment stream, the greater the present value effect caused by

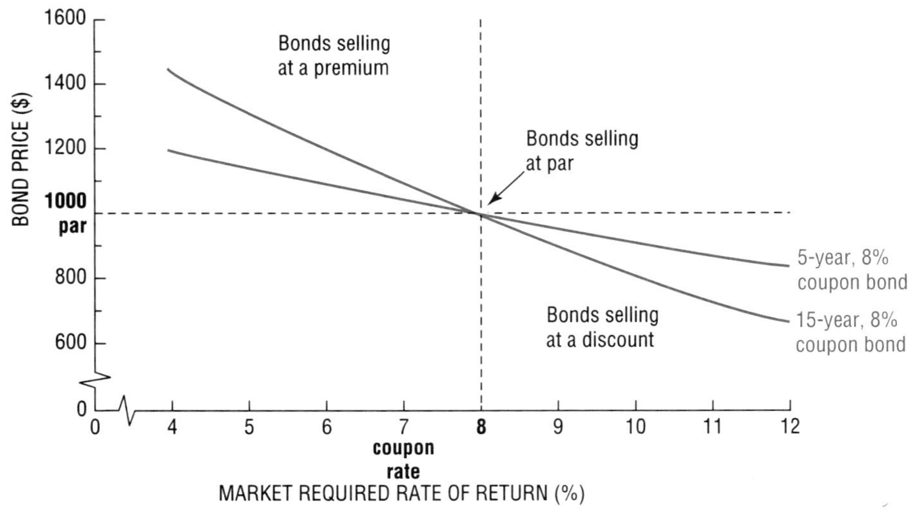

FIGURE 16-1
Price-yield relationship for two bonds where each price-yield curve represents a set of prices for that bond for different assumed market required rates of return (market yields)

a change in required return.[8] Even if high- and low-coupon-rate bonds have the same maturity, the price of the low-coupon-rate bond tends to be more volatile.

YTM and Semiannual Compounding. As previously mentioned, most domestic bonds pay interest twice a year, not once. This real-world complication is often ignored in an attempt to simplify discussion. We can take semiannual interest payments into account, however, when determining yield to maturity by replacing intrinsic value (V) with current market price (P_0) in bond valuation Eq. (16-8). The result is

$$P_0 = \sum_{t=1}^{2n} \frac{I/2}{(1 + k_d/2)^t} + \frac{MV}{(1 + k_d/2)^{2n}} \tag{16-24}$$

Solving for $k_d/2$ in this equation would give us the semiannual yield to maturity.

The practice of doubling the semiannual *YTM* has been adopted by convention in bond circles to provide the (annual) *YTM*. The appropriate procedure, however, would be to square "1 plus the semiannual *YTM*" and then subtract 1, that is,

$$(1 + \text{semiannual } YTM)^2 - 1 = (\text{true annual})\ YTM$$

[8]The interested reader is referred to James C. Van Horne, *Financial Market Rates and Flows*, 4th ed. (Englewood Cliffs, NJ: Prentice Hall, 1994), Chap. 6.

Yield on Preferred Stock

Substituting current market price (P_0) for intrinsic value (V) in preferred stock valuation Eq. (16-10), we have

$$P_0 = D_p/k_p \tag{16-25}$$

where D_p is still the stated annual dividend per share of preferred stock, but k_p is now the market required return for this stock, or simply the yield on preferred stock. Rearranging terms allows us to solve directly for the yield on preferred stock.

$$k_p = D_p/P_0 \tag{16-26}$$

To illustrate, assume that the current market price per share of Acme Zarf Company's 10 percent, \$100-par-value preferred stock is \$91.25. Acme's preferred stock is, therefore, priced to provide a yield of

$$k_p = \$10/\$91.25 = 10.96\%$$

Yield on Common Stock

The rate of return that sets the discounted value of the expected cash dividends from a share of common stock equal to the share's current market price is the yield on that common stock. If, for example, the constant dividend growth model was appropriate to apply to the stock of a particular company, the current market price (P_0) could be said to be

$$P_0 = D_1/(k_e - g) \tag{16-27}$$

Solving for k_e, which in this case is the market-determined yield on a company's common stock, we get

$$k_e = D_1/P_0 + g \tag{16-28}$$

From this last expression, it becomes clear that the yield on common stock comes from two sources. The first source is the expected *dividend yield*, D_1/P_0; while the second source, g, is the expected *capital gains yield*. Yes, g wears a number of hats. It is the expected compound annual growth rate in dividends. But given this model, it is also the expected annual percent change in stock price (that is, $P_1/P_0 - 1 = g$) and, as such, is referred to as the capital gains yield.

Q **What market yield is implied by a share of common stock currently selling for \$40 whose dividends are expected to grow at a rate of 9 percent per year and whose dividend next year is expected to be \$2.40?**

A The market yield, k_e, is equal to the dividend yield, D_1/P_0, plus the capital gains yield, g, as follows:

$$k_e = \$2.40/\$40 + .09 = .06 + .09 = \mathbf{15\%}$$

Summary Table of Key Present Value Formulas For Valuing Long-Term Securities (Annual Cash Flows Assumed)	
Securities	**Equation**
Bonds	
1. Perpetual	
$V = \sum_{t=1}^{\infty} \frac{I}{(1+k_d)^t} = \frac{I}{k_d}$	(16-1), (16-3)
2. Finite maturity, non-zero coupon	
$V = \sum_{t=1}^{n} \frac{I}{(1+k_d)^t} + \frac{MV}{(1+k_d)^n}$	(16-4)
$= I(PVIFA_{k_d,n}) + MV(PVIF_{k_d,n})$	(16-5)
3. Zero coupon	
$V = \frac{MV}{(1+k_d)^n}$	(16-6)
$= MV(PVIF_{k_d,n})$	(16-7)
Preferred Stock	
1. No call expected	
$V = \sum_{t=1}^{\infty} \frac{D_p}{(1+k_p)^t} = \frac{D_p}{k_p}$	(16-10)
2. Call expected at n	
$V = \sum_{t=1}^{n} \frac{D_p}{(1+k_p)^t} + \frac{\text{call price}}{(1+k_p)^n}$	
$= D_p(PVIFA_{k_p,n}) + (\text{call price})(PVIF_{k_p,n})$	
Common Stock	
Constant growth	
$V = \sum_{t=1}^{\infty} \frac{D_0(1+g)^t}{(1+k_e)^t} = \frac{D_1}{(k_e - g)}$	(16-14)

SUMMARY

- The concept of value includes *liquidation value, going-concern value, book value, market value,* and *intrinsic value.*
- The valuation approach taken in this chapter is one of determining a security's *intrinsic value*—what the security ought to be worth based on hard facts. This value is the present value of the cash-flow stream provided to the investor, discounted at a required rate of return appropriate for the risk involved.
- The intrinsic value of a *perpetual bond* is simply the capitalized value of an infinite stream of interest payments. This present value is the periodic interest payment divided by the investor's required rate of return.
- The intrinsic value of an *interest-bearing bond* with a finite maturity is equal to the present value of the interest payments plus the present value of principal payment at maturity, all discounted at the investor's required rate of return.

- The intrinsic value of a *zero-coupon bond* (a bond that makes no periodic interest payments) is the present value of the principal payment at maturity, discounted at the investor's required rate of return.
- The intrinsic value of *preferred stock* is equal to the stated annual dividend per share divided by the investor's required rate of return.
- Unlike bonds and preferred stock for which the future cash flows are contractually stated, much more uncertainty surrounds the future stream of returns connected with common stock
- The intrinsic value of a share of *common stock* can be viewed as the discounted value of all the cash dividends provided by the issuing firm.
- Dividend discount models are designed to compute the intrinsic value of a share of stock under specific assumptions as to the expected growth pattern of future dividends and the appropriate discount rate to employ.
- If dividends are expected to grow at a constant rate, the formula used to calculate the intrinsic value of a share of common stock is

$$V = D_1/(k_e - g) \quad (16\text{-}14)$$

- In the case of no expected dividend growth, the equation above reduces to

$$V = D_1/k_e \quad (16\text{-}19)$$

- Finally, when dividend growth is expected to differ during various phases of a firm's development, the present value of dividends for various growth phases can be determined and summed to produce the stock's intrinsic value.
- If intrinsic value (V) in our valuation equations is replaced with the security's market price (P_0), we can then solve for the *market required rate of return*. This rate, which sets the discounted value of the expected cash inflows equal to the security's market price, is also referred to as the security's (market) *yield*.
- *Yield to maturity* (*YTM*) is the expected rate of return on a bond if bought at its current market price and held to maturity. It is also known as the bond's *internal rate of return*.
- Interest rates and bond prices move in opposite directions.
- In general, the longer the maturity for a bond, the greater the bond's price fluctuation associated with a given change in market required return.
- The lower the coupon rate, the more sensitive that relative bond price changes are to changes in market yields.
- The yield on common stock comes from two sources. The first source is the expected *dividend yield*, while the second source is the expected *capital gains yield*.

QUESTIONS

1. What connection, if any, does a firm's *market value* have with its *liquidation* and/or *going-concern value?*
2. Could a security's *intrinsic value* to an investor ever differ from the security's *market value?* If so, under what circumstances?
3. In what sense is the treatment of bonds and preferred stock the same when it comes to valuation?
4. Why do bonds with long maturities fluctuate more in price than do bonds with short maturities, given the same change in yield to maturity?

5. A 20-year bond has a coupon rate of 8 percent, and another bond of the same maturity has a coupon rate of 15 percent. If the bonds are alike in all other respects, which will have the greater relative market price decline if interest rates increase sharply? Why?
6. Why are dividends the basis for the valuation of common stock?
7. Suppose that the controlling stock of IBM Corporation was placed in a perpetual trust with an irrevocable clause that cash or liquidating dividends would never be paid out of this trust. Earnings per share continued to grow. What would be the value of the company to the stockholders? Why?
8. Why is the growth rate in earnings and dividends of a company likely to taper off in the future? Could the growth rate increase as well? If it did, what would be the effect on stock price?
9. Using the constant perpetual growth dividend valuation model, could you have a situation in which a company grows at 30 percent per year (after subtracting out inflation) forever? Explain.
10. Tammy Whynot, a classmate of yours, suggests that when the constant growth dividend valuation model is used to explain a stock's current price, the quantity $(k_e - g)$ represents the expected dividend yield. Is she right or wrong? Explain.
11. **"$1,000 U.S. Government Treasury Bond FREE! with any $999 Purchase"** shouted the headline of an ad from a local furniture company. "WOW! Like, for sure, this is like getting the furniture like free," said your friend Heather Dawn Tiffany. What Heather overlooked was the fine print in the ad where you learned that the "free" bond was a zero-coupon issue with a 30-year maturity. Explain to Heather why the "free" $1,000 bond is more in the nature of an advertising "come-on" rather than something of large value.

SELF-CORRECTION PROBLEMS

1. Fast and Loose Company has outstanding an 8 percent, four-year, $1,000-par-value bond on which interest is paid annually.
   a. If the market required rate of return is 15 percent, what is the market value of the bond?
   b. What would be its market value if the market required return dropped to 12 percent? To 8 percent?
   c. If the coupon rate were 15 percent instead of 8 percent, what would be the market value (under Part (a))? If the required rate of return dropped to 8 percent, what would happen to the market price of the bond?
2. James Consol Company presently pays a dividend of $1.60 per share on its common stock. The company expects to increase the dividend at a 20 percent annual rate the first four years and at a 13 percent rate the next four years and then grow the dividend at a 7 percent rate thereafter. This phased-growth pattern is in keeping with the expected life cycle of earnings. You require a 16 percent return to invest in this stock. What value should you place on a share of this stock?
3. A $1,000-face-value bond has a current market price of $935, an 8 percent coupon rate, and 10 remaining years until maturity. Interest payments are made

semiannually. Before you do any calculations, decide if the yield to maturity is above or below the coupon rate. Why? What is the yield to maturity?

PROBLEMS

1. Gonzalez Electric Company has outstanding a 10 percent bond issue with a face value of $1,000 per bond and three years to maturity. Interest is payable annually. The bonds are privately held by Suresafe Fire Insurance Company. Suresafe wishes to sell the bonds and is negotiating with another party. It estimates that in current market conditions, the bonds should provide a return of 14 percent (yield to maturity). What price per bond should Suresafe be able to realize on the sale?
2. What would be the price per bond in Problem 1 if interest payments were made semiannually?
3. Superior Cement Company has an 8 percent preferred stock issue outstanding, with each share having a $100 face value. Currently, the yield is 10 percent. What is the market price per share? If interest rates in general should rise so that the required return becomes 12 percent, what will happen to the market price per share?
4. The stock of the Health Corporation is currently selling for $20 a share and is expected to pay a $1 dividend at the end of the year. If you bought the stock now and sold it for $23 after receiving the dividend, what rate of return would you earn?
5. Delphi Products Corporation currently pays a dividend of $2 per share, and this dividend is expected to grow at a 15 percent annual rate for three years, then at a 10 percent rate for the next three years, after which it is expected to grow at a 5 percent rate forever. What value would you place on the stock if an 18 percent rate of return was required?
6. North Great Timber Company will pay a dividend of $1.50 a share next year. After this, earnings and dividends are expected to grow at a 9 percent annual rate indefinitely. Investors presently require a rate of return of 13 percent. The company is considering several business strategies and wishes to determine the effect of these strategies on the market price per share of its stock.
   a. Continuing the present strategy will result in the expected growth rate and required rate of return stated above.
   b. Expanding timber holdings and sales will increase the expected dividend growth rate to 11 percent but will increase the risk of the company. As a result, the rate of return required by investors will increase to 16 percent.
   c. Integrating into retail stores will increase the dividend growth rate to 10 percent and increase the required rate of return to 14 percent.

   From the standpoint of market price per share, which strategy is best?
7. A share of preferred stock for the Buford Pusser Baseball Bat Company just sold for $100 and carries an $8 annual dividend.
   a. What is the yield on this stock?
   b. Now assume that this stock has a call price of $110 in five years, when the company intends to call the issue. (Note: The preferred stock in this case should not be treated as a perpetual—it will be bought back in five years for $110.) What is this preferred stock's *yield to call?*

SOLUTIONS TO SELF-CORRECTION PROBLEMS

1. a,b.

End of Year	Payment	Discount Factor, 15%	Present Value, 15%	Discount Factor, 12%	Present Value, 12%
1-3	$ 80	2.283	$182.64	2.402	$192.16
4	1,080	.572	617.76	.636	686.88
	Market value		**$800.40**		**$879.04**

Note: Rounding error incurred by use of tables may sometimes cause slight differences in answers when alternative solution methods are applied to the same cash flows.

The market value of an 8 percent bond yielding 8 percent is its face value, of **$1,000.**

c. The market value would be **$1,000** if the required return were 15 percent.

End of Year	Payment	Discount Factor, 8%	Present Value, 8%
1-3	$ 150	2.577	$ 386.55
4	1,150	.735	845.25
	Market value		**$1,231.80**

2.

Phases 1 & 2: Present Value of Dividends To Be Received Over First 8 Years

	End of Year	Present Value Calculation (Dividend	×	$PVIF_{16\%,t}$)		Present Value of Dividend
Phase 1	1	$\$1.60(1.20)^1 = \$1.92$	×	.862	=	$ 1.66
	2	$1.60(1.20)^2 = 2.30$	×	.743	=	1.71
	3	$1.60(1.20)^3 = 2.76$	×	.641	=	1.77
	4	$1.60(1.20)^4 = 3.32$	×	.552	=	1.83
Phase 2	5	$3.32(1.13)^1 = 3.75$	×	.476	=	1.79
	6	$3.32(1.13)^2 = 4.24$	×	.410	=	1.74
	7	$3.32(1.13)^3 = 4.79$	×	.354	=	1.70
	8	$3.32(1.13)^4 = 5.41$	×	.305	=	1.65
			or	$\left[\sum_{t=1}^{8} \frac{D_t}{(1.16)^t}\right]$	=	**$13.85**

Phase 3: Present Value of Constant Growth Component

Dividend at the end of year 9 $= \$5.41(1.07) = \$5.79$

Value of stock at the end of year 8 $= \dfrac{D_9}{(k_e - g)} = \dfrac{\$5.79}{(.16 - .07)} = \$64.33$

Present value of $64.33 at end of year 8 $= (\$64.33)(PVIF_{16\%,8})$

$= (\$64.33)(.305) =$ **$19.62**

Present Value of Stock

$V = \$13.85 + \$19.62 =$ **$33.47**

3. The yield to maturity is higher than the coupon rate of 8 percent because the bond sells at a discount from its face value. The yield to maturity as reported in bond circles is 9 percent (2 × semiannual YTM). (The true yield to maturity is 9.2025 percent—$(1 + .045)^2 - 1$.) The problem is set up as follows:

$$\$935 = \sum_{t=1}^{20} \frac{\$40}{(1 + k_d/2)^t} + \frac{\$1{,}000}{(1 + k_d/2)^{20}}$$
$$= (\$40)(PVIFA_{k_d/2,20}) + MV(PVIF_{k_d/2,20})$$

Solving for $k_d/2$ (the semiannual YTM) in this expression using a calculator, a computer routine, or present value tables yields 4.5 percent; the YTM is then 2 × 4.5 percent = **9%.**

SELECTED REFERENCES

Bauman, W. Scott. "Investment Returns and Present Values." *Financial Analysts Journal* 25 (November-December 1969), 107–18.

Chew, I. Keong, and Ronnie J. Clayton. "Bond Valuation: A Clarification." *The Financial Review* 18 (May 1983), 234–36.

Fuller, Russell J., and Chi-Cheng Hsia. "A Simplified Model for Estimating Stock Prices of Growth Firms." *Financial Analysts Journal* 40 (September–October 1984), 49–56.

Gordon, Myron J. *The Investment, Financing, and Valuation of the Corporation.* Homewood, IL: Richard D. Irwin, 1962.

Haugen, Robert A. *Modern Investment Theory,* 2nd ed. Englewood Cliffs, NJ: Prentice Hall, 1990.

Reilly, Frank K. *Investment Analysis and Portfolio Management,* 3rd ed. Hinsdale, IL: Dryden, 1988.

Sharpe, William F., and Gordon J. Alexander. *Investments,* 4th ed. Englewood Cliffs, NJ: Prentice Hall, 1990.

Siegel, Jeremy J. "The Application of the DCF Methodology for Determining the Cost of Equity Capital." *Financial Management* 14 (Spring 1985), 46–53.

Van Horne, James C. *Financial Market Rates and Flows,* 4th ed. Englewood Cliffs, NJ: Prentice Hall, 1994.

Williams, John B. *The Theory of Investment Value.* Cambridge, MA: Harvard University Press, 1938.

SECTION VII

Cost of Capital, Financing Mix and Dividend Policy

CHAPTER 17

Creating Shareholder Value

"Two years ago, Sears was the nation's largest retailer. It's now number three. Its share price today is less than it was in 1986. In my opinion the reputation of the Sears Board of Directors also has fallen, due largely to its lack of energy and interest in making management accountable to shareholders. Make no mistake, a board's value translates into stock price." So wrote Robert Monks, a Sears shareholder, urging all Sears shareholders to vote for proposals he had placed on the agenda for the next shareholders' meeting.[1] Robert Monk was actively soliciting votes to force Sears's management and board of directors to focus on creating shareholder value.

While many corporate executives talk about shareholder value in their annual reports and speeches, most have not made it part of their everyday business decisions. It is easier to state the objective than it is to fulfill it in practice. Companies take different approaches to increasing shareholder value. For example, the 1984 annual report of Coca-Cola states that "to increase shareholder value over time is the objective driving this enterprise." The next page of the report mentions that to accomplish this objective "growth in annual earnings per share and increased return on equity are still the names of the game." In contrast, Georgia-Pacific Corporation says the way to provide superior return to its shareholders is to focus on creating shareholder value through the generation of *free cash flow*, which is cash flow from operations less normal investments (see Figure 17-1). The 1984 annual report of Hillenbrand Industries takes a similar position. It explains that shareholder value "is created when a company generates free cash flow in excess of the shareholders' investment in the business."

The point is that although each company states that its objective is to increase shareholder value, Coca-Cola attempts to accomplish the objective by emphasizing

[1]See the proxy solicitation by Robert Monk in *The Wall Street Journal*, May 8, 1992, p. A13.

THE ONLY YARDSTICK THAT COUNTS.

Much has been written about various ways to measure corporate performance. But over the years, the odds-on favorite would have to be earnings.

We think that a focus on earnings misses a much more relevant factor.

Free cash flow.

And once again, we expect ours to remain strong. Extremely strong. In fact, in a year when business has certainly not been booming, our free cash flow will run close to $1 billion. And we expect that number to average substantially more in the coming years.

And the point?

Cash, not earnings, has put us on the fast track to debt reduction. In fact, between cash from operations and the sales of certain non-strategic assets, we're well ahead of schedule. Which means we're adding economic value to the company more quickly than many thought we could.

To be sure, there are as many opinions on the subject of how best to judge value as there are people to pen them. But we think we'll stick with cash. It sure works for us.

And we think it works for our shareholders.

Georgia-Pacific

FIGURE 17-1
The only yardstick that counts

accounting indicators, whereas Georgia-Pacific and Hillenbrand emphasize cash flow. The accounting approach is fraught with problems. Accounting numbers are fairly elastic, since management has much flexibility in how it wants to record transactions.[2] Cash flow, however, is the basis for valuing assets.

Our purpose in this chapter is to make the transition from the broader discussion of financial markets and the valuation of securities to the valuation of the firm. When you have completed this chapter, you should understand:

- How the firm's value is affected by the exchange of values between it and its customers and suppliers.
- The agency problem, or the series of conflicts that exist in the value-exchange system.
- How the interaction between the firm's investment opportunities and market rates affect the value of the firm.
- What causes a firm's value to increase, decline, or remain constant.
- How to calculate the value of the firm.

THE CORPORATE VALUE-EXCHANGE SYSTEM

A modern corporation is an interrelated set of contracts among several different groups: customers, employees, governments, investors, and vendors. Each group willingly enters into a contract with the expectation of receiving something of value from the arrangement. The exchange of values between the firm and the various parties can be summarized as follows. Suppliers provide inputs (values) to the firm, which are processed by the firm into products and services and ultimately supplied to customers in exchange for money. The firm uses the funds received from customers to help support its operations and satisfy obligations to suppliers: wages and benefits to employees in exchange for productive labor, technical skills, or management; payments to vendors for quality materials or services; interest and principal payments to creditors for use of their funds; taxes to governments; and dividends to shareholders.

The following Financial Reality article outlines how Cooper Industries, a firm with over $6 billion in sales, views its value-exchange system. The last sentence of the reading ends by stating that the key objective of the value-exchange system is to enhance shareholder wealth. This objective is not easy to meet. In reality, conflicts among various participants of the value-exchange system impede satisfying the shareholder-wealth-maximization objective.

The source of the conflict between consumers and the firm is rooted in whether the consumer can rely on the firm to fulfill its obligations in terms of providing adequate products or services now and in the future. The reputation of the firm, which translates into economic value for shareholders, is the issue at stake. A firm with a low reputation faces extreme difficulty in encouraging consumers to buy its products. For example, American Express lost more than two million cardholders in the early 1990s because management failed to understand that consumers preferred

[2]You may recall from your accounting classes that several different ways exist to record sales (percent of completion, installment, or point of sale). Each method results in different revenues for the period. Differences in recording costs also exist. Does the firm use straight-line depreciation or some accelerated method? Should bad debt expense be, say, 3 percent or 4 percent of sales? Should inventory be recorded using first-in, first-out or last-in, first-out methods? These are only a sample of the many alternatives available to management.

Financial Reality

BEST VALUE DELIVERED

Cooper Industries is in the business of creating value for its customers and shareholders. Management asserts that customers buy Cooper's products and shareholders invest in the company because they judge Cooper to provide value.

What constitutes value?

The word is elusive. It defies easy definition. The problem is that most efforts at definition make it seem very abstract or highly subjective, while to most customers, value is something much simpler. However hard to articulate, they know it when they see it.

Economists have attempted to quantify value by talking of "units of satisfaction" or "utils." While this may be helpful to economists, it is of little help to a manufacturer competing in the real world for a customer's order. The one clear message that emerges is that the customers are not just the ultimate judges of value, they are the only judges who count. The customers we know don't sit down and calculate the units of satisfaction they expect from a product, but they do look for value—and they either find it, or they don't. When they don't, we lose a customer.

In any case, the fact that something is hard to define doesn't mean it isn't quite real and very important.

Value comes in many forms. For some buyers, value simply means the lowest price; for them, that's the end of the discussion. Otherswill settle for nothing less than the highest quality, never mind the cost. Those are the extremes. More typically, price and quality are just two of the elements of value.

Customers also assign value to such criteria as design, performance, durability, delivery, safety and service or to less tangible factors, such as a manufacturer's reputation, or the comfort level that comes with doing business with one company with an established reputation rather than another. Since value reflects what something is worth to the customer *as seen through the customer's eyes,* success in manufacturing is determined by the ability to look outward to the marketplace. That's how manufacturers create value—by attending closely to the needs of their customers. An inward concentration on costs, organization, management, and facilities is also necessary—but only to the extent it adds or creates value for the customer.

There are, indeed, examples in which the sole determinant of value is cost or selling price. But they rarely involve manufactured products. They are more likely to be about commodities, such as copper, which have a world price that moves up or down depending on supply or demand. The copper one buys will be of a prescribed standard quality, no matter where it was mined, by whom, or how. Only when it passes through the hands of a fabricator and value is added does the raw material emerge as a unique and distinguishable product.

At Cooper, we are in the business of making products that deliver value. We add value to commodities by manufacturing thousands of useful and necessary products. Our challenge is to make them so different that our customers, for one reason or another, consider them to be of greater value than those available elsewhere. Our goal is to provide consistently the best value delivered.

We believe that a constant focus on providing value to our customers is the key to improved earnings and, consequently, to meeting our other objective of providing shareholders with a superior return on their investment.

Source: Cooper Industries 1991 Annual Report, pp. 13–15. Used by permission.

TABLE 17-1 Importance of Financial Objectives

Rank	Objective
1	Maximize percentage return on assets
2	Maximize earnings or earnings per share
3	Target share of the market
4	Maximize stock price
5	Target growth rate in earnings per share

Source: R. H. Pike, "Owner-Manager Conflict and the Role of the Payback Method," Accounting and Business Research *(Winter) 1985), pp. 47–51.*

value to prestige. Consumers wanted "plastic" that could be used anywhere, not just in fine restaurants and upscale retail stores. Consumer unrest was considered a major reason for significant decline in the stock price of American Express during this period.

Labor and vendor conflicts can cause serious problems for the firm. Lost production due to employee strikes or vendors' unwillingness to ship materials may result in lost customers because of unavailability of product. If the problems are well publicized, customers may also boycott the firm in sympathy with the employees or vendors.

Investor conflicts may arise if some investors perceive the firm to be less socially responsible than they would like. These investors are known to sell their securities because a company operates in a racially troubled country, because a firm manufactures war materials, or because it is a heavy industrial polluter. Johnson & Johnson Company created a dilemma for socially responsible investors. J&J has long been recognized as a business committed to its employees and communities. It was one of the first corporations to endorse the rights of individuals diagnosed with the AIDS virus. The company receives praise for its child-care programs, sick-care services, and flextime for employees. However, Johnson & Johnson is the fifth largest corporate user of animals in testing.[3] Can socially conscientious investors adversely affect the value of Johnson & Johnson's stock price? Unlikely, but the firm's management dislikes negative publicity.

COMPREHENSION CHECK

1. *Describe the corporate value-exchange system.*

PRINCIPAL-AGENT PROBLEMS

An aspect of the corporation's value-exchange system that is of great interest to the study of finance is the principal-agent problem that exists between shareholders and management. A survey of finance officers in the largest British companies found that maximization of shareholders' wealth is neither the only goal of management nor is it the most important. The results summarized in Table 17-1 show that maxi-

[3]The source of this information is John C. Harrington, *Investing with Your Conscience* (New York: John Wiley & Sons, Inc., 1992), p. 122.

mization of stock price (that is, shareholder wealth) ranks fourth. An earlier study in the United States found similar results.[4]

A much-debated reason that maximization of shareholder wealth may not be of top priority with many managers is because a *separation of ownership from management* exists in most publicly traded firms. Separation of ownership from management means that responsibility for administering companies is conferred to professional managers (agents). These managers effectively control the firm by their decisions, even though shareholders (principals) are the legal owners. Since the ownership of shares in large firms is often diffused, most individual shareholders have neither influence on, nor interest in, corporate governance issues such as the election of board members. Therefore, boards are largely responsive to management. Management, in turn, can ignore shareholders and run companies as it sees fit.

For example, the annual shareholder meeting is not an open forum for discussion. With the permission of the U.S. Securities and Exchange Commission (SEC), the firm places curbs on proposals made from the floor. In particular, unless a shareholder owns at least $1000 of the company's stock and has held it for at least one year, the shareholder is unable to file a resolution, no matter how much merit it might have, unless the issue relates to executive compensation.

There is much discussion in both practitioner and academic journals arguing that a number of factors exist to induce managers to act in the best interests of shareholders. These factors are derived from an assumption that the more unfavorable the expected consequences to the manager who decreases the wealth of shareholders, the less likely the manager will act against the interests of shareholders. The primary factors that are expected to induce management to align its interest with shareholders are:

- Management holds a relatively large ownership position.
- Management compensation is tied to shareholder return performance.
- Management faces loss of its position if the firm is taken over by another firm.
- Management faces a competitive labor market for its skills.

Ownership Position by Management

We would expect that managers with more stock ownership in the company would identify more closely with the shareholders' economic interests. However, a survey of *Fortune* 500 firms found that most chief executive officers do not have significant equity positions in their firms.[5] Even when managers own shares in their company, their perspective on risk may differ from that of shareholders. Managers, like most people, act in their own self-interest.

Compensation and Shareholder Return

A direct means of linking top management's interests with those of shareholders is to base management compensation, and particularly the incentive portion, on market returns realized by shareholders. In many cases, this linkage is accomplished by issu-

[4]See the article by J. W. Petty, D. F. Scott, and M. M. Bird, "The Capital Expenditure Decision-Making Process of Large Corporations," *The Engineering Economist* (Spring 1975), pp. 159–172.

[5]M. McComas, "Atop the *Fortune* 500: A Survey of the CEOs, "*Fortune,* 113 (April 28, 1986), 26–31. *Fortune* 500 refers to the 500 largest manufacturing companies included in the annual financial survey by *Fortune* magazine.

Basic Financial Management in Practice

THIS YEAR'S MODEL

Don't like the salary? Just change the formula.

For several years, the formula for determining a chief executive's bonus has been simple: As profits or stock prices rise, so does the bonus. But times are changing. Corporations are patching together innovative systems that take into account everything from quality improvement to buying and selling assets. The upshot: Executive pay can soar even when the company does poorly.

Chief executive bonuses typically are drawn from a pool made up of a percentage of net income that exceeds a certain return on equity; say 5 percent of the net that exceeds an 8 percent return on equity. But if net income falls, so does the bonus pool. Unless, that is, a company changes its absolute performance standards to relative ones. When companies compare performance with a group of competitors, the chief executive of the best-performing company would get a pay raise—even if every company in the group is doing poorly. Companies in troubled industries are especially likely to turn to this method.

Some companies are using flexible measures to compensate chief executives. Unlike the traditional fixed formulas, the flexible ones aren't spelled out in the corporate proxies, so it is harder to tell what the chief executive is being paid for. Among the objectives: divesting underperforming business units, synchronizing technology at diverse factories, laying off people, and restructuring money-losing operations.

Some companies are turning to a relatively new "sum of the awards" approach. Under the traditional formula, a CEO's entire bonus depends on a target return on equity or investment of the company. Using the new method, perhaps only 50 percent of the CEO's bonus would be based on return on equity or return on investment. Another 25 percent would be based on comparisons with competitors and a final 25 percent on successful restructuring of a troubled division. The percentages set by the board of directors can differ depending on a company's situation.

Adapted from Lee Berton, "This Year's Model," *The Wall Street Journal*, April 17, 1991, p. R5. Reprinted by permission of *The Wall Street Journal*,

ing the executives *stock options* on the company's common stock. These options have an expiration date sometime in the future, as determined by the board of directors.

The concept of stock options is that if the company does well, the executives can exercise their options. This means the executives can convert the options to common stock of the company by paying a price that is well below the market value of the shares. The executives receive immediate reward. If the company does not do well, the options lose their value and the executives are not rewarded. Although stock option compensation sounds like a good way to reward executives, stock options can encourage management to optimize performance in the short run before the options expire while ignoring the long run.

Rather than link incentive compensation directly to the market returns earned by shareholders, most *Fortune* 500 companies tie annual bonuses and long-term performance plans to internal financial goals, such as accounting earnings, accounting return on equity, or how the company compares to its competitors. Unfortunately, these criteria often conflict with how the financial market values common stock. If incentives are largely based on factors not determined by the market, such as accounting earnings, management might be motivated to pursue strategies shareholders view as unsound. In such a situation, what is economically irrational from the shareholder viewpoint may be perfectly rational for the executive.

Threat of Takeover

If managers are significantly exploiting shareholders, such action should be reflected automatically in a lower stock price of a publicly traded firm and, thereby, lower shareholder wealth. A lower price, relative to what it might be with more efficient management, offers an attractive takeover opportunity for another company, which usually replaces incumbent management. The threat of an unsolicited takeover and the possible loss of executive jobs is supposed to act as a constraint on corporate managers who might choose to pursue personal goals at the expense of shareholders.

In 1988, Coniston Partners initiated a shareholder revolt at Gillette, Inc. to force a sale of the business. Coniston had no complaint whatever with the excellent progress of Gillette, other than it thought Gillette management was not promoting the company vigorously enough in the financial markets. Coniston thought the company could be sold for more than its then trading price.[6]

In recent years, management has shown great ingenuity in escaping the clutches of unwanted suitors. Table 17-2 outlines the major defenses to thwart a takeover.

Possibly one of the greatest abuses of executive power in this antitakeover defense process is the changing of corporate bylaws to deprive or delay the transfer of control to an acquiring raider. The aim of the defensive bylaws changes is to retain present management's clout in the firm past the time it legally has a controlling interest. For instance, the elimination of *cumulative voting* in favor of *majority voting* can greatly diminish your voting power as a shareholder. Under *cumulative voting* you can allocate all your votes to just one candidate, thereby possibly helping to elect at least one member of the board of directors who is sympathetic to your concerns. Suppose there are four directors to be elected and you own 200 shares. Thus, you have a total of 800 votes: 4 directors × 200 shares. Under cumulative voting, you can cast all 800 votes for your favorite candidate. The alternative voting system is called *majority voting*. Under *majority voting*, you can cast a maximum of 200 shares for any one candidate.

Gulf Oil management, in defending its position against a takeover lead by T. Boone Pickens, convinced shareholders to approve a switch of its state of incorporation to Delaware which did not require cumulative voting. Gulf's stock price at the time was about $40 per share. Only the persistence of T. Boone Pickens enabled stockholders to eventually sell their Gulf stock to a white knight at a price near its true worth of $80 per share.

Other bylaws changes often used include the elimination of preemptive rights, the requirement that board of directors vacancies be filled by remaining directors, and an increased percentage of votes needed to call a shareholder meeting or approve a merger. The clear intent is to vest control in incumbent management. Sig-

[6]See Louis Lowenstein and Ira M. Millstein, "The American Corporation and the Institutional Investor: Are There Lessons from Abroad?" *Columbia Business and Law Review* (1988), pp. 744–745.

TABLE 17-2 Anti-takeover Defenses

Poison Pill. This technique triggers actions that make the target financially unattractive or by giving target shareholders rights to demand conversion into securities of the bidder on terms attractive to the target company but not to the bidder.

White Knight. Sometimes a company cannot resist a takeover attempt alone and resorts to offering itself to another company (the *white knight*) that it considers more suitable.

Shark Repellent. The directors amend the certificate of incorporation to permit additional defense measures if they feel they have sufficient votes to do so. For example, they might try an amendment requiring a supermajority ratification of any merger proposal, say, 75 percent.

Golden Parachute. Senior managers worried about losing their jobs as a result of a takeover contrive *golden parachutes* for themselves. The parachutes consist of lucrative bailout measures such as large severance pay or stock allowances in case of a takeover.

Dual Class Recapitalization. Management has the company distribute a second class of common stock that possesses superior voting rights (for example, 15 votes per share). The new shares can only be sold to the company. Over time, management's voting power increases as shareholders sell their shares.

Employee Stock Ownership Plan (ESOP). Management has the company purchase a large block of common stock (or voting preferred stock) in the secondary market and sells it to a company-sponsored ESOP. Management votes the ESOP's shares until they are distributed to employees, which typically takes place over several years.

Staggered Election of Directors. The company's board of directors is divided into three equal classes. Only one class stands for reelection each year. A hostile raider cannot obtain control through a single proxy contest.

Pac-Man Defense. The company under attack makes a counterbid for the common stock of the acquirer.

Standstill Agreement. Target company gets the prospective acquirer to agree, during the term of the agreement, (1) not to increase its share holdings above a specified percentage and, usually, (2) to vote its shares with management. The potential acquirer is often given a significant monetary amount, called *greenmail,* to agree to the agreement.

Leveraged Capitalization. The company borrows a large sum of money and distributes the loan proceeds, along with any other excess cash, to its shareholders as dividends. The additional debt on the company's balance sheet is designed to make it more difficult for a takeover raider to fund the acquisition with borrowed funds.

Litigation. The company files suit against the bidder alleging violation of state takeover statute(s), antitrust laws, securities laws, or other laws or regulations.

Share Repurchases or Sales. The company uses excess cash or borrows cash to repurchase a large number of its shares in the secondary market. Alternatively, the company repurchases shares from the takeover raider with any premium over fair market value representing greenmail. As a third alternative, the company sells shares to a "friendly" third party.

nificant costs can be incurred in pursuing anti-takeover measures. As the Financial Reality article on page 501 explains, a long-term employee and shareholder of a company lost most of his retirement savings as management tried to defend against an unwanted suitor.

Labor Market for Executives

Another often stated remedy for aligning management's interests with those of shareholders is the executive job market. Managerial labor markets are an essential mechanism for motivating managers to function in the best interests of shareholders, since managers compete for positions both within and outside of the firm. The increasing number of executive recruiting firms and the length of the "Who's News" column in *The Wall Street Journal* (see Figure 17-2) are evidence that the man-

The daily news indicates that the executive labor market is very active.

WHO'S NEWS

Tambrands Names as President, CEO Fogarty of Colgate-Palmolive U.S. Unit

By Suein L. Hwang
Staff Reporter of The Wall Street Journal

Tambrands Inc., struggling with shrinking market share and a perceived lack of direction, named Edward T. Fogarty, head of Colgate-Palmolive Co.'s U.S. unit, as its president and chief executive officer, ending a search that lasted nearly a year.

Colgate appointed Lois Juliber, its 45-year-old chief technological officer, to succeed Mr. Fogarty, whose appointment at Tambrands is effective May 31. The move makes Ms. Juliber the highest-ranking woman in the giant consumer-products company's history and puts her in line to possibly succeed Reuben Mark, Colgate's 55-year-old chairman and chief executive.

Edward T. Fogarty

As president of the unit, Ms. Juliber, like Mr. Fogarty, will have responsibility for Colgate's consumer-products businesses in the U.S. and Canada.

The changes come at a crucial time for both Colgate and Tambrands.

Long Vacancies

Mr. Fogarty, 57, is assuming two posts that have been vacant since last summer, when Martin F.C. Emmett was abruptly ousted as chief executive by the board and President and Chief Operating Officer Charles J. Chapman was demoted. At the time, the tampon maker was roiled by charges that Mr. Emmett spent company money lavishly and had questionable dealings with outside consultants who were also his friends. Mr. Emmett has denied any impropriety.

The White Plains, N.Y., maker of Tampax tampons hasn't regained market share lost during Mr. Emmett's regime, and its share price, which traded as high as $70 in 1992, has been in a steady decline. Tambrands stock closed yesterday at $36.875, up $1.125 or 3.1%, in New York Stock Exchange composite trading.

Wall Street's rather mild reaction to Mr. Fogarty's appointment indicates growing concern about the company's outlook. Tambrands' first-quarter earnings were nearly flat at $22 million, or 58 cents a share, compared with the year-earlier $21.9 million, or 56 cents a share. Excluding the effect of an accounting charge taken in 1993, operating profit fell 32%. Sales fell 10% to $139.2 million from $154.3 million.

Analysts worry about new competition from Kimberly-Clark Corp., which recently launched a new tampon with a curved applicator.

Still, hiring Mr. Fogarty is something of a coup for Tambrands. As the months wore on, industry executives say numerous candidates turned the job down, leading Tambrands to eventually switch executive-search firms early this year.

Doing 'the Search Right'

A Tambrands spokesman said the board simply "wanted to do the search right. The search lasted as long as it took to find the right candidate."

Tambrands' Chairman Howard B. Wentz Jr., who is also a Colgate board member, first contacted Mr. Mark about the possibility of hiring Mr. Fogarty. Tambrands' board approved Mr. Fogarty's appointment at a meeting Monday night, and Mr. Fogarty announced his move to his staff yesterday morning.

While they were surprised by his departure, Colgate executives say Mr. Fogarty was unlikely to succeed Mr. Mark, who shows no interest in retiring anytime soon. Mr. Fogarty couldn't be reached for comment.

When Mr. Fogarty, who had worked for New York-based Colgate in the 1960s and early 1970s, returned to Colgate in 1989, he was viewed by many as a possible heir-apparent to Mr. Mark. Analysts say that Colgate's U.S. business performed reasonably well for the first few years of his tenure, but by the end of 1993, Colgate's U.S. unit was suffering in a number of categories from market-share erosion, which company executives have blamed on overly aggressive cost-cutting that stifled new-product activity.

Colgate, with about $7 billion in annual sales, is in the midst of an offensive to increase ad spending and accelerate new-product activity. Colgate's stock rose 25 cents, or 0.4%, to $58.25 in Big Board trading yesterday.

Lois Juliber

Mr. Fogarty brings an extensive marketing background, which his CEO predecessor at Tambrands lacked. In the mid-1970s, he was a vice president and general manager of the predecessor to Playtex Products Inc., with responsibilities for marketing tampons there.

Outside director Mr. Wentz, who also serves as chairman of Esstar Inc. of New Haven, Conn., will continue as chairman of Tambrands.

* * *

SOUTHWESTERN PUBLIC SERVICE Co. (Amarillo, Texas) – C. Coney Burgess, 56 years old, was elected to the board of this utility company, increasing the number of members to 12. Mr. Burgess is chairman of Herring Bancorp of Vernon, Texas, and owns agricultural operations in the Texas Panhandle.

Wells-Gardner Names New Chief, Chairman, Posts 1st-Period Loss

By a Wall Street Journal *Staff Reporter*

CHICAGO—Wells-Gardner Electronics Corp. named Anthony Spier chairman and chief executive officer, effective immediately.

Mr. Spier, 50 years old, is former president and CEO of Oce-Bruning Inc., Itasca, Ill., an engineering-graphics company. He has been a Wells-Gardner director since 1990.

Mr. Spier succeeds Frank Myers, 64, who indicated he didn't wish to stand for re-election as a director or as chairman and CEO. Mr. Myers, who cited health reasons for his decision, joined the company as president in June 1989 and was named to the top post in April 1990.

Wells-Gardner, a maker of video monitors, also reported a widened first-quarter net loss of $1.3 million, or 33 cents a share, reflecting a $762,000 special charge for management reorganization. In the year-earlier quarter, the company had a loss of $236,000, or six cents a share. Sales slid 23% to $7.6 million from $9.9 million.

Management attributed the results to a decline in the market for coin-operated video-arcade games. Sales of video monitors to arcade-game customers fell 40%.

* * *

BANKAMERICA Corp. (San Francisco) – Joseph Bauman, head of business development for Citibank's derivatives business and chairman of the International Swaps and Derivatives Association, will join this bank as head of its U.S. financial engineering and risk management group, a newly created position. He will report to Robert D. McKnew, head of U.S. Capital Markets, and be based in San Francisco. The appointment of Mr. Bauman, 44 years old, reflects Bank of America's continued expansion of its derivatives business. Mr. Bauman had been with Citicorp's Citibank unit since 1992. Prior to that, he was a senior executive in global derivatives at Chemical Banking Corp. Mr. Bauman will have to resign as head of the ISDA trade group as a result of changing employers.

BORDEN Inc. (Columbus, Ohio) – Robert P. Magrann was named to the new position of senior vice president, sales, for Borden's North American foods division. He had been executive vice president of E.J. Brach Corp. Borden produces packaged foods, consumer products, packaging and industrial products.

BURLINGTON INDUSTRIES Inc. (Greensboro, N.C.) – John G. Medlin Jr. was elected a director of this textile company, expanding board membership to 10. Mr. Medlin, 60 years old, is chairman of Wachovia Corp., a banking company based jointly in Winston-Salem, N.C., and Atlanta.

CITICORP (New York) – This bank holding company named Michael Ricciardi, 38 years old, co-head of fixed income in the U.S. In this newly created position, Mr. Ricciardi will be responsible for developing Citicorp Securities Inc.'s investor base and jointly managing its fixed-income business. Mr. Ricciardi was most recently managing director of fixed-income sales at General Electric Co.'s Kidder, Peabody & Co. subsidiary.

FARR Co. (El Segundo, Calif.) – H.J. Meany was named chairman, president and chief executive officer. Mr. Meany, 71 years old, succeeds Charles R. Wofford, 61, who resigned to pursue other interests, the company said. Mr. Meany has been a Farr director since 1976, and Mr. Wofford joined Farr in 1991 from Texas Instruments Inc. Farr makes filters for particulate, liquid and gaseous filtration systems.

NETWORK GENERAL Corp. (Menlo Park, Calif.) – Charles J. Abbe, 53 years old, senior vice president for electronics at Raychem Corp., was elected a director of this software company, expanding board membership to seven.

THIOKOL Corp. (Ogden, Utah) – Richard L. Corbin was named senior vice president and chief financial officer, effective May 15. Mr. Corbin, 48 years old, succeeds James R. Wilson, 53, who was named president and chief executive last October. Mr. Corbin had served as chief financial officer and vice president, administration, for General Dynamics Corp.'s space systems division in San Diego. Thiokol makes solid-propulsion systems, ordinance and composite products for the space and defense industries.

WCT COMMUNICATIONS Inc. (Santa Barbara, Calif.) – Donald H. Sledge was named president of this long-distance telecommunications company, and will also hold the newly created position of chief operating officer. Mr. Sledge, 53 years old, assumes the president's position from Richard Frockt, 49, who remains chairman and chief executive. Mr. Sledge most recently served as interim head of operations of New T&T, a new telephone company in Hong Kong, and has held several other positions in various telecommunications concerns.

OLD AMERICA STORES Inc. (Howe, Texas) – The company said its president and chief executive officer, C. Wayne Brush, 54 years old, told it that he intends to step down from both posts when his employment agreement expires on Jan. 31, 1995. The home-decorating and arts and crafts retailer said Mr. Brush, the company's founder, will help hire and train a successor.

GTE Corp. (Stamford, Conn.) – Jeffrey S. Rubin, 50 years old, was named to the new position of senior vice president, corporate planning and development, at the telecommunications company.

ZENITH ELECTRONICS Corp. (Glenview, Ill.) – Ilene S. Gordon, vice president-operations for Tenneco Inc., was named a director of this maker of consumer electronic products. Ms. Gordon, 40 years old, succeeds G. Ralph Guthrie, retired chairman of Urban Investment & Development Co., who died last July.

FIGURE 17-2
"Who's News"

Financial Reality

ESOP'S FABLE, AN UNHAPPY ONE

Just before Halloween, the stockholders of the Harcourt Brace Jovanovich publishing company received in the mail a 264-page book explaining the ins and outs of a proposed merger between HBJ and General Cinema Corporation. I own 9839.55 shares, the rewards of working for HBJ for 26 years. As a member of the employee stock ownership plan, I never had control of those shares. I could not sell them when they were at $18, the high three years ago, unless I quit my job and thus gained control of the stock. Now General Cinema has bought them for 75 cents a share—payable not in cash but in chits convertible to GCC stock. The stockholders voted in favor of this offer at a special meeting on Saturday. HBJ advised a yes vote from the stockholders, saying 75 cents a share was about as much as we were going to get.

This was the second time around on the deal. The first time, this spring, GCC offered to pay HBJ bondholders certain fractional proportions, ranging from 32 to 91 cents on the dollar and give stockholders $1.30 a share. But the bondholders wanted more and scotched the deal. My nest egg, once worth $177,000, has just been marked down to about $6000.

Now, at least, it's under my control: On May 7, HBJ sold the magazine I edited for them, *Michigan Farmer,* and its ten other state farm magazines to Capital Cities/ABC, Inc. The new owner wanted the titles but not all the personnel, so HBJ terminated about 50 people, including me.

The chief culprit is William Jovanovich, now retired. In 1987, as chairman of the board of the company that has had his name on it since 1955, he led an ego-driven charge to keep it there. On May 18 that year, HBJ had received a letter from Robert Maxwell offering to buy HBJ for $44 a share in cash. I had 3000 shares then, so for me this deal was worth $132,000. Stockholders never got to vote on that. Mr. Jovanovich and the board turned the offer down.

The board opposed an alternate plan, the HBJ Recapitalization. Without stockholder vote, it declared a dividend of $40 a share in cash, plus one share of HBJ preferred stock, a new class worth $12 a share. Suddenly I was to get $52 for each of my 3000 shares, a deal now worth $156,000 for my retirement account. This was all done with borrowed money. Faced with buying a company with $1.6 billion in new debt, Mr. Maxwell bought Macmillan instead. HBJ had fended off the raider—but it was left hopelessly crippled. Employees were in a quandary. We could keep our jobs, and work to pay off this monstrous debt, or quit and cash in. The dividend was paid to ESOP members in new stock, bumping my numbers from 3000 shares to nearly 10,000. I liked my job, so I stayed. For a while, the stock went up, and my retirement account grew to a value of $177,111.90 before the precipitous slide began. But soon the unraveling began.

Adapted from Dick Hehnert, "ESOP's Fable, an Unhappy One," *The Wall Street Journal,* November 26, 1991, p. A14. Reprinted by permission of *The Wall Street Journal,*

agerial labor market is very active. What is less apparent is how the financial market evaluates managers. Within the firm, performance evaluation and incentive plans are the mechanisms for monitoring managerial performance. The unresolved issue is whether these measures are reliably linked to the market price of the company's stock.

COMPREHENSION CHECK

1. *Why is there a separation of control between management and ownership of large investor-owned corporations?*
2. *List the factors that may encourage corporate management to act in the interests of shareholders.*
3. *How have corporate top managements acted to prevent unsolicited (and unwanted) takeover attempts in recent years?*
4. *How can common stockholders possibly benefit from takeover attempts? What are possible disadvantages for shareholders of takeover attempts?*

HOW IS SHAREHOLDER VALUE CREATED?

Efforts to increase shareholder value can be hampered by conflicts within the firm's value-exchange system. Nevertheless, maximization of shareholder wealth is still the most appropriate objective management *should* pursue. Managerial finance is grounded on the premise that managers should be evaluated by the *economic returns* they generate for shareholders: *dividends* plus *share price appreciation*. As managers consider alternative business strategies, those strategies expected to develop the greatest sustainable competitive advantage are those that also create the greatest value for the firm and its shareholders.

Shareholders, both current and prospective, analyze information about the firm, including its successes, failures, and conflicts. Because financial markets in the United States and other economically developed nations are relatively efficient in processing information, we can think of the market value of the firm as equaling the market value of its financial securities issued to investors. Suppose the market value of debt and equity is \$3 million and \$10 million, respectively. Then the value of the firm is \$13 million:

$$\begin{aligned}
&\textbf{Market value of the firm}\\
&\quad = \textbf{Market value of debt} + \textbf{market value of equity}\\
&V = B + S \qquad (17\text{-}1)\\
&\quad = \$3{,}000{,}000 + \$10{,}000{,}000\\
&\quad = \$13{,}000{,}000
\end{aligned}$$

The equation shows that managers can increase shareholder wealth (equity) either by increasing the value of the firm or by decreasing the value of the debt with firm value staying constant. The second strategy results in value being transferred from debt investors to equity investors, which raises a conflict between creditors and shareholders.

The reality of the financial market is that all managers and companies are essentially in the business of allocating scarce funds to their most promising uses. To increase their company's stock price, managers must perform better than other com-

The financial market determines the company's risk which, in turn, determines the minimum rate of return the firm must earn on its investments. Management should accept all investments with expected returns in excess of the minimum required return.

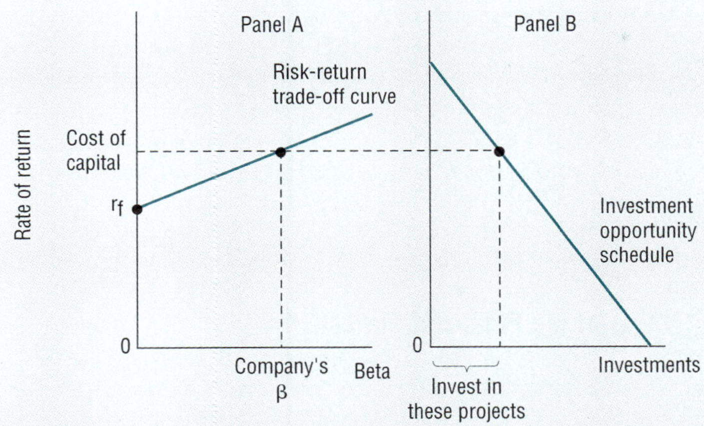

FIGURE 17-3
Economic model of value

petitors seeking investors' funds. The company must earn rates of return on investments that exceed the return offered by other companies of equal risk. If managers allocate resources efficiently, value is added to the funds placed at their disposal and the market value of the firm and its equity increase. If managers misallocate resources, the company's market value is less than the value a more competent management team could realize.

Interaction of the Investment Opportunity Schedule and the Cost of Capital

The allocation of scarce resources should work as follows. A firm's management ranks proposed investment projects according to their prospective rates of return, as depicted in Figure 17-3, Panel B, by the *investment opportunity schedule.* The downward-sloping *investment opportunity schedule* indicates that the most attractive investment opportunities are taken first and the least attractive ones last, if at all.

We can conceptualize the minimum required rate of return management should accept for creating value in the company by relating the investment opportunity schedule to risk-return concepts. Panel (a) of Figure 17-3 helps illustrate the relationship. Let's assume that we have determined the firm's risk to be as shown in panel (a). At the company's risk level in panel (a), we draw a vertical line that intersects the upward sloping risk-return trade-off curve. At the point of intersection, we draw a horizontal line to intersect the rate of return axis. The intersection at the axis represents the firm's minimum required market rate of return, that is, its *cost of capital,* a topic we will discuss extensively in the next chapter. The firm's *cost of capital* is equal to the minimum percentage return investors expect to earn by buying a portfolio of stocks and bonds of other companies of similar risk.

By extending the horizontal line into panel (b) in Figure 17-3, we find where it intersects the firm's investment opportunity schedule. Let's assume that the investments in the firm's portfolio are of risk equal to that of the firm. Only investments offering returns greater than or equal to the market rate of return (cost of capital) should be undertaken. *Managers should reject projects providing returns less than the cost of capital because the company's investors can do better with other investments.* Management measures the amount of funds needed to undertake the investments on the investment axis.

Distribution of Value in the Financial Market

Essentially, the financial markets distribute economic value created by the firm's production of goods and services. The financial securities of a firm that manufactures and sells quality, sought-after products gain in value as the firm becomes more profitable. A firm whose products are not as highly sought after will be less profitable and have lower cash flows. Its financial securities will lose value.

We can express the tendency of value to flow from low- to high-return companies by looking at the following equation for the market value of the firm:

$$\textbf{Market value of the firm} = \frac{\textbf{Corporate rate of return} \times \textbf{book value of assets}}{\textbf{Required market rate}} \quad \text{(17-2)}$$

We define the variables as follows:

Market value of the firm = Market value of debt + equity
Corporate rate of return = Economic profit ÷ book value of assets invested
Book value of assets = Accounting value of the firm, recorded at initial cost
Required market rate = Market determined rate (based on risk and diversification concepts)

Theoretically, both expressions for the value of the firm, Eq. (17-1 and 17-2) result in the same market value of the firm. Eq. (17-2) states that the relationship between the rate of return a company earns and the market return investors require is what determines whether the company's market value is at a premium or at a discount to the book value of assets invested in the business.[7] If the corporate rate of return exceeds the required market rate, market value of the firm exceeds the book value of the assets used in the firm. (See Illustration 17-1.)

[7]Eq. (17-2) is conceptually similar to the common stock model for perpetual cash flows:

$$P_0 = \frac{\text{Cash flows}}{\text{Required market rate}} = \frac{D_1}{r}$$

ILLUSTRATION 17-1

Value eroded; value created

Warren Buffett, chairman of Berkshire Hathaway, concluded in the company's 1984 annual report that if a company's rate of return does not at least equal that available to investors in the financial markets (adjusted for risk), the money should be distributed to shareholders. Otherwise, he says, the company might be invested to earn 8 percent when shareholders could on their own buy stocks with an average annual return of, say, 10 percent. The dollar that a company keeps won't be worth a dollar in the market price of its shares unless it can produce a return of 10 percent on that dollar. Dollars invested at 8 percent will soon be marked down in market price and the shareholders will have suffered a loss of $0.20 per $1.

Market value of the firm

$$= \frac{\textbf{Corporate rate of return} \times \textbf{book value of assets}}{\textbf{Required market rate}}$$

$$= \frac{\mathbf{8\% \times \$1}}{\mathbf{10\%}}$$

$$= \mathbf{\$0.80 \text{ per } \$1 \text{ of assets}}$$

If the firm is able to earn 15 percent on investments when investors require 10 percent, management's actions create value. For every dollar of invested assets, $1.50 appears in the stock market's valuation of the firm:

Market value of the firm

$$= \frac{\textbf{Corporate rate of return} \times \textbf{book value of assets}}{\textbf{Required market rate}}$$

$$= \frac{\mathbf{15\% \times \$1}}{\mathbf{10\%}}$$

$$= \mathbf{\$1.50 \text{ per } \$1 \text{ of assets}}$$

The moral is this: *If management is to create value, it must identify investments that promise expected returns in excess of the required market rate.* Failure to invest in such projects leads to erosion of firm value which, in turn, means erosion in value of either the firm's debt or equity, or both.

Change in Economic Value

Let's use our earlier formula in Eq. (17-1) for market value of the firm to discuss changes in that value. The formula shows that the firm's market value is the sum of its market values of equity (S) and debt (B). Change in the firm's value, ΔV, can be viewed from the perspective of change in market value of any financial securities issued by the company. We can express the relationship as:

Change in the firm's value

= Change in value of debt + change in value of equity (17-3)

$$\Delta V = \Delta B + \Delta S$$

Alternatively, we can express any change in value as investing in a new project, ΔI:

$$\textbf{Change in firm's value} \begin{matrix} > \\ = \\ < \end{matrix} \Delta I \begin{cases} \textbf{Value increases} \\ \textbf{No change in value} \\ \textbf{Value decreases} \end{cases} \tag{17-4}$$

or

$$\Delta V = \Delta B + \Delta S \begin{matrix} > \\ = \\ < \end{matrix} \Delta I \begin{cases} \textbf{Value increases} \\ \textbf{No change in value} \\ \textbf{Value decreases} \end{cases} \tag{17-5}$$

Eq. (17-5) shows that in the financial market, the contribution of new projects to a firm's value is reflected in the market values of the firm's debt and equity securities. Since the firm only promises debtholders a fixed return on their funds, most of the changing value of the firm is reflected in the changing value of the equity, ΔS; risk of debt default can change the value of debt ΔB.

For a new investment (ΔI) to enhance firm value, it is necessary for the expected change in value of the company (ΔV), as a result of undertaking a new investment, to exceed the cost of the new investment: $\Delta V - \Delta I > 0$. Or stated differently, $\Delta V/\Delta I > 1$. The firm's value increases:

- If net operating cash flows can be made to grow without tying up any more funds.
- If funds can be diverted or liquidated from business activities that do not provide adequate returns.
- If new funds can be invested in projects that earn more, in a time value of money framework, than the market cost of funds.

When the new investment neither contributes to an increase in shareholder wealth nor erodes such value, then $\Delta V/\Delta I = 1$. The new investment earns simply the cost of financing it; that is, the corporate rate of return equals the required market rate. Management erodes shareholder value if as a result of the investment, $\Delta V/\Delta I < 1$. The new investment fails to earn the minimum required return. Erosion of value happens when:

- Management passes over new investments likely to earn more than the required market rate.
- Management invests funds in projects that earn less than the required market rate.
- Management retains existing assets that earn less than the required market rate.

The change in shareholder value is also dependent upon whether management pursues a short-term or long-term investment strategy. Maximizing shareholder value often requires commitments for resources that may adversely affect short-run cash flows but contribute significantly to long-run cash flows. For instance, Merck & Company, Inc. spends about 11 percent of each sales dollar on research and development. Merck's R&D expenditures amount to over $1 billion annually. It can be years before successful products emerge from any R&D efforts. However, Merck must fund such large R&D expenditures if it is to retain its leadership position in the pharmaceutical industry. Other examples of long-term value-maximizing

TABLE 17-3 Long-term Value Index

Company	Recent Stock Price	Sum of Dividends for Next 5 Years	LVI
General Motors	$ 60.00	$ 4.00	93.3*
Exxon	66.75	14.75	77.9
Ford Motor	64.63	8.00	87.6
IBM	52.75	5.00	90.5
Mobil	80.88	17.00	79.0
General Electric	109.13	14.40	86.8
Texaco	66.88	16.00	94.8
AT&T	54.25	6.60	87.9
Du Pont	54.50	8.80	83.9
Chrysler	58.63	4.00	93.2
Chevron	89.00	18.50	79.2
Philip Morris	58.13	13.00	77.6
Amoco	53.00	11.00	79.2
United Technologies	70.63	9.00	87.3
Occidental Petroleum	18.38	5.00	72.8
Procter & Gamble	58.25	6.20	89.4
Atlantic Richfield	102.63	27.50	73.2
Boeing	47.75	5.00	89.5
Tenneco	56.38	8.00	85.9

*$[1 - (\$4/\$60)] \times 100 = 93.3$

Dividend data taken from Value Line Investors Survey, *February 11, 1994. Prices are taken from* The Wall Street Journal, *February 17, 1994.*

approaches faced by management may require product, market, or labor relations strategies that lead to higher expenses in the short run but superior-quality products, higher market share, improved employee productivity, and higher operating cash flow in the long run.

The financial market's pricing of common stock suggests that management should resist actions that boost only short-term profits. The results reported in Table 17-3 suggest that financial markets take a long-term perspective of five years or more to price common stock of firms. We calculate the *long-term value index (LVI)* as:[8]

$$\text{LVI} = \left(1 - \frac{\text{Sum of dividends for next 5 years}}{\text{Current stock price}}\right) \times 100 \qquad (17\text{-}6)$$

LVI provides an estimate of investors' confidence in the ability of management to create a sustainable long-term competitive advantage in its business. For instance, as of February 1994, the market was saying that only about 7 percent of the value of General Motors common stock was attributable to dividends over the next five years. Cash flows expected to occur beyond five years contribute about 93 percent of the stock's value.

[8]Alfred Rappaport developed the index. He discusses it in "Don't Sell Stock Market Horizons Short," *The Wall Street Journal*, June 27, 1983, p. 28. He assumes that the growth rate in dividends equals the market rate of return.

COMPREHENSION CHECK

1. *What is the purpose of a company's investment opportunity schedule? What does the schedule give as the minimum acceptable rate of return?*
2. *Explain how the formula for the market value of a firm (Eq. (17-2)) can result in an increase or decrease in investors' wealth.*
3. *Under what conditions does the value of a firm increase?*
4. *Based on Table 17-3, comment on the relative importance of short-term and long-term investment values.*

FINDING SHAREHOLDER VALUE IN THE BUSINESS ENVIRONMENT

Let's examine the creation of shareholder wealth more explicitly. Ownership of the company means ownership of the *net assets* (assets less liabilities) currently held by the company. Shareholders own any residual future cash returns which may arise either from use or sale of these net assets. The size and timing of any future cash returns are dependent upon the present and future investment decisions of management. At one extreme management could decide to sell all the firm's currently held assets and, after paying off all debtholders, give an immediate and final cash return (liquidating dividend) to shareholders. A more likely management investment policy is to replace and perhaps expand currently held assets at future points in time. This strategy is likely to result in shareholders receiving a continuing and perhaps increasing series of cash returns from ownership. The former policy yields a minimum value of the shares of a company as the current salable value of its currently held net assets. The latter policy yields the share value of a company at a point in time as the market value of the future cash returns to shareholders.

It is the ongoing strategy that interests us. First, we will explain the underlying basics of firm valuation by valuing a no-growth firm. Next, we will add more complex features to the problem.

Valuation of a No-Growth, All-Equity Financed Firm

The simplest valuation case is a firm without any growth prospects and financed entirely with equity.[9] Such a firm is also called an *unlevered firm*. We define a *no-growth firm* to include the following features.

- No investment opportunities exist that allow the firm to increase its market value and profitability.[10]
- Management makes necessary investments to replace assets used up so that the new investments simply maintain current profitability and assets levels.
- Any operating cash flows remaining after making necessary investments are paid as dividends to shareholders.

[9] The basis for much of the discussion on firm valuation is two articles by Franco Modigliani and Merton Miller. Although they were much criticized at the time, their theory is now accepted doctrine. For further information, see Franco Modigliani and Merton H. Miller, "The Cost of Capital, Corporation Finance and the Theory of Investment," *American Economic Review*, 48 (June 1958), 261–297, and "Corporate Income Taxes and the Cost of Capital: A Correction," *American Economic Review*, 53 (June 1963), 433–443.

[10] You can think of this feature in terms of our earlier discussion in this chapter where we stated $\Delta V/\Delta I = 1$; that is, change in value of the firm divided by new investment equals 1. The investment earns the minimum required rate of return and no more.

The existing cash operating profit of an unlevered, no-growth company determines its value. We obtain this value by capitalizing, or dividing, the constant after-tax perpetual cash operating profit at a market rate of return that compensates shareholders for bearing business risk.[11] The formula for *value of an unlevered firm* is:

Value of unlevered firm

$$= \frac{\textbf{Constant cash operating profit} \times \textbf{(1 - tax rate)}}{\textbf{Market rate that compensates for business risk}} \qquad \textbf{(17-7)}$$

$$V^u = \frac{\text{COP} \times (1 - \tau)}{r_u}$$

Business risk is the only risk affecting potential returns to shareholders of an unlevered firm. *Business risk,* also called *operating risk,* represents the uncertainty surrounding expected cash operating profit (COP). The following factors lead to high business risk:

- *The relationship between the firm's performance and the economy is high.* General Motors' profitability increases when the economy grows and falls when the economy slows.
- *The firm has a small market share in a competitive industry.* Digital Equipment Corporation has a market share in the personal computer industry of less than 1 percent. With such a small market share, Digital cannot dictate direction for the personal computer industry.
- *The firm is small relative to its major competitors.* Microbreweries, like San Francisco's Anchor Brewing, own less than 1 percent of the market. In 1993, Philip Morris's Miller Brewing introduced an all-barley Reserve Amber Ale to compete against the microbreweries.
- *The firm is not very well diversified.* It depends on one or two products for its income. American Power Conversion was founded in 1981 to make solar power products. The products flopped and the company nearly went out of business. However, American Power Conversion was able to become a profitable company by manufacturing backup power supply products for personal computers and minicomputers.
- *The firm's cost structure has significant fixed operating costs.* Public utilities, such as Long Island Lighting, have massive investment in plant and equipment with the result that much of its costs are fixed. Long Island Lighting must depend on a friendly New York state government regulatory agency to grant utility price increases to offset rising costs.

Shareholders incorporate their assessment of these business risk factors into the market discount rate r_u of Eq. (17-7). Illustration 17-2 outlines the procedure for capitalizing the cash operating profit to value an unlevered company.

[11]Think of *cash operating profit* as cash accounting profit as opposed to accrual accounting profit. *Accrual accounting* records revenues and expenses when management considers the transaction to be complete, whether or not money has been exchanged at the time of the transaction. *Cash accounting* requires an exchange of money before management considers the transaction completed.

ILLUSTRATION 17-2

Valuation of a no-growth unlevered firm

Let's suppose that Ethridge Publishing Company's cash operating profit is $2000 and its income tax rate is 28 percent. Management has financed investment in assets solely by issuing 1000 shares; it has not used debt. Shareholders of this unlevered company require a market rate of return (r_u) of 10 percent to compensate them for business risk.

Below is a partial income statement of expected cash earnings (or profit) based on cash and not accrual accounting.

Cash operating profit before interest and taxes (COP)	$2000
Interest expense	0
Cash earnings before taxes	$2000
Income taxes (28%)	560
Cash earnings after taxes	$1440
Number of shares outstanding	1000
Cash earnings per share ($1440/1000)	$1.44

Based on this information, the value of Ethridge Publishing is $14,400, computed as follows:[12]

$$V^u = \frac{\text{COP} \times (1 +- \tau)}{r_u}$$

$$V^u = \frac{\$2000 \times (1 - 0.28)}{0.10}$$

$$= \frac{\$1440}{0.10}$$

$$= \$14{,}400$$

With no debt financing, all of the company's $14,400 value belongs to its common shareholders. The stock price is $14.40 per share (= $14,400 ÷ 1000 shares) and cash earnings per share are $1.44. The firm's stock sells at a price-earnings (PE) ratio of 10 (= $14.40 ÷ $1.44). Stated differently, Ethridge Publishing stock sells for ten times expected cash earnings because each common share is worth $14.40. The firm does not have a $14.40 share price because it sells for ten times cash earnings.

Tax Benefit of Debt Financing

Suppose our no-growth, unlevered firm decides to change. Its managers wish to retire some equity and replace it with debt. Neither the assets of the firm nor the earning power of those assets change. The interest expense associated with debt financing is a tax-deductible expense to the business. For every $1 of interest cost incurred by the company, the government subsidizes the firm $1 × τ, where τ is the tax rate. This subsidy occurs because the tax statutes issued by the government allow interest expense as a deduction in computing taxable income. Thus, the company's after-tax interest cost is $1 × (1 − τ) per $1 of interest incurred. Alternatively, if the company finances with common stock and pays a dividend to shareholders,

[12]Because the firm is unlevered, COP × (1 − τ) equals *cash earnings after taxes*. This relationship does not hold if the firm finances with both debt and equity, as you will see shortly.

the government does not pay any part of the dividend. Hence, it is more expensive for management to finance the company with equity alone than with debt.

The value of the income tax saved by using some debt in place of some equity adds value to common share price. The additional value is the present value of the government "subsidy." Only the shareholders receive value from the subsidy because debt investors receive a fixed amount—their interest income. Illustration 17-3 shows the effects of debt financing. It causes earnings per share to increase.

ILLUSTRATION 17-3

Cash earnings with debt financing

Let's use the same information for Ethridge Publishing Company as in Illustration 17-2, but now assume that management replaces $7200 of financing, one half the equity ($14,400 ÷ 2) with debt, which costs 8 percent before taxes. Management uses the $7200 proceeds from debt financing to buy back 500 common shares at $14.40 each, the share price we calculated in Illustration 17-2.

	With No Debt	With $7200 Debt
Cash operating profit before interest and taxes	$2000	$2000.00
Interest expense ($7200 × 8%)	0	576.00
Cash earnings before taxes	$2000	$1424.00
Income taxes (28%)	560	398.72
Cash earnings after taxes	$1440	$1025.28
Number of shares outstanding	1000	500
Cash earnings per share: $1440/1000	$1.44	
$1025.28/500		$2.05

Cash *operating* profit after taxes—not cash earnings after taxes—for the levered firm is:

Cash earnings after taxes	$1025.28
+ Interest expense × (1 − τ) = $576 × (1 − 0.28)	414.72
= Cash operating profit after taxes	$1440.00

Cash operating profit after taxes (COPAT) for the levered firm equals the *cash earnings after taxes (CEAT)* for the unlevered firm. Since the unlevered firm has no debt, by definition, its CEAT is synonymous with its COPAT. The distinction between COPAT and CEAT for the levered firm is that COPAT excludes the debt's interest cost, whereas CEAT includes it.

The preceding result should not come as a surprise. If some debt simply replaces some equity in the financing of the company's assets, neither the assets nor the earning power of the assets are affected. Therefore, *cash operating profit after taxes* for the levered and unlevered firms must be the same, which is the case if you compare Illustrations 17-2 and 17-3.

We mentioned earlier that the government effectively subsidizes a firm $1 × τ per $1 of interest cost incurred when the firm uses debt financing. The amount of interest expense "paid" by the government increases the firm's market value of equity. Debt investors receive no part of the income tax savings because they are only promised a fixed payment (for example, 8 percent coupon rate). The cash flow saving to the firm is the difference in income taxes paid if management does not use debt to finance the firm versus the income taxes paid when management uses debt, that is, $1 × τ per $1 of interest. From Illustration 17-3:

Income taxes when no debt is issued	$560.00
Income taxes when debt is issued	398.72
Income tax saving	$161.28

Alternatively,

$$\begin{aligned}\textbf{Income tax savings} &= \textbf{Interest expense} \times \textbf{income tax rate} \\ &= \$576 \times 0.28 \\ &= \$161.28\end{aligned} \tag{17-8}$$

Notice in Illustration 17-3 that the levered firm could earn as little as $576 *cash operating profit before taxes* and still be able to pay the interest amount. In the absence of debt, with cash operating profit of $576, the firm would pay $161.28 in income taxes ($576 × 0.28). Thus, the risk associated with saving income taxes is the same risk of meeting the interest payment. Accordingly, the debt's market borrowing rate (r_d) of 8 percent is appropriate for discounting the income tax savings to a present value of $2016.

$$\begin{aligned}\textbf{Present value of tax savings} &= \frac{\textbf{Tax savings}}{r_d} \\ &= \frac{\$161.28}{0.08} \\ &= \$2016\end{aligned} \tag{17-9}$$

The specific meaning of the present value of tax savings, $2016, is as follows. A firm in the 28 percent income tax bracket, which incurs interest expense of $576 each year in perpetuity, is actually only paying $414.72 [= $576 × (1 − 0.28)] of this amount annually. The government "pays" the balance of $161.28 (= $576 × 0.28). The value of the annual government subsidy of $161.28 received in perpetuity is $2016, as shown by Equation 17-9.

Valuation of a Debt and Equity Financed Firm

How does the tax subsidy affect firm and shareholder values? Very simply; it increases both of them. The logic is as follows. The capitalized value of cash operating profit after taxes is the same whether or not debt is used; that is,

$$\frac{\textbf{COP} \times (1 - \tau)}{r_u} = \$14{,}400$$

which, as shown earlier, is the value of the unlevered firm. We find the value of the levered firm (V^L) by adding the present value of the tax savings (PVTS) to the capitalized cash operating profit after tax value:

$$\begin{aligned}V^L &= \frac{\textbf{COP} \times (1 - \tau)}{r_u} + \textbf{PVTS} \\ &= \$14{,}400 + \$2016 \\ &= \$16{,}416\end{aligned} \tag{17-10}$$

Stated differently, the value of the levered firm equals the value of the unlevered firm (V^u = COP × (1 − τ) ÷ r_u) plus the present value of the tax savings associated with debt financing:

$$V^L = V^u + \text{PVTS} \tag{17-11}$$

Alternatively, the value of the levered firm is:

$$\begin{aligned} V^L &= \text{Market value of debt + market value of equity} \\ &= B + S \end{aligned} \tag{17-12}$$

We calculate the market value of debt by discounting its future cash flows. To simplify the discussion, assume that all debt issued by the firm has no maturity date. If the required market rate of interest for the debt is 8 percent, which equals its coupon rate, the company's market value of outstanding debt *(B)* is $7200:

$$\begin{aligned} B &= \frac{\text{Coupon rate} \times \text{par value of debt}}{\text{Market rate of interest}} \\ &= \frac{0.08 \times \$7200}{0.08} \\ &= \$7200 \end{aligned} \tag{17-13}$$

(*Question:* What is the debt's value if the market interest rate is 7 percent and the coupon rate is 9 percent?[13])

We can calculate the equity value to be $9216 by rearranging Eq. (17-12) as the value of the levered firm minus the value of the debt:

$$\begin{aligned} S &= V^L - B \\ &= \$16{,}416 - \$7200 \\ &= \$9216 \end{aligned} \tag{17-14}$$

In our example, only 500 common shares remain outstanding after issuing debt. Thus, the stock price per share should be $18.43 (= $9216 ÷ 500 shares). The stock price increases from $14.40 for the unlevered situation to $18.43 for the levered case. Or look at the stock price from this perspective. Without debt financing, the stock price is $14.40. The use of debt financing results in a tax subsidy of $2016, or $4.03 per share (= $2016 ÷ 500 shares). Adding the tax subsidy of $4.03 to the old stock price of S14 results in the new stock price of $18.43.

The price-earnings (PE) ratio for the levered firm is approximately nine times:

$$\begin{aligned} \text{PE} &= \frac{\text{Price per share}}{\text{Earnings per share}} \\ &= \frac{\$18.43 \text{ (from the preceding paragraph)}}{\$2.05 \text{ (from Illustration 17-3)}} \\ &= 8.99 \end{aligned} \tag{17-15}$$

Without the use of debt financing, the PE ratio was ten times ($14.40 stock price ÷ $1.44 earnings per share, as given in Illustration 17-2). Thus, based on the PE ratio,

[13]If the coupon rate equals the market rate, then the par value of the debt equals the market value of the debt. The debt's market value exceeds its par value if the coupon rate exceeds the market rate. Finally, the debt's market value is less than its par value if the coupon rate is less than the market rate.

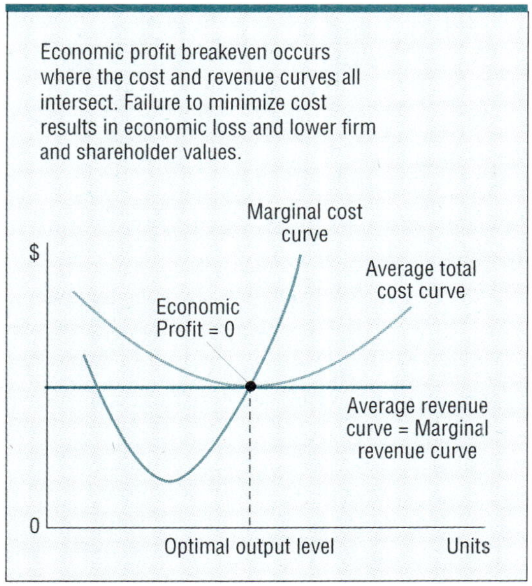

FIGURE 17-4
Operating in perfect competition

which is usually shown on the financial pages of the newspaper, this company's common stock appears to be worth less under debt financing than as an all-equity financed firm. Such a result is absurd. Cash operating profit of the firm has not changed and both price per share and total firm value increase. If management uses debt financing, this result suggests that the PE ratio is seriously deficient as a valuation tool.

Valuation of Growth Opportunities

To this point, we have based our discussion of creating shareholder value on two restrictive assumptions: Cash operating profit stays at a constant level in perpetuity; and cash operating profit results in the firm's investments earning only the market rates required by investors. We will now relax the restrictions and show how investment in growth opportunities, which have expected returns in excess of the minimum required market return, increase both firm and shareholder values.

In our context, no growth means that the ratio of the change in value of the firm to the change in the firm's investment (assets) equals 1, $\Delta V/\Delta I = 1$. Incremental investments add no value beyond their cost to either the firm or the equity when they only earn the minimum required return. Your microeconomics course labeled this type of environment *perfect competition.* As shown in Figure 17-4, in *perfect competition* firms break even in an economic setting; they do not earn any economic profit.[14]

[14]Firms make accounting profits, however.

Management should operate where marginal revenue equals marginal cost, not where the marginal cost curve intersects the average cost curve as in the case for perfect competition.

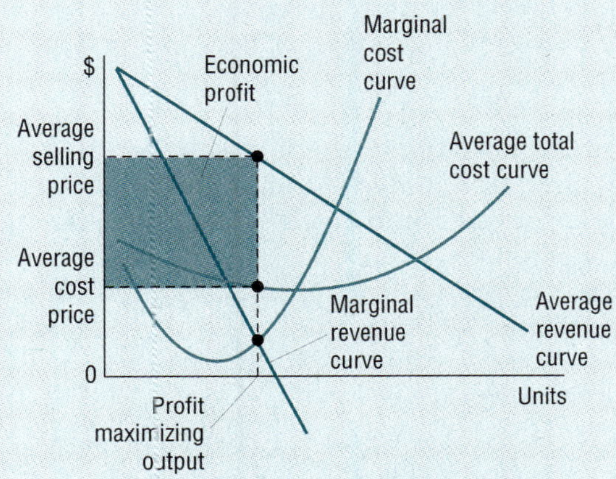

FIGURE 17-5
Operating in imperfect competition

If management can find a way to influence the price of the product or service, then the firm may be able to earn economic profit. For example, economic profit is present if the firm's investors require a return of 9 percent yet investments earn 15 percent. We call such an environment *imperfect competition*. In *imperfect competition* management's objective is to maximize economic profit, not to minimize cost. Management accomplishes the objective by operating the firm where marginal revenue equals marginal cost (see Figure 17-5).

Several reasons can account for the presence of economic profit.

- *Financing barriers to entry make it costly for new firms to enter the industry.* To start a new airplane manufacturing company to compete against Boeing or McDonnell Douglas costs a few billion dollars.
- *Legal barriers in the form of regulation keep some firms out of the industry.* Intel's patented microprocessors make it difficult for other firms to compete against it on a large scale. Intel successfully litigates most patent infringement suits.
- *Firm-specific competitive advantage factors exist for the firm.* The competitive edge may result from superior product differentiation, high research and development expenditures, and patent or trademark protection. Coca-Cola's patented formula and trademarked name Coke™ have made Coke the world's most recognized brand. Over the period 1981 through 1993, management enriched total shareholder value by $50 billion.[15]

[15] See John Huey, "The World's Best Brand," *Fortune*, May 31, 1993, pp. 44–54.

For firms operating in imperfect competition, investors attempt to estimate the length of time each firm can continue to earn superior returns on new investment. Unless the company benefits from extremely restrictive barriers to entry in its markets, other firms will enter the product market in an effort to also earn economic profit. Increased competition eventually results in erosion of the high returns. Competition may become so aggressive that some firms in the industry must exit the market. When only the stronger firms remain in the industry, economic profit levels usually have reached levels lower than existed before the fierce competition.

Apple Computer is an example of the struggle. Apple's management tries very hard to improve the company's market position and profitability in the personal computer industry. However, Apple's profit growth has been slowed considerably by Microsoft's Windows™ software, which allows DOS-based personal computers to look and handle more like Apple computers. In early 1993, John Sculley, then chairperson of Apple, proposed to IBM management that the two companies merge to form one strong competitive company. IBM was also struggling at the time but ignored Sculley's suggestion.

We can easily allow for growth circumstances in the valuation model. Simply add an expression to accommodate the value of the firm's growth opportunities. We call this expression the *present value of growth opportunities (PVGO).* The restated equation for value of the firm is:[16]

$$\begin{aligned} V^L &= \textbf{Value of unlevered firm + present value of tax savings} \\ &\quad \textbf{+ present value of growth opportunities} \qquad (17\text{-}16) \\ &= \frac{\text{COP} \times (1 - \tau)}{r_u} + \text{PVTS} + \text{PVGO} \end{aligned}$$

where we define PVGO as:

$$\text{PVGO} = \frac{\textbf{Investment} \times \textbf{(investment's rate of return)}}{\textbf{Required market return}} \qquad (17\text{-}17)$$

For simplicity, we state PVGO as a perpetuity. The numerator of the equation is equivalent to annual cash operating profit after taxes expected to be realized from investing in growth projects with perpetual life. We capitalize this forecasted profit at the market's required return, given in the denominator.

Illustration 17-4 shows how to apply the valuation models for PVGO investments. The process is an extension of our previous discussion.

ILLUSTRATION 17-4

Present value of growth opportunities

Earlier in Section 17.4.3, we found the value of the no-growth levered Ethridge Publishing Company to be \$16,416 (see Eq. (17-10)).

$$V^L = S + B \qquad \textit{or} \qquad V^L = \frac{\text{COP} \times (1 - \tau)}{r_u} = \text{PVTS}$$

$$= \$9216 + \$7200 \qquad\qquad = \$14{,}400 + \$2016$$

$$= \$16{,}416 \qquad\qquad = \$16{,}416$$

[16]The discussion also applies to the all-equity financed firm; in this case PVTS = 0.

Investments that have the potential to earn economic profit result in higher value for both the firm and the equity. The firm's value becomes

$$V^L = \$16{,}416 + \text{PVGO}$$

Suppose Ethridge Publishing invests \$1000 in new equipment today and expects a 15 percent return on the PVGO investment each year in perpetuity. If the minimum required market rate of return is 8.772 percent for the equipment, the value contributed to firm value is \$1710.

$$\begin{aligned}\text{PVGO} &= \frac{\text{Investment} \times (\text{investment's rate of return})}{\text{Required market rate}}\\ &= \frac{\$1000 \times 0.15}{0.08772}\\ &= \frac{\$150}{0.08772}\\ &= \$1710\end{aligned}$$

The \$150 in the numerator of the equation reflects the *investment's annual cash operating profit after taxes (IACOPAT)*. The present value of receiving these annual cash operating profits in perpetuity is \$150 ÷ 0.08772 = \$1710. After this investment, the value of Ethridge Publishing is \$16,416 + \$1710 = \$18,126.

The following table summarizes the effect of different growth opportunities (some of them negative) along several dimensions. Column *A* is the problem we have just solved. Column *B* shows results when the new investment's rate of return equals the market required rate (MRR) of 8.772 percent. In this case, IACOPAT = \$87.72 and PVGO = \$1000. The PVGO simply equals the \$1000 investment. Thus, the value of the firm increases by only \$1000. This situation is the no-growth scenario discussed earlier in the chapter. Column *C* shows that when the firm fails to earn the MRR of 8.772 percent on new investments, then IACOPAT and PVGO are both negative and the firm losses value.

Different Scenarios for a \$1000 Investment

	A	B	C
MRR	8.772%	8.772%	8.772%
Investment return	15.000%	8.772%	−11.228%
IACOPAT	\$150	\$87.72	−\$112.28
PVGO	\$1,710	\$1,000	−\$1,280
V^L	\$18,126	\$17,416	\$15,136

IACOPAT = investment × investment's rate of return
PVGO = IACOPAT ÷ MRR = IACOPAT ÷ 0.08872
V^L = \$16,416 + PVGO

Figure 17-6 aids in the explanation of the results in Illustration 17-4. A company's value is higher if expected PVGOs are positive. But any present value growth opportunity is dependent on the length of time that it takes the company to progress from a state of earning economic profit to a fully competitive equilibrium; that is, until PVGO = 0.

As PVGO values transfer to the COP expression in Equation 11.16, without management undertaking further new PVGO investments, the value of the firm declines until PVGO equals zero. At this point, the investments earn no economic profit and rate of return on investment equals market required rate, Although the company may continue to grow in size, the prospect of no further economic profit means that growth no longer adds additional value to either the firm or to shareholder wealth.

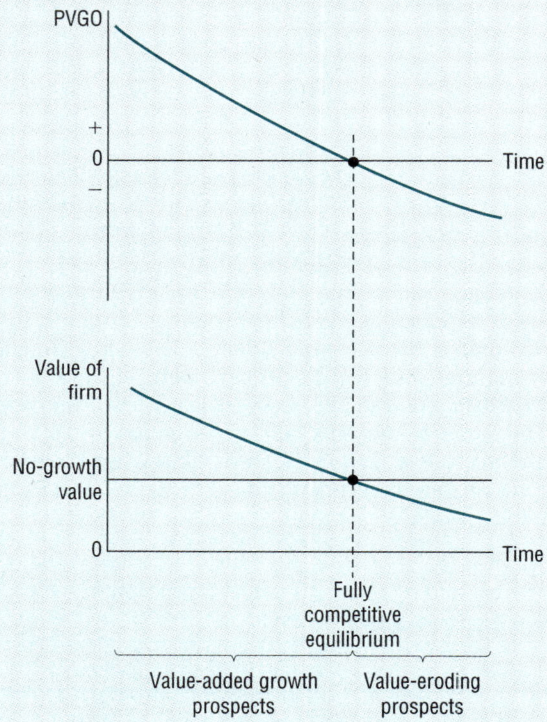

FIGURE 17-6
Contribution of PVGOs

In theory, the contribution of PVGO to firm and shareholder values grows smaller with each passing year, unless the firm invests in new growth projects that earn economic profit. As management makes new investments and the investments realize their forecasted potentials, economic value flows from present value of growth opportunities into cash operating profit in Eq. (17-16):

$$V^L = \frac{\mathbf{COP} \times (1 - \tau)}{r_u} + \mathbf{PVTS} + \mathbf{PVGO} \qquad \textbf{(17-16)}$$

PVGO becomes COP, which in turn earns the required market rate of return r_u but no excess return. That is to say, as PVGOs lose their economic profit, these projects move from an imperfect market environment of positive economic profit to a perfect market environment of zero economic profit.

COMPREHENSION CHECK

1. *How is the value of an unlevered firm calculated?*
2. *Under what conditions would a firm operate with a high degree of business risk? How could management reduce such a firm's business risk?*
3. *When a firm uses debt to finance part of its operations, what effect does this have on the firm's cash operating profit after taxes? What are the benefits of debt financing for the firm's shareholders?*
4. *How is the value determined for a firm that is financed with both debt and equity?*
5. *What conditions may limit a firm from earning economic profit indefinitely on its investments?*
6. *How many profitable growth opportunities be included in the valuation model of the firm?*

SUMMARY

- A corporation is an interrelated set of contracts among customers, employees, governments, investors, and vendors.
- Service values flow from the firm to the customer.
- Monetary amounts and customer and brand loyalty are the primary values flowing from customers to the firm.
- The supplier-firm value-exchange system consists of employees being fairly compensated in exchange for providing productive labor and skills to the firm, and investors earning a fair return given the risk of the firm.
- Any conflicts within the value-exchange system can result in lower value of both the firm and shareholder wealth.
- Principal-agent problems exist in that shareholder wealth maximization is not the primary objective of management.
- Theory suggests that managers act in the best interests of shareholders because of management's ownership position, compensation tied to performance, takeover threats, and the competitive labor market.
- The investment opportunity schedule and the market rate of return schedule interact to determine investments expected to increase firm value.
- The value of the firm declines if management invests in projects earning less than the market rate of return.
- The long-term value index suggests that the financial market prices common stock on the basis of long-term cash flow potential of the firm.
- A no-growth firm is one that invests in new plant and equipment to simply maintain current operating levels. Any cash flows remaining are paid as dividends to shareholders.
- Current after-tax cash operating profit, $COP \times (1 - \tau)$, is capitalized at a rate that compensates shareholders for bearing business risk, r_u.
- Financing the company with debt provides a tax benefit that increases both the value of the firm and shareholder wealth. This benefit is called the *present value tax savings (PVTS)*.
- Growth opportunities mean the firm can earn more than its minimum required market rate of return.

- Firms operating in perfect competition do not have growth opportunities since no firm is strong enough, or has a differentiated product, to command premium prices.
- Firms in imperfect competition can earn economic profit as a result of growth opportunities not available to other firms.
- The present value of growth opportunities is the economic profit capitalized by the market return:

$$PVGO = \frac{\text{Investment} \times \text{investment's rate of return}}{\text{Required market rate}}$$

- PVGO increase both the value of the firm and shareholder wealth, since debtholders receive a fixed return.

SELF-CORRECTION PROBLEMS

1. What is the market value of a corporation that has 2 million shares of common stock traded over the counter at $13 per share? Its debt is valued at $10 million.
2. Calculate the market value of a firm which earns 15 percent in perpetuity on its $80 million investment in assets, stated at book value. Investors require a return of 10 percent and there is no growth. Comment on the job that management is doing for the shareholders.
3. The future expected cash flow from operations of the Ridefast Company are $44,000 in perpetuity. The current liquidation value of the firm is estimated to be $400,000. If investors require a 13 percent return, should Ridefast continue operations?

PROBLEMS

1. a. It can be argued that economic profit maximization for the firm and wealth maximization for the owners are equivalent objectives. Discuss this issue. Identify your assumptions.
   b. Discuss an alternative to the corporate objective of maximizing share value.
2. Discuss examples of potential conflicts of interest between managers and shareholders. Why do managers generally work hard to make the firm successful?
3. As merger and takeover activity has increased in recent years, the issue of corporate ownership versus control has become more controversial. Discuss the principal-agent problem as it relates to shareholder-management relations. Why is there a potential conflict between the two groups? What steps can be taken to mitigate this problem?
4. The stated objective of commercial businesses is often taken to be the maximization of firm and equity valuation. Comment on the extent to which this objective is realistic and explain why management must be concerned with firm valuation. How can financial management techniques assist in meeting actual corporate objectives?
5. What is the market value of a corporation which has its 5 million shares of common stock listed on the American Stock Exchange and its bonds traded over the counter? The stock currently sells for $6 per share and the total value of the debt is $8 million.

6. Calculate the value of a public company. The asset value, as shown on the balance sheet, is \$10 million. The firm has \$5 million of debt, which is equal to its market value. There are 150,000 shares of common stock outstanding with a current market value of \$75 per share.
7. The GRT Corporation's common stock and bonds are traded on the New York Stock Exchange. The most recent balance sheet for GRT records the bonds at \$60 million, whereas equity has a value of \$240 million. There are 10 million shares of the company outstanding with a current market value of \$56 per share. GRT's bonds have a par value of \$1000 but are currently trading for 85 percent of par. Calculate the market value of GRT.
8. Royal Players, Inc. has 50 million shares of common stock outstanding, with a book value of \$900 million. The market price per share is \$44. Bonds are shown on the balance sheet at \$400 million. The noncallable bonds, which mature in 12 years, have a coupon rate of 10 percent with interest payable annually. The current market interest rate for similar risky debt is 9 percent. What is the market value of the company?
9. Use the following equation to answer the questions:

   Market value of the firm

   $$= \frac{\text{Corporate rate of return} \times \text{book value of assets}}{\text{Required market rate}}$$

   a. If investors increase the required market rate, what happens to the value of the firm, assuming all else remains constant?
   b. If the market value of the firm declines and the value of assets remain unchanged, what is the relationship between *corporate rate of return* and the *required market rate?*
   c. Management purchases some new assets that earn the *corporate rate of return.* However, the market value of the firm declines. Why?
10. Calculate the market value of a firm that earns 14 percent on its assets, which have a book value of \$144 million. The required rate of return by investors is 12 percent. Comment on the job that management is doing for its shareholders.
11. Warman Limited has assets with a book value of \$18 million on which management is currently earning a 15 percent return. Due to increasing concern over prospects for Warman's industry, investors have raised their rate of return expectations from 12 percent to 15 percent. Calculate the new market value of Warman given this change. What is the net change in Warman's value? Why did it occur?
12. Maui Sunset, Inc.'s assets have a book value of \$1.6 million. Management is able to earn a return of 20 percent on these assets. Because of a large increase in tourism and increased foreign investment in the area, investors have changed their rate of return expectation from 15 percent to 10 percent. Calculate the new market value of Maui Sunset. What is the net change in Maui Sunset's market value as a result of investors revising their rate?
13. Healthmax, Inc. is valued by the market at \$30 million. The firm's accounting records indicate that assets are recorded at a value of \$10 million. Investors require a market rate of 25 percent.
    a. What is the corporate rate of return that is necessary to maintain the firm's value at \$10 million?

b. What is the value of the firm if the assets earn a 60 percent rate of return? Does the value of the firm increase or decrease? Why?
c. At what point will loss of value occur?

14. Investment bankers believe the investors require a 12 percent market return to invest in Journal Press Corporation. For every $1 invested in assets of the firm, what is the contribution to the market value of the company if the corporate rate of return is 4 percent? 8 percent? 12 percent? 16 percent? 20 percent? Which corporate rates of return result in value being created, destroyed, or unchanged?
15. The management of Landstar Partners estimates that investors require a return of 15 percent to invest in the partnership. For each $1 invested in projects by the firm, what is the contribution to the value of the partnership if the rate of return on assets is 9 percent? 12 percent? 15 percent? 18 percent? 21 percent? Which rates of return on partnership assets result in value being created, destroyed, or unchanged?
16. When a firm uses a market rate of return that is too low for evaluating investment decisions, how is the firm's objective of value maximization affected?
17. In past years, Aerosouth Commuter Airline has earned 10 percent on its assets, which have a book value of $6 million. However, in the last recession Aerosouth's return fell to 2 percent on assets and has remained there as the economy started to improve. This airline is privately owned so there is no market value for its common stock. Investors of publicly owned commuter airlines have expected a rate of return of 12 percent. Estimate the value of Aerosouth before and after the recession. Comment on the company's condition.
18. Annual operating cash flows for Turborun Tracks, Inc. are expected to be $4.2 million. Management believes that the firm's required rate of return on investment is 12 percent. Calculate the value of the firm by capitalizing its operating cash flows. If management is correct, what will happen to the value of the firm if new investments are made that return 14 percent?
19. The value of a firm is given by capitalizing operating cash flow at an appropriate market rate of return; for example, $\$20 \div 0.10 = \$200$. Suppose management considers a new investment that requires an initial outlay of $100. The project is very risky and management estimates that if it is taken, the firm's market rate of return will increase to 0.20. Calculate the minimum required rate of return from the new project so that the value of the firm after the investment equals its preinvestment value plus the initial outlay for the investment.
20. Calculate the market value of Jayne Limited. It is expected to generate cash flow from operations of $3.8 million in perpetuity. Investors require an annual return of 19 percent.
21. What is the market value of Renner Company if investors require a 16 percent return? They believe the firm can earn annual cash flow from operations of $67 million.
22. How much in annual cash flows must McWilliams Company generate to maintain its market value of $100 million if management believes that investors require an 18 percent return?
23. The market value of Thomas II Mutual Fund is $45 million. If its annual cash flows are $3 million, what is the rate of return that investors require?
24. The future expected cash flow from operations for Packard Company is $35,000

in perpetuity. The liquidating value is estimated to be $200,000. If investors require a 15 percent return on their investment, should Packard continue operations?

25. What is the value of an unlevered firm where annual cash flow from operations is expected to remain constant at $430,000? The tax rate is zero. Owners of the firm require an 11 percent return for their exposure to business risk.
26. Calculate the value of an unlevered firm which has expected cash flow from operations of $120,000 annually. Cash flows are expected to remain constant for the foreseeable future. The firm's tax rate is 40 percent. Owners expect a rate of return on their investment of 9 percent to compensate them for the business risk.
27. What is the value of an all-equity firm where management expects no growth in cash earnings of $200,000 annually? The firm's owners expect a return of 14 percent on their investment. The tax rate for the business is 36 percent.
28. How much does the annual interest of $225,000 on a long-term loan actually cost a firm that is operating profitably? Assume the firm's marginal income tax rate is 36 percent.
29. If a corporation borrows money on a perpetual basis, which results in interest payments of $800,000 annually, what is the present value of the firm's income tax savings if the market rate on this debt is 12 percent? The firm's marginal tax rate is 28 percent.
30. A firm's management wants to substitute $100,000 of perpetual debt with an annual coupon interest rate of 9.5 percent for an equal amount of equity. The market rate for the debt will also be 9.5 percent. Presently, the firm is unleveraged. How much will the value of the firm be increased or decreased if business operations continue unchanged? The firm's tax rate is 36 percent.
31. a. What is the market value of a firm's perpetual debt which has a par value of $10.5 million? The debt's coupon rate is 9 percent and investors require a 12 percent return.
    b. What possible explanations are there for the present market value of the firm's debt?
32. Compute the value of the interest tax shield generated by the following debt issues. The marginal corporate tax rate is 34 percent and the market rate of interest is 8 percent.
    a. A $1000, one-year loan at 9 percent.
    b. A five-year balloon note of $1000 at 9 percent, with interest payable annually.
    c. A $1000 perpetuity at 9 percent.
33. Logic, Inc. is an unlevered firm with an expected net operating income of $10,000 per year. No growth in operating cash flow is expected. Shareholders require a 12 percent return on their investment. The tax rate is zero.
    a. Calculate the value of the firm.
    b. If the firm issues $25,000 of 7 percent perpetual bonds at face value, and retires $25,000 worth of stock with the proceeds, what is the value of the firm's equity?
    c. Now assume that the tax rate is 34 percent. Recalculate parts (a) and (b). Also calculate the value of the levered firm. You need to adjust operating income to an after-tax basis.
34. The book and market values for iTech Corporation are as follows:

Book value:	Net working capital	$ 30	Debt	$ 40
	Long-term assets	70	Equity	60
	Totals	$100		$100
Market value:	Net working capital	$ 30	Debt	$40
	Long-term assets	150	Equity	140
	Totals	$180		$180

The firm expects no growth. The $40 debt is permanent (that is, perpetual). The debt's coupon rate is 7 percent, which equals the required market rate. The tax rate is 34 percent.

a. How much does the tax shield from debt contribute to the value of the firm?
b. What happens to the value of the firm if Congress passes a law that eliminates the tax deductibility of interest? What is the new value?

35. Prime Box Company is an unlevered firm valued at $500,000. It has no growth prospects and there are 5000 shares outstanding. Investors require a 14 percent return on the stock and the firm's tax rate is 34 percent.
    a. How much is the firm's before-tax cash flow from operations?
    b. If the firm issues $200,000 of 8 percent debt at par and retires stock with the proceeds, what is the new value of the firm?
    c. What is the new value of the equity in part (b)?
    d. How much is the price per share before and after the debt swap?
    e. What is the price-earnings ratio before and after the debt swap?
36. The unlevered value of MacPower Corporation is $2 million. Operating cash flows are constant. The firm's marginal tax rate is 34 percent. Management is considering retiring some equity by issuing $600,000 of perpetual debt with a coupon rate of 9 percent.
    a. What is the firm's value after issuing the debt, if the required market rate for the debt is also 9 percent? What is the value of the equity?
    b. What is the value of the debt, the equity, and the firm if the required market rate for the debt is 8 percent? 10 percent?
37. Phoenix Enterprise, Inc. is an all-equity firm with a current market value of $80 million. This value reflects a required rate of return of 20 percent on its common stock. One million common shares are outstanding. Management of Phoenix has decided to undertake a project costing $6 million. The project's expected after-tax cash flow is $8 million at the end of the first year. (*Note:* The cash flows are not in perpetuity.) The required return on the nonrisk-changing investment is 20 percent.
    a. What is the value of Phoenix's shares after publicly announcing the decision to accept the investment, assuming the financial markets are efficient? The project will be financed with internally generated cash.
    b. What should be the new share price if the investment is financed by issuing 75,000 new shares?
    c. Suppose the level of interest rates increases and, consequently, the rate of return required on Phoenix's shares increases to 25 percent. What will be the value of each of Phoenix's shares if the project is financed with 75,000 new shares?
38. FastMicro, Inc. has a current market value of $2 million. The firm's present cash flow from operations is $200,000 annually. Management is considering investing in a new project which costs $1 million. This project is less risky than the exist-

ing projects and the discount rate for the firm would be reduced by 2 percentage points should management decide to make the investment.

a. Find the minimum required rate of return that should be attached to the new project.

b. Suppose the project's rate of return is larger by 9 percent in comparison to the minimum rate of return you calculate in part (a); that is, multiply your answer by 1.09 and then subtract 1. Calculate the value of the new project. What is the new value of the firm? (*Hint:* Add the current value of the firm to the value of the new project.)

39. Assume that two firms exist which differ only by how they are financed. The constant operating cash flows for both firms are equal. The unlevered firm is financed by 3 million shares of common stock with a market price per share of $10. The market discount rate for the unlevered firm is 15 percent. The levered firm has 2 million shares of stock and $10 million in long-term debt with an interest rate of 10 percent. The corporate tax rate is 40 percent.
    a. Calculate the value of each firm. (*Hint:* First calculate the unlevered firm's value and use your answer to value the levered firm.)
    b. Calculate the cash flow from operations (before taxes and interest payments) for each firm.
    c. How much is the net income for each firm? How much is each firm's earnings per share?

40. Two firms are identical except for how they are financed. One firm uses debt in its financing, whereas the other firm does not. At a tax rate of 34 percent and a discount rate of 10 percent, the value of the unlevered firm is $660, assuming the firm has no-growth opportunities.
    a. What is the amount of constant operating cash flow that is capitalized?
    b. If the tax rate increases from 34 percent to 46 percent, what is the value of the unlevered firm?
    c. If the levered firm is financed with $100 debt, what is the value of the firm before and after the tax rate change?

41. A company currently has no debt financing. The market value of each of its 5 million outstanding shares is $25. The new management of the company is convinced that debt financing increases the aggregate market value of the company's outstanding securities by the present value of the corporate tax shield on interest payments. In other words, they believe that $V^L = V^u + \tau B$. Cash flow from operations before taxes is expected to be constant at $35 million. The corporate tax rate is 30 percent. Management is considering a tender offer at $25 per share to repurchase 2.4 million of its own shares. The tender offer will be financed by issuing (at par) $60 million in 9 percent perpetual debentures.
    a. What is the current value of the firm?
    b. What is the required return on the company's stock?
    c. How much is the tax shield on the debt?
    d. If management is correct in believing that $V^L = V^u + PVTS\ B$, what is the likely market value per common share once the firm replaces some shares with debt financing?

42. Update Table 17-3 using the latest information available from Value Line Investment Services. Has the market's view changed much since February 1994?

43. An organization called CalPERS has been very active during the past few years monitoring actions of corporate executives performing below expectations. Based on a library search, write a short report outlining CalPERS's strategy to force management to improve returns to shareholders.

INTEGRATIVE PROBLEM

a. Increasing or maximizing share value is frequently expressed as the goal of corporate managements. What are some alternatives to this objective?
b. The separation of ownership and management in today's publicly owned corporations results in potential conflicts of interests between managers and shareholders. What factors induce management to align its interest with shareholders?
c. Takeover and merger activity has increased in recent years. This activity has increased the possible conflict between corporate management and owners. Discuss the principal-agent problem as it relates to shareholder-management relations. Why is there a potential conflict between the two groups? How can this conflict be reduced?
d. Why is the maximization of shareholder wealth the most appropriate objective for management to pursue?
e. Calculate the value of a publicly owned corporation. Its asset value, as shown on the balance sheet, is $98 million. The firm has $26 million of debt, which is equal to its market value. There are 5 million shares of common stock outstanding with a current market value of $33 per share.
f. Use the following equation to answer the questions:

Market value of the firm

$$= \frac{\text{Corporate rate of return} \times \text{book value of assets}}{\text{Required market rate}}$$

i. If investors increase the rate of return they require, what happens to the value of the firm, assuming all else remains constant?
ii. If the market value of the firm declines and the value of assets remains unchanged, what is the relationship between the corporate required rate of return and the required market rate of return?
iii. Management purchases new assets which earn the corporate rate of return. However, the market value of the firm declines. Why?

g. Using the equation in part (f), calculate the market value of a firm that earns 18 percent on its assets and has a book value of $100 million. Investors require a return of 12 percent. Comment on the job that management is doing in creating value for the firm's shareholders.
h. Jason Corporation, which has assets with a book value of $30 million, currently earns 10 percent. Due to increased concern over prospects for Jason's industry, investors have raised their required return from 10 percent to 15 percent. Calculate the new market value of the firm given this change. What is the net change in Jason's value? Why did it occur?

i. When a firm uses a rate of return that is too low for evaluating investments, how is the firm's objective of value maximization affected?

j. Calculate the market value of a firm that is expected to generate cash flow from operations of $5.6 million in perpetuity. Assume that investors require an annual return of 14 percent.

k. If the market value of a firm is $60 million and its annual cash flow from operations is $9 million, what is the rate of return investors require?

l. Zeron, Inc. issues $10 million of perpetual debt at a 9 percent annual interest rate. Its corporate income tax rate is 36 percent. How much is the annual income tax savings brought about by this borrowing? What is the present value of this savings?

m. Using the debt and tax rate for Zeron, Inc. in part (1), what is the value of Zeron if the cash operating profit before taxes is $4.2 million? The required rate of return for the unlevered operating cash flows is 12 percent.

n. A new corporate investment of $10 million has an expected rate of return of 14 percent. If the firm's required rate of return is 11 percent, what is the present value of the firm's growth opportunity if the project has a perpetual life expectancy?

SOLUTIONS TO SELF-CORRECTION PROBLEMS

1. Value of firm = Value of debt + value of equity

$$= \$10{,}000{,}000 + \$13 \times 2{,}000{,}000$$
$$= \$36{,}000{,}000$$

2. Value of firm

$$= \frac{\text{Corporate rate of return} \times \text{book value of assets}}{\text{Required market rate}}$$
$$= \frac{0.15 \times \$80{,}000{,}000}{0.10}$$
$$= \$120{,}000{,}000$$

Since the rate of return earned by the company is greater than the investors' required return, management is increasing common shareholders' wealth and acting in their best interests.

3. Value of firm

$$= \frac{\text{Corporate rate of return} \times \text{book value of assets}}{\text{Required market rate}}$$
$$= \frac{\text{Expected perpetual cash flows}}{\text{Required market rate}}$$
$$= \$44{,}000 \div 0.13$$
$$= \$338{,}462$$

Based on financial considerations, since the liquidation value exceeds the going-concern value by a considerable margin, the firm should discontinue operations, liquidate the assets, and distribute the proceeds to the owners.

SELECTED REFERENCES

Lowenstein, Louis, *Sense and Nonsense in Corporate Finance.* Reading, MA: Addison-Wesley Publishing Company, Inc., 1991. The author, a former executive, provides a thought-provoking discussion about financial theory.

Porter, Michael E., *Competitive Strategy: Techniques for Analyzing Industries and Competitors.* New York: The Free Press, 1980, and *Competitive Advantage: Creating and Sustaining Superior Performance.* New York: The Free Press, 1985. These two books provide much insight into factors affecting the long-term value of a firm.

Rappaport, Alfred, *Creating Shareholder Value: The New Standard for Business Performance.* New York: The Free Press, 1986. This book is widely acclaimed by practitioners.

CHAPTER 18

The Cost of Capital

"We would be much more modernized and therefore more competitive had the cost been lower."[1] James Geier, chief executive officer of Cincinnati Milacron, was expressing his concern that the high cost of financing has been one factor leading to the demise of many firms in the U.S. machine tool industry. Ken Olsen, former president of Digital Equipment Corporation, and Carl Ledbetter, former president of Control Data's abandoned supercomputer project, each claimed that if their company's financing costs had been lower, then their respective companies would have been more profitable.[2] These executives are saying that a firm's cost of funds, commonly called *cost of capital,* affects creation of shareholder value.

The cost of capital is made up of the return that both debt and equity investors expect to receive by investing in a firm's financial securities. In general, investors will demand a return equal to the return they could receive on an alternative set of cash flows carrying the same risk. Implicit in this statement is the fact that cost of capital is determined by the current market prices investors place on securities in their pursuit of risk-adjusted returns. Historical prices, including prices existing at the date the securities were originally issued, do not matter in calculating cost of capital. The cost of capital that results from investors' demands is, in turn, the minimum rate managers must receive on the firm's investments if they are to serve the investors' best interests.

Most corporate finance officers estimate the cost of capital by determining how much debt a firm can support and, by implication, how much equity capital must be invested. Then the yield to be paid on the debt and the required rate of return

[1]Joseph Morone and Albert Paulson, "Cost of Capital: The Managerial Perspective," *California Management Review* (Summer 1991), p. 15.

[2]See Peter Dunn, "DEC's Olsen: Capital Cost Hurting," *Electronic News,* March 29, 1989, p. 1, and Louis S. Richman, "How Capital Costs Cripple America," *Fortune,* August 4, 1989, p. 50.

demanded by shareholders on the equity can be combined for an estimate of cost of capital. Cost of capital is conceptually straightforward. As a practical matter, the numbers that actually can be used in the cost of capital calculation are necessarily approximate. The financial manager must make simplifying assumptions, looking backward in order to speculate about the future.

This chapter will examine how to calculate the cost of capital. When you have completed this chapter, you should understand:

- How to calculate the cost of debt and the cost of preferred stock.
- How to calculate the cost of equity financing.
- How to combine the costs of different forms of financing into a weighted average cost of capital, or WACC.
- How the weighted average cost of capital and firm value are related.

THE COST OF DEBT

In a world free of both taxes and risk, corporations could finance any and all investments through borrowing, provided that those investments were sure to return more than the interest rate demanded by lenders. In the real world, of course, taxes complicate the picture, and it is impossible to predict with absolute certainty that all required payments to creditors will be made on time. However, creditors are willing to bear a certain level of risk if the return is adequate. The return they demand is the *cost of debt* to the firm.

The *cost of debt* is the yield to maturity (YTM) to be realized by investors of the company's debt in the current market. In this discussion, we will focus on adjusting the YTM for taxes, a necessary step because debt interest payments are tax-deductible expenses to the issuing firm. The firm's after-tax cost of debt is:

$$\begin{aligned}\textbf{After-tax cost of debt} &= \textbf{YTM} \times \textbf{(1} - \textbf{tax rate)} \\ &= r_d \times (1 - t)\end{aligned} \qquad \textbf{(18-1)}$$

For example, if Ethridge Publishing's income tax rate is 28 percent and the bond's YTM is 8 percent, the cost of debt to the corporation is 5.76 percent: 8% × (1 – 0.28). It does not matter if the bond was originally issued to yield the investor, say, 9 percent. If Ethridge Publishing had to issue similar debt today, it would cost 5.76 percent after taxes. In the current market, Ethridge Publishing would pay debt investors 8 percent but would effectively reclaim 2.24 percentage points of interest payments on its tax return (= 8.00% – 5.76%).

Some people may question the use of the YTM in the cost of debt formula. Why not use the coupon rate stated on the bond instead? Isn't this the amount of interest expense actually incurred by the firm? Yes, the coupon amount is the interest expense incurred by the firm, but investors bid the price of the bond either up or down depending on market rates they can earn in alternative investments of equal risk. *Investors will earn the market interest rate, given the risk of the security, regardless of the stated coupon rate.* This fact is critical to understanding the cost of capital for all securities. It underscores our earlier point that the return to the investor is the cost to the firm.

COMPREHENSION CHECK

1. *State the equation to calculate the cost of debt.*
2. *Explain why the market value of debt is used to calculate the cost of debt.*

THE COST OF PREFERRED STOCK

If a firm issues preferred stock to help finance its assets, the cost is the market rate required by investors who buy the security. Since most preferred stock has a fixed dividend amount, investors bid the price up or down to earn the market rate, similar to how they price debt in the financial markets. Thus, the *cost of preferred stock* is its dividend yield:

Cost of preferred stock = Dividend ÷ market price of preferred stock (18-2)

If the firm's preferred stock pays a dividend of $3 per share, and shares sell for $24 each, the firm's cost of preferred stock is its dividend yield of 12.5 percent: $3 ÷ $24. Unlike debt interest, the preferred stock dividend is not a tax-deductible expense to the firm. Thus, we do not make any tax adjustment to the dividend yield.

COMPREHENSION CHECK

1. *Explain why market value is used to calculate the cost of preferred stock.*
2. *State the equation to calculate the cost of preferred stock.*

THE COST OF EQUITY

Like debt and preferred stock investors, common stock investors also require an appropriate market rate of return. Equity investors determine this market rate, or cost of equity, by bidding the price of the company's shares up or down until the share price reflects the rate of return participants willingly accept. But calculation of the cost of equity is more complicated than are the calculations for either the cost of debt or the cost of preferred stock because equity is not a fixed-income security. A number of methods exist to calculate the cost of equity. The predominant methods are the *dividend growth model*, the *security market line*, and the *inverted price-earnings ratio*.

The Cost of Equity Using the Dividend Growth Model

When we used the dividend growth model (DGM) to value common stock, we assumed that we knew the appropriate market rate. Now let's turn the problem around. Suppose we know the stock price but not the required market rate. We need to rearrange the DGM so that it is clear that the required market rate (cost of equity) is determined by the expected dividend next period, the current price of the stock, and the expected growth rate for dividends. For instance, the DGM is:

$$\textbf{Stock price} = \frac{\textbf{Expect dividend next year}}{\textbf{Required market rate} - \textbf{expected growth rate for dividends}} \qquad (18\text{-}3)$$

which, when rearranged, becomes:

$$\text{Required market rate} = \frac{\text{Expected dividend next year}}{\text{Stock price}} + \text{expected growth rate for dividends}$$

$$= \text{Dividend yield} + \text{expected growth rate for dividends} \qquad \textbf{(18-4)}$$

$$r_e = \frac{D_1}{P_0} + g$$

Calculation of the dividend yield, D_1/P_0, is usually straightforward. It is next year's expected dividend divided by the current common stock price. A good estimate of next year's dividend is this year's dividend, possibly increased a little to reflect any change in the dividend that has occurred in recent years. But how is growth, g, estimated?

A popular approach used to calculate g is to calculate the historical growth rate of dividends using the future value model. For example, assume that Ethridge Publishing, Inc. paid a dividend of $0.267 per share in year 1 (the earliest year) and paid $0.533 in year 10 (the latest year):

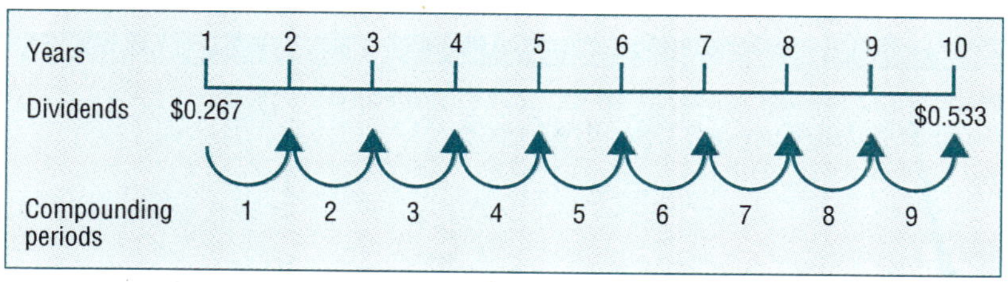

We find the annual compound growth rate in dividends by solving the future value equation:

Exercise:
If dividends were $0.10 for the year 1989 and $0.30 for the year 1995, what was the compounded annual growth rate in dividends? *Answer:* There are six compounding periods. $PV = FV \times (1 + g)^n \rightarrow 0.10 = 0.30 \times (1 + g)^6$. Solve for g and find it to be about 20 percent annually.

Exercise:
If the library subscribes to *Nelson's Directory of Investment Research,* have each student look up a company whose name starts with the first letter of her or his last name and report on the information found.

$$\text{Future value} = \text{Past value} \times (1 + \text{growth rate})^{n-1} \qquad \textbf{(18-5)}$$

$$\$0.533 = \$0.267 \times (1 + \text{growth rate})^9$$

$$(1 + \text{growth rate})^9 = \frac{\$0.533}{\$0.267} = 2$$

$$(1 + \text{growth rate}) = (2)^{1/9}$$

$$\text{Growth rate} = 0.08 \text{ or } 8 \text{ percent}$$

The exponent n in Eq. (18-5) is the number of years (10); n–1 represents the number of compounding periods (9). The calculation assumes that past growth is representative of future growth.[3]

A second approach to estimating growth is to learn what growth rates various securities analysts at brokerage houses project for the stock. Figure 18-1 is a sample from *Nelson's 1994 Directory of Investment Research.* In addition to other useful infor-

[3]When the table for the present value of $1 is available, an easy approximation of the growth rate between two periods of time is found by dividing the dividend for the earlier period by the dividend for the later period. Use the result as a present value interest factor to enter the present value table for the elapsed number of years and read up to the nearest whole percentage point. In the example given, enter the table for nine periods and read across the row until you find 0.500 (= $0.267 + $0.533), or a value close to it. From the table, the growth rate is 8 percent.

Nelson's 1994 Directory of Investment Research,

Section 6 - Company Profiles/Analyst Coverage:

In-depth corporate profiles of over 12,500 publicly-owned companies worldwide. Key executives, telephone number, five-year operations summary, key investment characteristics. . . . Plus the names and phone numbers of all security analysts who follow each company. Volume I includes over 6,000 companies whose principal equity trading market is in the United States; Volume II covers 6,500 companies traded outside the U.S., in 40 countries on six continents.

Capital Cities/ABC
77 W. 66th Street
New York, NY 10023
212 456-7777 fax (212) 456-1285

Headquarters address, phone & fax

Business Description:
Operates the ABC Television Network and eight TV stations, the ABC Radio Networks and 21 radio stations, and provides programming for cable television. The company publishes daily and weekly newspapers, shopping guides, and various specialty and business periodicals, books and records, and provides research services and distributes information from data bases.

Business description

Key Executives:
Chairman. . . . . Thomas S. Murphy, *67 (39 yrs)*
CEO. . . . . Thomas S. Murphy, *67 (39 yrs)*
CFO. . . . . Ronald J. Doerfler, *52 (24 yrs)*
Treasurer. . . . . David J. Vondrak, *48 (18 yrs)*
Controller . . . . Allan J. Edelson, *51 (13 yrs)*
Investor Relations. . . . . . .Joseph M. Fitzgerald, *44 (16 yrs)*
Corp. Communications . . . . Patricia J. Matson, *48 (16 yrs)*
Secretary . . . . .Phillip R. Farnsworth, *51 (16 yrs)*
General Counsel . . . . David Westin, *41 (3 yrs)*
Human Resources . . . . David J. Vondrak, *48 (18 yrs)*
Employee Benefits . . . . Warren Salerno
Real Estate . . . . .Bruce E. Phillips, *37 (17 yrs)*
MIS. John J. Wolters, *46 (15 yrs)*

Key Executives
Name, Age, Years with company

Summary of Opterations ($000)

Year	Sales	Net Income	$EPS
12/92	5,334,100	389,300	23.45
12/91	5,382,000	374,700	22.52
12/90	5,385,600	477,800	28.72
12/89	4,957,400	485,700	29.19
12/88	4,773,500	387,100	23
12/87	4,440,300	279,100	
5-yr. Growth Rate	3.8%	6.9%	

5-year operating summary - Sales, Net Income, and EPS as reported, without restatement for extraordinary items, discontinued operations, or changes in capitalization. (For banks, the "Sales" amount represents net interest income.)

Growth rates shown are compound annual rates, expressed as a percentage, computed over the period covered - usually five years - using the following formula, where...
RV = recent value,
PV = present value (base year), and
n = number of years;

$$\left[\left(\frac{RV}{PV}\right)^{\frac{1}{n-1}}\right]-1$$

Prim. Exchange: New York Stock Exchange
Ticker Symbol: CCB
Employees: 19,500
Shareholders: 9,600
Shares Outs.: 16,485,000
Market Val (Mil): $10,206
Auditor: Ernst & Young
Transfer Agent: Harris Trust & Savings Bank

Key corporate information

Institutional Ownership:

Institution	% Owned	$ Owned
Berskshire Hathaway	18.2%	1857.6 mil
State Farm Mutual Auto. Ins.	5.1%	520.5 mil
JP Morgan & Co.	4.9%	500.1 mil
Tukman Capital Management	3.0%	306.2 mil
Wells Fargo Institutional Trust Co.	2.2%	224.5 mil
Other Institutional Owners	43.7%	4460.2 mil
Total 357 Institutions	77.1%	7869.1 mil

Summary of institutional ownership - Largest holders, percent owned, total institutional holdings (Source: CDA/Spectrum)

Analyst Coverage:
Equity Analyst Coverage:
Sanford C.Bernstein . . . . *Tom Wolzien* (★) 212-486-5800
Alex. Brown . . . *Drew Marcus* 410-727-1700
Brown Brothers Harriman, *John G. Nelson* 212-483-1818
Buckingham Research, *David M.Goldsmith* 212-922-5500
Dillon Reed . . . .*Edward J. Atorino* 212-906-7000

"(★)" after analyst's name indicates membership on consensus all-star research teams of *Institutional Investor*, Extel Financial, and Nelson Publications.

Nelson Publications, 1 Gateway Plaza, Pt. Chester, NY 10573

FIGURE 18-1
Analyst coverage from *Nelson's 1994 Directory of Investment Research*

mation, this directory provides the names of analysts who follow publicly traded stocks. We can check the reports these analysts issue to obtain different growth rates for a given firm, or we can speak to them directly. Once all the estimated growth rates are collected, we can compute an average value and let it represent expected sustainable growth. If much variability exists among the estimates, the result will be a large range for the estimated cost of equity.

A third approach to estimating growth is to use the firm's sustainable growth rate, which we can approximate as:

Sustainable growth
= (1 − dividend payout ratio) × (return on beginning equity) **(18-6)**

The calculation for the dividend payout ratio is dividends per share ÷ earnings per share and *return on beginning equity* is net income ÷ beginning of period equity.[4] Much evidence exists to indicate that the use of sustainable growth as a proxy for g is appropriate. Illustration 18-1 provides an application of the technique.

ILLUSTRATION 18-1

Estimating the cost of equity using the DGM
Several security analysts hold a consensus view that Ethridge Publishing, Inc. will pay an expected dividend of \$0.576 per share next year. Analysts expect the dividend to grow 8 percent each year into the foreseeable future. Currently the stock price is \$18.43.

The dividend yield of the stock is \$0.576 ÷ \$18.43 = 0.03125, or 3.125 percent. Given that the growth rate is estimated to be 8 percent, the firm's cost of equity is 11.125 percent.

$$\begin{aligned}\text{Cost of equity} &= \text{Dividend yield} + \text{growth}\\ &= 0.03125 + 0.08\\ &= 0.11125\end{aligned}$$

Suppose the \$0.576 dividend per share represents 28 percent of earnings per share. Thus, earnings per share are \$0.576 ÷ 0.28 = \$2.06. If 500 shares are outstanding, net income of the firm is \$2.06 × 500 = \$1030. If the firm's beginning equity value is \$7410, *return on beginning equity* is \$1030 ÷ \$7410 = 0.139 or 13.9 percent.[5] Sustainable growth is 10 percent:

$$\begin{aligned}&\text{Sustainable growth}\\ &\quad= (1 - \text{dividend payout rate}) \times \text{return on beginning equity}\\ &\quad= (1 - 0.28) \times 0.139\\ &\quad= 0.10 \text{ or } 10 \text{ percent}\end{aligned}$$

Adding sustainable growth of 10 percent to the dividend yield of 3.125 percent results in a cost of equity of 13.125 percent.

The two approaches yield different answers because of disagreement over the expected growth rate. Which estimate is correct? Probably neither; however, the required cost of equity may be in the 11 to 13 percent range.

Exercise:
A firm earns \$1 million and pays out \$300,000 as dividends. Its equity at the beginning of the year was \$10 million. How much is the company's sustainable growth?
Answer: Retention rate = 1 − dividend payout = 0.70; return on beginning equity = 0.10; thus, sustainable growth = 0.70 × 0.10 = 0.07 or 7 percent.

[4] Return on equity is frequently calculated as profits ÷ ending equity. The sustainable growth Eq. (18-6) uses beginning equity to calculate return on equity.

[5] *Return on beginning equity* is an accounting measure of profitability; shareholders require a market rate.

The DGM (see Eq. (18-3)) reveals that the expected growth of dividends and common stock value are closely related. Increased dividends lead to higher stock price, and vice versa. However, there is *no relation* between growth and the cost of equity if the expected growth is *properly* reflected in the current share price. Illustration 18-2 demonstrates the apparent paradox of this statement using two different firms, both with the same cost of equity.

ILLUSTRATION 18-2

Growth and market returns to equity

Assume that the common stock of Jewell, Inc. and Nealon, Inc. are valued according to the dividend growth model of Eq. (18-3):

$$\text{Stock price} = \frac{\text{Expect dividend next period}}{\text{Required market rate} - \text{expected growth rate for dividends}}$$

Both firms have initial expected dividends of \$2 per share for period 1, and both firms have market rates for equity of 12 percent. Jewell expects a constant growth rate of 4 percent, whereas Nealon expects a constant growth rate of 8 percent. Each firm's share value is:

$$\text{Jewell } P_0 = \$2 \div (0.12 - 0.04) = \$25$$
$$\text{Nealon } P_0 = \$2 \div (0.12 - 0.08) = \$50$$

Market participants value Nealon, Inc. more highly because it has a higher growth rate.

At the end of one year, the values of the two securities are:

$$\text{Jewell } P_0 = \$2 \times 1.04 \div (0.12 - 0.04) = \$26$$
$$\text{Nealon } P_0 = \$2 \times 1.08 \div (0.12 - 0.08) = \$54$$

Nealon, Inc. has appreciated more in value than Jewell, Inc., but the total market return for each security (their respective equity cost) is still 12 percent! That is,

$$\text{Market return} = \frac{\text{Ending price} - \text{beginning price} + \text{dividend}}{\text{Beginning price}}$$

$$\text{Jewell total return} = (\$26 - \$25 + \$2) \div \$25 = 0.12$$
$$\text{Nealon total return} = (\$54 - \$50 + \$2) \div \$50 = 0.12$$

The reason the returns in Illustration 18-2 are the same is that share price reflects all anticipated growth. Thus, when the financial market anticipates the growth, higher-growth securities do not offer higher returns. It is only if the financial market does not anticipate high growth that higher-growth firms produce higher returns for their shareholders in excess of what they require.

The Cost of Equity Using the SML

A major limitation of deriving the cost of equity from the dividend growth model is that it offers no insight into the source of variation in market rates among dif-

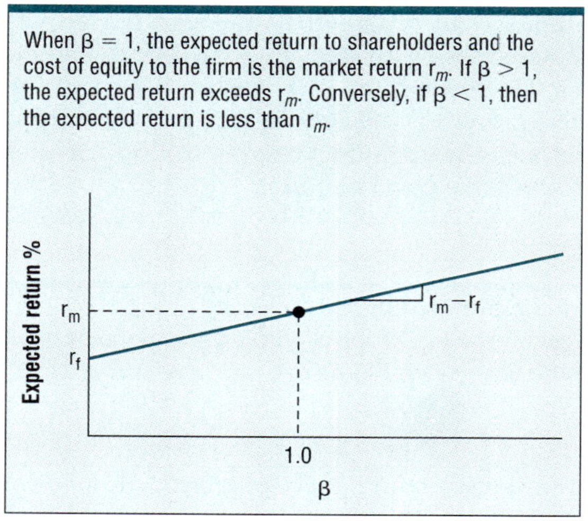

FIGURE 18-2
Risk-reward trade-off and the cost of equity

ferent securities. Conceptually, the appropriate market rate for a security is the sum of an interest rate on some safe investment plus a risk premium that is positively related to the risk of the stock. Capital asset pricing theory, discussed in Chapter 5, directs us to use the security market line (SML) for calculating the cost of equity:

Cost of equity
= Risk-free rate + beta × (expected market return − risk-free rate) (18-7)

$$r_e = r_f + \beta \times (r_m - r_f)$$

Figure 18-2 shows Eq. (18-7) graphically.

Although many theoretical arguments can be made in support of the SML, when it comes to plugging in the real numbers it can be a problem to implement. Should we use a Treasury bill or a Treasury bond to represent the risk-free rate? What stock index should we use to act as a proxy for the market return? Does β really capture the risk we need to be concerned with?

These issues are not inconsequential. Treasury bonds are likely a better choice than Treasury bills for the risk-free rate because the longer maturity of bonds better approximates the life of investments in the firm. The difference in yields between T-bills and T-bonds can be considerable, particularly if future expectations about future interest rates are very different than current short-term rates. And do we use already published betas or calculate our own? If we use published betas, whose do we use—Value Line's, Merrill Lynch's, or some other company's? The problem is that published betas differ from one source to another. If we calculate β, what do we use as the market return? Different market proxies can result in different β values.

However, let's assume that we can resolve any concerns about applying the SML for calculating cost of equity. Illustration 18-3 outlines the general procedure to use.

ILLUSTRATION 18-3

Cost of equity from a β perspective

Calculating beta requires the use of a statistical technique called *regression analysis.* We regress the daily differences between historical stock returns for firm i and the risk-free rate, $r_{it} - r_{ft}$, against the difference between historical returns for the market and the risk-free rate (that is, the market risk premium), $r_{mt} - r_{ft}$. Returns on the S&P 500 stock index represent market returns.

$$r_{it} - r_{ft} = \alpha_i + \beta_i \times (r_{mt} - r_{ft}) + \varepsilon_{it}$$

The subscript t means return for day t. Returns for r_{it}, r_{ft}, and r_{mt} for the past 250 days might be used in the regression. The parameters α_i and β_i are outputs from solving the regression. Since the regression does not explain all the variability that exists between actual returns for security i on day t and the market return on day t, the error term, ε_{it}, is nonzero. The intercept term, α_i, may also be nonzero. However, for our purpose we can safely ignore both α_i and ε_{it}.

Using the preceding methodology, assume we find that the beta for Ethridge Publishing is 0.36765. Suppose the risk-free rate r_f is 8 percent and the risk premium for common stocks, $r_m - r_f$, is 8.5 percent. Substituting these values into the equation for the SML results in Ethridge Publishing's cost of equity, r_e, being 0.11125, or 11.125 percent:

$$\begin{aligned} r_e &= r_f + \beta \times (r_m - r_f) \\ &= 0.08 + 0.36765 \times 0.085 \\ &= 0.11125 \end{aligned}$$

This return is the same as we calculated using the dividend growth model in Illustration 18-1.

In reality, the DGM and the SML provide different answers for r_e. The reason is because it is difficult to know whether the inputs to the models are correct; we don't operate in a world with perfect knowledge.[6] The nearby Financial Reality reading discusses how difficult practitioners find it to calculate the cost of equity. The article makes reference to several different approaches and concludes that calculating "the cost of equity is an art, not a science."

The management of Thermo Electron Corporation believes that there is much "art" associated with equity costs. Many years ago, its chief executive officer decided to drive the ownership of Thermo stock into the hands of individuals and institutions that were both interested in understanding Thermo's businesses and intent on investing for the long term. Management accomplished the task by keeping in almost daily contact with many of its stockholders to inform them of not only favorable but also unfavorable developments and to clearly articulate its strategy. By attracting investors who view management's forecasts as credible, Thermo management felt it was able to undertake longer-horizon projects.

One class of investors Thermo pursued was Europeans. They are typically more long-term oriented than Americans. Moreover, most Europeans pay no capital gains

[6]Theoretically, we can prove that the SML model provides the same answer as the dividend growth model if the cost of debt equals the risk-free rate ($r_d = r_f$) or the beta for debt is zero.

tax on the appreciation of equities, thereby making Thermo's nondividend-paying shares of particular interest.

The Effect of Debt on the Cost of Equity

If Ethridge Publishing finances entirely with common stock, assets equal equity. The only risk facing the shareholders is business risk, and the unlevered cost of equity is 10 percent.[7] But since management uses some debt to help finance the assets, this action exposes shareholders to *financial risk. Financial risk* exists whenever lenders require a firm to meet fixed finance payments on a security, such as debt interest. With debt financing, the levered return shareholders expect is 11.125 percent, as calculated in Illustration 18-3. The cost of equity is higher than when no debt is used because shareholders require higher returns given their greater exposure to business and financial risks.

Shareholders in Ethridge Publishing require a *default risk premium (DRP)* to offset the risk of default if the firm does not pay its debt obligations. This *default risk premium* is the difference between the cost of equity for the levered firm (r_e^l) and the cost of equity for the unlevered firm (r_e^u):

$$\begin{aligned}\textbf{Default risk premium} &= \textbf{Levered equity return} - \textbf{unlevered equity return}\\ \textbf{DRP} &= r_e^l - r_e^u\\ &= 0.11125 - 0.10\\ &= 0.01125\end{aligned} \qquad \textbf{(18-8)}$$

Shareholders require that their rate of return be increased 1.125 percentage points for a default risk premium.

An alternate way to calculate the cost of equity, which explicitly captures the DRP, is to use the following equation:

$$\begin{aligned}\textbf{Cost of equity} &= \textbf{Unlevered equity return} + \textbf{(1} - \textbf{tax rate)}\\ &\quad \times \textbf{(unlevered equity return} - \textbf{cost of debt)}\\ &\quad \times \frac{\textbf{market value of debt}}{\textbf{market value of equity}}\\ r_e^l &= r_e^u + (1 - \tau) \times (r_e^u - r_d) \times B/S\end{aligned} \qquad \textbf{(18-9)}$$

If Ethridge Publishing does not use debt financing, shareholders require a 10 percent return; that is, $r_e^u = 0.10$. However, as we discussed in the last chapter, Ethridge Publishing does use \$7200 of debt financing, the debt's YTM (r_d) is 0.08, and the market value debt-to-equity ratio (B/S) is \$7200/\$9216. The tax rate, τ, is 28 percent. Substituting these values into Eq. (18-9) results in a cost of equity of 11.125 percent:

$$\begin{aligned}r_e^l &= r_e^u + (1 - \tau) \times (r_e^u + r_d) \times B/S\\ &= 0.10 + (1 - 0.28) \times (0.10 - 0.08) \times \$7200/\$9216\\ &= 0.11125\end{aligned}$$

[7]This rate could be derived using the SML. Ethridge Publishing's beta would be 0.235, which is less than the current beta because the equity would be exposed to less risk if debt financing is not used.

Financial Reality

WHAT DOES EQUITY FINANCING REALLY COST?

Corporate America has a disdain for equity financing. The chief financial officer of Gannett Co. expresses a commonly held view about equity. "We borrow as cheaply as we can, and we pay it back rather rapidly. With equity, you've always got it out there, and you've got to cover it with earnings."

At first blush it may appear that issuing stock rather than bonds might appear to be a cheap way to raise money. The only perceived cost to the new shares is any dividends paid. The average dividend payment in the Standard & Poor's 500 stock index is 3.4 percent. That is lower than the cost of debt, even after the tax deductibility of interest.

But equity financing is more expensive than debt. How much more is the question debated among experts. The managing director of Prudential Securities, Inc. says, "We give clients three answers, and it doesn't matter which one they use as long as they understand the implications."

Those who view the dividend payout as the cost of equity point out that when stock is issued, new shareholders have a claim on both the current dividend and any future dividends, which likely will grow in amount. For instance, suppose Stupendous Corp. stock sells for $25 a share and has a $1 per share dividend. That's a 4 percent yield. Dividends are expected to grow at 10 percent a year into the future. That translates into a cost of equity of 14 percent.

Some companies do not pay any dividend, but their cost of equity is not zero. When a firm sells stock, there may not be any out-of-pocket dividend costs, but more people now have a stake in the company. The new shareholders have an equal claim to the earnings as possessed by old shareholders. To keep the stock price from falling, management must create additional earnings each year with the new shareholders' money. The rate that the company must earn on the new money is its "cost of equity."

Some managers determine the cost of equity using the so-called capital asset pricing model (CAPM). The CAPM is based on the idea that the greater the risk in holding a stock the greater the return—dividends + appreciation—investors must receive. If the required return is not received, then investors will dump the stock until the stock offers return in line with expected return-risk trade-off. Because all shareholders suffer if the stock price falls, the real cost of capital is the expected return. If the company can't meet the stock market's expectations, prices will fall.

The CAPM states that the required return depends on interest rates, the risk of owning stocks in general, and the risk of owning a specific company's stock. The calculation begins with the long-term, risk-free rate of return on a U.S. government bond. No one buys a stock if they think that the total return will be less than that of a Treasury bond.

To this figure is added the risk premium. The premium varies, depending on factors related to inflation outlook, recession, and investor sentiment toward stocks. Historically this premium runs 4 percent to 7 percent a year. This premium is the amount in excess of the risk-free rate that investors want to entice them into the market. This risk premium is adjusted for the risk of owning a specific stock. The risk adjustment is called beta. It measures the stock's volatility compared with the rest of the market. A beta of 1 means that a stock's price moves in tandem with the overall market. A beta of 2 means it moves twice as much as the market. To obtain

Financial Reality

the cost of equity, multiply the market risk premium by beta and add the result to the risk-free rate.

Whichever method is used to calculate the cost of equity, they're all based to some degree on numbers that can only be guessed at. John Lonski, senior economist for Moody's Investors Service, Inc., says, "Determining the cost of equity is an art, not a science."

Adapted from Jeffrey M. Laderman, "What Does Equity Financing Really Cost?" *Business Week,* December 7, 1988, pp. 146–147. Reprinted by permission, copyright © 1988 by McGraw-Hill, Inc.

Although the cost is the same as the one we calculated using DGM in Illustration 18-3, in the real world the two models would result in different numbers. In a perfect world, the two models would always give the same answer. However, our information is always imperfect. Because we do not know future cash flows with certainty, we must estimate values for the variables, and this leads to unknown errors creeping into the analysis.

If the firm is all-equity financed (or unlevered), the ratio of debt to equity (B/S) equals zero and $r_e^l = r_e^u = 0.10$, which is the appropriate rate of return shareholders expect to earn for business risk. However, when management uses debt financing, shareholders calculate the default risk premium of 1.125 percent as the after-tax difference in cost between the unlevered cost of equity and the cost of debt times the market valued debt-equity ratio: $(1 - \tau) \times (r_e^u - r_d) \times B/S$. Figure 18-3 graphs the effect debt has on the cost of equity.

The Cost of Equity and the PE Ratio

Business magazines and practitioners often refer to the cost of equity as the firm's inverted price-earnings (PE) ratio:

$$\textbf{Cost of equity} = \mathbf{1 \div PE\ ratio} \qquad \textbf{(18-10)}$$

For instance, if Ethridge Publishing, Inc.'s PE ratio is 8, then its cost of equity is 12.5 percent (= [1 ÷ 8] × 100). If the PE ratio is 20, then the cost of equity is 5 percent.

Any cost of equity calculation based on the PE ratio is suspect. The PE approach assumes that management undertakes only maintenance-type projects that result in neither appreciation nor depreciation in shareholder value. The board of directors authorizes payment of all cash flows remaining after making these value maintenance investments as dividends to shareholders. It is fair to say that such assumptions are inappropriate for about all firms. Illustration 18-4 explains the faulty logic some people use to justify the inverted PE ratio as the cost of equity.

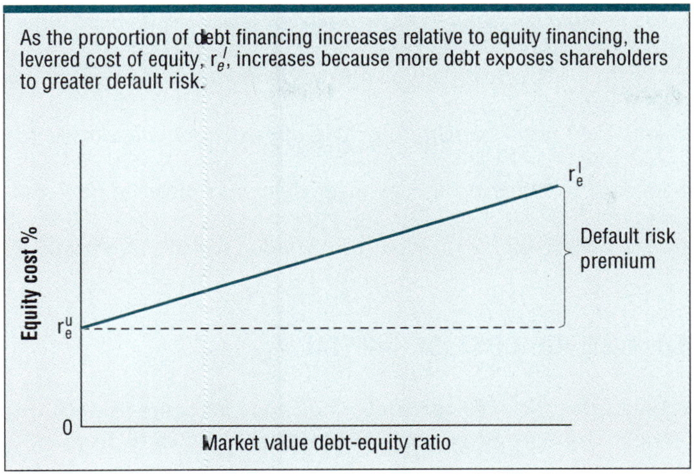

FIGURE 18-3
Cost of equity

ILLUSTRATION 18-4

Misguided use of the PE ratio
We can derive a firm's price-earnings ratio from the dividend growth model by dividing both sides of the model by next period's earnings:

$$\frac{P_0}{E_1} = \frac{D_1/E_1}{r_e - g}$$

P_0/E_1 is the price-earnings ratio (PE ratio) using expected earnings next year. The numerator on the right-hand side of the equation is the expected dividend payout ratio next period (D_1/E_1). The denominator is simply the difference between the required market rate and expected growth rate for dividends.

Now let's rearrange the preceding equation to state it in terms of r_e, the cost of equity:

$$r_e = \frac{D_1/E_1 1}{P_0/E_1} + g$$

$$= \frac{\text{Dividend payout ratio}}{\text{PE ratio}} + g$$

For the cost of equity to equal the inverted PE ratio (1/PE), the dividend payout ratio must equal 1. In other words, all earnings must be paid as dividends. If this is the case, then $g = 0$ because the firm has no earnings to reinvest in value-enhancing projects

COMPREHENSION CHECK

1. *How is the dividend growth model used to determine the cost of equity?*
2. *What approaches can be used to estimate the growth rate in the dividend growth model?*

3. *Explain how it is possible for stocks with similar growth rates to have different values but the same expected returns.*
4. *Why is the use of the SML conceptually superior to the dividend growth model for calculating cost of equity?*
5. *Describe problems with implementing the SML approach for calculating the cost of equity.*
6. *What is the relationship between the cost of equity of an unlevered firm and a levered firm of equal business risk?*
7. *When is it appropriate to use the inverted PE ratio to estimate the cost of equity?*

THE WEIGHTED AVERAGE COST OF CAPITAL

We have been discussing how to calculate the separate costs of debt, preferred stock, and common stock. If a company were able to use only debt financing, an impossible occurrence, its cost of capital is the after-tax cost of debt, $r_d \times (1 - \tau)$. If a company uses neither debt nor preferred stock financing, which is a possible but infrequent occurrence, the firm's cost of capital is the unlevered equity return required by the common shareholders, r_e^u. The most common practice is to use a combination of debt and equity financing, and possibly preferred stock. In the latter case, we need to combine the costs of the different forms of financing to calculate an overall cost. Such a cost is called the firm's *weighted average cost of capital.*

Calculating the Weighted Average Cost of Capital

To calculate Ethridge Publishing's weighted average cost of capital, we must first calculate the proportion that the market value of the firm's debt is to the total market value of the firm (W_d), the proportion that the market value of the firm's preferred stock is to the total market value of the firm (W_p), and the proportion that the market value of the firm's equity is to the total market value of the firm (W_e). The market value of the firm is the summation of the market values for its debt (B), preferred stock (P), and common stock (S). For Ethridge Publishing, $B = \$7200$, $P = \$0$, and $S = \$9216$.

$$W_d = \frac{\text{Market value of debt}}{\text{Market value of the firm}} \tag{18-11}$$

$$= \frac{B}{B + P + S}$$

$$= \frac{\$7200}{\$7200 + \$0 + \$9216}$$

$$= 0.4386$$

$$W_p = \frac{\text{Market value of preferred stock}}{\text{Market value of the firm}} \tag{18-12}$$

$$= \frac{P}{B + P + S}$$

Executive Commentary

THE ROLE OF COST OF CAPITAL

by A. James Ifflander, Ph.D., Principal, Ifflander & Associates Consulting

I previously taught the beginning corporate finance class some years ago. Students always wanted to know the practical application of the topic. A frequent question was, "What is the cost of capital used for?" Today much of my livelihood entails teaching the basic concepts that are related to the cost of capital to lawyers, judges, and others in the legal environment. I am a financial consultant who testifies in court in support of my opinion of a firm's cost of capital. Many times the only point of dispute between the parties is the cost of capital. In these court cases the cost of capital is the discount rate used to value the cash flows generated by the company's assets.

These assets can be quite varied. I have valued coal and gold mines, aluminum smelting facilities, paper and pulp mills, telecommunications companies including local, long-distance, and cellular companies, railroads, electric utilities, and natural gas pipelines, among others. As you can well imagine these all involve different problems and quite different answers. But the basic techniques are similar. In fact, you might be surprised to see a report prepared for the court and submitted as evidence that includes the formulas, methods, and even a basic discussion of each of the financial models that corresponds very closely to the materials you study in this chapter. Very often these court decisions discuss terms, such as beta, the risk-free rate, the risk premium, and the expected growth rate. More than one judge has commented on the need for a degree in finance to understand the testimony of the assorted experts.

Let me give some examples of the testimony that may be given in court. In a recent case the capital asset pricing model (CAPM) and the dividend growth model (DGM) were utilized by the experts for each side in the dispute. In this case, the CAPM gave much higher answers than the DGM. A large part of the testimony revolved around which model gave the better answer. In my opinion, the CAPM's answer was inferior because the risk premium and the beta were incorrectly calculated by the opposing expert. The case also involved discussions of the proper weights to use for the debt and equity costs. In fact, the experts disagreed over whether to use a company-specific debt-to-equity mix or a financing mix that was closer to the industry average.

The cost of capital is also examined at length in many government agencies. For instance, your electric bill to a certain extent is based on calculations of the cost of capital. A utility's approved customer rates are based on factoring in their cost of capital. And don't be surprised if new health-care regulations yet to be issued by the Clinton administration include required examinations of the cost of capital for a wide range of medical-related industries. How else could we tell if these industries are earning an abnormal profit, as claimed by the Clinton administration?

Investment bankers concerned with the valuation of companies for merger or other corporate purposes also calculate the cost of capital. I have seen presentations to the board of directors of various companies where the cost of capital and all the inputs such as beta and the dividend growth rate are clearly stated to facilitate discussion.

Hopefully, I've convinced you that the cost of capital is one of the most crucial calculations that affects all of us in some way. It is widely

Executive Commentary

used, discussed, and criticized in many different situations. It affects your electric and telephone bills. It is discussed by government officials and top managers of almost every company. Numerous court cases have examined various aspects of the cost of capital. Finally, millions of dollars are invested based on somebody's opinion of the cost of capital.

$$= \frac{\$0}{\$7200 + \$0 + \$9216}$$

$$= 0.0$$

$$W_e = \frac{\text{Market value of equity}}{\text{Market value of the firm}} \tag{18-13}$$

$$= \frac{S}{B + P + S}$$

$$= \frac{\$9216}{\$7200 + \$0 + \$9216}$$

$$= 0.5614$$

The proportions W_d, W_p, and W_e must sum to 1 (= 0.4386 + 0.0 + 0.5614) to indicate that all financing is considered in the calculation of the weighted average cost of capital. Multiplying these proportions by their respective after-tax costs and summing the results provides the firm's *weighted average cost of capital (WACC):*

$$\begin{aligned} \text{WACC} &= \text{After-tax cost of debt} \times \text{weight for debt} \\ &\quad + \text{cost of preferred stock} \times \text{weight for preferred stock} \\ &\quad + \text{cost of equity} \times \text{weight for equity} \\ &= r_d \times (1 - t) \times W_d + r_p \times W_p + r_e \times W_e \end{aligned} \tag{18-14}$$

Since debt interest is tax deductible, we adjust the cost of debt for taxes. Neither preferred stock nor common stock enjoy the same tax treatment. To calculate the WACC, we simply substitute the appropriate values into Eq. (18-14). In practice, the difficult part is determining these values.

Exercise:
If Ethridge Publishing reduces the proportion of equity from 56.14 percent to 50 percent and uses the 6.14 percent for 9 percent preferred stock, what would the new WACC be? *Answer:* 0.08 × (1 − 0.28) × 0.4386 + 0.09 × 0.0614 + 0.11125 × 0.50 = 0.08642 or 8.642 percent.

Let's continue with Ethridge Publishing to show how to apply Eq. (18-14). Previously, we found that: $r_d = 0.08$, $t = 0.28$, and $r_e = 0.11125$. Ethridge does not use any preferred stock financing; thus, $r_p = W_p = 0$. Eqs. (18-11) through (18-13) show the weights to use. After making the necessary substitutions, we find that the WACC is 8.772 percent:

$$\begin{aligned} \text{WACC} &= r_d \times (1 - t) \times W_d + r_p \times W_p + r_e \times W_e \\ &= 0.08 \times (1 - 0.28) \times 0.4386 + 0 \times 0 + 0.11125 \times 0.5614 \\ &= 0.08772 \end{aligned}$$

In reality, the WACC cannot continually decline. Beyond some level of debt to equity, the WACC will turn up, thereby suggesting that an optimal capital structure exists.

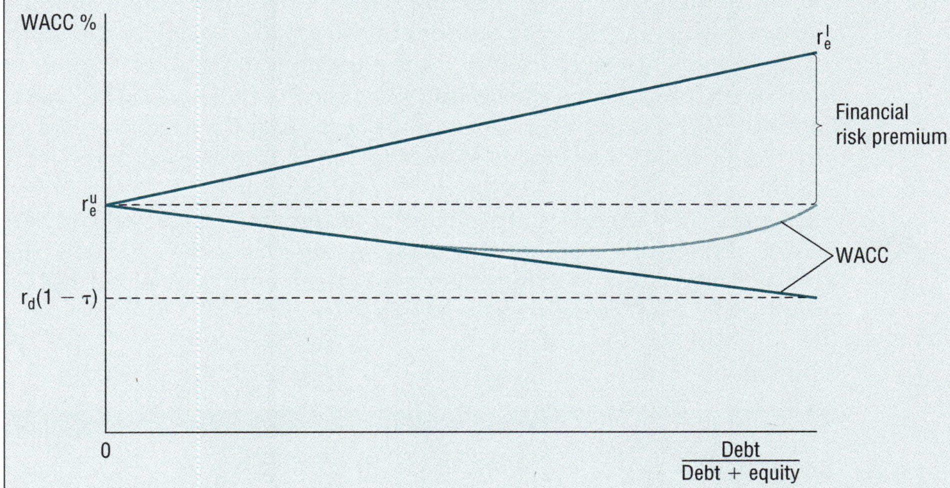

FIGURE 18-4
Weighted average cost of capital

Look at this WACC equation and consider how Ethridge Publishing should react to the increase in the corporate income tax rate enacted by the Clinton administration in 1993.[8] We should see Ethridge Publishing making greater use of debt because the government will now pay an even larger portion of each $1 of interest expense. The effect is to lower the after-tax cost of debt, and thereby the WACC, assuming that other factors affecting the cost of debt do not change.

Advantage of Debt Financing

A firm's cost of debt is *always* less than its cost of equity.[9] The reasons are twofold. First, debtholders are exposed to less risk than shareholders. Debtholders are the first investors (or are supposed to be) to receive cash distributions from the firm. Shareholders are last in priority to receive any cash distributions. Second, debt interest is a tax-deductible expense, thereby lowering its cost to the firm. Dividend payments are not tax-deductible expenses. Hence, the use of debt financing lowers the firm's WACC.

According to the WACC equation, as the firm finances with more debt and less equity, the WACC declines. The continually declining WACC curve in Figure 18-4 shows this phenomenon.

[8]Without the feature of tax deductibility of interest, the value of the firm is independent of its capital structure. As more debt is used, the cost of equity capital increases, which offsets any advantage of debt with the result that the WACC remains constant.

[9]We ignore preferred stock for this discussion. Few firms other than public utilities issue it. We could include it without changing our conclusions.

However, a continually falling WACC does not exist in the real world. A firm cannot be 100 percent debt financed. Lenders will not lend funds unless the owners of the firm have some of their own money (that is, equity) invested. Also, the Internal Revenue Service (IRS) has the authority to classify debt as equity if the firm uses too much debt financing. The IRS views abnormally high amounts of debt as attempts by management to take extraordinary advantage of the tax deductibility of interest payments. And we can see the government's point. Higher interest deductions mean lower tax payments and less revenue for Uncle Sam. These factors, along with others discussed shortly, cause the cost of capital to increase beyond some level of prudent debt financing, as shown by the saucer-shaped curve for WACC in Figure 18-4.

Figure 18-4 suggests that there is an *optimal capital structure* for minimizing WACC. First, let's examine the relationship that exists between firm value and WACC. Once you understand the link between firm value and WACC, the concept of optimal capital structure should be easier.

COMPREHENSION CHECK

1. *How is the weighted average cost of capital calculated?*
2. *Why is the calculation of the cost of debt treated differently from the cost of equity when calculating the weighted average cost of capital?*
3. *Explain why the weighted average cost of capital is lowered for a firm that uses debt to replace some of the equity in its capital structure.*
4. *What practical limitations prevent a firm from being 100 percent debt financed?*

THE RELATIONSHIP BETWEEN FIRM VALUE AND WACC

At the beginning of this chapter, we heard a few laments from business executives about the high cost of capital and the hardships it has caused for their firms. They believed that if capital costs were lower, then their firms would have been more competitive and valued more highly in the financial markets. Now let's formally tie together the concepts of valuation and cost of capital. We will continue to use Ethridge Publishing as our example. Table 18-1 summarizes important information about the company.

The $16,416 value of Ethridge Publishing (in Table 18-1) can be derived by using Ethridge Publishing's WACC of 8.772 percent. WACC replaces r_e^u in the equation for the value of the firm and we drop the expression for the present value of the interest tax shield. The valuation equation that uses the firm's WACC is:

$$V^L = \frac{\text{Cash operating profits after taxes}}{\text{Weighted average cost of capital}} \tag{18-15}$$

$$= \frac{\$2000 \times (1 - 0.28)}{0.08772}$$

$$= \$16{,}416$$

TABLE 18-1 Pertinent Information About Ethridge Publishing, Inc.

Cash operating profits before taxes (COP)	\$2,000
Debt financing	\$7,200
Interest rate on debt financing	8%
Interest expense (8% × \$7200)	\$576
Income tax rate (τ)	28%
Return to shareholders for business risk (r_e^u)	10%
Present value of tax shield provided by interest = Debt financing × tax rate	\$2,016
Value of the firm	
$= \dfrac{\text{COP} \times (1 - \tau)}{r_e^u} + \text{present value of tax shield}$	
$= \dfrac{\$2000 \times (1 - 0.28)}{0.10} + \$2016$	\$16,416

The WACC rate incorporates the tax shield provided by debt financing. It is important to realize that, although we get the same value for Ethridge Publishing using either Eq. (18-15) or

$$V^{L} = \frac{\textbf{COP} \times (1 - \tau)}{r_{e}^{u}} + \textbf{present value of the tax shield}$$

in Table 18-1, there is an important conceptual difference. The difference is this: *A firm derives its WACC from the value of the firm; the firm's value is not derived from its WACC.*

Consider the issue from the following perspective. The investors of a publicly traded company often number in the thousands. Most of these investors do not know each other, and generally investors in a company's stock are not investors in its bonds. When these investors buy and sell the firm's debt and equity securities, they do so in the expectation of earning a return that satisfies them for the amount of risk they are exposed to by owning these securities. Any buying and selling activity determines market prices for the securities. If the financial markets are efficient, then the securities prices and thereby their returns are satisfactory to the participants.

Given that investors do not buy the firm's debt and equity securities in the same proportion that the firm has issued them (although they could), the return that these investors seek is not the firm's WACC—because WACC is dependent on the proportions of debt to equity in the financing mix. Rather, investors demand the market-determined rates for the individual securities. Or think of the issue from another perspective. When we calculated the firm's WACC, we used costs and weights based on market values for all securities issued by the firm. Thus, we had to know the market valuations investors put on the securities before we could calculate the WACC. And the firm's value equals the market value of its debt plus the market value of its equity.

What is the significance of the WACC? *It is the minimum return that new investments with risk characteristics similar to the firm's present portfolio of assets should earn.* Illustration 18-5 elaborates on why the WACC represents the minimum return.

ILLUSTRATION 18-5

Firm value and the WACC

The current financial status of Ethridge Publishing is reflected in its balance sheet, as stated in market values. Management is considering investing $1000 in a new project to be financed in the same proportions as its market-based balance sheet.

Balance Sheet Stated in Market Values

				Financing Proportion	Costs
Assets	$16,416	Debt	$ 7,200	43.86%	8.000%
		Equity	9,216	56.14	11.125
			$16,416	100.00%	08.772%*

*WACC = 0.08 × (1 − 0.28) × 0.4386 + 0.11125 × 0.5614 = 0.08772

Project earns the WACC

Management believes the project will earn its WACC. Thus, the incremental amount of value that this investment should add to the value of the firm is $1000: $1000 investment × 8.772% expected return ÷ 8.772% WACC. By financing the investment in its market-valued balance sheet proportions, management will use $438.60 debt and $561.40 equity. The amount of cash operating profit before taxes (COP) that must be earned each year is $121.83. At this level of COP, debt investors earn their 8 percent and shareholders earn their 11.125 percent.

Cash operating profit before taxes	$121.83
Interest (8% × $438.60)	35.09
Cash profit before taxes	$ 86.74
Taxes (28%)	24.29
Cash profit after taxes	$ 62.45

Debtholders would receive $35.09, which represents an 8 percent return on their $438.60 investment. The $561.40 investment by shareholders would earn 11.125 percent: $62.45 ÷ $561.40 = 0.11125. The project's total return would be 8.772 percent; the after-tax cash operating profit divided by the initial investment: $121.83 × (1 − 0.28) ÷ $1000 = 0.08772 or 8.772 percent.

By earning the WACC, the project would increase the value of the firm from $16,416 to $17,416. The $1000 difference is the amount of the investment. Since the investment only earns its WACC, there is no value created beyond $1000.

Project's contribution to firm value

$$= \frac{\text{Cash operating profit after taxes from the project}}{\text{Required rate for business risk}}$$

$$+ \text{ present value of tax shield from debt financing}$$

$$= \frac{\$121.83 \times (1 - 0.28)}{0.10} + 0.28 \times \$438.60$$

$$= \$877.18 + \$122.81$$
$$= \$1000 \text{ (rounded)}$$

Project earns less than the WACC

Although the project is expected to earn 8.772 percent, what happens if it doesn't? Suppose the $1000 project only earns $100 cash operating profit before taxes? The project's total return would be 7.2 percent: $100 × (1 − 0.28) ÷ $1000. The debtholders would still receive $35.09 as interest payment, thereby earning their 8 percent. The shareholders who put up $561.40 as their share of the $1000 investment would only realize $46.74.

Cash operating profit before taxes	$100.00
Interest (8% × $438.60)	35.09
Cash profit before taxes	$ 64.91
Taxes (28%)	18.17
Cash profit after taxes	$ 46.74

The return to shareholders would be $46.74 ÷ $561.40 = 0.08326 or about 2.8 percentage points below what they require: 11.125% − 8.326%.

By only earning $100 of cash operating profit before taxes, the contribution of this $1000 project to the value of the firm would be $842.81.

Project's contribution to firm value

$$= \frac{\text{Cash operating profit after taxes from the project}}{\text{Required rate for business risk}}$$
$$+ \text{ present value of tax shield from debt financing}$$

$$= \frac{\$100 \times (1 - 0.28)}{0.10} + 0.28 \times \$438.60$$
$$= \$720 + \$122.81$$
$$= \$842.81$$

Thus, shareholders lose $157.19 of value ($1000 cost − $842.81 value) because the investment fails to earn the WACC.

Project earns more than the WACC

Suppose the project unexpectedly earns cash operating profit before taxes of $150. Value of the firm, and thereby shareholder value, should increase by $202.81 in excess of the project's $1000 cost. The total return in this case is 10.8 percent, about 2 percentage points greater than the firm's WACC. Can you derive these amounts?[10]

It is apparent from this illustration that cost of capital affects whether an investment makes any contribution to shareholder wealth. If management can lower cost of capital, projects become more valuable since they contribute value beyond their cost. This issue is at the heart of the point the executives quoted in our introduction were making. The remaining question to consider is *how much* debt to use.

AN OPTIMAL CAPITAL STRUCTURE

How much debt minimizes the firm's WACC? It is difficult to say exactly, although theory provides us with an understanding of important factors to consider: *agency*

[10]Solutions: Value of project = [$150 × (1 − 0.28)] ÷ 0.10 + 0.28 × $438.60 = $1202.81; total return = [$150 × (1 − 0.28)] ÷ $1000 = 0.108 or 10.8 percent.

costs, tax benefits, and *financial distress costs.* Debtholders, shareholders, and managers often have conflicting objectives. Let's briefly examine the conflicts as they pertain to capital structure.

Debtholder-Shareholder Conflicts

Why may debtholders and shareholders have different incentives? Debtholders are interested in safeguards for the firm's solvency to ensure repayment of funds they lent the firm. Shareholders invest in the firm with the understanding that getting an increased return on their equity investment requires taking risks; more risks than debt investors take. If the firm undertakes risky projects, shareholders reap most of the benefits from a successful project, while debt investors are paid a fixed return. On the other hand, if the project becomes unprofitable, debt investors may incur a portion of the loss due to the limited liability of the shareholders. Think of this situation as shareholders turning over their ownership interest in the firm to the debtholders. Such events occur whenever firms are unable to repay their creditors.

In an effort to prevent investment abuses by management, debt investors impose agency costs on the firm through the bond indenture, which restricts management's actions. For example, the indenture may place a ceiling on the dollar amount and a restriction on the type of new investment by the firm, the amount of total debt the firm can issue, or the amount of cash dividends the firm can pay common shareholders.

Management-Shareholder Conflicts

The conflict between management and shareholders arises because management does not always act in the best interest of shareholders. For most publicly traded firms, management's personal investment in the company's debt and equity financing is small. So instead of acting as investors, managers act as *agents* for investors. As agents their responsibility is to operate the firm to satisfy objectives of investors. However, many people hold the view that management's primary objective is to increase its compensation, its perquisites (such as lavish offices and company airplanes), and the size of the firm to provide executives with more status in the business community.

In an attempt to minimize such problems, shareholders incur *agency costs* to monitor management. Monitoring activities can range from something as simple as hiring certified public accountants to audit the company's financial statements to the more difficult task of determining whether management should be removed.

Trade-off of Agency Costs

Theory suggests that the smaller the proportion of the firm's equity financing owned by management, the larger the incentive for management to act in its own self-interest. By replacing some of the firm's equity with debt, management's proportionate equity ownership increases. The beneficial result should be a better align-

A trade-off of debt and equity agency costs suggests that some appropriate mix of debt and equity financing exists for minimizing total agency costs.

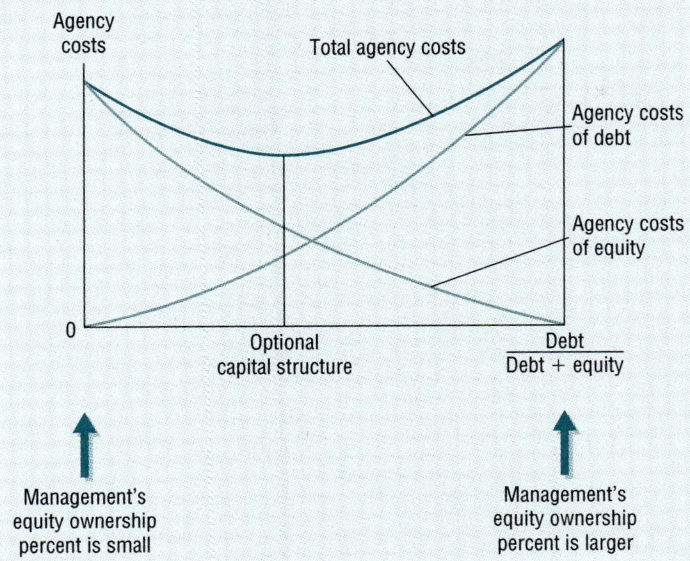

FIGURE 18-5
Agency costs and capital structure

ment of management and shareholders' objectives. However, greater use of debt to align the interest of management and shareholders puts debt investors at more risk. Thus, debt agency costs increase. Figure 18-5 graphs the problem.

Bankruptcy Costs Are Important

The trade-off of agency costs between debt and equity investors suggests that an optimal capital structure exists. However, the reality of an optimal capital structure is more complex. There is a trade-off between the present value tax saving of borrowing and the cost of financial distress or bankruptcy.[11] Bankruptcy costs can amount to millions of dollars in legal and administrative fees. For instance, one estimate of direct costs associated with the 1990 Allied Stores/Federated Department Stores bankruptcy proceedings was $60 million annually until completion of the bankruptcy.[12] Accountants and attorneys were the largest recipients of these funds. Beyond the legal and administrative costs are indirect costs associated with business operations. The operations can be disrupted with the possible loss of customers and skilled employees.

[11]Part of agency costs of debt are *bankruptcy costs*. However, we separate bankruptcy costs to simplify the discussion.

[12]Louis Lowenstein, *Sense and Nonsense in Corporate Finance* (Reading, MA: Addison-Wesley Publishing Company, 1991), p. 44.

Optimal capital structure occurs at the point where the value of the firm is maximized. At this point, WACC is minimized. Management must trade off benefits realized from the interest tax shield against financial distress and agency costs.

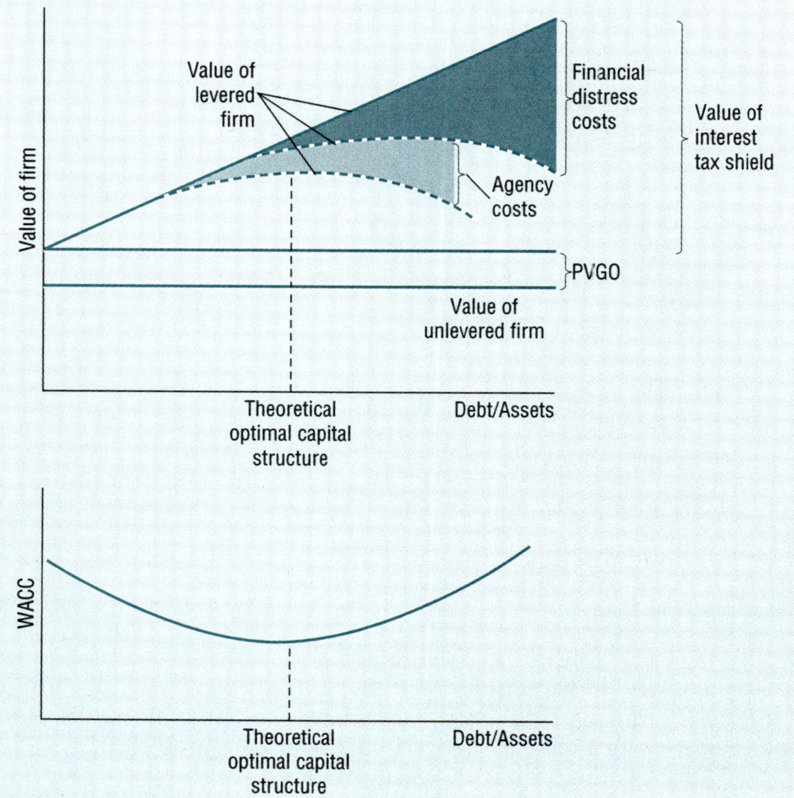

FIGURE 18-6
Theoretical optimal capital structure

However, a firm's bankruptcy does not have the same consequences for its investors as it does for its managers and employees. Investors can diversify their investment portfolios. They are concerned only with market risk of their investments; that is, the β risk. In contrast, managers, employees, and vendors are concerned with a larger risk. Managers and employees have so much of their investment in time and human capital tied up in the firm. They cannot diversify their efforts across other firms. Unless the firm represents a major portion of the vendor's business, a vendor is exposed to less risk than managers and employees. However, managers, employees, and vendors, in varying degrees, all concern themselves with the **total risk** of the firm defined as *diversifiable risk* plus *market risk.* Managers must balance the tax benefit of debt interest against their dual concern of financial distress costs and agency costs.

Figure 18-6 illustrates factors contributing to an optimal capital structure from the perspective of maximizing the firm's value. Value of the levered firm in the figure consists of several components:

Value of the firm with debt

$$\begin{aligned}&= \textbf{Value of the firm without debt}\\ &+ \textbf{present value of growth opportunities}\\ &+ \textbf{present value of the tax savings using debt}\\ &- \textbf{present value of the costs of financial distress}\\ &- \textbf{present value of agency costs}\end{aligned} \qquad (18\text{-}16)$$

$$V^{L} = \frac{\text{COP} \times (1 - \tau)}{r_u} + \text{PVGO} + \text{PVTS} - \text{PVFD} - \text{PVAC}$$

Eq. (18-16) is the valuation model (included in Table 18-1) with new expressions included for the *present value of financial distress costs (PVFD)* and the *present value of agency costs (PVAC)*. These costs are the expected discounted amounts incurred in avoiding bankruptcy and in minimizing agency problems between managers and investors and, at least theoretically, lead to an optimal capital structure.

The optimal capital structure exists at the point where the debt-equity financing mix maximizes the market value of the firm; at this point the firm minimizes its cost of capital. Maximization of firm value (Max V^L) occurs where the present value of the interest tax savings (PVTS) minus the sum of the present values of financial distress costs (PVFD) and agency costs (PVAC) is most positive, assuming the other expressions in Eq. (18-16) remain constant:

$$\text{Max } V^{L} = \text{Max }\{\text{PVTS} - \text{PVFD} - \text{PVAC}, 0\} \qquad (18\text{-}17)$$

If management's choice of capital structure results in PVTS – PVAD – PVAC being negative, then that capital structure should be rejected. A better one can be found for increasing value of the firm.

Illustration 18-6 provides a stylized example to show the tradeoff of various costs which result in maximization of firm value and minimization of WACC. In reality, it is extremely difficult to be as precise. For clarity, we assume that the present value of growth opportunities is zero.

ILLUSTRATION 18-6

Maximize value of the firm

Assume that Ethridge Publishing is all-equity financed with a market value of \$14,400. Management is considering issuing debt at par to repurchase common stock. The corporate income tax rate is 28 percent. An investment banker advises management that the present value of financial distress costs (PVFD) and the present value of agency costs (PVAC) can be estimated by the following equations:[13]

$$\text{PVFD} = 0.0001 \times (\text{debt financing})^2$$
$$\text{PVAC} = (\text{PVFD})^{1/2}$$

[13]These costs have been simplified greatly and are much more difficult to estimate than we assume in this illustration.

The investment banker calculates the estimated value of the levered firm, in the presence of financial distress costs and agency costs, using the equation:

$$V^L = V^u + \text{PVTS} - \text{PVFD} - \text{PVAC}$$

V^u is the value of the unlevered firm ($14,400) and PVTS is the present value of the interest tax saving.

Value of the firm for different debt amounts follows. The optimal amount of debt for maximizing firm value is about $1250. At this debt level, PVTS – PVFD – PVAC is larger than for any other debt level, resulting in the maximum value for the firm ($14,581.25) and the minimum WACC (9.876 percent).

Debt	WACC	V^L	=	V^u	+	PVTS	–	PVFD	–	PVAC
$ 0	10.000%	$14,400.00		$14,400		$ 0		$ 0.00		$ 0.00
1000	9.883	14,570.00		14,400		280		100.00		10.00
1250	9.876	14,581.25		14,400		350		156.25		12.50
1500	9.877	14,580.00		14,400		420		225.00		15.00
2000	9.904	14,540.00		14,400		560		400.00		20.00
4000	10.375	13,880.00		14,400		1120		1600.00		40.00
6000	11.594	12,420.00		14,400		1680		03600.00		60.00

$$\begin{aligned}\text{WACC} &= \text{Cash operating profit after taxes} \div V^L \\ &= \$2000 \times (1 - 0.28) \div V^L\end{aligned}$$

$$\begin{aligned}V^L &= \text{Cash operating profit after taxes} \div \text{unlevered equity cost} \\ &= \$2000 \times (1 - 0.28) \div 0.10 \\ &= \$14{,}400\end{aligned}$$

$$\begin{aligned}\text{PVTS} &= \text{Tax rate} \times \text{debt financing} \\ &= 0.28 \times \text{debt financing}\end{aligned}$$

COMPREHENSION CHECK

1. *Why is there a conflict between management and investors, and between debtholders and shareholders? How do these conflicts get resolved?*
2. *What factors affect the determination of a firm's optimal capital structure?*
3. *What is the interpretation of maximizing the value of the firm model, shown as Eq. (18-17)?*

SUMMARY

- The firm's cost of debt is its yield to maturity adjusted for corporate income taxes.
- The firm's cost of preferred stock is its market dividend yield.
- Analysts often use the dividend growth model, restated in terms of the required market return, to estimate the cost of equity.
- An accurate forecast of cost of equity depends on estimating the expected growth rate for dividends. The sustainable growth model and security analysts' forecasts are the primary means of estimating the growth component.

- Estimating the cost of equity from the dividend growth model fails to offer insight into the source of different cost-of-equity rates among firms.
- The SML model has a strong theoretical base for estimating cost of equity, but in practice it may be difficult to implement.
- A firm financed entirely with equity compensates shareholders for business risk. When the firm uses debt financing, it incurs financial risk (default risk).
- Financial risk causes the return expected by shareholders to increase.
- The inverted PE ratio provides a poor estimate of the cost of equity for all but the exceptional cases of no growth in the firm and all earnings are paid as dividends
- Weighted average cost of capital (WACC) sums the weighted after-tax costs for debt, preferred stock, and equity.
- Weights are based on market values for each type of financing used.
- WACC represents the minimum required return the firm must earn for non-risk-changing investments.
- Debt financing lowers the WACC (at least up to some point). Lower WACC means higher value for the firm. However, it is not feasible for a firm to be 100 percent debt financed.
- A firm derives its WACC from the value of the firm, not the other way around.
- Projects earning more than the WACC improve shareholder value and the value of the firm.
- Projects earning less than the WACC cause the value of the firm and shareholder value to decline.
- Conflicts between debt investors, shareholders, and management set the stage for agency costs.
- The trade-off of agency costs for debt against agency costs for equity suggest that an optimal mix of debt and equity financing exists for maximizing the value of the firm.
- The optimal capital structure is also affected by the trade-off of tax savings and financial distress costs.

SELF-CORRECTION PROBLEMS

1. Several years ago, General Motors sold preferred stock for $30 per share. The annual dividend is $1.98. If the current market price of this preferred stock is $26⅜ per share, what is the cost of this preferred stock to GM?
2. Photon Graphics Corporation's current stock price is $19.50, as quoted on the American Stock Exchange. Last year's dividend was $0.60. Dividends have grown 10 percent annually and are expected to continue to grow at this rate for the foreseeable future. What is Photon's cost of common stock?

PROBLEMS

1. What is the after-tax cost of debt for Starpoint Corporation if its borrowing cost is 11 percent and the firm's tax rate is 30 percent?

2. Morgan Stanley has an issue of preferred stock outstanding that pays an annual dividend of \$2.22 per share. The current market price of the stock is \$27.75. What is the company's cost of capital for preferred stock?
3. RJR Nabisco Limited has an issue of preferred stock outstanding that pays a dividend of \$0.84. If the current market price of the stock is \$7.75, what is the current cost of this preferred stock?
4. Is the preferred stock issued by Morgan Stanley (Problem 4) more or less risky than the preferred stock issued by RJR Nabisco (Problem 5)? Why?
5. A stock has a current market price of \$27.50 and is expected to grow at a constant rate of 4 percent in perpetuity. The *current* dividend is \$2.25. What is the required market rate that justifies this price? State any necessary assumptions.
6. Common dividends paid by Dime Department Store are expected to grow at a rate of 6 percent in perpetuity. Dividends are *currently* \$2.10 per share on stock traded at \$35. Calculate Dime's expected equity return.
7. The stock of ISG is selling for \$34.50 per share. The firm is expected to pay a dividend of \$2.50 per share next year and experience long-term growth of 6 percent. What is the firm's cost of equity?
8. Charlotte Luggage Company is planning to pay its initial common stock dividend next year. Total earnings this year are expected to be \$400,000. The common stock of the company is currently trading at \$7.25 per share and there are 200,000 shares outstanding. The company anticipates long-run growth of 8 percent each year. If investors want a return of at least 12 percent, what is the minimum dividend payout amount the firm should make?
9. The Southern Steel Company expects earnings per share of \$3 next year. Its retention ratio averages about 60 percent annually. If the expected dividend yield over the next year is 10 percent, and the growth rate in dividends is 5 percent, what is the cost of equity?
10. The cost of equity financing decreases as a firm employs more leverage. Is this statement correct? Discuss.
11. a. Determine the cost of equity capital for McEnroe Tennis Corporation. The company has a debt-to-equity ratio of 0.4, a 34 percent tax rate, a cost of debt of 12 percent, and an unlevered cost of equity of 15 percent.
    b. If the debt-to-equity ratio rose to 0.8 with no change in the cost of debt, what would be the cost of equity?
12. Assume that the risk-free rate of interest is 7 percent, the expected return on the market portfolio is 13 percent, and the betas for five companies are as follows: Firm 1 = 0.25; Firm 2 = 0.75; Firm 3 = 1.0; Firm 4 = 1.45; Firm 5 = 2.25.
    a. Calculate the cost of equity for each firm.
    b. Explain the relationship between beta and the cost of equity.
13. Calculate Quadra, Inc.'s cost of equity using the capital asset pricing model approach. The company's beta is 2.0, the risk-free rate is 6 percent, and the average return on the market is 12 percent.
14. The market return for Zisson Corporation is 18 percent, whereas the risk-free rate and the market portfolio yield are 6 percent and 12 percent, respectively. What is the value for Zisson's beta?
15. Renner Company's equity beta is 1.2. The dividend growth model suggests a cost of equity of 15 percent. If the cost of equity derived by the security market line and the dividend growth model are equal, and the return on the market portfolio is 14 percent, what is the risk-free rate?

16. MAG Computers is financed by 40 percent debt and 60 percent equity. There are 10,000 outstanding common shares valued at $30 each. Equityholders require a 16 percent return and debtholders require a 10 percent return. The tax rate is 34 percent. What is its weighted average cost of capital?
17. The management of Exclusive Designers has reason to believe that its current financing of 50 percent debt and 50 percent equity is optimal in a valuation sense. The firm pays 8 percent interest on its debt and estimates an equity cost of 14 percent. The company's tax rate is 34 percent. What is the weighted average cost of capital?
18. The Costello Company's debt-equity ratio is 0.6 using market values. Debt requires a 10 percent return, whereas equity requires a 17 percent return. The market value of common stock is $8 million. Calculate Costello's weighted average cost of capital assuming no change in the current financing mix and no sale of additional common stock. The tax rate is 34 percent.
19. Calculate the weighted average cost of capital for the Dryden Corporation using the following data. Market values represent value per bond and value per common and preferred share.

	Accounting Value	Market Value
Bonds, 9% coupon, $1000 par	$4,500,000	$1000
Preferred stock, 7%, $100 par	1,500,000	90
Common stock, 100,000 shares	1,000,000	65
Retained earnings	2,500,000	

Common stock dividends are expected to be $400,000 this year and grow at 5 percent per year. The firm's tax rate is 34 percent.
20. Calculate the weighted average cost of capital for a firm with the following financing:

- Debt: 40,000 bonds, par $1000, 8 percent interest in perpetuity
- Preferred stock: 250,000 shares, par $100, 10 percent interest
- Common equity: $75 million

The tax rate is 34 percent, the cost of equity is 15 percent, the market rate for debt is 10 percent, and the market rate for preferred stock is 12 percent.
21. The total assets of LEMA Company are expected to increase by $15 million during the next year. The firm's financing consists of the following amounts:

Debt, 9% coupon bonds, $1000 par	$ 7,000,000
Preferred stock, 12% coupon, $100 par	3,000,000
Common stock, $1 par	1,000,000
Retained earnings	9,000,000
Total financing	$20,000,000

Bonds with a 10 percent coupon can be sold at par and 12 percent preferred stock can be sold at a 10 percent discount from par. The risk-free rate is 6 percent and the return on the market is 13 percent. The beta for the common stock of LEMA is 1.4. The expansion is not expected to affect the beta. The corporate tax rate is 34 percent.

Compute the firm's weighted average cost of capital. The firm's target weights are the current accounting (that is, book) weights.

22. The Sale Co. is soon to be incorporated. Its promoters are considering five different possible capital structures for the new company. An analysis of comparable companies with equivalent business risks has been undertaken. This analysis shows that if the before-tax cost of debt is a constant 10 percent, regardless of the capital structure, then the cost of equity capital will be as follows:

Debt-Total Capital	Cost of Equity
0%	20.00%
20	21.25
40	23.33
50	25.00
60	27.50

The preceding predictions for the equity cost of capital also assume that the earnings of the Sale Co. will be taxed at a rate of 40 percent and that the debt interest is an allowable expense for tax purposes. The promoters expect that the company will generate a steady annual earnings stream of $12.6 million, before the payment of debt interest and taxes, for the foreseeable future.

a. Calculate the effective after-tax weighted average cost of capital for each of the five possible capital structures, assuming that the before-tax annual cost of debt will be a constant 10 percent, regardless of the capital structure chosen.

b. Discuss the possible consequences to a company of having a capital structure containing a high leverage ratio.

23. Assume that two firms exist which differ only by how they are financed. The constant operating cash flows for both firms are equal. The unlevered firm is financed by 3 million shares of common stock with a market price per share of $10. The market discount rate for the unlevered firm is 15 percent. The levered firm has 2 million shares of stock and $10 million in long-term debt with an interest rate of 10 percent. The corporate tax rate is 40 percent.

a. Calculate the value of the firm. (*Hint:* First calculate the unlevered firm's value and use your answer to value the levered firm.)

b. Calculate the operating cash flows (before taxes and interest payments) for each firm.

c. How much is the net income for each firm?

d. Calculate the cost of equity and the weighted average cost of capital for each firm.

e. Prove that your cost of capital figures in part (d) are correct by using them to capitalize each firm's after-tax operating cash flow to derive the firm's respective market value found in part (a).

24. Two firms are identical except for how they are financed. One firm uses debt in its financing, whereas the other firm does not. At a tax rate of 34 percent and a discount rate of 10 percent, the value of the unlevered firm is $660.
    a. How much is the amount of constant cash flow from operations for the unlevered firm?
    b. If the tax rate increases from 34 percent to 46 percent, what is the value of the unlevered firm?
    c. If the levered firm is financed with $100 debt, and the balance with equity, how much is the value of the firm before and after the tax rate change?
    d. How much is the levered firm's cost of capital before and after the tax rate increase?
25. The Rolf Company is all-equity financed. It has 750,000 shares outstanding with a market value of $10 each. The company earns an average of $2.5 million in annual operating cash flows before interest and taxes. Every year all earnings are paid out as dividends. Management is considering issuing (at par) $3 million in 15 percent perpetual debt to repurchase stock at $10 per share. The corporate tax rate is 30 percent.
    a. How much is the cost of equity if no debt is issued?
    b. If the firm issues debt to retire equity, how much is the value of the firm?
    c. If the firm issues debt to retire equity, how much is the firm's cost of capital?
26. Given that interest payments are tax deductible for a corporation while dividend payments are not, should companies finance all of their assets with debt?
27. Management of Mesa, Inc. is contemplating a leveraged buyout whereby it would acquire 100 percent of the 500,000 outstanding common shares of the all-equity financed firm. All shares are currently owned by one investor. The purchase price would be equal to the current fair market value of $30 per share. Management has a limited amount of cash it can commit to the purchase. Thus, management plans to recapitalize. Mesa would repurchase a portion of the shares initially acquired by management and issue debt to investors to finance the purchase. A possible consequence of indebtedness is the likelihood the firm will become bankrupt. Management's analysis suggests that different levels of debt would be associated with the following likelihood of bankruptcy costs:

Level of Debt	Likelihood of Bankruptcy	Present Value of Bankruptcy Costs If They Occur
$0 million	0.0000	$0.000 million
3 million	0.0537	2.795 million
6 million	0.1518	3.953 million
9 million	0.2789	4.841 million
12 million	0.4293	5.590 million
15 million	0.6000	6.250 million

The market value of interest tax shield is equal to τB—tax rate × market value of debt. Mesa's tax rate is 30 percent of taxable income.

a. If management wants to maximize the gain derived from the buyout, how much debt should it use? (*Hint:* Determine the expected present value bankruptcy costs and then apply the model Max {τB – present value of bankruptcy costs}).

b. What would the respective market values of debt and equity be? (*Hint:* First, find the value of the unlevered firm before the buyout. This value equals V^u. Next, find the value of the levered firm: $V^L = V^u + \tau B - \text{PVFD}$. Finally, use the equation V^L = Value of debt + value of equity.)

28. A new firm forecasts $900,000 in constant operating income before taxes. The chief financial officer is considering four separate alternatives for financing the firm's required investments:

- 100 percent equity ($4 million in shares of stock)
- $3 million in stock and $1 million of 7 percent bonds
- $2 million in stock and $2 million of 7 percent bonds
- $1 million in stock and $3 million of 7 percent bonds

The corporate tax rate is 34 percent. For each alternative, calculate the value of the firm and the weighted average cost of capital. The capitalization rate for the unlevered firm is 12 percent. The bonds are issued at par.

29. Select a company whose name begins with the first letter of your last name, and whose common stock trades on the New York Stock Exchange.

a. If the firm has publicly traded debt, what is its current internal rate of return (yield to maturity)?

b. If the firm issues preferred stock, what is the market cost of the stock?

c. Calculate the firm's cost of equity using both the dividend growth model and the security market line model. Use the yield of a 30-year Treasury bond as a proxy for the risk-free rate. Assume that the annualized yield for the Standard & Poor's 500 stock index is representative of the return on the market portfolio. Estimate the growth rate for the dividend growth model using the past ten-year growth in dividends per share. If the stock pays no dividends, then use the ten-year growth rate in earnings per share.

INTEGRATIVE PROBLEM

The capital structure of Xebys Corporation is shown below. It reflects management's desired proportions of debt and equity financing.

Debt, 8% coupon bonds, $1000 par	$10,000,000
Preferred stock, 7% coupon, $50 par	5,000,000
Common stock, $1 par	1,000,000
Retained earnings	34,000,000
Total	$50,000,000

New $1000 par-value bonds may be sold at par with a 9 percent coupon. New $25 par-value preferred stock may be sold at par with a dividend of $2.10. Cash dividends on the firm's common stock have grown at a rate of 12 percent, which is expected to continue. Next year's expected common stock dividend is $0.90. The company's common stock, with a beta of 1.2, sells over the counter for $18 per share. The risk-free rate is 5 percent and the market portfolio yields 15 percent. The company's tax rate is 34 percent.

a. Calculate the cost of debt for Xebys Corporation.
b. Calculate the cost of the company's preferred stock.
c. Calculate the company's cost of equity using both the dividend growth model and the security market line.
d. How much is the weighted average cost of capital?
e. What is the minimum expected rate of return for new investments by Xebys, assuming that the new projects do not change the overall risk of the company?

SOLUTIONS TO SELF-CORRECTION PROBLEMS

1.

$$\text{Cost of preferred stock} = \frac{\text{Dividend}}{\text{Market price of stock}}$$
$$= \$1.98 \div \$26.375$$
$$= 0.0751 \text{ or } 7.51 \text{ percent}$$

2. Use the dividend growth model to calculate the equity cost.

$$\text{Cost of equity} = \frac{\text{Dividend next period}}{\text{Current stock price}} + \text{expected growth}$$
$$= (\$0.60 \times (1 + 0.10)) \div \$19.50 + 0.10$$
$$= 0.1338 \text{ or } 13.38 \text{ percent}$$

SELECTED REFERENCES

Kester, W. Carl, and Timothy A. Luehrman, "The Myth of Japan's Low Cost Capital," *Harvard Business Review* (May–June 1992), pp. 130–138. This article discusses differences between cost of capital for U.S. and Japanese firms.

Lewellen, Wilbur G. *The Cost of Capital.* Dubuque, IA: Kendall/Hunt Publishing Company, 1976. This book clearly reveals an integrated view of the corporate financing decision, the cost of capital, and value of the firm.

CHAPTER 19

Capital Structure Management

Texas Instruments, Inc. (TI) is in the semiconductor memory business. Based on internal studies in the late 1980s, management concluded that if it did not reduce TI's cost of capital, the company would never regain its ability to be a world-class computer memory manufacturer. TI management concluded that the cost of capital of the U.S. semiconductor industry was roughly 75 percent higher than that of its Japanese counterpart. Such a large difference in cost of funds put the American firm at a clear and direct disadvantage in a business where success is in large measure determined by ability and willingness to invest. To overcome this disadvantage and regain its leadership in this capital-intensive business, TI management decided to pursue a more active role in managing its capital structure so as "to stimulate access to a low cost of capital environment."[1]

TI entered into a series of joint ventures in an effort to lower its cost of capital. Partners included the Italian government, Acer of Taiwan, and Kobe Steel of Japan, among others. The partners contributed millions of dollars, low-cost loans, tax incentives, and infrastructure improvements; TI contributed technical know-how and management expertise.

Texas Instruments had passively managed its capital structure for years—until management realized that a passive strategy would relegate the company to a less dominant status in the computer memory business. As we discussed in previous chapters, the cost of capital significantly affects the creation of firm and shareholder values. This is the biggest argument in support of an active capital structure management strategy. But management must exercise great care in choosing a capital structure. The debt versus equity choice is difficult because the factors involved are complex and the impact of each on firm and equity value is not obvious. Any advantage of additional debt must be balanced against any additional costs. Neither

[1]Joseph Morone and Albert Paulson, "Cost of Capital: The Managerial Perspective," *California Management Review* (Summer 1991), p. 15.

TABLE 19-1 Financing Policies and Practices

Selected Survey Questions:

Does your firm believe that there is a functional relationship between its capital costs and the amount of debt which it utilizes in its financial structure?

Yes responses: 92%

Does your firm believe that the use of an excessive amount of debt will eventually result in an increase in the yield (cost) of debt faced by your company?

Yes responses: 97%

Does your firm believe that the use of an excessive amount of debt will eventually result in the market price of your common stock being adversely affected?

Yes responses: 90%

Does your firm believe that there is some maximum amount of debt financing that should not be surpassed? (That is, does your firm subscribe to the concept of a corporate debt capacity?)

Yes responses: 87%

the advantages nor the costs lend themselves to precise measurement. In the end, the choice of capital structure requires expert judgment on the part of the chief financial officer and the firm's investment bankers.

This chapter examines some practical ways to manage the complex capital structure problem. When you have completed this chapter, you should understand:

- How the firm's ability to service debt, use tax shields, attain a desired bond rating, and manage subsidiaries affects the capital structure decision.
- How to measure business risk and financial risk using accounting data.
- How firms alter their capital structures over time to more desired debt levels.

PRACTICAL ISSUES ABOUT CAPITAL STRUCTURE

Are management's thoughts about capital structure consistent with the theoretical idea that an optimal debt-equity relationship exists. Apparently so, as suggested by one survey's results, summarized in Table 19-1. Practicing financial managers believe that debt must be managed carefully. Otherwise, they feel that financing costs will increase too much, and the result will be that value of the firm's securities will decline.

The nearby Financial Reality articles illustrate how debt helped focus management of Goodyear Tire & Rubber Company in its pursuit of improving shareholder value. On the other hand, too much debt financing led to the destruction of Harcourt Brace Jovanovich, Inc.

Some of the principal factors influencing management's decision about capital structure include the following:

- Ability to service debt.
- Ability to use tax-shield benefits.
- Desired bond rating category.
- Use of foreign and finance subsidiaries.

We will examine each of these factors in turn.

Financial Reality

DEBT FOCUSES THE MIND

Jimmy Goldsmith is not beloved at Goodyear Tire, but his thwarted raid of 1986 had some beneficial results.

Mark 1990 as the Year of the Blowout for Goodyear Tire & Rubber Co. It took its first annual loss since 1932. But 1990 was also the year that Goodyear began to put the rubber to the road. As a result, the company's future looks brighter than it has in years.

Goodyear's problems crystallized in 1986, when Sir James Goldsmith threatened to take over the company. To buy him off, Goodyear added $2.6 billion to its long-term debt, ransomed the raider's 12.5 million shares and bought back another 40 percent of its stock, reducing the total to near its current $58 million.

Goodyear's $3.3 billion in long-term debt remains a millstone. Debt service is over $300 million a year, equal to over $3 on every one of the tires Goodyear makes.

Say this for debt: It does focus the managerial mind on efficiency. During 1988 through 1990, Goodyear sold many of its nontire businesses and consolidated operations, modernized factories, and cut jobs—saving an estimated $250 million a year. It has grown more market sensitive at its 6300 outlets.

Also during 1988–1990, Goodyear invested $1.4 billion to upgrade its production facilities and switch almost exclusively to radial-tire production. The company has always been considered the low-cost producer but has improved on that.

In January 1990, after dropping two points of market share because of untimely price increases, Goodyear stopped trying to sell its tires at premium prices over competing brands. It cut prices on most tires by around $15 a tire. Result: Goodyear has recovered that lost market share, to about 28 percent of the North American business.

Adapted from Steve Weiner, "Debt Focuses the Mind," *Forbes,* January 7, 1991, pp. 40–41. Reprinted by permission of FORBES magazine.

Ability to Service Debt

The most direct and relevant measure of risk inherent in a leveraged capital structure is the projection of a firm's future cash flows and resources available to meet future cash requirements. A shortage of cash available to service debt is the most adverse possibility for any company. Thus, management must have:

- A strategy for selling future securities when the firm needs access to new financing.
- A plan for cutting dividends if cash flows decline too much and financial difficulty looms over the firm.
- A strategy for debt service in a worst-case economic scenario—in the worst set of economic conditions that is likely to occur.

Management's principal focus for the firm should be on minimizing the risk of *cash inadequacy*—the probability of running out of cash. The financial officer must

Financial Reality

DEBT MISMANAGED

Men such as Bruce Wasserstein, who with his partner, Joseph Perella, made hundreds of millions of dollars buying, selling and restructuring businesses through their investment-banking firm, Wasserstein Perella & Co.

In September 1987, during an appearance before a House Energy and Commerce subcommittee, Wasserstein discussed corporate debt and the unique abilities of sophisticated financial advisers to determine which companies were capable of carrying large amounts of debt.

He cited as an example Harcourt Brace Jovanovich Inc., a book publishing company that had expanded into other areas, including the Sea World theme parks and insurance.

In May 1987, British media mogul Robert Maxwell sought to buy Harcourt for about $2 billion, or $44 a share. To fend off the bid, Harcourt took on $2 billion in debt and distributed cash to stockholders.

Wasserstein approved of the move. "The shareholders have every reason to be ecstatic over what happened at Harcourt, because the offer that came in for the company was at something in the mid-$40, and the total value of the package shareholders received was something over $60 a share. We are confident that Harcourt will do very well, and that is reflected in the marketplace today."

Notwithstanding the sophisticated financial advice that Harcourt received, the company was unable to meet the interest payments on a staggering $2.5 billion debt without selling off properties, closing some operations, and laying off employees.

For 1987, the year it took on the new debt, Harcourt reported net income of $83.4 million. In 1988, the year after, the company lost $53.5 million. In 1989, Harcourt reported net income of $12.4 million. But that was due to the sale of its theme parks for $1.1 billion. Without the sale of assets, Harcourt would have lost $242.2 million on its operations.

As for the company's stock, in 1986—the year before the money industry moved in—it traded at a high of $104 a share. In late November 1991, it traded at 62.5 cents per share.

Ever since the restructuring that Wasserstein oversaw, Harcourt had been losing money, selling assets, scrambling to make ends meet. The company became a division of General Cinema Corp. in a $1.5 billion buyout. Harcourt disappeared as an independent company.

There is no mistaking the cause of Harcourt's demise: excessive debt made possible by a tax code that provides for a nearly unlimited interest deduction.

Source: *America: What Went Wrong?* Copyright 1992 by Donald L. Barlett and James B. Steele. Reprinted with permission of Andrews and McMeel.

have a detailed cash budget completed to identify cash inflows and outflows and establish their timing. Table 19-2 indicates several ways management can mobilize financial resources if a liquidity problem arises. The choices vary from using excess cash or unused lines of credit established with a bank; cutting production, dividends, or marketing activities; and selling assets. Associated with each activity is an estimate of the length of time it would take to mobilize the funds.

TABLE 19-2 Mobilization of Resources

Resources	Available for Use Within: One Quarter	One Year	Three Years
1. Uncommitted reserves			
Instant reserves:			
Surplus cash	$1,500		
Unused line of credit	2,000		
Negotiable reserves:			
Additional bank loans	1,200		
Issue of long-term debt		$ 4,000	
Issue of stock:			
Preferred stock		1,000	
Common stock		3,000	
2. Reduction of planned outflows			
Volume related:			
Change in production schedule	600		
Scale related:			
Marketing program		500	
R&D budget		200	
Administrative overhead		600	
Capital expenditures		2,000	
Value related:			
Dividend payments		200	
3. Liquidation of assets			
Sale of assets:			
Land and real estate		3,000	
Equipment		700	
Accounts receivable		600	
Inventory		400	
Sale of business units			$ 7,000
Total financial resources available	$5,300 ⇒	5,300	
		$21,500 ⇒	21,500
			$28,500

Source: Based on Gordon Donaldson, Strategy for Financial Mobility (Boston: Division of Research, Harvard Graduate School of Business Administration, 1969), p. 72.

There are two measures of debt-servicing capacity often used by external analysts; the *fixed-charge coverage (FCC) ratio* and the *interest coverage ratio.* The *fixed-charge coverage ratio* is an index of earnings available to pay interest, various fixed expenses management considers essential (such as rent and lease payments), debt principal payments, and preferred dividends. The formula is:

Fixed charge coverage

$$= \frac{\textbf{Earnings before interest, taxes and fixed charges}}{\textbf{Interest + fixed charges} + \dfrac{\textbf{principal repayment + preferred dividends}}{(1-t)}} \tag{19-1}$$

Exercise:
If Westinghouse declares a preferred dividend of $1 million, how much earnings before taxes must it realize to pay the dividend? Assume that earnings and operating cash flow are the same.
Answer: $1 million ÷ (1 – 0.35) = $1,538,462.

The larger the value of the index, the more *income* there is supposedly to pay the amounts included in the ratio.

Because debt principal payments and dividends are not tax-deductible expenses, it is necessary to divide them by 1 – tax rate (τ). A company pays debt principal and dividends out of after-tax dollars. For instance, assume that Westinghouse Corporation must make a $10 million principal payment. How much must earnings before taxes be if management uses the total net income amount as the source of funds to pay the principal amount? If the tax rate is 35 percent, management needs $15,384,615 income before taxes to pay $10,000,000 after taxes: $10,000,000 ÷ (1 – 0.35) = $15,384,615. We can verify that this amount is correct as follows: earnings before taxes ($15,384,615) – taxes (35% × $15,384,615) = net income ($10,000,000).

The *interest coverage ratio* is an index of earnings available to pay debt interest. Its definition is:

$$\textbf{Interest coverage} = \frac{\textbf{Earnings before interest and taxes}}{\textbf{Interest}} \tag{19-2}$$

We can derive this ratio from the FCC ratio by assuming that fixed charges, principal payments, and preferred dividends are zero.

Management and financial analysts use rules of thumb to assess the FCC and interest coverage risk. The interpretation of higher ratios is less risk. Illustration 19-1 shows calculations for both ratios.

ILLUSTRATION 19-1

Debt coverage ratios

Healey Manufacturing Company reports earnings before interest and taxes (EBIT) of $21 million. Included in the calculation of the EBIT balance is $5 million deducted for operating expenses (for example, operating lease payments) that management considers fixed and necessary to pay. Based on the firm's debt level, it incurs $2 million interest expense and $7 million in principal payment. The income tax rate is 30 percent.

The fixed-charge coverage ratio is 1.53:

$$\text{Fixed charge coverage} = \frac{\text{Earnings before interest, taxes and fixed charges}}{\text{Interest} + \text{fixed charges} + \dfrac{\text{principal payment}}{(1-t)}}$$

$$= \frac{\$21{,}000{,}000 + \$5{,}000{,}000}{\$2{,}000{,}000 + \$5{,}000{,}000 + \dfrac{\$7{,}000{,}000}{1-0.30}}$$

$$= 1.53$$

The interpretation of an FCC ratio of 1.53 is that the firm has $1.53 of *earnings* before interest, taxes, and operating fixed charges to pay for every $1 of interest, fixed operating charges, and principal due.

By ignoring the fixed charges and principal payments, the interest coverage ratio is $21 million ÷ $2 million = 10.5. The interpretation is similar to that for the FCC: $10.50 of earnings are available to pay for every $1 of interest.

Management and analysts use both the fixed-charge coverage ratio and the interest coverage ratio to evaluate the impact of different capital structures under different projected business scenarios. They then compare the calculated values for these ratios with benchmarks that reflect the company's desired credit rating. For example, if the firm's FCC ratio is 1.1 but the norm for firms with the same amount of risk is 2.5, then lenders may either refuse to lend or require a much higher interest rate to compensate for higher financial risk. *A problem with both of these ratios is that earnings are not cash flows. Debt obligations are paid with cash—not with earnings.* Thus, these coverage ratios misstate the true ability of the firm to meet its obligations.

Ability to Use Tax Benefits

A firm's taxable income is affected not only by the tax deductibility of interest, but also by other tax savings, such as the noncash charge for depreciation and tax loss from prior years, which reduce tax payments. These tax benefits represent savings as long as sufficient earnings exist or are expected to exist. When the current year's income is not large enough to allow the firm to take a tax deduction for all of its expenses, the tax law permits any unrecovered tax deductions (such as interest and depreciation) to be *carried back* to the three previous periods or *carried forward* for up to 15 future years.

For example, if Columbia Manufacturing Company has tax benefits totaling $1 million and income before considering these benefits of only $850,000, then the company cannot use $150,000 of the tax benefits this year. Columbia can recompute its taxable income in the earliest (third) prior year using the $150,000 as a tax deduction. The *carrybacks* allow the firm to claim a tax refund for taxes paid in previous years, since carrying back the deductions lowers income in the previous years. If no, or insufficient, taxable income exists in the third prior year, then the taxable income for two years ago is recomputed, and the same is done for one year ago if necessary.

If there are still unused tax deductions, the firm carries any excess deductions forward into future years to reduce taxable income. These tax *carryforwards* are also called *tax-loss carryovers.* The Financial Reality reading on page 460 outlines the importance of the carryovers to some firms. The essential point is that the firm can use tax-loss carryovers to reduce future tax payments. By reducing future cash outflows, the firm has more cash available to invest in growth opportunities to return the company to profitability.

If agency costs of debt and equity are immaterial, a company that currently pays no taxes (such as a bankrupt company) and does not expect to in the near future should not incur additional debt. Added debt increases the default risk with no additional interest tax benefit. If a company does not currently generate taxable income but expects to in the future, then management must consider whether to finance with additional debt. The added debt is beneficial only if the expected present value of the interest tax saving (PVTS) exceeds the expected present value of financial distress costs (PVFD) and the present value of agency costs (PVAC). In other words, it is necessary for PVTS > (PVFD + PVAC).

Desired Bond Rating

A company that forecasts substantial investments to expand its product line or undertake a massive national advertising campaign, for example, wants access to

Financial Reality

WHERE LOSSES ARE ASSETS

If a company suffering from poor profitability can be put back on a profitable trend, its tax-loss carryforward is like money in the bank.

Gone are the days when raiders captured companies for their tax-loss carryforwards. The 1986 tax act changed that by substantially limiting the use of the shelters when 50 percent or more of a company's stock changes hands. But carryforwards, a.k.a. net operating losses, still have value to companies that are not changing hands. Such corporations are sheltered from federal income tax until the loss carryforward is fully absorbed. Every dollar of past losses thus saves 34 cents in future taxes.

Chrysler and MCI Communications used carryforwards to get back on their feet. So have plenty of smaller companies. Fedders Corp., the air-conditioner manufacturer, ran into trouble, and by 1985 the company had stockpiled $139 million in carryforwards and the stock languished at around $4. But, a few years before, the company had begun a restructuring that included the elimination of the central air-conditioning line and the aggressive marketing of its room air conditioners. Today Fedders' tax losses are used up, but the stock has nearly quadrupled since 1985.

Other companies have used their tax credits by acquiring new profit-making businesses. An example includes Chicago Pacific. It emerged from bankruptcy in 1984 after disposing of all its railroad assets. The company had $135 million in loss carryforwards but no operating businesses. A string of acquisitions, including the Hoover vacuum cleaner line in 1985, turned the company into a consumer products manufacturer. Chicago Pacific's shares climbed seventeenfold between 1984 and 1988, when Maytag bought the company.

Adapted from Christopher Palmeri, "Where Losses Are Assets," *Forbes*, August 7, 1989, pp. 154–155. Reprinted by permission of FORBES magazine.

the financial markets on acceptable terms. To do so, it must have adequate credit strength, as measured by independent bond rating companies, such as Standard & Poor's or Moody's. An adequate bond rating is, in practice, a very important factor in a company's choice of capital structure. The distinction between investment-grade ratings (S&P's *BBB* rating or better) and speculative-grade ratings (below *BBB*) is important because of restrictions placed on certain classes of institutional investors. For instance, the U.S. comptroller of the currency allows commercial banks to invest only in investment-grade bonds. Various state laws impose minimum bond ratings (such as single *A*) and other standards that debt obligations must meet to qualify as legal investments for savings banks, trust companies, public pension funds, and insurance companies.

The issuance of high-rated bonds by a company also reduces the likelihood that creditors might impose restrictive covenants that could seriously impair the company's operating and financial flexibility. All in all, experience suggests that a single-*A* rating is a worthy rating target because it ensures reasonably good access

TABLE 19-3 Median Ratio Values by Rating Category, 1990–1992

Rating Category	AAA	AA	A	BBB	BB	B
Pretax interest coverage (×)	17.7	7.6	4.1	2.5	1.5	0.9
Funds from operations to total debt (%)	120.1	65.3	37.0	26.3	15.5	9.8
Total debt/capitalization (%)	21.9	32.7	40.3	48.8	66.2	71.5

Firms with *AAA* ratings have more than twice as much interest coverage as *AA*-rated companies, about three times as much funds from operations relative to total debt as single-*A* companies, and use much less debt, as a proportion of total financing to finance investments then all other rating categories.

Source: Standard & Poor's CreditStats, October 27, 1993, p. 12.

to the financial markets. However, managers must consider two factors in their decisions to set a bond-rating goal:

- The degree of risk of future financial distress the firm is willing to bear.
- The degree of future access to the financial markets the firm would like to achieve.

In reaching a judgment about the most appropriate rating, rating agencies apply a large number of criteria. While no all-purpose rating formula exists, the values of certain key credit statistics for comparable companies whose debt carries the target debt rating offer useful guidance. Table 19-3 shows how values of three key credit statistics vary across the six highest rating categories assigned by Standard & Poor's. The higher the firm's senior debt rating, the progressively better are *interest coverage, funds from operations relative to total debt*, and *total debt to all financing used to capitalize the firm*. These three elements represent measures of a company's ability to continue to service its debt on a current basis.

Financing Through Subsidiaries

Firms often have many different subsidiaries. Management establishes most subsidiaries as separate business units because their products are distinctive from other products of the company. However, two types of subsidiaries that can affect the capital structure decision are foreign subsidiaries and finance subsidiaries.

Foreign Subsidiaries. Firms with foreign subsidiaries must decide how to finance them. The parent company's worldwide capital structure dominates the subsidiary's capital structure. A subsidiary maintains a separate capital structure from the parent only if there is a reason management might allow the subsidiary to default with no recourse to corporate resources. If legal or ethical obligations exist to prevent default by a subsidiary, then the subsidiary does not have an independent capital structure. The subsidiary's true capital structure is equal to that of the whole enterprise. Thus, the parent company's worldwide capital structure dominates the foreign subsidiary's capital structure.

The firm typically finances its foreign subsidiary with a high proportion of debt. The parent company's equity investment in the subsidiary is generally small. The subsidiary usually obtains the debt financing from local sources. There are several reasons:

- Local funds are not subject to losses because of currency devaluations.
- Debt repayment is easier because there are no currency exchange costs or restrictions.
- Local financial institutions are happy when borrowing is done locally (although other businesses needing funds may not be happy if borrowing costs increase).
- The political risk of investing in countries where the threat of expropriation of foreign assets is significant is reduced. If the host government takes over the subsidiary, the parent corporation's loss of investment is relatively minimal because it invested very little equity.
- In countries with minimal threat of expropriation of assets, the parent company may still use much debt, but if it guarantees the subsidiary's debts, then host-country lenders usually provide loans to the subsidiary at favorable rates.

Finance Subsidiary. Where credit is important to a firm's marketing efforts, it is not unusual for the firm to form its own *finance subsidiary.* Generally, the *finance subsidiary's* sole purpose is to buy the accounts receivable of the parent company. The subsidiary pays for the receivables by borrowing from banks or issuing commercial paper in the money market. A prominent finance subsidiary is General Motors' General Motors Acceptance Corporation, or GMAC. It finances GM's auto and truck sales.

The parent company is usually able to improve the total company's (parent plus subsidiary) debt capacity by establishing a finance subsidiary. This happens because lenders base the incremental debt capacity of the subsidiary on the highly marketable accounts receivable rather than on the standard cash operating profit. Illustration 19-2 demonstrates how a financial subsidiary increases the firm's debt capacity.

ILLUSTRATION 19-2

How a finance subsidiary works

Suppose the expected sales volume of Arneson Marketing Limited is unable to generate enough earnings before interest to take advantage of any additional interest tax savings. To overcome this problem, management of Arneson establishes a finance subsidiary to buy its receivables. Arneson finances the subsidiary entirely with 8 percent debt.[2] Management expects the receivables to be collected every three months.

The subsidiary relies on the collection of the receivables to repay principal and interest to lenders. Arneson must sell the receivables to the subsidiary at a discount large enough to provide cash operating profit to the subsidiary to be able to meet payments to the lenders. Since the receivables have an average life of three months and the effective annual interest rate is 8 percent, a 2 percent discount on the sale of the receivables to the subsidiary is necessary (one quarter of the annual rate).[3]

During the year the parent company expects credit sales of $107.1 million. The subsidiary buys the receivables for $107.1 ÷ 1.02, or $105 million, which represents a $2.1 million discount. At any one time, about $26.25 million of receivables (at cost) will be uncollected: ($105 million ÷ 12 months) × 3 months outstanding. Thus, the subsidiary requires $26.25 million of debt to support its operations. The annual

[2]Normally the parent company has a small equity investment in the subsidiary.

[3]The correct quarterly rate is $(1 + 0.08)^{1/4} - 1 = 0.0194$, or 1.94 percent. The use of 2 percent is satisfactory for explaining the concept.

interest expense is 8% × \$26.25 million = \$2.1 million. With discount income of \$2.1 million (the difference between what the sub collects and what it pays for the receivables) and interest expense of \$2.1 million, the subsidiary reports no taxable income.

For Arneson the net effect of this arrangement is the addition of \$26.25 million of debt capacity and realization of the attendant interest tax savings.

COMPREHENSION CHECK

1. *Based on Table 19-1, discuss practicing managers' views on whether there is an optimal capital structure for business firms.*
2. *Briefly list the four basic considerations involved in choosing a firm's capital structure.*
3. *Explain how federal income tax law helps corporations that borrow money, even for those firms which have operating losses and are not able to benefit from the tax deductibility of interest payments in the current accounting period.*
4. *What is the general relationship between the ratings on a corporation's debt and the firm's interest cost?*
5. *How can foreign and finance subsidiaries affect the firm's capital structure?*

BUSINESS RISK VERSUS FINANCIAL RISK

Underlying capital structure decisions about the firm's ability to service debt, to use all its tax benefits, to obtain its desired bond ratings, or to use foreign or finance subsidiaries is the issue of *business risk* versus *financial risk.* Recall that a firm's business risk arises from investment in plant and equipment and technology to make its products and from the markets in which it sells the finished products. Financial risk arises from how management finances the firm.

Most firms with high business risk fall into at least one of the following categories:[4]

- *Products that require costly repairs.* Customer demand drops for a product when consumers feel the product cannot be serviced if the firm encounters financial difficulty. Caterpillar Inc. has an excellent worldwide reputation for its heavy equipment. A long and violent labor strike against Caterpillar in 1992 caused the firm to lose market share to a Japanese manufacturer, thereby increasing its business risk.
- *Goods or services whose quality is difficult to determine before buying.* The concern is that firms in financial difficulty will reduce quality in an effort to conserve funds. Consumers levied this criticism against the U.S. automotive manufacturers during the 1980s. With increasing costs and lagging sales because of Japanese competition, the quality of American-made cars declined as the Big 3 U.S. auto companies tried to improve profits. Business risk increased as consumers purchased more foreign-made cars and trucks.
- *Products that have significant switching costs.* If customers must encounter large costs to switch suppliers (for example, mainframe computer suppliers), they will buy from the financially strong company.

[4]See Sheridan Titman, "The Effect of Capital Structure on a Firm's Liquidation Decision," *Journal of Financial Economics,* 13 (1984), 137–151.

TABLE 19-4 Median Industry Debt-to-total Capital Ratios in 1992

Aerospace/defense	38%
Aluminum	27
Beverages, alcoholic	32
Broadcasting, media	69
Chemicals, diversified	28
Entertainment	20
Foods	31
Hardware and tools	51
Health care drugs	12
Medical products and supplies	32
Oil and gas drilling	20
Pollution control	41
Publishing, newspapers	32
Retail stores general merchandise	46
Steel producers	64
Telecommunications, long distance	33

Source: Standard & Poor's Analyst's Handbook Official Series, 1993 Annual Edition.

Management usually tries to trade off business risk against financial risk. A company operating in an industry with low business risk can support greater financial leverage. On the other hand, a firm operating in an industry with high business risk generally takes on lower financial risk. Debt ratios summarized in Table 19-4 suggest that capital structure choices by management differ across industries. Why do you suppose broadcasting and health care drugs are so different? Broadcasting's exposure to business risk is much less. A few dominant firms control the broadcasting industry. Neither the broadcasting industry's technology nor exposure to government regulation is as risky as in the drug industry. A health care firm developing a new drug may find that it takes five or more years to develop the drug, only to have the Federal Drug Administration deny the firm the right to sell it in the United States. Thus, to offset high business risk, health care drug firms reduce their exposure to financial risk.

Management attempts to quantify business and financial risks. Two popular techniques for this process are analysis of *trading on the equity* and *degree of leverage.* These techniques evaluate whether the firm can realize *favorable, neutral,* or *unfavorable financial leverage. Favorable financial leverage* results if the firm's assets earn more on the use of debt than the debt's after-tax cost. *Unfavorable financial leverage* means the firm's assets earn less on the use of debt funds than their after-tax cost. *Neutral financial leverage* is the result of the assets simply earning the after-tax cost of debt.

Trading on the Equity

No creditor is willing to put up loan funds without the safety provided by the owners' equity capital. Thus, management *trades on the equity;* that is, a given amount of equity capital contributed by shareholders acts as a base against which to borrow debt funds. The two ratios used to analyze trading on the equity are *return on equity*

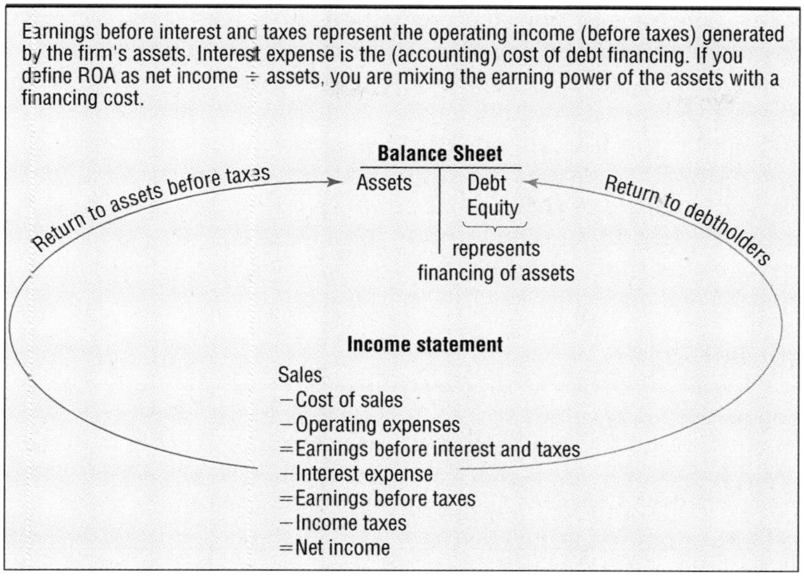

FIGURE 19-1
A firm's financial statements

and *return on assets. Return on equity* is the return shareholders earn on their investment—the firm's equity financing:

$$\textbf{Return on equity} + \frac{\textbf{Net income}}{\textbf{Equity}} \tag{19-3}$$

Return on assets measures the accounting profitability, or earning power, of the assets used by the company in its business. Its formula is:

$$\begin{aligned}\textbf{Return on assets} &= \frac{\textbf{Earnings before interest and taxes} \times (1 - \textbf{tax rate})}{\textbf{Assets}} \\ &= \frac{\textbf{Net income} + \textbf{interest} \times (1 - \textbf{tax rate})}{\textbf{Assets}}\end{aligned} \tag{19-4}$$

We must measure return on assets (ROA) before any deductions for interest cost, since we want to calculate the earning power of the assets.[5] For instance, consider the firm's balance sheet and income statement in Figure 19-1. Interest expense in the income statement is the financing cost for the debt appearing in the balance sheet. Because ROA seeks to determine the earning power of the assets, it is necessary to exclude interest expense in the calculation. Unlike cost of sales and operat-

[5]Many managers, accountants, and academicians incorrectly calculate ROA as:

$$\text{ROA} = \frac{\text{Net income}}{\text{Assets}}$$

This definition mixes earning power of the assets with the financing of the assets and understates the actual return on assets.

ing expenses, which result from the production, advertising, and administration of the firm's products, interest expense arises from using debt financing.

If management decides to finance the assets entirely with equity capital, the interest cost would be zero but the ability of the assets to produce the firm's products would not be affected. Although we discussed in the last chapter that interest expense provides a tax saving that adds value to both the firm and shareholders' wealth, *interest expense does not affect the earning power of the assets.* We work through the consequences of trading on the equity in Illustration 19-3. *An important assumption of trading on the equity analysis is that asset size remains constant while management looks at different debt and equity financing combinations.*

ILLUSTRATION 19-3

Trading on the equity

Two companies with identical assets and *accounting* earnings before interest expense and taxes (EBIT) are financed differently. Levered Company finances 40 percent of its assets with debt; Unlevered Company does not use debt.

	Company	
	Levered	**Unlevered**
Assets	$1000.0	$1000.0
Debt (8% interest)	$ 400.0	$ 0.0
Equity	600.0	1000.0
Total	$1000.0	$1000.0
Favorable financial leverage case:		
EBIT	$ 200.0	$ 200.0
Interest (8%)	32.0	0.0
Earnings before taxes	$ 168.0	$ 200.0
Taxes (30%)	50.4	60.0
Net income	$ 117.6	$ 140.0

Return on assets

$$= \frac{\text{Net income + interest} \times (1 - \tau)}{\text{Assets}}$$

	Levered	Unlevered
$\frac{\$117.6 + \$32(1 - 0.30)}{\$1000}$		14.0%
$\frac{\$140.0}{\$1000}$	14.0%	

Return on equity

$$= \frac{\text{Net income}}{\text{Equity}}$$

	Levered	Unlevered
$117.6 ÷ $600	19.6%	
$140.0 ÷ $1000		14.0%

Return on assets is 14 percent for both firms. The return on equity is higher for Levered Company than it is for Unlevered Company. The reason is because the assets of Levered Company earn more (14 percent) for the use of debt than its after-tax cost (5.6% = 8% × [1 – 0.30]). For Unlevered Company, the return on assets always equals the return on equity because management does not use debt financing.

Neutral financial leverage case:

	Company	
	Levered	**Unlevered**
EBIT*	$80.0	$80.0
Interest (8%)	32.0	0.0
Earnings before taxes	$48.0	$80.0
Taxes (30%)	14.4	24.0
Net income	$33.6	$56.0

**EBIT has decreased relative to the first situation. The assets generate less operating income than in the favorable case.*

Return on assets

$$= \frac{\text{Net income} + \text{interest} \times (1 - t)}{\text{Assets}}$$

$$\frac{\$33.6 + \$32.0(1 - 0.30)}{\$1000} \quad 5.6\%$$

$$\frac{\$56.0}{\$1000} \quad 5.6\%$$

Return on equity

$$= \frac{\text{Net income}}{\text{Equity}}$$

	Levered	Unlevered
\$33.6 ÷ \$600	5.6%	
\$56.0 ÷ \$1000		5.6%

Return on assets equals the return on equity for both companies. We should expect this result for Unlevered Company, since it does not use debt. However, for Levered Company return on assets and return on equity are equal. The reason is that the firm's assets earn the same return (5.6 percent) from the use of debt as the after-tax cost of debt. The equal returns neutralize financial leverage.

Unfavorable financial leverage case:

	Company	
	Levered	**Unlevered**
EBIT*	$60.0	$60.0
Interest (8%)	32.0	0.0
Earnings before taxes	$28.0	$60.0
Taxes (30%)	8.4	18.0
Net income	$19.6	$42.0

**EBIT is decreased again because assets continue to generate less operating profit.*

Return on assets

$$= \frac{\text{Net income} + \text{interest} \times (1 - \tau)}{\text{Assets}}$$

	Levered	Unlevered
$\frac{\$19.6 + 32.0(1 - 0.30)}{\$1000}$	4.2%	
$\frac{\$42.0}{\$1000}$		4.2%

Return on equity

$$= \frac{\text{Net income}}{\text{Equity}}$$

	Levered	Unlevered
$19.6 ÷ $600	3.3%	
$42.0 ÷ $1000		4.2%

These results show leverage to be a double-edged sword. When return on assets (4.2 percent) is below the after-tax cost of debt (5.6 percent), Levered Company's return on equity is less than that of Unlevered Company. Levered Company experiences unfavorable financial leverage.

What have we just learned? Different debt and equity financing mixes result in different accounting results. If the firm's assets can earn more on the use of debt funds than their after-tax cost, then profitability increases as a result of favorable financial leverage. Of course, the reverse situation could also occur.[6] Figure 19-2 plots the different scenarios of Illustration 19-3. The graph shows the trade-off between EBIT and return on equity (ROE) and return on assets (ROA) for an all-equity financing alternative versus a capital structure including both debt and equity financing.

In Figure 19-2, the line *OU* represents the different EBIT-ROE combinations for the illustration's unlevered firm. This line also represents the ROAs for both firms because changes in the capital structure do not affect the earning power of the assets. Possibly you noticed the constant earning power of assets in Illustration 19-3. Both firms have equal ROAs for each scenario. The line *IL* in the figure represents the EBIT-ROE combinations when management uses debt financing. The line intercepts the EBIT-axis at the (before-tax) level of interest costs ($32) incurred. When interest cost exceeds the level of EBIT, then ROE is negative.

Where lines *IL* and *OU* intersect, ROA = ROE = after-tax interest rate of debt. We call the intersection the *indifference point,* the point at which assets earn only the cost

[6]A comparison of the correct calculation Eq. (19-4) and the incorrect calculation (see footnote 5) for ROA shows a significant error exists when you use the wrong equation. For our two firms, the error is $32.0 × (1 − 0.30) ÷ $1000 = 0.022 or 2.2 percent, which is the difference between the following two ROA columns.

	Incorrect ROA	Correct ROA
Favorable leverage	$117.6 ÷ $1000 = 11.8%	14.0%
Neutral leverage	$33.6 ÷ $1000 = 3.4%	5.6%
Unfavorable leverage	$19.6 ÷ $1000 = 2.0%	4.2%

When EBIT is below the level of $80, the firm will be more profitable if management finances with an all-equity capital structure. Above the indifference point, a combination of debt and equity financing improves profitability.

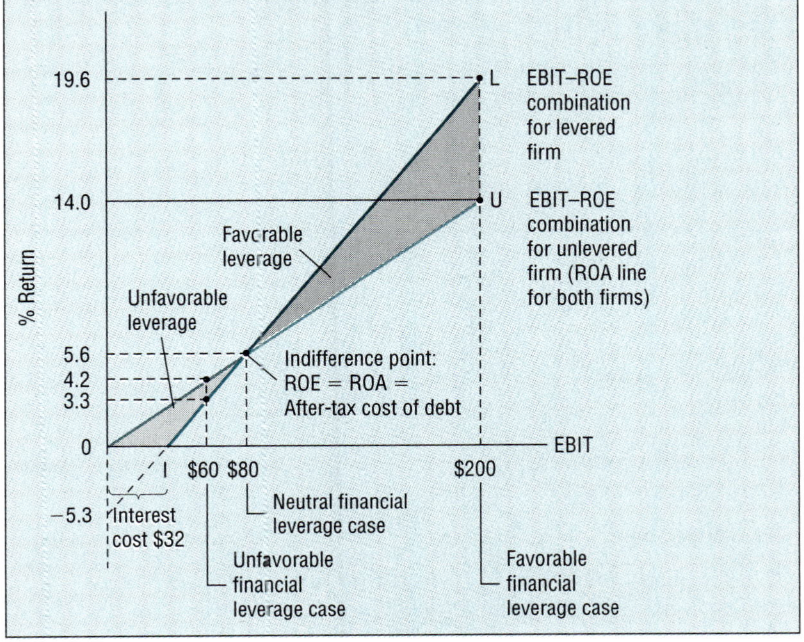

FIGURE 19-2
EBIT-profitability analysis

of financing and financial leverage is neutral between some debt and no debt at all. We can calculate the amount of EBIT for which management is indifferent between alternative capital structures. This level is called the *EBIT indifference level:*

EBIT indifference level

$$= \frac{\begin{array}{c}\textbf{Equity of alternative \#1} \times \textbf{interest cost of alternative \#2} \\ - \textbf{equity of alternative \#2} \times \textbf{interest cost of alternative \#1}\end{array}}{\textbf{Equity of alternative \#1} - \textbf{equity of alternative \#2}} \qquad \textbf{(19-5)}$$

$$= \frac{E_1 \times I_2 - E_2 \times I_1}{E_1 - E_2}$$

$$= \frac{\$600 \times \$0 - \$1000 \times \$32}{\$600 - \$1000}$$

$$= \$80$$

The answer we found for the neutral case in Illustration 19-3 and plotted in Figure 19-2 is the *indifference level* of $80. If EBIT is expected to be above $80, management should chose the debt and equity alternative. Favorable financial leverage will result in higher return on both assets and equity.

What if the firm is considering an all-equity capital structure versus some different scenarios for debt? Illustration 19-4 provides an example of the necessary calculations. You will find some subtle differences compared to the problem we have just solved.

ILLUSTRATION 19-4

EBIT indifference level for capital structure

Financial data for three different capital structures under consideration by managers at Deguzman Enterprises are as follows:

	Possible Capital Structures #1	#2	#3
Debt	$ 0	$ 300	$ 600
Equity	1000	700	400
Assets	$1000	$1000	$1000
Interest (9%)		$ 27	
Interest (10%)			$ 60

Management is indifferent between capital structures #1 and #2 when earnings before interest and taxes (EBIT) are $90.

EBIT indifference level

$$= \frac{\text{Equity of alternative \#1} \times \text{interest cost of alternative \#2} - \text{equity of alternative \#2} \times \text{interest cost of alternative \#1}}{\text{Equity of alternative \#1} - \text{equity of alternative \#2}}$$

$$= \frac{E_1 \times I_2 - E_2 \times I_1}{E_1 - E_2}$$

$$= \frac{\$700 \times \$0 - \$1000 \times \$27}{\$700 - \$1000}$$

$$= \$90$$

Similar calculations provide EBIT of $100 as the indifference level between capital structures #1 and #3. The EBIT indifference level between capital structures #2 and #3 is $104. Can you derive these answers?[7]

Let's calculate ROA and ROE for an EBIT level of $104. You can do similar calculations for the other levels. (See the capital structure comparisons following these calculations.)

$$\text{ROA} = \frac{\text{Net income} + \text{interest} \times (1 - t)}{\text{Assets}}$$

$$\text{ROA \#2} = \frac{\$53.9 + \$27.0 \times (1 - 0.30)}{\$100} = 0.0728 \text{ or } 7.28\%$$

$$\text{ROA \#3} = \frac{\$30.8 + \$60.0 \times (1 - 0.30)}{\$100} = 0.0728 \text{ or } 7.28\%$$

$$\text{ROE} = \text{Net income} \div \text{equity}$$

$$\text{ROE \#2} = \$53.9 \div \$700 = 0.077 \text{ or } 7.7\%$$

$$\text{ROE \#3} = \$30.8 \div \$400 = 0.077 \text{ or } 7.7\%$$

[7]Solutions: EBIT indifference level for #1 and #3 = ($1000 × $60 – $400 × $0)/($1000 – $400) = $100; EBIT indifference level for #2 and #3 = ($700 × $60 – $400 × $27)/($700 – $400) = $104.

	#1	vs.	#2	#1	vs.	#3	#2	vs.	#3
				Capital Structure Comparisons					
EBIT$	$ 90.0		$ 90.0	$ 100.0		$ 100.0	$104.0		$104.0
Interest	0.0		27.0	$ 0.0		60.0	27.0		60.0
Earnings before tax	$ 90.0		$ 63.0	100.0		$ 40.0	$ 77.0		$ 44.0
Taxes (30%)	27.0		18.9	$ 30.0		12.0	23.1		13.2
Net income$	$ 63.0		$ 44.1	$ 70.0		$ 28.0	$ 53.9		$ 30.8
Debt$	0.0		$300.0	$ 0.0		$ 600.0	$300.0		$600.0
Equity	1000.0		700.0	1000.0		400.0	700.0		400.0
ROA	6.3%		6.3%	7.0%		7.0%	7.28%		7.28%
ROE	6.3%		6.3%	7.0%		7.0%	7.70%		7.70%
After-tax debt cost	6.3%		6.3%	7.0%		7.0%	6.30%		7.00%

Notice that when a capital structure with debt (either #2 or #3) is compared against an all-equity capital structure (#1), ROA = ROE = after-tax debt cost at the level of EBIT for which management is indifferent between the capital structures. This relationship does not hold when two capital structures both using debt are compared (#2 versus #3). The reason is that capital structures #2 and #3 have different interest rates for debt. If interest rates for both capital structures were 9 percent, the EBIT indifference level would be $90, and ROA = ROE = after-tax debt cost = 6.3%. Again, see if you can get this result.[8]

Let's return to our assumption of different interest rates for the debt. We can verify that if EBIT exceeds $104, then capital structure #3 is better. For example, if EBIT is $150, ROE #2 is 12.30 percent, ROE #3 is 15.75 percent, and ROA for both capital structures is 10.5 percent. Therefore, if EBIT exceeds the EBIT indifference amount of $104, then management should use capital structure #3, which makes greater use of debt.

What financing mix should management use if EBIT is less than $90? Any EBIT amount less than $90 will do to show the concept, but let's choose $80. You should be able to calculate the following amounts for ROA, ROE, and after-tax cost of debt:

Capital Structure	ROA	ROE	After-tax Cost of Debt
#1—no debt	5.6%	5.6%	–
#2—$300 debt	5.6%	3.7%	6.3%
#3—$600 debt	5.6%	1.4%	7.0%

We see that the firm should not use debt if EBIT is less than $90. Debt financing causes ROE < ROA < after-tax cost of debt. Unfavorable financial leverage has resulted; the assets earn less than the after-tax cost of debt.

Finally, what capital structure should management use if EBIT is greater than $90 but less than $104? Suppose EBIT is $95. At this level of EBIT, we calculate the following amounts for ROA, ROE, and after-tax cost of debt for different capital structures:

[8]Solutions: EBIT indifference level = ($700 × $54 − $400 × $27)/($700 − $400) = $90; ROE = ($90 − $54) × (1 − 0.30)/$400 = 0.063; cost of debt = 0.09 × (1 − 0.30) = 0.063; ROA = $90 × (1 − 0.30)/$1000 = 0.063.

Capital Structure	ROA	ROE	After-tax Cost of Debt
#1—no debt	6.65%	6.65%	—
#2—$300 debt	6.65%	6.80%	6.3%
#3—$600 debt	6.65%	6.13%	7.0%

The results indicate that capital structure #2 is the best choice. Its ROE exceeds the ROEs for the other two capital structures and ROE > ROA > after-tax cost of debt.

Figure 19-3 graphs the three capital structure choices examined in Illustration 19-4. Management wants to follow the thick curve, which represents the best ROE-EBIT combinations. The decision should be as follows:

Level of EBIT	Capital Structure Choice
EBIT < $90	#1—$1000 equity; no debt
EBIT = $90	Indifferent between #1 and #2
$90 < EBIT < $104	#2—$300 debt; $700 equity
EBIT = $104	Indifferent between #2 and #3
EBIT > $104	#3—$600 debt; $400 equity

As Illustrations 19-3 and 19-4 show, ROE usually differs from ROA. Why? Because debt financing results in default risk, which is not present with an all-equity capital structure. If the firm defaults on any debt payments, shareholders could lose their entire investment. Therefore, with debt financing shareholders expect ROE > ROA > after-tax cost of debt. Eq. (19-6) is an alternative way to define ROE to show the relationship that exists between return on equity, return on assets, and the after-tax cost of debt as the mix of debt and equity in the capital structure changes.

$$\begin{aligned}&\textbf{Return on equity}\\&\quad= \textbf{Return on assets}\\&\qquad + \textbf{(return on assets + after-tax cost of debt)}\ \frac{\textbf{debt}}{\textbf{equity}}\end{aligned} \tag{19-6}$$

$$\mathrm{ROE} = \mathrm{ROA} + [\mathrm{ROA} - i(1 - t)]\ \frac{\text{debt}}{\text{equity}}$$

Let's substitute values from Illustration 19-4 into Eq. (19-6) to calculate ROE for each capital structure for the case of EBIT = $150, or $105 after taxes.

$$\begin{aligned}\mathrm{ROE}\ \#2 &= 0.105 + [0.105 - 0.09 \times (1 - 0.30)]\ \frac{\$300}{\$700}\\&= 0.105 + 0.018\\&= 0.123 \text{ or } 12.3 \text{ percent}\end{aligned}$$

$$\begin{aligned}\mathrm{ROE}\ \#3 &= 0.105 + [0.105 - 0.10 \times (1 - 0.30)]\ \frac{\$600}{\$400}\\&= 0.105 + 0.0525\\&= 0.1575 \text{ or } 15.75 \text{ percent}\end{aligned}$$

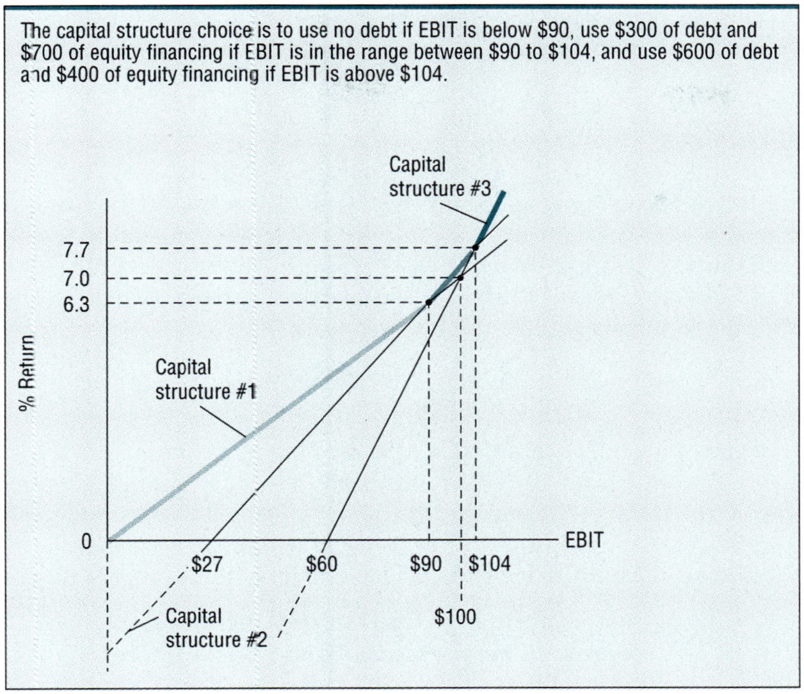

FIGURE 19-3
Choice among different capital structures

Without the use of financial leverage (Case #1), shareholders only require a 10.5 percent return, which is the return on assets number. Shareholders require a higher debt default risk premium (5.25 percent) under capital structure #3 than they require under capital structure #2 (1.8 percent).

Let's look at a slightly different situation but maintain the assumption that the earning power of the assets stays constant; that is, ROA still equals 10.5 percent. Suppose interest rates were to return to their 1981–1982 heights of about 22 percent. For our example, ROEs would shrink to 8.4 percent and 3.15 percent for capital structures #2 and #3, respectively.

$$\begin{aligned}\textbf{ROE \#2} &= \mathbf{0.105 + [0.105 - 0.22 \times (1 - 0.30)]\,\frac{\$300}{\$700}} \\ &= \mathbf{0.105 - 0.021} \\ &= \mathbf{0.084 \text{ or } 8.4 \text{ percent}}\end{aligned}$$

$$\begin{aligned}\textbf{ROE \#3} &= \mathbf{0.105 + [0.105 - 0.22 \times (1 - 0.30)]\,\frac{\$600}{\$400}} \\ &= \mathbf{0.105 - 0.0735} \\ &= \mathbf{0.0315 \text{ or } 3.15 \text{ percent}}\end{aligned}$$

The result is unfavorable financial leverage—ROA is less than the after-tax interest cost of 15.4 percent: 0.22 × (1 – 0.30). Also ROE of either 8.4 percent or 3.15 percent is less than the ROA of 10.5 percent. In this case, the firm would be better off without debt financing. *Thus, as the interest-rate environment changes, management should be prepared to alter the firm's capital structure in an effort to protect profitability.* However, this task is harder than it sounds, as we will discuss later in this chapter.

Degree of Leverage

An alternative approach managers use to assess the trade-off between debt and equity financing is to measure the volatility of net income available for shareholders. This volatility is affected by the *degree of financial leverage* and the *degree of operating leverage. Degree of financial leverage (DFL)* calculates the change in net income for a given change in earnings before interest and taxes:

$$\text{DFL} = \frac{\%\Delta \textbf{ Net income}}{\%\Delta \textbf{ Earnings before interest and taxes}} \tag{19-7}$$

where %Δ means percentage change. Recall our income statement in Figure 19-3. It shows that to proceed from EBIT to net income we must deduct interest expense and income taxes. Thus, DFL measures the significance of after-tax interest expense on profit.

An alternative calculation for DFL, which provides the same result, is:

$$\text{DFL} = \frac{\textbf{Earnings before interest and taxes}}{\textbf{Earnings before interest and taxes} - \textbf{interest}} \tag{19-8}$$

This formula shows that interest expense is the cause of financial leverage, as measured by DFL. If the firm is unlevered, interest expense in the denominator of Eq. (19-8) is zero with the result that the DFL = 1 because the numerator equals the denominator. As the firm adds debt to its capital structure, the DFL increases above 1. Thus, 1 is the minimum value for DFL and indicates an all-equity financed firm with no financial risk.

Regardless of whether management uses debt financing, the firm still faces business risk. We can analyze business risk in terms of the volatility of numbers contained in a firm's income statement. We call this volatility the *degree of operating leverage (DOL)* and define it as:

$$\text{DOL} = \frac{\%\Delta \textbf{ Earnings before interest and taxes}}{\%\ \Delta\textbf{Sales}} \tag{19-9}$$

Again, an alternate definition provides the same result, but gives insight into what causes operating leverage:

$$\text{DOL} = \frac{\textbf{Sales} - \textbf{variable operating costs}}{\textbf{Sales} - \textbf{variable operating costs} - \textbf{fixed operating costs}} \tag{19-10}$$

Notice that the only difference between the numerator and the denominator of Eq. (19-10) is the *fixed operating costs.* Fixed operating costs are expenses for items that do not change as sales volume changes. Examples include the salary of administrative employees, property taxes, and depreciation for plant and equipment. If a firm has no fixed operating costs—an unlikely situation—then DOL = 1. In this case, as long as revenues from sales exceed the variable operating costs incurred in manufacturing and selling the products, the firm will always show a profit. However, as management adds fixed operating costs to business operations, the firm's profit declines and it becomes possible for total costs—variable plus fixed—to exceed sales and the firm to report a loss. On the other hand, it is also possible for the firm to greatly expand its output and profits with the addition of fixed costs. The firm may be able to realize economies of scale with these fixed costs and generate a significantly higher amount of output. In either case, the inclusion of fixed costs exposes the firm's profits to operating risk. As management adds fixed costs, DOL increases above 1 signifying higher operating leverage, that is, business risk. Illustration 19-5 reveals the problem of putting financial risk on top of business risk. Although both the unlevered and levered firms have equal business risk, as indicated by the degree of operating leverage, the levered firm is in a riskier situation because of its financial risk.

When both DFL and DOL are present, the resulting *degree of total leverage* captures both business risk and financial risk from an accounting perspective. We define the *degree of total leverage (DTL)* as:

$$\text{DTL} = \frac{\text{Sales} - \text{variable operating costs}}{\text{Sales} - \text{variable operating costs} - \text{fixed costs} - \text{interest}} \qquad (19\text{-}11)$$

which can be restated as:

$$\text{DTL} = \text{DFL} \times \text{DOL} \qquad (19\text{-}12)$$

Thus, DTL is not a simple addition of the separate risks; rather it is multiplicative. An alternative definition of DTL is:

$$\text{DTL} = \%\Delta \text{ Net income} \div \%\Delta \text{ Sales} \qquad (19\text{-}13)$$

ILLUSTRATION 19-5

Total risk = business risk × financial risk

	Unlevered Firm			Levered Firm		
	Present	Expected	%Δ	Present	Expected	%Δ
Sales	$1000	$1200	20.00%	$1000	$1200	20.00%
Costs:						
Variable (60%)	$ 600	$ 720		$ 600	$ 720	
Fixed	100	100		100	100	
Total	$ 700	$ 820		$ 700	$ 820	
EBIT	$ 300	$ 380	26.67	$ 300	$ 380	26.67
Interest	0	0		50	50	
EBT	$ 300	$ 380		$ 250	$ 330	
Taxes (30%)	90	114		75	99	
Net income	$ 210	$ 266	26.67	$ 175	$ 231	32.00
DOL = %ΔEBIT ÷ %ΔSales						
= 26.67 ÷ 20.00			1.33			1.33
DFL = %ΔNet income ÷ %ΔEBIT						
= 26.67 ÷ 26.67			1.00			
= 32.00 ÷ 26.67						1.20
DTL = %ΔNet income ÷ %ΔSales						
= 26.67 ÷ 20.00			1.33			
= 32.00 ÷ 20.00						1.60

When we use the alternative formulas, we use the present (base) period to calculate business and financial risk.

$\text{DOL} = \dfrac{\text{Sales} - \text{variable operating costs}}{\text{Sales} - \text{variable operating costs} - \text{fixed costs}}$		
$= \dfrac{\$1000 - \$600}{\$1000 - \$600 - \$100}$	1.33	1.33
$\text{DFL} = \dfrac{\text{EBIT}}{\text{EBIT} - \text{interest}}$		
$= \dfrac{\$300}{\$300 - \$0}$	1.00	
$= \dfrac{\$300}{\$300 - \$50}$		1.20
$\text{DTL} = \text{DOL} \times \text{DFL}$		
$= 1.33 \times 1.00$	1.33	
$= 1.33 \times 1.20$		1.60

COMPREHENSION CHECK

1. *Distinguish between favorable, unfavorable, and neutral financial leverage.*
2. *Explain the correct calculation of return on assets, or ROA, for a levered firm. Why is this calculation different from the ROA calculation for an unlevered firm?*
3. *What is the significance of the financing indifference point?*
4. *How can you calculate the influence of debt financing on a firm's return on equity?*
5. *Define: the degree of financial leverage (DFL); the degree of operating leverage (DOL); the degree of total leverage (DTL).*

EFFECTING CHANGES IN CAPITAL STRUCTURE

The firm's investment in plant and equipment and technology, and its type of industry and the markets it has chosen to serve, determine its level of business risk. It is costly and difficult to change factors affecting business risk. However, it is relatively easy for a firm to modify its financial risk to change total risk. We will consider changing financial risk for two types of firms: a financially healthy firm and a financially distressed firm.

Capital Structure Changes in a Healthy Firm

Suppose management of a financially healthy firm decides that the desired capital structure for the firm differs significantly from the current capital structure. What should management do? It can decide on one of two general strategies: slow adjustment or quick adjustment.

Management can slowly alter the capital structure over several years by adjusting the future financing mix. For example, suppose the target capital structure of DeGroot Electrical Components, Inc. consists of 30 percent debt and 70 percent equity, whereas the current capital structure is 65 percent debt and 35 percent equity. Management can change the overleveraged condition by financing with, say, 10 percent debt and 90 percent equity whenever it needs funds until its debt ratio reaches 30 percent. However, this tactic means that the capital structure continues to be above target proportions for as long as it takes the company to correct the condition.

A number of strategies are available to alter the capital structure more quickly, say, within one month to a year. However, the firm usually incurs significant transaction costs with these alternatives.

- *Exchange offer.* Current debt investors can be offered shares of common stock to replace some of their debt.
- *Debt repurchase program.* The firm may buy its own debt in the financial markets and retire it.
- *Debt defeasance.* The firm may transfer debt from its balance sheet to a trustee. In this instance, the firm is still obligated for the debt but it does not appear on the balance sheet. This is called *off-balance sheet debt.* (See the nearby Financial Reality reading.)
- *Sale-leaseback agreement.* The firm may sell assets and lease them back under an operating lease agreement. Management uses proceeds from the sale of assets to retire debt.[9]
- *Private placement.* Equity securities may be placed with private investors. The securities do not have to be registered with the U.S. Securities and Exchange Commission.
- *Sale of subsidiary.* All or part of a subsidiary may be taken public. Management then uses proceeds from the stock issue to pay down the debt.

Is a slow adjustment to the targeted capital structure better than a quick approach? If a company's capital structure deviates from its target debt-equity proportions to the extent that it is one or more categories away from its bond-rating objective, an exchange offer or some other type of transaction designed to effect an immediate change in capital structure is probably justified. If the company is less than one category away from its bond-rating objective, then changing the firm's dividend payout ratio may be more appropriate. Increasing the amount of profits paid as dividends results in less earnings for the firm to retain. The effect is that equity on the balance sheet will not increase as much with the result that the debt-to-equity ratio increases.

Capital Structure Changes in a Distressed Firm

When financial distress sets in, it typically does so over an extended period. Any financial deterioration eventually reveals itself in the company's published balance sheet and income statement. It is possible to build predictive models to detect the onset of financial distress. These models use a variety of financial ratios to detect the significant deterioration in profitability and liquidity and the significant increase in financial leverage that typically signal bankruptcy.

Arthur Andersen, the public accounting firm, uses the Z-score model when auditing firms. Many credit analysts use similar models when evaluating credit applicants. The Z-score model, or variants of it, has been applied in Australia, Brazil, Canada, England, France, Germany, Ireland, Japan, the Netherlands, and the United States to measure the likelihood of bankruptcy by firms. Although considerable variation exists among the scores of the different countries, in all cases finan-

[9]From an accounting perspective, operating leases show neither the asset value nor the associated liability on the balance sheet. If the asset is leased under a financial (capital) lease, then both the asset value and the associated liability appear on the balance sheet.

Financial Reality

Predicting Bankruptcy

The detection of company operating and financial difficulties is a subject susceptible to financial ratio analysis. The following discussion briefly reviews a quantitative model for predicting corporate bankruptcies.

Several years ago, Edward Altman developed a model for predicting corporate bankruptcy. His model was the forerunner of many studies for predicting corporate bankruptcy.

After careful consideration of the nature of the problem, Altman chose a multiple discriminant analysis (MDA) model as the appropriate statistical technique.

MDA is a technique used to classify an observation into one of sever *a priori* groupings dependent upon the observation's individual characteristics. MDA has the advantage of considering an entire profile of characteristics common to the relevant firms, as well as the interaction of these properties. The best combination of variables Altman tested for his MDA model follows at the end of this reading.

Altman found the model to have high predictive ability. One year before bankruptcy, it correctly predicted 95 percent of the firms that went bankrupt. Two years before bankruptcy, 72 percent of the firms were predicted correctly. The model predicted 36 percent of the firms correctly up to five years before ultimate bankruptcy.

Application of the model requires calculating the indicated ratios for a firm and substituting them into the equation. Each ratio is multiplied by its coefficient, shown in the model. Results are then summed to get the overall index, frequently referred to as the *Z-score.*

Firms with Z-scores greater than 2.99 fall into the nonbankrupt sector, while those with a Z below 1.81 are considered bankrupt. The area between 1.81 and 2.99 is a gray area and requires more analysis.

Subsequent authors were critical of this methodology. However, variations of it are used by many firms today.

Z-score = 0.012 × [working capital ÷ total assets] + 0.014 × [retained earnings ÷ total assets] + 0.033 × [EBIT ÷ total assets] + 0.006 × [market value equity ÷ book value of total debt] + 0.999 × [sales ÷ total assets]

The model is from Edward I. Altman, "Financial Ratios, Discriminant Analysis and the Prediction of Corporate Bankruptcy," *Journal of Finance* (September 1968), pp. 589–609.

Note:
The Altman Z-score model was derived in 1968. Since that time many variations of this model have been published, some by Altman. The coefficients of the model have changed since 1968.

cially distressed firms have much lower Z-scores than nondistressed firms. For each country, the overall average Z-score of firms that subsequently fail is below the critical Z-score value of 1.8.[10]

A company that finds itself in financial distress has four basic alternatives.

- It can seek to sell some of its assets in order to raise cash to pay its lenders.
- It can ask its lenders to renegotiate the terms of their loans or to exchange voluntarily some portion of their debt holdings for equity instruments of the distressed company.
- It may seek a merger with a company that is strong financially.

[10]Edward I. Altman, "The Success of Business Failure Prediction Models: An International Survey," Occasional Paper, No. 5, Salomon Brothers Center for the Study of Financial Institutions, Graduate School of Business Administration, New York University, 1983.

- If the company's situation is acute and the first three alternatives are unavailable or unworkable, the company may have to seek bankruptcy protection from its creditors under the provisions of the U.S. bankruptcy code.

The first three alternatives are reasonably straightforward. But bankruptcy is more complex.

What is Bankruptcy? *Bankruptcy* is a judicial process through which debtors can obtain relief from their indebtedness. It gives debtors a fresh start, but it also provides for equal treatment of various creditors. There are two basic forms of bankruptcy: *reorganization* and *liquidation*. *Reorganization,* as governed by Chapter 11 of the U.S. bankruptcy code, restrains the creditors while the debtor works out a plan to settle its debt obligations, usually for less than 100 cents on the dollar. The debtor's business continues to operate under the supervision of the bankruptcy trustee. Under a *liquidation,* as governed by Chapter 7 of the U.S. bankruptcy code, the bankruptcy court liquidates the debtor's business in an orderly manner and distributes the proceeds to creditors according to a strict order of priority. Shareholders receive any residual proceeds.

Reorganization or Liquidation? A company that seeks protection from its creditors under the bankruptcy laws must choose between reorganization and liquidation. If the company's creditors believe that the value of the payments they will realize if the bankruptcy court liquidates the company exceeds the present value of the payments they could expect to receive in the future if the company is reorganized, they will seek to have the company liquidated. If the bankruptcy court liquidates the company under Chapter 7 of the U.S. bankruptcy code, the legal rules observed in the distribution of proceeds normally leaves nothing for shareholders. Consequently, shareholders usually prefer a reorganization under Chapter 11 to a liquidation under Chapter 7. However, a reorganization can be mutually beneficial to stockholders and creditors if the company's difficulties are only temporary. For example, new management might be able to revitalize the business by correcting the excesses of prior management and by operating the business more efficiently.

Certain types of businesses are more difficult to reorganize than others. For example, a company in a high-technology industry that is dependent on a few critical employees for its competitive edge, or a company in heavy equipment manufacturing that is dependent on a network of independent dealers for distributing its products may cease to be viable if its key personnel and distributors leave. On the other hand, a retailing company competes more on price than on technical superiority and its sales do not require a specialized distribution network. Such a firm is more likely to emerge from reorganization successfully.

When Congress adopted the Bankruptcy Reform Act of 1978, it expressed concern that liquidations destroy corporate assets and are costly for stockholders, bondholders, employees, suppliers, and customers. Therefore, it changed Chapter 11 to make it significantly easier for managers to obtain protection from creditors and give them more control over reorganizations.

COMPREHENSION CHECK

1. *When management determines that the firm needs an adjustment in its capital structure, what are the relative merits of a quick adjustment compared with a slow adjustment?*

Financial Reality

REDUCE LEVERAGE AND INCREASE PROFITS

In 1983, the Financial Accounting Standards Board decided to permit companies to consider their fixed-rate known maturity debt to be extinguished for financial reporting purposes even though the debt is not extinguished. The transaction is called *insubstance defeasance of debt.*

Defeasance of debt can be an attractive way for companies with low coupon debt outstanding to boost earnings and improve their debt-equity ratio. Indeed, Standard & Poor's disregards any debt issue defeased, and its related interest and escrowed assets, when computing financial ratios for debt-rating purposes.

The company irrevocably segregates assets with a third party. The third party invests them in direct obligations of the U.S. government, U.S. government guaranteed obligations, or securities backed by U.S. government obligations as collateral under which the interest and principal payments on the collateral generally flow immediately to the holder of the security.

The investment and the interest on it are then used to satisfy scheduled debt payments of principal and interest on the outstanding debt. The outstanding debt has a lower coupon yield than the segregated assets, so less funds must be set aside to satisfy the outstanding lower coupon debt obligation than would be required if management just retired the debt. If management is virtually assured that no further funds will need to be transferred to the third party, the firm can account for the transaction as an extinguishment of debt. The firm can then take any difference between the face value of the outstanding debt and the funds set aside as a gain, to be reported in the income statement. For tax purposes, the company continues to deduct interest expense but also pays tax on the income from trust securities. The gain from defeasance is not taxed until the debt actually matures.

Defeased debt must be disclosed in the annual report's footnotes through a description of the transaction as long as the debt is outstanding.

With defeasance, the firm gives up present liquidity to enhance profitability and lower perceived financial risk as measured by the debt-equity ratio.

George W. Gallinger and P. Basil Healey, *Liquidity Analysis and Management* (Reading, MA: Addison-Wesley, 1991), pp. 135–138.

2. *What are the alternatives for a company that finds itself in financial distress?*
3. *What is bankruptcy? Explain the two basic forms of bankruptcy.*
4. *What factors can influence whether owners, seeking protection from a firm's creditors, will choose reorganization or liquidation?*

SUMMARY

- Financial managers believe that capital structure is important to the cost of capital and value of the firm.
- The most direct approach to understanding risk associated with debt financing is to evaluate the potential for cash inadequacy. This requires evaluation of sources and uses of cash.

Financial Reality

USES AND ABUSES OF CHAPTER 11

Charles Lamb, an eighteenth-century English essayist, reckoned that all bankrupts should be hanged. Fortunately for Mr. Frank Lorenzo, former chairman of Texas Air, American law is lenient. In 1983 Continental Airlines, which was owned by Texas Air, filed under Chapter 11 of the bankruptcy code. In March 1989 another part of Mr. Lorenzo's empire, Eastern Air Lines, followed suit. Today, Continental is one of America's most profitable airlines. But how can America have a system where going bankrupt does not mean going bust?

The reason is Chapter 11. Many other countries' laws aim to protect creditors rather than debtors: If a company runs into trouble and is unable to reach a deal with its creditors, it has to apply for liquidation. A liquidator is appointed and the company is wound up. American companies can do this as well under Chapter 7 of the bankruptcy code. But they can also file under Chapter 11. Japan and West Germany have similar laws.

Chapter 11 gives a company protection from its creditors until it proposes a reorganization plan. That plan has to be passed by all the creditor committees (secured, unsecured, trade, and so on). If the company's plan is accepted, it can trade again, even if some of its creditors have not been paid in full.

Filing for Chapter 11 is relatively easy. A company is only refused if there is evidence of fraud or if there are no jobs at stake (and thus no reason to give the debtor a second chance). The company can also file before if defaults on any debt. Both Continental and Eastern had enough cash to meet their immediate obligations. Two other big Chapter 11 cases, Manville, an asbestos maker, and A.H. Robins, a drugs firm, were profitable when they filed. Both took this action because they faced a host of consumer lawsuits—Manville for asbestos, A.H. Robins for allegedly harmful birth control devices.

Technically a company that has filed under Chapter 11 has a set period—usually 120 days—in which to propose a reorganization plan. But the bankruptcy judge can grant extensions. Manville filed in 1982; it emerged only in November 1988. In the interim, a company's hands look tied: It cannot sell an important asset without the court's permission.

On the other hand, Chapter 11 allows a company's managers to stay on. And a company can do anything to survive that the judge decides is in its interests. This can help a great deal, as Mr. Lorenzo demonstrated at Continental. Arguing that the airline could not survive without lower wage costs, he tore up its union contracts, sacked two-thirds of the work force and forced the remaining third to accept 50 percent wage cuts. By offering extremely cheap flights Continental won back customers and paid back its creditors. Mr. Lorenzo emerged with a low-cost, nonunion airline.

Partly because of what Lorenzo did at Continental, Congress has changed the rules to stop companies abrogating labor contracts while in Chapter 11.

America's biggest bankrupt, Texaco, which owned some $35 billion of assets when it filed in 1987, also used Chapter 11 to attack an old foe: Pennzoil, which had just won damages of $10.5 billion because Texaco had "stolen" Getty Oil from under its nose a year earlier. Texaco managed to reduce its damages to $3 billion.

Mr. Lorenzo or Texaco claim that their use of Chapter 11 is defensive, but it doesn't look that way. "What was designed as a shield has become a sword," argued Mr. Marc Hyman of

Financial Reality

Business Bankruptcy Report, a trade magazine. In 1987, 17,500 companies filed under Chapter 11; in 1988 the figure may have topped 20,000. Many of those companies, particularly the largest ones, filed in order to defy their creditors, not to help them.

Is there, then, a case for reforming Chapter 11? There is—and a powerful one. Critics point out, first, that its provisions help big companies more than small ones. In 1987, 69 percent of companies with annual sales of over $100 million survived; only 30 percent of those with sales under $25 million did. The cost of lawyers and accountants needed to supervise Chapter 11 can cripple small firms.

Second, Chapter 11 cases often attract investors whose actions, while legal, can be seen as inimical to the aims to the provision. Some arbitragers specialize in buying out weak-kneed creditors at low prices in order to dominate the creditor committees. And Chapter 11 firms are now being hyped as a cheap alternative to putting money in venture capital funds. In 1988 Wall Street raised around $500 million for Chapter 11 funds.

Profits from this sort of activity can be big. In 1986 Manville's bond issues were trading at around 40 percent of their face value. By mid-1988 they traded at 140 percent because the reorganization plan offered an equity bonus to bondholders on top of full repayment of principal.

Given this sort of thing, some lawyers think that "bust-or-nothing" bankruptcy is better. In some respects, no doubt it is. But not in all. To see the good and bad sides of America's system, consider the example of Manville. Had it gone into liquidation in the early 1980s, the company's 30,000 workers would have lost their jobs and the asbestosis sufferers would also have lost out.

Instead Manville has shed a third of its work force. The asbestosis sufferers, through two trust funds currently worth $935 million, now own 50 percent of the company. The company's profits will feed the fund and should meet the $3 billion of expected claims over the next 25 years. Secured creditors have been paid in full. Unsecured creditors who did not sell the debt have got all of their principal with much of the interest. The losers are the common equity holders: they may receive as little as 2 percent of their original holding. If a company goes bankrupt, there are, inevitably, losers. What is unusual about Chapter 11 is that it creates winners, too.

Source: "American Bankruptcy: The Uses and Abuses of Chapter 11," *The Economist*, March 18, 1989, p. 72.

- The fixed-charge coverage and the interest coverage ratios are often used to measure financial risk. Higher ratios mean less risk.
- If a firm cannot generate enough income to take advantage of tax-deductible expenses, managers should consider using less debt.
- A firm's managers often determine the debt-equity mix that leads to a desired bond rating.
- Foreign and finance subsidiaries allow the firm to increase its debt capacity.
- Business risk is a function of the firm's investment in production and technology and its markets. Business risk increases as production technology becomes more complex and markets become more competitive. Products that require costly repair, are difficult to determine their quality before buying, and have significant switching costs lead to higher business risk.

- Financial risk arises when a firm uses debt financing.
- Financial leverage represents the relationship between the after-tax cost of debt and the return the borrowed funds earn in the business.
- Favorable leverage results when a firm's assets earn more than its after-tax cost of debt. Unfavorable leverage results when the return on assets is less than the after-tax cost of debt.
- The financing indifference point indicates the level of earnings before interest and taxes where two different capital structures result in equal return-on-asset ratios and equal return-on-equity ratios.
- Financial leverage can also be measured by the degree of financial leverage ratio. The ratio shows the impact of interest expense on net income.
- The degree of operating leverage provides an index for business risk. It shows the impact of fixed operating costs on the firm's financial results.
- Total business risk can be measured by multiplying the degree of financial leverage by the degree of operating leverage.
- A firm's mix of debt and equity can be changed quickly or slowly to meet management's desired capital structure.
- Some strategies for changing capital structure include exchange offers, debt repurchase plans, sale-leaseback agreements, private placements, and sale of subsidiaries.
- Financially distressed firms encounter the threat of bankruptcy. The outcome of bankruptcy is either a liquidation of the firm or a reorganization of the debt structure so the firm can survive without a burdensome debt repayment problem.

SELF-CORRECTION PROBLEMS

1. PCG Manufacturing Company has just reported annual earnings before interest and taxes (EBIT) of $25 million. Included in the calculation of EBIT is $5 million of operating lease payments. Annual interest payments are $8 million and preferred dividend payments are $6.6 million. The firm's income tax rate is 34 percent.
   a. Calculate the interest coverage ratio.
   b. Calculate the fixed-charge coverage ratio.
2. a. Calculate the return on equity and return on assets for the two corporations whose partial financial statements follow.

	Javier Corp.	Crystal Corp.
Assets	$10,000,000	$10,000,000
Debt (10% interest)	$ 0	$ 3,000,000
Equity	10,000,000	7,000,000
Total	$10,000,000	$10,000,000
EBIT	$ 1,500,000	$ 1,500,000
Interest	0	300,000
Earnings before taxes	$ 1,500,000	$ 1,200,000
Taxes (40%)	600,000	480,000
Net income	$ 900,000	$ 720,000

b. How do you account for the differences, if any, in the return on equity and return on assets for these two corporations?

3. a. Calculate the degree of operating leverage for a firm that has fixed operating costs of \$1,200,000. Variable costs are \$5 per unit of production. Sales revenue is \$20 per unit. Total sales for the year amount to \$4 million. The firm's income tax rate is estimated to be 28 percent. Based on its debt, the firm pays annual interest of \$600,000.
   b. Based on the information in part (a), calculate the firm's degree of financial leverage at its current level of sales.
   c. Based on the information in part (a) or your calculations for parts (a) and (b), what is the firm's degree of total leverage at its current level of sales?

PROBLEMS

1. Given that interest payments are tax deductible for a corporation whereas dividend payments are not, should companies finance all of their assets with debt?
2. Jamison Company had earnings before interest and taxes (EBIT) of \$450,000 for the year just ended. No significant fixed charges were included in calculating EBIT. Based on current borrowing, Jamison's annual interest payments are \$180,000; no principal payment is due on the debt. The firm's directors have called for a preferred dividend payment of \$250,000. The firm's income tax rate is 25 percent.
   a. Calculate the interest coverage ratio.
   b. Calculate the fixed-charge coverage ratio.
3. Flagstaff Tool & Die, Inc. has widely fluctuating sales. The firm has just reported annual earnings before interest and taxes (EBIT) of \$6 million. Included in the calculation of EBIT is \$2 million of operating lease payments. Annual interest payments are \$1.5 million. The firm must make a debt principal payment of \$3 million. The firm's income tax rate is 28 percent.
   a. Calculate the interest coverage ratio.
   b. Calculate the fixed-charge coverage ratio.
   c. What conclusions might you draw about this firm from the ratios computed in parts (a) and (b)?
4. Surefire Electric Company's management reported earnings before interest and taxes (EBIT) of \$37 million for the year just ended. Management also reported that the public utility had interest payments of \$10 million and paid principal and preferred dividend payments amounting to \$6 million in total. The firm's income tax rate is 35 percent.
   a. Calculate the interest coverage ratio.
   b. Calculate the fixed-charge coverage ratio.
5. Royal Manufacturing Corporation reports earnings before interest and taxes (EBIT) of \$24 million. Included in the firm's EBIT balance is \$2 million deducted from operating lease payments, which management considers as fixed expenses. Royal's long-term debt provides for the annual payment of \$3 million in interest and \$4 million in principal. Royal's income tax rate is 35 percent.
   a. Calculate the interest coverage ratio.
   b. Calculate the fixed-charge coverage ratio.

6. Compare the two sets of ratios for Surefire Electric and Royal Manufacturing computed in Problems 19-4 and 19-5. If you were a bondholder of these two corporations, which investment would you consider more secure? Explain your answer.

Use the following data for Problems 7–11.

Renaldo Corporation's earnings before taxes (EBT) and tax liabilities for the years 1985 through 1994 follow. Renaldo's tax rate is 30 percent.

Year	EBT	Tax Liability
1985	$1,000,000	$300,000
1986	1,500,000	450,000
1987	800,000	240,000
1988	500,000	150,000
1989		
1990	700,000	210,000
1991	1,000,000	300,000
1992	1,200,000	360,000
1993	400,000	120,000
1994	200,000	60,000

7. Calculate Renaldo's tax liability after considering any tax carryback or carryforward for each year if in 1989 the company had earnings before taxes of $300,000. What would be the total change in taxes for the ten-year period as a result of using carrybacks or carryforwards?
8. Calculate Renaldo's tax liability after considering any tax carryback or carryforward for each year if in 1989 the company had an operating loss before taxes of $1.8 million.
9. Calculate Renaldo's tax liability after considering any tax carryback or carryforward for each year if in 1989 the company had $0 earnings before taxes.
10. Calculate Renaldo's tax liability after considering any tax carryback or carryforward for each year if in 1989 the company had an operating loss before taxes of $4.5 million.
11. Calculate Renaldo's tax liability after considering any tax carryback or carryforward for each year if in 1989 the company had an operating loss before taxes of $7.3 million.
12. Influtex, Inc., a biotech research and development corporation started ten years ago, has had operating losses since its origin. Today, the firm has a number of products in the development pipeline that management believes have prospects for commercial application at some unknown time in the future. The firm has no long-term debt. When the firm was started, management decided to finance operations with common stock sales to the founders and a small group of private investors. As an outside consultant, would you advise management to raise financing now through the sale of long-term bonds? Explain your answer so that management, whose expertise is in science and not finance, can easily understand it.
13. Based on Table 19-3, what bond rating would you assign the following corporation's bonds?

	Company A	B	C	D	E
Pretax interest coverage (×)	5.10	16.51	1.17	10.95	2.90
Funds from operations to total debt (%)	34.18	135.90	18.53	56.01	22.59
Total debt/capitalization (%)	41.47	17.35	59.87	29.79	52.15

14. What reasons would a financial officer give to a firm's board of directors for financing a foreign subsidiary's operations mostly with debt denominated in the currency of the country of the subsidiary?
15. Why might a manufacturing corporation establish its own finance subsidiary?
16. a. Based on Table 19-4, rank the following industries according to debt-to-total capital ratios. Show the debt percentages in your answer.

    Hardware and tools
    Aerospace/defense
    Telecommunications, long distance
    Broadcasting, media
    Steel producers
    Foods

    b. How do you account for the difference in these capital structures?
17. a. Calculate the return on equity and the return on assets for the companies whose accounting statements follow.

	Company A	Company B
Assets	$4,000,000	$4,000,000
Debt (9% interest)	$ 0	$1,000,000
Equity	4,000,000	3,000,000
Total	$4,000,000	$4,000,000
EBIT	$ 500,000	$ 500,000
Interest	0	90,000
Earnings before taxes	$ 500,000	$ 410,000
Taxes (35%)	175,000	143,500
Net income	$ 325,000	$ 266,500

    b. How do you account for the differences, if any, in the return on equity and return on assets for these two companies?
18. a. Calculate the return on equity and the return on assets for the companies whose accounting statements follow.

	Company C	Company D
Assets	$5,000,000	$5,000,000
Debt (10% interest)	$ 0	$2,000,000
Equity	5,000,000	3,000,000
Total	$5,000,000	$5,000,000
EBIT	$ 300,000	$ 300,000
Interest	0	200,000

Earnings before taxes	$ 300,000	$ 100,000
Taxes (30%)	90,000	30,000
Net income	$ 210,000	$ 70,000

b. How do you account for the differences, if any, in the return on equity and return on assets for these two companies?

19. a. Calculate the return on equity and the return on assets for the companies whose accounting statements follow.

	Company E	Company F
Assets	$2,000,000	$2,000,000
Debt (7.5% interest)	$ 0	$ 500,000
Equity	2,000,000	1,500,000
Total	$2,000,000	$2,000,000
EBIT	$ 150,000	$ 150,000
Interest	0	37,500
Earnings before taxes	$ 150,000	$ 112,500
Taxes (20%)	30,000	22,500
Net income	$ 120,000	$ 90,000

b. How do you account for the differences, if any, in the return on equity and return on assets for these two companies?

20. Following are the simplified balance sheet and income statement for Wal-Mart Stores, Inc. Calculate Wal-Mart's return on equity and return on assets. Is Wal-Mart realizing favorable or unfavorable financial leverage? Dollar amounts are in millions.

Balance Sheet

Current assets	$10,198	Current liabilities	$ 6,754
Net fixed assets	9,792	Long-term debt	5,052
Other assets	575	Equity	8,759
Total	$20,565	Total	$20,565

Income Statement

Total revenues	$55,985
Cost of sales	44,175
Gross income	$11,810
Selling, general and administrative expenses	8,321
Earnings before interest and taxes	$ 3,489
Interest	323
Earnings before taxes	$ 3,166
Taxes	1,171
Net income	$ 1,995

21. LaserMicro, Inc. has debt of $40,000 and equity of $60,000. Its debt has an average interest cost of 10 percent before taxes; equity earns a 12 percent return. Given a tax rate of 34 percent, how much is the firm's return on assets.

22. Learner Corporation has equity of $70,000 and debt of $30,000. The before tax cost of debt is 9 percent and the return on equity is 10 percent. The firm's income tax rate is 28 percent. Calculate the company's return on assets rate.
23. Wyatt Oil Company has assets of $50 million, which are financed 45 percent by debt and 55 percent by equity. The firm currently earns 8 percent on its assets and 12 percent on its equity. The tax rate is 40 percent.
    a. How much is Wyatt's net income?
    b. How much is interest expense? (*Hint:* Use the ROA equation.)
24. ATech, Inc. is considering the following alternative financing arrangements:

	Alternative A	Alternative B
Market values:		
Bonds (8%)	$200,000	
Common stock	400,000	$600,000
Assets	$600,000	$600,000

Management estimates that earnings before interest and taxes (EBIT) for this year will be $40,000. The company's income tax rate is 34 percent. Assume that the degree of economic risk associated with the sources of funds remains the same for both alternatives.
    a. Calculate return on assets and return on equity under both alternatives and decide which alternative management should select.
    b. If EBIT doubles next year, what happens to return on assets and return on equity?
    c. Calculate the EBIT indifference level for the two financing alternatives. Construct partial income statements and calculate return on assets, return on equity, and the after-tax cost of debt to prove that your EBIT indifference level is correct.
25. Rearden Metal, Inc. has assets of $100 million financed with $25 million of debt and $75 million of equity. The debt has an average cost of 9 percent before taxes. Hank Rearden, owner of the business, is considering replacing $30 million of equity financing with $30 million of debt financing. There would be no change in the capabilities of the assets to generate earnings. He expects the average cost of all debt financing to increase to 9.25 percent if the change is made. Earnings before interest and taxes (EBIT) are $20 million and should not change as a result of the new capital structure. The income tax rate is 34 percent.
    a. Calculate the current net income, return on assets, and return on equity.
    b. Calculate net income, return on assets, and return on equity if Rearden adopts the new capital structure.
    c. Compare your answers for parts (a) and (b). Why are return-on-asset numbers unchanged?
    d. Does Rearden Metal currently enjoy favorable financial leverage? Will the financial leverage be favorable if the new capital structure is adopted?
26. a. Use Eq. (19-5) to calculate the EBIT indifference level between the two capital structures in Problem 25.

b. Verify your answer to part (a) by calculating return on assets, return on equity, and the after-tax cost of debt for each capital structure when the firm operates at the EBIT indifference level.

27. How much is the incremental tax-shield benefit from using additional debt financing in Problem 19-25?

28. Rearden Metal in Problem 25 earns 19-2 percent return on assets. Its return on equity is 15.62 percent when the debt-equity ratio is 1/3 (that is, $25 million debt ÷ $75 million equity).

a. Use Eq. (19-6) to solve for return on equity under each of the following debt-equity ratio cases. The tax rate is 34 percent.

Debt-equity Ratio	% Interest Cost
0.333	9.00%
1.222	9.25
1.500	10.50
2.333	15.00
4.000	20.00
9.000	24.00

b. What is the best capital structure, given these six alternatives?

c. At what debt-equity ratio is financial leverage neutral?

d. At what debt-equity ratio is financial leverage unfavorable? What is the relationship between return on assets, return on equity, and the after-tax cost of debt at this point?

29. Supra, Inc. is an unlevered firm earning 14 percent return on assets. What will be the firm's return on equity if the income tax rate is 34 percent, the interest rate on debt financing is 8 percent, and the proportion of debt to equity is either 0.25, 0.667, 1.50, or 4.0?

30. Discuss the factors which might influence a firm's managers to increase or decrease the use of interest-bearing debt to finance operations. Build your discussion around the concepts of degree of operating leverage and the degree of financial leverage.

31. Over a rather wide range of production, Smythe Company has fixed operating costs of $100,000. Variable costs are $3 per unit of production and the company's product is sold for $7 each. Smythe pays annual interest of $60,000 and incurs an income tax rate of 30 percent.

a. What is the company's EBIT and net income if 50,000 units are sold annually?

b. Calculate the degree of operating leverage at the current sales level.

c. Calculate the degree of financial leverage at the current sales level.

d. Calculate the degree of total leverage at the current sales level.

32. Gitman Limited has fixed operating costs of $480,000, and variable costs are $10 per unit of production. Sales revenue is $19 per unit with total sales for the year amounting to $1,520,000. The firm's income tax rate is 25 percent. The firm pays annual interest of $100,000.

a. Calculate the firm's degree of operating leverage at the current sales level.

b. Calculate the firm's degree of financial leverage at the current sales level.

c. Calculate the firm's degree of total leverage at the current sales level.

d. Calculate net income for the current year.
e. If units sold decline 25 percent to 60,000, how much should earnings before interest and taxes decline?
f. Construct an income statement to prove your answer to part (e).
g. What advice do you have for management regarding its operating and financing policies?

33. The Harper Corporation sold 100,000 units last year at $11 each. Its income statement is shown below.

Sales	$1,100,000
Variable costs	550,000
Contribution margin	$ 550,000
Fixed operating costs	150,000
Earnings before interest and taxes	$ 400,000
Interest expense	50,000
Income before taxes	$ 350,000
Income taxes	119,000
Net income	$ 231,000

a. Calculate the degree of financial leverage at the current level of sales.
b. Calculate the degree of operation leverage at the current level of sales.
c. Determine the degree of total leverage at the current level of sales.

34. Harper Corporation's sales manager in Problem 33 forecasts sales growth of 12 percent next year over the current sales of $1.1 million. Variable costs are expected to remain at 50 percent of sales and no additional fixed costs or interest expense are expected to be incurred. The tax rate remains at 34 percent.
a. Calculate the expected income statement for next year.
b. Calculate the degree of financial leverage, the degree of operating leverage, and the degree of total leverage at next year's forecasted sales level.
c. Is total risk expected to be more or less than the levels found in Problem 19-33? If risk changes, what is the reason(s)?

35. Let's change the assumptions for the analysis in Problem 34. Sales are still forecasted to grow 12 percent and variable costs remain at 50 percent of sales. However, fixed operating costs and interest expense should increase $20,000 and $5,000, respectively. The tax rate remains at 34 percent.
a. Calculate the new income statement.
b. Calculate the degree of financial leverage, the degree of operating leverage, and the degree of total leverage for the new income statement.
c. Why are each of the firm's risk components in this problem's analysis expected to increase over the forecast in Problem 19-34?
d. Using the current year's activity in Problem 19-33 as the base period, calculate the degree of operating leverage, the degree of financial leverage, and the degree of total leverage.

INTEGRATIVE PROBLEM

Smart Manufacturing Corporation's accounting statements for the year just ended follow.

Balance Sheet

Assets	$100,000,000	Debt (10% interest)	$ 40,000,000
		Equity	60,000,000
		Total	$100,000,000

Income Statement

Sales revenue	$150,000,000
Variable operating costs	90,000,000
Fixed operating costs	35,000,000
EBIT	$ 25,000,000
Interest	4,000,000
Earnings before taxes	$ 21,000,000
Taxes (30%)	6,300,000
Net income	$ 14,700,000

a. Calculate the interest coverage ratio and the fixed-charge coverage ratio for Smart Manufacturing. Annual principal payments on debt are $4.2 million.
b. How much is the tax-shield benefit to Smart from its use of long-term debt?
c. Calculate the return on equity and the return on assets for the company.
d. How much is the default risk premium? Compare the return on equity against the return on assets.
e. Calculate the degree of operating leverage, the degree of financial leverage, and the degree of total leverage based on the current sales level.
f. Comment on Smart Manufacturing's capital structure. The company produces industrial goods where demand is highly sensitive to economic conditions. The year just ended was a good one for the company and the industry.

SOLUTIONS TO SELF-CORRECTION PROBLEMS

1. a. Interest coverage ratio $= \dfrac{\text{Earnings before interest and taxes}}{\text{Interest}}$

$$= \$25{,}000{,}000 \div \$8{,}000{,}000$$
$$= 3.125 \text{ times}$$

b. Fixed-charge coverage ratio

$$= \frac{\text{Earnings before interest, taxes and fixed charges}}{\text{Interest} + \text{fixed charges} + \dfrac{\text{preferred dividends}}{(1 - \text{tax rate})}}$$

$$= \frac{\$25{,}000{,}000 + \$5{,}000{,}000}{\$8{,}000{,}000 + \$5{,}000{,}000 + \dfrac{\$6{,}600{,}000}{(1 - 0.34)}}$$

$= 1.30$

2. a. Return on equity = Net income ÷ equity
   Javier: \$900,000 ÷ \$10,000,000 = 0.09 or 9 percent
   Crystal: \$720,000 ÷ \$7,000,000 = 0.1029 or 10.29 percent
   Return on assets = EBIT × (1 – tax rate) ÷ assets
   Javier: \$1,500,000 × (1 – 0.40) ÷ \$10,000,000
   = 0.09 or 9 percent
   Crystal: \$1,500,000 × (1 – 0.40) ÷ \$10,000,000
   = 0.09 or 9 percent

   b. The return on assets is the same for both companies because EBIT, the tax rate, and assets are identical. However, return on equity is greater for Crystal Corp. in view of the favorable employment of debt. The after tax cost of debt is 0.10 × (1 – 0.40) = 0.06 or 6 percent, which is less than the return on assets of 9 percent. Thus, leverage works in favor of Crystal's stockholders.

3. a. Degree of operating leverage (DOL)

$$= \frac{\text{Sales} - \text{variable costs}}{\text{Sales} - \text{variable costs} - \text{fixed costs}}$$

$$= \frac{\$4{,}000{,}000 - (\$5 \times 200{,}000)}{\$4{,}000{,}000 - \$1{,}000{,}000 - \$1{,}200{,}000}$$

$= 1.667$

   b. Degree of financial leverage (DFL) $= \dfrac{\text{EBIT}}{\text{EBIT} - \text{interest}}$

$$= \frac{\$1{,}800{,}000}{\$1{,}800{,}000 - \$600{,}000}$$

$= 1.50$

   c. Degree of total leverage = DOL × DFL
   = 1.667 × 1.50
   = 2.50

SELECTED REFERENCES

Friedman, Benjamin M., *The Changing Roles of Debt and Equity in Financing United States Capital Formation.* Chicago: University of Chicago Press, 1982. This book provides broad coverage of the capital structure issue.

Friedman, Benjamin M., *Corporate Capital Structures in the United States.* Chicago: University of Chicago Press, 1985. This is another book providing broad coverage of capital structure issues.

CHAPTER 20

Dividend Policy

Dividend policy is an integral part of the firm's financing decision. The **dividend payout ratio** determines the amount of earnings that can be retained in the firm as a source of financing. However, retaining a greater amount of current earnings in the firm means that fewer dollars will be available for current dividend payments. A major aspect, then, of the dividend policy of the firm is to determine the appropriate allocation of profits between dividend payments and additions to the firm's retained earnings. But also important are other issues pertaining to a firm's overall dividend policy: legal, liquidity, and control issues; stability of dividends; stock dividends and splits; stock repurchase; and administrative considerations.

Dividend-payout ratio Annual cash dividends divided by annual earnings; or alternatively, dividends per share divided by earnings per share. The ratio indicates the percentage of a company's earnings that is paid out to shareholders in cash.

PASSIVE VERSUS ACTIVE DIVIDEND POLICIES

Dividends as a Passive Residual

We focus first on a two-part question. Can the payment of cash dividends affect shareholder wealth and if so, what dividend-payout ratio will maximize shareholder wealth? As we did when studying the effects of financial leverage, we again assume that business risk is held constant. To evaluate the question of whether the dividend-payout ratio affects shareholder wealth, it is necessary to first examine the firm's dividend policy as solely a financing decision involving the retention of earnings. Each period, the firm must decide whether to retain its earnings or to distribute part or all of them to shareholders as cash dividends. (We rule out share repurchase for now.) As long as the firm is faced with investment projects having returns exceeding those that are required, the firm will use earnings, plus the amount of senior securities the increase in the equity base will support, to finance these projects. If the firm has earnings left after financing all acceptable investment opportunities, these earnings would then be distributed to shareholders in the form of cash dividends. If not, there would be no dividends. If the number of acceptable investment opportunities involves a total dollar amount that exceeds the amount of retained earnings plus the senior securities these retained earnings will support, the firm would finance the excess needs with a combination of a new equity issue and senior securities.

When we treat dividend policy as strictly a financing decision, the payment of cash dividends is a passive residual. The percentage of earnings paid out as dividends will fluctuate from period to period in keeping with fluctuations in the amount of acceptable investment opportunities available to the firm. If these opportunities abound, the percentage of earnings paid out is likely to be zero. On the other hand, if the firm is unable to find profitable investment opportunities, dividends paid out will be 100 percent of earnings. For situations between these two extremes, the dividend-payout ratio will be a fraction between zero and one.

The treatment of dividend policy as a passive residual, determined solely by the availability of acceptable investment proposals, implies that dividends are irrelevant. Are dividends really just a means of distributing unused funds? Instead, should dividend payments be an active decision variable with earnings retentions as a residual? To answer these questions, we must examine the argument that dividends are irrelevant, so that changes in the dividend-payout ratio (holding investment opportunities constant) do not affect shareholder wealth.

Irrelevance of Dividends

Modigliani and Miller (M & M) provide the most comprehensive argument for the irrelevance of dividends.[1] They assert that, given the investment decision of the firm, the dividend-payout ratio is a mere detail. It does not affect the wealth of shareholders. M & M argue that the value of the firm is determined solely by the earning power of the firm's assets, or its investment policy, and that the manner in which the earnings stream is split between dividends and retained earnings does not affect this value. As in the previous chapter, when we considered the capital structure decision, M & M assume perfect capital markets where there are no transactions costs, no flotation costs to companies issuing securities, and no taxes. Moreover, the future profits of the firm are assumed to be known with certainty. (Later this last assumption is removed.)

Current Dividends Versus Retention of Earnings. The crux of M & M's position is that the effect of dividend payments on shareholder wealth is exactly offset by other means of financing. Let us first consider selling additional common stock to raise equity capital instead of simply retaining earnings. After the firm has made its investment decision, it must decide whether (1) to retain earnings or (2) to pay dividends and sell new stock in the amount of these dividends in order to finance the investments. M & M suggest that the sum of the discounted value per share of com-

[1]Merton H. Miller and Franco Modigliani, "Dividend Policy, Growth, and the Valuation of Shares," *Journal of Business* 34 (October 1961), 411–33.

mon stock after financing plus current dividends paid is exactly equal to the market value per share of common stock before the payment of current dividends. In other words, the common stock's decline in market price because of the **dilution** caused by external equity financing is exactly offset by the payment of the dividend. Thus, the shareholder is said to be indifferent between receiving dividends and having earnings retained by the firm

Dilution A decrease in the proportional claim on earnings and assets of a share of common stock because of the issuance of additional shares.

At this point, one might rightfully ask, How does all of this relate to our earlier chapters, when we said that dividends are the foundation for the valuation of common stock? Is there some contradiction? Although it is still true that the market value of a share of common stock is the present value of all expected future dividends, the timing and magnitude of the dividends can vary. The dividend-irrelevance position simply argues that the present value of future dividends remains unchanged even though dividend policy may change the timing and magnitude of dividends It does not argue that dividends, including a liquidating dividend, are never paid. On the contrary, it argues only that dividend postponement (but where the future dividend magnitude is allowed to grow) is a matter of indifference when it comes to the market price of common stock.

Conservation of Value. Given M & M's assumptions of certainty and perfect capital markets, the irrelevance of dividends naturally follows. The *total-value principle* ensures that the sum of the market value plus current dividends of two firms identical in all respects other than dividend-payout ratios will be the same.

Investors are able to replicate any dividend stream the corporation might be able to pay but currently is not. If dividends are lower than desired, investors can sell some shares of stock to obtain their desired cash distribution. If dividends are higher than desired, investors can use dividends to purchase additional shares of stock in the company. Thus, investors are able to manufacture "homemade" dividends in the same way that they could devise "homemade" financial leverage if they were unhappy with a firm's current capital structure. For a corporate decision to have value, the company must be able to do something for shareholders that they cannot do for themselves. Because investors can manufacture homemade dividends, which are perfect substitutes for corporate dividends under the preceding assumptions, dividend policy is irrelevant. As a result, one dividend policy is as good as the next. The firm is unable to create value simply by altering the mix of dividends and retained earnings. As in capital structure theory, there is a conservation of values so that the sum of the parts is always the same. The total size of the pie is not changed by the slicing.

Arguments for Dividend Relevance

A number of arguments have been advanced in support of the contrary position, namely, that dividends are relevant under conditions of uncertainty. In other words, investors are not indifferent as to whether they receive returns in the form of dividend income or share price appreciation. We shall examine these arguments under conditions of uncertainty.

Preference for Dividends. Certain investors may have a preference for dividends over capital gains. The payment of dividends may resolve uncertainty in their minds concerning company profitability. Dividends are received on a current, ongoing basis, while the prospect of realizing capital gains is in the future. Therefore, investors in a dividend-paying company resolve their uncertainty earlier than those investing in a non-dividend-paying company. To the extent that investors prefer the early resolution of uncertainty, they may be willing to pay a higher price for the stock that offers the greater dividend, all other things held constant. If, in fact, investors can manufacture homemade dividends, such a preference is irrational. Nonetheless, sufficient statements from investors make it difficult to dismiss this argument. Perhaps, for either psychological reasons or reasons of inconvenience, investors prefer not to manufacture homemade dividends but to get the "real thing" directly from the company.

Taxes on the Investor. When we allow for taxes, there are a variety of effects. To the extent that the personal tax rate on capital gains is less than that on dividend income, there may be an advantage to the retention of earnings. In addition, the capital gains tax is deferred until the actual sale of stock (when any gain is then *realized*). Effectively, the shareholder is given a valuable timing option when the firm retains earnings as opposed to pays dividends. Also, the capital gains tax may be avoided altogether if appreciated securities are given as gifts to charitable causes or if the security owner dies. For these reasons, the effective tax on capital gains (in present value terms) is less than that on dividend income, even when the federal tax rate on the two types of income is the same. This would suggest that a dividend-paying stock will need to provide a higher expected before-tax return than a non-dividend-paying stock of the same risk. According to this notion, the greater the **dividend yield** on a stock, the higher the required-before-tax return, all other things being the same.

Dividend yield
Anticipated annual dividend divided by the market price of the stock.

However, all investors do not experience the same taxation on the two types of income just discussed. Certain institutional investors, such as retirement and pension funds, pay no tax on either dividend income or realized capital gains. Such investors would be indifferent from a tax standpoint between a dollar of dividend income and a dollar of capital gains. For corporate investors intercompany dividends are taxed at an effective rate below that applicable to capital gains. For example, if Alpha Corporation owns 100 shares of Omega Corporation, which pays a $1 per share annual dividend, 70 percent of the dividend income to Alpha Corporation is tax exempt. In other words, Alpha Corporation would pay taxes on $30 of dividend income at the corporate tax rate. The overall tax effect will be less than if Omega Corporation had share appreciation of $100 and all of this were taxed at the capital gains rate. Accordingly, there may be a preference for current dividends on the part of corporate investors. Also, there are a growing number of institutional investors.

If there are clienteles of investors having different dividend preferences, corporations could adjust their dividend-payout ratio to take advantage of the situation. Suppose that two-fifths of all investors prefer a zero-dividend-payout ratio, one-fifth prefer a 25 percent payout ratio, and the remaining two-fifths prefer a 50 percent payout ratio. If most companies pay out 25 percent of their earnings in dividends, there will be excess demand for the shares of companies paying zero dividends and for the shares of companies whose dividend-payout ratio is 50 percent. Presumably, a number of companies will recognize this excess demand and adjust their payout ratios in order to increase share price. The action of these companies will eliminate the excess demand. In equilibrium, the dividend-payout ratios of corporations will match the desires of investor groups. At this point, no company would be able to affect its share price by altering its dividend. As a result, even with taxes, the dividend-payout ratio would be irrelevant.

In actuality, we are left with an unsettled situation in which the effect of taxes on dividends is not clear. Before considering some of the empirical evidence on the effect that dividends have on share price, we must look at other factors that may influence the payment of dividends.

Flotation Costs. The irrelevance of the dividend payout is based on the idea that when favorable investment opportunities exist and yet dividends are paid, the funds paid out of the firm must be replaced by funds acquired through external financing. The introduction of flotation costs favors the retention of earnings in the firm. For each dollar paid out in dividends, the firm nets less than a dollar after flotation costs per dollar of external financing.

Transactions Costs and Divisibility of Securities. Transactions costs involved in the sale of securities tend to restrict the arbitrage process in the same manner as that described for debt. Shareholders who desire current income must pay brokerage fees on the sale of portions of their stock ownership if the dividend paid is not sufficient to satisfy their current desire for income. This fee, per dollar of shares sold, varies inversely with the size of the sale. For a small sale, the brokerage fee can be a rather significant percentage of the total sale. As a result of this fee, shareholders with consumption desires in excess of current dividends will prefer that the company pay additional dividends. Perfect capital markets also assume that securities are infinitely divisible. The fact that the smallest equity-security unit is one share may result in "lumpiness" with respect to selling shares for current income. This, too, acts as a deterrent to the sale of stock in lieu of dividends. On the other hand, shareholders not desiring dividends for current consumption purposes will need to reinvest their dividends. Here, again, transactions costs and divisibility problems work to the disadvantage of the shareholder, although this time as a deterrent to the purchase of stock. Thus, transactions costs and divisibility problems cut both ways, and one is not able to draw directional implications regarding paying dividends versus retaining earnings.

Institutional Restrictions. Certain institutional investors are restricted in the types of common stock they can buy or in the portfolio percentages they can hold in various types of common stock. The prescribed list of eligible securities for these investors is determined in part by the length of time over which dividends have been paid. If a company does not pay dividends or has not paid them over a sufficiently long period, certain institutional investors are not permitted to invest in the stock of that company.

Universities, on the other hand, sometimes have restrictions on the expenditure of capital gains from their endowments. Also, a number of trusts have a prohibition against the liquidation of principal. In the case of common stocks, the trust beneficiary is entitled to dividend income but not to the proceeds from the sale of common stock. As a result of this stipulation, the trustee who manages the investments may feel constrained to pay particular attention to dividend yield and seek stocks paying reasonable dividends. Though the two influences described are small in aggregate, they work in the direction of a preference for dividends as opposed to earnings retention and capital gains.

Financial Signaling. Financial signaling is different from the other arguments presented in this section in that it depends on imperfections in the market for financial information. It suggests that dividends have an impact on share price because they communicate information, or signals, about the firm's profitability. Presumably, firms with good news about their future profitability will want to tell investors. Rather than make a simple announcement, dividends may be increased to add conviction to the statement. When a firm has a target dividend-payout ratio that has been stable over time and the firm increases this ratio, investors may believe that management is announcing a positive change in the expected future profitability of the firm. The signal to investors is that management and the board of directors truly believe that things are better than the stock price reflects.

Accordingly, the price of the stock may react favorably to this increase in dividends. The idea here is that the reported accounting earnings of a company may not be a proper reflection of the company's economic earnings. To the extent that dividends provide information on economic earnings not provided by reported earnings, share price will respond. Put another way, cash dividends speak louder than words. Thus, dividends are said to be used by investors as predictors of the firm's future performance. Dividends convey management's expectations of the future.

Empirical Testing of Dividend Policy

While there are a number of factors that may explain dividends' impact on valuation, many are difficult to test. Most empirical testing has concentrated on the tax effect and on financial signaling.[2] This is not to say that such things as preference for dividends, flotation costs, transactions costs, and institutional restrictions have no effect. Rather, whatever result these factors may have is sampled by tax and financial signaling effects.

With a tax effect, where dividends are taxed more heavily (in present value terms) than are capital gains, stock prices and before-tax returns should reflect this differential taxation. Empirical results have been mixed as to whether high-dividend stocks provide higher expected before-tax returns than low-dividend stocks to offset the tax effect. Certain evidence suggests such a "negative" (anti-dividend-paying) effect, but other studies are consistent with neutrality.

Therefore, the question of the effect of taxes and payment of dividends is in an unsettled state empirically. It may be that such a tax effect, if any, is too sensitive to be picked up by economic models. After the passage of the 1986 Tax Reform Act, dividend-payout ratios of American corporations increased somewhat. This increase is consistent with a tax effect lessening as the differential between taxation of dividends and capital gains narrows. Under the 1993 Revenue Reconciliation Act, this differential widened as personal income tax rates increased and the maximum capital gains tax rate stayed at 28 percent. While this most recent tax change should logically lead to lower dividend-payout ratios, it is too early to tell.

[2]For a detailed review of the empirical evidence, see James C. Van Horne, *Financial Management and Policy*, 10th ed. (Englewood Cliffs, NJ: Prentice-Hall, 1995), Chap. 11.

In contrast to the results for a tax effect, the evidence on financial signaling is consistent in support of a dividend announcement effect: increases in dividends lead to positive excess stock returns, while decreases in dividends lead to negative excess returns. Therefore, dividends would appear to convey information.

A Summing Up

A company should endeavor to establish a dividend policy that will maximize shareholder wealth. Most everyone agrees that if a company does not have sufficiently profitable investment opportunities, it should distribute any excess funds to its shareholders. The firm need not pay out the exact unused portion of earnings each period. Indeed, it may wish to stabilize the absolute amount of dividends paid from period to period. But over the longer run the total earnings retained, plus the additional senior securities the increasing equity base will support, will correspond to the amount of new profitable investment opportunities. Dividend policy would still be a passive residual determined by the amount of investment opportunities.

For the firm to be justified in paying a dividend larger than that dictated by the amount of earnings left over after making all acceptable investment opportunities, there must be a net preference for dividends in the market. It is very difficult to "net out" the arguments just discussed to arrive at the bottom line. Only institutional restrictions and some investors' preferences for dividends argue for dividends. The other arguments suggest either a neutral effect or a bias favoring earnings retention. There does appear to be some positive value associated with a modest dividend as opposed to none at all. This occurrence may be due to institutional restrictions and a signaling effect. Beyond that, the picture is very cloudy, and some argue that even a modest dividend has no effect on valuation. Few academic scholars argue that dividends significantly in excess of what a passive policy would dictate will lead to share price improvement. With personal taxes and flotation costs, shareholders are "money behind" when a company issues stock to pay dividends. Before making a final observation, let us look at some practical things to consider in approaching a dividend policy decision.

FACTORS INFLUENCING DIVIDEND POLICY

So far we have discussed only the theoretical aspects of dividend policy. Yet when a company establishes a dividend policy, it looks at a number of other matters. These additional considerations should be related to the theoretical concepts surrounding dividend payout and the valuation of the firm. In what follows, we take up various practical factors that firms actually do (and should) analyze when approaching a dividend policy decision.

Legal Rules

The legal rules that we discuss below are important in establishing the legal boundaries within which a firm's finalized dividend policy can operate. These legal rules have to do with capital impairment, insolvency, and undue retention of earnings.

Capital Impairment Rule. Although state laws vary considerably, most states prohibit the payment of dividends if these dividends impair capital. *Capital* is defined in some states as the total par value of the common stock. If a firm has 1 million common shares outstanding with a $2 par value per share, total capital would be $2 million. If the shareholders' equity of this company were $2.1 million, the company could not pay a cash dividend totaling more than $100,000 without impairing capital.

Other states define *capital* to include not only the total par value of the common stock but also the additional paid-in capital. Under such state statutes, dividends can be paid only "to the extent of retained earnings." Notice, we did not say that dividends can be paid only "out of retained earnings." A company pays dividends "out of cash," while incurring a corresponding reduction in the retained earnings account.

The purpose of the capital impairment laws is to protect creditors of a corporation, and these laws may have some effect when a corporation is relatively new. With established companies that have been profitable in the past and have built up retained earnings, substantial losses will usually have to be incurred before the restriction has an effect on curbing dividend payments. By this time, the situation may be sufficiently hopeless that the restriction gives creditors little protection.

Insolvency Rule. Some states prohibit the payment of cash dividends if the company is insolvent. *Insolvency* is defined either, in a legal sense, as the recorded value of liabilities exceeding the recorded value of assets or, in a technical sense, as the firm's inability to pay its creditors as obligations come due. As the firm's ability to pay its obligations is dependent on its liquidity rather than on its capital, the technical insolvency restriction gives creditors a good deal of protection. When cash is limited, a company is restricted from favoring shareholders to the detriment of creditors.

Undue Retention of Earnings Rule. The Internal Revenue Code prohibits the undue retention of earnings. Although *undue retention* is vaguely defined, it is usually thought to mean retention significantly in excess of the present and future investment needs of the company. The purpose of the law is to prevent companies from retaining earnings for the sake of avoiding taxes. For example, a company might retain all if its earnings and build up a substantial cash and marketable securities position. The entire company could then be sold, and shareholders would be subject to only a capital gains tax, which is postponed relative to what would occur if dividends were paid. If the Internal Revenue Service can prove unjustified retention, it can impose penalty tax rates on the earnings accumulation. Whenever a company does build up a substantial liquid position, it has to be sure that it can justify the retention of these funds to the IRS. Otherwise, it may be more prudent to pay the excess funds as dividends to shareholders.

Funding Needs of the Firm

Once the legal boundaries for the firm's dividend policy have been established, the next step involves an assessment of the funding needs of the firm. In this regard, cash budgets, projected sources and uses of funds statements, and projected cash flow statements are of particular use. The key is to determine the likely cash flows and cash position of the company in the absence of a change in dividend policy. In addition to looking at expected outcomes, we should factor in business risk, so that we may obtain a range of possible cash-flow outcomes.

In keeping with our earlier discussion of the theoretical aspects of dividend policy, the firm would wish to determine if anything is left over after servicing its funding needs, including funding acceptable investment projects. In this regard, the firm should look at its situation over a reasonable number of future years to iron out fluctuations. The likely ability of the firm to sustain a dividend should be analyzed relative to the probability distributions of possible future cash flows and cash balances. On the basis of this analysis, a company can determine its likely future residual funds.

Liquidity

The liquidity of a company is a prime consideration in many dividend decisions. Because dividends represent a cash outflow, the greater the cash position and overall liquidity of a company, the greater its ability to pay a dividend. A company that is growing and profitable may not be liquid since its funds may go into fixed assets and permanent working capital. Because the management of such a company usually desires to maintain some liquidity cushion to give it financial flexibility and protection against uncertainty, it may be reluctant to jeopardize this position in order to pay a large dividend.

Ability to Borrow

A liquid position is not the only way to provide for financial flexibility and thereby protect against uncertainty. If a firm has the ability to borrow on comparatively short notice, it may be relatively financially flexible. This ability to borrow can be in the form of a line of credit or a revolving credit agreement from a bank, or simply the informal willingness of a financial institution to extend credit. In addition, financial flexibility can come from the ability of a firm to go to the capital market with a bond issue. The larger and more established a company, the better its access to the capital market. The greater the ability of the firm to borrow, the greater its financial flexibility, and the greater its ability to pay a cash dividend. With ready access to debt funds, management should be less concerned with the effect that a cash dividend has on its liquidity.

Restrictions in Debt Contracts

The protective convenants in a bond indenture or loan agreement often include a restriction on the payment of dividends. The restriction is employed by the lenders to preserve the company's ability to service debt. Usually it is expressed as a maximum percentage of cumulative earnings retained (reinvested) in the firm. When such a restriction is in force, it naturally influences the firm's dividend policy. Sometimes the management of a company welcomes a dividend restriction imposed by lenders, because then it does not have to justify the retention of earnings to its shareholders. It only needs to point to the restriction.

Control

If a company pays substantial dividends, it may need to raise capital at a later time through the sale of stock in order to finance profitable investment opportunities. Under such circumstances, the controlling interest of the company may be diluted if controlling shareholders do not or cannot subscribe for additional shares. These shareholders may prefer a low dividend payout and the financing of investment needs by retaining earnings. Such a dividend policy may not maximize overall shareholder wealth, but it still may be in the best interests of those in control.

Control can operate in another, very different, way. When a company is being sought for acquisition by another company or by individuals, a low dividend payout may work to the advantage of the "outsiders" seeking control. The outsiders may be able to convince shareholders that the company is not maximizing shareholder wealth and that they (the outsiders) can do a better job. Consequently, companies in danger of being acquired may establish a high dividend payout in order to please shareholders.

Some Final Observations

In determining a dividend payout, the typical company will analyze a number of the factors just described. These factors largely dictate the legal and other boundaries within which a dividend can be paid. When a company pays a dividend in excess of its residual funds, it implies that management and the board of directors believe that the payment has a favorable effect on shareholder wealth. The frustrating thing is that we have so little in the way of clear generalizations from the empirical evidence. The lack of a firm footing for predicting the long-run effect of a specific dividend policy on valuation makes the dividend choice a most difficult policy decision.

Considerations taken up in this section allow a company to determine with reasonable accuracy what would be an appropriate passive dividend strategy. An active dividend policy involves an act of faith, because it demands that a portion of the cumulative dividends paid out ultimately be replaced with common stock financing. Such a strategy is undertaken in a foggy area, but one in which most academics have difficulty believing that shareholder wealth will be enhanced. Notwithstanding, many companies profess a belief that dividend payout affects share price and behave in a manner consistent with dividend importance.

DIVIDEND STABILITY

Stability of dividend payments is an attractive feature to many investors. By *stability* we mean maintaining the position of the firm's dividend payments in relation to a trend line, preferably one that is upward sloping. All other things being the same, a share of stock may command a higher price if it pays a stable dividend over time than if it pays out a fixed percentage of earnings. Suppose that Company A has a long-run dividend-payout ratio of 50 percent of earnings. It pays out this percentage every year, despite the fact that its earnings are cyclical. The earnings and dividends, per share of Company A are shown in Fig. 20-1. Company B, on the other hand, has exactly the same earnings and a long-run dividend-payout ratio of 50 percent, but it maintains a relatively stable dividend over time. It changes the absolute amount of dividend payment only in keeping with the underlying trend of earnings. The earnings and dividends per share of Company B are shown in Fig. 20-2.

Over the long run, the total amount of dividends paid by these two firms is the same. However, the market price per share of Company B may be higher than that of Company A, all other things being the same. Investors may well place a positive utility on dividend stability and pay a premium for the company that offers it. To the extent that investors value dividend stability, the overall dividend policy of Company B would be better than that of Company A. This policy encompasses not only the percentage of dividend payout in relation to earnings but also the manner in which the actual dividends are paid. Rather than vary dividends directly with changes in earnings per share, Company B raises the dividend only when reasonably confident a higher dividend can be maintained.

Valuation of Dividend Stability

Investors may be willing to pay a premium for stable dividends because of the informational content of dividends, the desire of investors for current income, and certain institutional considerations.

Informational Content. When earnings drop and a company does not cut its dividend, the market may have more confidence in the stock than it would have if the dividend were cut. The stable dividend may convey management's view that the future of the company is better than the drop in earnings suggests. Thus, management may be able to affect the expectations of investors through the informational content of dividends. Management will not be able to fool the market permanently. If there is a downward trend in earnings, a stable dividend will not convey forever an impression of a promising future. Moreover, if a firm is in an unstable business with wide swings in earnings, a stable dividend cannot give the illusion of underlying stability.

Current Income Desires. A second factor may favor stable dividends. Investors who desire a specific periodic income will prefer a company with stable dividends to one with unstable dividends, even though both companies may have the same pattern of earnings and long-run dividend payout. Although investors can always sell a portion of their common stock for income when the dividend is not sufficient to meet their current needs, many investors have an aversion to dipping into principal. Moreover, when a company reduces its dividend, earnings are usually down and the market price of the common stock depressed. Overall, income-conscious investors place a positive utility on stable dividends, even though they can always sell a few shares of stock for income.

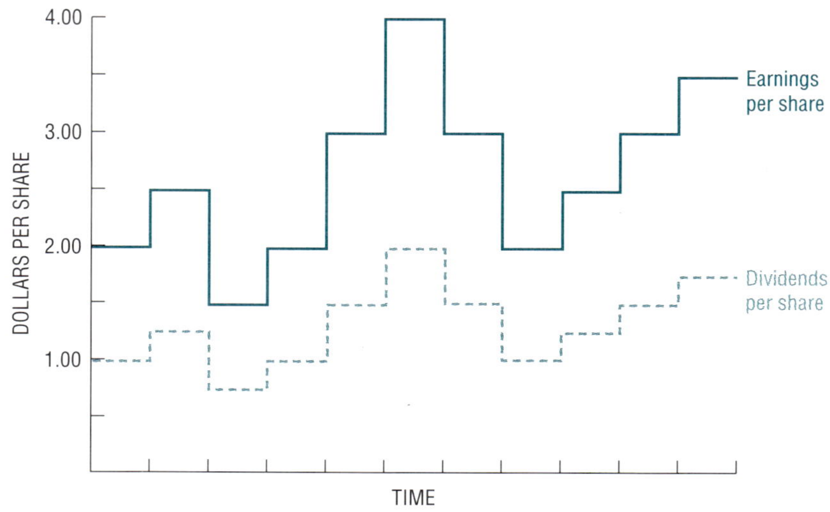

FIGURE 20-1
Dividend policy of Company A showing strict adherence to a constant 50 percent dividend-payout ratio

Institutional Considerations. A stable dividend may be advantageous from the legal standpoint of permitting certain institutional investors to buy the common stock. Various governmental bodies prepare *approved (or legal) lists* of securities in which pension funds, savings banks, trustees, insurance companies, and certain other institutions may invest. To qualify, a company often must have an uninterrupted pattern of dividends. A cut in dividends may result in the removal of a company from these approved lists.

The argument presented in support of the notion that stable dividends have a positive effect on the market price of the stock are only suggestive. Little empirical evidence sheds light on the question. Although studies of individual stocks often suggest that stable dividends buffer the market price of the stock when earnings are down, there have been no comprehensive studies of a large sample of stocks dealing with the relationship between dividend stability and valuation. Nevertheless, most companies strive for stability in their dividend payments. This is consistent with a belief that stable dividends have a positive effect on value.

Target Payout Ratios

A number of companies appear to follow the policy of a target dividend-payout ratio over the long run. John Lintner contends that dividends are adjusted to changes in earnings, but only with a lag.[3] When earnings increase to a new level, a company increases dividends only when it feels it can maintain the increase in earnings. Companies are also reluctant to cut the absolute amount of their cash dividend. Both of these factors help explain why dividend changes often lag behind

[3]See John Lintner, "Distribution of Income of Corporations," *American Economic Review* 46 (May 1956), 97–113.

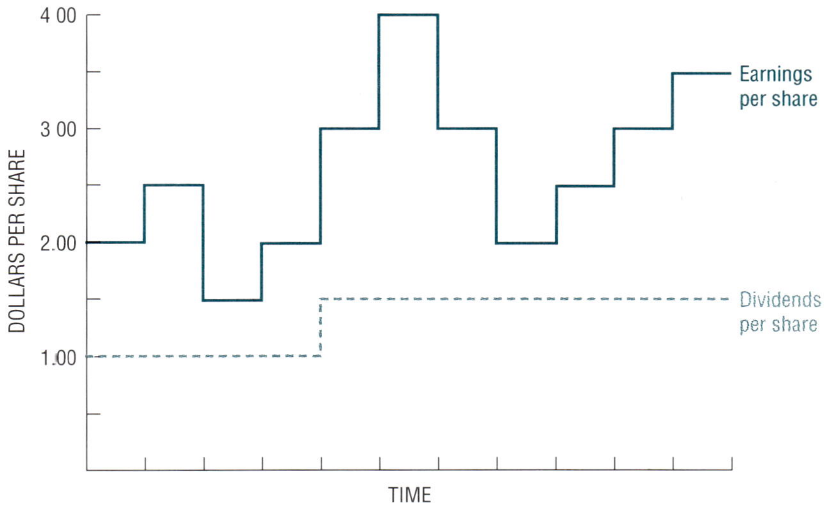

FIGURE 20-2
Dividend policy of Company B showing a long-run 50 percent dividend-payout ratio but dividend increases only when supported by growth in earnings

changes in earnings. In an economic upturn, the lag relationship becomes visible when retained earnings increase in relation to dividends. In a contraction, retained earnings will decrease relative to dividends.

Regular and Extra Dividends

One way for a company to increase its cash distribution to shareholders in periods of prosperity is to declare an **extra dividend** in addition to the **regular dividend** which is generally paid on a quarterly or semiannual basis. By declaring an extra dividend, the company warns investors that the dividend is not an increase in the established dividend rate. The declaration of an extra dividend is particularly suitable for companies with fluctuating earnings. General Motors, for example, has declared extra dividends in good years. The use of extra dividends enables the company to maintain a stable record of regular dividends and also to distribute some of the rewards of prosperity. If a company pays extra dividends continuously, it defeats its purpose. The extra dividend becomes expected. When properly labeled, however, an extra, or special, dividend still conveys positive information to the market concerning the firm's present and future performance.

Extra dividend
A nonrecurring dividend paid to shareholders in addition to the regular dividend. It is brought about by special circumstances.

Regular dividend
The dividend that is normally expected to be paid by the firm.

STOCK DIVIDENDS AND STOCK SPLITS

Stock dividends and stock splits are often used for different purposes. In an economic sense, there is little difference between the two. Only from an accounting standpoint is there a significant difference.

Stock Dividends

Stock dividend A payment of additional shares of stock to shareholders. Often used in place of or in addition to a cash dividend.

A **stock dividend** is simply the payment of additional shares of common stock to shareholders. It represents nothing more than a bookkeeping shift within the shareholders' equity account on the firm's balance sheet. A shareholder's proportional ownership in the firm remains unchanged. Accounting authorities make a distinction between small-percentage stock dividends and large-percentage stock dividends.

Small-Percentage Stock Dividends. If a stock dividend represents an increase of less than (typically) 20 percent of the previously outstanding common stock, it is referred to as a *small-percentage stock dividend.* Accounting for this type of stock dividend entails transferring an amount from retained earnings to common stock and additional paid-in capital.

Suppose that Chen Industries had a total shareholders' equity account—before issuing a stock dividend—as shown on the left-hand side of Table 20-1. Chen Industries then pays a 5 percent stock dividend, amounting to 20,000 additional shares (400,000 × .05) of stock. The fair market value of the stock is $40 per share. For each 20 shares of common stock owned, the shareholder receives an additional share. The total shareholder's equity account after the stock dividend is pictured on the right-hand side of Table 20-1.

With a 5 percent stock dividend, $800,000 ($40 × 20,000 shares) in market value of the additional shares is transferred (on paper) from retained earnings to the common stock and additional paid-in capital accounts. Because the par value per share stays the same, the increase in number of shares is reflected in a $100,000 ($5 × 20,000 shares) increase in the common stock account. The residual of $700,000 is entered into the additional paid-in capital account. The total shareholders' equity of the company remains the same, namely $10 million.

Because the number of shares of common stock outstanding is increased by 5 percent, earnings per share of the company are reduced proportionately. Assume that net profit after taxes for the period just ended is $1 million. Before the stock dividend, earnings per share were $2.50 ($1,000,000/400,000 shares). After the stock dividend, earnings per share would be $2.38 ($1,000,000/420,000 shares). Shareholders have more shares of stock but lower earnings per share. However, each shareholder's proportionate ownership claim against total earnings available to common shareholders remains unchanged.

Large-Percentage Stock Dividends. *Large-percentage stock dividends* (typically 20 percent or higher of previously outstanding common stock) must be accounted for differently. While small-percentage stock dividends are not expected to have much effect on the market value per share of stock, large-percentage stock dividends are expected to materially reduce the market price per share of stock. In the case of large-percentage stock dividends, therefore, conservatism argues for reclassifying an amount limited to the par value of additional shares rather than an amount related to the pre-stock-dividend market value of the stock.

Suppose that Chen Industries decided to issue a 100 percent stock dividend instead of the 5 percent stock dividend originally discussed. In Table 20-2 we see what the total shareholders' equity section of Chen Industries' balance sheet looks like both before and after the 100 percent stock dividend.

TABLE 20-1 5% Stock Dividend for Chen Industries

Before		After	
Common stock		Common stock	
($5 par; 400,000 shares)	$ 2,000,000	($5 par; **420,000** shares)	**$ 2,100,000**
Additional paid-in capital	1,000,000	Additional paid-in capital	**1,700,000**
Retained earnings	7,000,000	Retained earnings	**6,200,000**
Total shareholders' equity	$10,000,000	Total shareholders' equity	$10,000,000

Note: Current market price per share = $40.

TABLE 20-2 100% Stock Dividend for Chen Industries

Before		After	
Common stock		Common stock	
($5 par; 400,000 shares)	$ 2,000,000	($5 par; **800,000** shares)	**$ 4,000,000**
Additional paid-in capital	1,000,000	Additional paid-in capital	1,000,000
Retained earnings	7,000,000	Retained earnings	**5,000,000**
Total shareholders' equity	$10,000,000	Total shareholders' equity	$10,000,000

Because of the 100 percent stock dividend, $2,000,000 ($5 × 400,000 shares) in par value of the additional 400,000 shares is transferred from retained earnings to the common stock (at par) account. The total shareholders' equity of the company remains unchanged at $10 million.

Stock Splits

With a **stock split** the number of shares is increased through a proportional reduction in the par value of the stock. In our last example, Chen Industries issued a 100 percent stock dividend. A 2-for-1 stock split would have similar economic consequences to a 100 percent stock dividend but would require different accounting treatment. Table 20-3 shows us the total shareholders' equity account for Chen Industries both before and after a 2-for-1 stock split.

Stock split
An increase in the number of shares outstanding by reducing the par value of the stock; for example, a 2-for-1 stock split where par value per share is reduced by one-half.

With a stock dividend, the par value of common stock is not reduced, whereas with a stock split, it is. As a result, the common stock, additional paid-in capital, and retained earnings accounts remain unchanged with a stock split. The total shareholders' equity, of course, also stays the same. The only change is in the par value of the common stock which, on a per-share basis, is now half of what it once was. Except in accounting treatment, then, the stock dividend and stock split are very similar. A stock split (or alternatively, a large-percentage stock dividend) is usually reserved for occasions when a company wishes to achieve a substantial reduction in the market price per share of common stock. A principal purpose of a split is to place the stock in a more popular trading range, thereby (hopefully) attracting more buyers.

A company will seldom maintain the same cash dividend per share before and after a stock split. But, it might increase the effective dividend to shareholders. For

TABLE 20-3 2-for-1 Stock Split for Chen Industries

Before		After	
Common stock		Common stock	
($5 par; 400,000 shares)	$ 2,000,000	(**$2.50** par; **800,000** shares)	$ 2,000,000
Additional paid-in capital	1,000,000	Additional paid-in capital	1,000,000
Retained earnings	7,000,000	Retained earnings	7,000,000
Total shareholders' equity	$10,000,000	Total shareholders' equity	$10,000,000

example, a company may split its common stock 2 for 1 and establish an annual dividend rate of $1.20 a share, whereas before, the rate might have been $2 a share. A shareholder owning 100 shares before the stock split would receive $200 in cash dividends per year. After the stock split, the shareholder would own 200 shares and would receive $240 in dividends per year.

Value to Investors of Stock Dividends and Stock Splits

Theoretically, a stock dividend or stock split is not a thing of value to investors. They receive ownership of additional shares of common stock, but their proportionate ownership of the company is unchanged. The market price of the stock should decline proportionately, so that the total value of each shareholder's holdings stays the same. To illustrate with a stock dividend, suppose that you held 100 shares of common stock worth $40 per share or $4,000 in total. After a 5 percent stock dividend, share price should drop to $38.10 ($40/1.05). The total value of your holdings, however, would still be worth $4,000 ($38.10 × 105 shares). Under these conditions, the stock dividend does not represent a thing of value to you. You merely have a greater number of shares of stock evidencing the same ownership interest. In theory, the stock dividend or split is a purely cosmetic change.

To the extent that an investor wishes to sell a few shares of stock for income, the stock dividend/split may make it easier to do so. Without the stock dividend/split, of course, shareholders could also sell a few shares of their original holdings for income. In either case, the sale of stock represents the sale of principal and is subject to the capital gains tax. It is probable that certain investors do not look at the sale of additional stock resulting from a stock dividend/split as a sale of principal. To them, the stock dividend/split represents a windfall gain. They can sell the additional shares and still retain their original holdings. The stock dividend/split may have a favorable psychological effect on these shareholders.

Effect on Cash Dividends. The stock dividend or stock split may be accompanied by an increased cash dividend. For the former, suppose that an investor owns 100 shares of a company paying a $1 annual dividend. The company declares a 10 percent stock dividend and, at the same time, announces that the cash dividend per share will remain unchanged. The investor will then have 110 shares, and total cash dividends will be $110 rather than $100, as before. In this case, a stock dividend increases the total cash dividends. Whether this increase in cash dividend has a positive effect on shareholder wealth will depend on the trade-off between current dividends and the retention of earnings, which we discussed earlier. Clearly, the stock dividend in this case represents a decision by the firm to moderately increase the amount of cash dividends. However, the firm does not need the stock dividend to do so. The firm could merely increase its cash dividend per share from $1.00 to $1.10.

Sometimes a stock dividend is employed to conserve cash. Instead of increasing the cash dividend as earnings rise, a company may desire to retain a greater portion of its earnings and declare a modest stock dividend. This decision effectively amounts to lowering the dividend-payout ratio: as earnings rise and the dividend remains approximately the same, the dividend-payout ratio will decline. Whether shareholder wealth is increased by this action will depend on considerations previously discussed. The decision to retain a higher proportion of earnings, of course, could be accomplished without a stock dividend. Although he stock dividend may tend to please certain investors by virtue of its psychological impact, the substitution of common stock for cash dividends involves a sizable administrative cost. Stock dividends are simply much more costly to administer than are cash dividends. This out-of-pocket expense works to the disadvantage of stock dividends.

More Popular Trading Range. A stock split and, to a lesser extent, a stock dividend are used to place a stock in a lower, more popular trading range that may attract more buyers and may also affect the mix of stockholders as individual holdings are increased and institutional holdings are decreased.

Informational Content. The declaration of a stock dividend or a stock split may convey information to investors. As taken up earlier, there may be a situation in which management possesses more favorable information about the company than investors. Instead of simply issuing an announcement to the press, management may use a stock dividend or stock split to more convincingly state its belief about the favorable prospects of the company. Whether such a signal has a positive share price effect is an empirical question. Here the evidence is overwhelming. There is a statistically significant, positive stock price reaction around the announcement of a stock dividend or a stock split.[4] The information effect is that the stock is undervalued and should be higher priced. But we must be careful in how we interpret these results. As it turns out, stock dividends and stock splits generally precede cash dividend and earnings increases. The market appears to be viewing stock dividends and stock splits as leading indicators of greater cash dividends and earning power. Thus, it is not the stock dividend or stock split itself that causes a positive share price reaction, but rather it is the positive information that these signals convey. Also, the company must eventually deliver improved dividends and earnings if the stock price is to remain higher.

[4]See Guy Charest, "Split Information, Stock Returns and Market Efficiency," *Journal of Financial Economics* 6 (June–September 1978), 265–96; Eugene F. Fama, Lawrence Fisher, Michael Jensen, and Richard Roll. "The Adjustment of Stock Prices to New Information," *International Economic Review* 10 (February 1969), 1–21: Mark S. Grinblatt, Ronald W. Masulis, and Sheridan Titman, "The Valuation Effects of Stock Splits and Stock Dividends," *Journal of Financial Economics* 13 (December 1984), 461–90; and J. Randall Woolridge, "Stock Dividends as Signals," *Journal of Financial Research* 6 (Spring 1983), 1–12.

Reverse Stock Split

Reverse stock split A stock split in which the number of shares outstanding is decreased; for example, a 1-for-2 reverse stock split where each shareholder receives one new share in exchange for every two old shares held.

Rather than increase the number of shares of common stock outstanding, a company may want to reduce the number. It can accomplish this with a **reverse stock split.** If the firm in our previous examples, Chen Industries, had engaged in a 1-for-4 reverse stock split, for each four shares held, the shareholder would receive one new share in exchange. The new par value per share would become \$20 (\$5 × 4), and there would be 100,000 shares outstanding (400,000 shares/4) rather than 400,000. Reverse stock splits are employed to increase the market price per share when the stock is considered to be selling at too low a price. Many companies have an aversion to seeing their stock fall significantly below \$10 per share.

As with stock dividends and straight stock splits, there is likely to be an information or signaling effect associated with the announcement of a reverse stock split. Usually the signal is negative, such as would accompany the admission by a company that it is in financial difficulty. However, financial difficulty need not be the underlying motivating factor for the reverse split. The company may simply want to move the stock price into a higher trading range where total trading costs and servicing expenses are lower. Nevertheless, the empirical evidence is consistent with a statistically significant decline in share price around the reverse stock split announcement date, holding other things constant.[5] The decline is tempered by the company's past earnings performance, but a healthy company should think twice before undertaking a reverse stock split. There are too many bad apples in the barrel not to be tainted by association.

STOCK REPURCHASE

Stock repurchase The repurchase (buyback) of stock by the issuing firm, either in the open (secondary) market or by *self-tender offer*.

In recent years a number of companies have repurchased a portion of their outstanding common stock. Some companies repurchase stock in order to have it available for management stock-option plans. In this way, the total number of shares is not increased with the exercise of the options. Another reason for **stock repurchase** is to have shares available for the acquisition of other companies. In certain cases, companies no longer wishing to be publicly owned "go private" by purchasing all of the stock of outside shareholders. In still other situations, stock is repurchased with the full intention of retiring it. When you look at the total cash distributed to shareholders by corporations—cash dividends, share repurchases, and cash tender offers in connection with acquisitions—dividends are simply one (and not always the primary) mechanism for cash distribution.

Method of Repurchase

Self-tender offer An offer by a firm to repurchase some of its own shares at a specified price.

The two most common methods of repurchase are through a **self-tender offer** and through the purchase of stock in the marketplace. With a self-tender offer, the company makes a formal offer to shareholders to purchase a certain number of shares,

[5]See J. Randall Woolridge and Donald R. Chambers, "Reverse Splits and Shareholder Wealth," *Financial Management* 12 (Autumn 1983), 5–15; and R. C. Radcliffe and W. Gillespie, "The Price Impact of Reverse Splits," *Financial Analysts Journal* 35 (January–February 1979), 63–67.

typically at a set price. This bid price is above the current market price. Shareholders can elect either to sell their shares at the specified price or to continue to hold them. Usually the tender-offer period is between two and three weeks. If shareholders tender more shares than originally sought by the company, the company may elect to purchase all or part of the excess. However, it is under no obligation to do so. In general, the transactions costs to the firm in making a tender offer are higher than those incurred in the purchase of stock in the open market.

In open-market purchases, a company buys its stock as any other investor does—through a brokerage house. Usually, the brokerage fee is negotiated. Certain Securities and Exchange Commission rules restrict the manner in which a company bids for its own shares. As a result, it takes an extended period of time for a company to accumulate a relatively large block of stock. For this reason, the self-tender offer is more suitable when the company seeks a large amount of stock.

Before the company repurchases its stock, shareholders must be informed of the company's intentions. In a self-tender offer, these intentions are announced by the other itself. Even here, the company must not withhold other information. It would be unethical for a mining company, for example, to withhold information of a substantial ore discovery while making a self-tender offer to repurchase shares. In open-market purchases, especially, it is necessary to disclose the company's repurchase intentions. Otherwise, shareholders may sell their stock not knowing about a repurchase program that will increase earnings per share. Given full information about the amount of repurchase and the objective of the company, the shareholders can sell their shares if they so choose. Without proper disclosure, the selling shareholder may be penalized. When the amount of the stock repurchase is substantial, a self-tender offer is particularly suitable, for it gives all shareholders equal treatment.

Repurchasing as Part of Dividend Policy

If a firm has excess cash and insufficient profitable investment opportunities to justify the use of these funds, it may be in the shareholders' interests to distribute the funds. The distribution can be accomplished either by the repurchase of stock or by paying the funds out in increased dividends. In the absence of personal income taxes and transactions costs, the two alternatives should theoretically make no difference to shareholders. With repurchase, fewer shares remain outstanding, and earnings per share and, ultimately, dividends per share rise. As a result, the market price per share should rise as well. In theory, the capital gain arising from repurchase should equal the dividend that otherwise would have been paid.

Suppose Deuce Hardware Company is considering the distribution of $1.5 million, either in cash dividends or in the repurchase of its own stock. Key company figures just prior to the $1.5 million distribution are as follows:

Earnings after taxes	$2,000,000
Number of common shares outstanding	÷ 500,000
Earnings per share (EPS)	$ 4
Current market price per share	$ 63
Expected dividend	$ 3

Since investors are expecting a \$3-per-share cash dividend (\$1,500,000/500,000 shares), the \$63 value of a share of stock before the dividend is paid consists of the \$3-per-share expected dividend plus the \$60 market price expected to occur after the cash dividend distribution.

Alternatively, the firm could choose to repurchase some of its stock and make a self-tender offer to shareholders at \$63 a share. It then would be able to repurchase 23,810 shares (\$1,500,000/\$63). Earnings per share after repurchase would be

$$EPS = \$2{,}000{,}000/(500{,}000 - 23{,}810) = \$4.20$$

If the firm chooses to pay a cash dividend, its price/earnings ratio after the dividend would be 15 (\$60/\$4). If this price/earnings ratio stays at 15 after a stock repurchase, the total market price per share will be \$63 (\$4.20 × 15). The firm's shareholders are equally well-off with either a cash dividend or stock repurchase. Under the cash dividend option, current shareholders end up with \$3 in dividends per share plus stock worth \$60 a share, while under the repurchase option, current shareholders have stock worth \$63 a share. Thus, the amount of distribution to shareholders is \$3 per share—either in the form of dividends or share price appreciation (and resulting capital gain).

To the extent that the personal tax rate on capital gains is less than that on dividend income, the repurchase of stock offers a tax advantage over the payment of dividends to the taxable investor. Currently, for individuals, realized capital gains are taxed at the ordinary tax rates, or at a maximum of 28 percent. However, the capital gains tax is postponed until the stock is sold, whereas with dividends the tax must be paid on a current basis.

The repurchase of stock seems particularly appropriate when the firm has a large amount of excess cash to distribute. To pay these funds out through an extra dividend would result in a nonpostponable tax to shareholders. The tax effect could be alleviated somewhat by paying the funds out as extra dividends over a period of the, but this action might result in investors' counting on the extra dividend to be maintained continuously into the future. Also, the firm must be careful not to undertake a steady program of stock repurchase in lieu of paying dividends. The Internal Revenue Service will regard regularly occurring repurchases as the equivalent of cash dividends and not allow shareholders redeeming their shares any capital gains tax advantages.

Investment or Financing Decision?

Treasury stock Common stock that has been repurchased and is held by the issuing company.

Some regard the repurchase of stock as an investment decision instead of a financing decision. Indeed, in a strict sense, it is, even though shares held as **treasury stock** do not provide an expected return as do other investments. No company can exist by "investing" only in its own stock. The decision to repurchase stock should involve distribution of excess funds when the firm's investment opportunities are not sufficiently attractive to warrant employing those funds, either now or in the foreseeable future. Thus, the repurchase of stock cannot really be treated as an investment decision as we define the term.

Stock repurchase is best regarded as a type of financing decision possessing capital structure or dividend policy motivations. For example, sometimes the purpose of a stock repurchase is to alter the capital structure of the firm. By issuing debt and repurchasing stock, a firm can immediately change its debt-to-equity ratio toward a greater proportion of debt. At other times, when there is excess cash, the repurchase of stock can be viewed as part of the firm's overall dividend policy.

Possible Signaling Effect

Stock repurchases may also have a positive signaling effect. For example, suppose management believed that the firm's common stock was undervalued and that they were personally constrained in not being able to respond to a self-tender offer with shares that they owned individually. In such a case, the self-tender offer bid premium (amount by which the repurchase price exceeds the existing share price) would reflect management's belief about the degree of undervaluation. The idea is that concrete actions speak louder than words.[6]

While cash dividends and stock repurchases are similar in informational content in that they both use cash to send a positive signal, they also provide some dissimilar information. The regular cash dividend provides ongoing reinforcement of the underlying ability of the firm to generate cash. It is like a quarterly news release and can be habit-forming. In contrast, share repurchase is not a regular event. It may be viewed more as an "extra" news bulletin used on occasions when management believes that the firm's common stock is greatly undervalued.[7] Because both cash dividends and stock repurchases are done with money, management has a disincentive to give false signals and implicitly pledges itself to provide cash-flow results consistent with the signal.

ADMINISTRATIVE CONSIDERATIONS

Procedural Aspects

When the board of directors of a corporation declares a cash dividend, it specifies a **record date.** At the close of business on that date, a list of shareholders is drawn up by the company from its stock-transfer books. Shareholders on the list are entitled to the dividend, whereas shareholders who come on the books after the record date are not entitled to the dividend. For example, suppose that when the board of directors of United Chemical Company met on May 8, it declared a dividend of $1 per share payable June 15 to shareholders of record on May 31. Beth Broach owned some United Chemical stock on May 31, so she is entitled to the dividend even though she might sell her stock prior to the dividend actually being paid on June 15.

Record date
The date, set by the board of directors when a dividend is declared, on which an investor must be a shareholder of record to be entitled to the upcoming dividend.

A problem can develop in the sale of stock in the days immediately prior to the record date. The buyer and the seller of the stock have several days to *settle,* that is, to pay for the stock or to deliver it, in the case of the seller. To avoid confusion about

[6]In separate empirical studies Dann and Vermaelen find evidence supporting the positive signaling effect of stock repurchases, particularly for self-tender offers as opposed to open-market purchases. See Larry Y. Dann, "Common Stock Repurchases: An Analysis of Returns to Bondholders and Stockholders," *Journal of Financial Economics* 9 (June 1981), 113–38; and Theo Vermaelen, "Common Stock Repurchases and Market Signaling," *Journal of Economics* 9 (June 1981), 139–83.

[7]See Paul Asquith and David W. Mullins, Jr., "Signalling with Dividends, Stock Repurchases, and Equity Issues," *Financial Management* 15 (Autumn 1986), 27–44.

Dividends and Share Repurchases at Georgia-Pacific

Managing and reinvesting in our core businesses to add value for the shareholder is our primary responsibility. To the extent that we cannot identify satisfactory investment opportunities, however, we are committed to returning cash to our shareholders through dividends or share repurchases.

Our policy is to pay dividends at a rate of approximately one-third of sustainable earnings. We consider sustainable earnings to be the average earnings expected over a cycle. Recognizing the cyclical nature of our business, we do not intend to adjust dividends based on short-term swings in earnings.

Our board of directors authorized a share repurchase program that began in 1987 as a means of distributing cash to our shareholders and of maintaining our ratio of debt to capital within a target range. During 1987, 1988 and 1989, we repurchased 26.2 million shares of common stock at a total cost of $1.1 billion. In 1989, we suspended our share repurchase program, anticipating the higher leverage that resulted from the GNN acquisition. We anticipate that share repurchases will again be an option for the use of excess cash after we reduce debt to an appropriate level.

which investors are entitled to dividends when shares are sold just prior to the record date, the brokerage community has a rule whereby new shareholders are entitled to dividends only if they purchase the stock at least four business days prior to the record date. If the stock is purchased after that time, the shareholder is not entitled to the dividend. The date itself is known as the **ex-dividend date.**

Ex-dividend date
The first date on which a stock purchaser is no longer entitled to the recently declared dividend.

Declaration date
The date that the board of directors announces the amount and date of the next dividend.

Payment date
The date when the corporation actually pays the declared dividend.

Figure 20-3 shows the important dividend dates in our examples on a time line. May 8 was the date on which the board of directors declared a dividend (the **declaration date**), payable June 15 (the **payment date**) to shareholders of record as of May 31 (the record date). If May 31 were a Friday, four business days before would be May 27 (the ex-dividend date). To receive the dividend, a new shareholder must purchase the stock on May 26 or before. If purchased on May 27 or after, the stock is said to be *ex-dividend*. That is, it trades without the right to the declared dividend.

Dividend Reinvestment Plans

Dividend reinvestment plan (DRIP)
An optional plan allowing shareholders to automatically reinvest dividend payments in additional shares of the company's stock.

A number of large companies have established **dividend reinvestment plans (DRIPs).** Under these plans, shareholders have the option to reinvest their cash dividends in additional shares of the company's stock. There are two basic types of DRIPs, characterized by whether the additional shares come from already existing common stock or newly issued common stock. If existing common stock is used, the company transfers the cash dividends from all shareholders wishing to reinvest to a bank, which acts as a trustee. The bank then purchases shares of the company's common stock in the open market. Some companies even absorb any brokerage costs involved with purchasing the common stock required for reinvestment. For DRIPs in which the shareholder must bear the brokerage costs, these costs are relatively low, however, because the trustee buys stock in volume.

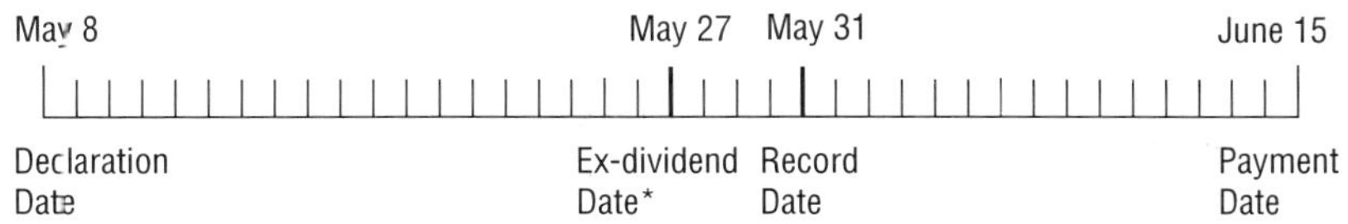

*A stock that has gone ex-dividend is marked with an "x" in newspaper price listings.

FIGURE 20-3
Important dividend dates for United Chemical Company

The other type of reinvestment plan involves having the firm issue new common stock. Only under this method can the firm actually raise new funds. This type of plan has proven especially popular with companies in need of new capital for construction and improvements. Effectively, such a plan reduces a firm's cash dividend payout. For example, suppose that a firm using a "new-stock" DRIP currently reports a 60 percent dividend-payout ratio. But after subtracting all cash dividends that are reinvested in new common stock, the "actual" payout may drop to only 40 percent. The cash savings to a large firm could easily amount to millions of dollars. With a new-stock DRIP the shares come directly from the company, so there are no brokerage costs involved. Some of these new-stock plans even allow participants to buy additional shares at a discount from the current market price of the stock. Commonly the discount is 3 to 5 percent, and it serves as an inducement for reinvestment. Even though reinvested, the dividend is taxable to the shareholder as ordinary income, and this is a major disadvantage to the taxable shareholder. Companies offering DRIPs range from utilities to banks to industrial concerns.

SUMMARY

- The critical question in dividend policy is, given the investment decision of the firm, do dividends have an influence upon the value of the firm?
- If dividends are irrelevant, as argued by Modigliani and Miller (M & M), the firm should retain earnings only in keeping with the availability of acceptable investment proposals. If there are not sufficient investment opportunities to provide returns in excess of those that are required, the unused funds should be paid out as dividends.
- With perfect capital markets and an absence of taxes, shareholders can manufacture "homemade" dividends, making the firm's dividend payout irrelevant. With differential taxes (in present value terms) on cash dividends and capital gains, there seemingly is a bias in favor of earnings retention.
- The market imperfection of flotation costs biases things in favor of earnings retention because this "internal" equity financing is less expensive than "external" equity financing (issuance of new common stock) used to replace the funds lost to the cash dividend. On the other hand, restrictions on the investment behavior of financial institutions work in the direction of a preference for dividends. Other market imperfections are also part of the picture.
- Empirical testing of dividend policy has focused on whether there is a tax effect and whether dividends serve as a signal in conveying information. The evidence is conflicting with respect to the tax effect, ranging from a neutral effect

to a negative (anti-dividend-paying) effect. However, there seems to be agreement that dividends provide financial signals.

- In the final analysis, finance experts are unable to state unequivocally whether the dividend payout of the firm should be more than a passive decision variable. Most academics think not. Admittedly, many companies behave as if dividend policy is relevant, but the case for it is not conclusive.
- When a company is faced with a dividend decision, managerial considerations include legal rules, the funding needs of the firm, business risk, liquidity, ability to borrow, assessment of any valuation information, control, and restrictions in debt contracts.
- Many people feel that the stability of dividends has a positive effect on the market price of the stock. Stable dividends may tend to resolve uncertainty in the minds of investors, particularly when earnings per share drop. Stable dividends may also have a positive utility to investors interested in current periodic income. Many companies appear to follow the policy of a target dividend-payout ratio, increasing dividends only when they feel that an increase in earnings can be maintained. The use of an *extra dividend* permits a cyclical company to maintain a stable record of *regular dividends* while paying additional dividends whenever earnings are unusually high.
- A *stock divided* pays additional common stock to shareholders. It is frequently used to conserve cash and to reduce the cash-dividend-payout ratio of the firm. Theoretically, a stock dividend/split per se is not a thing of value to the shareholder unless total cash dividends paid increase.
- When the intent is to materially reduce the market price per share of stock, either a *stock split* or *large-percentage stock dividend* is used. With a split, the number of shares is increased by the terms of the split. For example, a 3-for-1 split means that the number of shares outstanding is tripled.
- Both stock dividends and stock splits appear to have an informational or signaling effect. Share price tends to rise around the time of a stock dividend/split announcement, consistent with a positive signal. The market appears to view the stock dividend/split as a leading indicator of greater cash dividends and earning power. In a *reverse stock split*, the number of shares outstanding is reduced, and the signal to the market usually is negative.
- A company's repurchase of its own stock should be treated as part of the firm's dividend policy when the firm has funds in excess of present and foreseeable future investment needs. The use of these excess funds to repurchase stock is an alternative to distributing them in the form of cash dividends.
- With a tax differential (in present value terms) between cash dividends and capital gains, there is a tax advantage to the repurchase of dividends. Because of objections by the Internal Revenue Service, regularly occurring repurchases of common stock cannot be used in lieu of regular dividends.
- The dividend payment process begins with the firm's board of directors, which on a particular date (the *declaration date*) declares a dividend, payable on a later date (the *payment date*) to shareholders of record as of a particular date the (*record date*). On the fourth business date before the record date (the *ex-dividend date*), the stock goes "ex-dividend"—meaning that the stock trades without the right to the declared dividend.
- *Dividend reinvestment plans (DRIPs)* allow shareholders to automatically reinvest dividend payments in additional shares of the company's stock.

QUESTIONS

1. Contrast a passive dividend policy with an active one.
2. How does an investor manufacture "homemade" dividends? What is the effect of the actions of a number of investors doing so, all other things held constant?
3. How do taxes affect the return to different investors? Are taxes a consideration in the dividend policy decision?
4. Why do companies with high growth rates tend to have low dividend-payout ratios and companies with low growth rates tend to have high dividend-payout ratios?
5. What is financial signaling as it relates to cash dividends, stock dividends/splits, and stock repurchase?
6. From a managerial standpoint, how does a firm's liquidity and ability to borrow affect its dividend-payout ratio?
7. As the firm's financial manager, would you recommend to the board of directors that the firm adopt as policy a stable dividend payment per share or a stable dividend-payout ratio? What are the disadvantages of each? Would the firm's industry influence your decision? Why?
8. What is a *target dividend-payout ratio?* An *extra cash dividend?*
9. Define a *stock dividend* and a *stock split*. What is the impact of each on share value?
10. Are *stock dividends* valuable to investors? Why or why not?
11. If we wish to raise share price, is it a good idea to have a *reverse stock split?* Explain.
12. As an investor, would you prefer the firm to repurchase its common stock by means of a *self-tender offer* or through open-market operations? Why?
13. If repurchase of stock has a favorable tax effect, why would a company ever want to pay a cash dividend?
14. When earnings falter, why are boards of directors of companies reluctant to reduce the dividend?
15. Why do lenders frequently place a formal restriction in the debt contract on the amount of dividends that can be paid?
16. What is a *dividend reinvestment plan (DRIP)* and how might it help shareholders?
17. Is dividend policy a type of financing decision or is it a type of investment decision? Explain.

SELF-CORRECTION PROBLEMS

1. The Borowiak Rose Water Company expects with some degree of certainty to generate the following net income and to have the following capital expenditures during the next five years (in thousands of dollars):

	Year				
	1	2	3	4	5
Net income	$2,000	$1,500	$2,500	$2,300	$1,800
Capital expenditures	1,000	1,500	2,000	1,500	2,000

The company currently has 1 million shares of common stock outstanding and pays annual dividends of $1 per share.

a. Determine dividends per share and external financing required in each year if dividend policy is treated as a residual decision.
b. Determine the amounts of external financing that will be necessary in each year if the present annual dividend per share is maintained.
c. Determine dividends per share and the amounts of external financing that will be necessary if a dividend-payout ratio of 50 percent is maintained.
d. Under which of the three dividend policies are aggregate dividends (total dividends over five years) maximized? External required financing (total financing over five years) minimized?

2. Dew Drop Inn, Inc.'s earnings per share over the last 10 years were the following:

	Year									
	1	2	3	4	5	6	7	8	9	10
EPS	$1.70	$1.82	$1.44	$1.88	$2.18	$2.32	$1.84	$2.23	$2.50	$2.73

a. Determine annual dividends per share under the following policies:
   (1) A constant dividend-payout ratio of 40 percent (to the nearest cent).
   (2) A regular dividend of 80 cents and an extra dividend to bring the payout ratio to 40 percent if it otherwise would fall below.
   (3) A stable dividend that is occasionally raised. The payout ratio may range between 30 percent and 50 percent in any given year, but it should average approximately 40 percent.
b. What are the valuation implications of each of these policies?

3. The Klingon Fastener Company has the following shareholders equity account:

Common stock ($8 par value)	$ 2,000,000
Additional paid-in capital	1,600,000
Retained earnings	8,400,000
Total shareholders' equity	$12,000,000

The current market price of the stock is $60 per share.

a. What will happen to this account and to the number of shares outstanding with (1) a 10 percent stock dividend? (2) a 2-for-1 stock split? (3) a 1-for-2 reverse stock split?
b. In the absence of an informational or signaling effect, at what share price should the common stock sell after the 10 percent stock dividend? What might happen to stock price if there were a signaling effect?

PROBLEMS

1. The DeWitt Company's shareholders' equity account (book value) as of December 31, 19X1, is as follows:

Common stock ($5 par value; 1,000,000 shares)	$ 5,000,000
Additional paid-in capital	5,000,000
Retained earnings	15,000,000
Total shareholders' equity	$25,000,000

   Currently, DeWitt is under pressure from shareholders to pay some dividends, DeWitt's cash balance is $500,000, all of which is needed for transactions purposes. The stock is trading for $7 a share.

   a. What is the legal limit that can be paid in cash dividends? (Treat additional paid-in capital as part of *capital*.)
   b. Reformulate the shareholders' equity account if the company pays a 15 percent stock dividend.
   c. Reformulate the shareholders' equity account if the company pays a 25 percent stock dividend.
   d. Reformulate the shareholders' equity account if the company declares a 5-for-4 stock split.

2. Tijuana Brass Instruments Company treats dividends as a residual decision. It expects to generate $2 million in net earnings after taxes in the coming year. The company has an all-equity capital structure, and its cost of equity capital is 15 percent. The company treats this cost as the opportunity cost of "internal" equity financing (retained earnings). Because of flotation costs and underpricing, "external" equity financing (new common stock) is not relied on until internal equity financing is exhausted.
   a. How much in dividends (out of the $2 million in earnings) should be paid if the company has $1.5 million in projects whose expected returns exceed 15 percent?
   b. How much in dividends should be paid if it has $2 million in projects whose expected returns exceed 15 percent?
   c. How much in dividends should be paid if it has $3 million in projects whose expected returns exceed 16 percent? What else should be done?

3. For each of the companies described here, would you expect it to have a low, medium, or high dividend-payout ratio? Explain why.
   a. A company with a large proportion of inside ownership, all of whom are high-income individuals.
   b. A growth company with an abundance of good investment opportunities.
   c. A company that has high liquidity and much unused borrowing capacity and is experiencing ordinary growth.
   d. A dividend-paying company that experiences an unexpected drop in earnings from an upward-sloping trend line.
   e. A company with volatile earnings and high business risk.

4. Jumbo Shrimp Corporation and Giant Shrimp Company are in the same industry; both are publicly held with a large number of shareholders; and they have the following characteristics:

	Jumbo	Giant
Expected annual cash flow (in thousands)	$50,000	$35,000
Standard deviation of cash flow (in thousands)	30,000	25,000
Annual capital expenditures (in thousands)	42,000	40,000
Cash and marketable securities (in thousands)	5,000	7,000
Existing long-term debt (in thousands)	100,000	85,000
Unused short-term line of credit (in thousands)	25,000	10,000
Flotation costs and underpricing on common stock issues as a percent of proceeds	.05	.08

On the basis of this information, which company is likely to have the higher dividend-payout ratio? Why?

5. The Oprah Corporation and the Harpo Corporation have had remarkably similar earnings patterns over the last five years. In fact, both firms have had identical earnings per share. Further, both firms are in the same industry, produce the same product, and face the same business and financial risks. In short, these firms are carbon copies of each other in every respect but one: Oprah paid out a constant percentage of its earnings (50 percent) in dividends, while Harpo has paid a constant cash dividend. The financial manager of the Oprah Corporation has been puzzled by the fact that the price of her firm's stock has been generally lower than the price of Harpo's stock, even though in some years Oprah's dividend was substantially larger than Harpo's.
   a. What might account for the condition that has been puzzling the financial manager of Oprah?
   b. What might be done by both companies to increase the market prices of their stock?

	Oprah			Harpo		
Years	EPS	Dividend	Market Price	EPS	Dividend	Market Price
1	$1.00	$.50	$6	$1.00	$.23	$4 7/8
2	.50	.25	4	.50	.23	4
3	–.25	nil	2	–.25	.23	4 1/4
4	.50	.25	3 1/2	.50	.23	4 1/2

6. The Chris Clapper Copper Company declared a 25 percent stock dividend on March 10 to shareholders of record on April 1. The market price of the stock is $50 per share. You own 160 shares of the stock.
   a. If you sold your stock on March 20, what would be the price per share, all other things the same (no signaling effect)?
   b. After the stock dividend is paid, how many shares of stock will you own?

c. At what price would you expect the stock to sell on April 2, all other things the same (no signaling effect)?
d. What will be the total value of your holdings before and after the stock dividend, all other things the same?
e. If there were an informational or signaling effect, what would be the effect on share price?

7.

Sherill Corporation Shareholders' Equity as of December 30, 19X3

Common stock ($1 par value; 1,000,000 shares)	$1,000,000
Additional paid-in capital	300,000
Retained earnings	1,700,000
Total shareholders' equity	$3,000,000

The firm earned $300,000 after taxes in 19X3 and paid out 50 percent of these earnings as cash dividends. The price on the firm's stock on December 30 was $5.

a. If the firm declared a stock dividend of 3 percent on December 31, what would be the reformulated shareholders' equity account?
b. Assuming the firm paid no stock dividend, how much would earnings per share be for 19X3? Dividends per share?
c. Assuming a 3 percent stock dividend, what would happen to earnings per share (EPS) and dividends per share (DPS) for 19X3?
d. What would the price of the stock be after the 3 percent stock dividend if there were no signaling or other effects?

8. Johore Trading Company has 2.4 million shares of common stock outstanding, and the present market price per share is $36. Its equity capitalization is as follows:

Common stock ($2.00 par; 2,400,000 shares)	$ 4,800,000
Additional paid-in capital	5,900,000
Retained earnings	87,300,000
Total shareholders' equity	$98,000,000

a. If the company were to declare a 12 percent stock dividend, what would happen to these accounts? A 25 percent stock dividend? A 5 percent stock dividend?
b. If, instead, the company declared a 3-for-2 stock split, what would happen to the accounts? A 2-for-1 stock split? A 3-for-1 split?
c. What would happen if there were a reverse stock split of 1 for 4? 1 for 6?

9. The H. M. Hornes Company is primarily owned by several wealthy Texans. The firm earned $3,500,000 after taxes this year. With 1 million shares outstanding, earnings per share were $3.50. The stock recently has traded at $72 per share, among the current shareholders. Two dollars of this value is accounted for by investor anticipation of a cash dividend. As financial manager of H. M. Hornes,

you have contemplated the alternative of repurchasing some company common stock by means of a tender offer at $72 per share.

a. How much common stock could the firm repurchase if this alternative were selected?
b. Ignoring taxes, which alternative should be selected?
c. Considering taxes, which alternative should be selected?

SOLUTIONS TO SELF-CORRECTION PROBLEMS

1. a.

Year	Income Available For Dividends (in thousands)	Dividends Per share	External Financing Required (in thousands)
1	$1,000	$1.00	$ 0
2	0	0	0
3	500	.50	0
4	800	.80	0
5	0	0	200
	$2,300		$200

b. (in thousands)

Year	(1) Net Income	(2) Dividends	(3) Capital Expenditures	(4) External Financing Required (2) + (3) − (1)
1	$2,000	$1,000	$1,000	$ 0
2	1,500	1,000	1,500	1,000
3	2,500	1,000	2,000	500
4	2,300	1,000	1,500	200
5	1,800	1,000	2,000	1,200
		$5,000		$2,900

c.

Year	(1) Net Income (in thousands)	(2) Dividends (in thousands)	(3) Dividends Per Share	(4) Capital Expenditures (in thousands)	(5) External Financing Required (2) + (4) − (1) (in thousands)
1	$2,000	$1,000	$1.00	$1,000	$ 0
2	1,500	750	.75	1,500	750
3	2,500	1,250	1.25	2,000	750
4	2,300	1,150	1.15	1,500	350
5	1,800	900	.90	2,000	1,100
		$5,050			$2,950

d. Aggregate dividends are highest under Alternative C, which involves a 50 percent dividend-payout ratio. However, they are only slightly higher than that which occurs under Alternative B. External financing is minimized under Alternative A, the residual dividend policy.

2. a.

Year	Policy 1	Policy 2	Policy 3
1	$ .68	$ .80	$ .68
2	.73	.80	.68
3	.58	.80	.68
4	.75	.80	.80
5	.87	.87	.80
6	.93	.93	.80
7	.74	.80	.80
8	.89	.89	1.00
9	1.00	1.00	1.00
10	1.09	1.09	1.00

Other dividend streams are possible under Policy 3. This solution is but one.

b. Policy 1 and, to a much lesser degree, Policy 2 result in fluctuating dividends over time, as the company is cyclical. Because of the $.80 minimum regular dividend, Policy 2 results in an average payout ratio in excess of 40 percent. Shareholders may come to count on the extra dividend and be disappointed when it is not paid, such as in year 7. To the extent that investors value stable dividends and periodic rising dividends over time and that 40 percent is an optimal average payout ratio, dividend Policy 3 would be preferred and would likely maximize share price.

3. a. Present number of shares = $2,000,000/$8 par value = 250,000.

	(1) Stock Divided	(2) Stock Split	(3) Reverse Split
Common stock (par)	$ 2,200,000 ($8)	$ 2,000,000 ($4)	$ 2,000,000 ($16)
Additional paid-in capital	2,900,000	1,600,000	1,600,000
Retained earnings	6,900,000	8,400,000	8,400,000
Tota shareholders' equity	$12,000,000	$12,000,000	$12,000,000
Number of shares	275,000	500,000	125,000

b. The total market value of the firm before the stock dividend is $60 × 250,000 shares = $15 million. With no change in the total value of the firm, market price per share after the stock dividend should be $15,000,000/275,000 shares = *$54.55 per share.* If there is a signaling effect, the total value of the firm might rise and share price be somewhat higher than $54.55 per share. The magnitude of the effect would probably be no more than several dollars a share, based on empirical findings.

SELECTED REFERENCES

Asquith, Paul, and David W. Mullins, Jr. "The Impact of Initiating Dividend Payments on Shareholders' Wealth." *Journal of Business* 56 (January 1983), 77–96.

______. "Signalling with Dividends, Stock Repurchases, and Equity Issues." *Financial Management* 15 (Autumn 1986), 27–44.

Bagwell, Laurie Simon, and John B. Shoven. "Cash Distributions to Shareholders." *Journal of Economic Perspectives* 3 (Summer 1989), 129–40.

Black, Fischer. "The Dividend Puzzle." *Journal of Portfolio Management* 2 (Winter 1976), 5–8.

______, and Myron Scholes. "The Effects of Dividend Yield and Dividend Policy on Common Stock Prices and Returns." *Journal of Financial Economics* 1 (May 1974), 1–22.

Brennan, Michael J., and Thomas E. Copeland. "Stock Splits, Stock Prices, and Transaction Costs." *Journal of Financial Economics* 22 (October 1988), 83–101.

Chang, Rosita P., and S. Ghon Rhee. "The Impact of Personal Taxes on Corporate Dividend Policy and Capital Structure Decisions." *Financial Management* 19 (Summer 1990), 21–31.

Charest, Guy. "Split Information, Stock Returns and Market Efficiency." *Journal of Financial Economics* 6 (June–September 1978), 265–96.

Dann, Larry Y. "Common Stock Repurchases: An Analysis of Returns to Bondholders and Stockholders." *Journal of Financial Economics* 9 (June 1981), 113–38.

Eades, Kenneth M., Patrick J. Hess, and E. Han Kim. "On Interpreting Security Returns During the Ex-Dividend Period." *Journal of Financial Economics* 13 (December 1984), 461–90.

Fama, Eugene F., Lawrence Fisher, Michael Jensen, and Richard Roll. "The Adjustment of Stock Prices to New Information." *International Economic Review* 10 (February 1969), 1–21.

Grinblatt, Mark S., Ronald W. Masulis, and Sheridan Titman. "The Valuation Effects of Stock Splits and Stock Dividends." *Journal of Financial Economics* 13 (December 1984), 461–90.

Healy, Paul M., and Krishna G. Palepu. "Earnings Information Conveyed by Dividend Initiations and Omissions." *Journal of Financial Economics* 21 (September 1988), 149–75.

Lakonishok, Josef, and Theo Vermaelen. "Anomalous Price Behavior Around Repurchase Tender Offers." *Journal of Finance* 45 (June 1990), 455–78.

Lintner, John. "Distribution of Income of corporations Among Dividends, Retained Earnings, and Taxes." *American Economic Review* 46 (May 1956), 97–113.

Litzenberger, Robert H., and Krishna Ramiswamy. "Dividends, Short Selling Restrictions, Tax Induced Investor Clienteles and Market Equilibrium." *Journal of Finance* 35 (May 1980), 469–82.

______. "The Effects of Dividends on Common Stock Prices: Tax Effects or Information Effects?" *Journal of Finance* 37 (May 1982), 429–44.

Litzenberger, Robert H., and James C. Van Horne. "Elimination of the Double Taxation of Dividends and Corporate Financial Policy." *Journal of Finance* 33 (June 1978), 737–49.

Markese, John. "Common Stock Dividends: What Are They Worth?" *AAII Journal* 11 (July 1989), 29–33.

McNichols, Maureen, and Ajay Dravid. "Stock Dividends, Stock Splits, and Signaling." *Journal of Finance* 45 (July 1990), 857–79.

Miller, Merton H. "Behavioral Rationality in Finance: The Case of Dividends." *Midland Corporate Finance Journal* 4 (Winter 1987), 6–15.

______, and Franco Modigliani. "Dividend Policy, Growth, and the Valuation of Shares." *Journal of Business* 34 (October 1961), 411–33.

Miller, Merton, H., and Kevin Rock. "Dividend Policy under Asymmetric Information." *Journal of Finance* 40 (September 1985), 1031–51.

Van Horne, James C., and John G. McDonald. "Dividend Policy and New Equity Financing." *Journal of Finance* 26 (May 1971), 507–19.

Vermalelen, Theo. "Common Stock Repurchases and Market Signalling." *Journal of Financial Economics* 9 (June 1981), 139–83.

Woolridge, J. Randall. "Stock Dividends as Signals." *Journal of Financial Research* 6 (Spring 1983), 1–12.

______, and Donald R. Chambers. "Reverse Splits and Shareholder Wealth." *Financial Management* 12 (Autumn 1983), 5–15.

SECTION VIII

Fundamentals of Capital Budgeting

CAPITAL BUDGETING AND ESTIMATING CASH FLOWS

CAPITAL BUDGETING TECHNIQUES AND PRACTICE

CAPITAL BUDGETING AND RISK ANALYSIS

CHAPTER 21

Capital Budgeting and Estimating Cash Flows

THE CAPITAL BUDGETING PROCESS: AN OVERVIEW

Having explored ways to efficiently manage working capital (current assets and their supporting financing), we now turn our attention to decisions that involve long-lived assets. These decisions involve both investment and financing choices, the first of which takes up the next three chapters.

When a business makes a capital investment, it incurs a current cash outlay in the expectation of future benefits. Usually, these benefits extend beyond one year in the future. Examples include investment in assets such as equipment, buildings, and land, as well as the introduction of a new product, a new distribution system, or a new program for research and development. In short, the firm's future success and profitability depend on long-term decisions currently made.

An investment proposal should be judged in relation to whether or not it provides a return equal to, or greater than, that required by investors. To simplify our investigation of the methods of **capital budgeting** in this and the following chapter, we assume that the required return is given and is the same for all investment projects. This assumption implies that the selection of any investment project does not alter the operating, or business-risk, complexion of the firm as perceived by financing suppliers.

Capital budgeting The process of identifying, analyzing, and selecting investment projects whose returns (cash flows) are expected to extend beyond one year.

Capital budgeting involves

- Generating investment project proposals consistent with the firm's strategic objectives
- Estimating after-tax incremental operating cash flows for the investment projects
- Evaluating project incremental cash flows

- Selecting projects based on a value-maximizing acceptance criterion
- Reevaluating implemented investment projects continually and performing postaudits for completed projects

In this chapter, we restrict ourselves to a discussion of the first two items on this list.

GENERATING INVESTMENT PROJECT PROPOSALS

Investment project proposals can stem from a variety of sources. For purposes of analysis, projects may be classified into one of five categories:

1. New products or expansion of existing products
2. Replacement of equipment or buildings
3. Research and development
4. Exploration
5. Other (for example, safety-related or pollution-control devices)

For a new product, the proposal usually originates in the marketing department. A proposal to replace a piece of equipment with a more sophisticated model, however, usually arises from the production area of the firm. In each case, efficient administrative procedures are needed for channeling investment requests. All investment requests should be consistent with corporate strategy in order to avoid needless analysis of projects incompatible with this strategy. (McDonald's probably would not want to install cigarette vending machines in its restaurants, for example.)

Most firms screen proposals at multiple levels of authority. For a proposal originating in the production area, the hierarchy of authority might run (1) from section chiefs, (2) to plant managers, (3) to the vice president for operations, (4) to a capital expenditures committee under the financial manager, (5) to the president, (6) to the board of directors. How high a proposal must go before it is finally approved usually depends on its cost. The greater the capital outlay, the greater the number of "screens" usually required. Plant managers may be able to approve moderate-sized projects on their own, but only higher levels of authority approve larger ones. Because the administrative procedures for screening investment proposals vary from firm to firm, it is not possible to generalize. The best procedure will depend on the circumstances. It is clear, however, that companies are becoming increasingly sophisticated in their approach to capital budgeting.

ESTIMATING PROJECT "AFTER-TAX INCREMENTAL OPERATING CASH FLOWS"

Cash-Flow Checklist

One of the most important tasks in capital budgeting is estimating future cash flows for a project. The final results we obtain from our analysis are no better than the accuracy of our cash-flow estimates. Since cash, not accounting income, is central to all decisions of the firm, we express whatever benefits we expect from a project in terms of *cash flows* rather than income flows. The firm invests cash now in the hope of receiving even greater cash returns in the future. Only cash can be reinvested in the firm or paid to shareholders in the form of dividends. In capital budgeting, good guys may get credit, but effective managers get cash. In setting up the cash flows for analysis, a computer spreadsheet program is invaluable. It allows one to change assumptions and quickly produce a new cash-flow stream.

For each investment proposal we need to provide information on *operating*, as opposed to financing, cash flows. Financing flows such as interest payments, principal payments, and cash dividends are excluded from our cash-flow analysis. However, the need for an investment's return to cover capital costs is not ignored. The use of a discount (or hurdle) rate equal to the required rate of return of capital suppliers will capture the financing cost dimension. We will discuss the mechanics of this type of analysis in the next chapter.

Cash flows should be determined on an *after-tax* basis. The initial investment outlay, as well as the appropriate discount rate, will be expressed in after-tax terms. Therefore, all forcasted flows need to be stated on an equivalent, after-tax basis.

In addition, the information must be presented on an *incremental* basis, so that we analyze only the difference between the cash flows of the firm with and without the project. For example, if a firm contemplates a new product that is likely to compete with existing products, it is not appropriate to express cash flows in terms of estimated total sales of the new product. We must take into account the probable "cannibalization" of existing products and make our cash-flow estimates on the basis of incremental sales. When continuation of the status quo results in loss of market share, we must take this into account when analyzing what happens if we do not make a new investment. That is, if cash flows will erode if we do not invest, we must factor this into our analysis. The key is to analyze the situation with and without the new investment and where all relevant costs and benefits are brought into play. Only incremental cash flows matter.

In this regard, **sunk costs** must be ignored. Our concern lies with incremental costs and benefits. Unrecoverable past costs are irrelevant and should not enter into the decision process. Also, we must be mindful that certain relevant costs do not necessarily involve an actual dollar outlay. If we have allocated plant space to a project and this space can be used for something else, its **opportunity cost** must be included in the project's evaluation. If a presently unused building needed for a project can be sold for $300,000, that amount (net of any taxes) should be treated *as if it were a cash outlay* at the outset of the project. Thus, in deriving cash flows we need to consider any appropriate opportunity costs.

Sunk costs Unrecoverable past outlays that, since they cannot be recovered, should not affect present actions or future decisions.

Opportunity cost What is lost by not taking the next-best investment alternative.

When a capital investment contains a current asset component, this component (net of any spontaneous changes in current liabilities) is treated as part of the capital investment and not as a separate working capital decision. For example, with the acceptance of a new project it is sometimes necessary to carry additional cash, receivables, or inventories. This investment in working capital should be treated as a cash outflow at the time it occurs. At the end of a project's life, the working capital investment is presumably returned in the form of an additional cash inflow.

In estimating cash flows, *anticipated inflation must be taken into account.* Often there is a tendency to erroneously assume that price levels will remain unchanged throughout the life of a project. If the required rate of return for a project to be accepted embodies a premium for inflation (as it usually does), then estimated cash flows must also reflect inflation. Such cash flows are affected in several ways. If cash inflows ultimately arise from the sale of a product, expected future prices affect these inflows. As for cash outflows, inflation affects both expected future wages and material costs.

Table 21-1 summarizes the major concerns to keep in mind as we prepare to actually determine project "after-tax incremental operating cash flows." It provides us with a "checklist" for determining cash-flow estimates.

TABLE 21-1 Cash-Flow Checklist

Basic characteristics of relevant project flows

- ✓ ***Cash*** (not accounting income) flows
- ✓ ***Operating*** (not financing) flows
- ✓ ***After-tax*** flows
- ✓ **Incremental** flows

Basic principles that must be adhered to in estimating "after-tax incremental operating cash flows"

- ✓ Ignore ***sunk costs***
- ✓ Include ***opportunity costs***
- ✓ Include project-driven ***changes in working capital*** net of spontaneous changes in current liabilities
- ✓ Include effects of ***inflation***

Tax Considerations

Method of Depreciation. *Depreciation* is the systematic allocation of the cost of a capital asset over a period of time for financial reporting purposes, tax purposes, or both. Since depreciation deductions taken on a firm's tax return are treated as expense items, depreciation lowers taxable income. Everything else being equal, the greater the depreciation charges, the lower the taxes paid. While depreciation itself is a noncash expense, it does affect the firm's cash flow by directly influencing the cash outflow of taxes paid.

There are a number of alternative procedures that may be used to depreciate capital assets. These include straight-line and various accelerated depreciation methods. Most profitable firms prefer to use an accelerated depreciation method *for tax purposes*—one that allows for a more rapid write-off and, therefore, a lower tax bill.

Q **Can MACRS depreciation be utilized by U.S. companies on equipment used outside the United States?**

A No. Generally, MACRS depreciation is not allowed for equipment that is used predominantly outside of the United States during the taxable year. For such equipment, the Alternative Depreciation System (ADS) is required. ADS is a straight-line method of depreciation (determined without regard to estimated future salvage value).

The Tax Reform Act of 1986 allows companies to use a particular type of accelerated depreciation for tax purposes known as the Modified Accelerated Cost Recovery System (MACRS). Under MACRS, machinery, equipment, and real estate are assigned to one of eight classes for cost recovery (depreciation) purposes. The property category in which an asset falls determines its depreciable life for tax purposes. As also described in that chapter, the *half-year convention* must generally be applied to all machinery and equipment. There is a half-year of depreciation in the year an asset is acquired and in the final year that depreciation is taken on the asset. The Treasury publishes depreciation percentages of original cost for each property class, which incorporate the half-year conventions. Table 21-2 presents the depreciation percentages for the first four property classes.

Depreciable Basis. Computing depreciation for an asset requires a determination of the asset's **depreciable basis.** This is the amount that taxing authorities allow to be written off for tax purposes over a period of years. The cost of the asset, including any other **capitalized expenditures**—such as shipping and installation—that are incurred in order to prepare the asset for its intended use, constitutes the asset's depreciable basis under MACRS. Notice that under MACRS the asset's depreciable basis is *not* reduced by the estimated salvage value of the asset.

Depreciable basis In tax accounting, the fully installed cost of an asset. This is the amount that, by law, may be written off over time for tax purposes.

Capitalized expenditures Expenditures that may provide benefits into the future and therefore are treated as capital outlays and not as expenses of the period in which they were incurred.

Sale or Disposal of a Depreciable Asset. In general, if a depreciable asset used in business is sold for more than its depreciated (tax) book value, any amount realized in excess of book value but less than the asset's depreciable basis is considered a "recapture of depreciation" and is taxed at the firm's ordinary income tax rate. This effectively reverses any positive tax benefits of having taken "too much" depreciation in earlier years—that is, reducing (tax) book value below market value. If the asset happens to sell for more than its depreciable basis (which, by the way, is not too likely), the portion of the total amount in excess of the depreciable basis is taxed at the capital gains tax rate (which currently is equal to the firm's ordinary income tax rate, or a maximum of 35 percent).

If the asset sells for less than (tax) book value, a loss is incurred equal to the difference between sales price and (tax) book value. In general, this loss is deducted from the firm's ordinary income. In effect, an amount of taxable income equal to the loss is "shielded" from being taxed. The net result is a tax-shield savings equal to the firm's ordinary tax rate multiplied by the loss on the sale of the depreciable asset. Thus, a "paper" loss is cause for a "cash" savings.

Our discussion on the tax consequences of the sale of a depreciable asset has assumed no additional complicating factors. In actuality, a number of complications can and often do occur. Therefore, the reader is cautioned to refer to the tax code and/or a tax specialist when faced with the tax treatment of a sale of an asset. In examples and problems, for ease of calculation we will generally use a 40 percent marginal ordinary income tax rate.

Calculating the Incremental Cash Flows

We now face the task of identifying the specific components that determine a project's relevant cash flows. We need to keep in mind both the concerns enumerated in our "Cash-Flow Checklist" (Table 21-1) as well as the various tax considera-

TABLE 21-2 MACRS Depreciation Percentages

Recovery Year	Property Class 3-Year	5-Year	7-Year	10-Year
1	33.33%	20.00%	14.29%	10.00%
2	44.45	32.00	24.49	18.00
3	14.81	19.20	17.49	14.40
4	7.41	11.52	12.49	11.52
5		11.52	8.93	9.22
6		5.76	8.92	7.37
7			8.93	6.55
8			4.46	6.55
9				6.56
10				6.55
11				3.28
TOTALS	100.00%	100.00%	100.00%	100.00%

tions just discussed. It is helpful to place project cash flows into three categories based on timing:

1. *Initial cash outflow*—the initial net cash investment.
2. *Interim incremental net cash flows*—those net cash flows occurring after the initial cash investment but not including the final period's cash flow.
3. *Terminal-year incremental net cash flow*—the final period's net cash flow. (This period's cash flow is singled out for special attention because a particular set of cash flows often occurs at project termination.)

Initial Cash Outflow. In general, the initial cash outflow for a project is determined as follows in Table 21-3. As seen, the cost of the asset is subject to adjustments in order to reflect the totality of cash flows associated with its acquisition. These cash flows include installation costs, changes in net working capital, sale proceeds from the disposition of any assets replaced, and tax adjustments.

Interim Incremental Net Cash Flows. After making the initial cash outflow that is necessary to begin implementing a project, the firm hopes to benefit from the future cash inflows generated by the project. Generally, these future cash flows can be determined by following the step-by-step procedure outlined in Table 21-4.

Notice that we first deduct any increase (add any decrease) in incremental tax depreciation related to project acceptance—see step (b)—in determining the "net change in income before taxes." However, a few steps later we add back any increase (deduct any decrease) in tax depreciation—see step (f)—in determining "incremental net cash flow for the period." What is going on here? Well, tax depreciation itself, as you may remember, is a noncash charge against operating income that lowers taxable income. So we need to consider it as we determine the incremental effect that project acceptance has on the firm's taxes. However, we ultimately

TABLE 21-3 Basic Format for Determining Initial Cash Outflow

a)		Cost of "new" asset(s)
b)	+	Capitalized expenditures (for example, installation costs, shipping expenses, etc.)*
c)	+(−)	Increased (decreased) level of "net" working capital**
d)	−	Net proceeds from sale of "old" asset(s) if the investment is a replacement decision
e)	+(−)	Taxes (tax savings) due to the sale of "old" asset(s) if the investment is a replacement decision
f)	=	Initial cash outflow

Asset cost plus capitalized expenditures from the basis upon which tax depreciation is computed.

***Any change in working capital should be considered "net" of any spontaneous changes in current liabilities that occur because the project is implemented.*

TABLE 21-4 Basic Format for Determining Interim Incremental Net Cash Flow (per Period)

a)		Net increase (decrease) in operating revenue less (plus) any net increase (decrease) in operating expenses, excluding depreciation
b)	−(−)	Net increase (decrease) in tax depreciation charges
c)	=	Net change in income before taxes
d)	−(−)	Net increase (decrease) in taxes
e)	=	Net change in income after taxes
f)	+(−)	Net increase (decrease) in tax depreciation charges
g)	=	Incremental net cash flow for the period

need to add back any increase (subtract any decrease) in tax depreciation to our resulting "net change in income after taxes" figure so as not to understate the project's effect on cash flow. If we somehow knew in advance the incremental effect on taxes caused by project acceptance, we could simply skip steps (b), (c), (e), and (f) entirely. An example may help to clarify the issue.

Assume that we apply the step-by-step framework outlined in Table 21-4 to the purchase of a new machine with the following results for year 2 of the project's life:

			Cash And/Or Noncash Figures	Cash Figures Only
a)		Net increase in operating revenue less any net increase in operating expenses, excluding depreciation	$7,410	$7,410
b)	−	Net increase in tax depreciation charges	(4,000)	
c)	=	Net change in income before taxes	$3,410	
d)	−	Net increase in taxes (40% rate)	(1,364)	(1,364)
e)	=	Net change in income after taxes	$2,046	
f)	+	Net increase in tax depreciation charges	4,000	
g)	=	Incremental net cash flow for the period	$6,046	$6,046

Notice how advance knowledge of the machine's effect on the "net increase in taxes" would allow us to skip four calculation steps. In most cases, however, you will probably have to rely on the longer step-by-step procedure because such "advance knowledge" about taxes will not be available.

Terminal-Year Incremental Net Cash Flow. Finally, we turn our attention to determining the project's incremental cash flow in its final, or terminal, year of existence. We apply the same step-by-step procedure for this period's cash flow as we did to those in all the interim periods. In addition, we give special recognition to a few cash flows that are often connected only with project termination. These potential project windup cash flows are (1) the salvage value of any sold or disposed assets, (2) taxes (tax savings) related to asset sale or disposal, and (3) any project-termination-related change in working capital—generally, any initial working capital investment is now returned as an additional cash inflow. Table 21-5 summarizes all the necessary steps and highlights in color those steps that are reserved especially for project termination.

Example of Asset Expansion

To illustrate the information needed for a capital budgeting decision, we examine the following situation. The Faversham Fish Farm is considering the introduction of a new fish-flaking facility. To launch the facility, it will need to spend $90,000 for special equipment. The equipment has a useful life of four years and is in the three-year property class for tax purposes. Shipping and installation expenditures equal $10,000, and the machinery has an expected final salvage value, four years from now, of $15,000. The machinery is to be housed in an abandoned warehouse next to the main processing plant. The old warehouse has no alternative economic use. No additional "net" working capital is needed. The marketing department envisions that use of the new facility will generate additional net operating revenue cash flows, before consideration of depreciation and taxes, as follows:

	End of Year			
	1	2	3	4
Net cash flows	$35,167	$36,250	$55,725	$32,258

Assuming that the marginal tax rate equals 40 percent, we now need to estimate the project's relevant incremental cash flows.

The first step is to estimate the project's initial cash outflow:

Step A: Estimating initial cash outflow

	Cost of "new" asset(s)	$ 90,000
+	Capitalized expenditures (shipping and installation)	10,000
=	Initial cash outflow	$100,000

TABLE 21-5 Basic Format for Determining Terminal Year Incremental Net Cash Flow

a)		Net increase (decrease) in operating revenue less (plus) any net increase (decrease) in operating expenses, excluding depreciation
b)	−⊇(+)	Net increase (decrease) in tax depreciation charges
c)	=⊇	Net change in income before taxes
d)	−⊇(+)	Net increase (decrease) in taxes
e)	=	Net change in income after taxes
f)	−⊇(−)	Net increase (decrease) in tax depreciation charges
g)	=⊇	Incremental cash flow for the terminal year before project windup considerations
h)	+	Final salvage value of "new" asset(s)
i)	−⊇(+)	Taxes (tax savings) due to sale or disposal of "new" asset(s)
j)	+⊇(−)	Decreased (increased) level of "net" working capital*
k)	=	Terminal year incremental net cash flow

**Any change in working capital should be considered "net" of any spontaneous changes in current liabilities that occur because the project is terminated.*

The next steps involve calculating the incremental future cash flows.

		End of Year			
		1	2	3	4
Step B: Calculating interim incremental net cash flows (years 1 to 3)					
	Net change in operating revenue, excluding depreciation	$ 35,167	$ 36,250	$ 55,725	$ 32,258
−	Net increase in tax depreciation charges[a]	(33,330)	(44,450)	(14,810)	(7,410)
=	Net change in income before taxes	$ 1,837	$ (8,200)	$ 40,915	$ 24,848
−(+)	Net increase (decrease) in taxes (40% rate)	(735)	3,280[b]	(16,366)	(9,939)
=	Net change in income after taxes	$ 1,102	$ (4,920)	$ 24,549	$ 14,909
+	Net increase in tax depreciation charges	33,330	44,450	14,810	7,410
=	Incremental net cash flow for years 1 to 3	$ 34,432	$ 39,530	$ 39,359	
Step C: Calculating terminal-year incremental net cash flow					
=	Incremental cash flow for the terminal year before project windup considerations				$ 22,319
+	Final salvage value of "new" asset(s)				16,500[c]
−	Taxes due to sale or disposal of "new" asset(s)				(6,600)
=	Terminal-year incremental net cash flow				$ 32,219

[a]MACRS depreciation percentages for 3-year property class asset applied against asset with a depreciable basis of $100,000.

[b]Assumes that tax loss shields other income of the firm.

[c]Assumes salvage value is recapture of depreciation and taxed at ordinary income rate of 40 percent.

The expected incremental net cash flows from the project are

	End Of Year				
	0	1	2	3	4
Net cash flows	($100,000)	$34,432	$39,530	$39,359	$32,219

Thus, for an initial cash outflow of $100,000, the firm expects to generate net cash flows of $34,432, $39,530, $39,359, and $32,219 over the next four years. This data represents the relevant cash-flow information that we need in order to judge the attractiveness of the project.

By now, you are probably dying to know whether the Faversham Fish Farm should favor the fish-flaking facility. However, we will leave the analysis of these cash flows until the next chapter. Our concern here has been simply to determine the relevant cash-flow information needed.

Example of Asset Replacement

To go to a somewhat more complicated example, we suppose that we are considering the purchase of a new automotive-glass mold to replace an old mold and that we need to obtain cash-flow information in order to evaluate the attractiveness of this project. The purchase price of the new mold is $18,500, and it will require an additional $1,500 to install, bringing the total cost to $20,000. The old mold, which has a remaining useful life of four years, can be sold for its depreciated (tax) book value of $2,000. The old mold would have no salvage value if held to the end of its useful life. Notice that since salvage value equals tax book value, taxes due to the sale of the old asset are zero. The initial cash outflow for the investment project, therefore, is $18,000 as follows:

	Cost of "new" asset	$18,500
+	Capitalized expenditures (shipping and installation)	1,500
−	Net proceeds from sale of "old" asset	(2,000)
+	Taxes (tax savings) due to sale of "old" asset	0
=	Initial cash outflow	$18,000

The new machine should cut labor and maintenance costs and produce other cash savings totaling $7,100 a year before taxes for each of the next four years, after which it will probably not provide any savings nor have a salvage value. These savings represent the net operating revenue savings to the firm if it replaces the old mold with the new one. Remember, we are concerned with the differences in the cash flows resulting from continuing to use the old mold versus replacing it with a new one.

Suppose that the new mold we are considering falls into the three-year property category for MACRS depreciation. Moreover, assume the following in regards to the old mold:

1. The original depreciable basis was $9,000.
2. The mold fell into the three-year property class.
3. The remaining depreciable life is two years.

Because we are interested in the incremental impact of the project, we must subtract depreciation charges on the old mold from depreciation charges on the new one to obtain the incremental depreciation charges associated with the project. Given the information provided plus the appropriate MACRS depreciation percentages, we are able to calculate the difference in depreciation charges resulting from the acceptance of the project. The necessary calculations are as follows:

		YEAR			
		1	2	3	4
a)	New mold's depreciable basis	$20,000	$20,000	$20,000	$20,000
b) ×	MACRS depreciation (%)	× .3333	× .4445	× .1481	× .0741
c) =	New mold's periodic depreciation	$ 6,666	$ 8,890	$ 2,962	$ 1,482
d)	Old mold's depreciable basis	$ 9,000	$ 9,000	$ 9,000	$ 9,000
e) ×	MACRS depreciation (%)	× .1481	× .0741	× 0	× 0
f) =	Old mold's *remaining* periodic depreciation	$ 1,333	$ 667	$ 0	$ 0
g)	Net increase in tax depreciation charges Line (c) – Line (f)	$ 5,333	$ 8,223	$ 2,962	$ 1,482

We can now calculate the future incremental cash flows as follows:

		End Of Year			
		1	2	3	4
Interim incremental net cash flows (years 1 to 3)					
	Net change in operating revenue, excluding depreciation	$ 7,100	$ 7,100	$ 7,100	$ 7,100
–	Net increase in tax depreciation charges	(5,333)	(8,223)	(2,962)	(1,482)
=	Net change in income before taxes	$ 1,767	$(1,123)	$ 4,138	$ 5,618
–(+)	Net increase (decrease) in taxes (40% rate)	(707)	449[a]	(1,655)	(2,247)
=	Net change in income after taxes	$ 1,060	$ (674)	$ 2,483	$ 3,371
+	Net increase in tax depreciation charges	5,333	8,223	2,962	1,482
=	Incremental net cash flow for years 1 to 3	$ 6,393	$ 7,549	$ 5,445	
Terminal-year incremental net cash flow					
=	Incremental cash flow for the terminal year before project windup considerations				$ 4,853
+	Final salvage value of "new" asset				0
–	Taxes (tax savings) due to sale or disposal of "new" asset				0
=	Terminal-year incremental net cash flow				$ 4,853

[a]*Assumes that tax loss shields other income of the firm.*

The expected incremental net cash flows from the replacement project are:

	End Of Year				
	0	1	2	3	4
Net cash flows	($18,000)	$6,393	$7,549	$5,445	$4,853

For an initial cash outflow of $18,000, then, we are able to replace an old glass mold with a new one that is expected to result in net cash flows of $6,393, $7,549, $5,445, and $4,853 over the next four years. As in the previous example, the relevant cash-flow information for capital budgeting purposes is expressed on an incremental, after-tax basis.

SUMMARY

- *Capital budgeting* is the process of identifying, analyzing, and selecting investment projects whose returns (cash flows) are expected to extend beyond one year.
- Specifically, capital budgeting involves (1) generating investment project proposals consistent with the firm's strategic objectives; (2) estimating after-tax incremental operating cash flows for the investment projects; (3) evaluating project incremental cash flows; (4) selecting projects based on a value-maximizing acceptance criterion; and (5) continually reevaluating implemented investment projects and performing postaudits for completed projects.
- Since cash, not accounting income, is central to all decisions of the firm, we express the benefits we expect to receive from a project in terms of *cash flows*-rather than income flows.
- Cash flows should be measured on an *incremental, after-tax* basis. In addition, our concern is with *operating*, not financing, flows.
- Tax depreciation under the Modified Accelerated Cost Recovery System (1986 Tax Reform Act) has a significant effect on the size and pattern of cash flows. Also affecting the size and pattern of cash flows is the presence of salvage value and project-driven changes in working capital requirements.
- It is helpful to place project cash flows into three categories based on timing: (1) the initial cash outflow, (2) interim incremental net cash flows, and (3) the terminal-year incremental net cash flow.

QUESTIONS

1. When relevant cash flows are examined, why is an increase in tax depreciation at first deducted and then later added back in determining incremental net cash flow for a period?
2. In capital budgeting, should the following be ignored, or rather added or subtracted from the new machine's purchase price when estimating initial cash outflow? When estimating the machine's depreciable basis?

a. The market value of the old machine is $500, the old machine has a remaining useful life, and the investment is a replacement decision.
b. An additional investment in inventory of $2,000 is required.
c. $200 is required to ship the new machine to the plant site.
d. A concrete foundation for the new machine will cost $250.
e. Training of the machine operator will cost $300.

3. In determining the expected cash flows from a new investment project, why should past sunk costs be ignored in the estimates?
4. Discuss the adjustments in the capital budgeting process that should be made to compensate for expected inflation.
5. What is the purpose of requiring more levels of management approval, the larger the proposed capital expenditure? Is more information also required in support of the request?
6. What is the difference between a product expansion and an equipment replacement investment?

SELF-CORRECTION PROBLEMS

1. Pilsudski Coal Company is considering the replacement of two machines that are three years old with a new, more efficient machine. The two old machines could be sold currently for a total of $70,000 in the secondary market, but they would have a zero final salvage value if held to the end of their remaining useful life. Their original depreciable basis totaled $300,000. They have a depreciated tax book value of $86,400, and a remaining useful life of eight years. MACRS depreciation is used on these machines, and they are five-year property class assets. The new machine can be purchased and installed for $480,000. It has a useful life of eight years, at the end of which a salvage value of $40,000 is expected. The machine falls into the five-year property class for accelerated cost recovery (depreciation) purposes. Due to its greater efficiency, the new machine is expected to result in incremental annual operating savings of $100,000. The company's corporate tax rate is 40 percent, and if a loss occurs in any year on the project, it is assumed that the company can offset the loss against other company income.

   What are the incremental cash inflows over the eight years, and what is the incremental cash outflow at time 0?

2. The Fresno Finial Fabricating Works is considering automating its existing finial casting and assembly department. The plant manager, Mel Content, has accumulated the following information for you:
   - The automation proposal would result in reduced labor costs of $150,000 per year.
   - The cost of defects is expected to remain at $5,000 even if the new automation proposal is accepted.
   - New equipment costing $500,000 would need to be purchased. For financial reporting purposes, the equipment will be depreciated on a straight-line basis over its useful four-year life. For tax purposes, however, the equipment falls into the three-year property class and will be depreciated using the MACRS depreciation percentages. The estimated final salvage value of the new equipment is $50,000.

- Annual maintenance costs will increase from $2,000 to $8,000 if the new equipment is purchased.
- The company is subject to a marginal tax rate of 40 percent.

What are the relevant incremental cash inflows over the proposal's useful life, and what is the incremental cash outflow at time 0?

PROBLEMS

1. Thoma Pharmaceutical Company may buy DNA-testing equipment costing $60,000. This equipment is expected to reduce labor costs of the clinical staff by $20,000 annually. The equipment has a useful life of five years but falls in the three-year property class for cost recovery (depreciation) purposes. No salvage value is expected at the end. The corporate tax rate for Thoma (combined federal and state) is 38 percent, and its required rate of return is 15 percent. (If profits after taxes on the project are negative in any year, the firm will offset the loss against other firm income for that year.) On the basis of this information, what are the relevant cash flows?
2. In Problem 1, suppose that 6 percent inflation in savings from labor costs is expected over the last four years, so that savings in the first year are $20,000, savings in the second year are $21,200, and so forth.
   a. On the basis of this information, what are the relevant cash flows?
   b. If working capital of $10,000 were required in addition to the cost of the equipment and this additional investment were needed over the life of the project, what would be the effect on the relevant cash flow? (All other things are the same as in Problem 2, part (a).)
3. The City of San Jose must replace a number of its concrete-mixer trucks with new trucks. It has received two bids and has evaluated closely the performance characteristics of the various trucks. The Rockbuilt truck, which costs $74,000, is top-of-the-line equipment. The truck has a life of eight years, assuming that the engine is rebuilt in the fifth year. Maintenance costs of $2,000 a year are expected in the first four years, followed by total maintenance and rebuilding costs of $13,000 in the fifth year. During the last three years, maintenance costs are expected to be $4,000 a year. At the end of eight years the truck will have an estimated scrap value of $9,000.

   A bid from Bulldog Trucks, Inc., is for $59,000 a truck. Maintenance costs for the truck will be higher. In the first year they are expected to be $3,000, and this amount is expected to increase by $1,500 a year through the eighth year. In the fourth year the engine will need to be rebuilt, and this will cost the company $15,000 in addition to maintenance costs in that year. At the end of eight years the Bulldog truck will have an estimated scrap value of $5,000.
   a. What are the relevant cash flows related to the trucks of each bidder? Ignore tax considerations, as the City of San Jose pays no taxes.
   b. Using the figures determined in part (a), what are the cash-flow savings each year that can be obtained by going with the more expensive truck rather than the less expensive one? (That is, calculate the periodic cash-flow differences between the two cash-flow streams—assume that any net cost savings are positive benefits.)
4. U.S. Blivet is contemplating the purchase of a more advanced blivet-extrusion

machine to replace the machine currently being used in its production process. The firm's production engineers contend that the newer machine will turn out the current volume of output more efficiently. They note the following facts in support of their contention.

- The old machine can be used for four more years. It has a *current* salvage value of $8,000; but if held to the end of its useful life, the old machine would have an estimated *final* salvage value of $2,000. This is the final year that tax depreciation will be taken on the machine, and the amount of depreciation is equal to the machine's remaining depreciated (tax) book value of $4,520.
- The new, advanced blivet-extrusion machine costs $60,000. Its final salvage value is projected to be $15,000 at the end of its four-year useful life. The new machine falls into the three-year property category for MACRS depreciation.
- The new machine will reduce labor and maintenance usage by $12,000 annually.
- Income taxes on incremental profits are paid at a 40 percent rate.

Calculate the expected annual incremental cash flows for years 1 through 4, as well as the estimated initial cash outflow.

5. In Problem 4, suppose that you just discovered that the production engineers had slipped up twice in their statement of the relevant facts concerning the potential purchase of the new machine:
   - The engineers failed to note that in addition to the $60,000 invoice price for the new machine, $2,000 must be paid for installation.
   - The *current* salvage value of the old machine is not $8,000, but rather only $3,000.

   On the basis of this new information, what are the relevant cash flows for this replacement problem?

SOLUTIONS TO SELF-CORRECTION PROBLEMS

1. Incremental cash inflows:

	End Of Year			
	1	2	3	4
1. Savings	$100,000	$100,000	$100,000	$100,000
2. Depreciation, new	96,000	153,600	92,160	55,296
3. Depreciation, old	34,560	34,560	17,280	0
4. Incremental depreciation Line (2) – Line (3)	61,440	119,040	74,880	55,296
5. Profit change before tax Line (1) – Line (4)	38,560	(19,040)	25,120	44,704
6. Taxes Line (5) × (40%)	15,424	(7,616)	10,048	17,882
7. Profit change after tax Line (5) – Line (6)	23,136	(11,424)	15,072	26,822
8. Operating cash-flow change Line (7) + Line (4) *or* Line (1) – Line (6)	84,576	107,616	89,952	82,118
9. Salvage value × (1 – .40)	0	0	0	0
10. Net cash flow Line (8) + Line (9)	**$ 84,576**	**$ 107,616**	**$ 89,952**	**$ 82,118**

	End Of Year			
	5	6	7	8
1. Savings	$100,000	$100,000	$100,000	$100,000
2. Depreciation, new	55,296	27,648	0	0
3. Depreciation, old	0	0	0	0
4. Incremental depreciation Line (2) – Line (3)	55,296	27,648	0	0
5. Profit change before tax Line (1) – Line (4)	44,704	72,352	100,000	100,000
6. Taxes Line (5) × (40%)	17,882	28,941	40,000	40,000
7. Profit change after tax Line (5) – Line (6)	26,822	43,411	60,000	60,000
8. Operating cash-flow change Line (7) + Line (4) *or* Line (1) – Line (6)	82,118	71,059	60,000	60,000
9. Salvage value × (1 – .40)	0	0	0	24,000
10. Net cash flow Line (8) + Line (9)	**$ 82,118**	**$ 71,059**	**$ 60,000**	**$ 84,000**

Incremental cash outflow at time 0 (initial cash outflow)

Cost – Sale of old machines – Tax savings on book loss
$480,000 – $70,000 – (.40)($86,400 – $70,000) = **$403,440**

2. Incremental cash inflows:

	End Of Year			
	1	2	3	4
1. Labor savings	$150,000	$150,000	$150,000	$150,000
2. Incremental maintenance	6,000	6,000	6,000	6,000
3. Depreciation	166,650	222,250	74,050	37,050
4. Profit change before tax Line (1) − Line (2) − Line (3)	(22,650)	(78,250)	69,950	106,950
5. Taxes Line (4) × (40%)	(9,060)	(31,300)	27,980	42,780
6. Profit change after tax Line (4) − Line (5)	(13,590)	(46,950)	41,970	64,170
7. Operating cash-flow change Line (6) + Line (3) *or* Line (1) − Line (2) − Line (5)	153,060	175,300	116,020	101,220
8. Salvage value × (1 − .40)	0	0	0	30,000
9. Net cash flow Line (7) + Line (8)	**$153,060**	**$175,300**	**$116,020**	**$131,220**

Incremental cash outflow at time 0 (initial cash outflow) = **$500,000** (in this case, simply the cost of the project).

SELECTED REFERENCES

Barwise, Patrick, Paul R. Marsh, and Robin Wensley. "Must Finance and Strategy Clash?" *Harvard Business Review* 67 (September–October 1989), 85–90.

Bierman, Harold, Jr., and Seymour Smidt. *The Capital Budgeting Decision: Economic Analysis of Investment Projects*, 8th ed. New York: Macmillan, 1993.

Hong, Hai. "Inflation and the Market Value of the Firm: Theory and Tests." *Journal of Finance* 32 (September 1977), 1031–48.

Kim, Suk H. "A Summary of Empirical Studies on Capital Budgeting Practices." *Business and Public Affairs* 13 (Fall 1986), 21–25.

Levy, Haim, and Marshall Sarnat. *Capital Investment and Financial Decisions*, 5th ed. Englewood Cliffs, NJ: Prentice Hall, 1994.

Marshuetz, Richard J. "How American Can Allocates Capital." *Harvard Business Review* 63 (January–February 1985), 82–91.

Rappaport, Alfred, and Robert A. Taggart, Jr. "Evaluation of Capital Expenditure Proposals Under Inflation." *Financial Management* 11 (Spring 1982), 5–13.

Seitz, Neil E. *Capital Budgeting and Long-term Financing Decisions.* Hinsdale, IL: Dryden, 1990.

Shapiro, Alan C. "Corporate Strategy and the Capital Budgeting Decision." *Midland Corporate Finance Journal* 3 (Spring 1985), 22–36.

Van Horne, James C. "A Note on Biases in Capital Budgeting Introduced by Inflation." *Journal of Financial and Quantitative Analysis* 6 (January 1971), 653–58.

CHAPTER 22

Capital Budgeting Techniques and Practice

In the previous chapters we developed tools for comparing cash flows that occur in different periods. This chapter uses these techniques in conjunction with additional decision rules to determine when to invest money in long-term assets, a process called *capital budgeting*. In evaluating capital investment proposals, we compare the costs and benefits of each in a number of ways. Some of these methods take into account the time value of money, others do not; however, each of these methods is used frequently in the real world. As you will see, our preferred method of analysis will be the net present value (NPV) method that compares the present value of inflows and outflows.

Capital budgeting is a decision-making process for investment in fixed assets; specifically, it involves measuring the incremental cash flows associated with investment proposals and evaluating the attractiveness of these cash flows relative to the project's cost. Typically these investments involve rather large cash outlays at the outset and commit the firm to a particular course of action over a relatively long period. Thus, if a capital-budgeting decision is incorrect, reversing it tends to be costly.

For example, about 35 years ago the Ford Motor Company's decision to produce the Edsel entailed an outlay of $250 million to bring the car to market and losses of approximately $200 million during the 2 ½ years it was produced—in all, a $450 million mistake.[1] This type of decision is costly to reverse. Fortunately for Ford, it was able to convert Edsel production facilities to produce the Mustang,

[1]"The Edsel Dies, and Ford Regroups Survivors," *Business Week*, November 28, 1959, p. 27.

thereby avoiding an even larger loss. In the 1980s General Motors made a major capital-budgeting decision by investing $3.5 billion to construct its Saturn automobile plant. As of 1993 sales looked good, but only time will tell if this decision proves to be profitable in the long run.

In this chapter we look first at the difficulties associated with finding profitable projects. Four capital-budgeting criteria are subsequently provided for evaluating capital investments, followed by a discussion of the problems created when the number of projects that can be accepted or the total budget is limited. This chapter closes with an examination of capital budgeting in practice.

FINDING PROFITABLE PROJECTS

Without question it is easier to evaluate profitable projects than it is to find them. In competitive markets, generating ideas for profitable projects is extremely difficult. The competition is brisk for new profitable projects, and once they have been uncovered competitors generally rush in, pushing down prices and profits. For this reason a firm must have a systematic strategy for generating capital-budgeting projects. Without this flow of new projects and ideas, the firm cannot grow or even survive for long, being forced to live off the profits from existing projects with limited lives. So where do these ideas come from for new products, for ways to improve existing products, or for ways to make existing products more profitable? The answer is from inside the firm—from everywhere inside the firm.

Typically a firm has a research and development department that searches for ways of improving on existing products or finding new products. These ideas may come from within the R&D department or be based on referral ideas from executives, sales personnel, or anyone in the firm. For example, at Ford Motor Company prior to the 1980s, ideas for product improvement had typically been generated in Ford's research and development department. Unfortunately, this strategy was not enough to keep Ford from losing much of its market share to the Japanese. In an attempt to cut costs and improve product quality, Ford moved from strict reliance on an R&D department to seeking the input of employees at all levels for new ideas. Bonuses are now provided to workers for their cost-cutting suggestions, and assembly line personnel who can see the production process from a hands-on point of view are now brought into the hunt for new projects. The effect on Ford has been positive and significant. Although not all suggested projects prove to be profitable, many new ideas generated from within the firm turn out to be good ones. The best way to evaluate new investment proposals is the topic of the remainder of this chapter.

CAPITAL-BUDGETING DECISION CRITERIA

In deciding whether to accept a new project we will focus on the cash flows. Cash flows represent the benefits generated from accepting a capital-budgeting proposal. In this chapter we will assume a given cash flow is generated by a project and work on determining whether that project should be accepted.

We will consider four commonly used criteria for determining acceptability of investment proposals. The first one is the least sophisticated, in that it does not incorporate the time value of money into its calculations; the other three do take it into account.

Financial Management in Practice

FINDING PROFITABLE PROJECTS IN COMPETITIVE MARKETS—CREATING THEM BY DEVELOPING A COST ADVANTAGE

Iowa Beef Packers and Federal Express have been able to win strong competitive positions by restructuring the traditional production-cost chains in their industries. In beef packing the traditional production sequence involved raising cattle on scattered farms and ranches, shipping them live to labor-intensive unionized slaughtering plants, and then transporting whole sides of beef to grocery retailers, whose butcher departments cut them into smaller pieces and packaged them for sale to grocery shoppers. Iowa Beef Packers revamped the traditional chain with a radically different strategy: Large automated plants employing nonunion labor were built near economically transportable supplies of cattle, and the meat was partially butchered at the processing plant into smaller high-yield cuts (sometimes sealed in plastic casing ready for purchase), boxed, and shipped to retailers. IBP's inbound cattle transportation expenses, traditionally a major cost item, were cut significantly by avoiding the weight losses that occurred when live animals were shipped long distances. Major outbound shipping cost savings were achieved by not having to ship whole sides of beef, with their high waste factor. Iowa Beef's strategy was so successful that it was, in 1985, the largest U.S. meatpacker, surpassing former industry leaders Swift, Wilson, and Armour.

Federal Express redefined the production-cost chain for rapid delivery of small parcels. Traditional firms like Emery and Airborne Express operated by collecting freight packages of varying sizes, shipping them to their destination points via air freight and commercial airlines, and then delivering them to the addressee. Federal Express opted to focus only on the market for overnight delivery of small packages and documents. These were collected at local drop points during the late afternoon hours; flown on company-owned planes during early evening hours to a central hub in Memphis, where from 11 p.m. to 3 a.m. each night all parcels were sorted; and then reloaded on company planes and flown during the early morning hours to their destination points, from which they were delivered that morning by company personnel using company trucks. The cost structure thus achieved by Federal Express was low enough to permit guaranteed overnight delivery of a small parcel anywhere in the United States for a price as low as $11. In 1986 Federal Express had a 58 percent market share of the air-express package-delivery market, versus a 15 percent share for UPS, 11 percent for Airborne Express, and 10 percent for Emery/Purolator.

Source: Arthur A. Thompson, Jr., *Economics of the Firm: Theory and Practice* (Englewood Cliffs, NJ: Prentice Hall, 1989), p. 451. Based on information in Michael E. Porter, *Competitive Advantage* (New York: Free Press, 1985), p. 109.

Payback Period

The *payback period* is the number of years needed to recover the initial cash outlay. As this criterion measures how quickly the project will return its original investment, it deals with cash flows rather than accounting profits. It also ignores the time value of money and does not discount these cash flows back to the present. The accept-reject criterion involves whether the project's payback period is less than or equal to the firm's maximum desired payback period. For example, if a firm's maximum desired payback period is three years and an investment proposal requires an initial cash outlay of $10,000 and yields the following set of annual cash flows, what is its payback period? Should the project be accepted?

Year	After Tax Cash Flow
1	$2,000
2	4,000
3	3,000
4	3,000
5	1,000

In this case, after three years the firm will have recaptured $9,000 on an initial investment of $10,000, leaving $1,000 of the initial investment to be recouped. During the fourth year a total of $3,000 will be returned from this investment, and, assuming it will flow into the firm at a constant rate over the year, it will take one-third of the year ($1,000/$3,000) to recapture the remaining $1,000. Thus, the payback period on this project is three and a third years, which is more than the desired payback period. Using the payback period criterion, the firm would reject this project.

Although the payback period is used frequently, it does have some rather obvious drawbacks, which can best be demonstrated through the use of an example. Consider two investment projects, A and B, which involve an initial cash outlay of $10,000 each and produce the annual cash flows shown in Table 22-1. Both projects have a payback period of two years; therefore, in terms of the payback period criterion both are equally acceptable. However, if we had our choice, it is clear we would select A over B, for at least two reasons. First, regardless of what happens after the payback period, project A returns our initial investment to us earlier within the payback period. Thus, if there is a time value of money, the cash flows occurring within the payback period should not be weighted equally, as they are. In addition, all cash flows that occur after the payback period are ignored. This violates the principle that investors desire more in the way of benefits rather than less—a principle that is difficult to deny, especially when we are talking about money.

To deal with the criticism that the payback period ignores the time value of money, some firms use the *discounted payback period* approach. The discounted payback period method is similar to the traditional payback period except that it uses discounted net cash flows rather than actual undiscounted net cash flows in calculating the payback period. The discounted payback period is defined as the number of years needed to recover the initial cash outlay from the *discounted net cash flows.* The accept-reject criterion then becomes whether the project's discounted payback period is less than or equal to the firm's maximum desired dis-

TABLE 22-1 Payback Period Example

	Projects A	Projects B
Initial cash outlay	–$10,000	–$10,000
Annual net cash inflows:		
Year 1	$ 6,000	$ 5,000
2	4,000	5,000
3	3,000	0
4	2,000	0
5	1,000	0

counted payback period. Using the assumption that the required rate of return on projects A and B illustrated in Table 22-1 is 17 percent, the discounted cash flows from these projects are given in Table 22-2. The discounted payback period for Project A is 3.07 years, calculated as follows:

$$\textbf{Discounted Payback Period}_A = 3.0 + \$74/\$1{,}068 = 3.07 \textbf{ years.}$$

If Project A's discounted payback period was less than the firm's maximum desired discounted payback period, then Project A would be accepted. Project B, on the other hand, does not have a discounted payback period because it never fully recovers the project's initial cash outlay, and thus should be rejected. The major problem with the discounted payback period comes in setting the firm's maximum desired discounted payback period. This is an arbitrary decision that affects which projects are accepted and which ones are rejected. Thus, while the discounted payback period is superior to the traditional payback period, in that it accounts for the time value of money in its calculations, its use is limited by this problem in selecting a maximum desired payback period. Moreover, as we will soon see, the net present value criterion is theoretically superior and no more difficult to calculate.

Although these deficiencies limit the value of the payback period and discounted payback period as tools for investment evaluation, these methods do have several positive features. First, they deal with cash flows, as opposed to accounting profits, and therefore focus on the true timing of the project's benefits and costs, even though the traditional payback period does not adjust the cash flows for the time value of money. Second, they are easy to visualize, quickly understood, and easy to calculate. Finally, although the payback period and discounted payback period methods have serious deficiencies, they are often used as rough screening devices to eliminate projects whose returns do not materialize until later years. These methods emphasize the earliest returns, which in all likelihood are less uncertain, and provide for the liquidity needs of the firm. Although their advantages are certainly significant, their disadvantages severely limit their value as discriminating capital-budgeting criteria.

Net Present Value

The *net present value (NPV)* of an investment proposal is equal to the present value of its annual net cash flows after tax less the investment's initial outlay. The net present value can be expressed as follows:

TABLE 22-2 Discounted Payback Period Example Using a 17 Percent Required Rate of Return

Project A

Year	Undiscounted Cash Flows	$PVIF_{17\%,n}$	Discounted Cash Flows	Cumulative Discounted Cash Flows
0	–$10,000	1.0	–$10,000	–$10,000
1	6,000	.855	5,130	–4,870
2	4,000	.731	2,924	–1,946
3	3,000	.624	1,872	–74
4	2,000	.534	1,068	994
5	1,000	.456	456	1,450

Project B

Year	Undiscounted Cash Flows	$PVIF_{17\%,n}$	Discounted Cash Flows	Cumulative Discounted Cash Flows
0	–$10,000	1.0	–$10,000	–$10,000
1	5,000	.855	4,275	–5,725
2	5,000	.731	3,655	–2,070
3	0	.624	0	–2,070
4	0	.534	0	–2,070
5	0	.456	0	-2,070

$$NPV = \sum_{t=1}^{n} \frac{ACF_t}{(1+k)^t} - IO \tag{22-1}$$

where ACF_t = the annual after-tax cash flow in time period t (this can take on either positive or negative values)

k = the appropriate discount rate that is; the required rate of return or cost of capital[2]

IO = the initial cash outlay

n = the project's expected life

The project's net present value gives a measurement of the *net value* of an investment proposal in terms of today's dollars. Because all cash flows are discounted back to the present, comparing the difference between the present value of the annual cash flows and the investment outlay does not violate the time value of money assumption. The difference between the present value of the annual cash flows and the initial outlay determines the net value of accepting the investment proposal in terms of today's dollars. Whenever the project's NPV is greater than or equal to zero, we will accept the project; and whenever there is a negative value associated with the acceptance of a project, we will reject the project. If the project's net present value is zero, then it returns the required rate of return and should be accepted. This accept-reject criterion is illustrated below:

NPV ≥ 0.0: Accept
NPV < 0.0: Reject

[2]The required rate of return or cost of capital is the rate of return necessary to justify raising funds to finance the project or, alternatively, the rate of return necessary to maintain the firm's current market price per share.

The following example illustrates the use of the net present value capital-budgeting criterion.

EXAMPLE

A firm is considering new machinery, for which the after-tax cash flows are shown in Table 22-3. If the firm has a 12 percent required rate of return, the present value of the after-tax cash flows is $47,678, as calculated in Table 22-4. Furthermore, the net present value of the new machinery is $7,678. Because this value is greater than zero, the net present value criterion indicates that the project should be accepted.

Note that the worth of the net present value calculation is a function of the accuracy of cash flow predictions. Before the NPV criterion can reasonably be applied, incremental costs and benefits must first be estimated, including the initial outlay, the differential flows over the project's life, and the terminal cash flow.

The NPV criterion is the capital budgeting decision tool we will find most favorable for several reasons. First of all, it deals with cash flows rather than accounting profits. In this regard it is sensitive to the true timing of the benefits resulting from the project. Moreover, recognizing the time value of money allows comparison of the benefits and costs in a logical manner. Finally, because projects are accepted only if a positive net present value is associated with them, the acceptance of a project using this criterion will increase the value of the firm, which is consistent with the goal of maximizing the shareholders' wealth.

The disadvantage of the NPV method stems from the need for detailed, long-term forecasts of the incremental cash flows accruing from the project's acceptance. Despite this drawback, the net present value is the most theoretically correct criterion that we will examine. The following example provides an additional illustration of its application.

EXAMPLE

A firm is considering the purchase of a new computer system, which will cost $30,000 initially, to aid in credit billing and inventory management. The incremental after-tax cash flows resulting from this project are provided in Table 22-5. The required rate of return demanded by the firm is 10 percent. To determine the system's net present value, the three-year $15,000 cash flow annuity is first discounted back to the present at 10 percent. From Appendix E in the back of this book, we find that $PVIFA_{10\%,3\ yr}$ is 2.487 Thus, the present value of this $15,000 annuity is $37,305.

Because the cash inflows have been discounted back to the present, they can now be compared with the initial outlay. This is because both of the flows are now stated in terms of today's dollars. Subtracting the initial outlay ($30,000) from the present value of the cash inflows ($37,305), we find that the system's net present value is $7,305. Because the NPV on this project is positive, the project should be accepted.

Profitability Index (Benefit/Cost Ratio)

The *profitability index* (PI), or *benefit/cost ratio,* is the ratio of the present value of the future net cash flows to the initial outlay. Although the net present value investment criterion gives a measure of the absolute dollar desirability of a project, the

TABLE 22-3 NPV Illustration of Investment in New Machinery

	After-Tax Cash Flow
Initial outlay	–$40,000
Inflow year 1	15,000
Inflow year 2	14,000
Inflow year 3	13,000
Inflow year 4	12,000
Inflow year 5	11,000

TABLE 22-4 Calculation for NPV Illustration of Investment in New Machinery

	After-Tax Cash Flow	Present Value Factor at 12 Percent	Present Value
Inflow year 1	15,000	.893	$13,395
Inflow year 2	14,000	.797	11,158
Inflow year 3	13,000	.712	9,256
Inflow year 4	12,000	.636	7,632
Inflow year 5	11,000	.567	6,237
Present value of cash flows			$47,678
Investment initial outlay			–40,000
Net present value			$ 7,678

profitability index provides a relative measure of an investment proposal's desirability—that is, the ratio of the present value of its future net benefits to its initial cost. The profitability index can be expressed as follows:

$$PI = \frac{\sum_{t=1}^{n} \frac{ACF_t}{(1+k)^t}}{IO} \tag{22-2}$$

where ACF_t = the annual after-tax cash flow in time period t (this can take on either positive or negative values)
k = the appropriate discount rate; that is, the required rate of return or cost of capital
IO = the initial cash outlay
n = the project's expected life

The decision criterion with respect to the profitability index is to accept the project if the PI is greater than or equal to 1.00, and to reject the project if the PI is less than 1.00.

PI ≥ 1.0: Accept
PI < 1.0: Reject

TABLE 22-5 NPV Example Problem of Computer System

	After-Tax Cash Flow
Initial outlay	–$30,000
Inflow Year 1	15,000
Inflow Year 2	15,000
Inflow Year 3	15,000

Looking closely at this criterion, we see that it yields the same accept-reject decision as does the net present value criterion. Whenever the present value of the project's net cash flows is greater than its initial cash outlay, the project's net present value will be positive, signaling a decision to accept. When this is true, then the project's profitability index will also be greater than 1, as the present value of the net cash flows (the PI's numerator) is greater than its initial outlay (the PI's denominator). Although these two decision criteria will always yield the same decision, they will not necessarily rank acceptable projects in the same order. This problem of conflicting ranking will be dealt with at a later point.

Because the net present value and profitability index criteria are essentially the same, they have the same advantages over the other criteria examined. Both employ cash flows, recognize the timing of the cash flows, and are consistent with the goal of maximization of shareholders' wealth. The major disadvantage of this criterion, similar to the net present value criterion, is that it requires long, detailed cash flow forecasts.

EXAMPLE

A firm with a 10 percent required rate of return is considering investing in a new machine with an expected life of six years. The after-tax cash flows resulting from this investment are given in Table 22-6. Discounting the project's future net cash flows back to the present yields a present value of $53,667; dividing this value by the initial outlay of $50,000 gives a profitability index of 1.0733, as shown in Table 22-7. This tells us that the present value of the future benefits accruing from this project is 1.0733 times the level of the initial outlay. Because the profitability index is greater than 1.0, the project should be accepted.

Internal Rate of Return

The *internal rate of return (IRR)* attempts to answer this question: What rate of return does this project earn? For computational purposes, the internal rate of return is defined as the discount rate that equates the present value of the project's future net cash flows with the project's initial cash outlay. Mathematically, the internal rate of return is defined as the value *IRR* in the following equation:

$$IO = \sum_{t=1}^{n} \frac{ACF_t}{(1+IRR)^t} \tag{22-3}$$

TABLE 22-6 PI Illustration of Investment in New Machinery

	After-Tax Cash Flow
Initial outlay	–$50,000
Inflow year 1	15,000
Inflow year 2	8,000
Inflow year 3	10,000
Inflow year 4	12,000
Inflow year 5	14,000
Inflow year 6	16,000

where ACF_t = the annual after-tax cash flow in time period t (this can take on either positive or negative values)
IO = the initial cash outlay
n = the project's expected life
IRR = the project's internal rate of return

A project's internal rate of return is simply the rate of return that the project earns.

The decision criterion associated with the internal rate of return is to accept the project if the internal rate of return is greater than or equal to the required rate of return. We reject the project if its internal rate of return is less than this required rate of return. This accept-reject criterion is illustrated below:

IRR ≥ required rate of return: Accept
IRR < required rate of return: Reject

If the internal rate of return on a project is equal to the shareholders' required rate of return, then the project should be accepted. This is because the firm is earning the rate that its shareholders are requiring. However, the acceptance of a project with an internal rate of return below the investors' required rate of return will decrease the firm's stock price.

If the NPV is positive, then the IRR must be greater than the required rate of return, k. Thus, all the discounted cash flow criteria are consistent and will give similar accept-reject decisions. In addition, because the internal rate of return is another discounted cash flow criterion, it exhibits the same general advantages and disadvantages as both the net present value and profitability index, but has an additional disadvantage of being tedious to calculate if a financial calculator is not available.

Computing the IRR for Even Cash Flows

In this section we are going to put our calculators aside and examine the mathematical process of calculating internal rates of return for a better understanding of the IRR.

TABLE 22-7 Calculation for PI Illustration of Investment in New Machinery

	After-Tax Cash Flow	Present Value Factor at 10 Percent	Present Value
Initial outlay	–$50,000	1.000	–$50,000
Inflow year 1	15,000	0.909	13,635
Inflow year 2	8,000	0.826	6,608
Inflow year 3	10,000	0.751	7,510
Inflow year 4	12,000	0.683	8,196
Inflow year 5	14,000	0.621	8,694
Inflow year 6	16,000	0.564	9,024

$$PI = \frac{\sum_{t=1}^{n} \frac{ACF_t}{(1+k)^t}}{IO}$$

$$= \frac{\$13{,}635 + \$6{,}608 + \$7{,}510 + \$8{,}196 + \$8{,}694 + \$9{,}024}{\$50{,}000}$$

$$= \frac{\$53{,}667}{\$50{,}000}$$

$$= 1.0733$$

The calculation of a project's internal rate of return can either be very simple or relatively complicated. As an example of a straightforward solution, assume that a firm with a required rate of return of 10 percent is considering a project that involves an initial outlay of \$45,555. If the investment is taken, the after-tax cash flows are expected to be \$15,000 per annum over the project's four-year life. In this case, the internal rate of return is equal to *IRR* in the following equation:

$$\$45{,}555 = \frac{\$15{,}000}{(1+IRR)^1} + \frac{\$15{,}000}{(1+IRR)^2} + \frac{\$15{,}000}{(1+IRR)^3} + \frac{\$15{,}000}{(1+IRR)^4}$$

From our discussion of the present value of an annuity we know that this equation can be reduced to

$$\$45{,}555 = \$15{,}000 \left[\sum_{t=1}^{4} \frac{1}{(1+IRR)^t}\right]$$

Appendix E gives values for the $\text{PVIFA}_{i,n}$ for various combinations of i and n, which further reduces this equation to

$$\$45{,}555 = \$15{,}000\ (PVIFA_{i,\ 4\ yr})$$

Dividing both sides by \$15,000, this becomes

$$3.037 = PVIFA_{i,\ 4yr}$$

Hence, we are looking for $\text{PVIFA}_{i,\ 4\ yr}$ of 3.037 in the four-year row of Appendix E. This value occurs when i equals 12 percent, which means that 12 percent is the internal rate of return for the investment. Therefore, since 12 percent is greater than the 10 percent required return, the project should be accepted.

Computing the IRR for Uneven Cash Flows

Unfortunately, although solving for the IRR is quite easy when using a financial calculator or spreadsheet, it can be solved directly in the tables only when the future after-tax net cash flows are in the form of an annuity or a single payment. With a calculator the process is simple: One need only key in the initial cash outlay, the cash flows and their timing, and press the *IRR* button. When a financial calculator is not available and these flows are in the form of an uneven series of flows, a trial-and-error approach is necessary. To do this, we first determine the present value of the future after-tax net cash flows using an arbitrary discount rate. If the present value of the future cash flows at this discount rate is larger than the initial outlay, the rate is increased; if it is smaller than the initial outlay, the discount rate is lowered and the process begins again. This search routine is continued until the present value of the future after-tax cash flows is equal to the initial outlay. The interest rate that creates this situation is the internal rate of return. This is the same basic process that a financial calculator uses to calculate an IRR.

To illustrate the procedure, consider an investment proposal that requires an initial outlay of $3,817 and returns $1,000 at the end of year 1, $2,000 at the end of year 2, and $3,000 at the end of year 3. In this case, the internal rate of return must be determined using trial and error. This process is presented in Table 22-8, in which an arbitrarily selected discount rate of 15 percent was chosen to begin the process. The trial-and-error technique slowly centers in on the project's internal rate of return of 22 percent. The project's internal rate of return is then compared with the firm's required rate of return, and if the *IRR* is the larger, the project is accepted.

EXAMPLE

A firm with a required rate of return of 10 percent is considering three investment proposals. Given the information in Table 22-9, management plans to calculate the internal rate of return for each project and determine which projects should be accepted.

Because project A is an annuity, we can easily calculate its internal rate of return by determining the $PVIFA_{i,\,4\,yr}$ necessary to equate the present value of the future cash flows with the initial outlay. This computation is done as follows:

$$IO = \sum_{t=1}^{n} \frac{ACF_t}{(1 + IRR)^t}$$

$$\$10{,}000 = \sum_{t=1}^{4} \frac{\$3{,}362}{(1 + IRR)^t}$$

$$\$10{,}000 = \$3{,}362\ (PVIFA_{i,\,4\,yr})$$

$$2.974 = (PVIFA_{i,\,4\,yr})$$

We are looking for a $PVIFA_{i,\,4\,yr}$ of 2.974, in the four-year row of Appendix E, which occurs in the i = 13 percent column. Thus, 13 percent is the internal rate of return. Because this rate is greater than the firm's required rate of return of 10 percent, the project should be accepted.

TABLE 22-8 Computing IRR for Uneven Cash Flows Without a Financial Calculator

Initial outlay	−$3,817
Inflow year 1	1,000
Inflow year 2	2,000
Inflow year 3	3,000

Solution:

Step 1: Pick an arbitrary discount rate and use it to determine the present value of the inflows.

Step 2: Compare the present value of the inflows with the initial outlay; if they are equal you have determined the IRR.

Step 3: If the present value of the inflows is larger (less than) than the initial outlay, raise (lower) the discount rate.

Step 4: Determine the present value of the inflows and repeat Step 2.

1. Try i = 15 percent:

	Net Cash Flows	Present Value Factor at 15 Percent	Present Value
Inflow year 1	$1,000	.870	$ 870
Inflow year 2	2,000	.756	1,512
Inflow year 3	3,000	.658	1,974
Present value of inflows			$4,356
Initial outlay			−$3,817

2. Try i = 20 percent:

	Net Cash Flows	Present Value Factor at 20 Percent	Present Value
Inflow year 1	$1,000	.833	$ 833
Inflow year 2	2,000	.694	1,388
Inflow year 3	3,000	.579	1,737
Present value of inflows			$3,958
Initial outlay			−$3,817

3. Try i = 22 percent:

	Net Cash Flows	Present Value Factor at 22 Percent	Present Value
Inflow year 1	$1,000	.820	$ 820
Inflow year 2	2,000	.672	1,344
Inflow year 3	3,000	.551	1,653
Present value of inflows			$3,817
Initial outlay			−$3,817

Project B involves a single future cash flow of $13,605, resulting from an initial outlay of $10,000; thus, its internal rate of return can be determined directly from the present-value table in Appendix C as follows:

$$IO = \frac{ACF_1}{(1 + IRR)^t}$$

$$\$10{,}000 = \frac{\$13{,}605}{(1 + IRR)^4}$$

$$\$10{,}000 = \$13{,}605\ (PVIF_{i,\ 4\ yr})$$

$$.735 = (PVIF_{i,\ 4\ yr})$$

This tells us that we should look for a $\text{PVIF}_{i,\ 4\ yr}$ of .735 in the four-year row of Appendix C, which occurs in the $i = 8$ percent column. We may therefore conclude that 8 percent is the internal rate of return. Because this rate is less than the firm's required rate of return of 10 percent, project B should be rejected.

The uneven nature of the future cash flows associated with project C necessitates the use of the trial-and-error method. The internal rate of return for project C is equal to the value of *IRR* in the following equation:

$$\$10{,}000 = \frac{\$1{,}000}{(1 + IRR)^1} + \frac{\$3{,}000}{(1 + IRR)^2} + \frac{\$6{,}000}{(1 + IRR)^3} + \frac{\$7{,}000}{(1 + IRR)^4} \quad \textbf{(22-4)}$$

Arbitrarily selecting a discount rate of 15 percent and substituting it into Eq. (22-4) for IRR reduces the right-hand side of the equation to $11,090, as shown in Table 22-10. Therefore, because the present value of the future cash flows is larger than the initial outlay, we must raise the discount rate to find the project's internal rate of return. Substituting 20 percent for the discount rate, the right-hand side of Eq. (22-4) now becomes $9,763. As this is less than the initial outlay of $10,000, we must now decrease the discount rate. In other words, we know that the internal rate of return for this project is between 15 and 20 percent. Because the present value of the future flows discounted back to present at 20 percent was only $237 too low, a discount rate of 19 percent is selected. As shown in Table 22-10, a discount rate of 19 percent reduces the present value of the future inflows down to $10,009, which is approximately the same as the initial outlay. Consequently, project C's internal rate of return is approximately 19percent.[7] Because the internal rate of return is greater than the firm's required rate of return of 10 percent, this investment should be accepted.

[7]If desired, the actual rate can be more precisely approximated through interpolation as follows:

Discount Rate	Present Value		
19%	$10,009	difference $9	difference $246
IRR	10,000		
20%	9,763		

Thus, IRR = 19% + ($9/246) • 1% = 19.04%

TABLE 22-9 Three IRR Investment Proposal Examples

	A	B	C
Initial outlay	$10,000	$10,000	$10,000
Inflow year 1	3,362	0	1,000
Inflow year 2	3,362	0	3,000
Inflow year 3	3,362	0	6,000
Inflow year 4	3,362	13,605	7,000

TABLE 22-10 Computing IRR for Project C

Try i = 15 percent:

	Net Cash Flows	Present Value Factor at 15 Percent	Present Value
Inflow year 1	$1,000	.870	$ 870
Inflow year 2	3,000	.756	2,268
Inflow year 3	6,000	.658	3,948
Inflow year 4	7,000	.572	4,004
Present value of inflows			$11,090
Initial outlay			–$10,000

Try i = 20 percent:

	Net Cash Flows	Present Value Factor at 20 Percent	Present Value
Inflow year 1	$1,000	.833	$ 833
Inflow year 2	3,000	.694	2,082
Inflow year 3	6,000	.579	3,474
Inflow year 4	7,000	.482	3,374
Present value of inflows			$9,763
Initial outlay			–$10,000

Try i = 19 percent:

	Net Cash Flows	Present Value Factor at 19 Percent	Present Value
Inflow year 1	$1,000	.840	$840
Inflow year 2	3,000	.706	2,118
Inflow year 3	6,000	.593	3,558
Inflow year 4	7,000	.499	3,493
Present value of inflows			$10,009
Initial outlay			–$10,000

Complications with IRR: Multiple Rates of Return

Although any project can have only one NPV and one PI, a single project under certain circumstances can have more than one IRR. The reason for this can be traced to the calculations involved in determining the IRR. Eq. (22-3) states that the IRR is the discount rate that equates the present value of the project's future net cash flows with the project's initial outlay:

$$IO = \sum_{t=1}^{n} \frac{ACF_t}{(1 + IRR)^t} \tag{22-3}$$

However, because Eq. (22-3) is a polynomial of a degree n, it has n solutions. Now if the initial outlay (IO) is the only negative cash flow and all the annual after-tax cash flows (ACF_t) are positive, then all but one of these n solutions is either a negative or imaginary number and there is no problem. But problems occur when there are sign reversals in the cash flow stream; in fact there can be as many solutions as there are sign reversals. Thus, a normal pattern with a negative initial outlay and positive annual after-tax cash flows after that (–, +, +, +, . . . , +) has only one sign reversal, hence only one positive IRR. However, a pattern with more than one sign reversal can have more than one IRR. Consider, for example, the following pattern of cash flows.[8]

	After-Tax Cash Flow
Initial outlay	–$ 1,600
Year 1	+$10,000
Year 2	–$10,000

In this pattern of cash flows there are two sign reversals, from –$1,600 to +$10,000 and then from +$10,000 to –$10,000, so there can be as many as two positive IRRs that will make the present value of the future cash flows equal to the initial outlay. In fact two internal rates of return solve this problem, 25 and 400 percent. Graphically what we are solving for is the discount rate that makes the project's NPV equal to zero; as Figure 22-1 illustrates, this occurs twice.

Which solution is correct? The answer is that neither solution is valid. Although each fits the definition of IRR, neither provides any insight into the true project returns. In summary, when there is more than one sign reversal in the cash flow stream, the possibility of multiple IRRs exists, and the normal interpretation of the IRR loses its meaning.

CAPITAL RATIONING

The use of our capital-budgeting decision rules developed in this chapter implies that the size of the capital budget is determined by the availability of acceptable investment proposals. However, a firm may place a limit on the dollar size of the

[8]This example is taken from James H. Lorie and Leonard J. Savage, "Three Problems in Rationing Capital," *Journal of Business* 28 (October 1955), pp. 229-39.

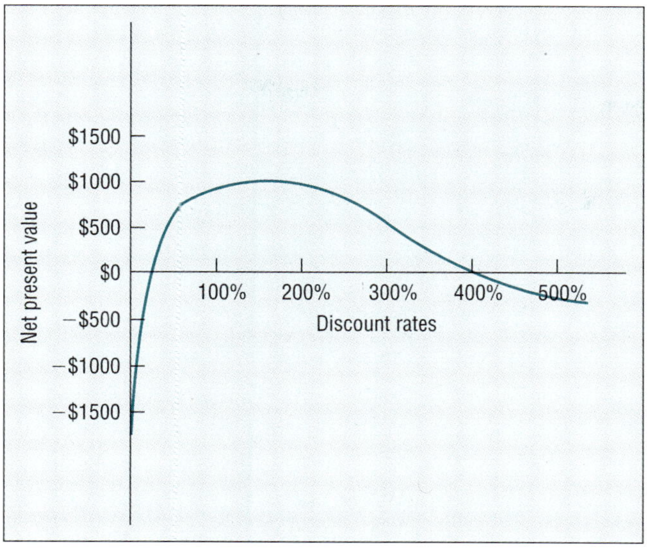

FIGURE 22-1
Multiple IRRs

capital budget. This situation is called *capital rationing*. As we will see, an examination of capital rationing will not only enable us to deal with complexities of the real world better but will serve to demonstrate the superiority of the NPV method over the IRR method for capital budgeting as well.

Using the internal rate of return as the firm's decision rule, a firm accepts all projects with an internal rate of return greater than the firm's required rate of return. This rule is illustrated in Figure 22-2, where projects A through E would be chosen. However, when capital rationing is imposed, the dollar size of the total investment is limited by the budget constraint. In Figure 22-2 the budget constraint of $\$X$ precludes the acceptance of an attractive investment, project E. This situation obviously contradicts prior decision rules. Moreover, the solution of choosing the projects with the highest internal rate of return is complicated by the fact that some projects may be indivisible; for example, it is meaningless to recommend that half project D be acquired.

PERSPECTIVE IN FINANCE

It is always somewhat uncomfortable to deal with problems associated with capital rationing because, under capital rationing, projects with positive net present values are rejected. This is a situation that violates the firm's goal of shareholder wealth maximization. However, in the real world capital rationing does exist, and managers must deal with it. Often when firms impose capital constraints they are recognizing that they do not have the ability to handle more than a certain number or dollar value of new projects profitably.

Rationale for Capital Rationing

We will first ask why capital rationing exists and whether it is rational. In general, three principal reasons are given for imposing a capital-rationing constraint. First,

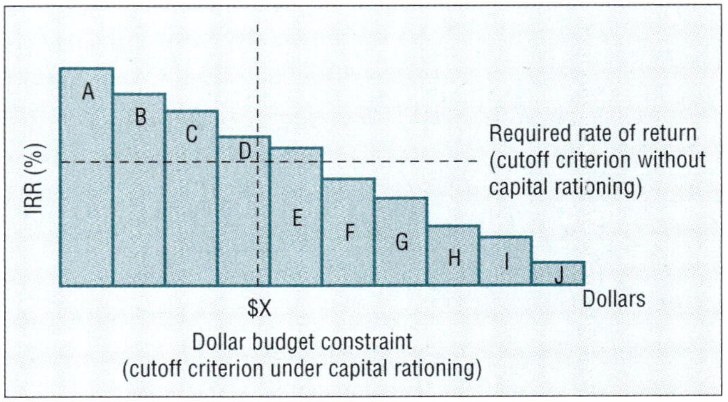

FIGURE 22-2
Projects ranked by IRR

management may think market conditions are temporarily adverse. In the period surrounding the stock market crash of 1987 this reason was frequently given. At that time interest rates were high, and stock prices were depressed. Second, there may be a shortage of qualified managers to direct new projects; this can happen when projects are of a highly technical nature. Third, there may be intangible considerations. For example, management may simply fear debt, wishing to avoid interest payments at any cost. Or perhaps issuance of common stock may be limited to maintain a stable dividend policy.

Despite strong evidence that capital rationing exists in practice, the question remains as to its effect on the firm. In brief, the effect is negative, and to what degree depends on the severity of the rationing. If the rationing is minor and short-lived, the firm's share price will not suffer to any great extent. In this case capital rationing can probably be excused, although it should be noted that any capital rationing that rejects projects with positive net present values is contrary to the firm's goal of maximization of shareholders' wealth. If the capital rationing is a result of the firm's decision to limit dramatically the number of new projects or to limit total investment to internally generated funds, then this policy will eventually have a significantly negative effect on the firm's share price. For example, a lower share price will eventually result from lost competitive advantage if, owing to a decision to limit arbitrarily its capital budget, a firm fails to upgrade its products and manufacturing process.

Capital Rationing and Project Selection

If the firm decides to impose a capital constraint on investment projects, the appropriate decision criterion is to select the set of projects with the highest net present value subject to the capital constraint. This guideline may preclude merely taking the highest-ranked projects in terms of the profitability index or the internal rate of return. If the projects shown in Figure 22-2 are divisible, the last project accepted may be only partially accepted. Although partial acceptances may be possible in some cases, the indivisibility of most capital investments prevents it. If a project is a sales outlet or a truck, it may be meaningless to purchase half a sales outlet or half a truck.

TABLE 22-11 Capital-Rationing Example of Five Indivisible Projects

Project	Initial Outlay	Profitability Index	Net Present Value
A	$200,000	2.4	$280,000
B	200,000	2.3	260,000
C	800,000	1.7	560,000
D	300,000	1.3	90,000
E	300,000	1.2	60,000

To illustrate this procedure, consider a firm with a budget constraint of $1 million and five indivisible projects available to it, as given in Table 22-11. If the highest-ranked projects were taken, projects A and B would be taken first. At that point there would not be enough funds available to take project C; hence, projects D and E would be taken. However, a higher total net present value is provided by the combination of projects A and C. Thus projects A and C should be selected from the set of projects available. This illustrates our guideline: to select the set of projects that maximizes the firm's net present value.

Project Ranking

In the past, we have proposed that all projects with a positive net present value, a profitability index greater than 1.0, or an internal rate of return greater than the required rate of return be accepted, assuming there is no capital rationing. However, this acceptance is not always possible. In some cases, when two projects are judged acceptable by the discounted cash flow criteria, it may be necessary to select only one of them, as they are mutually exclusive. *Mutually exclusive projects* occur when a set of investment proposals perform essentially the same task; acceptance of one will necessarily mean rejection of the others. For example, a company considering the installation of a computer system may evaluate three or four systems, all of which may have positive net present values; however, the acceptance of one system will automatically mean rejection of the others. In general, to deal with mutually exclusive projects, we will simply rank them by means of the discounted cash flow criteria and select the project with the highest ranking. On occasion, however, problems of conflicting ranking may arise. As we will see, in general the net present value method is the preferred decision-making tool because it leads to the selection of the project that increases shareholder wealth the most.

Problems in Project Ranking

There are three general types of ranking problems: the size disparity problem, the time disparity problem, and the unequal lives problem. Each involves the possibility of conflict in the ranks yielded by the various discounted cash flow capital-budgeting criteria. As noted previously, when one discounted cash flow criterion gives

TABLE 22-12 Size Disparity Ranking Problem

Project A	*Project B*
(inflow) $300 at 1 year	(inflow) $1,900 at 1 year
$200 (outflow)	$1500 (outflow)
NPV = $72.70	*NPV* = $227.10
PI = 1.36	*PI* = 1.15
IRR = 50%	*IRR* = 27%

an accept signal, they will all give an accept signal, but they will not necessarily rank all projects in the same order. In most cases this disparity is not critical; however, for mutually exclusive projects the ranking order is important.

Size Disparity

The *size disparity problem* occurs when mutually exclusive projects of unequal size are examined. This problem is most easily clarified with an example.

EXAMPLE

Suppose a firm is considering two mutually exclusive projects, A and B, both with required rates of return of 10 percent. Project A involves a $200 initial outlay and cash inflow of $300 at the end of one year, whereas project B involves an initial outlay of $1,500 and a cash inflow of $1,900 at the end of one year. The net present value, profitability index, and internal rate of return for these projects are given in Table 22-12.

In this case, if the net present value criterion is used, project B should be accepted, whereas if the profitability index or the internal rate of return criterion is used, project A should be chosen. The question now becomes: Which project is better? The answer depends on whether capital rationing exists. Without capital rationing, project B is better because it provides the largest increase in shareholders' wealth; that is, it has a larger net present value. If there is a capital constraint, the problem then focuses on what can be done with the additional $1,300 that is freed if project A is chosen (costing $200, as opposed to $1,500). If the firm can earn more on project A plus the project financed with the additional $1,300 than it can on project B, then project A and the marginal project should be accepted. In effect, we are attempting to select the set of projects that maximize the firm's NPV. Thus, if the marginal project has a net present value greater than $154.40 ($277.10 – $72.70), selecting it plus project A with a net present value of $72.70 will provide a net present value greater than $227.10, the net present value for project B.

In summary, whenever the size disparity problem results in conflicting rankings between mutually exclusive projects, the project with the largest net present value will be selected, provided there is no capital rationing. When capital rationing exists, the firm should select the set of projects with the largest net present value.

Time Disparity

The *time disparity problem* and the conflicting rankings that accompany it result from the differing reinvestment assumptions made by the net present value and internal rate of return decision criteria. The NPV criterion assumes that cash flows over the life of the project can be reinvested at the required rate of return or cost of capital, whereas the IRR criterion implicitly assumes that the cash flows over the life of the project can be reinvested at the internal rate of return. Again, this problem may be illustrated through the use of an example.

EXAMPLE

Suppose a firm with a required rate of return or cost of capital of 10 percent and with no capital constraint is considering the two mutually exclusive projects illustrated in Table 22-13. The net present value and profitability index indicate that project A is the better of the two, whereas the internal rate of return indicates that project B is the better. Project B receives its cash flows earlier than project A, and the different assumptions made as to how these flows can be reinvested result in the difference in rankings. Which criterion should be followed depends on which reinvestment assumption is used. The net present value criterion is preferred in this case because it makes the most acceptable assumption for the wealth-maximizing firm. It is certainly the most conservative assumption that can be made, because the required rate of return is the lowest possible reinvestment rate. Moreover, as we have already noted, the net present value method maximizes the value of the firm and the shareholders' wealth.

Unequal Lives

The final ranking problem to be examined centers on the question of whether it is appropriate to compare mutually exclusive projects with different life spans.

EXAMPLE

Suppose a firm with a 10 percent required rate of return is faced with the problem of replacing an aging machine and is considering two replacement machines, one with a three-year life and one with a six-year life. The relevant cash flow information for these projects is given in Table 22-14.

Examining the discounted cash flow criteria, we find that the net present value and profitability index criteria indicate that project B is the better project, whereas the internal rate of return favors project A. This ranking inconsistency is caused by the different life spans of the projects being compared. In this case the decision is a difficult one because the projects are not comparable.

The problem of incomparability of projects with different lives arises because future profitable investment proposals may be rejected without being included in the

TABLE 22-13 Time Disparity Ranking Problem

	Project A	*Project B*
0	$1000	$1000
1	$100	$650
2	$200	$650
3 years	$2,000	$650
NPV	$758.10	$616.55
PI	1.758	1.617
IRR	35%	43%

analysis. This can easily be seen in a replacement problem such as the present example, in which two mutually exclusive machines with different lives are being considered. In this case a comparison of the net present values alone on each of these projects would be misleading. If the project with the shorter life were taken, at its termination the firm could replace the machine and receive additional benefits, whereas acceptance of the project with the longer life would exclude this possibility, a possibility that is not included in the analysis. The key question thus becomes: Does today's investment decision include all future profitable investment proposals in its analysis? If not, the projects are not comparable. In this case, if project B is taken, then the project that could have been taken after three years when project A terminates is automatically rejected without being included in the analysis. Thus, acceptance of project B not only forces rejection of project A, but also forces rejection of any replacement machine that might have been considered for years 4 through 6 without including this replacement machine in the analysis.

There are several methods to deal with this situation. The first option is to assume that the cash inflows from the shorter-lived investment will be reinvested at the required rate of return until the termination of the longer-lived asset. Although this approach is the simplest, merely calculating the net present value, it actually ignores the problem at hand—that of allowing for participation in another replacement opportunity with a positive net present value. The proper solution thus becomes the projection of reinvestment opportunities into the future—that is, making assumptions about possible future investment opportunities. Unfortunately, while the first method is too simplistic to be of any value, the second is extremely difficult, requiring extensive cash flow forecasts. The final technique for confronting the problem is to assume that reinvestment opportunities in the future will be similar to the current ones. The two most common ways of doing this are by creating a replacement chain to equalize life spans or calculating the project's Equivalent Annual Annuity (EAA). Using a replacement chain, the present example would call for the creation of a two-chain cycle for project A; that is, we assume that project A can be replaced with a similar investment at the end of three years. Thus, project A would be viewed as two A projects occurring back to back, as illustrated in Figure 22-3. The net present value on this replacement chain is $426.50, which is comparable with project B's net present value. Therefore, project A should be accepted because the net present value of its replacement chain is greater than the net present value of project B.

One problem with replacement chains is that depending on the life of each project, it can be quite difficult to come up with equivalent lives. For example, if the two

TABLE 22-14 Unequal Lives Ranking Problem

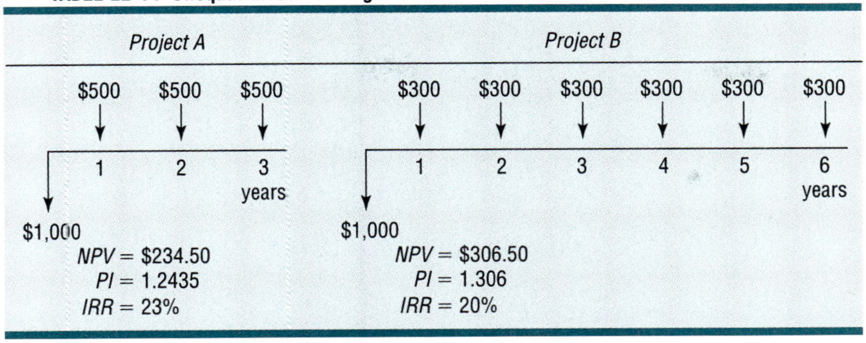

projects had 7- and 13-year lives, a 91-year replacement chain would be needed to establish equivalent lives. In this case it is easier to determine the project's *equivalent annual annuity (EAA)*. A project's EAA is simply an annuity cash flow that yields the same present value as the project's NPV. To calculate a project's EAA we need only calculate a project's NPV and then divide that number by the PVIFA, $_{i,n}$ to determine the dollar value of an n-year annuity that would produce the same NPV as the project. This can be done in two steps as follows:

Step 1: *Calculate the project's NPV.* In Table 22-14 we determined that project A had an NPV of $234.50, whereas project B had an NPV of $306.50.

Step 2: *Calculate the EAA.* The EAA is determined by dividing each project's NPV by the $PVIFA_{i,n}$ where i is the required rate of return and n is the project's life. This determines the level of an annuity cash flow that would produce the same NPV as the project. For project A the $PVIFA_{10\%,\ 3\ yr}$ is equal to 2.487, whereas the $PVIFA_{10\%,\ 6\ yr}$ for project B is equal to 4.355. Dividing each project's NPV by the appropriate $PVIFA_{i,n}$ we determine the EAA for each project:

$$
\begin{aligned}
EAA_A &= NPV/PVIFA_{i,n} \\
&= \$234.50/2.487 \\
&= \$94.29 \\
EAA_B &= \$306.50/4.355 \\
&= \$70.38
\end{aligned}
$$

How do we interpret the EAA? For a project with an n-year life, it tells us what the dollar value is of an n-year annual annuity that would provide the same NPV as the project. Thus, for project A it means that a three-year annuity of $94.29 given a discount rate of 10 percent would produce a net present value the same as project A's net present value, which is $234.50. We can now compare the equivalent annual annuities directly to determine which project is better. We can do this because we now have found the level of annual annuity that produces an NPV equivalent to the project's NPV. Thus, because they are both annual annuities they are comparable. An easy way to see this is to use the EAAs to create infinite-life replacement chains. To do this we need only calculate the present value of an infinite stream of perpetuity of equivalent annual annuities. This is done by using the present value of an infinite annuity formula, that is, simply dividing the equivalent annual annuity by the appropriate discount rate. In this case we find:

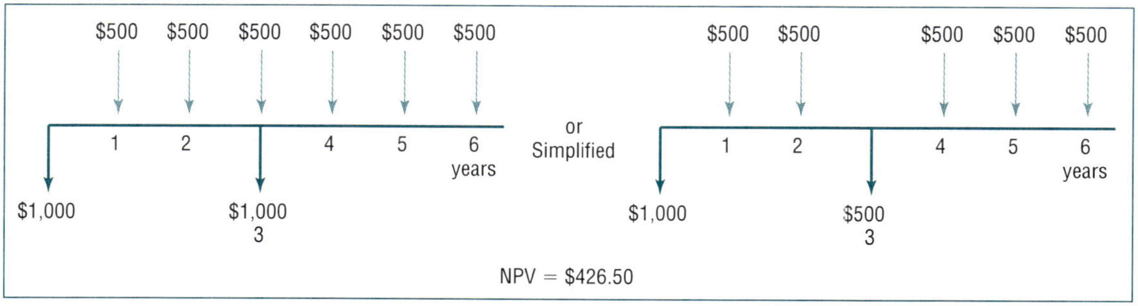

FIGURE 22-3
Replacement chain illustration: two a Project A's back to back

$$
\begin{aligned}
NPV_{\infty, A} &= \$94.29/.10 \\
&= \$942.90 \\
NPV_{\infty, B} &= \$70.38/.10 \\
&= \$703.80
\end{aligned}
$$

Here we have calculated the present value of an infinite-life replacement chain. Because the EAA method provides the same results as the infinite-life replacement chain, it really doesn't matter which method you prefer to use.

ETHICS IN CAPITAL BUDGETING

Although it may not seem obvious, ethics has a role in capital budgeting. Beech-Nut provides an example of how these rules have been violated in the past and what the consequences can be. No doubt this project appeared to have a positive net present value associated with it, but in fact, it cost Beech-Nut tremendously. The *Ethics in Financial Management* insert, "Bad Apple for Baby," tells what occurred.

A GLANCE AT ACTUAL CAPITAL-BUDGETING PRACTICES

During the past 35 years the popularity of each of the capital-budgeting methods has shifted rather dramatically. In the 1950s the payback period method dominated capital budgeting, but through the 1960s and 1970s the discounted cash flow decision techniques slowly displaced the nondiscounted techniques. This movement from the payback period to net present value and the internal rate of return is shown in Table 22-15, which indicates the growth in popularity of these techniques as reflected in surveys of practices over the years. Interestingly, although most firms use the NPV and IRR as their primary techniques, most firms also use the payback period as a secondary decision method for capital budgeting. In a sense they are using the payback period to control for risk. The logic behind this is that because the payback period dramatically emphasizes early cash flows, which are presumably more certain—that is, have less risk—than cash flows occurring later in a project's life, managers believe its use will lead to projects with more certain cash flows.

Ethics in Financial Management

BAD APPLE FOR BABY

It's a widely held but hard to prove belief that a company gains because it is perceived as more socially responsive than its competitors. Over the years, the three major manufacturers of baby food—Gerber Products, Beech-Nut Nutrition and H. J. Heinz—had, with almost equal success, gone out of their way to build an image of respectability.

Theirs is an almost perfect zero-sum business. They know, at any given time, how many babies are being born. They all pay roughly the same price for their commodities, and their manufacturing and distribution costs are almost identical. So how does one company gain a market share edge over another, especially in a stagnant or declining market?

The answer for Beech-Nut was to sell a cheaper, adulterated product. Beginning in 1977, the company began buying a chemical concoction, made up mostly of sugar and water, and labeling it as apple juice. Sales of that product brought Beech-Nut an estimated $60 million between 1977 and 1982, while reducing material costs about $250,000 annually.

When various investigators tried to do something about it, the company stonewalled. Among other things, they shipped the bogus juice out of a plant in New York to Puerto Rico to put it beyond the jurisdiction of federal investigators, and they even offered the juice as a giveaway to reduce their stocks after they were finally forced to discontinue selling it.

In the end, the company pleaded guilty to 215 counts of introducing adulterated food into commerce and violating the Federal Food Drug and Cosmetic Act. The FDA fined Beech-Nut $2 million.

In addition, Beech-Nut's president, Neils Hoyvald, and its vice president of operations, John Lavery, were found guilty of similar charges. Each was sentenced to a year and one day in jail and fined $100,000. Both are now out on appeal on a jurisdiction technicality.

Why did they do it? The Fort Washington, Pa.-based company will not comment. But perhaps some portion of motive can be inferred from a report Hoyvald wrote to Nestle, the company that had acquired Beech-Nut in the midst of his coverup. "It is our feeling that we can report safely now that the apple juice recall has been completed. If the recall had been effectuated in early June [when the FDA had first ordered it], over 700,000 cases in inventory would have been affected. Due to our many delays, we were only faced with having to destroy 20,000 cases."

One thing is clear: Two executives of a company with an excellent reputation breached a trust and did their company harm.

Since 1987, when the case was brought to a close, Beech-Nut's share of the overall baby food market has fallen from 19.1% to 15.8%. So what was gained in the past has been lost in the present, and perhaps for the future as well.

Source: Stephen Kindel, "Bad Apple for Baby," *Financial World*, June 27, 1989, p. 48.

TABLE 22-15 Past Surveys of Capital-Budgeting Practices—Percent of Respondents Using Each Technique

Capital-Budgeting Technique	Klammer, 1959	Klammer, 1964	Klammer, 1970	Petty et al., 1972	Kim and Farragher, 1975	Gitman and Forrester, 1977	Kim and Farragher 1979	Kim, Crick and Kim 1986
Primary method:								
NPV	5%	15%	27%	15%	26%	13%	19%	21%
IRR	8	17	30	41	37	53	49	49
Payback	34	24	12	11	15	9	12	19
Secondary method:								
NPV	2%	3%	7%	14%	7%	28%	8%	24%
IRR	1	2	6	19	7	14	8	15
Payback	18	21	32	37	33	44	39	35

Sources: Thomas Klammer, "Empirical Evidence of the Adoption of Sophisticated Capital Budgeting Techniques," Journal of Business *(July 1972), pp. 387-397; J. William Petty, David F. Scott, Jr., and Monroe M. Bird, "The Capital Expenditure Decision-Making Process of Large Corporations,"* Engineering Economist *(Spring 1975), pp. 159-172; S. H. Kim and E. J. Farragher, "Capital Budgeting Practices in Large Industrial Firms,"* Baylor Business Studies *(November 1976), pp. 19-25; Lawrence J. Gitman and John R. Forrester, Jr., "Forecasting and Evaluation Practices and Performance: A Survey of Capital Budgeting,"* Financial Management *(Fall 1977), pp. 66-71; S. H. Kim and E. J. Farragher, "Current Capital Budgeting Practices," Management Accounting(June 1981), pp. 26-30; and Suk H. Kim, T. Crick, and Sesung H. Kim, "Do Executives Practice What Academics Preach?"* Management Accounting *(November 1986); pp. 49-52.*

A reliance on the payback period came out even more dramatically in a study of the capital-budgeting practices of 12 large manufacturing firms.[9] Information for this study was gathered from interviews over one to three days in addition to an examination of the records of about 400 projects. This study revealed several points of interest. First, firms were typically found to categorize capital investments as mandatory (regulations and contracts, capitalized maintenance, replacement of antiqued equipment, produce quality) or discretionary (expanded markets, new businesses, cost cutting), with the decision-making process being different for mandatory and discretionary projects. Second, it was found that the decision-making process was different for projects of differing size. In fact, approval authority tended to rest in different locations, depending on the size of the project. Table 22-16 provides the typical levels of approval authority.

The study also showed that while the discounted cash flow methods are used at most firms, the simple payback criterion was the measure relied on primarily in one-third of the firms examined. The use of the payback period seemed to be even more common for smaller projects, with firms severely simplifying the discounted cash flow analysis or relying primarily on the payback period. Thus, although discounted cash flow decision techniques have become more widely accepted, their use depends to an extent on the size of the project and where within the firm the decision is being made.

SUMMARY

- The process of capital budgeting involves decision making with respect to investment in fixed assets. We examine four commonly used criteria for deter-

[9]Marc Ross, "Capital Budgeting Practices of Twelve Large Manufacturers," *Financial Management,* 15 (Winter 1986), pp. 15-22.

TABLE 22-16 Project Size and Decision-Making Authority

Project Size	Typical Boundaries	Primary Decision Site
Very small	Up to $100,000	Plant
Small	$100,000 to $1,000,000	Division
Medium	$1 million to $10 million	Corporate investment committee
Large	Over $10 million	CEO & board

mining the acceptance or rejection of capital-budgeting proposals. The first method, the payback period, does not incorporate the time value of money into its calculations, although a variation of it, the discounted payback period, recognizes the time value of money. The discounted methods, the net present value, profitability index, and internal rate of return, do account for the time value of money. These methods are summarized in Table 22-17.

- This chapter introduces several complications into the capital-budgeting process. First, we examine capital rationing and the problems it can create by imposing a limit on the dollar size of the capital budget. Although capital rationing does not, in general, lead to the goal of maximization of shareholders' wealth, it does exist in practice. We also discuss problems associated with the evaluation of mutually exclusive projects. Mutually exclusive projects occur when a set of investment proposals perform essentially the same task. In general, to deal with mutually exclusive projects, we rank them by means of the discounted cash flow criteria and select the project with the highest ranking. Conflicting rankings may arise because of the size disparity problem, the time disparity problem, and unequal lives. The problem of incomparability of projects with different lives is not simply a result of the different lives; rather, it arises because future profitable investment proposals may be rejected without being included in the analysis. Replacement chains and equivalent annual annuities are presented as possible solutions to this problem.

QUESTIONS

1. Why is the capital-budgeting decision such an important process? Why are capital-budgeting errors so costly?
2. What are the criticisms of the use of the payback period as a capital-budgeting technique? What are its advantages? Why is it so frequently used?
3. In some countries, expropriation of foreign investments is a common practice. If you were considering an investment in one of those countries, would the use of the payback period criterion seem more reasonable than it otherwise might? Why?
4. Briefly compare and contrast the NPV, PI and IRR criteria. What are the advantages and disadvantages of using each of these methods?
5. What are mutually exclusive projects? Why might the existence of mutually exclusive projects cause problems in the implementation of the discounted cash flow capital-budgeting criteria?

TABLE 22-17 Capital-Budgeting Criteria

1. Payback period = number of years required to recapture the initial investment

Accept if payback ≤ maximum acceptable payback period
Reject if payback > maximum acceptable payback period

Advantages:
- Uses cash flows.
- Is easy to calculate and understand.
- May be used as rough screening device.

Disadvantages:
- Ignores the time value of money.
- Ignores cash flows occurring after the payback period.
- Selection of the maximum acceptable payback period is arbitrary.

2. Discounted Payback period—the number of years needed to recover the initial cash outlay from the *discounted net cash flows.*

Accept if discounted payback ≤ maximum acceptable discounted payback period
Reject if discounted payback > maximum acceptable discounted payback period

Advantages:
- Uses cash flows.
- Is easy to calculate and understand.
- Consider time value of money.

Disadvantages:
- Ignores cash flows occurring after the payback period.
- Selection of the maximum acceptable payback period is arbitrary.

3. Net present value = present value of the annual cash flows after tax less the investment's initial outlay.

$$NPV = \sum_{t=1}^{n} \frac{ACF_t}{(1+k)^t} - IO$$

where ACF_t = the annual after-tax cash flow in time period t (this can take on either positive or negative values)
k = the appropriate discount rate; that is, the required rate of return or the cost of capital
IO = the initial cash outlay
n = the project's expected life

Accept if $NPV \geq 0.0$
Reject if $NPV < 0.0$

Advantages:
- Uses cash flows.
- Recognizes the time value of money.
- Is consistent with the firm goal of shareholder wealth maximization.

Disadvantages:
- Requires detailed long-term forecasts of the incremental benefits and costs.

6. What are common reasons for capital rationing? Is capital rationing rational?
7. How should managers compare two mutually exclusive projects of unequal size? Would your approach change if capital rationing existed?
8. What causes the time disparity ranking problem? What reinvestment rate assumptions are associated with the net present value and internal rate of return capital-budgeting criteria?
9. When might two mutually exclusive projects having unequal lives be incomparable? How should managers deal with this problem?

TABLE 22-17 Capital-Budgeting Criteria (*continued*)

- Profitability index = ratio of the present value of the future net cash flows to the initial outlay.

$$PI = \frac{\sum_{t=1}^{n} \frac{ACF_t}{(1+k)^t}}{IO}$$

Accept if $PI \geq 1.0$
Reject if $PI < 1.0$

Advantages:
Uses cash flows.
- Recognizes the time value of money.
- Is consistent with the firm goal of shareholder wealth maximization.

Disadvantages:
- Requires detailed long-term forecasts of the incremental benefits and costs.

- Internal rate of return = the discount rate that equates the present value of the project's future net cash flows with the project's initial outlay.

$$IO = \sum_{t=1}^{n} \frac{ACF_t}{(1+IRR)^t}$$

Where IRR = the project's internal rate of return
Accept if $IRR \geq$ required rate of return
Reject if $IRR <$ required rate of return

Advantages:
- Uses cash flows.
- Recognizes the time value of money.
- Is in general consistent with the firm goal of shareholder wealth maximization.
- Possibility of multiple IRRs.

Disadvantages:
- Requires detailed long-term forecasts of the incremental benefits and costs.
- Can involve tedious calculations.

SELF-CORRECTION PROBLEMS

1. You are considering a project that will require an initial outlay of $54,200. This project has an expected life of 5 years and will generate after-tax cash flows to the company as a whole of $20,608 at the end of each year over its five-year life. In addition to the $20,608 cash flow from operations during the fifth and final year, there will be an additional cash inflow of $13,200 at the end of the fifth year associated with the salvage value of the machine, making the cash flow in year 5 equal to $33,808. Thus the cash flows associated with this project look like this:

Year	Cash Flow
0	–$54,200
1	20,608
2	20,608
3	20,608
4	20,608
5	33,808

Given a required rate of return of 15 percent, calculate the following:

a. Payback Period
b. Net present value
c. Profitability index
d. Internal rate of return
Should this project be accepted?

2. The J. Serrano Corporation is considering signing a one-year contract with one of two computer-based marketing firms. Although one is more expensive, it offers a more extensive program and thus will provide higher after-tax net cash flows. Assume these two options are mutually exclusive and that the required rate of return is 12 percent. Given the following after-tax net cash flows:

Year	Option A	Option B
0	–$50,000	–$100,000
1	70,000	130,000

a. Calculate the net present value.
b. Calculate the profitability index.
c. Calculate the internal rate of return.
d. If there is no capital-rationing constraint, which project should be selected? If there is a capital-rationing constraint, how should the decision be made?

PROBLEMS

1. Determine the internal rate of return on the following projects:
   a. An initial outlay of $10,000 resulting in a single cash flow of $17,182 after 8 years.
   b. An initial outlay of $10,000 resulting in a single cash flow of $48,077 after 10 years.
   c. An initial outlay of $10,000 resulting in a single cash flow of $114,943 after 20 years.
   d. An initial outlay of $10,000 resulting in a single cash flow of $13,680 after 3 years.

2. Determine the internal rate of return on the following projects:
   a. An initial outlay of $10,000 resulting in a cash flow of $1,993 at the end of each year for the next 10 years.
   b. An initial outlay of $10,000 resulting in a cash flow of $2,054 at the end of each year for the next 20 years.
   c. An initial outlay of $10,000 resulting in a cash flow of $1,193 at the end of each year for the next 12 years.
   d. An initial outlay of $10,000 resulting in a cash flow of $2,843 at the end of each year for the next 5 years.
3. Determine the internal rate of return to the nearest percent on the following projects:
   a. An initial outlay of $10,000 resulting in a cash flow of $2,000 at the end of year 1, $5,000 at the end of year 2, and $8,000 at the end of year 3.
   b. An initial outlay of $10,000 resulting in a cash flow of $8,000 at the end of year 1, $5,000 at the end of year 2, and $2,000 at the end of year 3.
   c. An initial outlay of $10,000 resulting in a cash flow of $2,000 at the end of years 1 through 5 and $5,000 at the end of year 6.
4. Fijisawa, Inc., is considering a major expansion of its product line and has estimated the following cash flows associated with such an expansion. The initial outlay associated with the expansion would be $1,950,000 and the project would generate incremental after-tax cash flows of $450,000 per year for six years. The appropriate required rate of return is 9 percent.
   a. Calculate the net present value.
   b. Calculate the profitability index.
   c. Calculate the internal rate of return.
   d. Should this project be accepted?
5. You are considering a project with an initial cash outlay of $80,000 and expected after-tax cash flows of $20,000 at the end of each year for 6 years. The required rate of return for this project is 10 percent.
   a. What are the project's payback and discounted payback periods?
   b. What is the project's NPV?
   c. What is the project's PI?
   d. What is the project's IRR?
6. You are considering two independent projects, Project A and Project B. The initial cash outlay associated with Project A is $50,000 and the initial cash outlay associated with Project B is $70,00. The required rate of return on both projects is 12 percent. The expected annual after-tax cash inflows from each project are as follows:

Year	Project A	Project B
0	$12,000	$13,000
1	12,000	13,000
2	12,000	13,000
3	12,000	13,000
4	12,000	13,000
5	12,000	13,000
6	12,000	13,000

Calculate the NPV, PI, and IRR for each project and indicate if the project should be accepted.

7. You are considering three independent projects, Project A, Project B, and Project C. The required rate of return is 10 percent on each. Given the following cash flow information calculate the payback period and discounted payback period for each.

Year	Project A	Project B	Project C
0	–$1,000	–$10,000	–$5,000
1	600	5,000	1,000
2	300	3,000	1,000
3	200	3,000	2,000
4	100	3,000	2,000
5	500	3,000	2,000

If you require a 3-year payback for both the traditional and discounted payback period methods before an investment can be accepted, which projects would be accepted under each criterion?

8. Dowling Sportswear is considering building a new factory to produce aluminum baseball bats. This project would require an initial cash outlay of $5,000,000 and will generate annual after-tax cash inflows of $1,000,000 per year for 8 years. Calculate the project's NPV given:
   a. A required rate of return of 9 percent.
   b. A required rate of return of 11 percent.
   c. A required rate of return of 13 percent.
   d. A required rate of return of 15 percent.
9. Given the following cash flows, determine the internal rate of return for the three independent projects A, B, and C.

	Project A	Project B	Project C
Initial Investment:	–$50,000	–$100,000	–$450,000
Cash Inflows:			
Year 1	$10,000	25,000	200,000
Year 2	15,000	25,000	200,000
Year 3	20,000	25,000	200,000
Year 4	25,000	25,000	—
Year 5	30,000	25,000	—

10. Big Steve's, makers of swizzle sticks, is considering the purchase of a new plastic stamping machine. This investment requires an initial outlay of $100,000 and will generate after-tax cash inflows of $18,000 per year for 10 years. For each of the listed required rates of return, determine the project's net present value.
    a. The required rate of return is 10 percent.
    b. The required rate of return is 15 percent.

c. Would the project be accepted under part (a) or (b)?
d. What is this project's internal rate of return?

11. The D. Dorner Farms Corporation is considering purchasing one of two fertilizer-herbicides for the upcoming year. The more expensive of the two is better and will produce a higher yield. Assume these projects are mutually exclusive and that the required rate of return is 10 percent. Given the following after-tax net cash flows:

Year	Project A	Project B
0	–$500	–$5,000
1	700	6,000

a. Calculate the net present value.
b. Calculate the profitability index.
c. Calculate the internal rate of return.
d. If there is no capital-rationing constraint, which project should be selected? If there is a capital-rationing constraint, how should the decision be made?

12. The State Spartan Corporation is considering two mutually exclusive projects. The cash flows associated with those projects are as follows:

Year	Project A	Project B
0	–$50,000	–$ 50,000
1	15,625	0
2	15,625	0
3	15,625	0
4	15,625	0
5	15,625	$100,000

The required rate of return on these projects is 10 percent.
a. What is each project's payback period?
b. What is each project's net present value?
c. What is each project's internal rate of return?
d. What has caused the ranking conflict?
e. Which project should be accepted? Why?

13. The B. T. Knight Corporation is considering two mutually exclusive pieces of machinery that perform the same task. The two alternatives available provide the following set of after-tax net cash flows:

Year	Equipment A	Equipment B
0	–$20,000	–$20,000
1	12,590	6,625
2	12,590	6,625
3	12,590	6,625
4		6,625
5		6,625
6		6,625
7		6,625
8		6,625
9		6,625

Equipment A has an expected life of three years, whereas equipment B has an expected life of nine years. Assume a required rate of return of 15 percent.

a. Calculate each project's payback period.
b. Calculate each project's net present value.
c. Calculate each project's internal rate of return.
d. Are these project's comparable?
e. Compare these projects using replacement chains and EAA. Which project should be selected? Support your recommendation.

14. The Andrzejewski Corporation is considering two mutually exclusive projects, one with a 3-year life and one with a 7-year life. The after-tax cash flows from the two projects are as follows:

Year	Project A	Project B
0	–$50,000	–$50,000
1	20,000	36,000
2	20,000	36,000
3	20,000	36,000
4	20,000	
5	20,000	
6	20,000	
7	20,000	

a. Assuming a 10 percent required rate of return on both projects, calculate each project's EAA. Which project should be selected?
b. Calculate the present value of an infinite-life replacement chain for each project.

15. The Cowboy Hat Company of Stillwater, Okla., is considering seven capital investment proposals, for which the funds available are limited to a maximum of $12 million. The projects are independent and have the following costs and profitability indexes associated with them:

Project	Cost	Profitability Index
A	$4,000,000	1.18
B	3,000,000	1.08
C	5,000,000	1.33
D	6,000,000	1.31
E	4,000,000	1.19
F	6,000,000	1.20
G	4,000,000	1.18

a. Under strict capital rationing, which projects should be selected?
b. What problems are there with capital rationing?

SOLUTIONS TO SELF-CORRECTION PROBLEMS

1. a. Payback period $= \dfrac{\$54{,}200}{\$20{,}608} = 2.630$ years

b. $$NPV = \sum_{t=1}^{n} \frac{ACF_t}{(1+k)^t} - IO$$

$$= \sum_{t=1}^{4} \frac{\$20{,}608}{(1+.15)^t} + \frac{\$33{,}808}{(1+.15)^5} - \$54{,}200$$

$= \$20{,}608\ (2.855) + \$33{,}808\ (.497) - \$54{,}200$
$= \$58{,}836 + \$16{,}803 - \$54{,}200$
$= \$21{,}439$

c. $$PI = \frac{\sum_{t=1}^{n} \frac{ACF_t}{(1+k)^t}}{IO}$$

$$= \frac{\$75{,}639}{\$54{,}200}$$

$= 1.396$

d. $$IO = \sum_{t=1}^{n} \frac{ACF_t}{(1+\text{IRR})^t}$$

$\$54{,}200 = \$20{,}608\ (PVIFA_{IRR\%,4yr}) + \$33{,}808\ (PVIF_{IRR\%,5yr})$
Try 29 percent
$\$54{,}200 = \$20{,}608\ (2.203) + \$33{,}808\ (.280)$
$= \$45{,}399 + 9{,}466$
$= \$54{,}865$
Try 30 percent
$\$45{,}200 = \$20{,}608\ (2.166) + \$33{,}808\ (.269)$
$= \$44{,}637 + 9{,}094$
$= \$53{,}731$

Thus, the IRR is just below 30 percent and the project should be accepted because the NPV is positive, the PI is greater than 1.0, and the IRR is greater than the required rate of return of 15 percent.

2. a. $NPV_A = \$70,000 \left[\frac{1}{(1+.12)^1}\right] - \$50,000$

$$= \$70,000\ (.893) - \$50,000$$
$$= \$62,510 - \$50,000$$
$$= \$12,510$$

$$NPV_B = \$130,000 \left[\frac{1}{(1+.12)^1}\right] - \$100,000$$

$$= \$130,000\ (.893) - \$100,000$$
$$= \$116,090 - \$100,000$$
$$= \$16,090$$

b. $PI_A = \frac{\$62,510}{\$50,000}$

$$= 1.2502$$

$$PI_B = \frac{\$116,090}{\$100,000}$$

$$= 1.1609$$

c. $\$50,000 = \$70,000\ (PVIF_{i,\,1\,yr})$

$$.7143 = PVIF_{i,\,1\,yr}$$

Looking for a value of $\text{PVIF}_{i,\,1\,\text{yr}}$ in Appendix C, a value of .714 is found in the 40 percent column. Thus, the IRR is 40 percent.

$$\$100,000 = \$130,000\ (\text{FVIF}_{i,\,1\,\text{yr}})$$
$$.7692 = \text{PVIF}_{i,\,1\,\text{yr}}$$

Looking for a value of $\text{PVIF}_{i,\,1\,\text{yr}}$ in Appendix C a value of .769 is found in the 30 percent column. Thus, the IRR is 30 percent.

d. If there is no capital rationing, project B should be accepted because it has a larger net present value. If there is a capital constraint, the problem focuses on what can be done with the additional $50,000 (the additional money that could be invested if project A, with an initial outlay of $50,000, were selected over project B, with an initial outlay of $100,000). In the capital constraint case, if Serrano can earn more on project A plus the marginal project financed with the additional $50,000 than it can on project B, then project A and the marginal project should be accepted.

ALTERNATIVE PROBLEMS

1. Determine the internal rate of return on the following projects:
   a. An initial outlay of $10,000 resulting in a single cash flow of $19,926 after 8 years.
   b. An initial outlay of $10,000 resulting in a single cash flow of $20,122 after 12 years.

c. An initial outlay of $10,000 resulting in a single cash flow of $121,000 after 22 years.
d. An initial outlay of $10,000 resulting in a single cash flow of $19,254 after 5 years.

2. Determine the internal rate of return on the following projects:
   a. An initial outlay of $10,000 resulting in a cash flow of $2,146 at the end of each year for the next 10 years.
   b. An initial outlay of $10,000 resulting in a cash flow of $1,960 at the end of each year for the next 20 years.
   c. An initial outlay of $10,000 resulting in a cash flow of $1,396 at the end of each year for the next 12 years.
   d. An initial outlay of $10,000 resulting in a cash flow of $3,197 at the end of each year for the next 5 years.
3. Determine the internal rate of return to the nearest percent on the following projects:
   a. An initial outlay of $10,000 resulting in a cash flow of $3,000 at the end of year 1, $5,000 at the end of year 2, and $7,500 at the end of year 3.
   b. An initial outlay of $12,000 resulting in a cash flow of $9,000 at the end of year 1, $6,000 at the end of year 2, and $2,000 at the end of year 3.
   c. An initial outlay of $8,000 resulting in a cash flow of $2,000 at the end of years 1 through 5, and $5,000 at the end of year 6.
4. Gecewich, Inc., is considering a major expansion of its product line and has estimated the following cash flows associated with such an expansion. The initial outlay associated with the expansion would be $2,500,000 and the project would generate incremental after-tax cash flows of $750,000 per year for six years. The appropriate required rate of return is 11 percent.
   a. Calculate the net present value.
   b. Calculate the profitability index.
   c. Calculate the internal rate of return.
   d. Should this project be accepted?
5. No alternative problem available.
6. No alternative problem available.
7. No alternative problem available.
8. No alternative problem available.
9. Given the following cash flows, determine the internal rate of return for projects A, B, and C.

	Project A	Project B	Project C
Initial Investment:	$75,000	$95,000	$395,000
Cash Inflows:			
Year 1	$10,000	25,000	150,000
Year 2	10,000	25,000	150,000
Year 3	30,000	25,000	150,000
Year 4	25,000	25,000	
Year 5	30,000	25,000	

10. Bert's, makers of gourmet corn dogs, is considering the purchase of a new plastic stamping machine. This investment requires an initial outlay of $150,000 and will generate after-tax cash inflows of $25,000 per year for 10 years. For each of the listed required rates of return, determine the project's net present value.
    a. The required rate of return is 9 percent.
    b. The required rate of return is 15 percent.
    c. Would the project be accepted under part (a) or (b)?
    d. What is the project's internal rate of return?
11. The Unk's Farms Corporation is considering purchasing one of two fertilizer-herbicides for the upcoming year. The more expensive of the two is the better and will produce a higher yield. Assume these projects are mutually exclusive and that the required rate of return is 10 percent. Given the following after-tax net cash flows:

Year	Project A	Project B
0	–$650	–$4,000
1	800	5,500

    a. Calculate the net present value.
    b. Calculate the profitability index.
    c. Calculate the internal rate of return.
    d. If there is no capital-rationing constraint, which project should be selected? If there is a capital-rationing constraint, how should the decision be made?
12. The Z. Bello Corporation is considering two mutually exclusive projects. The cash flows associated with those projects are as follows:

Year	Project A	Project B
0	–$50,000	–$ 50,000
1	16,000	0
2	16,000	0
3	16,000	0
4	16,000	0
5	16,000	$100,000

    The required rate of return on these projects is 11 percent.
    a. What is each project's payback period?
    b. What is each project's net present value?
    c. What is each project's internal rate of return?
    d. What has caused the ranking conflict?
    e. Which project should be accepted? Why?
13. The Battling Bishops Corporation is considering two mutually exclusive pieces of machinery that perform the same task. The two alternatives available provide the following set of after-tax net cash flows:

Year	Equipment A	Equipment B
0	–$20,000	–$20,000
1	13,000	6,500
2	13,000	6,500
3	13,000	6,500
4		6,500
5		6,500
6		6,500
7		6,500
8		6,500
9		6,500

Equipment A has an expected life of three years, whereas equipment B has an expected life of nine years. Assume a required rate of return of 14 percent.

a. Calculate each project's payback period.
b. Calculate each project's net present value.
c. Calculate each project's internal rate of return.
d. Are these projects comparable?
e. Compare these projects using replacement chains and EAAs. Which project should be selected? Support your recommendation.

14. The Anduski Corporation is considering two mutually exclusive projects, one with a 5-year life and one with a 7-year life. The after-tax cash flows from the two projects are as follows:

Year	Project A	Project B
0	–$40,000	–40,000
1	20,000	25,000
2	20,000	25,000
3	20,000	25,000
4	20,000	25,000
5	20,000	25,000
6	20,000	
7	20,000	

a. Assuming a 10 percent required rate of return on both projects, calculate each project's EAA. Which project should be selected?
b. Calculate the present value of an infinite-life replacement chain for each project.

15. The Taco Toast Company is considering seven capital investment proposals, for which the funds available are limited to a maximum of $12 million. The projects are independent and have the following costs and profitability indexes associated with them:

Project	Cost	Profitability Index
A	$4,000,000	1.18
B	3,000,000	1.08
C	5,000,000	1.33
D	6,000,000	1.31
E	4,000,000	1.19
F	6,000,000	1.20
G	4,000,000	1.18

a. Under strict capital rationing, which projects should be selected?
b. What problems are associated with imposing capital rationing?

CHAPTER 23

Capital Budgeting and Risk Analysis

INTRODUCTION

As international competition increases and technology changes at an ever quickening pace, risk and uncertainty play an increasingly important role in business decisions. In this chapter, we will examine problems in measuring risk and approaches for dealing with it as it affects business decisions.

We will look at the problems facing Judy Lewent, the Chief Financial Officer at Merck & Co., the giant pharmaceutical firm. As we will see, it takes Merck an average of ten years and an investment of $359 million to bring a new drug to market. Quite an investment, particularly when you consider the uncertainty involving what the competition will be like in ten years and what constraints surrounding pricing might be in place as a result of possible health care reform. Moreover, not all new drugs introduced are profitable. In fact, only three out of ten new drugs that Merck introduces produce a positive net present value. How should Merck evaluate projects with uncertain returns that stretch out well into the future? Certainly, they shouldn't treat all projects in the same way, but how should they insure that the decisions they make correctly reflect a project's uncertainty? Complicating Merck's task is the question of what is the appropriate measure of risk for a new project.

RISK AND THE INVESTMENT DECISION

Up to this point, we have ignored risk in capital budgeting; that is, we have discounted expected cash flows back to present and ignored any uncertainty that there might be surrounding that estimate. In reality, the future cash flows associated with the introduction of a new sales outlet or a new product are estimates of what is expected to happen in the future, not necessarily what will happen in the future. For example, when the Ford Motor Company made its decision to introduce the Edsel, you can bet that the expected cash flows it based its decision on were nothing like the cash flows it realized. In effect, the cash flows we have discounted back to the present have been our best estimate the expected future cash flows. A cash flow diagram based on the possible outcomes of an investment proposal rather than the expected values of these outcomes appears in Figure 23-1.

In this section, we will assume that under conditions of risk we do not know beforehand what cash flows will actually result from a new project. However, we do have expectations concerning the possible outcomes and are able to assign probabilities to these outcomes. Stated another way, although we do not know the cash flows resulting from the acceptance of a new project, we can formulate the probability distributions from which the flows will be drawn.

Risk occurs when there is some question as to the future outcome of an event. We will now proceed with an examination of the logic behind this definition. Again, risk is defined as the potential variability in future cash flows.

The fact that variability reflects risk can easily be shown with a coin toss. Consider the possibility of flipping a coin—heads you win, tails you lose—for 25 cents with your finance professor. Most likely, you would be willing to take on this game because the utility gained from winning 25 cents is about equal to the utility lost if you lose 25 cents. Conversely, if the flip is for $1,000 you may be willing to play only if you are offered more than $1,000 if you win—say, you win $1,500 if it turns out heads and lose $1,000 if it turns out tails. In each case, the probability of winning and losing is the same; that is, there is an equal chance that the coin will land heads or tails. In each case, however, the width of the dispersion changes, which is why the second coin toss is more risky and why you may not take the chance unless the payoffs are altered. The key here is the fact that only the dispersion changes; the probability of winning or losing is the same in each case. Thus the potential variability in future returns reflects the risk.

The final question to be addressed is whether or not individuals are in fact risk averse. Although we do see people gambling where the odds of winning are against them, it should be stressed that monetary return is not the only possible return they may receive. A nonmonetary, psychic reward accrues to some gamblers, allowing them to fantasize that they will break the bank, never have to work again, and retire to some offshore island. Actually, the heart of the question is how wealth is measured. Although gamblers appear to be acting as risk seekers, they actually attach an additional nonmonetary return to gambling; the risk is in effect its own reward. When this is considered, their actions seem totally rational. It should also be noted that although gamblers appear to be pursuing risk on one hand, on the other hand they are also eliminating some risk by purchasing insurance and diversifying their investments.

In the remainder of this chapter we assume that although future cash flows are not known with certainty, the probability distribution from which they come is known. Also, since the dispersion of possible outcomes reflects risk, we are prepared to use a measure of dispersion or variability later in the chapter when we quantify risk.

In the pages that follow, there are only two basic issues that we address: (1) What is risk in terms of capital-budgeting decisions, and how should it be measured? (2) How should risk be incorporated into capital-budgeting analysis?

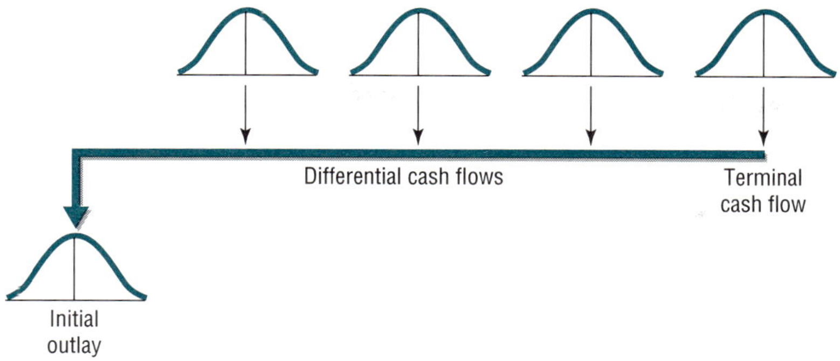

FIGURE 23-1
Cash flow diagram based on possible outcomes

What Measure of Risk Is Relevant in Capital Budgeting

Before we begin our discussion of how to adjust for risk, it is important to determine just what type of risk we are to adjust for. In capital budgeting, a project's risk can be looked at on three levels. First, there is the **project standing alone risk,** which is a project's risk ignoring the fact that much of this risk will be diversified away as the project is combined with the firm's other projects and assets.

Second, we have the project's **contribution-to-firm risk,** which is the amount of risk that the project contributes to the firm as a whole; this measure considers the fact that some of the project's risk will be diversified away as the project is combined with the firm's other projects and assets, but *ignores* the effects of diversification of the firm's shareholders. Finally, there is **systematic risk,** which is the risk of the project from the viewpoint of a well-diversified shareholder; this measure considers the fact that some of a project's risk will be diversified away as the project is combined with the firm's other projects, and, in addition, some of the remaining risk will be diversified away by shareholders as they combine this stock with other stocks in their portfolio. Graphically, this is shown in Figure 23-2.

Should we be interested in the project standing alone risk? The answer is no. Perhaps the easiest way to understand why not is to look at an example. Let's take the case of research and development projects at Johnson & Johnson. Each year Johnson & Johnson takes on hundreds of new R&D projects, knowing that they only have about a 10 percent probability of being successful. If they are successful, the profits can be enormous; if they fail, the investment is lost. If the company has only one project, and it is an R&D project, the company would have a 90 percent chance of failure. Thus, if we look at these R&D projects individually and measure their project standing alone risk, we would have to judge them to be enormously risky. However, if we consider the effect of the diversification that comes about from taking on several hundred independent R&D projects a year, all with a 10 percent chance of success, we can see that these R&D projects do not add much in the way of risk to Johnson & Johnson. In short, because much of a project's risk is diversified away within the firm, project standing alone risk is an inappropriate measure of the level of risk of a capital-budgeting project.

Project standing alone risk
The risk of a project standing alone is measured by the variability of the asset's expected returns. That is, it is the risk of a project ignoring the fact that it is only one of many projects within the firm, and the firm's stock is but one of many stocks within a stockholder's portfolio.

Project's contribution-to-firm risk
The amount of risk that a project contributes to the firm as a whole. That is, a project's risk considering the effects of diversification among different projects within the firm, but ignoring the effects of shareholder's diversification within his or her portfolio.

Systematic risk
The risk of a project measured from the point of view of a well-diversified shareholder. That is, a project's risk taking into account the fact that this project is only one of many projects within the firm, and the firm's stock is but one of many stocks within a stockholder's portfolio.

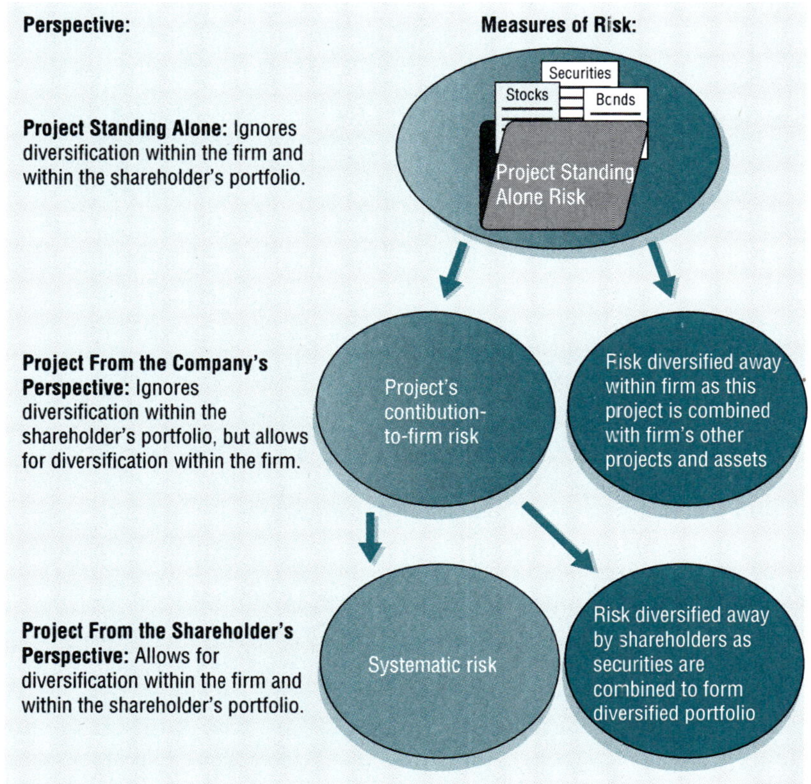

FIGURE 23-2
Looking at three measures of a project's risk

Should we be interested in the project's contribution-to-firm risk? Once again, the answer is no, provided investors are well diversified, and there is no chance of bankruptcy. As shareholders, if we combined our stocks with other stocks to form a diversified portfolio, much of the risk of our security would be diversified away. Thus all that affects the shareholders is the systematic risk of the project, and as such is all that is theoretically relevant for capital budgeting.

Measuring Risk for Capital-Budgeting Purposes and a Dose of Reality—Is Systematic Risk All There Is?

According to the Capital Asset Pricing Model (CAPM), systematic risk is the only relevant risk for capital-budgeting purposes; however, reality complicates this somewhat. In many instances, a firm will have undiversified shareholders including owners of small corporations. Because they are not diversified, for those shareholders the relevant measure of risk is the project's contribution-to-firm risk.

The possibility of bankruptcy also affects our view of what measure of risk is relevant. Because the project's contribution-to-firm risk can affect the possibility of bankruptcy, this may be an appropriate measure of risk if there are costs associated with bankruptcy. Quite obviously, in the real world, there is a cost associated with

Financial Management in Practice

PLIGHT AT THE END OF THE TUNNEL

FOLKSTONE, ENGLAND—Hailing what they called the engineering marvel of the century, Queen Elizabeth II and French President Francois Mitterrand inaugurated the Channel Tunnel crossing today and formally marked the end of Britain's physical isolation from the continent since the last Ice Age.

In a historic celebration that began in the French seacoast village of Coquelles and ended here near the white cliffs of Dover, the two heads of state pledged that the successful completion of the project that eluded visionary builders since Napoleon's time would now bind Britain irrevocably to Europe.

The queen paid tribute to the 15,000 workers on both sides of the channel who toiled for the past seven years and surmounted countless obstacles in finishing Europe's largest construction project "for the benefit of all humanity."**(A)**

Mitterrand too saluted the crowning example of French-British cooperation that aides say has been one of the most gratifying events of his presidency.

"We now have a land frontier," Mitterrand said. "This prodigious work, full of imagination and invention, shows what France and Britain can do when they put together their talent, energy and resources. We can achieve even greater things, so let us vow to do more for the cause of Europe."

Yet even before it enters into service, the Channel Tunnel is being lambasted by critics as a potential white elephant. The undersea link, which features two tubular train lines each running for a length of more than 31 miles, cost $16 billion to build, more than twice the original estimate.

The Anglo-French consortium Eurotunnel, the private enterprise in charge of tunnel operations, is already burdened by $10 billion in debt and expects to runs out of cash by June unless a bank rescue can be arranged.**(B)** Eurotunnel was supposed to start service a year ago, but security checks and other delays will postpone regular traffic for at least another four months. Each day lost is costing an extra $2 million.

Ferry companies, fearing possible extinction, have vowed to launch a price war that could sink the tunnel's hopes of breaking even by the year 2000. Round-trip tunnel fares for a single car, which will start at $330 in the winter and run to $460 in summer, are deemed too high by experts to justify crossing the channel in 35 minutes, half the time it takes with the cheaper ferry crossing.**(C)**

Source: Excerpted from William Drozdiak, "Plight at End of Tunnel," *Washington Post* (May 7, 1994): A1, 14.

bankruptcy. First, if a firm fails, its assets, in general, cannot be sold for their true economic value. Moreover, the amount of money actually available for distribution to stockholders is further reduced by liquidation and legal fees that must be paid. Finally, the opportunity cost associated with the delays related to the legal process further reduces the funds available to the shareholder. Therefore, because there are costs associated with bankruptcy, reduction of the chance of bankruptcy has a very real value associated with it.

Financial Management in Practice

ANALYSIS AND IMPLICATIONS . . .

A. This project illustrates just how large a capital-budgeting project can be. In this case the cost of the Channel Tunnel was $16 billion. Where is the risk? In this case, the risk is that the estimated initial outlay and annual cash flows are not reliable. Given the fact that the initial outlay ran double the estimate, this project could face some serious problems in the years to come.

B. As is evident in this case, not only the future cash flows but the initial outlay estimates can have uncertainty associated with them. Throughout this chapter try to keep in mind that the value of any capital-budgeting decision is dependent on the quality of the inputs. As the old saying goes, "Junk in, junk out."

C. Capital budgeting in the public sector is always difficult. What exactly happens to the Eurotunnel, only time will tell. But as with most capital budgeting projects, it will be difficult to reverse—and if it proves to be unprofitable, it will drain resources for years to come.

Indirect costs of bankruptcy also affect other areas of the firm, including production, sales, and the quality and efficiency of management. For example, firms with a higher probability of bankruptcy may have a more difficult time recruiting and retaining quality managers because jobs with that firm are viewed as being less secure. Suppliers also may be less willing to sell on credit. Finally, customers may lose confidence and fear that the firm may not be around to honor the warranty or to supply spare parts for the product in the future. As a result, as the probability of bankruptcy increases, the eventual bankruptcy may become self-fulfilling as potential customers and suppliers flee. The end result is that the project's contribution-to-firm risk is also a relevant risk measure for capital budgeting.

Finally, problems in measuring a project's systematic risk make its implementation extremely difficult. As we will see later on in this chapter, it is much easier talking about a project's systematic risk than it is measuring it.

Given all this, what do we use? The answer is that we will give consideration to both measures. We know in theory systematic risk is correct. We also know that bankruptcy costs and undiversified shareholders violate the assumptions of the theory, which brings us back to the concept of a project's contribution-to-firm risk. Still, the concept of systematic risk holds value of capital-budgeting decisions, because that is the risk for which shareholders are compensated. As such, we will concern ourselves with both the project's contribution-to-firm risk and the project's systematic risk, and not try to make any specific allocation of importance between the two for capital-budgeting purposes.

METHODS FOR INCORPORATING RISK INTO CAPITAL BUDGETING

In the previous chapter, we ignored any risk differences between projects. This assumption is simple but not valid; different investment projects do in fact contain different levels of risk. We will now look at two methods for incorporating risk into the analysis. The first technique, the *certainty equivalent approach,* attempts to incorporate the manager's utility function into the analysis. The second technique, the *risk-adjusted discount rate,* is based on the notion that investors require higher rates of return on more risky projects.

Certainty Equivalent Approach

The **certainty equivalent approach** involves a direct attempt to allow the decision maker to incorporate his or her utility function into the analysis. The financial manager is allowed to substitute the certain dollar amount that he or she feels is equivalent to the expected but risky cash flow offered by the investment for that risky cash flow in the capital-budgeting analysis. In effect, a set of riskless cash flows is substituted for the original risky cash flows, between both of which the financial manager is indifferent. To a certain extent this process is like the old television program "Let's Make a Deal." On that show, Monty Hall asked contestants to trade certain outcomes for uncertain outcomes. In some cases, contestants were willing to make a trade, and in some cases, they were not; it all depended upon how risk averse they were. The main difference between what we are doing and what was done on "Let's Make a Deal" is that on the TV show contestants were in general not indifferent with respect to the certain outcome and the risky outcome, whereas in the certainty equivalent approach managers are indifferent.

Certainty equivalent approach
A technique for incorporating risk into the capital-budgeting decision in which the decision maker substitutes a set of equivalent riskless cash flows for the expected cash flows and then discounts these cash flows back to the present.

To illustrate the concept of a **certainty equivalent,** let us look at simple coin toss. Assume you can play the game only once and if it comes out heads, you win $10,000, and if it comes out tails you win nothing. Obviously, you have a 50 percent chance of winning $10,000 and a 50 percent chance of winning nothing, with an expected value of $5,000. Thus, $5,000 is your uncertain expected value outcome. The certainty equivalent then becomes the amount you would demand to make you indifferent with regard to playing and not playing the game. If you are indifferent with respect to receiving $3,000 for certain and not playing the game, then $3,000 is the certainty equivalent.

Certainty equivalents
The amount of cash a person would require with certainty to make him or her indifferent between this certain sum and a particular risky or uncertain sum.

To simplify future calculations and problems, let us define certainty equivalent coefficient (α_t) that represents the ratio of the certain outcome to the risky or expected outcome, between which the financial manager is indifferent. In equation form, α_t can be represented as follows:

$$\alpha_t = \frac{\text{certain cash flow}_t}{\text{risky or expected cash flow}_t} \tag{23-1}$$

Thus the alphas (α_t) can vary between 0, in the case of extreme risk, and 1, in the case of certainty. To obtain the value of the equivalent certain cash flow, we need only multiply the risky cash flow in years t times the α_t. When this is done we are indifferent with respect to this certain cash flow and the risky cash flow. In the preceding example of the simple coin toss, the certain cash flow was $3,000, while the risky cash flow was $5,000, the expected value of the coin toss; thus the certainty equivalent coefficient is $3000/$5000 = 0.6. In summary, by multiplying the certainty equivalent coefficient (α_t) times the expected but risky cash flow, we can determine and equivalent certain cash flow.

Once this risk is taken out of the project's cash flows, those cash flows are discounted back to present at the risk-free rate of interest, and the project's net present value or profitability index is determined. If the internal rate of return is calculated, it is then compared with the risk-free rate of interest rather than the firm's required rate of return in determining whether or not it should be accepted or rejected. The certainty equivalent method can be summarized as follows:

$$NPV = \sum_{t=1}^{n} \frac{\alpha_t ACF_t}{(1 + k_{rf})^t} - IO \qquad (23\text{-}2)$$

where α_t = the certainty equivalent coefficient in period t
ACF_t = the annual after-tax expected cash flow in period t
IO = the initial cash outlay
n = the project's expected life
k_{rf} = the risk-free interest rate

The certainty equivalent approach can be summarized as follows:

- Step 1: Risk is removed from the cash flows by substituting equivalent certain cash flows for the risky cash flows. If the certainty equivalent coefficient (α_t) is given, this is done by multiplying each risky cash flow by the appropriate α_t value.
- Step 2: These riskless cash flows are then discounted back to the present at the riskless rate of interest.
- Step 3: The normal capital-budgeting criteria are then applied, except in the case of the internal rate of return criterion, where the project's internal rate of return is compared with the risk-free rate of interest rather than the firm's required rate of return.

EXAMPLE

A firm with a 10 percent required rate of return is considering building new research facilities with an expected life of five years. The initial outlay associated with this project involves a certain cash outflow of $120,000. The expected cash inflows and certainty equivalent coefficients, α_t are as follows:

Year	Expected Cash Flow	Certainty Equivalent Coefficient, α_t
1	$10,000	0.95
2	20,000	0.90
3	40,000	0.85
4	80,000	0.75
5	80,000	0.65

The risk-free rate of interest is 6 percent. What is the project's net present value?

To determine the net present value of this project using the certainty equivalent approach, we must first remove the risk from the future cash flows. We do so by multiplying each expected cash flow by the corresponding certainty equivalent coefficient, α_t, as shown on the following page:

Expected Cash Flow	Certainty Equivalent Coefficient, α_t	α_t (Expected Cash Flow) = Equivalent Riskless Cash Flow
$10,000	0.95	$ 9,500
20,000	0.90	18,000
40,000	0.85	34,000
80,000	0.75	60,000
80,000	0.65	52,000

The equivalent riskless cash flows are then discounted back to the present at the riskless interest rate, not the firm's required rate of return. The required rate of return would be used if this project had the same level of risk as a typical project for this firm. However, these equivalent cash flows have no risk at all; hence, the appropriate discount rate is the riskless rate of interest. The equivalent riskless cash flows can be discounted back to present at the riskless rate of interest, 6 percent, as follows:

Year	Equivalent Riskless Cash Flow	Present Value Factor at 6 Percent	Present Value
1	$ 9,500	0.943	$ 8,958.50
2	18,000	0.890	16,020.00
3	34,000	0.840	28,560.00
4	60,000	0.792	47,520.00
5	52,000	0.747	38,844.00

NPV = −$120,000 + $8958.50 + $16,020 + $28,560 + $47,520 + $38,844 = $19,902.50

Applying the normal capital-budgeting decision criteria, we find that the project should be accepted, as its net present value is greater than zero.

Risk-Adjusted Discount Rates

The use of risk-adjusted discount rates is based on the concept that investors demand higher returns for more risky projects. This is the basic principle behind the CAPM, and the relationship between risk and return is illustrated graphically in Figure 23-3.

The required rate of return on any investment should include compensation for delaying consumption equal to the risk-free rate of return, plus compensation for any risk taken on. If the risk associated with the investment is greater than the risk involved in a typical endeavor, the discount rate is adjusted upward to compensate for this added risk. Once the firm determines the appropriate required rate of return for a project with a given level of risk, cash flows are discounted back to present at the **risk-adjusted discount rate.** Then the normal capital-budgeting criteria are applied, except in the case of the internal rate of return. For the IRR, the hurdle rate with which the project's internal rate of return is compared now becomes the risk-adjusted discount rate. Expressed mathematically, the net present value using the risk-adjusted discount rates becomes

Risk-adjusted discount rate
A method for incorporating the project's level of risk into the capital-budgeting process, in which the discount rate is adjusted upward to compensate for higher than normal risk or downward to adjust for lower than normal risk.

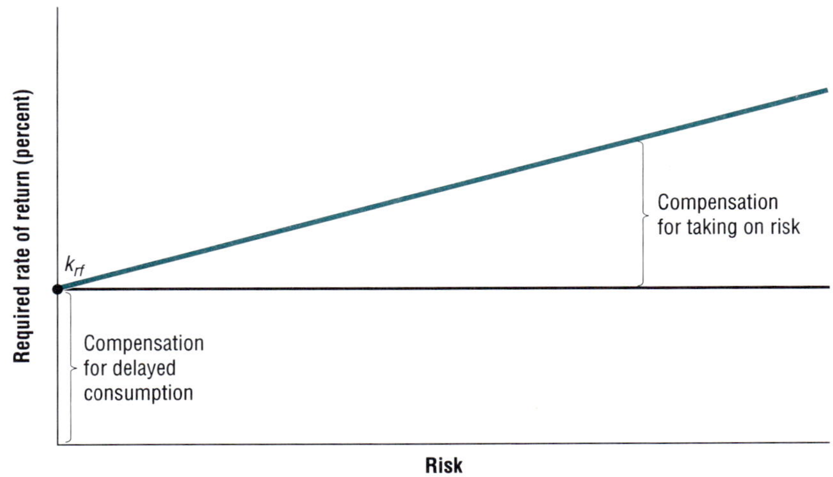

FIGURE 23-3
Risk-return relationship

$$NPV = \sum_{t=1}^{n} \frac{ACF_t}{(1 + k^*)^t} - IO \qquad (23\text{-}3)$$

where ACF_t = the annual after-tax expected cash flow in time period t
IO = the initial cash outlay
k^* = the risk-adjusted discount rate
n = the project's expected life

The logic behind the risk-adjusted discount rate stems from the idea that if the level of risk in a project is different from that in the firm's typical project, then management must incorporate the shareholders' probable reaction to this new endeavor into the decision-making process. If the project has more risk than a typical project, then a higher required rate of return should apply. Otherwise, marginal projects will lower the firm's share price—that is, reduce shareholders' wealth. This will occur as the market raises its required rate of return on the firm to reflect the addition of a more risky project, whereas the incremental cash flows resulting from the acceptance of the new project are not large enough to offset this change fully. By the same logic, if the project has less than normal risk, a reduction in the required rate of return is appropriate. Thus, the risk-adjusted discount method attempts to apply more stringent standards—that is, require a higher rate of return—to projects that will increase the firm's risk level.

EXAMPLE

A toy manufacturer is considering the introduction of a line of fishing equipment with an expected life of five years. In the past, this firm has been quite conservative in its investment in new products, sticking primarily to standard toys. In this context, the introduction of a line of fishing equipment is considered an abnormally risky project. Management thinks that the normal required rate of return for the firm

Financial Management in Practice

SCIENTIFIC MANAGEMENT AT MERCK: AN INTERVIEW WITH CFO JUDY LEWENT

"People who don't practice finance properly have done a great disservice to U.S. industry. Too often, when finance people are unleashed on operating people, an unhealthy tension develops between the need to invest in new projects and the need to have tight controls on spending. For that reason, finance people are often viewed as traffic cops: "You can't do this or go there." **(A)** They keep the records straight, and that's that.

"At Merck, we certainly work with a very sharp pencil. We are not lax. But instead of being an impediment to business, we attempt to work with the operating units and, in many cases, have been accepted as a partner in the business. I think that finance departments can take the nuances, the intuitive feelings that really fine businesspeople have and quantify them. In that way, they can capture both the hard financials of a project and the strategic intent.

"For example, we had a development project for a nontraditional market segment, an antiparasitic agent called Avid that everyone was excited about. We collected the manufacturing and marketing elements and the research inputs, but the financial evaluation of the model showed a negative net present value for the project. **(B)** If we were traffic cops, we would have blown our whistle and gone home.

"But instead, we started to take the project apart and talk more in-depth with marketing and with manufacturing. It turned out that the packaging costs were eating up the gross margins on the project.**(C)** This was something that the original sponsors of the project had feared all along, but only on a conceptual level. We were able to give the project's sponsors, the marketing department, and manufacturing people a framework for talking about the product, and it suddenly became clear to all involved that the packaging size had to change. In this case, then, finance was a real resource in problem solving."

Source: Reprinted by permission of *Harvard Business Review*. An excerpt from "Scientific Management at Merck: An Interview with CFO Judy Lewent," by Nancy A. Nichols.

of 10 percent is not sufficient. Instead, the minimally acceptable rate of return on this project should be 15 percent. The initial outlay would be $110,000, and the expected cash flows from this project are as follows:

Year	Expected Cash Flow
1	$30,000
2	30,000
3	30,000
4	30,000
5	30,000

Financial Management in Practice

ANALYSIS AND IMPLICATIONS . . .

A. For Merck and other pharmaceutical firms, taking on risk is simply part of the game. New products can only be generated through research and there is no guarantee that an R&D project will result in a profitable project. Complicating all this is the fact that after a large investment in research, a good project may not generate profits for ten to fifteen years.

B. In evaluating projects, Merck relies on a simulation approach. In fact, since 1989, every significant research and development project at Merck has been analyzed using a simulation approach over a twenty-year time horizon.

C. Merck uses the simulation approach not only to make decisions, but also to find areas causing financial concern to the project. This is done by performing sensitivity or "What if?" analysis—changing one input while holding other inputs constant to determine what the effect is on the distribution of possible returns. In this case, Merck was able to spot an area in which the costs were so large as to turn a good project into a bad one. Once the problem area was spotted, it could be corrected. In this way, finance served not only as a method to evaluate and control the project, but also to refine it.

Discounting this annuity back to the present at 15 percent yields a present value of the future cash flows of $100,560. Because the initial outlay on this project is $110,000, the net present value becomes –$9,440, and the project should be rejected. If the normal required rate of return of 10 percent had been used as the discount rate, the project would have been accepted with a net present value of $3,730.

In practice, when the risk-adjusted discount rate is used, projects are generally grouped according to purpose, or risk class; then the discount rate preassigned to that purpose or risk class is used. For example, a firm with an overall required rate of return of 12 percent might use the following rate-of-return categorization:

Project	Required Rate of Return
Replacement decision	12%
Modification or expansion of existing product line	15
Project unrelated to current operations	18
Research and development operations	25

The purpose of this categorization of projects is to make their evaluation easier, but it also introduces a sense of the arbitrary into the calculations that makes the evaluation less meaningful. The tradeoffs involved in the classification above are obvious; time and effort are minimized, but only at the cost of precision.

Certainty Equivalent Versus Risk-Adjusted Discount Rate Methods

The primary difference between the certainty equivalent approach and the risk-adjusted discount rate approach involves the point at which the adjustment for risk is incorporated into the calculations. The certainty equivalent penalizes or adjusts downward the value of the expected annual after-tax cash flows, ACF_t which results in a lower net present value for a risky project. The risk-adjusted discount rate, conversely, leaves the cash flows at their expected value and adjusts the required rate of return, k, upward to compensate for added risk. In either case the project's net present value is being adjusted downward to compensate for additional risk. The computational differences are illustrated in Table 23-1.

In addition to the difference in point of adjustment for risk, the risk-adjusted discount rate makes the implicit assumption that risk becomes greater as we move further out in time. Although this is not necessarily a good or bad assumption, we should be aware of it and understand it. Let's look at an example in which the risk-adjusted discount rate is used and then determine what certainty equivalent coefficients, α_t, would be necessary to arrive at the same solution.

EXAMPLE

Assume that a firm with a required rate of return of 10 percent is considering introducing a new product. This product has an initial outlay of $800,000, an expected life of fifteen years, and after-tax cash flows of $100,000 each year during its life. Because of the increased risk associated with this project, management is requiring a 15 percent rate of return. Let us also assume that the risk-free rate of return is 6 percent.

If the firm chose to use the certainty equivalent method, the certainty equivalent cash flows would be discounted back to the present at 6 percent, the risk-free rate of interest. The present value of the $100,000 cash flow occurring at the end of the first year discounted back to present at 15 percent is $87,000. The present value of this $100,000 flow discounted back to present at the risk-free rate of 6 percent is $94,300. Thus, if the certainty equivalent approach were used, a certainty equivalent coefficient, α_1, of .9226 ($87,000 ÷ $94,300 = 0.9226) would be necessary to produce a present value of $87,000. In other words, the same results can be obtained in the first year by using the risk-adjusted discount rate and adjusting the discount rate up to 15 percent or by using the certainty equivalent approach and adjusting the expected cash flows by a certainty equivalent coefficient of 0.9226.

Under the risk-adjusted discount rate, the present value of the $100,000 cash flow occurring at the end of the second year becomes $75,600, and to produce an identical present value under the certainty equivalent approach, a certainty equivalent coefficient of 0.8494 would be needed. Following this through for the life of the project yields the certainty equivalent coefficients given in Table 23-2.

TABLE 23-1 Computational Steps in Certainty Equivalent and Risk-Adjusted Discount Rate Methods

Certainty Equivalent		Risk-Adjusted Discount Rate	
Step 1:	Adjust the expected cash flows, ACF_t, downward for risk by multiplying them by the corresponding certainty equivalent, coefficient, α_t.	Step 1:	Adjust the discount rate upward for risk.
Step 2:	Discount the certainty equivalent, riskless, cash flows back to the present using the risk-free rate of interest.	Step 2:	Discount the expected cash flows back to present using the risk-adjusted discount rate.
Step 3:	Apply the normal decision criteria, except in the case of the internal rate of return, where the risk-free rate of interest replaces the required rate of return as the hurdle rate.	Step 3:	Apply the normal decision criteria except in the case of the internal rate of return, where the risk-adjusted discount rate replaces the required rate of return as the hurdle rate.

TABLE 23-2 Certainty Equivalent Coefficients Yielding Same Results as Risk-Adjusted Discount Rate of 15 Percent in Illustrative Example

Year	1	2	3	4	5	6	7	8	9	10
α_t:	0.9226	0.8494	0.7833	0.7222	0.6653	0.6128	0.5654	0.5215	0.4797	0.4427

What does this analysis suggest? It indicates that if the risk-adjusted discount rate method is used, we are adjusting downward the value of future cash flows that occur further in the future more severely than earlier cash flows.

In summary, the use of the risk-adjusted discount rate assumes that risk increases over time and that cash flows occurring further in the future should be more severely penalized.

STOP AND THINK

If performed properly, either of these methods can do a good job of adjusting for risk. However, by far, the most popular method of risk adjustment is the risk-adjusted discount rate. The reason for the popularity of the risk-adjusted discount rate over the certainty equivalent approach is purely and simply its ease of implementation.

Risk-Adjusted Discount Rate and Measurement of a Project's Systematic Risk

When we initially talked about systematic risk or a beta, we were talking about measuring it for the entire firm. As you recall, although we could estimate a firm's beta using historical data, we did not have complete confidence in our results. As we will see, estimating the appropriate level of systematic risk for a single project is even more fraught with difficulties. To truly understand what it is that we are trying to do and the difficulties that we will encounter let us step back a bit and examine systematic risk and the risk adjustment for a project.

What we are trying to do is to use the CAPM to determine the level of risk and the appropriate risk-return tradeoffs for a particular project. We will then take the expected return on this project and compare it to the risk-return tradeoffs suggested by the CAPM to determine whether or not the project should be accepted. If the project appears to be a typical one for the firm, using the CAPM to determine the appropriate risk-return tradeoffs and then judging the project against them may be a warranted approach. But if the project is not a typical project, what do we do? Historical data generally do not exist for a new project. In fact, for some capital investments, for example, a truck or a new building, historical data would not have much meaning. What we need to do is make the best out of a bad situation. We either (1) fake it—that is, use historical accounting data, if available, to substitute for historical price data in estimating systematic risk; or (2) we attempt to find a substitute firm in the same industry as the capital-budgeting project and use the substitute firm's estimated systematic risk as a proxy for the project's systematic risk.

Beta Estimation Using Accounting Data When we are dealing with a project that is identical to the firm's other projects, we need only estimate the level of systematic risk for the firm and use that estimate as a proxy for the project's risk. Unfortunately, when projects are not typical of the firm, this approach does not work. For example, when R. J. Reynolds introduces a new food through one of its food products divisions, this new product most likely carries with it a different level of systematic risk than is typical for Reynolds as a whole.

To get a better approximation of the systematic risk level on this project we could estimate the level of systematic risk for the food division and use that as a proxy for the project's systematic risk. Unfortunately, historical stock price data are available only for the company as a whole, and as you recall historical stock return data are generally used to estimate a firm's beta. Thus we are forced to use *accounting return data* rather than historical stock return data for the division to estimate the division's systematic risk. To estimate a project's beta using accounting data we need only run a time series regression of the division's return on assets (net income/ total assets) on the market index (the S&P 500). The regression coefficient from this equation would be the project's accounting beta and would serve as an approximation for the project's true beta or measure of systematic risk. Alternatively, a multiple regression model based on accounting data could be developed to explain betas. The results of this model could then be applied to firms which are not publicly traded to estimate their betas.

How good is the accounting beta technique? It certainly is not as good as a direct calculation of the beta. In fact, the correlation between the accounting beta and the beta calculated on historical stock return data is only about 0.6; however, better luck has been experienced with multiple regression models used to predict betas. Unfortunately, in many cases there may not be any realistic alternative to the calculation of the accounting beta. Owing to the importance of adjusting for a project's risk, the accounting beta method is much preferred to doing nothing.

The Pure Play Method for Estimating a Project's Beta

Pure play method
A method of estimating a project's beta that attempts to identify a publicly traded firm that is engaged solely in the same business as the project, and uses that beta as a proxy for the project's beta.

Whereas the accounting beta method attempts to directly estimate a project or division's beta, the **pure play method** attempts to identify publicly traded firms that are engaged solely in the same business as the project or division. Once the proxy or pure play firm is identified, its systematic risk is determined and then used as a proxy for the project or division's level of systematic risk. What we are doing is looking for a publicly traded firm on the outside that looks like our project, and using that firm's required rate of return to judge our project. In doing so, we are presuming that the systematic risk and the capital structure of the proxy firm are identical to those of the project.

In using the pure play method, it should be noted that a firm's capital structure is reflected in its beta. When the capital structure of the proxy firm is different from that of the project's firm, some adjustment must be made for this difference. Although not a perfect approach, it does provide some insights as to the level of systematic risk a project might have.

OTHER APPROACHES TO EVALUATING RISK IN CAPITAL BUDGETING

Simulation

Simulation
The process of imitating the performance of an investment project under evaluation using a computer. This is done by randomly selecting observations from each of the distributions that affect the outcome of the project, combining those observations to determine the final output of the project, and continuing with this process until a representative record of the project's probable outcome is assembled.

Another method for evaluating risk in the investment decision is through the use of **simulation.** The certainty equivalent and risk-adjusted discount rate approaches provided us with a single value for the risk-adjusted net present value, whereas a simulation approach gives us a probability distribution for the investment's net present value or internal rate of return. Simulation imitates the performance of the project under evaluation. This is done by randomly selecting observations from each of the distributions that affect the outcome of the project, combining those observations to determine the final output of the project, and continuing with this process until a representative record of the project's probable outcome is assembled.

The easiest way to develop an understanding of the computer simulation process is to follow through an example simulation for an investment project evaluation. Suppose Merck is considering a new drug for the treatment of Alzheimers disease. The simulation process is portrayed in Figure 23-4. First, the probability distributions are determined for all the factors that affect the project's returns; in this case, let us assume there are nine such variables:

1. Market size
2. Selling price
3. Market growth rate
4. Share of market (which results in physical sales volume)
5. Investment required
6. Residual value of investment
7. Operating costs
8. Fixed costs
9. Useful life of facilities

Then the computer randomly selects one observation from each of the probability distributions, according to its chance of actually occurring in the future. These nine observations are combined, and a net present value or internal rate of return figure is calculated. This process is repeated as many times as desired, until a representative distribution of possible future outcomes is assembled. Thus, the inputs to a simulation include all the principal factors affecting the project's profitability, and the simulation output is a probability distribution of net present values or internal rates of return for the project. The decision maker bases the decision on the full range of

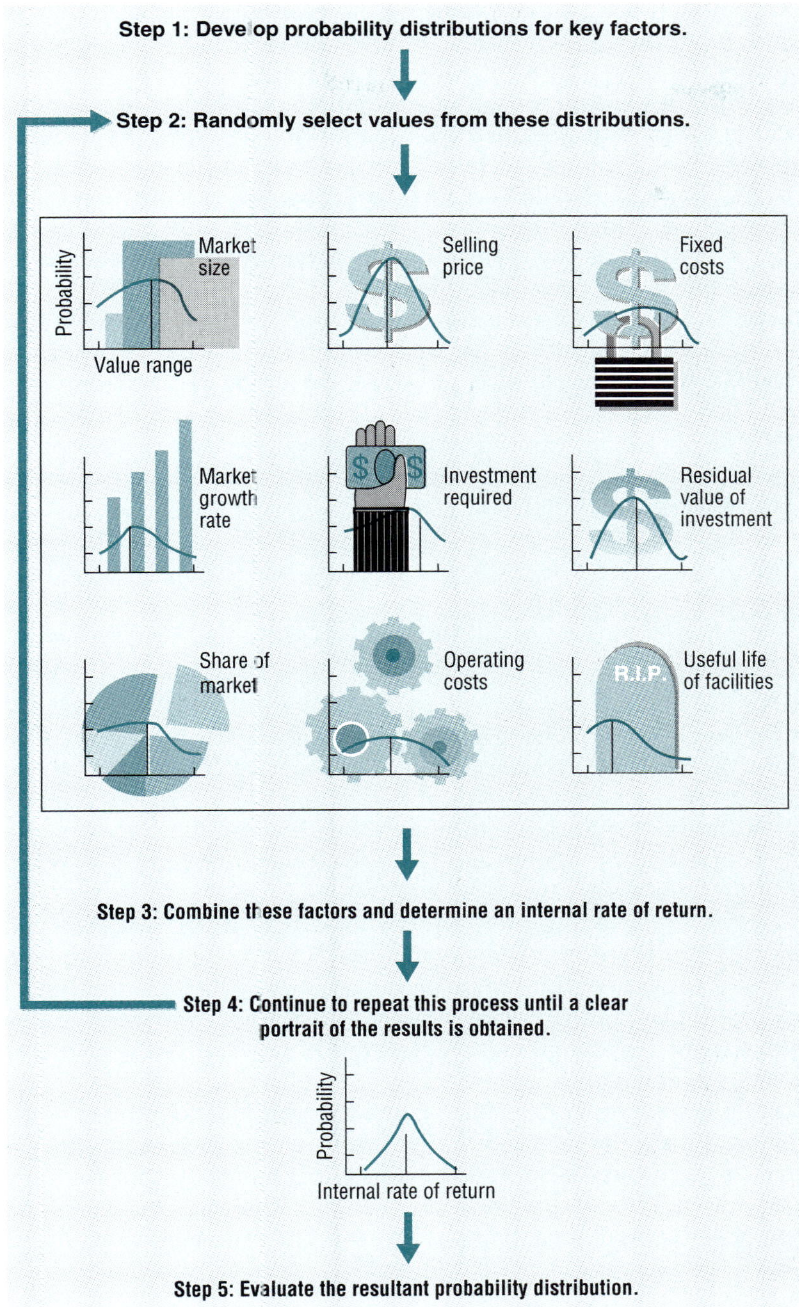

FIGURE 23-4
Capital-budgeting simulation for proposed new Alzheimers drug

possible outcomes. The project is accepted if the decision maker feels that enough of the distribution lies above the normal cutoff criteria ($NPV \geq 0$, $IRR \geq$ required rate of return).

Suppose that the output from the simulation of Merck's Alzheimers disease drug project is as given in Figure 23-5. This output provides the decision maker with the probability of different outcomes occurring in addition to the range of possible outcomes. Sometimes called **scenario analysis,** this examination identifies the range of possible outcomes under the worst, best, and most likely case. Merck's management will examine the distribution to determine the project's level of risk and then make the appropriate adjustment.

Scenario analysis
Simulation analysis that focuses on an examination of the range of possible outcomes.

You'll notice that although the simulation approach helps us to determine the amount of total risk that a project has, it does not differentiate between systematic and unsystematic risk. Because systematic risk cannot be diversified away for free, the simulation approach does not provide a complete method of risk assessment. However, it does provide important insights as to the total risk level of a given investment project. Now we will look briefly at how the simulation approach can be used to perform sensitivity analysis.

Sensitivity Analysis through Simulation Approach

Sensitivity analysis
The process of determining how the distribution of possible returns for a particular project is affected by a change in one particular input variable.

Sensitivity analysis involves determining how the distribution of possible net present values or internal rates of return for a particular project is affected by a change in one particular input variable. This is done by changing the value of one input variable while holding all other input variables constant. The distribution of possible net present values or internal rates of return that is generated is then compared with the distribution of possible returns generated before the change was made to determine the effect of the change. For this reason sensitivity analysis is commonly called *"What if?" Analysis.*

For example, in analyzing the proposal for a new drug for the prevention of Alzheimers disease, Merck's management may wish to determine the effect of a more pessimistic forecast of the anticipated market growth rate. After the more pessimistic forecast replaces the original forecast in the model, the simulation is rerun. The two outputs are then compared to determine how sensitive the results are to the revised estimate of the market growth rate.

By modifying assumptions made about the values and ranges of the input factors and rerunning the simulation, management can determine how sensitive the outcome of the project is to these changes. If the output appears to be highly sensitive to one or two of the input factors, the financial managers may then wish to spend additional time refining those input estimates to make sure they are accurate.

Probability Trees

Probability tree
A schematic representation of a problem in which all possible outcomes are graphically displayed.

A **probability tree** is a graphic exposition of the sequence of possible outcomes; it presents the decision maker with a schematic representation of the problem in which all possible outcomes are pictures. Moreover, the computations and results of

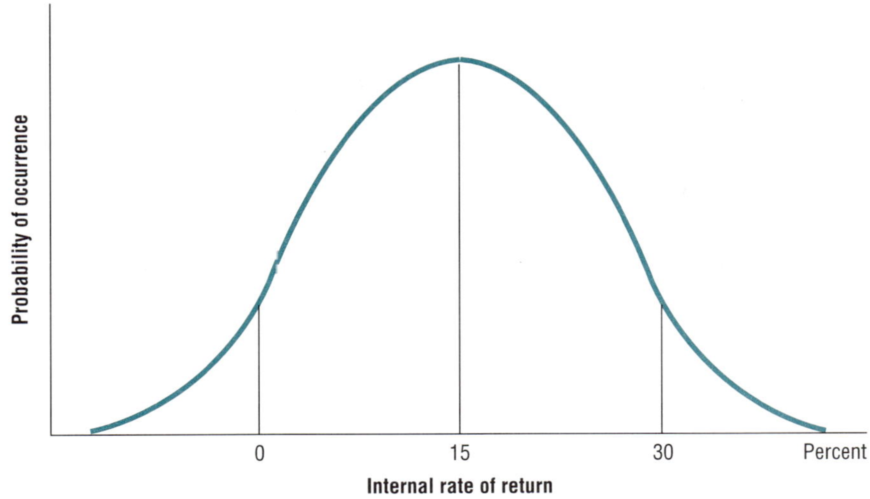

FIGURE 23-5
Output from simulation of a proposed new drug for the prevention of Alzheimers disease

TABLE 23-3 Possible Outcomes in Year 1

	Probability		
	.5 Outcome 1	.3 Outcome 2	.2 Outcome 3
Cash flow	$600,000	$700,000	$800,000

the computations are shown directly on the tree, so that the information can be easily understood.

To illustrate the use of a probability tree, suppose a firm is considering an investment proposal that requires an initial outlay of $1 million and will yield cash flows for the next two years. During the first year let us assume there are three possible outcomes, as shown in Table 23-3. Graphically, each of these three possible alternatives is represented on the probability tree in Figure 23-6 as one of the three possible branches.

The second step in the probability tree is to continue drawing branches in a similar manner so that each of the possible outcomes during the second year is represent by a new branch. For example, if outcome 1 occurs in year 1, then there would be a 20 percent chance of a $300,000 cash flow and an 80 percent chance of a $600,000 cash flow in year 2 as shown in Table 23-4. Two branches would be sent out from the outcome 1 node, reflecting these two possible outcomes. The cash flows that occur if outcome 1 takes place and the probabilities associated with them are called *conditional outcomes* and *conditional probabilities* because they can occur only if outcome 1 occurs during the first year. Finally, to determine the prob-

First Stage of a Probabliity-Tree Diagram

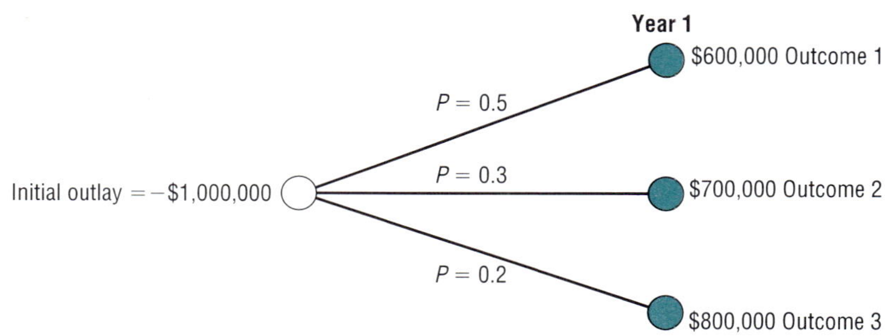

FIGURE 23-6
First stage of a probability-tree diagram

Joint probability The probability of two different sequential outcomes occurring.

ability of the sequence of a $600,000 flow in year 1 and a $300,000 outcome in year 2, the probability of the $600,000 flow (.5) is multiplied by the conditional probability of the second flow (.2), telling us that this sequence has a 10 percent chance of occurring; this is called its **joint probability.** Letting the values in Table 23-4 represent the conditional outcomes and their respective conditional probabilities, we can complete the probability tree, as shown in Figure 23-7.

The financial manager, by examining the probability tree, is provided with the expected internal rate of return for the investment, the range of possible outcomes, and a listing of each possible outcome with the probability associated with it. In this case, the expected internal rate of return is 14.74 percent, and there is a 10 percent chance of incurring the worst possible outcome with an internal rate of return of –7.55 percent. There is a 2 percent probability of achieving the most favorable outcome, an internal rate of return of 37.98 percent.

Decision making with probability trees does not mean simply the acceptance of any project with an internal rate of return greater than the firm's required rate of return, because the project's required rate of return has not yet been adjusted for risk. As a result, the financial decision maker must examine the entire distribution of possible internal rates of return. Then, based on that examination, he or she must decide, given her or his aversion to risk, if enough of this distribution is above the appropriate (risk-adjusted) required rate of return to warrant acceptance of the project. Thus the probability tree allows the manager to quickly visualize the possible future events, their probabilities, and their outcomes. In addition, the calculation of the expected internal rate of return and enumeration of the distribution should aid the financial manager in determining the risk level of the project.

Other Sources of Risk: Time Dependence of Cash Flows

Up to this point, in all approaches other than the probability tree, we have assumed that the cash flow in one period is independent of the cash flow in the previous

TABLE 23-4 Conditional Outcomes and Probabilities for Year 2

	If Outcome 1		If Outcome 2		If Outcome 3	
Year 1	ACF_1 = \$600,000 Then		ACF_1 = \$700,000 Then		ACF_1 = \$800,000 Then	
Year 2	ACF_2	Probability	ACF_2	Probability	ACF_2	Probability
	\$300,000	.2	\$300,000	.2	\$400,000	.2
	600,000	.8	500,000	.3	600,000	.7
			700,000	.5	800,000	.1

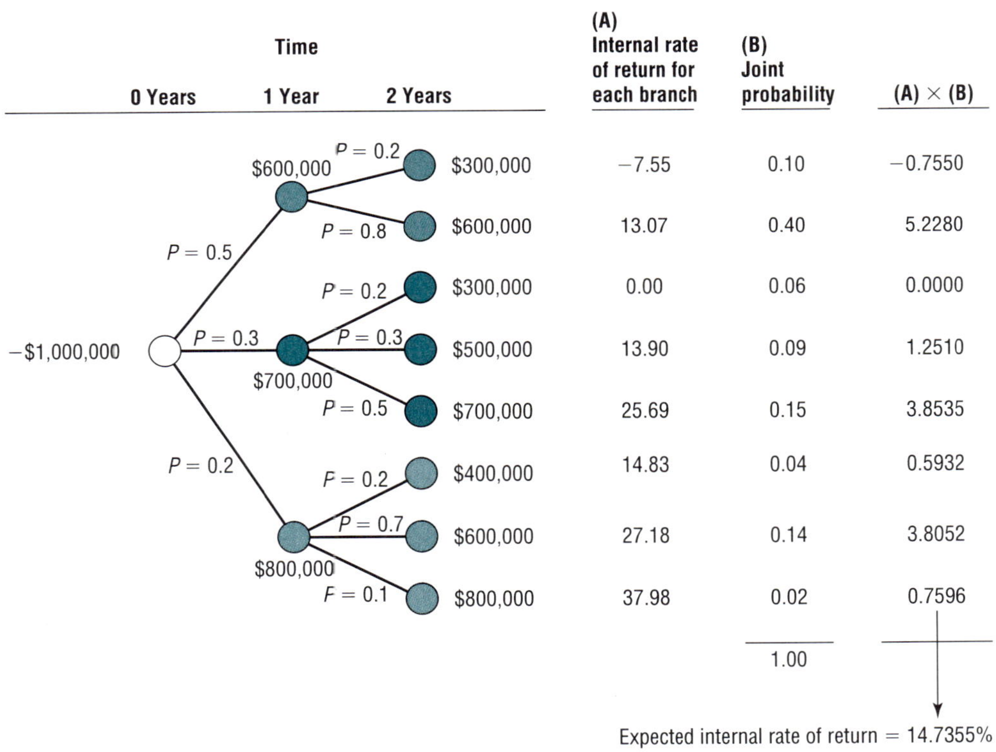

FIGURE 23-7
Probability tree

period. Although this assumption is appealing because it is simple, in many cases it is also invalid. For example, if a new product is introduced and the initial public reaction is poor, resulting in low initial cash flows, then cash flows in future periods are likely to be low. An extreme example of this is Ford's experience with the Edsel. Poor consumer acceptance and sales in the first year were followed by even poorer results in the second year. If the Edsel had been received favorably during its first year, it quite likely would have done well in the second year. The end effect of time dependence of cash flows is to increase the risk of the project over time. That is,

Financial Management in Practice

FINANCIAL ENGINEERING AT MERCK

Last year Merck & Co., Inc., invested well over $2 billion in R&D and capital expenditures combined. The company spent much of the money on risky, long-term projects that are notoriously difficult to evaluate. Indeed, the critics of modern finance would argue that such projects should not be subjected to rigorous financial analysis, because such analysis fails to reflect the strategic value of long-term investments. **(A)** Yet at Merck, it is those projects with the longest time horizon that receive the most intense and financially sophisticated analyses. In fact, Merck's financial function is active and influential with a highly quantitative, analytical orientation. The company is seldom, if ever, criticized for being shortsighted.

Why doesn't all this analysis choke off long-term investing, as critics of modern finance theory say it should? In part because Merck is a leader in building financial models of scientific and commercial processes and in using those models to improve business decisions. Rather than relying on static, single-point forecasts, Merck's models use probability distributions for numerous variables and come up with a range of possible outcomes that both stimulate discussion and facilitate decision making.**(B)**

For example, Merck's Research Planning Model, now ten years old, and its Revenue Hedging Model, now four years old, integrate economics, finance, statistics, and computer science to produce disciplined, quantitative analyses of specific elements of Merck's business. These models do not make decisions. Instead, they provide Merck executives with cogent information both about risks and returns and about financial performance for specific projects and activities.**(C)**

Source: Reprinted by permission of *Harvard Business Review*. An excerpt from "Financial Engineering at Merck" by Timothy A. Luehrman. *Harvard Business Review* (January-February 1994): 93.

ANALYSIS AND IMPLICATIONS . . .

A. The risks that pharmaceutical firms face in product development are great. It costs $359 million and takes ten years to bring a new drug to market. Then, once the drug has reached the market, 70 percent of the new drugs introduced do not cover their costs.

B. Rather than simply using an estimate of the project's expected net present value, Merck relies on a simulation approach. They examine the returns on proposed new drugs over a twenty-year period, allowing for any and all complexities that they can foresee.

C. One of the key aspects of the simulation approach used by Merck is the ability to perform sensitivity analysis by changing the value of specific variables and seeing how the results are affected. In this way, Merck can determine where to spend more time in forecasting and where they should spend time and money trying to improve efficiency.

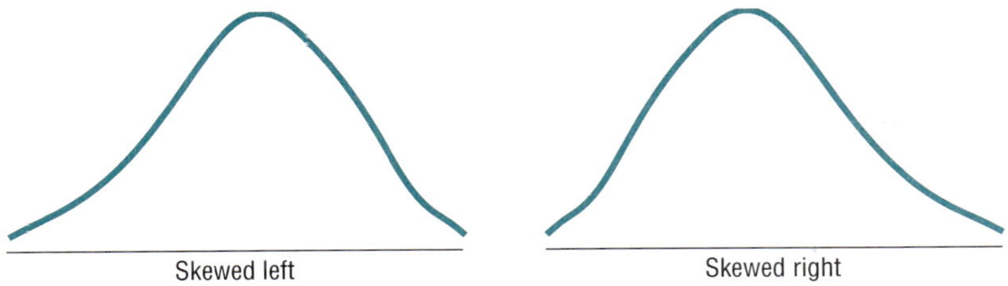

FIGURE 23-8
Examples of skewed distributions

because large cash flows in the first period lead to large cash flows in the second period, and low cash flows in the first period lead to low cash flows in the second period, the probability distribution of possible net present values tends to be wider than if the cash flows were not dependent over time. The greater the degree of correlation between flows over time, the greater will be the dispersion of the probability distribution.

Other Sources of Risk: Skewness

In all previous approaches other than simulation and probability trees, we have assumed that the distributions of net present values for projects being evaluated are normally distributed. This assumption is not always valid. When it is true, the standard deviation provides an adequate measure of the distribution's dispersion; however, when the distribution is not normally distributed, reliance on the standard deviation can be misleading.

A distribution that is not symmetric is said to be skewed. A **skewed distribution** has either a longer "tail" to the right or to the left. For example, if a distribution is skewed to the right, most values will be clustered around the left end, and the distribution will appear to have a long tail on the right end of the range of values. Graphic illustrations of skewed distributions are presented in Figure 23-8.

Skewed distribution a distribution that has a longer "tail" to the right or the left.

The difficulty associated with skewed distributions arises from the fact that the use of the expected value and standard deviation alone may not be enough to differentiate properly between two distributions. For example, the two distributions shown in Figure 23-9 have the same expected value and the same standard deviation; however, distribution A is skewed to the left while B is skewed to the right. If a financial manager were given a choice between these two distributions, assuming they are mutually exclusive, he or she would most likely choose distribution B, because it involves less chance of a negative net present value. Thus, skewness can affect the level of risk and the desirability of a distribution.

SUMMARY

- In this chapter, we example the problem of incorporating risk into the the capital-budgeting decision. First we explore just what type of risk to adjust for: project standing alone risk, the project's contribution-to-firm risk, or the project's systematic risk. In theory, systematic risk is the appropriate risk measure, but

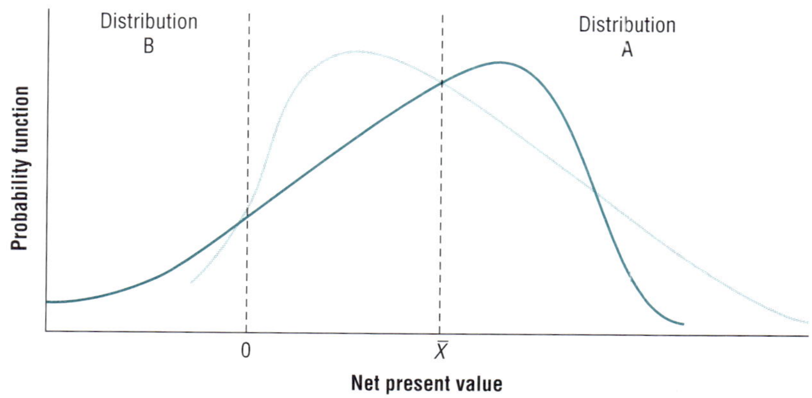

FIGURE 23-9
Two distributions with identical expected values and standard deviations but different skewness

bankruptcy costs and the issue of undiversified shareholders also give weight to considering a project's contribution-to-firm risk as the appropriate risk measure. Both measures of risk have merit and we avoid making any specific allocation of importance between the two in capital budgeting.

- Two commonly used methods for incorporating risk into capital budgeting are (1) the certainty equivalent method and (2) risk-adjusted discount rates. The certainty equivalent approach involves a direct attempt to incorporate the decision maker's utility function into the analysis. Under this method, cash flows are adjusted downward by multiplying them by certainty equivalent coefficients, α_t's which transform the risky cash flows into equivalent certain cash flows in terms of desirability. A project's net present value using the certainty equivalent method for adjusting for risk becomes

$$NPV = \sum_{t=1}^{n} \frac{\alpha_t ACF_t}{(1 + k_{rf})^t} - IO \qquad (23\text{-}2)$$

- The risk-adjusted discount rate involves an upward adjustment of the discount rate to compensate for risk. This method is based on the concept that investors demand higher returns for riskier projects.
- The simulation and probability tree methods are used to provide information as to the location and shape of the distribution of possible outcomes. Decisions could be based directly on these methods, or they could be used to determine input into either certainty equivalent or risk-adjusted discount method approaches.

QUESTIONS

1. In Chapter 22, we examined the payback period capital-budgeting criterion. Often this capital-budgeting criterion is used as a risk-screening device. Explain the rationale behind its use.

2. The use of the risk-adjusted discount rate assumes that risk increases over time. Justify this assumption.
3. What are the similarities and differences between the risk-adjusted discount rate and certainty equivalent methods for incorporating risk into the capital-budgeting decision?
4. What is the value of using the probability tree technique for evaluating capital-budgeting projects?
5. Explain how simulation works. What is the value in using a simulation approach?
6. What does time dependence of cash flows mean? Why might cash flows be time dependent? Give some examples.
7. What does skewness mean? If a distribution is skewed, how does this affect the significance of its standard deviation and mean?

SELF-CORRECTION PROBLEM

G. Norohna and Co. is considering two mutually exclusive projects. The expected values for each project's cash flows are given below.

Year	Project A	Project B
0	–$300,000	–$300,000
1	100,000	200,000
2	200,000	200,000
3	200,000	200,000
4	300,000	300,000
5	300,000	400,000

The company has decided to evaluate these projects using the certainty equivalent method. The certainty equivalent coefficients for each project's cash flows are given below:

Year	Project A	Project B
0	1.00	1.00
1	.95	.90
2	.90	.80
3	.85	.70
4	.80	.60
5	.75	.50

Given that this company's normal required rate of return is 15 percent and the after-tax risk-free rate is 8 percent, which project should be selected?

PROBLEMS

1. The Hokie Corporation is considering two mutually exclusive projects. Both require an initial outlay of $10,000 and will operate for five years. The probability distributions associated with each project for years 1 through 5 are given as follows:

Probability Distribution for Cash Flow Years 1–5 (the same cash flow each year)

Project A		Project B	
Probability	Cash Flow	Probability	Cash Flow
.15	$4,000	.15	$ 2,000
.70	5,000	.70	6,000
.15	6,000	.15	10,000

Because project B is the riskier of the two projects, the management of Hokie Corporation has decided to apply a required rate of return of 15 percent to its evaluation but only a 12 percent required rate of return to project A.

a. Determine the expected value of each project's cash flows.
b. Determine each project's risk-adjusted net present value.
c. What other factors might be considered in deciding between these two projects?

2. The Goblu Corporation is evaluating two mutually exclusive projects, both of which require an initial outlay of $100,000. Each project has an expected life of five years. The probability distributions associated with the annual cash flows from each project follow:

Probability Distribution for Cash Flow Years 1–5 (the same cash flow each year)

Project A		Project B	
Probability	Cash Flow	Probability	Cash Flow
.10	$35,000	.10	$10,000
.40	40,000	.20	30,000
.40	45,000	.40	45,000
.10	50,000	.20	60,000
		.10	80,000

The normal required rate of return for Goblu is 10 percent, but because these projects are riskier than most, they are requiring a higher-than-normal rate of return on them. On project A they are requiring a 12 percent and on project B a 13 percent rate of return.

a. Determine the expected value for each project's cash flows.

b. Determine each project's risk-adjusted net present value.
c. What other factors might be considered in deciding between these projects?

3. The V. Coles Corp. is considering two mutually exclusive projects. The expected values for each project's cash flows are given below:

Year	Project A	Project B
0	–$1,000,000	–$1,000,000
1	500,000	500,000
2	700,000	600,000
3	600,000	700,000
4	500,000	800,000

The management has decided to evaluate these projects using the certainty equivalent method. The certainty equivalent coefficients for each project's cash flows are given below:

Year	Project A	Project B
0	1.00	1.00
1	.95	.90
2	.90	.70
3	.80	.60
4	.70	.50

Given that this company's normal required rate of return is 15 percent and the after-tax risk-free rate is 5 percent, which project should be selected?

4. Neustal, Inc., has decided to use the certainty equivalent method in determining whether or not a new investment should be made. The expected cash flows associated with this investment and the estimated certainty equivalent coefficients are as follows:

Year	Expected Values for Cash Flows	Certainty Equivalent Coefficients
0	–$90,000	1.00
1	25,000	0.95
2	30,000	0.90
3	30,000	0.83
4	25,000	0.75
5	20,000	0.65

Given that Neustal's normal required rate of return is 18 percent and that the after-tax risk free rate is 7 percent, should this project be accepted?

5. The G. Wolfe Corporation is examining two capital-budgeting projects with five-year lives. The first, project A, is a replacement project; the second, project B, is a project unrelated to current operations. The G. Wolfe Corporation uses the risk-adjusted discount rate method and groups projects according to purpose and then uses a required rate of return or discount rate that has been preassigned to that purpose or risk class. The expected cash flows for these projects are given below:

	Project A	Project B
Initial Investment:	$250,000	$400,000
Cash inflows:		
Year 1	$ 30,000	$135,000
Year 2	40,000	135,000
Year 3	50,000	135,000
Year 4	90,000	135,000
Year 5	130,000	135,000

The purpose/risk classes and preassigned required rates of return are as follows:

Purpose	Required Rate of Return
Replacement decision	12%
Modification or expansion of existing product line	15
Project unrelated to current operations	18
Research and development operations	20

Determine the project's risk-adjusted net present value.

6. Nacho Nachtmann Company uses the certainty equivalent approach when it evaluates risky investments. The company presently has two mutually exclusive investment proposals, with an expected life of four years each, to choose from with money it received from the sale of part of its toy division to another company. The expected net cash flows are given below:

Year	Project A	Project B
0	–$50,000	–$50,000
1	15,000	20,000
2	15,000	25,000
3	15,000	25,000
4	45,000	30,000

The certainty equivalent coefficients for the net cash flows are as follows:

Year	Project A	Project B
0	1.00	1.00
1	.95	.90
2	.85	.85
3	.80	.80
4	.70	.75

Which of the two investment proposals should be chosen, given that the after-tax risk-free rate of return is 6 percent?

7. The M. Solt Corporation is evaluating an investment proposal with an expected life of two years. This project will require an initial outlay of $1,200,000. The resultant possible cash flows are given below:

Possible Outcomes in Year 1

	Probability		
	.6 Outcome 1	.3 Outcome 2	.2 Outcome 3
Cash flow =	$700,000	$850,000	$1,000,000

Conditional Outcomes and Probabilities for Year 2

If ACF_1 = $700,000		If ACF_1 = $850,000		ACF_1 = $1,000,000	
ACF_2	Probability	ACF_2	Probability	ACF_2	Probability
$ 300,000	.2	$ 400,000	.2	$ 600,000	.1
700,000	.6	500,000	.5	900,000	.5
1,100,000	.1	1,000,000	.2	1,100,000	.4
		1,300,000	.1		

a. Construct a probability tree representing the possible outcomes.
b. Determine the joint probability of each possible sequence of events taking place.
c. What is the expected IRR of this project?
d. What is the range of possible IRRs for this project?

8. V. Janjigian, Inc., is considering expanding its operations into computer-based basketball games. Janjigian feels that there is a three-year life associated with this project, and it will initially involve an investment of $100,000. It also believes there is a 60 percent chance of success and a cash flow of $100,000 in year 1 and a 40 percent chance of failure and a $10,000 cash flow in year 1. If the project fails in year 1, there is a 60 percent chance that it will produce cash flows of only $10,000 in years 2 and 3. There is also a 40 percent chance that it will *really* fail and Janjigian will earn nothing in year 2 and get

out of this line of business, with the project terminating and no cash flow occurring in year 3. If, conversely, this project succeeds in the first year, then cash flows in the second year are expected to be $200,000, $175,000, or $150,000 with probabilities of .30, .50, and .20, respectively. Finally, if the project succeeds in the third and final year of operation, the cash flows are expected to be either $30,000 more or $20,000 less than they were in year 2, with an equal chance of occurrence.

a. Construct a probability tree representing the possible outcomes.
b. Determine the joint probability of each possible sequence of events.
c. What is the expected IRR?
d. What is the range of possible IRRs for this project?

INTEGRATIVE PROBLEM

It's been four months since you took a position as an assistant financial analyst at Caledonia Products. During that time, you've had a promotion and now are working as a special assistant for capital budgeting to the CEO of Caledonia Products. Your latest assignment involves the analysis of several risky projects. Since this is your first assignment dealing with risk analysis, you have been asked not only to provide a recommendation on the projects in question, but also to respond to a number of questions aimed at judging your understanding of analysis and capital budgeting. The memorandum you received outlining your assignment follows:

TO: The Special Assistant for Capital Budgeting
FROM: Mr. V. Morrison, CEO, Caledonia Products
RE: Capital Budgeting and Risk Analysis

Provide a written response to the following questions:

a. In capital budgeting, risk can be measured from three perspectives. What are those three measures of a project's risk?
b. According to the CAPM, which measurement of a project's risk is relevant? What complications does reality introduce into the CAPM view of risk and what does that mean for our view of the relevant measure of a project's risk?
c. What are the similarities and differences between the risk-adjusted discount rate and certainty equivalent methods for incorporating risk into the capital-budgeting decision?
d. Why might we use the probability-tree technique for evaluating capital-budgeting projects?
e. Explain how simulation works. What is the value in using a simulation approach?
f. What is sensitivity analysis and what is its purpose?
g. What does time dependence of cash flows mean? Why might cash flows be time dependent? Give some examples.
h. Caledonia Products is using the certainty equivalent approach to evaluate two mutually exclusive investment proposals with an expected life of four years. The expected net cash flows are given below:

Year	Project A	Project B
0	–$150,000	–$200,000
1	40,000	50,000
2	40,000	60,000
3	40,000	60,000
4	100,000	50,000

The certainty equivalent coefficients for the net cash flows are as follows:

Year	Project A	Project B
0	1.00	1.00
1	.90	.95
2	.85	.85
3	.80	.80
4	.70	.75

Which of the two investment proposals should be chosen, given that the after-tax risk-free rate of return is 7 percent?

i. Caledonia is considering an additional investment project with an expected life of two years and would like some insights on the level of risk this project has using the probability tree method. The initial outlay on this project would be $600,000, and the resultant possible cash flows are given below:

Possible Outcomes in Year 1

	Probability		
	.4 Outcome 1	.4 Outcome 2	.2 Outcome 3
Cash flow =	$300,000	$350,000	$450,000

Conditional Outcomes and Probabilities for Year 2

If ACF_1 = $300,000		If ACF_1 = $350,000		If ACF_1 = $450,000	
ACF_2	Probability	ACF_2	Probability	ACF_2	Probability
$200,000	.3	$250,000	.2	$ 300,000	.2
300,000	.7	450,000	.5	500,000	.5
		650,000	.3	700,000	.2
				1,000,000	.1

1. Construct a probability tree representing the possible outcomes.
2. Determine the joint probability of each possible sequence of events taking place.
3. What is the expected IRR of this project?
4. What is the range of possible IRRs for this project?

SOLUTION TO SELF-CORRECTION PROBLEM

Project A:

Year	(A) Expected Cash Flow	(B) α_t	(A • B) (Expected Cash Flow) x (α_t)	Present Value Factor at 8%	Present Value
0	–$300,000	1.00	–$300,000	1.000	–$300,000
1	100,000	.95	95,000	0.926	87,970
2	200,000	.90	180,000	0.857	154,260
3	200,000	.85	170,000	0.794	134,980
4	300,000	.80	240,000	0.735	176,400
5	300,000	.75	225,000	0.681	153,225
					NPV_A = $406,835

Project B:

Year	(A) Expected Cash Flow	(B) α_t	(A • B) (Expected Cash Flow) x (α_t)	Present Value Factor at 8%	Present Value
0	–$300,000	1.00	–$300,000	1.000	–$300,000
1	200,000	.90	180,000	0.926	166,680
2	200,000	.80	160,000	0.857	137,120
3	200,000	.70	140,000	0.794	111,160
4	300,000	.60	180,000	0.735	132,300
5	400,000	.50	200,000	0.681	136,200
					NPV_A = $383,460

Thus project A should be selected since it has the higher NPV.

Case Problem

MADE IN THE U.S.A.: DUMPED IN BRAZIL, AFRICA . . .

Ethics in Dealing with Uncertainty in Capital Budgeting, or What Happens When a Project is No Longer Sellable

In an uncertain world, capital budgeting attempts to determine what the future of a new product will bring and how then to act on that forecast. We never know for certain what the future will bring, but we do arrive at some idea of what the distribution of possible outcomes looks like. Unfortunately, when there is uncertainty, the outcome is not always a good one. For example, what happens if the government rules that our product is not safe? The answer is that we must abandon the product. The question then becomes what to do with the inventory we currently have on hand. We certainly want to deal with it in a way that is in the best interests of our shareholders. We also want to obey the law and act ethically. As with most ethical questions, there isn't necessarily a right or wrong answer.

When it comes to the safety of young children, fire is a parent's nightmare. Just the thought of their young ones trapped in their cribs and beds by a raging nocturnal blaze is enough to make most mothers and fathers take every precaution to ensure their children's safety. Little wonder that when fire-retardant children's pajamas hit the market in the mid-1970s, they proved an overnight success. Within a few short years, more than 200 million pairs were sold, and the sales of millions more were all but guaranteed. For their manufacturers, the future could not have been been brighter. Then, like a bolt from the blue, came word that the pajamas were killers.

In June 1977, the U.S. Consumer Product Safety Commission (CPSC) banned the sale of these pajamas and ordered the recall of millions of pairs. Reason: The pajamas contained the flame-retardant chemical Tris (2,3-dibromoprophyl), which had been found to cause kidney cancer in children.

Whereas just months earlier the 100 medium- and small-garment manufacturers of the Tris-impregnated pajamas couldn't fill orders fast enough, suddenly they were worrying about how to get rid of the millions of pairs now sitting in warehouses. Because of its toxicity, the sleepwear couldn't even be thrown away, let alone be sold. Indeed, the CPSC left no doubt about how the pajamas were to be disposed of—buried or burned or used as industrial wiping cloths. All meant millions of dollars in losses for manufacturers.

The companies affected—mostly small, family-run operations employing fewer than 100 workers—immediately attempted to shift blame to the mills that made the cloth. When the attempt failed, they tried to get the big department stores that sold the pajamas and the chemical companies that produced Tris to share the financial losses. Again, no sale. Finally, in desperation, the companies lobbied in Washington for a bill making the federal government partially responsible for the losses. It was the government, they argued, that originally had required the companies to add Tris to pajamas and then had prohibited their sale. Congress was sympathetic; it passed a bill granting companies relief. But President Carter vetoed it.

While the small firms were waging their political battle in the halls of Congress, ads began appearing in the classified pages of *Women's Wear Daily*. "Tris-Tris-Tris . . . We will buy any fabric containing Tris," read one. Another said, "Tris—we will purchase any large quantities of garments containing Tris."[1] The ads had been placed

[1]Mark Hosenball, "Karl Marx and the pajamas Game," *Mother Jones* (November 1979):47.

by exporters, who began buying up the pajamas, usually at 10 to 30 percent of the normal wholesale price. Their intent was clear: to dump[2] the carcinogenic pajamas on overseas markets.[3]

Tris is not the only example of dumping. In 1972, 400 Iraqis died and 5,000 were hospitalized after eating wheat and barely treated with a U.S.-banned organic mercury fungicide. Winstrol, a synthetic male hormone that had been found to stunt the growth of American children, was made available in Brazil as an appetite stimulant for children. Depo-Provera, an injectable contraceptive known to cause malignant tumors in animals, was shipped overseas to seventy countries where it was used in U.S.-sponsored population control programs. And 450,000 baby pacifiers, of the type known to have caused choking deaths, were exported for sale overseas.

Manufacturers that dump products abroad clearly are motivated by profit or at least by the hope of avoiding financial losses resulting from having to withdraw a product from the market. For government and health agencies that cooperate in the exporting of dangerous products, the motives are more complex.

For example, as early as 1971, the dangers of the Dalkon Shield intrauterine device were well documented.[4] Among the adverse reactions were pelvic inflammation, blood poisoning, pregnancies resulting in spontaneous abortions, tubal pregnancies, and uterine perforations. A number of deaths were even attributed to the device. Faced with losing its domestic market, A. H. Robins Co., manufacturer of the Dalkon Shield, worked out a deal with the Office of Population within the U.S. Agency for International Development (AID), whereby AID bought thousands of the devices at a reduced price for use in population-control programs in forty-two countries.

Why do governmental and population-control agencies approve for sale and use overseas birth control devices proved dangerous in the United States? They say their motives are humanitarian. Since the rate of dying in childbirth is high in Third World countries, almost any birth control device is preferable to none. Third World scientists and government officials frequently support this argument. They insist that denying their countries access to the contraceptives of their choice is tantamount to violating their countries' national sovereignty.

Apparently this argument has found a sympathetic ear in Washington, for it turns up in the "notification" system that regulates the export of banned or dangerous products overseas. Based on the principles of national sovereignty, self-determination, and free trade, the notification system requires that foreign governments be notified whenever a product is banned, deregulated, suspended, or canceled by an American regulatory agency. The State Department, which implements the system, has a policy statement on the subject that reads in part: "No country should establish itself as the arbiter of others' health and safety standards. Individual governments are generally in the best position to establish standards of public health and safety."

Critics of the system claim that notifying foreign health officials is virtually useless. For one thing, other governments rarely can establish health standards or even control imports into their countries. Indeed, most of the Third World countries were banned or dangerous products are dumped lack regulatory agencies, adequate testing facilities, and well-staffed customs departments.

Then there's the problem of getting the word out about hazardous products. In theory, when a government agency such as the Environmental Protection Agency or the Food and Drug Administration (FDA) finds a product hazardous, it is supposed to inform the State Department, which is to notify local health officials. But agencies often fail to inform the State Department of the product they have banned or found harmful. And when it is notified, its communiqués typically go no further than the U.S. embassies abroad. One embassy official even told the General Accounting Office that he "did not routinely forward notification of chemicals

[2]"Dumping" is a term apparently coined by *Mother Jones* magazine to refer to the practice of exporting to overseas countries products that have been banned or declared hazardous in the United States.

[3]Unless otherwise noted, the facts and quotations reported in this case are based on Mark Dowie, "The Corporate Crime of the Century," *Mother Jones* (November 1971) and Russell Mokhiber, *Corporate Crime and Violence* (San Francisco: Sierra Club Books, 1988), 181–95. See also Jane Kay, "Global Dumping of U.S. Toxics Is Big Business," *San Francisco Examiner* (September 23, 1990): A2.

[4]See Mark Dowie and Tracy Johnston, "A Case of Corporate Malpractice," *Mother Jones* (November 1976).

not registered in the host country because it may adversely affect U.S. exporting." When foreign officials are notified by U.S. embassies, they sometimes find the communiqués vague or ambiguous or too technical to understand.

In an effort to remedy these problems, at the end of his term in office, President Jimmy Carter issued an executive order that (1) improved export notice procedures; (2) called for publishing an annual summary of substances banned or severely restricted for domestic use in the United States; (3) directed the State Department and other federal agencies to participate in the development of international hazards alert systems; and (4) established procedures for placing formal export licensing controls on a limited number of extremely hazardous substances. In one of this first acts as president, however, Ronald Reagan rescinded the order. Later in his administration, the law that formerly prohibited U.S. pharmaceutical companies from exporting drugs that are banned or not registered in this country was weakened to allow the export to twenty-one countries of drugs not yet approved for use in the United States.

But even if communication procedures were improved or the export of dangerous products forbidden, there are ways that companies can circumvent these threats to their profits—for example, by simply changing the name of the product or by exporting the individual ingredients of a product to a plant in a foreign country. Once there, the ingredients can be reassembled and the product dumped.[5] Upjohn, for example, through its Belgian subsidiary, continues to produce Depo-Provera, which the FDA has consistently refused to approve for use in this country. And the prohibition on the export of dangerous drugs is not that hard to sidestep. "Unless the package bursts open on the dock," one drug company executive observes, "you have no chance of being caught."

Unfortunately for us, in the case of pesticides the effects of overseas dumping are now coming home. The Environmental Protection Agency bans from the United States all crop uses of DDT and Dieldrin, which kill fish, cause tumors in animals, and build up in the fatty tissue of humans. It also bans heptachlor, chlordane, leptophos, endrin, and many other pesticides, including 2,4,5-T (which contains the deadly poison dioxin, the active ingredient in Agent Orange, the notorious defoliant used in Vietnam) because they are dangerous to human beings. No law, however, prohibits the sale of DDT and these other U.S.-banned pesticides overseas, where thanks to corporate dumping they are routinely used in agriculture. The FDA now estimates, through spot checks, the 10 percent of our imported food is contaminated with illegal residues of banned pesticides. And the FDA's most commonly used testing procedure does not even check for 70 percent of the pesticides known to cause cancer.

Questions

1. Was the dumping in this case ethical? Those involved in the dumping might have argued that the people receiving the pajamas would not have otherwise had access to such clothing and were notified of the health and safety hazards. Does this affect your feelings about the case? What do you think about the exportation of the Dalkon Shield? Can it be justified because the rate of dying during childbirth in Third World Countries is extremely high, and, as such, any effective birth control device is better than none?
2. What obligations did the financial managers have to their shareholders to do whatever is possible to avoid major financial losses associated with these products?
3. Is it still immoral or unethical to dump goods when doing so does not violate any U.S. laws? How about when those receiving the goods know the dangers? Why do you think dumpers dump? Do you think they believe what they are doing is ethically acceptable?

[5]Mark Dowie, "A Dumper's Guide to Tricks of the Trade," *Mother Jones* (November 1979):25

Source: Adapted by permission from William Shaw and Vincent Barry, *Moral Issues in Business*, 5th ed. (New York: Wadsworth, 1992), 28–31.

SECTION IX

Convertible Securities, Warrants, Options, and Restructuring and Reorganization

CHAPTER 24

Convertibles, Exchangeables, and Warrants

In addition to **straight debt** and **equity** instruments, a company may finance with an *option*, a contract giving its holder the right to buy common stock or to exchange something for it within a specific period of time. As a result, the value of the option instrument is strongly influenced by changes in value of the stock. In this chapter, we consider three specific types of options employed by business firms in their financing—the convertible security, the exchangeable bond, and the warrant. In the addendum to the chapter, a detailed discussion of option pricing theory appears.

Straight debt (or equity) Debt (or equity) that cannot be exchanged for another asset.

Convertible security A bond or a preferred stock that is convertible into a specified number of shares of common stock at the option of the holder.

Conversion price The price per share at which common stock will be exchanged for a convertible security. It is equal to the face value of the convertible security divided by the conversion ratio.

Conversion ratio The number of shares of common stock into which a convertible security can be converted. It is equal to the face value of the convertible security divided by the conversion price.

CONVERTIBLE SECURITY FEATURES

A **convertible security** is a bond or a share of preferred stock that can be converted at the option of the holder into common stock of the same corporation. Once converted into common stock, the stock cannot be exchanged again for bonds or preferred stock. The ratio of exchange between the convertible security and the common stock can be stated in terms of either a **conversion price** or a **conversion ratio.** McKesson Corporation's 9.75 percent convertible subordinated debentures ($1,000 face value) have a conversion price of $43.75, meaning that each debenture is convertible into 22.86 shares of common stock. We simply divide the face value of the security ($1,000) by the conversion price ($43.75) to obtain the conversion ratio, *22.86 shares.* The conversion privilege can be stated in terms of either the conversion price or the conversion ratio.

The conversion terms are not necessarily constant over time. Some convertible issues provide for increases or step-ups in the conversion price at periodic intervals. For example, a $1,000-face-value bond might have a conversion price of $40 a share for the first five years, $45 a share for the second five years, $50 for the third five years, and so on. In this way, the bond converts into fewer shares of common stock as time goes by. Usually, the conversion price is adjusted for any stock splits or stock dividends that occur after the securities are sold. If the common stock were split 2 for 1, the conversion price would be halved. This provision protects the convertible bondholder and is known as an *antidilution clause.*

Conversion Value and Premium Over Conversion Value

Conversion value
The value of the convertible security in terms of the common stock into which the security can be converted. It is equal to the conversion ratio times the current market price per share of the common stock.

Premium over conversion value
The market price of a convertible security minus its conversion value; also called *conversion premium.*

The **conversion value** of a convertible security is the conversion ratio of the security times the market price per share of the common stock. If McKesson stock were selling for $50, the conversion value of one convertible subordinated debenture would be 22.86 × $50 = *$1,143.*

The convertible security provides the investor with a fixed return from a bond or with a specified dividend from preferred stock. In addition, the investor receives an option to convert the security into common stock and thereby participates in the possibility of capital gains associated with being a residual owner of the corporation. Because of this option, the company is able to sell the convertible security at a lower yield than it would have to pay on a straight bond or preferred stock issue.

At the time of issuance, the convertible security will be priced higher than its conversion value. The differential is known as the **premium over conversion value.** The McKesson convertible subordinated debentures were sold to the public for $1,000 a bond. The market price of the common stock at the time of issuance of the convertibles was approximately $38.50 per share. Therefore, the conversion value of each bond was 22.86 × $38.50 = *$880,* and the differential of $120 between this value and the $1,000 issuing price represented the premium over conversion value. Frequently, this premium is expressed as a percentage of the conversion value. In our example the conversion premium is $120 divided by $880, or *13.6 percent.* For most issues of convertibles, the conversion premium ranges from 10 to 20 percent. For a growth company, the conversion premium can be in the upper part of this range, or perhaps even higher in the case of "super-growth." For companies with more moderate growth, the conversion premium may be closer to 10 percent. The range itself is established mainly by market tradition, in keeping with the idea that the issuer should be in a position to force conversion within a reasonable period of time. (Forcing conversion will be illustrated shortly.)

Almost without exception, convertible securities provide for a *call price.* As was true with the straight bond or preferred stock, the call feature enables the corporation to call the security for redemption. Few convertible securities, however, are ever redeemed. Instead, the purpose of the call is usually to force conversion when the conversion value of the security is significantly above its call price.

Other Features

Almost all convertible bond issues are subordinated to other creditors. That fact permits the lender to treat convertible subordinated debt or convertible preferred stock as a part of the equity base when evaluating the financial condition of the issuer. In the event of liquidation, it makes no difference to the creditor if the issue is actually converted. In either case, the lender has a prior claim. The situation is different with a convertible bond that is not subordinate. As long as the bond is not converted, its holder would be a general creditor in the event of liquidation. For this reason, there is a strong incentive from other creditors for the company to make the issue subordinated.

Investors in a company's common stock tend to recognize the potential **dilution** in their position before actual conversion takes place. For accounting reporting purposes, a company with convertible securities or warrants outstanding is required to report earnings per share in such a way that the reader of the financial statement can visualize the potential dilution. More specifically, it must report earnings per share on two bases. The first is *primary earnings per share,* where earnings per share is calculated "as if" *common stock equivalents* (securities whose primary value is due to their ability to be converted to or exchanged for common stock) that dilute earnings per share were converted or exercised. The second is *fully diluted earnings per share,* which assumes conversion of *all* potentially dilutive securities. For companies with sizeable financing involving potentially dilutive securities other than common stock equivalents, the difference between the two earnings per share figures can be substantial.

Dilution
A decrease in the proportional claim on earnings and assets of a share of common stock because of the issuance of additional shares.

USE OF CONVERTIBLES

In many cases, convertible securities are employed as "deferred" common stock financing. Technically these securities represent debt or preferred stock, but in essence they are delayed common stock. Companies that issue convertibles expect them to be converted in the future. By selling a convertible security instead of common stock, companies create less dilution in earnings per share, both now and in the future. The reason is that the conversion price on a convertible security is higher than the issuing price on a new issue of common stock.

The current market price of the common stock of the mythical ABC Corporation is $40 per share. If the company raises capital with an issue of common stock, it will have to underprice the issue in order to sell it in the market. The company can sell the stock through underwriters and thus realize net proceeds of $36 per share. If the company wishes to raise $18 million, the issue will involve 500,000 shares of additional stock. On the other hand, if ABC Corporation sells a convertible issue, it is able to set the conversion price above the current market price per share. If the conversion premium is 15 percent, the conversion price will be $46 per share. Assuming an $18 million issue of convertibles, the number of shares of additional common stock after conversion will be

$$\frac{\$18 \text{ million}}{\$46} = 391{,}305$$

We see that potential dilution with a convertible issue is less than that with a common stock issue because 500,000 minus 391,305 leaves **108,695** fewer shares to be added.

Another advantage to the company in using convertible securities is that the interest rate or preferred dividend rate is lower than the rate the company would have to pay on a straight bond or a straight preferred stock issue. The conversion feature makes the issue more attractive to investors. The greater the value of the conversion feature to investors, the lower the yield the company will need to pay in order to sell the issue. The lower interest payments may be particularly useful to a company in a growth phase, because lower payments allow the firm to keep more cash for growth. Moverover, companies with relatively low credit ratings but good prospects for growth may find it extremely difficult to sell a straight issue of bonds or preferred stock. The market may respond favorably to convertible issues of these companies, not because of the quality of the convertible bonds or the convertible preferred stock per se but because of the quality of the underlying common stock.

Forcing or Stimulating Conversion

Companies usually issue convertible securities with the expectation that these securities will be converted within a certain length of time. Investors can *exercise* their options voluntarily at any time and exchange the convertible security for common stock. However, they may prefer to hold the security, for its price will increase if the price of the common stock increases. Also, during this time, they receive regular interest payments or preferred stock dividends. For the security convertible into common stock that pays no dividend, it is to the holder's advantage never to convert voluntarily. In other words, the investor should delay conversion as long as possible. (When a company pays a common stock dividend, it may be in the interest of the convertible security holder to convert voluntarily.) On the other hand, it is in the company's interest, on behalf of its current shareholders, to force conversion as soon as the conversion value exceeds the call price—thereby taking the option away from the option's holder. In doing so, the firm also eliminates the cost of paying interest on the convertible debentures or dividends on the convertible preferred stock.

To force conversion, companies issuing convertible securities must usually call the issue. If the call is to succeed, the market price of the security must be significantly higher than the call price so that investors will convert rather than accept the lower call price. Many companies regard a 15 percent premium of conversion value over call price as a sufficient cushion for possible resulting declines in market price and for enticing investors to convert their securities. The conversion price of a convertible debenture ($1,000 face value) might be $50 and the call price $1,080. For the conversion value of the bond to equal the call price, the market price of the stock must be $1,080 dividend by 20, or $54 a share. If the bonds are called when the market price is $54, many investors might choose to accept the call price rather than convert. The company would then have to redeem many of the bonds for cash, in part defeating the purpose of the original financing. In order to ensure almost complete conversion, the company might wait to call the debentures until the conversion value of the bond was 15 percent above the call price, a value that corresponds to a common stock market price of approximately $62 a share. At this price, the investor who accepts the call price suffers a significant opportunity loss. Studies show that companies tend to call their convertibles after a period of rise in their common stock price relative to the market. As a result, the opportunity loss to the holder for not converting is pronounced.

Market Price Reaction. Upon announcement that a convertible bond issue is to be called, the market price of the company's common stock typically declines by a small but significant amount. This decline may be due to several reasons, though all are somewhat ambiguous. It is clear that the company will have lower interest expenses after conversion than before. As a result, it loses a tax shield, which as we know may have value to the common shareholders. However, this argument supposes that investors are surprised by the call and that they do not expect the company to replace the called debt. Another reason for the decline in share price might be the dilution in earnings per share, which results from an increased number of shares. However, the potential dilution is surely recognized in the marketplace before the convertible bond is called, although the timing of the call may be somewhat uncertain. Finally, there may be a wealth transfer from shareholders to senior-security holders if the calling of the convertible bond issue is unexpected. The senior claims simply become more creditworthy with the elimination of a debt issue. Wayne H. Mikkelson tested these notions and found that convertible bond calls result in a decline in share price at the announcement date, but convertible preferred stock calls do not result in a decline.[1] He speculated that there may be an information effect at play and that the calling of a convertible bond conveys unfavorable information about the company's earnings prospects.

Stimulating Conversion. Other means are available for a company to "stimulate," as opposed to "force," conversion. By establishing an acceleration of "step-up" in the conversion price at steady intervals in the future, the company places persistent pressure on bondholders to convert, assuming that the conversion value of the security is relatively high. If the conversion price is scheduled to increase from $50 to $56 at the end of next month, convertible bondholders have an incentive to convert prior to that time, all other things being the same. If the holders wait, they receive fewer shares of common stock. The step-up provision must be established at the time the convertible issue is sold. It cannot be used for purposes of stimulating conversion at a particular moment.

Another means for stimulating conversion is to increase the dividend on the common stock, thereby making the common stock more attractive. In certain cases, the dividend income available on the common stock may exceed interest income on the convertible security. Although these two stimulants enhance conversion, invariably a portion of the convertible bondholders will not convert, owing to the downside protection of the bond, the superior legal claim on assets, and other reasons. Consequently, calling the issue may be the only means for ensuring that the issue will be substantially converted.

Debt-Plus-Option Characteristic. The simplistic view that a convertible bond is the best of all possible worlds for the issuing firm—because it offers a lower interest cost than straight debt and less dilution than equity financing—overlooks the option nature of the contract. The convertible bond may be viewed as straight debt plus an option to purchase common stock. The greater the uncertainty, or risk, of the firm's cash flow, the less the value of the debt, all other things the same. Expressed differently, the greater the risk, the higher the interest rate necessary to attract lenders. On the other hand, the greater the uncertainty or volatility of cash flow, the greater the value of the option (see the addendum at the end of the chapter.)

[1]Wayne H. Mikkelson, "Convertible Calls and Security Returns," *Journal of Financial Economics* 9 (September 1981), 237–64.

Thus, risk cuts both ways when it comes to convertibles. As its operating risk increases, a firm incurs higher interest costs on new straight debt. However, with convertible debt the option component becomes more valuable to the option holder as a firm's operating risk increases. This suggests that when a company's future is highly uncertain, a convertible security may be the financing method of choice. Whereas a high-risk company may be unable to sell straight debt at a reasonable price, the option characteristic in a convertible security makes the debt-plus-option characteristic attractive in the marketplace. Thus, the convertible security serves an important role for the company faced with operating uncertainty.

VALUE OF CONVERTIBLE SECURITIES

Hedge
(Noun) Something which reduces the risk of future price movements.

As we know, the value of a convertible security to an investor is twofold—its value as a bond or preferred stock and its potential value as common stock. (Because the principles of valuation of a convertible bond and of a convertible preferred stock are nearly the same, our subsequent discussion will refer to convertible bonds.) Investors obtain a **hedge** when they purchase a convertible bond. If the market price of the stock rises, the value of the convertible is determined largely by its conversion value. If the market for the stock turns down, the investor still holds a bond whose value provides a floor below which the price of the convertible is unlikely to fall.

Straight Bond Value

Straight bond value
The value of a convertible bond if the convertible feature were valueless; in other words, the value of a nonconvertible bond with the same coupon rate, maturity, and default risk as the convertible bond.

The **straight bond value** of a convertible security is the price at which a similar but nonconvertible bond of the same company would sell in the open market. For semiannual compounding, it can be determined by solving the following equation for V_{SB}:

$$V_{SB} = \sum_{t=1}^{2n} \frac{I/2}{(1 + i/2)^t} + \frac{F}{(1 + i/2)^{2n}} \quad \textbf{(22-1)}$$

$$= (I/2)(PVIFA_{i/2,2n}) + F(PVIF_{i/2,2n}) \quad \textbf{(22-2)}$$

where V_{SB} = straight bond value of the convertible
$I/2$ = semiannual interest payments determined by the coupon rate
F = face value of the bond
$2n$ = number of semiannual periods until final maturity
$i/2$ = market semiannual yield to maturity on a similar but nonconvertible bond of the same company

In Eqs. (22-1) and (22-2), we assume semiannual interest payments, which are typical with U.S. corporate bonds, so the total number of interest payments is 2 times the years to maturity.

Fawlty Food Company has outstanding a 9 percent convertible debenture with a final maturity 20 years hence. This corresponds to a semiannual coupon payment of 4.5 percent of the bond's face value of $1,000, or $45. If the company is to sell a straight 20-year debenture in the current market, the semiannual yield will have to be 6 percent to be attractive to investors. For a 20-year bond with a 9 percent coupon to provide a 6 percent semiannual yield to maturity, the bond has to sell at a discount. Using Eq. (22-2) and rounding, we have

$$V_{SB} = (\$45)(PVIFA_{6\%,40}) + \$1{,}000(PVIF_{6\%,40}) = \$774$$

Thus the straight bond floor value of Fawlty Food Company's convertible bonds would be \$774. This floor value suggests that if the price of the common stock were to fall sharply so that the conversion feature had negligible value, the price of the convertible would fall only to \$774. At that price, the security would sell as a straight bond in keeping with prevailing bond yields for that grade of security.

The straight bond value of a convertible is not constant over time. It varies with (1) interest-rate movements in the capital market and (2) changes in the financial risk of the company involved. If interest rates in general rise, the straight bond value of a convertible bond will decline. If the semiannual yield to maturity on a straight bond in our example increases from 6 to 7 percent, the straight bond value of the convertible will drop from \$774 to \$667. Moreover, the company's credit rating can either improve or deteriorate over time. If it improves and the company is able to sell a straight bond at a lower yield to maturity, the straight bond value of the convertible security will increase, all other things held constant. If the company's credit standing deteriorates and the yield on a straight bond increases, the straight bond value will decline. Unfortunately for the investor, when the market price of the stock falls because of poor earnings and/or increased risk, the company's credit standing may suffer. As a result, the straight bond value of the convertible may decline along with the decline in its conversion value, giving investors less downside protection than they might have originally expected.[2]

Premiums

Convertible securities frequently sell at premiums over both their straight bond value and their conversion value. Recall that the conversion value of a convertible is simply the current market price per share of the company's common stock times the number of shares into which the security is convertible. The fact that the convertible bond provides the investor with a degree of downside protection, given the qualifications mentioned, often results in its selling at a market price somewhat higher than its conversion value. In general, the more volatile the price movements of the stock, the more valuable is the downside protection afforded by the straight bond value floor. For this reason, as well as for additional reasons discussed later, the market price of a convertible security frequently is above its conversion value. The difference is known as the *premium over conversion value.*

Moreover, a convertible bond will typically sell at a **premium over straight bond value,** primarily because of the conversion feature. Unless the market price of the stock is very low relative to the conversion price, the conversion feature will usually have value, in that investors may eventually find it profitable to convert the securities. To the extent that the conversion feature does have value, the convertible security will sell at a premium over its straight bond value. The higher the market price of the common stock relative to the conversion price, the greater this premium.

Premium over straight bond value Market price of a convertible bond minus its straight bond value.

[2]Mathematically, the straight bond value of a convertible will rise over time, all other things held constant, if the face value of the convertible is above the straight bond value at the time of issuance. At final maturity, the straight bond value will equal the face value of the convertible, assuming the company is not in default.

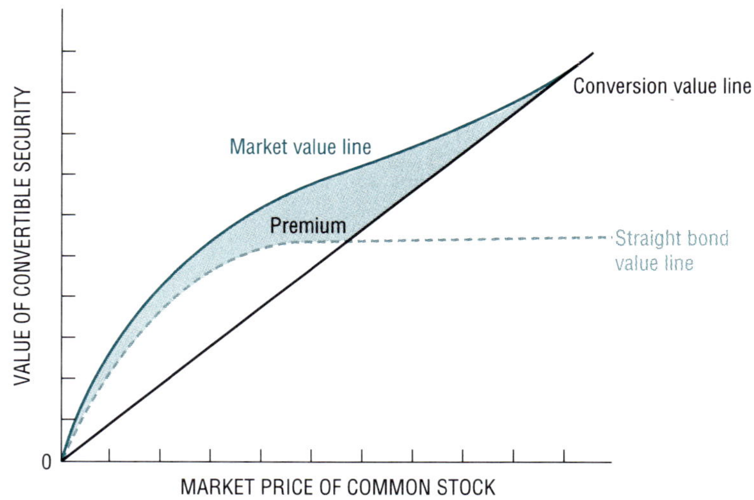

FIGURE 24-1
Relationships among the various types of bond values and premiums

Relationships Among Premiums

The trade-off between the two premiums depicts the value of the option to investors and is illustrated in Fig. 24-1. The market price of the common stock is on the horizontal axis. The value of the convertible security is on the vertical. It should be pointed out that the two axes are on different scales. The diagonal line, which starts at the origin, represents the conversion value of the bond. It is linear, as the conversion ratio is invariant with respect to the market price of the stock.

The straight bond value line, however, is related to the market price of the common stock. If a company is doing badly financially, the prices of both its common stock and its bonds are likely to be low. At the extreme, if the total value of the company were zero, both the bonds and the common stock would have a value of zero. As the company becomes sounder financially and the common stock increases in price, bond value increases but at a decreasing rate. After a point, the straight bond value line becomes flat, and further increases in common stock price are unrelated to it. At this point, the straight bond value is determined by what other similar high-grade bonds sell for in the market. The upper curved line in the figure represents the market price of the convertible security. The distance between this line and the straight bond value line is the premium over straight bond value, while the distance between the market value line and the conversion value line represents the premium over conversion value. Finally, if we consider the convertible bond's *floor value* to be the higher of its conversion value or straight bond value, the shaded area in Fig. 24-1 represents the "overall" premium, or *premium over floor value.*

We see that at relatively high common stock price levels, the value of the convertible as a bond is insignificant. Consequently, its premium over straight bond value is high, whereas its premium over conversion value is negligible. The security sells mainly for its common stock equivalent. Investors are unwilling to pay a significant premium over conversion value for the following reasons. First, the greater the premium of market price of the convertible over its straight bond value, the less valuable the straight bond value protection is to the investor. Second, when the conversion value is high, the convertible may be called. If it is, the investor will want to convert rather than redeem the bond for the call price. Upon conversion, of course, the bond is worth only its conversion value.

On the other hand, when the market value of the convertible is close to its straight bond value, the conversion feature has little value. At this level, the convertible security is valued primarily as a straight bond. Under these circumstances, the market price of the convertible is likely to exceed its conversion value by a significant premium.

The principal reason for premiums in market price over both conversion value and straight bond value is the unusual appeal of a convertible as both a bond and an option on common stock. A convertible security offers the holder partial protection on the downside together with participation in upward movements in common stock price. Thus, the distribution of possible outcomes is skewed to the right, and this characteristic finds favor with investors. Option pricing theory allows a deeper understanding of the valuation of this characteristic, and that is the subject of the addendum to this chapter.

EXCHANGEABLE BONDS

An **exchangeable bond** is like a convertible bond, but the common stock involved is that of another corporation. For example, National Distillers and Chemical Corporation issued $49 million in 6 percent subordinated debentures exchangeable into common stock of Cetus Corporation, a biotechnology firm. While still not a widespread means of financing, exchangeables are increasing in importance.

Exchangeable bond A bond that allows the holder to exchange the security for common stock of another company—generally, one in which the bond issuer has an ownership interest.

Features

Like the conversion price and conversion ratio for a convertible security, the *exchange price* and *exchange ratio* must be set at the time of issuance. The National Distillers debentures have an exchange price of $49, which translates into 20.41 shares of Cetus for each $1,000-face-value debenture. At the time of issuance, Cetus was selling for $37.50 per share. Therefore, the *exchange premium* was 30.7 percent, which is very high as conversion premiums go. This reflected the nature of Cetus—lots of potential but having little revenue and much uncertainty. The more variable the outcome, of course, the higher the option value. As with convertible bonds, there is typically a call feature with an exchangeable bond, and most issues are subordinated.

Use in Financing

Exchangeable bond issues usually occur only when the issuer owns common stock in the company in which the bonds can be exchanged. National Distillers, for example, owned 4 percent of the outstanding stock of Cetus Corporation. Exchange requests presumably will be satisfied from this holding, as opposed to acquiring stock in the open market. Therefore, the decision to go with an exchangeable bond issue may bring with it the reduction in or elimination of stock ownership in another company. A conscious decision of this sort is embodied in the financing.

As with a convertible security, interest costs of exchangeable bonds are lower because of the option value of the instrument. So far, most companies issuing exchangeables have been large and would not have experienced difficulty financing with a straight debt issue. The attraction is a lower interest cost together with the possibility of disposing of a common stock investment at a premium above the present price. Finally, some exchangeable issues of U.S. companies have been placed with investors outside the United States.

Valuation of an Exchangeable

The valuation of an exchangeable security is identical in most respects to that of a convertible security. However, there are some differences. Instead of the bond and the common stock being in the same company, the bond is in one company and the common stock is in another. Therefore, the investor must analyze and track both components. One advantage with this arrangement is diversification. The straight bond value and the stock value are not directly linked. Poor earnings and financial performance in one company will not lead to a simultaneous decline in straight bond value and the common stock value. If the companies are in unrelated industries, the investor achieves diversification. With market imperfections, this may lead to a higher valuation for an exchangeable than for a convertible, all other things the same.

Because option values are driven by the volatility of the associated asset, differences in volatility may affect the choice between an exchangeable and a convertible bond issue. If the common stock of the company in exchange is more volatile than that of the issuer, the option value will be greater with an exchangeable bond issue than it will with a convertible bond issue, all other things the same.

A relative disadvantage has to do with taxation. The difference between the market value of the common stock at the time of exchange and the cost of the bond is treated as a capital gain for tax purposes. In the case of a convertible, this gain goes unrecognized until the common stock is sold. The net effect of these factors is unclear. In summary, exchangeable securities are a variant of convertible securities that may increase in use, what with the rapid innovation now occurring in corporate financing.

WARRANTS

Warrant
A relatively long-term option to purchase common stock at a specified exercise price over a specified period of time.

A **warrant** is an option to purchase common stock at a specified exercise price (usually higher than the market price at the time of warrant issuance) for a specified period (often lasting for years and, in some cases, in perpetuity). In contrast, a *right* is also an option to buy common stock, but normally it has a subscription price lower than the market value of the common stock and very short life (often two to four weeks).

Features

The warrant itself contains the provisions of the option. It states the number of shares the holder can buy for each warrant. Frequently, a warrant will provide the option to purchase 1 share of common stock for each warrant held, but it might be 2 shares, 3 shares, or 2.54 shares. Another important provision is the price at which the warrant is exercisable, such as $12 a share. This means that in order to buy 1 share, the warrant holder must put up $12 a share. This **exercise price** may either be fixed or stepped up over time. For example, the exercise price might increase from $12 to $13 after three years and to $14 after another three years.

Exercise price
The price at which the common stock associated with a warrant or call option can be purchased over a specified period.

The warrant must specify the date that the option expires unless it is perpetual, having no expiration date, such as warrants of Alleghany Corporation. Because a warrant is only an option to purchase stock, warrant holders are not entitled to any cash dividends paid on the common stock, nor do they have voting power. If the common stock is split or a stock dividend is declared, the option price of the warrant is usually adjusted to take this change into account.

Exercise of Warrants. When warrants are *exercised,* the common stock of the company is increased. Moreover, the debt that was issued in conjunction with the warrants remains outstanding, assuming that the warrants are detachable. At the time of the issue of the warrants, the exercise price is usually set in excess of the market price of the common stock. The premium is often 15 percent or so above the stock's value. If the share price is $40, this translates into an exercise price of $46.

To see how new capital can be infused with the exercise of warrants, let us take a company we shall call Black Shoals, Inc. It has just raised $25 million in debt funds with warrants attached. The debentures carry an 11 percent coupon rate. With each debenture ($1,000 face value) investors receive one warrant entitling them to purchase four shares of common stock at $30 a share. The capitalization of the company before financing, after financing, and after complete exercise of the warrant options is as follows (in millions):

	Before Financing	After Financing	After Exercise
Debentures		$25	$25
Common stock ($10 par value)	$10	$10	$11
Additional paid-in capital			2
Retained earnings	40	40	40
Shareholders' equity	$50	$50	$53
Total capitalization	$50	$75	$78

The retained earnings of the company remain unchanged, and the debenture issue has neither matured nor been called. Exercising their warrant options, the warrant holders purchase 100,000 shares of stock at $30 a share, or $3 million in total. Consequently, the total capitalization of the company is increased by that amount.

A company cannot force the exercise of the warrant option as it can force the exercise of the conversion option by calling a convertible security. Consequently, it is unable to control when, if ever, the warrants will be exercised and there will be an infusion of new equity capital into the corporation. Only the expiration date sets a limit on how long the warrants can remain outstanding and unexercised. As with convertibles, it is necessary for companies to report earnings per share on a fully diluted basis. Full dilution means the maximum possible dilution if all convertible securities were converted into common stock and all warrants or options to purchase common stock were exercised, as long as they are dilutive. As a result of this requirement, the common stock investor is not likely to overlook the potential dilution inherent in a company's financing with convertible securities and warrants.

Valuation of a Warrant

The theoretical value of a warrant can be determined by

$$(N)(P_s) - E \tag{22-3}$$

where N = the number of shares that can be purchased with one warrant
P_s = the market price of one share of stock
E = the exercise price associated with the purchase of N shares

The theoretical value of a warrant is the lowest level at which the warrant will generally sell. If, for some reason, the market price of a warrant were to go lower than its theoretical value, arbitragers would eliminate the differential by buying the warrants, exercising them, and selling the stock.

When the market value of the associated stock is less than the exercise price, the theoretical value of the warrant is zero, and it is said to be trading "out of the money." When the value of the associated common stock is greater than the exercise price, the theoretical value of the warrant is positive, as depicted by the solid line in Fig. 24-2. Under these circumstances, the warrant is said to be trading "in the money."

Premium Over Theoretical Value

The primary reason that a warrant sells at a price higher than its theoretical value is the opportunity for leverage. To illustrate the concept of leverage, consider the Textron warrants. For each warrant held, one share of common stock can be purchased, and the exercise price is $10. If the common stock were selling at $12 a share, the theoretical value of the warrant would be $2. Suppose, however, that the common stock increased by 25 percent in price to $15 a share. The theoretical value of the warrant would go from $2 to $5, a gain of 150 percent.

The opportunity for increased gain is attractive to investors when the common stock is selling near its exercise price. For a particular dollar investment, the investor can buy more warrants than common stock. If the stock moves up in price, the investor will make more money on the warrants than on an equal dollar investment in common stock. Of course, leverage works both ways. The percentage change can be almost as pronounced on the downside. However, there is a limit to how far the warrant can fall in price because it is bounded at zero. Moreover, for the market price to drop to zero, there would have to be no probability that the market

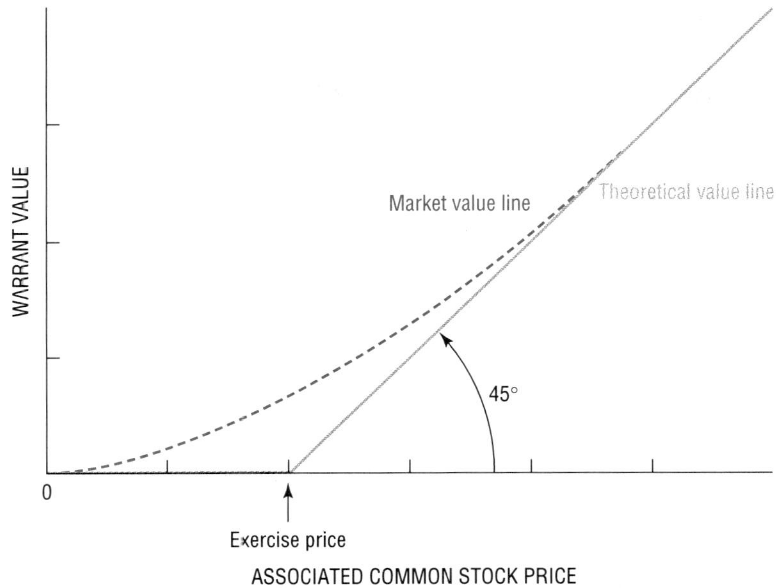

FIGURE 24-2
Relationship between the theoretical value and the market value of a warrant

price of the stock would exceed the exercise price during the exercise period. Usually there is some probability.

The market prices of many warrants are in excess of their theoretical values because of the potential for upside movements in the value of the warrant while, at the same time, downside movements are cushioned. In particular, this event occurs when the market price of the associated common stock is near the exercise price of the warrant.

Relationship Between Values

The typical relationship between the market value of a warrant and the price of the associated common stock is shown in Fig. 24-2. The theoretical value of the warrant is represented by the solid line in the figure and the actual market value by the dashed line. One might think of the theoretical value line as representing the values a warrant might take with only a moment to expiration of the warrant. When there is a reasonable amount of time to expiration of the warrant, the relationship between warrant value and stock price is better depicted by the dashed line in Fig. 24-2. The greater the length of time to expiration, the more time the investor has in which to exercise the warrant, and the more valuable it becomes. As a result, the further in the future the expiration date of the warrant, the higher the market value line tends to be in relation to the theoretical value line.

We note in the figure that when the market price of the associated common stock is low in relation to the exercise price, the actual market value of a warrant exceeds its theoretical value. As the market price of the associated stock rises, the market value of the warrant usually approaches its theoretical value. This simply suggests that a warrant has the greatest value, relative to its theoretical value, when it has the greatest potential in terms of percentage for upside movements and where the amount of funds invested is not all that great. The valuation of options, of which warrants are one form, is explored in more depth in the addendum to this chapter.

SUMMARY

- Convertible securities, exchangeable securities, and warrants are options under which the holder can obtain common stock.
- A *convertible security* is a bond or a share of preferred stock that can be converted at the option of the holder into common stock of the same corporation. For the issuing corporation, convertibles often represent "delayed" common stock financing. For a given amount of financing, there will be less dilution with a convertible issue than with a common stock issue, assuming that the convertible is eventually converted and is not simply left "overhanging."
- As a hybrid security, a convertible bond has a straight bond value floor and a conversion, or stock, value. As a result, the distribution of possible returns to the security holder is skewed to the right, and there is a trade-off between the two factors.
- An *exchangeable bond* may be exchanged for common stock in another corporation. It is like the convertible security in its valuation underpinnings with a couple of exceptions. This method of financing is applicable to companies that have stock holdings in another company.
- A *warrant* is an option to purchase common stock at a specified exercise price (usually higher than the market price at the time of warrant issuance) for a specified period (often lasting for years and, in some cases, in perpetuity).
- The conversion or exchange feature enables the investor to transfer a debt instrument or preferred stock into common stock, whereas a warrant attached to a bond enables the holder to purchase a specified number of shares at a specified price. With a warrant, the exercise of the option does not result in the elimination of the bonds.
- Normally, warrants are employed as a "sweetener" for a public or private issue of debt. The market price of a warrant is usually higher than its theoretical value when the market price of the stock is close to the exercise price. When the market price of the stock is high relative to the exercise price, warrants tend to sell at about their theoretical values.

ADDENDUM: OPTION PRICING

Call option
A contract that gives the holder the right to *purchase* a specified quantity of the underlying asset at a predetermined price (the *exercise price*) on or before a fixed expiration date.

An *option* is simply a contract that gives the holder the right to buy or sell the common stock of a company at some specified price. Among a variety of option contracts, the most prevalent are the *call option* and the *put option*. The **call option** gives the holder the right to buy a share of stock at a specified price, known as the exercise price. We might have a call option to buy one share of ABC Corporation's common stock at $10 through December 31, which is the expiration date. The party which provides the option is known as the *option writer*. In the case of a call option, the writer must deliver stock to the option holder when the latter exercises the option.

As is evident from our discussions in the chapter, a warrant is a form of call option, as is a convertible security. Both give the holder an option on the company's stock. In contrast to a call option, a **put option** gives the holder the right to sell a share of stock at a specified price up to the expiration date. It is the mirror image of a call option. In what follows, we will focus only on the valuation of call options.

Put option
A contract that gives the holder the right to *sell* a specified quantity of the underlying asset at a predetermined price (the *exercise price*) on or before a fixed expiration date.

Valuation on Expiration Date

Suppose that we are concerned with the value of a call option (hereafter simply called an option) on its expiration date. The value of the option, V_o is simply

$$V_o = \max(P_s - E, 0) \tag{24A-1}$$

where P_s is the market price of one share of stock, E is the exercise price of the option, and max means the maximum value of $(P_s - E)$, or zero, whichever is greater. To illustrate the formula, suppose that one share of Lindahl Corporation's common stock is \$25 at the expiration date and that the exercise price of an option is \$15. The value of the option would be \$25 – \$15 = **\$10.** Note that the value of the option is determined solely by the price of the common stock less the exercise price. However, the value of the option cannot have a negative value. When the exercise price exceeds the price of the common stock, the price of the option becomes zero.

This notion is illustrated graphically in Fig. 24-2, where the theoretical value of a warrant is shown. The expiration value of the option lies along the theoretical value line. The horizontal axis represents the price of a share of common stock at the expiration date.

Valuation Prior to Expiration

Consider now the value of the option with one period to expiration. For simplicity, let us assume that it can be exercised only on the expiration date. The price of the common stock at the expiration date is not known but rather is subject to probabilistic beliefs. As long as there is some time to expiration, it is possible for the market value of the option to be greater than its theoretical value. The reason is that the option *may* have value in the future. This idea was explored when we discussed warrants, so further discussion here is not necessary. The actual value of the option might be described by the dashed line in Fig. 24-2.

The Effect of Time of Expiration. In general, the longer the period of time to expiration, the greater the value of the option relative to its theoretical value. This makes sense in that there is more time in which the option may have value. Moreover, the further in the future one pays the exercise price, the lower its present value, and this too enhances the option's value. As the expiration date of an option approaches, the relationship between the option value and the common stock price becomes more convex (rounded outward) This is illustrated in Fig. 24A-1. Market value line 1 represents an option with a shorter time to expiration than that for market value line 2, and market value line 2 represents an option with a shorter time to expiration than that for market value line 3.

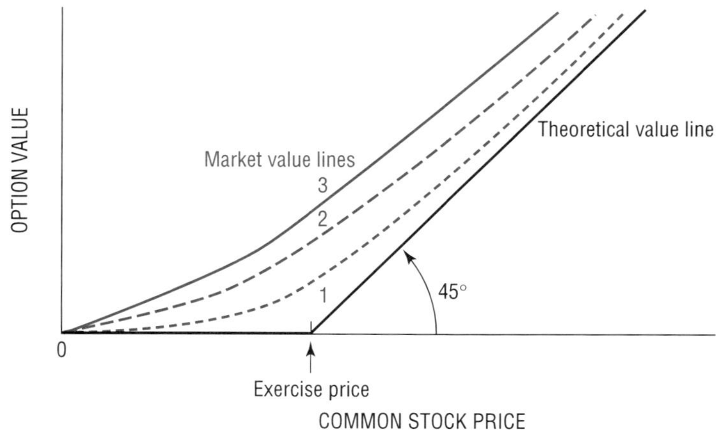

FIGURE 24A-1
Relationship between common stock price and option value for various expiration dates

The Interest Rate Employed. Another feature crucial to option valuation is the time value of money. When an investor acquires a share of common stock by means of an option, he or she makes an initial "down payment" on the total price to be paid for the exercised option. The "final installment" (i.e., the exercise price) is not due until the option is exercised sometime in the future. The higher that interest rates are in the market, the more valuable this delay (until the time the exercise price is paid) is to the investor. Thus, an option will be more valuable the longer the time to its expiration and the higher the interest rate.

The Influence of Volatility. Usually the most important factor in the valuation of options is the price volatility of the associated common stock. More specifically, the greater the possibility of extreme outcomes, the greater the value of the option to the holder, all other things the same. We may, at the beginning of a period, be considering options on two common stocks that have the following probability distributions of possible values at the expiration of the option:

Probability of Occurrence	Price of Common Stock A	Price of Common Stock B
.10	$30	$20
.25	36	30
.30	40	40
.25	44	50
.10	50	60
1.00		

The expected stock price at the end of the period is the same for both common stocks, namely $40. For common stock B, however, there is a much larger dispersion of possible outcomes. Suppose that the exercise prices of options to purchase common stock A and common stock B at the end of the period are also the same, say, \$38. Thus, the two common stocks have the same expected values at the end of the period, and the options have the same exercise price. The expected value of the option, $\overline{V}_o$, for common stock A at the end of the period, however, is

(1) Probability of Occurrence	(2) Price of Common Stock A, P_s	(3) max(P_s − \$38, 0)	(4) (1) × (3)
.10	\$30	\$ 0	\$ .00
.25	36	0	.00
.30	40	2	.60
.25	44	6	1.50
.10	50	12	1.20
1.00			$\overline{V}_o$ = **\$3.30**

Whereas that for common stock B is

(1) Probability of Occurrence	(2) Price of Common Stock B, P_s	(3) max(P_s − \$38, 0)	(4) (1) × (3)
.10	\$20	\$ 0	\$ .00
.25	30	0	.00
.30	40	2	.60
.25	50	12	3.00
.10	60	24	2.20
1.00			$\overline{V}_o$ = **\$5.80**

Thus, the greater dispersion of possible outcomes for common stock B leads to a greater expected value of option price on the expiration date. The reason is that values for the option cannot be negative. As a result, the greater the dispersion, the greater the magnitude of favorable outcomes as measured by the common stock price minus the exercise price. Increases in the volatility of the common stock price therefore increase the magnitude of favorable outcomes for the option buyer and, hence, increase the value of the option.

This effect of stock price volatility on option value is illustrated in Fig. 24A-2. Two common stocks with different end-of-period share price distributions are shown. The exercise price is the same for each stock, so the lower boundary for expiration-date option values (theoretical values is also the same. This is shown by the hockey-stick-shaped portion of the one at the bottom of the figure. The probability distribution of end-of-period share price is wider for common stock W than it is for common stock N, reflecting greater price volatility for stock W. Since common stock W provides a greater chance for a big payoff (i.e., one that is far to the right of the exercise price), its option is worth more than that for common stock N.

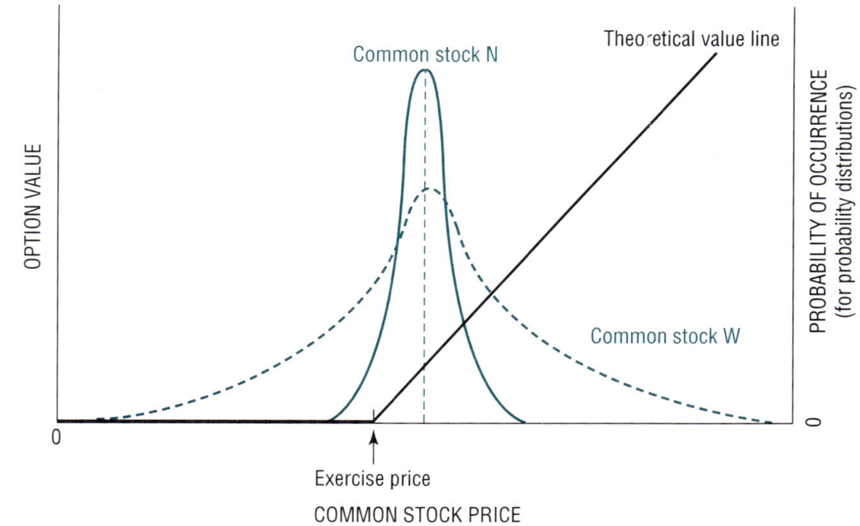

FIGURE 24A-2
Stock price volatility and option values for two common stocks

To summarize where we are, we note that the value (or price) of a call option will change as follows when the variables listed below increase:

Increase in Variable	Resulting Change in Option Value
Stock price volatility	Increase
Time to option expiration	Increase
Interest rate	Increase
Exercise price	Decrease
Current stock price	Increase

Keeping these relationships in mind will help us as we probe deeper into option valuation.

Hedging With Options

Having two related financial assets—a common stock and an option on that common stock—we can set up a risk-free *hedged position.* Price movements in one of the financial assets will be offset by opposite price movements in the other. A hedged position can be established by buying the common stock (termed *holding it long*) and by writing options. If the common stock goes up in price, we gain in our long position, that is, in the value of the common stock we hold. We lose in the options we have written, because the price we must pay for the common stock in order to deliver to the person exercising the option is higher than it was when the option was written.

Thus, when one holds a combination of common stock and options written, movements upward or downward in the price of the common stock are offset by opposite movements in the value of the option position written. If one does this properly, one can make the overall position (long in common stock coupled with options written) approximately risk free. In market equilibrium, one would expect to earn only the risk-free rate on a perfectly hedged position.

Black-Scholes Option Model

In a landmark paper, Fischer Black and Myron Scholes developed a precise model for determining the equilibrium value of an option.[3] This model is based on the hedging notion just discussed. Black-Scholes assume an option that can be exercised only at maturity; no transactions costs or market imperfections; a common stock that pays no dividend; a known short-term interest rate at which market participants can both borrow and lend; and finally, changes to common stock prices that follow a random pattern.

Given these assumptions, we can determine the equilibrium value of an option. Should the actual price of the option differ from that given by the model, we could establish a riskless hedged position and earn a return in excess of the short-term interest rate. As arbitragers enter the scene, the excess return would eventually be driven out, and the price of the option would equal that value given by the model.

To illustrate a hedged position, suppose that the appropriate relationship between the option and the common stock of XYZ Corporation is that shown in Fig. 24A-3. Suppose further that the current market price of the common stock is $20 and the price of the option $7. At $20 a share, the slope (rise over run) of the *market value line* in Fig. 24A-3 is one-half, or 1 to 2. The slope determines the appropriate hedged position. Therefore, in this particular situation a hedged position could be undertaken by buying *one* share of stock for $20 and writing *two* options at $7 each. The "net money" invested in this position would be $20 – 2($7) = **$6.**

The combination of holding one share of common stock long and two options short leaves us essentially hedged with respect to risk. If the common stock drops slightly in price, the value of the short position goes up by approximately an equal amount. We say *approximately* because with changes in the price of the common stock and with changes in time, the ideal hedge ratio changes. With a common stock price increase, for example, the slope of the market value line in Fig. 24A-3 increases. Therefore, fewer options would need to be written. If the common stock price declines, the slope decreases, and more options would need to be written to maintain a hedge. In addition to modifications to the slope of the line caused by stock price changes, the line itself will shift downward as time goes on and the expiration date approaches. This is illustrated in Fig. 24A-1.

Thus, one's short position in options must be continually adjusted for changes in the common stock price and for changes in time if a riskless hedged position is to be maintained. The assumptions of the model make this possible. But in the real world, transactions costs make it impractical to adjust one's short position continuously. Even here, however, the risk that will appear as a result of moderate changes

[3]Fischer Black and Myron Scholes, 'The Pricing of Options and Corporate Liabilities," *Journal of Political Economy* 81 (May-June 1973), 637–54.

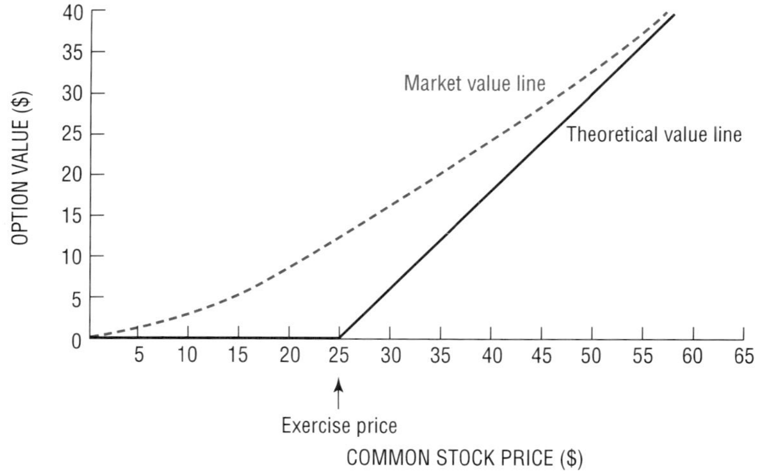

FIGURE 24A-3
Relationship between the option value and the common stock price for XYZ Corporation

in common stock price or of the passage of time will be small. Moreover, it can be diversified away. For practical purposes, then, it is possible to maintain a hedged position that is approximately risk free. Arbitrage will ensure that the return on this position is approximately the short-term, risk-free rate.

If the price of the option gets out of line with that of the common stock, it would be possible for a person to earn more than the short-term rate on a hedged position. In the example, remember the "net money" invested in the position was \$20 – 2(\$7) = **\$6.** As the total hedged position is riskless, the "net money" invested should provide a return equal only to the short-term rate. If for some reason the prices on the two instruments get out of line with each other, it would be possible to earn a return on the total position in excess of the short-term interest rate times the "net money" invested. In other words, excess returns would be possible on a position perfectly hedged for risk.

As a result, arbitragers would enter the picture and would borrow large sums of money, establish hedged positions, and reap the excess returns available. This action would continue until the buying or selling pressure on the prices of the common stock and the option drove such prices into "equilibrium" with each other. At such time, the return on the "net money" invested in a fully hedged position would once again be the short-term rate. Thus, there are equilibrium forces that cause a riskless hedge to provide a return equal to the short-term rate.

The Exact Formula and Implications. In this context, the equilibrium value of the option, V_o, that entitles the holder to buy one share of stock is shown by Black and Scholes to be

$$V_o = (P_s)(N(d_1)) - (E/e^{rt})(N(d_2)) \qquad \textbf{(24A-2)}$$

where P_s = the current price of the underlying common stock
E = the exercise price of the option
e = 2.71828, the base of the natural system of logarithms
r = the short-term, risk-free interest rate, continuously compounded

t = the length of time in years to the expiration of the option

$N(d)$ = the probability that a standardized, normally distributed random variable will have a value less than d

$$d_1 = \frac{\ln(P_s/E) + [r + (.5)\sigma^2]t}{\sigma\sqrt{t}}$$

$$d_2 = \frac{\ln(P_s/E) + [r - (.5)\sigma^2]t}{\sigma\sqrt{t}}$$

ln = the natural logarithm

σ = the standard deviation of the continuously compounded annual rate of return on the stock

The important implication of this formula is that the value of the option is a function of the short-term, risk-free interest rate; of the time to expiration; and of the variance of the rate of return on the stock but that it is *not* a function of the expected return on the stock. The value of the option in Eq. (24A-2) increases with the increase of the time to expiration, t, the standard deviation, σ, and the short-term, risk-free interest rate, r. The reasons for these relationships were discussed earlier in this addendum.

In solving the formula, we know the current common stock price, the time to expiration, the exercise price, and the short-term interest rate. The key unknown, then, is the standard deviation of the annual rate of return of the common stock. This must be estimated. The usual approach is to use the past volatility of the common stock's return as a proxy for the future. Black and Scholes, as well as others, have tested the model using standard deviations estimated from past data with some degree of success. Given the valuation equation for options, Black and Scholes have derived the ratio of shares of common stock to options necessary to maintain a fully hedged position. It is shown to be $N(d_1)$, which was defined earlier. Thus, the Black-Scholes model permits the quantification of the various factors that affect the value of an option. As we saw, the key factor is estimating the future volatility of the common stock.

SUMMARY

In summary, it is possible to establish a riskless hedged position by buying a common stock and by writing options. The hedge ratio determines the portion of stock held long in relation to the options that are written. In efficient financial markets, the rate of return on a perfectly hedged position would be the risk-free rate. If this is the case, it is possible to determine the appropriate value of the option at the beginning of the period. If the actual value is above or below this value, arbitrage should drive the price of the option toward the correct price.

The Black-Scholes option pricing model provides an exact formula for determining the value of an option based on the volatility of the common stock, the price of the common stock, the exercise price of the option, the time to expiration of the option, and the short-term, risk-free interest rate. The model is based on the notion that investors are able to maintain reasonably hedged positions over time and that arbitrage will drive the return on such positions to the risk-free rate. As a result, the option price will bear a precise relationship to the common stock price. The Black-Scholes model provides considerable insight into the valuation of options.

QUESTIONS

1. Define the *conversion price* of a convertible debenture, the *conversion ratio*, the *conversion value*, the *premium over conversion value*, and the *premium over straight bond value*.
2. This chapter argues that convertible securities are a form of delayed equity financing allowing the sale of equity at a 10 to 20 percent premium over current market price. Yet most convertibles are finally called only if the current market price is well in excess of the conversion price. Would the firm have been better off to simply wait and sell the common stock later? Explain your position.
3. If convertible securities can be issued at a lower effective interest rate than long-term bonds, why would a company ever issue straight debt?
4. Some warrants have a current theoretical value of zero and yet sell for positive prices. Explain why.
5. Suppose that you are the financial manager of a closely held (owned by few shareholders), small electronics firm. You have a favorable investment opportunity and are considering raising funds to finance it, using subordinated convertible debentures or straight bonds with warrants attached. Equity funds are not a possibility, as you feel the current stock price has been unnecessarily penalized for recent start-up expenses and the firm's high debt ratio (relative to the industry). If you expect additional large future funds requirements, which financing alternative would you adopt? Why?
6. Why might the holder of a convertible bond elect to convert voluntarily?
7. What reasons can you offer for the use of warrants by small, rapidly growing companies?
8. Why does the market price of an option such as a warrant usually exceed its value as common stock?
9. When a convertible security is converted into common stock, there is dilution in earnings per share. Would you expect the market price of the stock to decline as a result of this dilution? Explain.
10. If the desire of a company in selling convertible securities is delayed equity financing, would it be wise to establish at the time the security is initially sold a step-up in conversion price every few years?
11. Why would an investor want to invest in warrants as opposed to common stock?
12. As a lender, how attractive are warrants to you as a "sweetener"? Will you give terms more favorable than you otherwise would? Explain.
13. Why is unlimited upside potential and a lower (price) boundary of zero attractive to investors in a warrant? If the common stock were highly volatile, would this be a good or a bad thing?
14. With option financing, such as convertible securities and debt issues with warrants attached, does the company get something (a lower interest cost) for nothing?
15. How does an exchangeable bond differ from a convertible bond? How is the bond the same?

16. With respect to valuation, is the investor better off with an exchangeable bond or with a convertible bond?

SELF-CORRECTION PROBLEMS

1. The Barnaby Boat Company has current earnings of $3 a share with 500,000 shares of common stock outstanding. The company plans to issue 40,000 shares of 7 percent, $50-par-value convertible preferred stock at par. The preferred stock is convertible into two shares of common for each preferred share held. The common stock has a current market price of $21 per share.
   a. What is the preferred stock's conversion value?
   b. What is its premium over conversion value?
   c. Assuming that total earnings stay the same, what will be the effect of the issue on earnings per share (i) before conversion? (ii) on a fully diluted basis?
   d. If profits after taxes increase by $1 million, what will be earnings per share (i) before conversion? (ii) on a fully diluted basis?
2. Phlogiston Chemical Company plans to issue $10 million in 10 percent convertible subordinated debentures. Currently, the common stock price is $36 per share, and the company believes it could obtain a conversion premium (issuing price in excess of conversion value) of approximately 12 percent. The call price of the debenture in the first 10 years is $1,060 per bond, after which it drops to $1,030 in the next 10 years and to $1,000 in the last 10 years. To allow for fluctuations in the market price of the stock, the company does not want to call the debentures until their conversion value is at least 15 percent in excess of the call price. Earnings per share are expected to grow at an 8 percent compound annual rate in the foreseeable future, and the company envisions no change in its price/earnings ratio.
   a. Determine the expected length of time that must elapse before the company is in a position to force conversion.
   b. Is the issuance of a convertible security a good idea for the company?
3. Red Herring Pizza has outstanding warrants, where each warrant entitles the holder to purchase two shares of stock at $24 per share. The market price per share of stock and market price per warrant were the following over the last year:

	Observation					
	1	2	3	4	5	6
Stock price	$20	$18	$27	$32	$24	$38
Warrant price	5	3	12	20	8	29

Determine the theoretical value per warrant for each of these observations. Then plot the market value per warrant in relation to this theoretical value. At what price per common share is the warrant premium over theoretical value the greatest? Why?

PROBLEMS

1. The common stock of the Blue Sky Corporation earns $3.00 per share, has a 60 percent dividend payout, and sells at a P/E ratio of 8.333. Blue Sky wishes to offer $10 million of 9 percent, 20-year convertible debentures with an initial conversion premium of 20 percent and a call price of 105 ($1,050 per $1,000 face value). Blue Sky currently has 1 million common shares outstanding and has a 40 percent tax rate.
   a. What is the conversion price?
   b. What is the conversion ratio per $1,000 debenture?
   c. What is the initial conversion value of each debenture?
   d. How many new shares of common stock must be issued if all debentures are converted?
   e. If Blue Sky can increase operating earnings (before taxes) by $1 million per year with the proceeds of the debenture issue, compute the new earnings per share and earnings retained before and after conversion.
2. Assume that the Blue Sky Corporation (in Problem 1) could sell $10 million in straight debt at 12 percent as an alternative to the convertible issue. Compute the earnings per share and earnings retained after issuance of the straight debt under the assumption of a $1 million increase in operating earnings, and compare your answers with those obtained in Problem 1, Part (e).
3. Faversham Fish Farm has outstanding a 7.75 percent, 20-year convertible debenture issue. Each $1,000 debenture is convertible into 25 shares of common stock. The company also has a straight debt issue outstanding of the same approximate maturity, so it is an easy matter to determine the straight bond value of the convertible issue. The market price of Faversham common stock is volatile. Over the last year, the following was observed:

	Observation				
	1	2	3	4	5
Market price per share	$ 40	$ 45	$ 32	$ 23	$ 18
Straight bond value	690	700	650	600	550
Market price of convertible debenture	1,065	1,140	890	740	640

   a. Compute the premium over conversion value (in dollars) and the premium over straight bond value for each of the observations.
   b. Compare the two premiums either visually or by graph. What do the relationships tell you with respect to the valuation of the convertible debenture?
4. The following year, Faversham Fish Farm (see Problem 3) flounders. Its stock price drops to $10 per share and the market price of the convertible debentures to $440 per debenture. The straight bond value goes to $410. Determine the premium over conversion value and the premium over straight bond value. What can you say about the bond value floor?
5. The Rambutan Fruit Company needs to raise $10 million by means of a debt issue. It has the following two alternatives: a 20-year, 8 percent convertible debenture issue with a $50 conversion price and $1,000 face value; or a 20-year,

12 percent straight debt issue. Each $1,000 bond has a detachable warrant to purchase four shares of stock for a total of $200. The company has a 40 percent tax rate, and its stock is currently selling at $40 per share. Its net income before interest and taxes is a constant 20 percent of its total capitalization, which currently appears as follows:

Common stock (par $5)	$ 5,000,000
Additional paid-in capital	10,000,000
Retained earnings	15,000,000
Total capitalization	$30,000,000

a. Show the capitalization from each alternative, both before and after conversion or exercise (a total of four different capitalizations).
b. Compute earnings per share currently and under each of the four capitalizations determined in Part (a).
c. If the price of Rambutan stock went to $75, determine the theoretical value of each warrant issued under the second alternative.

6. Singapore Enterprise is considering an exchangeable bond issue where each bond can be exchanged for $16\frac{2}{3}$ shares of Malaysian Palm Oil Company. The latter company's stock is presently selling for $50 a share. At what premium over exchange value (expressed as a percentage) will the bonds be sold if they are sold for $1,000 a bond? Are there advantages to this type of financing versus a convertible issue?
7. Using Eq. (24-2), compute the theoretical value of each of the following warrants:

Warrant	N	P_s	E
(a)	5	$100	$400
(b)	10	10	60
(c)	2.3	4	10
(d)	3.54	27.125	35.40

8. Alexander Zinc Company called its 7 percent convertible subordinated debentures for redemption at the end of last month. The call price was 106 ($1,060 per $1,000 face value). A holder of a $1,000 bond was entitled to convert into 34.7 shares of stock. At the time of the call announcement, the common stock of Alexander Zinc was selling at $43 per share.
   a. What is the approximate market price at which the debentures would be selling at the time of the announcement?
   b. By what percentage would market price per share need to drop before bondholders would rationally accept the call price?
9. Jenni Shover, Inc., has warrants outstanding that allow the holder to purchase three shares of common stock for a total $60 for each warrant that is held. Currently, the market price per share of Jenni Shover common stock is $18. How-

ever, investors hold the following probabilistic beliefs about the stock six months hence.

Market price per share	$16	$18	$20	$22	$24
Probability	.15	.20	.30	.20	.15

a. What is the present theoretical value of the warrant?
b. What is the expected value of stock price six months hence?
c. What is the expected theoretical value of the warrant six months hence?
d. Would you expect the present market price of the warrant to equal its theoretical value? If not, why not?

10. Suppose you have just bought a warrant that entitles you to purchase two shares of common stock for $45. The market price of the common stock is $26 per share, whereas the market price of the warrant is $10 in excess of its theoretical value. One year later the common stock has risen in price to $50 per share. The warrant now sells for $2 more than its theoretical value.
    a. If the common stock paid $1 in dividends for the year, what is the return on investment in the common stock?
    b. What is the return on investment in the warrant?
    c. Why do the two rates of return differ?

SOLUTIONS TO SELF-CORRECTION PROBLEMS

1. a. Conversion value = Conversion ratio × market price per share
   $= 2 \times \$21 =$ **$42**
   b. Premium over conversion value = $50 − $42 = **$8**
   (or, expressed as a percentage = $8/$42 = 19.05%)
   c. Earnings per share:

Total after-tax earnings ($3 × 500,000 shares)	$1,500,000
Preferred stock dividend	140,000
Earnings available to common shareholders	$1,360,000
Number of shares	÷ 500,000
Earnings per share	**$2.72**
Total after-tax earnings	$1,500,000
Number of shares (500,000 + 80,000)	÷ 580,000
Earnings per share	**$2.59**

   d. Earnings per share after profit increase:

Total after-tax earnings	$2,500,000
Preferred stock dividend	140,000
Earnings available to common shareholders	$2,360,000
Number of shares	÷ 500,000
Earnings per share	**$4.72**
Total after-tax earnings	$2,500,000
Number of shares (500,000 + 80,000)	÷ 580,000
Earnings per share	**$4.31**

2. a. Conversion price = $36 × 1.12 = $40.32
   Call price per share the first 10 years = $40.32 × 1.06 = $42.74
   Price to which the common must rise before company will be in a position to force conversion = $42.74 × 1.15 = $49.15
   Increase from present price = ($49.15/$36) – 1 = 36.5%
   At an 8 percent compound growth rate, earnings per share will grow to 36 percent in 4 years—this is simply $(1.08)^4 - 1$. If the price/earnings ratio stays the same, it will take approximately *four years* before the company will be in a position to force conversion.
   b. This period is somewhat longer than the two to three years that market participants have come to expect for the convertible security. Still, it is not far out of line, and the company may wish to go ahead. However, if uncertainty as to earnings per share increases with the length of time in the future, there may be considerable risk of an "overhanging" issue. This may cause the company to reconsider.
3. Market price of warrant and theoretical value at various common stock prices (in ascending order):

Common stock	$18	$20	$24	$27	$32	$38
Warrant price	3	5	8	12	20	29
Theoretical value	0	0	0	6	16	28

When plotted, the relationship is of the same pattern as shown in Fig. 24-1. The maximum premium over theoretical value occurs when share price is $24 and the warrant has a theoretical value of zero. Here the greatest leverage occurs, and since volatility is what gives an option value, the premium over theoretical value tends to be the greatest at this point.

SELECTED REFERENCES

Black, Fischer, "How to Use the Holes in Black-Scholes." *Journal of Applied Corporate Finance* 1 (Winter 1989), 67–73.

______, and Myron Scholes. "The Pricing of Options and Corporate Liabilities." *Journal of Political Economy* 81 (May-June 1973), 637–54.

Brennan, Michael J., and Eduardo S. Schwartz. "Convertible Bonds: Valuation and Optimal Strategies for Call and Conversion." *Journal of Finance* 32 (December 1977), 1699–1715.

______. "Analyzing Convertible Bonds." *Journal of Financial and Quantitative Analysis* 15 (November 1980), 907–29.

______. "The Case for Convertibles." *Journal of Applied Corporate Finance* 1 (Summer 1988), 55–64.

Ferri, Michael G., Joseph W. Kremer, and H. Dennis Oberhelman. "An Analysis of Corporate Warrants." *Advances in Futures and Options Research* 1 (1986), 201–26.

Finnerty, John D. "The Case for Issuing Synthetic Convertible Bonds." *Midland Corporate Finance Journal* 4 (Fall 1986), 73–82.

Green, Richard C. "Investment Incentives, Debt, and Warrants." *Journal of Financial Economics* 13 (March 1984), 115–36.

Haugen, Robert A. *Modern Investment Theory,* 3rd ed. Englewood Cliffs, NJ: Prentice Hall, 1994, Chap. 17–18.

Hull, John. *Options, Futures, and Other Derivative Securities.* Englewood Cliffs, NJ: Prentice Hall, 1989.

Jones, E. Philip, and Scott P. Mason. "Equity-Linker Debt." *Midland Corporate Finance Journal* 3 (Winter 1986), 47–58.

Marr, M. Wayne, and G. Rodney Thompson. "The Pricing of New Convertible Bond Issues." *Financial Management* 13 (Summer 1984), 31–37.

Mikkelson, Wayne H. "Convertible Calls and Security Returns." *Journal of Financial Economics* 9 (September 1981), 237–64.

Rubinstein, Mark, and John C. Cox. *Option Markets.* Englewood Cliffs, NJ: Prentice Hall, 1985.

Sharpe, William F., and Gordon J. Alexander. *Investments,* 4th ed. Englewood Cliffs, NJ: Prentice Hall, 1990, Chap. 18.

Van Horne, James C. "Warrant Valuation in Relation to Volatility and Opportunity Costs." *Industrial Management Review* 10 (Spring 1969), 19–32.

______. *Financial Market Rates and Flows,* 4th ed. Englewood Cliffs, NJ: Prentice Hall, 1994. Chap. 10–11.

CHAPTER 25

Corporate Restructuring: Combinations and Divestitures

INTRODUCTION

On the whole, mergers and acquisitions during the 1980s were motivated by change. Specifically, this period saw some of the largest corporate giants taken private through leveraged buyouts, then dismembered and sold off piecemeal. What emerged from the process was a leaner and far more profitable corporation. Investors and the investment bankers that served them applauded these reformations, while bondholders and employees frequently decried what they saw as unwarranted attempts by shareholders to capture a larger portion of the firm's value. Shareholders, on the other hand, simply said they were reclaiming what was theirs all along.

A breed of specialists has been created to remake staid old corporations and return them to financial health. One such individual is Albert J. Dunlap, who now heads Scott Paper Company's efforts to restructure itself.[1] Mr. Dunlap developed his reputation for turning around poor performing companies working for Sir James Goldsmith (a British takeover specialist), where he turned around Crown Zellerbach and Diamond International. So what does Mr. Dunlap (known by some as "Rambo in Stripes" and to others simply as "Chainsaw") have in mind to reengineer Scott paper? The answer is quite simple. Learn to do more with less (cut the labor force by one third or lay off 10,500 workers) and focus on the firm's core businesses. Sounds simple. So why was it necessary to bring in Mr. Dunlap to accomplish the task? The answer is that the job of downsizing a firm is not a pleasant task, and few have the stomach for the trauma that it creates within an organization. Some, like Mr. Dunlap, do and they become turnaround specialists.

[1]Based on Glenn Collins, "Tough Leader Wields the Ax at Scott," *New York Times* (August 15, 1994):C1, C6.

Ethics In Financial Management

WERE EARLY CORPORATE TYCOONS BENEFACTORS OR ROBBER BARONS?

Management practices at the turn of the century were not always conducted with the highest of integrity. People like Cornelius Vanderbilt and John D. Rockefeller built immensely successful railroads and oil companies by engaging in activities that some have described as unethical and irresponsible.

Vanderbilt gained control of the New York and Harlem railroad lines by bribing the New York state legislature and by stock manipulation. Rockefeller conspired with the railroads to extract rebates on his freight and obtained kickbacks on the oil that his rivals shipped. Rockefeller also engaged in ruthless competition, driving his competitors out of business and then buying their assets at a fraction of their value.

Despite their unsavory practices, these early tycoons built companies that created tens of thousands of jobs and provided the industrial base for U.S. manufacturing preeminence during the first sixty years of this century. At one point, for instance, Vanderbilt employed more people than anyone in the United States. Some of these tycoons also returned a large portion of the profits they made back to society through their philanthropic efforts. Rockefeller, for instance, endowed the University of Chicago, gave millions to education, and established the Rockefeller Foundation, which continues to give away tens of millions of dollars each year.

STOP AND THINK

Mergers and acquisitions are usually justified by management on the grounds that merging diversifies the firm, thus reducing risk. However, since the stockholder can diversify personally with more ease and less expense by buying stock in the two companies, there must be other reasons for the merger if it is to add value.

WHY MERGERS MIGHT CREATE WEALTH

Clearly, for a merger to create wealth, it would have to provide shareholders with something they could not get by merely holding the individual shares of the two firms.

Economies of Scale

Wealth can be created in a merger through economies of scale. For example, administrative expenses including accounting, data processing, or simply top-management costs, may fall as a percentage of total sales as a result of sharing these resources.

Financial Management in Practice

OF TOADS AND PRINCES

Many managements apparently were overexposed in impressionable childhood years to the story in which the imprisoned handsome prince is released from a toad's body by a kiss from a beautiful princess. Consequently, they are certain their managerial kiss will do wonders for the profitability of Company T(arget) . . . investors can always buy toads at the going price for toads. If investors instead bankroll princesses who wish to pay double for the right to kiss the toad, those kisses had better pack some real dynamite. We've observed many kisses but very few miracles. Nevertheless, many managerial princesses remain serenely confident about the future potency of their kisses—even after their corporate backyards are knee-deep in unresponsive toads . . . (**A**)

We have tried occasionally to buy toads at bargain prices with results that have been chronicled in past reports. Clearly, our kisses felt flat. We have done well with a couple of princes—but they were princes when purchased. At least our kisses didn't turn them into toads. And, finally, we have occasionally been quite successful in purchasing fractional interests in easily identifiable princes at toad-like prices. (**B**)

Source: Warren Buffett, *1981 Annual Report of Berkshire Hathaway*, 4–5.

ANALYSIS AND IMPLICATIONS. . .

A. A wide variety of "strategies" have been tried in attempting to acquire companies that add value. On average, the stockholders of acquiring firms merely break even, and the acquired firm's stockholders realize an average return of 30 percent. So where is the logic to making corporate acquisitions of other corporations? For Berkshire Hathaway and Warren Buffet, the preferred strategy has been to acquire good companies, not "fixer uppers."

B. The key to success in corporate acquisitions is acquiring a business for the right price. The same is true for any business. The simple truth is that if the acquisition does not offer a positive net present value to the acquiring firm's stockholders, it should not be made.

Restating the question: What benefits are there to shareholders from holding the stock of a new, single firm that has been created through a merger as opposed to holding stock in the two individual firms prior to their merger? Let's consider some of these benefits.

Tax Benefits

If a merger were to result in a reduction of taxes that is not otherwise possible, then wealth is created by the merger. This can be the case with a firm that has lost money and thus generated tax credits but does not currently have a level of earnings sufficient to use those tax credits. Operating losses can be carried back three years and forward a total of fifteen years. As a result, tax credits that cannot be used and have no value to one firm can take on value when that firm is acquired by another firm that has earnings sufficient enough to employ the tax credits. In addition, a merger allows for previously depreciated assets to be revalued; wealth is created from the tax benefits arising from the increased depreciation associated with this revaluation of assets.

The sharing of resources can also lead to an increase in the firm's productivity. For example, if two firms sharing the same distribution channels merge, distributors carrying one product may now be willing to carry the other, thereby increasing the sales outlets for the products.

Unused Debt Potential

Some firms simply do not exhaust their debt capacity. If a firm with unused debt capacity is acquired, the new management can then increase debt financing, and reap the tax benefits associated with the increased leverage.

Complementarity in Financial Stack

When cash-rich bidders and cash-poor targets are combined, wealth may be created. This is particularly true where the cash-poor firm is a small business with limited access to capital markets. In effect, the merger allows positive NPV projects to be accepted that would have been rejected if the merger had not occurred.

Removal of Ineffective Management

A merger can result in the replacement of inefficient operations, whether in production or management. If a firm with ineffective management can be acquired, it may be possible to replace the current management with a more efficient management team, and thereby create wealth. This may be the case with firms that have grown from solely production into production and distribution companies, or R & D firms that have expanded into production and distribution; the managers simply may not know enough about the new aspects of the firm to manage it effectively.

Increased Market Power

The merger of two firms can result in an increase in market or monopoly power. Although this can result in increased wealth, it may also be illegal. The Clayton Act, as amended by the Celler-Kefauver Amendment of 1950, makes any merger illegal that results in a monopoly or substantially reduces competition. The Justice Department and the Federal Trade Commission monitor all mergers to ensure that they do not result in a reduction of competition.

Reduction in Bankruptcy Costs

There is no question that diversification can reduce the chance of financial failure and bankruptcy. Furthermore, there is a cost associated with bankruptcy. First, if a firm fails, its assets frequently cannot be sold for their true economic value. Moreover, the amount of money actually available for distribution to stockholders is further reduced by selling costs and legal fees that must be paid. Finally, the opportunity cost associated with the delays related to the legal process further reduces the funds available to the shareholder. Therefore, because costs are associated with bankruptcy, reduction of the chance of bankruptcy adds value.

The risk of bankruptcy also entails indirect costs associated with changes in the firm's debt capacity and the cost of debt. As the firm's cash flow patterns stabilize, the risk of default will decline, giving the firm an increased debt capacity and possibly reducing the cost of its debt. Because interest payments are tax deductible, they provide valuable tax savings. Thus monetary benefits are associated with an increased debt capacity. These indirect costs of bankruptcy also spread out into other areas of the firm, affecting things like production and the quality and efficiency of management. Firms with higher probabilities of bankruptcy may have a more difficult time recruiting and retaining quality managers and employees because jobs with that firm are viewed as less secure. This in turn may result in less productivity for these firms. In addition, firms with higher probabilities of bankruptcy may have a more difficult time marketing their product because of customer concern over future availability of the product. In short, there are real costs to bankruptcy. If a merger reduces this possibility of bankruptcy, it creates wealth.

"Chop-Shop" Approach—Buying Below Replacement Cost

The "chop-shop" approach, which will be discussed more fully later, suggests that the sum of the individual parts of a firm may be worth more than the current value of the whole. In the 1980s, many corporate raiders were driven by the fact that it was less expensive to purchase assets through an acquisition than it was to obtain those assets in any other way. This was particularly true of both conglomerates and oil companies. For conglomerates, corporate raiders found that they often sold for less than the sum of the market value of their parts. Much of the merger and acquisition activity associated with oil companies was driven by the fact that it was cheaper to acquire new oil reserves by purchasing a rival oil company than it was through exploration. If assets are mispriced, as this approach seems to suggest, then identifying those assets and revealing this information about the undervalued assets to an investor may result in the creation of wealth.

It should be noted that the free cash flow theory could explain this creation of wealth as easily as a mispricing theory. In particular, the oil industry was characterized in the late 1970s and early 1980s by overexploration and drilling activity in the face of reduced consumption while oil price increases created large cash flows. During this period, managers attempted to increase reserves to protect them from possible future market fluctuations. As mergers and restructuring raged through the oil industry, wealth was created. Again, this creation of wealth did not necessarily come about through any correction of mispricing. It may have been the elimination of wasteful exploration expenditures that created the wealth.

DETERMINATION OF A FIRM'S VALUE

One of the first problems in analyzing a potential merger involves placing a value on the acquired firm. This task is not easy. The value of a firm depends not only on its cash flow generation capabilities, but also upon the operating and financial characteristics of the acquiring firm. As a result, no single dollar value exists for a company. Instead, a range of values is determined that would be economically justifiable to the prospective acquirer. The final price is then negotiated by the two managements within this range.

To determine an acceptable price for a corporation, several factors are carefully evaluated. We know that the objective of the acquiring firm should be maximization of the stockholders' wealth (stock price). However, quantifying the relevant variables for this purpose is difficult at best. For instance, the primary reason for a merger might be to acquire managerial talent, or to complement a strong sales staff with an excellent production department. These *synergistic effects* are difficult to measure using the historical data of the companies involved. Even so, several quantitative variables are frequently used in an effort to estimate a firm's value. These factors include (1) book value, (2) appraisal value, (3) market price of the firm's common stock, and (4) expected cash flows.

Book Value

Book value
Generally used in this context to refer to the book or historical cost value of the firm's net worth.

The **book value** of a firm's net worth is the balance sheet amount of the assets less its outstanding liabilities or the owners' equity. For example, if a firm's historical cost less accumulated depreciation is $10 million and the firm's debt totals $4 million, the aggregate book value is $6 million. Furthermore, if 100,000 shares of common stock are outstanding, the book value per share is $60 ($6 million ÷ 100,000 shares).

Book value does not measure the market value of a company's net worth because it is based on the historical cost of the firm's assets. Seldom do such costs bear a relationship to the value of the organization or its ability to produce earnings.

Although the book value of an enterprise is clearly not the most important factor, it should not be overlooked. It can be used as a starting point to be compared with other analyses. Also, a study of the firm's working capital is particularly important to acquisitions involving a business consisting primarily of liquid assets like financial institutions. Furthermore, in industries where the ability to generate earnings requires large investments in such items as steel, cement, and petroleum, the book value could be a critical factor, especially where plant and equipment are relatively new.

Appraisal Value

An *appraisal value* of a company may be acquired from an independent appraisal firm. The techniques used by appraisers vary widely; however, this value is often closely tied to replacement cost. This method of analysis is not adequate by itself, since the value of individual assets may have little relation to the firm's overall ability to generate earnings, and thus the going-concern value of the firm. However, the

Financial Management in Practice

CORPORATE RESTRUCTURING: THE NEW THINKING

The fundamental assumptions about how businesses should be organized have changed significantly from what they were several years ago. Financial market behavior, economic logic and plain common sense suggest that focusing on a single business, or on a very small number of genuinely linked businesses, is the only way to build the value of a company in the long term. The tempting, even seductive, aphorisms of the past—diversify to reduce risk; diversify for higher growth; manage a balanced portfolio of businesses—are about as useful on today's corporate battlefield as is a horse cavalry in a modern tank war. Sadly, these old assumptions are still cherished by some corporate managers today.

The Financial Rules of the Game

The financial markets, however, have imposed their own set of rules on corporate management. Two key points highlight the difference between the old and new thinking:

(1) Managements cannot create value by doing what shareholders can do for themselves. (**A**) Unless there are real economic and business connections that lead to sustainable improvements in operating performance, managements do nothing by making acquisitions that investors cannot do for themselves by making a telephone call to a broker. Investors can diversify their risks by investing at the market price. They do not want corporate managements to do it for them by paying acquisitions premiums of 50 to 100 percent above the going rate.

This sounds straightforward enough, but it actually strikes at the heart of many, if not most, of the reasons given for corporate acquisitions in the United States and United Kingdom. Many managements seem to operate under the illusion that they should act as a substitute for the capital markets, making resource-allocation decisions that take them well beyond the activities in which they enjoy true operating advantages.

Few topics have been subjected to as much measurement and analysis as corporate diversification, and there is a large body of evidence that points to one conclusion: Unless an acquired business gains a sustainable operating advantage from becoming part of another company, no value for the acquiror's shareholders will be created by the acquisition. The fact that two businesses operate in adjacent or apparently similar areas of activity is not enough to justify the acquisition of one by the other. In fact, much of the restructuring we have seen over the past several years has been the unwinding of grandiose schemes devised by those self-deluding managements that have confused their own role with that of the financial markets. The markets are now exhibiting a healthy impatience with such fantasies.

(2) Shareholders will unlock values suppressed by management. (**B**) If investors notice that a particular company's strategy is causing it to trade at a discount to its true value, the defenses installed by managements will not, in the long run, stop the investors from getting their way. Investors can be misled, and they frequently misprice securities; however, years of bitter experience and their increasing sophistication (particularly in the United States) have made investors far less willing to accept management rationales for diversifying acquisitions. They are

Financial Management in Practice

much more likely to seek ways to evade the various barriers erected by managements to protect their empires.

Furthermore, size is no longer a barrier. Some corporate managements acquire businesses as part of a defensive strategy, believing that bigger is, if not better, at least tougher to knock over. However, unless such acquisitions achieve sustainable operating advantages for the company, they only put off the evil day. Indeed, all such acquisitions really do is increase the size of the discount in absolute dollars and make the acquiring company even more attractive to well-financed or imaginative predators.

The New Business Environment

The changes in the ground rules mentioned above show that if companies do not restructure themselves, the financial markets will do it for them. (**C**) Even without the prodding from the financial markets, however, there are compelling business reasons for companies to restructure:

(1) Competition. In a fiercely competitive environment, a broad span of businesses is a luxury that is less and less affordable. Indeed, today's managers are seeing a heightened sense of competitor performance. Absolute measures of success mean much less. Whatever the subject—whether product cost or quality, the rate of innovation, quality of service, or almost any other dimension of business—it is all relative to the competition.

(2) Flexibility. The quick and the dead. Rapidity of response is becoming crucial to corporate survival and success. Technological developments in information, production and distribution systems, and an increased consumer demand for variety are causing major shifts in the pattern of business activity. As a result, diversified firms are in for a tough time. It is hard to jump in several directions at once.

(3) Excessive corporate overhead. Too much value is absorbed by unnecessary corporate expense. Such expense is often worse than unnecessary; it can be positively damaging. In order to justify their existence, corporate headquarters frequently embark upon acquisition programs that create no value for their shareholders. After all, acquisitions are exciting, dramatic, and glamorous.

For example, the financial statements of one major diversified corporation reveal an item called "corporate expense" that totals slightly under $200 million. Compare this amount to the company's net income, which (after various adjustments for extraordinary items) totals about $1.3 billion. While adjusted net income has grown at slightly under 15 percent per annum over the past few years, corporate expense has been growing at the staggering rate of just under 50 percent per annum over the same period. Adjusting the corporate expense to an after-tax figure and applying the company's price earnings ratio to the net expense produces a cost of over $1.4 billion. Even assuming that some of the expense is necessary, there is clearly a lot of value being wasted by excessive overhead. [Editor's note: The company in question is RJR Nabisco. Duffy's article was written prior to the buyout.]

The Role of Finance

Under these new ground rules, the CFO must play a more active role in planning the direction of the company. However, good finance is not a substitute for good strategy and operations. The CFO's role is overlapping more and more with those of the CEO and COO because of the growing interconnectedness of finance, strategy, and operations. Unless this interconnectedness is acknowledged and encouraged, the best finance function in the world will not be able to

Financial Management in Practice

make up for poor strategy or inferior performance.

Therefore, the CFO needs to be centrally involved in strategy formulation, not just to ensure that the strategy is financially sound, but to bring a financial market perspective and ensure that strategic plans translate directly into shareholder value. He also needs to be more closely involved in operations, if only to ensure that the operators are fully aware of the financial dimension of operating decisions and make certain that the real causes of poor financial performance are addressed and remedied.

Source: Simon Duffy, "Corporate Restructuring: The New Thinking," *Business International Money* (January 9, 1989):1–3.

ANALYSIS AND IMPLICATIONS. . .

A. You may recall that this simple logic was used earlier when we discussed the relevance of dividend and financing policies to firm valuation. The idea is simple. Management should go about doing those things that it can do better (at lower cost and with higher value added) than the firm's shareholders.

B. Why would management want to suppress the values of the firms they manage? One possible answer is, **managers won't work for the owners unless it's in their best interest.** Consider the situation faced by a firm's top executives. They have invested a disproportionate amount of their personal wealth (including the value of their human capital as managers) in a single firm. Consequently, if something were to happen to the firm and if it should go bankrupt, they would not only lose the money they have invested over the years in corporate stock options but would find themselves at the helm of a failed firm (not a very good recommendation for a future employer). This circumstance suggests that the top management may want to diversify the firm's investments so as to reduce the risk of financial failure of the firm and the consequent losses they would suffer. Stockholders, on the other hand, can diversify their own equity portfolio easily and cheaply and consequently would not be supportive of management's efforts to "protect themselves" through corporate diversification.

C. The takeover wave of the 1980s has faded, however, the pressures for restructuring did not disappear. The new impetus for performance improvements has come from various institutional investors. Specifically, public employee pension funds such as the California Public Employees Retirement System (CalPERS) and State of Wisconsin Investment Board (SWIB) have become increasingly more active in identifying poor performing companies and pressuring their management for change. The power of these pension funds in combination with other institutional investors is formidable since institutions hold over 50 percent of all publicly traded shares of common stock and constitute approximately 80 percent of all trades.

appraised value of an enterprise may be beneficial when used in conjunction with other valuation methods. Also, the appraised value may be an important factor in special situations, such as in financial companies, natural resource enterprises, or organizations that have been operating at a loss.[2]

The use of appraisal values does yield several additional advantages. The value according to independent appraisers may permit the reduction of a counting goodwill by increasing the recognized worth of specific assets. *Goodwill* results when the purchase price of a firm exceeds the book value of the assets. Consider a company having a book value of $60,000 that is purchased for $100,000 (the $40,000 difference is goodwill). The $60,000 book value consists of $20,000 in working capital and $40,000 in fixed assets. However, an appraisal might suggest that the current values of these assets are $25,000 and $55,000, respectively. The $15,000 increase ($55,000 – $40,000) in fixed assets permits the acquiring firm to record a larger depreciation expense than would otherwise be possible, thereby reducing taxes. A second reason for an appraisal is to provide a test of the reasonableness of results obtained through methods based upon the going-concern concept. Third, the appraiser may uncover strengths and weaknesses that otherwise might not be recognized, such as in the valuation of patents, secret processes, and partially completed R & D expenditures.

Thus the appraisal is generally worthwhile if performed with additional evaluation processes. In specific instances, it may be an important instrument for valuing a corporation.

Stock Market Value

The stock market value, as expressed by stock market quotations, is another approach to estimating the net worth of a business. If the stock is listed on a major securities exchange, such as the New York Stock Exchange, and is widely traded, an approximate value can be established on the basis of the market value. The justification is based on the fact that the market quotations indicate the consensus of investors as to a firm's cash flow potential and the corresponding risk.

The market-value approach is the one most frequently used in valuing large corporations. However, this value can change abruptly. Analytical factors compete with purely speculative influences and are subject to people's sentiments and personal decisions. Thus the market is not a weighing machine, on which the value of each issue is recorded by an exact and impersonal mechanism, in accordance with the specific qualities. Rather should we say that the market is a voting machine, whereon countless individuals register choices which are the product partly of reason and partly of emotion.[3]

In short, the market-value approach is probably the one most widely used for determining the worth of a firm; a 10 to 20 percent premium above the market price is often required as an inducement for the current owners to sell their stock. Even

[2] The assets of a financial company and a natural resources firm largely consist of securities and natural reserves, respectively. The value of these individual assets has a direct bearing on the firm's earning capacity. Also, a company operating at a loss may only be worth its liquidation value, which would approximate the appraisal value.

[3] Benjamin Graham, David L. Dodd, and Sidney Cottle, *Security Analysis*, 4th ed. (New York: McGraw-Hill, 1962), 42.

so, executives who place their entire reliance upon this are subject to an inherent danger of market psychology.

"Chop-Shop" Value

The "chop-shop" approach to valuation was first proposed by Dean Lebaron and Lawrence Speidell of Batterymarch Financial Management. Specifically, it attempts to identify multi-industry companies that are undervalued and would be worth more if separated into their parts. This approach conceptualizes the practice of attempting to buy assets below their replacement cost.

Any time we confront a technique that suggests that stocks may be inefficiently priced, we must be a bit skeptical. In the case of a multi-industry firm, inefficiency in pricing may be brought on by the high cost of obtaining information. Alternatively, these firms may be worth more if split up because of agency problems. Shareholders of multi-industry companies may feel they have less control of the firm's managers, since additional layers of management may have developed with multi-industry firms. These agency costs may take the form of increased expenditures necessary to monitor the managers, costs associated with organizational change, and opportunity costs associated with poor decisions made as a result of the manager acting in his or her own best interests rather than the best interest of the shareholders.

The "chop-shop" approach attempts to value companies by their various business segments. As it is implemented by Batterymarch, it first attempts to find "pure-play" companies—that is, companies in a single industry from which it computes average "valuation ratios." The ratios frequently used compare total capitalization (debt plus equity) to total sales, to assets, and to income. In effect, these ratios represent the average value of a dollar of sales, a dollar of assets, and a dollar of income for a particular industry based on the average of all pure play companies in that industry. Assuming that these ratios hold for the various business segments of a multi-industry firm, the firm can then be valued by its parts.

For the chop-shop valuation technique to be feasible, we must naturally have information about the various business segments within the firm. This requirement is fulfilled, at least in part, by the reporting rules set forth in *Statement 14* of the Financial Accounting Standards Board (the public accountants governing group). This standard requires that firms provide detailed accounting statements along the various lines of business or what is called Standard Industrial Codes (SIC). Of course, we know that not all firms in the same industry are in fact the same—some have more growth potential or earning ability than others. As such, this methodology should be viewed cautiously. However, it is in use by financial managers, and we should understand it.

The "chop-shop" approach is actually a three-step process:

Step 1: Identify the firm's various business segments and calculate the average capitalization ratios for firms in those industries.

Step 2: Calculate a "theoretical" market value based upon each of the average capitalization ratios.

Step 3: Average the "theoretical" market values to determine the "chop-shop" value of the firm.

EXAMPLE

To illustrate the chop-shop approach, consider Cavos, Inc., with common stock currently trading at a total market price of $13 million. For Cavos, the accounting data set forth four business segments: industrial specialties, basic chemicals, consumer specialties, and basic plastics. Data for these four segments are as follows:

Business Segment	Segment Sales ($000)	Segment Assets ($000)	Segment Income ($000)
Industrial specialties	$ 2,765	$2,206	$186
Basic chemicals	5,237	4,762	165
Consumer specialties	2,029	1,645	226
Basic plastics	1,506	1,079	60
Total	$11,537	$9,692	$637

The three steps for valuing Cavos would be

Step 1: We first identify "pure" companies, that being firms that operate solely in one of the above industries; we then calculate the average capitalization ratios for those firms. This could easily be done using a computer data base, such as the Compustat tapes, which provide detailed financial information on most publicly traded firms. The average capitalization ratios for Cavos's four business segments have been determined and are as shown in Table 25-1.

Step 2: Once we have calculated the average market capitalization ratios for the various market segments, we need only multiply Cavos's segment values (that is, segment sales, segment assets, and segment income) times the corresponding capitalization ratios to determine the theoretical market values. This is done in Table 25-2.

Step 3: Finally, the theoretical values must be averaged to calculate the "chop-shop" value of the firm. The average of the three theoretical values in Table 25-3 is $18,923,000, computed as follows:

$$\frac{\text{value based on sales} + \text{value based on assets} + \text{value based on income}}{3}$$

or

$$\frac{(\$23{,}518{,}500 + \$21{,}087{,}700 + \$12{,}132{,}800)}{3}$$

$$= \$18{,}913{,}000$$

Hence Cavos, Inc. is selling for significantly less than its chop-shop value—$13 million compared with $18.9 million.

The major limitation of a valuation model such as the chop-shop approach is that it is not derived from any theoretical basis. What it does is assume that average industry capitalization relationships—in this case, ratios of capitalization to sales, assets, and operating income—hold for all firms or conglomerate subsidiaries in that particular industry. Of course, this is frequently not the case. It is easy to identify specific companies that simply produce superior products and whose

TABLE 25-1 Average Capitalization Ratios for Industries in Which Cavos, Inc., Is Active

Business Segment	Capitalization Sales	Capitalization Assets	Capitalization Operating Income
Industrial specialties	0.61	1.07	21.49
Basic chemicals	2.29	2.43	17.45
Consumer specialties	3.58	2.92	19.26
Basic plastics	1.71	2.18	15.06

future earnings growth is, as a result, brighter. These companies, because of their expected future growth, should have their sales, assets, and operating income valued higher.

Given this limitation of the chop-shop valuation approach, why have we dealt with it in such detail? The reason is that it reflects a view among some investors and corporate raiders that the replacement value of a firm's assets may exceed the value placed on the firm as a whole in the market. The chop-shop method attempts to value the multi-industry firm by its parts. Moreover, as we will see when we explore the cash flow approach to valuation, there simply is no way to estimate the value of a takeover candidate with complete confidence. Thus, this method provides the decision maker with additional information.

The Cash Flow Value

Our last look at valuation models should be familiar to us, given our prior work in finding the present value of cash flows, when we studied capital budgeting. Using the cash flow approach to merger valuation requires that we estimate the incremental net cash flows available to the bidding firms as a result of the merger or acquisition. The present value of these cash flows then will be determined, and this will be the maximum amount that should be paid for the target firm. The initial outlay then can be subtracted out to calculate the net present value from the merger. Although this is very similar to a capital-budgeting problem, there are differences, particularly in estimating the initial outlay.

Finding the present value of the cash flows for a merger involves a five-step process:

Step 1: Estimate the incremental after-tax cash flows available from the target firm. This includes all synergistic cash flows (including those to both the bidding and target firms) created as a result of the acquisition. It should also be noted that interest expenses are not included in these cash flows, as they are accounted for in the required rate of return.

Step 2: Estimate the after-tax risk-adjusted discount rate associated with cash flows from the target firm. The target firm's, not the bidding firm's, required rate of return is appropriate here. If there is any anticipated change in financing associated with the target firm as a result of the acquisition, this change should also be considered.

Step 3: Calculate the present value of the incremental cash flows from the target firm.

TABLE 25-2 Calculation of the "Theoretical Values" for Cavos, Inc., Using Market Capitalization Ratios

	Value Based on Market Capitalization/Sales		
Business Segment	(A) Market Capitalization Sales	(B) Segment Sales	(A) × (B) Theoretical Market Value
Industrial specialties	0.61	$2,765	$ 1,686.7
Basic chemicals	2.29	5,237	11,992.7
Consumer specialties	3.58	2,029	7,263.8
Basic plastics	1.71	1,506	2,575.3
Total			$23,518.5

	Value Based on Market Capitalization/Sales		
Business Segment	(A) Market Capitalization Assets	(B) Segment Assets	(A) × (B) Theoretical Market Value
Industrial specialties	1.07	$2,206	$ 2,360.4
Basic chemicals	2.43	4,762	11,571.7
Consumer specialties	2.92	1,645	4,803.4
Basic plastics	2.18	1,079	2,352.2
Total			$21,087.7

	Value Based on Market Capitalization/Sales		
Business Segment	(A) Market Capitalization Income	(B) Segment income	(A) × (B) Theoretical Market Value
Industrial specialties	21.49	$186	$ 3,997.1
Basic chemicals	17.45	165	2,879.3
Consumer specialties	19.26	226	4,352.8
Basic plastics	15.06	60	903.6
Total			$12,132.8

Step 4: Estimate the initial outlay associated with the acquisition. The initial outlay is defined here as the market value of all securities and cash paid out plus the market value of all liabilities assumed.

Step 5: Calculate the net present value of the acquisition by subtracting the initial outlay from the present value of the incremental cash flows from the target firm.

Estimation of the incremental after-tax cash flows resulting from an acquisition can be extremely difficult. A certain lack of precision is inherent in these calculations because of the problem of estimating the synergistic gains from combining the two firms. For example, it is very difficult to estimate the gains that might be expected from any reduction in bankruptcy costs, increased market power, or reduction in agency costs that might occur. Still, it is imperative to estimate these gains if we are to place a value on the target firm. Once the required rate of return is determined, the present value of the incremental cash flows from acquiring the target firm can then be calculated. The final step then becomes the calculation of the initial outlay associated with the acquisition.

EXAMPLE

Let's look at the example of Tabbypaw Pie, Inc., which is being considered as a possible takeover target by ALF, Inc. Currently, Tabbypaw Pie uses 30 percent debt in its capital structure, but ALF plans on increasing the debt ratio to 40 percent (we will assume that only debt and equity are used) once the acquisition is completed. The after-tax cost of debt capital for Tabbypaw Pie is estimated to be 7 percent, and we will assume that this rate does not change as Tabbypaw's capital structure changes. The cost of equity after the acquisition is expected to be 20.8 percent. The current market value of Tabbypaw's debt outstanding is $110 million, all of which will be assumed by ALF. Also, let's assume that ALF intends to pay $260 million in cash and common stock for all of Tabbypaw Pie's stock in addition to assuming all of Tabbypaw's debt. Currently, the market price of Tabbypaw Pie's common stock is $210 million.

Step 1: Estimate the incremental cash flows from the target firm, including the synergistic flows, such as any possible flows from tax credits. This estimation for Tabbypaw is provided in Table 25-3. Here we are assuming that any cash flows after 1999 will be constant at $75 million. Also, we subtract any funds that must be reinvested in the firm in the form of capital expenditures that are required to support the firm's increasing profits.

Step 2: Determine an appropriate risk-adjusted discount rate for evaluating Tabbypaw. Here we will use the weighted cost of capital (k_0) for Tabbypaw as our discount rate, where the weighted cost of capital is calculated as

$$k_0 = W_d K_d + W_c K_c$$

where W_d, W_c = the percentage of funds provided by debt and common, respectively

K_d,K_c = **the cost of debt and common, respectively**

For Tabbypaw,

$$K_0 = (.40)(.07) + (.60)(.208) = .1528, \text{ or } 15.28\%$$

Step 3: Next we must calculate the present value of the incremental cash flows expected from the target firm, as given in Table 21-3. Assuming that cash flows do not change after 1999, but continue at the 1999 level in perpetuity, and discounting these cash flows at the 15.28 percent, we get

$$\begin{pmatrix}\text{present value}\\ \text{of all cash flows}\end{pmatrix} = \begin{pmatrix}\text{present value}\\ \text{of 1995–1998}\\ \text{cash flows}\end{pmatrix} = \begin{pmatrix}\text{present value}\\ \text{of cash flows}\\ \text{after 1998}\end{pmatrix}$$

where the present value of cash flows for 1995 through 1998 would be $190.772 million, determined as follows:

$$\frac{\$63}{(1+.1528)} + \frac{\$66}{(1+.1528)^2} + \frac{\$70}{(1+.1528)^3} + \frac{\$72}{(1+.1528)^4}$$

TABLE 25-3 Estimated Incremental Cash Flows from Tabbypaw Pie, Inc. ($ millions)

	1995	1996	1997	1998	1999 and Thereafter
Net sales	$496	$536	$606	S670	$731
Cost of goods sold	354	385	444	500	551
Administrative and selling expenses	28	30	32	35	38
Earnings before depreciation and interest	114	121	130	135	142
Depreciation	39	40	41	42	43
Earnings before interest and taxes	75	81	89	93	99
Taxes (incremental)	27	30	34	36	39
Net income	48	51	55	57	60
Net income	48	51	55	57	60
+Depreciation	39	40	41	42	43
−Capital expenditures	24	25	26	27	28
Net after-tax cash flow (before interest)	$ 63	$ 66	$ 70	S 72	$ 75

and the present value of the $75 million cash flow stream, beginning in 1999, is computed to be $277.921 million.[4]

$$\frac{\frac{\$75}{.1528}}{(1+.1528)^4} = \$277.921$$

Thus the present value of the cash inflows associated with the acquisition of Tabbypaw Pie by ALF is $468.693 million, or $468,693,000; that is, the sum of $190.772 million and $277.921 million.

Step 4: Next, we estimate the initial outlay associated with the acquisition. As already noted, the initial outlay is defined as the market value of all securities and cash paid out plus the market value of all debt liabilities assumed. In this case, the market value of the assumed debt obligations is $110 million. This amount, along with the acquisition price of $260 million, comprise the initial outlay of $370 million.

Step 5: Finally, the net present value of the acquisition is calculated by subtracting the initial outlay (calculated in step 4) from the present value of the incremental cash flows from the target firm (calculated in step 3):

$$\begin{aligned}\text{NPV acquisition} &= \text{PV inflows} - \text{initial outlay}\\ &= \$468{,}693{,}000 - \$370{,}000{,}000\\ &= \$98{,}693{,}000\end{aligned}$$

Thus the acquisition should be undertaken because it has a positive net present value. In fact, ALF could pay up to $468.693 million for Tabbypaw Pie.

[4]Remember that we can find the present value of an infinite stream of cash flows, where the amount is constant in each year, as follows:

$$\text{value} = \frac{\text{annual cash flow}}{\text{required rate of return}}$$

Because the cash flows do not begin until the fifth year, our equation is finding the value at the end of the fourth year; thus, we must discount the value back for four years.

Financial Management in Practice

TOUGH LEADER WIELDS THE AX AT SCOTT

The two brass ornaments that decorate the desk of Albert J. Dunlap are circling sharks. A pouncing brass lion rules his conference table. And a brass eagle stoops to its prey in his reception room. "I like predators," said Mr. Dunlap, the chief executive of the Scott Paper Company, fixing an officer visitor with steely blue eyes. "I like them because they live by their wits."

To be sure, the 57-year-old turn-around specialist, who announced the biggest corporate revamping in Scott's history, has acquired a few predatory nicknames himself. When asked about them, he smiled, paused, and said: "On the whole, I prefer to be called Rambo in Pinstripes rather than Chainsaw. That makes me sound like a serial killer, don't you think?"

Mr. Dunlap said both sobriquets were quite popular in England, where he lived for eight years while turning around Crown Zellerbach and Diamond International for Sir James Goldsmith, the British-French financier. Then Mr. Dunlap restructured units of Consolidated Press Holdings, the Australian media company led by Kerry Packer. (**A**)

Cutting 10,500 Jobs

Now Mr. Dunlap, a perpetual-motion machine with a bull-dozer voice and a caustic wit, is applying for intensity to the world's largest producer of tissue products. In early August, Mr. Dunlap announced that 10,500 jobs—nearly a third of the company's work force—would be eliminated by the end of the year. The cutback superseded the more gradual three-year reduction of 8,300 jobs announced last November. In scope and in number of jobs, Mr. Dunlap said, this is the largest revamping he has ever tried.

Mr. Dunlap, who came out of retirement to join Scott in April, trained as a paratrooper before he graduated from West Point in 1960. (He continues to wear his class ring.) And though he no longer jumps out of airplanes, he is still "taking frightening jumps out of the sky into strange corporations," he said.

After touchdown, instead of sinking in the quicksands of corporate culture, Mr. Dunlap has sought to transform the companies he heads. "You must get rid of the people who represent the old culture, or they will fight you," he said. "And you have to get rid of all the old symbols." (**B**)

Many Scott employees are in a state of shock, dread, and anger as they wait for their managers to decide who will go and who will stay. "Hundreds of people are already cleaning out their offices, and most people are assuming they're not staying," said Susan Kent, a 10-year employee on the corporate human relations staff. Ms. Kent has already learned her fate: she was let go last week.

Dottie Carrigan, a purchasing specialist who has worked for Scott for 19 years, did not know if she would be dismissed but found the courage to say that Mr. Dunlap "has no idea of the quality or the spirit or the integrity of the people he's letting go." "It's a very painful thing," she said.

But Mr. Dunlap says he sympathizes with the pain of his workers. "I come from a working-class family, and lots of times my father was out of work due to no fault of his own," referring to Albert Sr., a shop steward at Todd Shipyards in Hoboken, N.J. where Mr. Dunlap survived what he called an inner-city childhood.

"They call me abrasive, but I'm really just a catalyst," Mr. Dunlap added. "It doesn't make any sense to sacrifice 100 percent of the people at

Financial Management in Practice

this company to save 30 percent of the people we have to let go."

When he came aboard at Scott, Mr. Dunlap bought $2 million worth of stock at $38 a share. When the stock price rose above $50 in June, he bought another $2 million, because he believed in the company.

Praise from Wall Street

The stock is now trading for more than $69, not only because Wall Street loves blood, but because Mr. Dunlap "has been extremely successful in restructuring and is very conservative about the balance sheet," said Kathryn McAuley, an analyst who follows Scott for Brown Brothers Harriman & Company. (**C**)

Mr. Dunlap said earlier this month that this shrinking of Scott would save $420 million in operating costs next year before taxes. Scott's second-quarter earnings rose 71 percent, to $40.2 million, or 54 cents a share, from $23.5 million, or 32 cents per share, in the quarter a year earlier. Sales, however, declined 2 percent, to $1.18 billion in the quarter.

Scott "was a stodgy old company, and they decided to go outside to someone from a totally different management culture," Mr. Dunlap said. The tough, brash raider described his arrival in the comfortable, patrician offices of Scott as "a strange marriage, born out of desperation."

"It was call me, or call Dr. Kevorkian," he added.

Scott was "in jeopardy of losing our investment-grade rating on our bonds," he asserted. Annual shareholder returns were down 1.9 percent, in comparison with returns in the rest of the paper and forest-products industry, which were up 9.6 percent. "Debt had ballooned, there was a high cost structure, there was no vision and no leadership," he said. "If you ask me about the shareholders, they would have been abused less if they had been captured by terrorists."

A Hands-On Manager

Since his arrival, Mr. Dunlap has been a ubiquitous presence in Scott's corporate suites as he charges down corridors for face-to-face meetings with his managers. "I walked into my office today, and Al was there, sitting in my chair," said Basil L. Anderson, Scott's chief financial officer, one of the few former senior Scott executives to make the new team. (Seven other senior executives were not so lucky.) Mr. Dunlap sat to scribble out a memo.

Internationally, Scott is the market leader in sales of toilet paper, facial tissues, paper towels, napkins, and wet wipes. But domestically, it has been vying for second place with James River, the maker of Northern brand products, while Proctor & Gamble is No. 1.

Mr. Dunlap has already put up for sale Scott's S. D. Warren subsidiary, which produces coated printing papers, and other paper-industry businesses, because, he said, "our emphasis will no longer be as a forest-products company." (**D**)

"We are no longer solely in the business of pumping out tons of paper," he said.

Also on the block is the 55-acre Scott World Headquarters, a symbol of the order he is changing. "It has lovely walking paths, fountains, a pond and geese, too," Mr. Dunlap said of the corporate park with its three squat, modernistic buildings that sit like three boxes of Scott tissues adjacent to the Philadelphia airport. Everything must go: "The pond, the flags, and we'll throw in the geese."

The corporate headquarters staff will be reduced to 200 from 1,600 initially, employees will be consolidated in a building in Philadelphia. Mr. Dunlap would not say how long the company would honor its marriage vows to Philadelphia.

Financial Management in Practice

Focus on Signature Brands

Beyond cost-cutting, Mr. Dunlap's vision is to focus on Scott signature brands, he said, reorienting the corporation as a global consumer-product company selling not only to individuals but also to offices, factories, institutions and hotels, a market that accounts for 40 percent of domestic sales.

Emphasizing this core business will enable Scott "to work out our debt reduction and future possible stock buybacks," he said, adding that he intends to create a new corporate culture from the ground up, "building on the adversity that the new team has shared."

There is a belief among workers at Scott that Mr. Dunlap is a short-time hit man who will not fulfill his five-year contract and who took the job to make a lot of money. Their view is that Salomon Brothers and Coopers & Lybrand, the reorganization consultants, are calling the tune.

"Al is hardly a puppet dancing to our tune—boy, let me tell you, with Al, it's just the opposite," said C. Don Burnett, a senior partner at Coopers & Lybrand. "There's no question that Al is in charge."

By the accounts of executives who have worked for him, Mr. Dunlap is an exacting leader whose dressing-down of a manager can be as surgical as his rejuggling of a balance sheet.

Mr. Dunlap "Is No Diplomat"

Mr. Dunlap "is no diplomat," Sir James Goldsmith said in a telephone interview from Spain.

Sir James also has high praise for Mr. Dunlap's skills. "At the particular task of repositioning a company, and taking the hard decisions to get it right, I've never met anyone better," Sir James said. "He is a surgeon in the sense that he has to cause bleeding to get the patient right."

To Mr. Dunlap, the huge work-force reduction is not uninhibited bloodletting, but carefully targeted laser surgery. Those who survive it can reap great rewards. More then a decade ago, when Mr. Dunlap brought the near-moribund Lily-Tulip Inc., the paper cup maker, back from the living dead, "Everyone was shaking in their boots," said John P. Murtagh, whom Mr. Dunlap brought in as Scott's general counsel in June. "I thought my number was up. But he took me from a low-level lawyer and elevated me above my boss."

"It's a Sin to Lose Money"

As for charges that he is making money off the painful restructuring Mr. Dunlap said: "Scott should be making money for its shareholders. It's a sin to lose money, a mortal sin."

Mr. Dunlap is not among the sinners but the saved. He denied published reports that his net worth is $50 million; he put it at twice that, and several executives he has worked with confirmed that figure.

His wealth gave him a lavish retirement. But by all accounts, Mr. Dunlap did not flourish in it for long. "Al gets bored when all he has to do is go to the golf course or play tennis," Judy, his wife of 26 years, said.

Why, then, did he come out of retirement to head Scott? "He wants to show people, this time, that he is more than Rambo in Pinstripes," said Mr. Burnett of Coopers & Lybrand. "He wants to show the world that he knows how to build a company."

Standing at parade rest behind his desk with the circling sharks, Mr. Dunlap supplied his own answer. "Jimmy said to me once, 'You have a fire in the belly,'" he said, referring to Sir James. "I feel that he was absolutely right."

Source: Glen Collins, *New York Times* (August 15, 1994):C1, C6.

Financial Management in Practice

ANALYSIS AND IMPLICATIONS. . .

A. Corporate restructuring is simply another term for change, major change to the business. In this instance Scott Paper Company is downsizing its workforce dramatically to improve its profitability.

B. The human side of restructuring can be devastating. When a firm finds itself no longer able to compete effectively with its industry peers, drastic measures are frequently required to make the firm competitive again. In this instance, one third of the firm's workforce will be eliminated.

C. When drastic cost cutting is undertaken, the result is improved earnings and improved prospects of future cash flow. Wall Street discounts these additional expected cash flows back to the present, and the resulting present value becomes the basis for an increase in the firm's stock price. In this instance, the source of the increase in share price can be traced directly to the firm's cost cutting efforts which focus primarily on reducing the firm's workforce.

D. In addition to reductions in workforce, other tools of restructuring typically include refocusing on the firm's core business by selling off subsidiaries and divisions that are not tied directly on the core business. In addition, lavish corporate assets like corporate jets, apartment complexes in resort areas, and plush corporate headquarters, are frequently sold.

FINANCING AND CORPORATE RESTRUCTURING[5]

In recent years, we have seen significant changes in the financing practices of U.S. firms, in part the result of the restructuring of corporate America. The outstanding debt of many companies increased as they borrowed heavily to finance restructuring activity. As part of this restructuring, three popular types of highly leveraged transactions have developed: MBO, LBO, and the leveraged Employee Stock Ownership Plan (ESOP). How significant are these financing techniques? The use of LBOs increased from less than $5 billion in 1983 to more than $60 billion in 1989. These three financing approaches are described subsequently.[6] Following a discussion of these techniques, we will look at the use of a bond that has drawn great attention during the 1980s—the junk bond.

MBO
A management buyout or MBO involves a purchase of a firm from its stockholders by a small group of investors that includes a group from the firm's management.

MBOs

An **MBO** occurs when a group of investors form a shell corporation to acquire the target firm or buy the target firm directly. The distinguishing features of an MBO are (1) the group of investors includes members of the management of the target com-

[5]The ideas in this section come largely from Leland Crabbe, Margaret Pickering, and Stephen Prowse, "Recent Developments in Corporate Finance," *Federal Reserve Bulletin* (August 1990): 595–603.

[6]Taken from John D. Martin and John W. Kensinger, *Exploring the Controversy Over Corporate Restructuring* (Morristown, NJ: Financial Executive Institute Research Foundation, 1990), 46.

pany; (2) following the acquisition the newly formed company goes private; and (3) the acquisition is financed primarily by debt, so the resulting firm is much more highly leveraged than most publicly traded companies.

LBOs

An **LBO** is a more general type of restructuring device that can be distinguished from an MBO in that the new owners do not necessarily have to include members of the original management team, and the firm is not necessarily taken private following the acquisition. Most LBOs are also MBOS, and the term LBO is more generally used in describing high-leverage acquisitions and restructurings. Table 25-4 illustrates the process of an LBO, using the events surrounding the RJR Nabisco LBO as an example.

LBO
An LBO or leveraged buyout involves a purchase of a firm from its stockholders by a small group of investors (which includes members of the firm's management in the case of an MBO). Usually the acquisition will be financed largely by debt financing, hence the term "leveraged" buyout.

Leveraged ESOPs

In a leveraged **ESOP**, the rank-and-file employees participate with management in the purchase of stock in their corporation. In these arrangements, a special trust is formed to borrow money to purchase the firm's stock. The loan is then repaid from the employees' retirement funds, and the shares are credited to the employees' retirement account. The employer corporation typically guarantees the loan. The stock is held in trust until the participating employee retires or terminates employment. There are three distinct tax advantages with an ESOP: (1) Dividends paid by the company to stock owned by an ESOP are tax deductible; (2) the institution lending the money to create the ESOP has to pay income tax on only half of the interest received from the ESOP, and thus the plan allows borrowing at low interest rates; and (3) the employer corporation is allowed to make tax-deductible contributions of cash or stock to the ESOP.

ESOP
Employee stock option plan whereby the employees of the firm can acquire shares of their employer. In a leveraged ESOP, employees set up a trust to borrow the funds needed to acquire shares. The loan is repaid from the employees' retirement funds and the shares are credited to the employees' retirement account.

Junk Bonds

Junk bonds, which have been described in several earlier chapters, have been closely linked to the large, and at times unsuccessful, mergers of the 1980s. The use of these bonds has been viewed as a common element in some of the country's worst financial disasters in the late 1980s. Examples include the failure of the Campeau retailing empire and the bankruptcy of Drexel, Burnham, Lambert.

Junk bonds
Below investment grade bonds (BB or below). These bonds are generally associated with the funding of corporate takeovers during the eighties.

Some critics blame many of the market ills on junk bonds. According to these critics, junk bonds fueled the merger mania of the 1980s, caused the excessive use of debt, and created instability in the financial markets. Although these opinions are certainly understandable, the evidence does not support these extreme charges against junk bonds.[7] Junk bonds align with our expectations, as studied in chapter 6, in terms of risk and expected returns. They are not inherently different from other securities—they have greater risk but also greater expected return. Also, the junk bond market, although significant, was too small to have caused the 1980s merger boom, nor was it large enough to account directly for the growth in corporate debt.

[7]These ideas come from Sean Beckett, "The Truth About Junk Bonds," Federal Reserve Bank of Kansas City, *Economic Review* (July–August 1990): 45–54.

TABLE 25-4 An LBO: The Case of RJR Nabisco Corp.

First indication per share	October 21, 1988, F. Ross Johnson, CEO or RJR, announced a proposed MBO for $75.
Completion date	December 1, 1988, KKR won a bidding war for RJR for $109 per share.
Major events	
10/21/88	RJR announced a proposed MBO.
10/27/88	KKR began a $20.8 billion tender offer for RJR.
11/8/88	RJR management was joined by Shearson Lehman Hutton and Salomon on a buyout offer of $21.16 billion ($92 per share). RJR opened the bidding process for sealed bids.
11/30/88	KKR appeared to have won the bidding contest for RJR with a bid of $23.7 billion ($103 per share).
12/1/88	KKR officially named the winner of the bidding war with a bid of $109 per share, or $25 billion.
2/7/89	Swiss Bank and J. P. Morgan (Switzerland) demanded that RJR call its Swiss Franc Bonds at face value because of losses incurred by bondholders due to the LBO financing.
2/10/89	KKR completed the takeover.
3/23/89	Swiss court issues temporary order to stop the completion of the RJR takeover. The order is on behalf of Swiss bondholders who have seen the value of their RJR bonds decrease due to the buyout.
4/6/89	RJR plans to sell $5.5 to $6 billion in assets. RJR also files prospectus for $4 billion bond issue. These bonds are to be used to pay interest on current debt.
4/28/89	Shareholders vote final approval of RJR buyout.
5/12/89	$4 billion bridge loan refinanced.
6/1/89	Federal judge rejects Metropolitan Life's claims that RJR had violated an unwritten requirement to treat bondholders fairly.
6/7/89	RJR sells five of its European food businesses for $2.5 billion.
6/12/89	Federal judge rules that RJR can sell off assets to help pay debt incurred by LBO. Met Life files suit to protect bondholder's rights.
6/21/89	Chung King sold for $52 million.
7/28/89	Scandinavian food unit sold for $20.4 million.
8/1/89	Several corporate apartments and houses sold for $8.6 million.
9/7/89	Del Monte Tropical Fruit sold for $875 million. Negotiations underway for the sale of Del Monte Foods canned food unit for $1.5 billion.

Source: John D. Martin and John W. Kensinger, Exploring the Controversy over Corporate Restructuring (Morristown, NJ: Financial Executive Institute Research Foundation, 1990), 11.

Junk bonds in fact accounted for only 14 percent of the growth in corporate debt during the 1980s. Nevertheless, the financing that had been available through the junk bond market essentially evaporated at the conclusion of the 1980s. Merger activity accordingly declined noticeably during the first part of 1990 as a consequence of the virtual unavailability of new financing in the low-grade bond market. Also, the more cautious attitude of commercial banks and the weakening in the market for asset sales contributed to the decline. Nevertheless, well-structured acquisition proposals, especially those aimed at enhancing a firm's competitive position within its own lines of business, continue today.

TENDER OFFER

Tender offer A bid by an interested party, usually a corporation, for controlling interest in another corporation.

As an alternative approach in purchasing another firm, the acquiring corporation may consider using a **tender offer.** A tender offer involves a bid by an interested party of controlling interest in another corporation. The prospective purchaser approaches the stockholders of the firm, rather than the management, to encourage them to sell their shares, typically at a premium over the current market price. For instance, in late 1990, AT&T made a $6.1 billion tender offer for NCR, or $90 per share. NCR's management quickly responded by telling the stockholders they should refuse the offer because the stock was worth $125, even though it had only been selling for $48 per share before AT&T's tender offer. After a real dog fight, the final agreement was for $110 per share.

Because the tender offer is a direct appeal to the stockholders, prior approval is not required by the management of the target firm. However, the acquiring firm may choose to approach the management of the target firm. If the two managements are unsuccessful in negotiating the terms, a tender offer may then be attempted. Alternatively, a firm's management that is interested in acquiring control of a second corporation may try a surprise takeover without contacting the management of the latter company. T. Boone Pickens of Mesa Petroleum is a prime example of someone who has used the tender offer in his efforts to acquire such firms as Cities Service and Gulf.

RESISTANCE TO MERGERS

In response to unfriendly merger attempts, especially tender offers, the management of the firm under attack will frequently strike back. Several defense tactics are used to counter tender offers. These defensive maneuvers include white knights, shark repellents, poison pills, and golden parachutes. Let us examine these more closely.

A *white knight* is a company that comes to the rescue of a corporation that is being targeted for a takeover. For example, when Pennzoil made a tender offer for Getty Oil, the Getty management opposed the Pennzoil attempt. To prevent the takeover, Texaco, at the encouragement of Getty's management, made its own tender offer for Getty at a higher price. Texaco was the white knight for Getty. However, Pennzoil later received a $10 billion judgment against Texaco for its action in the Getty acquisition.

PacMan defense
A defensive tactic used in response to a tender offer in which the firm under attack makes a bid for the firm that is attempting the takeover.

PacMan, the name taken from the video game, is another defensive tactic to tender offers, where the firm under attack becomes the attacker. For instance, Bendix Corporation tried to take control of Martin-Marietta by a tender offer. When the takeover effort failed, Martin-Marietta counterattacked the buying Bendix stock in an attempt to take control of Bendix. Martin-Marietta became the PacMan. To recounter, Bendix successfully courted Allied Corporation to come to its rescue. Allied bought Bendix so that Martin-Marietta could not buy enough for control. Allied was a white knight.

Shark repellents are policy changes or legal manipulations that can be used to discourage unfriendly takeovers. As an example, a firm may revise its bylaws to stagger the terms of directors so that only a few come up for election in any one year. A firm making a tender offer would have to wait at least two years before gaining a majority of board members. Another ploy is to reincorporate in a state with rules that favor existing management. Gulf Oil was incorporated in Pennsylvania, where minority stockholders could use cumulative voting to gain a voice on the board of directors. When T. Boone Pickens began buying major blocks of Gulf stock, Gulf reincorporated in Delaware, where cumulative voting could not be used, making it more difficult for Pickens to have any impact on the management of Gulf.

Poison pill
A tactic used by the target of a hostile takeover which involves triggering a very unfavorable event for the takeover firm should it win the struggle for control of the firm. Examples include the sale of a large block of newly issued shares to a friendly party at a very low price.

Another tactic is the **poison pill,** an action initiated automatically if an unfriendly party tries to acquire a firm. For instance, management might devise a plan whereby all the firm's debt becomes due if the management is removed. Still another tactic is the *golden parachute,* which stipulates that the acquiring company must pay the executives of the acquired firm a substantial sum of money to "let them down easy" as new management is brought into the company.

The disadvantages of the unfriendly takeover are readily apparent from the preceding examples. If the target firm's management attempts to block it, the costs of executing the offer may increase significantly. Also, the purchasing company may fail to acquire a sufficient number of shares to meet the objective of controlling the firm. Conversely, if the offer is not strongly contested,it may possibly be less expensive than the normal route for acquiring a company, in that it permits control by purchasing a smaller portion of the firm. Also, the tender offer has proven somewhat less susceptible to judicial inquiries regarding the fairness of the purchase price, because each stockholder individually decides the fairness of the price.

DIVESTITURES

Although the merger-and-acquisition phenomenon has been a major influence in restructuring the corporate sector, divestitures, or what we might call "reverse mergers," may have become an equally important factor. In fact, preliminary research to date would suggest that we may be witnessing a "new era" in the making—one where the public corporation has become a more efficient vehicle for increasing and maintaining stockholder wealth.[8] Whereas corporate management once seemed to behave as if 2 + 2 were equal to 5, especially during the conglomerate heyday of the '60s, the wave of reverse mergers seems based on the counter proposition that 5 – 1 is 5. And the market's consistently positive response to such deals seems to be providing broad confirmation of the "new math."[9]

Selloff
The sale of a subsidiary, division, or product line by one firm to another.

Spinoff
The separation of a subsidiary from its parent, with no change in the equity ownership. The management of the parent company gives up operating control over the assets involved in the spin-off but the stockholders retain ownership, albeit through shares of the newly created spin-off company.

A successful divestiture allows the firm's assets to be used more efficiently and therefore to be assigned a higher value by the market forces. It essentially eliminates a division or subsidiary that does not fit strategically with the rest of the company; that is, it removes an operation that does not contribute to the company's basic purposes.

The different types of divestitures may be summarized as follows:

1. **Selloff.** A selloff is the sale of a subsidiary, division, or product line by one company to another. For example, Radio Corporation of America (RCA) sold its finance company and General Electric sold its metallurgical coal business.
2. **Spinoff.** A spinoff involves the separation of a subsidiary from its parent, with no change in the equity ownership. The management of the parent company gives up operating control of the subsidiary, but the shareholders retain the same percentage ownership in both firms. New shares representing ownership in the diverted assets are issued to the original shareholders on a pro-rata basis.

[8]See Robert Comment and Gregg A. Jarrell, 1995, "Corporate focus and stock returns," *Journal of Financial Economics* 37:67–87; and Kose John and Eli Ofek, 1995, "Asset sales and increase in focus," *Journal of Financial Economics* 37: 105–126.

[9]Joel M. Stern, and Donald H. Chew, Jr. (eds.), *The Revolution in Corporate Finance* (New York: Basis Blackwell, 1986), 416.

Financial Management in Practice

KKR LEARNS ABCS OF LBOS, 1977

Kohlberg Kravis Roberts & Co. on April 7, 1977, used mostly bank loans to buy a small truck-suspension maker, thus launching the leveraged buyout's modern era.

Such buyouts by a few investors using loans date back to obscure transactions in the late 1940s, but KKR gave them prominence in the late 1970s. And new twists: Buy a public company with bank loans and high-interest junk bonds; sell off parts of it to reduce the debt; and then resell the company to the public or to another firm. (**A**) LBO makers gain whopping profits from the later sale, plus fees along the way.

KKR, formed by three former Bear Stearns partners in May 1976 with $120,000 in capital, set up in spartan Manhattan offices and became by far the No. 1 LBO firm of the 200 or so firms in the hot field in the mid-1980s.

In that first $25.6 million KKR buyout of A.J. Industries in 1977, KKR partners invested only $1.7 million; they sold it in 1985 for $75 million. KKR has since done more than 30 LBOS.

Within seven years KKR—especially aided since 1981 by big state employee pension plan investors—was buying companies totaling more than $1 billion in size. And early this year it bought RJR Nabisco for a record takeover tag of $25 billion, picking up $75 million in fees.

KKR's managing partners became wealthy. Henry Kravis pledged $10 million in 1987 to the Metropolitan Museum of Art to complete the Henry R. Kravis Wing by 1990. As to criticism that LBOs only line their makers' pockets, Kravis, in a *Fortune* interview, said: "Greed really turns me off. To me, money means security."

Recently, LBOs have been tested by the weakness in junk bonds, the souring of some debt-plagued LBOs and the failure of banks to provide the financing for UAL's planned LBO. But LBOs have bounced back before; so experts aren't predicting their end. (**B**)

Source: "KKR Learns ABCs of LBOS, 1977," *Wall Street Journal* (November 6, 1989): B1.

ANALYSIS AND IMPLICATIONS. . .

A. The leveraged buyout or LBO was used during the '80s as a transitional organizational form. That is, large diversified corporations such as RJR Nabisco were purchased through the use of a lot of borrowed money (primarily junk or "below investment grade" bonds). The new management then sold off divisions and operating units and used the proceeds to retire debt. When the LBO firm was reduced down to its core business it was either sold to another company or resold to the public through a stock offering. In a sense the LBO was a "corporate undertaker."

B. We now know that although LBOs decreased dramatically in the late eighties with the collapse of the market for junk bonds, they experienced a resurgence in the mid-nineties.

3. **Liquidation.** A liquidation in this context is not a decision to shut down or abandon an asset. Rather, the assets are sold to another company, and the proceeds are distributed to the stockholders.
4. **Going private.** A company goes private when its stock that has traded publicly is purchased by a small group of investors, and the stock is no longer bought and sold on a public exchange. The ownership of the company is transferred from a diverse group of outside stockholders to a small group of private investors, usually including the firm's management. The leveraged buyout is a special case of going private. As noted earlier in the chapter, the existing shareholders sell their shares to a small group of investors. The purchasers of the stock use the firm's unused debt capacity to borrow the funds to pay for the stock. Thus the new investors acquire the firm with little, if any, personal investment. However, the firm's debt ratio may increase by as much as tenfold.

SUMMARY

- Business combinations historically have represented a major influence in the growth of firms the United States. This avenue for growth has been particularly important during select periods, such as in the 1980s.
- The assertion that merger activity creates wealth for the shareholder cannot be maintained with certainty. Only if the merger provides something that the investor cannot do on his or her own can a merger or acquisition be of financial benefit.
- Determining the value of a firm is a difficult task. In addition to projecting the firm's future profitability, which is a cornerstone in valuation, the acquirer must consider the effects of joining two businesses into a single operation. What may represent a good investment may not be a good merger.

  In estimating a firm's worth several factors are frequently considered, including (1) the firm's book value, (2) its appraisal value, (3) the stock market value of a firm's common shares, (4) its chop-shop value, and (5) the present value of future free cash flows.
- Financial innovation frequently has come in conjunction with corporate restructuring; most notable examples include MBOs, LBOs, and leveraged ESOPs. Certainly these concepts are not new, but the extent of their application has increased significantly. In more recent years, we have seen a marked increase in the use of debt. Before the takeovers of the 1980s, managers strove to maintain a targeted capital structure mix. In the 1980s, the use of an LBO sometimes meant that an acquired firm's debt might be increased tenfold; the intent was not to maintain that high level of debt but rather to bring it down to more acceptable norms as soon as possible. As the 1990s began, the failure of some large firms to meet their large debt obligations brought on by mergers has recently led to the use of equity as a favored way to finance a merger.
- Normally, the purchaser approaches the management of the firm to be acquired. Alternatively, the purchasing firm can directly approach the stockholders of the firm under consideration. This bid for ownership, called a tender offer, has been used with increasing frequency. This approach may be cheaper, but often the managers of the target firm attempt to block it.

- A divestiture represents a variety of ways to let go of a portion of the firm's assets It has become an important vehicle in restructuring the corporation into a more efficient operation.
- Some of the most interesting and colorful language of finance has arisen out of the attempts of target firms to resist an unwanted takeover. For example, when firm A is under attack from hostile takeover firm B, it may seek out a more friendly arrangement by seeking out a third bidder who will come in and purchase the firm. In the jargon of the merger literature, the third firm is called a white knight (for obvious reasons). Another popular tactic, the poison pill, comes right out of the spy novel tradition. In this instance, the target firm puts in place a set of conditions that are triggered only in the event that the firm is taken over by an unfriendly suitor. For example, the firm might arrange for the issuance of new common stock to be distributed to everyone other than the hostile takeover firm, or the firm's debt might be made due and payable immediately should the firm fall victim to an unwanted takeover. The list goes on, and the techniques that might be devised to resist an unwanted takeover are limited only the imaginations of the management of the firm and the boundaries set by state and local law.

QUESTIONS

1. Why might merger activities create wealth?
2. Why is book value alone an imperfect measure of the worth of a company?
3. What advantages are provided by the use of an appraisal value in valuing a firm?
4. What is the concept of the chop-shop valuation procedure?
5. Compare the NPV approach used in valuing a merger with the same approach in capital budgeting.
6. Describe an MBO, LBO, and leveraged ESOP.
7. What are the disadvantages of the tender offer?
8. Explain the different types of divestitures.

SELF-CORRECTION PROBLEM

Using the chop-shop approach, assign a value for the Calvert Corporation, where its common stock is currently trading at a total market price of $5 million. For Calvert, the accounting data set forth two business segments: auto sales and auto specialties. Data for the firm's two segments are as follows:

Business Segment	Segment Sales ($000)	Segment Assets ($000)	Segment Income ($000)
Auto sales	$3,000	$1,000	$150
Auto specialties	2,500	3,000	500
Total	$5,500	$4,000	$650

Industry data for "pure-play" firms have been compiled and are summarized as follows:

Business Segment	Capitalization Sales	Capitalization Assets	Capitalization Operating Income
Auto sales	1.40	3.20	18.00
Auto specialties	.80	.90	8.00

PROBLEMS

1. Using the chop-shop approach, assign a value for Dabney, Inc., whose common stock is currently trading at a total market price of $7 million. For Dabney, the accounting data sets forth three business segments: consumer wholesaling, specialty services, and retirement center's. Data for the firm's three segments are as follows:

Business Segment	Segment Sales ($000)	Segment Assets ($000)	Segment Income ($000)
Industrial specialties	$ 2,765	$2,206	$186
Basic chemicals	5,237	4,762	165
Consumer specialties	2,029	1,645	226
Basic plastics	1,506	1,079	60
Total	$11,537	$9,692	$637

Industry data for "pure-play" firms have been compiled and are summarized as follows:

Business Segment	Capitalization Sales	Capitalization Assets	Capitalization Operating Income
Consumer wholesaling	0.80	.70	12.00
Specialty services	1.20	1.00	6.00
Retirement centers	1.20	.70	7.00

2. Using the chop-shop method, determine a value for Aramus, Inc., whose common stock is trading at a total market price of $15 million. For Aramus, the accounting data are divided into three business segments: sunglasses distribution, reading glasses distribution, and technical products. Data for the firm's three segments are as follows:

Business Segment	Segment Sales ($000)	Segment Assets ($000)	Segment Income ($000)
Sunglasses distribution	$ 3,500	$ 1,000	$ 350
Reading glasses distribution	2,000	1,500	250
Technical products	6,500	8,500	1,200
Total	$12,000	$11,000	$1,800

Industry data for "pure-play" firms have been computed and are summarized as follows:

Business Segment	Capitalization Sales	Capitalization Assets	Capitalization Operating Income
Sunglasses distribution	1.0	.8	8.0
Reading glasses distribution	.9	.8	10.0
Technical products	1.2	1.0	7.0

3. The Argo Corporation is viewed as a possible takeover target by Hilary, Inc. Currently, Argo uses 20 percent debt in its capital structure, but Hilary plans to increase the debt ratio to 30 percent if the acquisition is consummated. The after-tax cost of debt capital for Argo is estimated to be 8 percent, with either 20 or 30 percent debt financing. The cost of equity after the acquisition is expected to be 18 percent. The current market value of Argo's outstanding debt is $40 million, all of which will be assumed by Hilary. Hilary intends to pay $250 million in cash and common stock for all of Argo's stock in addition to assuming all of Argo's debt. Currently, the market price of Argo's common stock is $200 million. Selected items from Argo's financial data are as follows:

	1995	1996	1997	1998	Thereafter
			(Millions)		
Net sales	$200	$225	$240	$250	$275
Administrative and selling expenses	15	20	27	28	30
Depreciation	10	15	17	20	24
Capital expenditures	12	13	15	17	20

In addition, the cost of goods sold runs 60 percent of sales and the marginal tax rate is 34 percent. Compute the net present value of the acquisition.

4. The Prime Corporation is viewed as a possible takeover target by Big Boy, Inc. Currently, Prime uses 25 percent debt in its capital structure, but Big Boy plans

to increase the debt ratio to 40 percent if the acquisition is expected to be 20 percent. The current market value of Prime's debt outstanding is $30 million, all of which will be assumed by Big Boy. Big Boy intends to pay $150 million in cash and common stock for all of Prime's stock in addition to assuming all of its debt. Currently, the market price of Prime's common stock is $125 million. Selected items from Prime's financial data are as follows:

	1995	1996	1997	1998	Thereafter
			(Millions)		
Net sales	$300	$330	$375	$400	$425
Admininstrative and selling expenses	40	50	58	62	65
Depreciation	25	30	35	38	40
Capital expenditures	30	37	45	48	50

In addition, the cost of goods sold runs 60 percent of sales, and the marginal tax rate is 34 percent. Compute the NPV of the acquisition.

SOLUTION TO SELF-CORRECTION PROBLEM

	Capital-to-Sales	Segment Sales	Theoretical Values
Auto sales	1.40	$3,000	$4,200
Auto specialties	0.80	2,500	2,000
			$6,200

	Capital-to-Assets	Segment Assets	Theoretical Values
Auto sales	3.20	$1,000	$3,200
Auto specialties	0.90	3,000	2,700
			$5,900

	Capital-to-Income	Segment Income	Theoretical Values
Auto sales	18.00	$ 150	$2,700
Auto specialties	8.00	500	4,000
			$6,700

Theoretical based on	
Sales	$6,200
Assets	5,900
Income	6,700
Average value	$6,267

CHAPTER 26

Business Failure and Reorganization

Businesses fail by having negative or low returns, being unable to pay liabilities as they come due, or having more liabilities than assets, for a variety of reasons. What do you think are some of the major causes of business failure? Take a few moments to answer this question before reading further.

A business failure is an unfortunate circumstance. Although the majority of firms that fail do so within the first year or two of life, other firms grow, mature, and fail much later. The failure of a business can be viewed in a number of ways and can result from one or more causes.

TYPES OF BUSINESS FAILURE

A firm may fail because its *returns are negative or low.* A firm that consistently reports operating losses will probably experience a decline in market value. If the firm fails to earn a return that is greater than its cost of capital, it can be viewed as having failed. Negative or low returns, unless remedied, are likely to result eventually in one of the following more serious types of failure.

A second type of failure, **technical insolvency,** occurs when a firm is unable to pay its liabilities as they come due. When a firm is technically insolvent, its assets are still greater than its liabilities, but it is confronted with a *liquidity crisis.* If some of its assets can be converted into cash within a reasonable period, the company may be able to escape complete failure. If not, the result is the third and most serious type of failure, **bankruptcy.** Bankruptcy occurs when a firm's liabilities exceed the fair market value of its assets. A bankrupt firm has a *negative* stockholders'

Technical insolvency Business failure that occurs when a firm is unable to pay its liabilities as they come due.

Bankruptcy Business failure that occurs when a firm's liabilities exceed the fair market value of its assets.

equity.[1] This means that the claims of creditors cannot be satisfied unless the firm's assets can be liquidated for more than their book value. Although bankruptcy is an obvious form of failure, *the courts treat technical insolvency and bankruptcy in the same way.* They are both considered to indicate the financial failure of the firm.

MAJOR CAUSES OF BUSINESS FAILURE

The primary cause of business failure is *mismanagement,* which accounts for more than 50 percent of all cases. Numerous specific managerial faults can cause the firm to fail. Overexpansion, poor financial actions, an ineffective sales force, and high production costs can all singly or in combination cause the ultimate failure of the firm. Since all major corporate decisions are eventually measured in terms of dollars, the financial manager may play a key role in avoiding or causing a business failure. It is his or her duty to monitor the firm's financial pulse.

Economic activity—especially economic downturns—can contribute to the failure of a firm.[2] If the economy goes into a recession, sales may decrease abruptly, leaving the firm with high fixed costs and insufficient revenues to cover them. In addition, rapid rises in interest rates just prior to a recession can further contribute to cash flow problems and make it more difficult for the firm to obtain and maintain needed financing. If the recession is prolonged, the likelihood of survival decreases even further. Recently, a number of major business failures such as those of Olympia and York (real estate), America West Airlines, and Southmark Corporation (convenience stores) have resulted from overexpansion and a recessionary economy.

A final cause of business failure is *corporate maturity.* Firms, like individuals, do not have infinite lives. Like a product, a firm goes through the stages of birth, growth, maturity, and eventual decline. The firm's management should attempt to prolong the growth stage through research, the development of new products, and mergers. Once the firm has matured and has begun to decline, it should seek to be acquired by another firm or liquidate before it fails. Effective management planning should help the firm to postpone decline and ultimate failure.

VOLUNTARY SETTLEMENTS

Voluntary settlement An arrangement between a technically insolvent or bankrupt firm and its creditors enabling it to bypass many of the costs involved in legal bankruptcy proceedings.

When a firm becomes technically insolvent or bankrupt, it may arrange with its creditors a **voluntary settlement,** which enables it to bypass many of the costs involved in legal bankruptcy proceedings. The settlement is normally initiated by the debtor firm, since such an arrangement may enable it to continue to exist or to

[1]Since on a balance sheet the firm's assets equal the sum of its liabilities and stockholders' equity, the only way a firm that has more liabilities than assets can balance its balance sheet is to have a *negative* stockholders' equity.

[2]The success of some firms runs countercyclical to economic activity, and other firms are unaffected by economic activity. For example, the sale of sewing machines is likely to increase during a recession, since people are more willing to make their own clothes and less willing to pay for the labor of others. The sale of boats and other luxury items may decline during a recession, while sales of staple items such as electricity are likely to be unaffected. In terms of beta, the measure of nondiversifiable risk, a negative-beta stock would be associated with a firm whose behavior is generally countercyclical to economic activity.

be liquidated in a manner that gives the owners the greatest chance of recovering part of their investment. The debtor, possibly with the aid of a key creditor, arranges a meeting between itself and all its creditors. At the meeting, a committee of creditors is selected to investigate and analyze the debtor's situation and recommend a plan of action. The recommendations of the committee are discussed with both the debtor and the creditors, and a plan for sustaining or liquidating the firm is drawn up.

Voluntary Settlement to Sustain the Firm

Normally, the rationale for sustaining a firm is that it is reasonable to believe that the firm's recovery is feasible. By sustaining the firm the creditor can continue to receive business from it. A number of strategies are commonly used. An **extension** is an arrangement whereby the firm's creditors receive payment in full, although not immediately. Normally, when creditors grant an extension, they agree to require cash payments for purchases until all past debts have been paid. A second arrangement, called **composition,** is a pro rata cash settlement of creditor claims. Instead of receiving full payment of their claims, as in the case of an extension, creditors receive only a partial payment. A uniform percentage of each dollar owed is paid in satisfaction of each creditor's claim. A third arrangement is **creditor control.** In this case the creditor committee may decide that the only circumstance in which maintaining the firm is feasible is if the operating management is replaced. The committee may then take control of the firm and operate it until all claims have been settled. Sometimes, a plan involving some combination of extension, composition, and creditor control will result. An example of this would be a settlement whereby the debtor agrees to pay a total of 75 cents on the dollar in three annual installments of 25 cents on the dollar, while the creditors agree to sell additional merchandise to the firm on 30-day terms if the existing management is replaced by new management that is acceptable to them.

Extension
An arrangement whereby the firm's creditors receive payment in full, although not immediately.

Composition
A pro rata cash settlement of creditor claims by the debtor firm; a uniform percentage of each dollar owed is paid.

Creditor control
An arrangement in which the creditor committee replaces the firm's operating management and operates the firm until all claims have been settled.

Voluntary Settlement Resulting in Liquidation

After the situation of the firm has been investigated by the creditor committee, recommendations have been made, and talks among the creditors and the debtor have been held, the only acceptable course of action may be liquidation of the firm. Liquidation can be carried out in two ways—privately or through the legal procedures provided by bankruptcy law. If the debtor firm is willing to accept liquidation, legal procedures may not be required. Generally, the avoidance of litigation enables the creditors to obtain *quicker* and *higher* settlements. However, all the creditors must agree to a private liquidation for it to be feasible.

The objective of the voluntary liquidation process is to recover as much per dollar owed as possible. Under voluntary liquidation, common stockholders, who are the firm's true owners, cannot receive any funds until the claims of all other parties have been satisfied. A common procedure is to have a meeting of the creditors at which they make an **assignment** by passing the power to liquidate the firm's assets to an adjustment bureau, a trade association, or a third party, which is designated

Assignment
A voluntary liquidation procedure by which a firm's creditors pass the power to liquidate the firm's assets to an adjustment bureau, a trade association, or a third party, which is designated the *assignee*.

the *assignee.* The assignee's job is to liquidate the assets, obtaining the best price possible. The assignees is sometimes referred to as the *trustee,* since it is entrusted with the title to the company's assets and the responsibility to liquidate them efficiently. Once the trustee has liquidated the assets, it distributes the recovered funds to the creditors and owners (if any funds remain for the owners). The final action in a private liquidation is for the creditors to sign a release attesting to the satisfactory settlement of their claims.

BANKRUPTCY LEGISLATION

As was already stated, *bankruptcy* in the legal sense occurs when the firm cannot pay its bills or when its liabilities exceed the fair market value of its assets. In either of these situations a firm may be declared legally bankrupt. However, creditors generally attempt to avoid forcing a firm into bankruptcy if it appears to have opportunities for future success.

Bankruptcy Reform Act of 1978
The current governing bankruptcy legislation in the United States.

Chapter 7
The portion of the *Bankruptcy Reform Act of 1978* that details the procedures to be followed in liquidating a failed firm.

Chapter 11
The portion of the *Bankruptcy Reform Act of 1978* that outlines the procedures for reorganizing a failed (or failing) firm, whether its petition is filed voluntarily or involuntarily.

The governing bankruptcy legislation in the United States today is the **Bankruptcy Reform Act of 1978,** which significantly modified earlier bankruptcy legislation. This law contains eight odd-numbered (1 through 15) chapters and one even-numbered (12) chapter. A number of these chapters would apply in the instance of failure; the two key ones are Chapters 7 and 11. **Chapter 7** of the Bankruptcy Reform Act of 1978 details the procedures to be followed in liquidating a failed firm. This chapter typically comes into play once it has been determined that a fair, equitable, and feasible basis for the reorganization of a failed firm does not exist (although a firm may of its own accord choose not to reorganize and may instead go directly into liquidation). **Chapter 11** outlines the procedures for reorganizing a failed (or failing) firm, whether its petition is filed voluntarily or involuntarily. If a workable plan for reorganization cannot be developed, the firm will be liquidated under Chapter 7.

REORGANIZATION IN BANKRUPTCY

Voluntary reorganization
A petition filed by a failed firm on its own behalf for reorganizing its structure and paying its creditors.

Involuntary reorganization
A petition initiated by an outside party, usually a creditor, for the reorganization and payment of creditors of a failed firm.

There are two basic types of reorganization petitions—voluntary and involuntary. Any firm that is not a municipal or financial institution can file a petition for **voluntary reorganization** on its own behalf.[1] **Involuntary reorganization** is initiated by an outside party, usually a creditor. An involuntary petition against a firm can be filed if one of three conditions is met:

1. The firm has past-due debts of $5,000 or more.
2. Three or more creditors can prove that they have aggregate unpaid claims of $5,000 against the firm. If the firm has fewer than 12 creditors, any creditor that is owed more than $5,000 can file the petition.
3. The firm is *insolvent,* which means (a) that it is not paying its debts as they come due, (b) that within the immediately preceding 120 days a custodian (a third party) was appointed or took possession of the debtor's property, or (c) that the fair market value of the firm's assets is less than the stated value of its liabilities.

[1]Firms sometimes file a voluntary petition to obtain temporary legal protection from creditors or from prolonged litigation. Once they have straightened out their financial or legal affairs—prior to further reorganization or liquidation actions—they will have the petition dismissed. Although such actions are not the intent of the bankruptcy law, difficulty in enforcing the law has allowed this abuse to occur.

Concept in Practice

R-TEK and 96,000 Other Firms. R-Tek Corporation, a record and video marketer, has the distinction of being the worst-performing stock in 1992. The company lost millions of dollars when a German subsidiary went into receivership and its share price fell from $7.75 to pennies per share. R-Tek was not alone. According to Dun & Bradstreet Information Services, business failures in 1992 were more common than ever. Approximately 96,000 businesses closed their doors, 9 percent more than in 1991 and 30 percent more than in 1990. The dollar value of unpaid liabilities associated with these failures amounted to $105 billion. The one bright spot was that the number of bankruptcies leaving liabilities greater than $1 million dropped.

Procedures. The procedures for initiation and execution of corporate reorganizations entail five separate steps: filing, appointment, development and approval of a reorganization plan, acceptance of the plan, and payment of expenses.

Filing. A reorganization petition under Chapter 11 must be filed in a federal bankruptcy court. In the case of an involuntary petition, if it is challenged by the debtor, a hearing must be held to determine whether the firm is insolvent. If it is, the court enters an "Order for Relief" that formally initiates the process.

Appointment. Upon the filing of a reorganization petition, the filing firm becomes the **debtor in possession (DIP)** of the assets. If creditors object to the filing firm being the debtor in possession, they can ask the judge to appoint a trustee.

Debtor in possession (DIP)
The term assigned to a firm that files a reorganization petition under Chapter 11 and then develops, if feasible, a reorganization plan.

Reorganization Plan. After reviewing its situation the debtor in possession submits a plan of reorganization to the court. The plan and a disclosure statement summarizing the plan are filed. A hearing is held to determine whether the plan is *fair, equitable,* and *feasible* and whether the disclosure statement contains adequate information. The court's approval or disapproval is based on its evaluation of the plan in light of these standards. A plan is considered *fair and equitable* if it *maintains the priorities* of the contractual claims of the creditors, preferred stockholders, and common stockholders. The court must also find the reorganization plan *feasible,* meaning that it must be *workable.* The reorganized corporation must have sufficient working capital, sufficient funds to cover fixed charges, sufficient credit prospects, and sufficient ability to retire or refund debts as proposed by the plan.

Acceptance of the Reorganization Plan. Once approved, the plan, along with the disclosure statement, is given to the firm's creditors and shareholders for their acceptance. Under the Bankruptcy Reform Act, creditors and owners are separated into groups with similar types of claims. In the case of creditor groups, approval by holders of at least two-thirds of the dollar amount of claims as well as numerical majority of creditors in the group is required. In the case of ownership groups (preferred and common stockholders), two-thirds of the shares in each group must approve the reorganization plan for it to be accepted. Once accepted and confirmed by the court, the plan is put into effect as soon as possible.

Payment of Expenses. After the reorganization plan has been approved or disapproved, all parties to the proceedings whose services were beneficial or contributed to the approval or disapproval of the plan file a statement of expenses. If the court finds these claims acceptable, the debtor must pay these expenses within a reasonable period of time.

Role of the Debtor in Possession (DIP)

Since reorganization activities are largely in the hands of the debtor in possession (DIP), it is useful to understand the DIP's responsibilities. The DIP's first responsibility is the valuation of the firm to determine whether reorganization is appropriate. To do this, the DIP must estimate both the *liquidation value* of the business and its value as a *going concern.* If the DIP finds that its value as a going concern is less than its liquidation value, it will recommend liquidation. If the opposite is found to be true, the DIP will recommend reorganization. If the reorganization of the firm is recommended by the DIP, a plan of reorganization must be drawn up. The key portion of the reorganization plan generally concerns the firm's capital structure. Since most firms' financial difficulties result from high fixed charges, the company's capital structure is generally *recapitalized,* or altered, to reduce these charges. Under **recapitalization,** debts are generally exchanged for equity, or the maturities of existing debts are extended. The DIP, in recapitalizing the firm, places a great deal of emphasis on building a mix of debt and equity that will allow the firm to meet its debts and provide a reasonable level of earnings for its owners.

Recapitalization
The reorganization procedure under which a failed firm's debts are generally exchanged for equity or the maturities of existing debts are extended.

Once the optimal capital structure has been determined, the DIP must establish a plan for exchanging outstanding obligations for new securities. The guiding principle is to *observe priorities.* Senior claims (those with higher legal priority) must be satisfied before junior claims (those with lower legal priority). To comply with this principle, senior suppliers of capital must receive a claim on new capital equal to their previous claims. The common stockholders are the last to receive any new securities. (It is not unusual for them to receive nothing.) Security holders do not necessarily have to receive the same type of security they held before; often they receive a combination of securities. Once the debtor in possession has determined the new capital structure and distribution of capital, it will submit the reorganization plan and disclosure statement to the court as described.

LIQUIDATION IN BANKRUPTCY

The liquidation of a bankrupt firm usually occurs once the courts have determined that reorganization is not feasible. A petition for reorganization must normally be filed by the managers or creditors of the bankrupt firm. If no petition is filed, if a petition is filed and denied, or if the reorganization plan is denied, the firm must be liquidated. Three important aspects of liquidation in bankruptcy are the procedures, the priority of claims, and the final accounting.

Procedures

When a firm is adjudged bankrupt, the judge may appoint a *trustee* to perform the many routine duties required in administering the bankruptcy. The trustee takes charge of the property of the bankrupt firm and protects the interest of its creditors.

Once the firm has been adjudged bankrupt, a meeting of creditors must be held between 20 and 40 days thereafter. At this meeting, the creditors are made aware of the prospects for the liquidation. The meeting is presided over by the bankruptcy court clerk. The trustee is then given the responsibility to liquidate the firm, keep records, examine creditors' claims, disburse money, furnish information as required, and make final reports on the liquidation. In essence the trustee is responsible for the liquidation of the firm. Occasionally, the court will call subsequent creditor meetings, but only a final meeting for closing the bankruptcy is required.

Priority of Claims

It is the trustee's responsibility to liquidate all the firm's assets and to distribute the proceeds to the holders of *provable claims*. The courts have established certain procedures for determining the provability of claims. The priority of claims, which is specified in Chapter 7 of the Bankruptcy Reform Act, must be maintained by the trustee in distributing the funds from liquidation. It is important to recognize that any **secured creditors** have specific assets pledged as collateral and, in liquidation, receive proceeds from the sale of those assets. If these proceeds are inadequate to meet their claim, the secured creditors become **unsecured, or general, creditors** for the unrecovered amount, since specific collateral no longer exists. These and other unsecured creditors will divide up, on a pro rata basis, any funds remaining after all prior claims have been satisfied. If the proceeds from the sale of secured assets are in excess of the claims against them, the excess funds become available to meet claims of unsecured creditors. The complete order of priority of claims is as follows:

Secured creditors
Creditors who have specific assets pledged as collateral and in liquidation of the failed firm receive proceeds from the sale of those assets.

Unsecured, or general, creditors
Creditors who have a general claim against all the firm's assets other than those specifically pledged as collateral.

1. The expenses of administering the bankruptcy proceedings.
2. Any unpaid interim expenses incurred in the ordinary course of business between filing the bankruptcy petition and the entry of an Order for Relief in an involuntary proceeding. (This step is *not* applicable in a voluntary bankruptcy.)
3. Wages of not more than $2,000 per worker that have been earned by workers in the 90-day period immediately preceding the commencement of bankruptcy proceedings.
4. Unpaid employee benefit plan contributions that were to be paid in the 180-day period preceding the filing of bankruptcy or the termination of business, whichever occurred first. For any employee, the sum of this claim plus eligible unpaid wages (item 3) cannot exceed $2,000.
5. Claims of farmers or fishermen in a grain-storage or fish-storage facility, not to exceed $2,000 for each producer.
6. Unsecured customer deposits, not to exceed $900 each, resulting from purchasing or leasing a good or service from the failed firm.
7. Taxes legally due and owed by the bankrupt firm to the federal government, state government, or any other governmental subdivision.
8. Claims of secured creditors, who receive the proceeds from the sale of collateral held, regardless of the priorities above. If the proceeds from the liquidation of the collateral are insufficient to satisfy the secured creditors' claims, the secured creditors become unsecured creditors for the unpaid amount.
9. Claims of unsecured creditors. The claims of unsecured, or general, creditors and unsatisfied portions of secured creditors' claims (item 8) are all treated equally.

TABLE 26-1 Balance Sheet for Cambridge Company

Assets		Liabilities and Stockholders' Equity	
Cash	$ 10,000	Accounts payable	$ 200,000
Marketable securities	5,000	Notes payable—bank	1,000,000
Accounts receivable	1,090,000	Accrued wages[a]	320,000
Inventories	3,100,000	Unpaid employee benefits[b]	80,000
Prepaid expenses	5,000	Unsecured customer deposits[c]	100,000
Total current assets	$4,210,000	Taxes payable	300,000
Land	$2,000,000	Total current liabilities	$2,000,000
Net plant	1,810,000	First mortgage[d]	$1,800,000
Net equipment	80,000	Second mortgage[d]	1,000,000
Total fixed assets	$3,890,000	Unsecured bonds	800,000
Total	$8,100,000	Total long-term debt	$3,600,000
		Preferred stock (5,000 shares)	$ 400,000
		Common stock (10,000 shares)	500,000
		Paid-in capital in excess of par	1,500,000
		Retained earnings	100,000
		Total shareholders' equity	$2,500,000
		Total	$8,100,000

[a] *Represents wages of $800 per employee earned within 90 days of filing bankruptcy for 400 of the firm's employees.*

[b] *These unpaid employee benefits were due in the 180-day period preceding the firm's bankruptcy filing, which occurred simultaneously with the termination of its business.*

[c] *Unsecured customer deposits not exceeding $900 each.*

[d] *The first and second mortgages are on the firm's total fixed assets.*

10. Preferred stockholders, who receive an amount up to the par, or stated, value of their preferred stock.
11. Common stockholders, who receive any remaining funds, which are distributed on an equal per-share basis. If different classes of common stock are outstanding priorities may exist.

In spite of the priorities listed in items 1 through 7, secured creditors have first claim on proceeds from the sale of their collateral. The claims of unsecured creditors, including the unpaid claims of secured creditors, are satisfied next and, finally, the claims of preferred and common stockholders. The application of these priorities by the trustee in bankruptcy liquidation proceedings can be illustrated by a simple example.

EXAMPLE

Cambridge Company, a manufacturer of portable computers, has the balance sheet presented in Table 26-1. The trustee, as was her obligation, has liquidated the firm's assets, obtaining the highest amounts she could get. She managed to obtain $2.3 million for the firm's current assets and $2 million for the firm's fixed assets. The total proceeds from the liquidation were therefore $4.3 million. It should be clear that the firm is legally bankrupt, since its liabilities of $5.6 million dollars exceed the $4.3 million fair market value of its assets.

The next step is to distribute the proceeds to the various creditors. The only liability that is not shown on the balance sheet is $800,000 in expenses for administer-

TABLE 26-2 Distribution of the Liquidation Proceeds of Cambridge Company

Proceeds from liquidation	$4,300,000
—Expenses of administering bankruptcy and paying interim bills	$ 800,000
—Wages owed workers	320,000
—Unpaid employee benefits	80,000
—Unsecured customer deposits	100,000
—Taxes owed governments	300,000
Funds available for creditors	**$2,700,000**
—First mortgage, paid from the $2 million proceeds from the sale of fixed assets	$ 1,800,000
—Second mortgage, partially paid from the remaining $200,000 of fixed assets proceeds	200,000
Funds available for unsecured creditors	**$ 700,000**

TABLE 26-3 Pro Rata Distribution of Funds Among Unsecured Creditors of Cambridge Company

Unsecured creditors' claims	Amount	Settlement at 25%[a]
Unpaid balance of second mortgage	$ 800,000[b]	$200,000
Accounts payable	200,000	50,000
Notes payable—bank	1,000,000	250,000
Unsecured bonds	800,000	200,000
Totals	$2,800,000	$700,000

[a] *The 25 percent rate is calculated by dividing the $700,000 available for unsecured creditors by the $2.8 million owed unsecured creditors. Each is entitled to a pro rata share.*

[b] *This figure represents the difference between the $1 million second mortgage and the $200,000 payment on the second mortgage from the proceeds from the sale of the collateral remaining after satisfying the first mortgage.*

ing the bankruptcy proceedings and satisfying unpaid bills incurred between the time of filing the bankruptcy petition and the entry of an Order for Relief. The distribution of the $4.3 million among the firm's creditors is shown in Table 26-2. The table shows that once all prior claims on the proceeds from liquidation have been satisfied, the unsecured creditors get the remaining funds. The pro rate distribution of the $700,000 among the unsecured creditors is given in Table 26-3. The disposition of funds in the Cambridge Company liquidation should be clear from Tables 26-2 and 26-3. Since the claims of the unsecured creditors have not been fully satisfied, the preferred and common stockholders receive nothing.

Final Accounting

After the trustee has liquidated all the bankrupt firm's assets and distributed the proceeds to satisfy all provable claims in the appropriate order of priority, he or she makes a final accounting to the bankruptcy court and creditors. Once the court approves the final accounting, the liquidation is complete.

SUMMARY

- **Types and major causes of business failure and the use of voluntary settlements to sustain or liquidate the failed firm.** A firm may fail because it has negative or low returns, because it is technically insolvent, or because it is bankrupt. The major causes of business failure are mismanagement, downturns in economic activity, and corporate maturity. Voluntary settlements are initiated by the debtor and can result in sustaining the firm through an extension, a composition, creditor control of the firm, or a combination of these strategies. If creditors do not agree to a plan to sustain a firm, they may recommend voluntary liquidation, which bypasses many of the legal requirements and costs of bankruptcy proceedings.
- **Bankruptcy legislation and the procedures involved in reorganizing or liquidating a bankrupt firm.** A failed firm that cannot or does not want to arrange a voluntary settlement can voluntarily or involuntarily file in federal bankruptcy court for reorganization under Chapter 11 or liquidation under Chapter 7 of the Bankruptcy Reform Act of 1978. Under Chapter 11 the judge will appoint the debtor in possession, who with court supervision develops, if feasible, a reorganization plan. A firm that cannot be reorganized under Chapter 11 of the bankruptcy law or does not petition for reorganization is liquidated under Chapter 7. The responsibility for liquidation is placed in the hands of a court-appointed trustee, whose duties include the liquidation of assets, the distribution of the proceeds, and making a final accounting. Liquidation procedures follow a priority of claims for distribution of the proceeds from the sale of assets.

QUESTIONS

1. What is the concern of Chapter 11 of the Bankruptcy Reform Act of 1978? How is the *debtor in possession (DIP)* involved in (a) the valuation of the firm, (b) the recapitalization of the firm, and (c) the exchange of obligations using the priority rule?
2. What is the concern of Chapter 7 of the Bankruptcy Reform Act of 1978? Under which conditions is a firm liquidated in bankruptcy? Describe the procedures (including the role of the *trustee*) involved in liquidating the bankrupt firm.
3. In which order would the following claims be settled in distributing the proceeds from liquidating a bankrupt firm?
   a. Claims of preferred stockholders
   b. Claims of secured creditors
   c. Expenses of administering the bankruptcy
   d. Claims of common stockholders
   e. Claims of unsecured, or general, creditors
   f. Taxes legally due
   g. Unsecured deposits of customers
   h. Certain eligible wages
   i. Unpaid employee benefit plan contributions
   j. Unpaid interim expenses incurred between the time of filing and the entry of an Order for Relief
   k. Claims of farmers or fishermen in a grain-storage facility

SELF-CORRECTION PROBLEM

The Leto Company recently failed and was left with the balance sheet shown below. The trustee liquidated the firm's assets, obtaining net proceeds of $2.2 million from the current assets and $2.5 million from the fixed assets. In the process of liquidating the assets, the trustee incurred expenses totaling $400,000. Because of the speed with which the Order for Relief was entered, no interim expenses were incurred.

a. Prepare a table indicating the amount, if any, to be distributed to each claimant except unsecured creditors. Indicate the amount to be paid, if any, to the group of unsecured creditors.
b. After all claims other than those of unsecured creditors have been satisfied, how much, if any, is still owed to the second-mortgage holders? Why?
c. Prepare a table showing how the remaining funds, if any, would be distributed to the firm's unsecured creditors.

Balance Sheet of Leto Company

Assets		Liabilities and Stockholders' Equity	
Cash	$ 80,000	Accounts payable	$ 400,000
Marketable securities	10,000	Notes payable—bank	800,000
Accounts receivable	1,090,000	Accrued wages[a]	500,000
Inventories	2,300,000	Unpaid employee benefits[b]	100,000
Prepaid expenses	20,000	Unsecured customer deposits[c]	50,000
Total current		Taxes payable	250,000
assets	$3,500,000	Total current liabilities	$2,100,000
Land	$1,000,000	First mortgage[d]	$2,000,000
Net plant	2,000,000	Second mortgage[d]	800,000
Net equipment	1,500,000	Unsecured bonds	500,000
Total fixed		Total long-term debt	$3,300,000
assets	$4,500,000	Preferred stock (10,000	
Total	$8,000,000	shares)	$300,000
		Common stock (5,000 shares)	300,000
		Paid-in capital in excess of par	1,500,000
		Retained earnings	500,000
		Total stockholders' equity	$2,600,000
		Total	$8,000,000

[a] *Represents wages of $250 per employee earned within 90 days of filing bankruptcy for 2,000 of the firm's employees.*

[b] *these unpaid employee benefits were due in the 180-day period preceding the firm's bankruptcy filing, which occurred simultaneously with the termination of its business.*

[c] *Unsecured customer deposits not exceeding $900 each.*

[d] *The first and second mortgages are on the firm's total fixed assets.*

PROBLEM

Keck Business Forms recently failed and was liquidated by a court-appointed trustee who charged $200,000 for her services. Between the time of filing of the bankruptcy petition and the entry of an Order for Relief, a total of $100,000 in unpaid bills was incurred and remain unpaid. The preliquidation balance sheet follows.

Assets		Liabilities and Stockholders' Equity	
Cash	$ 40,000	Accounts payable	$ 200,000
Marketable securities	30,000	Notes payable—bank	300,000
Accounts receivable	620,000	Accrued wages[a]	50,000
Inventories	1,200,000	Unsecured customer deposits[b]	30,000
Prepaid expenses	10,000	Taxes payable	20,000
Total current assets	$1,900,000	Total current liabilities	$ 600,000
		First mortgage[c]	$ 700,000
Land	$ 300,000	Second mortgage[c]	400,000
Net plant	400,000	Unsecured bonds	300,000
Net equipment	400,000	Total long-term debt	$1,400,000
Total fixed assets	$1,100,000	Preferred stock (15,000 shares)	$ 200,000
Total	$3,000,000	Common stock (10,000 shares)	200,000
		Paid-in capital in excess of par	500,000
		Retained earnings	100,000
		Total stockholders' equity	$1,000,000
		Total	$3,000,000

[a]*Represents wages of $500 per employee earned within 90 days of filing bankruptcy for 100 of the firm's employees.*

[b]*Unsecured customer deposits not exceeding $900 each.*

[c]*The first and second mortgages are on the firm's total fixed assets.*

a. Assume that the trustee liquidates the assets for $2.5 million—$1.3 million from current assets and $1.2 million from fixed assets.
   (1) Prepare a table indicating the amount to be distributed to each claimant. Indicate whether the claimant is an unsecured creditor.
   (2) Before satisfying unsecured creditor claims, how much is owed to first-mortgage holders and second-mortgage holders?
   (3) Do the firm's owners receive any funds? Is so, in what amounts?

b. Assume the trustee liquidates the assets for $1.8 million—$1.2 million from current assets and $600,000 from fixed assets; rework your answers in a.

c. Compare, contrast, and discuss your findings in a and b.

SOLUTION TO SELF-CORRECTION PROBLEM

a.

Proceeds from liquidation	$4,700,000
—Trustee's expenses	$400,000
—Wages owed workers	500,000
—Unpaid employee benefits	100,000
—Unsecured customer deposits	50,000
—Taxes owed governments	250,000
Funds available for creditors	$3,400,000
—First mortgage, paid from the $2 5 million proceeds from the sale of fixed assets	$2,000,000
—Second mortgage, partially paid from the remaining $500,000 of fixed assets proceeds	500,000
Funds available for unsecured creditors	$ 900,000

b. The second-mortgage holders are *still owed $300,000,* since they have recovered from the sale of the fixed assets $500,000 of the $800,000 owed them.

c.

Unsecured Creditors' Claims	**Amount**	**Settlement at 45%[a]**
Unpaid balance of second mortgage	$ 300,000[b]	$135,000
Accounts payable	400,000	180,000
Notes payable—bank	800,000	360,000
Unsecured bonds	500,000	225,000
Totals	$2,000,000	$900,000

[a] *The 45 percent rate is calculated by dividing the $900,000 available for unsecured creditors by the $2,000,000 owed unsecured creditors. Each is entitled to a pro rata share.*

[b] *Value calculated in part b.*

SECTION X

International Finance

INTERNATIONAL FINANCE:
CONCEPTS AND APPLICATIONS

CHAPTER 27

International Finance: Concepts and Applications

INTRODUCTION

Today, international economic boundaries no longer exist. In financial management, when we ask, Where can funds be raised least expensively? Where can this new product be produced least expensively? Where will our major competition come from? The answer will quite likely involve a foreign country. If we are going to be successful in business, we must have an international perspective in our decision making.

The case of the biotechnology industry typifies how the internationalization of business coupled with recent technological breakthroughs have created both competition and opportunities for U.S. firms. Here, we as financial managers must be able to look at new projects and see both their potential and risks from an international perspective.

One business battle presently being fought in the international arena is for dominance in biotechnology products. Not only are the profits from success going to come from sales around the world, but the competition is also international in perspective. The United States have been at the forefront of biotechnology, but Japanese companies are quickly gaining ground. Drawing on a strategy that has served them well in other industries, the Japanese are heavily relying on "piggybacking." The key to this strategy is to use their considerable financial assets to supply needed cash to biotechnology laboratories around the world, which then grant the Japanese access to technological breakthroughs. By riding "piggyback" on basic research conducted in other countries, the Japanese companies, in effect, augment their own research budgets, freeing resources for perfecting products that have the best chance of dominating markets around the world. Takeda, for example, which has a joint venture with Abbott Labs and alliances in West Germany, France, and Italy, funds research at Harvard University.

Today, the United States is spending three times the Japanese investment per year on biotech R&D and still holds a considerable lead in most areas of research. However, only time will tell how this will all turn out. What is important to us is that we recognize that businesses are no longer bound by international boundaries, and that we must be able to apply our trade around the world.

THE GLOBALIZATION OF PRODUCT AND FINANCIAL MARKETS

World trade has grown much faster over the last few decades than world aggregate output (global gross national product or GNP). The dollar value of world exports has grown from $129.5 billion in 1962 to $3.3 *trillion* in 1990. This remarkable increase in international trade is reflected in the increased openness of almost all national economies to international influences. For example, the proportion of U.S. GNP accounted for by exports and imports (about one fifth) is now double what it was two decades ago, and is even higher for manufactured goods (see Figure 27-1). The U.S. Department of Commerce estimates that the United States exports about one fifth of its industrial production and that about 70 percent of all U.S. goods compete directly with foreign goods.

Some industries and states are highly dependent on the international economy. For example, the electronic consumer products and automobile industries are widely considered to be global industries. Ohio ranks fourth in terms of manufactured exports, and more than half of all Ohio workers are employed by firms that depend to some extent on exports.

There has also been a rise in the global level of international portfolio and direct investment. Both direct and portfolio investment in the United States have been increasing faster than U.S. investment overseas. Direct investment occurs when the **multinational corporation (MNC)** has control over the investment, such as when it builds an offshore manufacturing facility. Portfolio investment involves financial assets with maturities greater than one year, such as the purchase of foreign stocks and bonds. Total foreign investment in the U.S. now exceeds such U.S. investment overseas.

Multinational corporation (MNC) A corporation with holdings and/or operations in one or more countries.

A major reason for long-run overseas investments of United States companies is the high rates of return obtainable from these investments. The amount of United States *direct foreign investments (DFI)* abroad is large and growing. Significant amounts of the total assets, sales, and profits of American MNCs are attributable to foreign investments and foreign operations. Direct foreign investment is not limited to American firms. Many European and Japanese firms have operations abroad, too. During the last decade, these firms have been increasing their sales and setting up production facilities abroad, especially in the United States.

Capital flows between countries for international financial investment purposes have also been increasing. Many firms, investment companies, and individuals invest in the capital markets in foreign countries. The motivation is twofold: to obtain returns higher than those obtainable in the domestic capital markets, and to reduce portfolio risk through international diversification. The increase in world trade and investment activity is reflected in the recent globalization of financial markets. The Eurodollar market is larger than any domestic financial market. U.S. companies are increasingly turning to this market for funds. Even companies and public entities that have no overseas presence are beginning to rely on this market for financing.

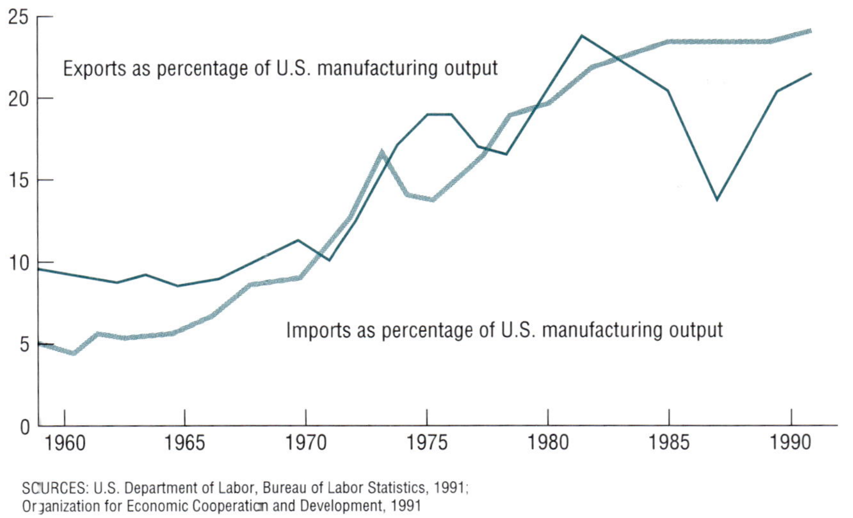

FIGURE 27-1
U.S. trade as a share of U.S. manufacturing output

In addition, most national financial markets are becoming more integrated with global markets because of the rapid increase in the volume of interest rate and currency swaps. Because of the widespread availability of these swaps, the currency denomination and the source country of financing for many globally integrated companies are dictated by accessibility and relative cost considerations regardless of the currency ultimately needed by the firm.

The foreign exchange markets have also grown rapidly, and the weekly trading volume in these globally integrated markets, between $3 and $5 trillion, exceeds the annual trading volume on the world's securities markets. Even a *purely domestic firm* that buys all its inputs and sells all its output in its home country is not immune to foreign competition, nor can it totally ignore the workings of the international financial markets.

EXCHANGE RATES

Recent History of Exchange Rates

Between 1949 and 1970, the exchange rates between the major currencies were fixed. All countries were required to set a specific *parity rate* for their currency vis-à-vis the United States dollar. For example, consider the German currency, the Deutsche mark (DM). In 1949, the parity rate was set at 4.0 DM to $1. The actual exchange rate prevailing on any day was allowed to lie within a narrow band around the parity rate. The DM was allowed to fluctuate between 4.04 and 3.96 per dollar. A country could effect a major adjustment in the exchange rate by changing its parity rate with respect to the dollar. When the currency was made cheaper with respect to the dollar, this adjustment was called a *devaluation*. A *revaluation* resulted when a currency became more expensive with respect to the dollar. In 1969, the DM parity rate was adjusted to 3.66 per dollar. This adjustment was a revaluation of the DM parity by 9.3 percent.

The new bands around the parity were 3.7010 and 3.6188 DM per dollar. The DM strengthened against the dollar since fewer DM were needed to buy a dollar.

Since 1973, a *floating-rate* international currency system has been operating. For most currencies, there are no parity rates and no bands within which the currencies fluctuate.[1] Most major currencies, including the United States dollar, fluctuate freely, depending upon their values as perceived by the traders in foreign exchange markets. The country's relative economic strengths, its level of exports and imports, the level of monetary activity, and the deficits or surpluses in its balance of payments (BOP) are all important factors in the determination of exchange rates.[2] Short-term, day-to-day fluctuations in exchange rates are caused by changing supply and demand conditions in the foreign exchange market.

The Foreign Exchange Market

The foreign exchange market provides a mechanism for the transfer of purchasing power from one currency to another. This market is not a physical entity like the New York Stock Exchange; it is a network of telephone and computer connections among banks, foreign exchange dealers, and brokers. The market operates simultaneously at three levels. At the first level, customers buy and sell foreign exchange (that is, foreign currency) through their banks. At the second level, banks buy and sell foreign exchange from other banks in the same commercial center. At the last level, banks buy and sell foreign exchange from banks in commercial centers in other countries. Some important commercial centers for foreign exchange trading are New York, London, Zurich, Frankfurt, Hong Kong, Singapore, and Tokyo.

An example will illustrate this multilevel trading. A trader in Texas may buy foreign exchange (pounds) from a bank in Houston for payment to a British supplier against some purchase made. The Houston bank, in turn, may purchase the foreign currency (pounds) from a New York bank. The New York bank may buy the pounds from another bank in New York or from a bank in London.

Because this market provides transactions in a continuous manner for a very large volume of sales and purchases, the currency markets are *efficient*. In other words, it is difficult to make a profit by shopping around from one bank to another. Minute differences in the quotes from different banks are quickly eliminated. Because of the arbitrage mechanism, simultaneous quotes to different buyers in London and New York are likely to be the same.

Two major types of transactions are carried out in the foreign exchange markets: *spot* and *forward transactions.*

Spot Exchange Rates

Spot transaction
A transaction made immediately in the market place at the market price.

A typical spot transaction involves an American firm buying foreign currency from its bank and paying for it in dollars. The price of foreign currency in terms of the domestic currency is the *exchange rate.* Another type of spot transaction is when an American firm receives foreign currency from abroad. The firm typically would sell the foreign currency to its bank for dollars. These are both **spot transactions** because

[1] The system of floating rates is referred to as the "floating-rate regime."

[2] The balance of payments for the United States reflects the difference between the imports and exports of goods (the trade balance) and services. Capital inflows and outflows are tabulated in the capital account.

one currency is exchanged for another currency today. The actual exchange rate quotes are expressed in several different ways, as discussed later. To allow time for the transfer of funds, the *value date* when the currencies are actually exchanged is two days after the spot transaction occurs. Four banks could easily be involved in the transactions: the local banks of the buyer and seller of the foreign exchange, and the money-center banks that handle the purchase and sale in the interbank market. Perhaps the buyer or seller will have to move the funds from one of its local banks to another, bringing even more banks into the transaction.

On the spot exchange market the quoted exchange rate is typically called a direct quote. A **direct quote** indicates the number of units of the home currency required to buy one unit of the foreign currency. That is, in New York the typical exchange-rate quote indicates the number of dollars needed to buy one unit of a foreign currency: dollars per pound, dollars per mark, and so on. The spot rates in columns 2 and 3 of Table 27-1 are the direct exchange quotes taken from *The Wall Street Journal* on July 19, 1994. To buy one pound on July 18, 1994, 1.5615 dollars were needed. To buy one franc and one mark, 18.848 cents and 64.66 cents were needed, respectively. The quotes in the spot market in Paris are given in terms of francs and those in Frankfurt in terms of Deutsche marks.

Direct quote The exchange rate that indicates the number of units of the home currency required to buy one unit of foreign currency.

An **indirect quote** indicates the number of units of foreign currency that can be bought for one unit of the home currency. This reads as pounds per dollar, francs per dollar, and so on. Indirect quotes are given in the last two columns of Table 27-1.

Indirect quote The exchange rate that expresses the required number of units of foreign currency to buy one unit of home currency.

In summary, a direct quote is the dollar/foreign currency rate ($/FC), and an indirect quote is the foreign currency/dollar rate (FC/$). Therefore, an indirect quote is the reciprocal of a direct quote and vice versa. The following example illustrates the computation of an indirect quote from a given direct quote.

EXAMPLE

Suppose you want to compute the indirect quotes from the direct quotes of spot rates for pounds, francs, and marks given in column 2 of Table 27-1. The direct quotes are: pound, 1.5615; French franc, .18848; and Deutsche mark, .6466. The related indirect quotes are calculated as the *reciprocal* of the direct quote as follows:

$$\text{indirect quote} = \frac{1}{\text{direct quote}}$$

Thus

pounds: $$\frac{1}{\$1.5615/£} = £.6404/\$$$

francs: $$\frac{1}{\$.18848/FF} = FF5.3055/\$$$

Deutsche marks: $$\frac{1}{\$.6466/DM} = DM1.5465/\$$$

Notice that the above direct quotes and indirect quotes are identical to those shown in columns 2 and 4 of Table 27-1.

Direct and indirect quotes are useful in conducting international transactions, as the following examples show.

TABLE 27-1 Foreign Exchange Rates Reported on July 19, 1994

	U.S. $ equiv.		Currency[a] per U.S. $	
Country	**Mon.**	**Fri.**	**Mon.**	**Fri.**
Argentina (Peso)	1.01	1.01	.99	.99
Australia (Dollar)	.7303	.7335	1.3693	1.3633
Austria (Schilling)	.09187	.09146	10.88	10.93
Belgium (Franc)	.03137	.03122	31.88	32.03
Brazil (Real)	1.0989011	1.0729614	.91	.93
Britain (Pound)	1.5615	1.5607	.6404	.6407
30-Day Forward	1.5609	1.5601	.6407	.6410
90-Day Forward	1.5605	1.5597	.6408	.6411
180-Day Forward	1.5603	1.5595	.6409	.6412
Canada (Dollar)	.7265	.7260	1.3765	1.3775
30-Day Forward	.7256	.7251	1.3782	1.3792
90-Day Forward	.7236	.7231	1.3820	1.3830
180-Day Forward	.7196	.7191	1.3896	1.3906
China (Renminbi)	.115221	.115221	8.6790	8.6790
France (Franc)	.18848	.18758	5.3055	5.3310
30-Day Forward	.18829	.18739	5.3110	5.3365
90-Day Forward	.18809	.18719	5.3167	5.3422
180-Day Forward	.18795	.18706	5.3205	5.3460
Germany (Mark)	.6466	.6433	1.5465	1.5545
30-Day Forward	.6450	.6416	1.5505	1.5585
90-Day Forward	.6467	.6434	1.5462	1.5542
180-Day Forward	.6480	.6447	1.5431	1.5511
Hong Kong (Dollar)	.12945	.12945	7.7250	7.7250
India (Rupee)	.03212	.03212	31.13	31.13
Ireland (Punt)	1.5406	1.5372	.6491	.6505
Israel (Shekel)	.3298	.3298	3.0320	3.0320
Italy (Lira)	.0006447	.0006452	1551.14	1549.86
Japan (Yen)	.010168	.010220	98.35	97.85
Mexico (Peso)				
Floating rate	.2943341	.2942475	3.3975	3.3985
Netherland (Guilder)	.5765	.5737	1.7346	1.7431
Norway (Krone)	.1477	.1470	6.7721	6.8033
Philippines (Peso)	.03821	.03861	26.17	25.90
Portugal (Escudo)	.006277	.006249	159.30	160.04
Saudi Arabia (Riyal)	.26667	.26665	3.7500	3.7503
South Korea (Won)	.0012392	.0012408	807.00	805.90
Spain (Peseta)	.007824	.007783	127.82	128.48
Sweden (Krona)	.1300	.1292	7.6900	7.7414
Switzerland (Franc)	.7664	.7642	1.3048	1.3085
Taiwan (Dollar)	.037622	.037509	26.58	26.66
SDR[b]	1.46680	1.46321	.68176	.68343
ECU[c]	1.23320	1.22950	—	—

[a]*Exchange Rates: Monday, July 18, 1994. The New York foreign exchange selling rates apply to trading among banks in amounts of $1 million and more, as quoted at 3* P.M. *Eastern time by Bankers Trust Co., Dow Jones Telerate Systems, Inc, and other sources.*

Retail transactions provide fewer units of foreign currency per dollar.

[b]*Special Drawing Rights (SDR) are based on exchange rates for the U.S., German, British, French and Japanese currencies. SOURCE: International Monetary Fund.*

[c]*European Currency Unit (ECU) is based on a basket of community currencies. SOURCE: European Community Commission.*

EXAMPLE

An American business must pay 1,000 marks to a German firm on July 18, 1994. How many dollars will be required for this transaction?

$$\$.6466/\text{DM} \times \text{DM}1000 = \$646.60$$

EXAMPLE

An American business must pay $2,000 to a British resident on July 18, 1994. How many pounds will the British resident receive?

$$£.6406/\$ \times \$2000 = £1281.20$$

Exchange Rates and Arbitrage

The foreign exchange quotes in two different countries must be in line with each other. The direct quote for U.S. dollars in London is given in pounds/dollar. Because the foreign exchange markets are efficient, the direct quotes for the United States dollar in London, on July 18, 1994, must be very close to the indirect rate of .6406 pounds/dollar prevailing in New York on that date.

If the exchange-rate quotations between the London and New York spot exchange markets were *out of line,* then an enterprising trader could make a profit by buying in the market where the currency was cheaper and selling it in the other. Such a buy-and-sell strategy would involve a zero net investment of funds and no risk bearing yet would provide a sure profit. Such a person is called an **arbitrager,** and the process of buying and selling in more than one market to make a riskless profit is called *arbitrage.* Spot exchange markets are efficient in the sense that arbitrage opportunities do not persist for any length of time. That is, the exchange rates between two different markets are quickly brought *in line,* aided by the arbitrage process. *Simple arbitrage* eliminates exchange rate differentials across the markets for a single currency, as in the preceding example for the New York and London quotes. *Triangular arbitrage* does the same across the markets for all currencies. Covered interest arbitrage eliminates differentials across currency and interest rate markets.

Arbitrager
A person involved in the process of buying and selling in more than one market to make riskless profits.

Suppose that London quotes £.6600/$ instead of £.6406/$. If you simultaneously bought a pound in New York for £.6406/$ and sold a pound in London for £.6600/$, you would have (1) taken a zero net investment position since you bought £1 and sold £1, (2) locked in a sure profit of £.0194/$ *no matter which way* the pound subsequently moves, and (3) set in motion the forces that will eliminate the different quotes in New York and London. As others in the marketplace learn of your transaction, they will attempt to make the same transaction. The increased demand to buy pounds in New York will lead to a higher quote there and the increased supply of pounds will lead to a lower quote in London. The workings of the market will produce a new spot rate that lies between £.6406/$ and £.6600/$ and is the same in New York and in London.

Asked and Bid Rates

Two types of rates are quoted in the spot exchange market: the asked and the bid rates. The *asked rate* is the rate the bank or the foreign exchange trader "asks" the customer to pay in home currency for foreign currency when the bank is selling and the customer is buying. The asked rate is also known as the *selling rate* or the *offer rate.* The *bid rate* is the rate at which the bank buys the foreign currency from the customer by paying in home currency. The bid rate is also known as the *buying rate.* Note that Table 27-1 contains only the selling, offer, or asked rates, and not the buying rate.

Bid-asked spread The difference between the asked quote and the bid quote.

The bank sells a unit of foreign currency for more than it pays for it. Therefore the direct asked quote ($/FC) is greater than the direct bid quote. The difference is known as the **bid-asked spread.** When there is a large volume of transactions and the trading is continuous, the spread is small and can be less than .5% (.005) for the major currencies. The spread is much higher for infrequently traded currencies. The spread exists to compensate the banks for holding the risky foreign currency and for providing the service of converting currencies.

Cross Rates

A *cross rate* is the computation of an exchange rate for a currency from the exchange rates of two other currencies. The following example illustrates how this works.

EXAMPLE

Taking the dollar/pound and the mark/dollar rates from columns 2 and 4 of Table 27-1, determine the mark/pound and pound/mark exchange rates. We see that

$$(\$/£) \times (DM/\$) = (DM/£)$$

or

$$1.5615 \times 1.5465 = DM2.4149/£$$

Thus the pound/mark exchange rate is

$$1/2.4149 = £.4141/DM$$

Cross-rate computations make it possible to use quotations in New York to compute the exchange rate between pounds, marks, and francs. Arbitrage conditions hold in cross rates, too. For example, the pound exchange rate in Frankfurt (the direct quote marks/pound) must be 2.4149. The mark exchange rate in London must be .4141 pounds/mark. If the rates prevailing in Frankfurt and London were different from the computed cross rates, using quotes from New York, a trader could use three different currencies to lock in arbitrage profits through a process called *triangular arbitrage.*

Forward Exchange Rates

A forward exchange contract requires delivery, at a specified future date, of one currency for a specified amount of another currency. The exchange rate for the forward transaction is agreed on today; the actual payment of one currency and the receipt of another currency take place at the future date. For example, a thirty-day contract on March 1 is for delivery on March 31. Note that the forward rate is not the same as the spot rate that will prevail in the future. The actual spot rate that will prevail is not known today; only the forward rate is known. The actual spot rate will depend on the market conditions at that time; it may be more or less than today's forward rate. **Exchange rate risk** is the risk that tomorrow's exchange rate will differ from today's rate.

Exchange rate risk
The risk that tomorrow's exchange rate will differ from today's.

As indicated earlier, it is extremely unlikely that the future spot rate will be exactly the same as the forward rate quoted today. Assume that you are going to receive a payment denominated in pounds from a British customer in thirty days. If you wait for thirty days and exchange the pounds at the spot rate, you will receive a dollar amount reflecting the exchange rate thirty days hence (that is, the future spot rate). As of today, you have no way of knowing the exact dollar value of your future pound receipts. Consequently, you cannot make precise plans about the use of these dollars. If, conversely, you buy a future contract, then you know the exact dollar value of your future receipts, and you can make precise plans concerning their use. The forward contract, therefore, can reduce your uncertainty about the future, and the major advantage of the forward market is that of *risk reduction*.

Forward contracts are usually quoted for periods of 30, 90, and 180 days. A contract for any intermediate date can be obtained, usually with the payment of a small premium. Forward contracts for periods longer than 180 days can be obtained by special negotiations with banks. Contracts for periods greater than one year can be costly.

Forward rates, like spot rates, are quoted in both direct and indirect form. The direct quotes for the thirty-day and ninety-day forward contracts on pounds, francs, and marks are given in column 2 of Table 27-1. The indirect quotes for forward contracts, like spot rates, are reciprocals of the direct quotes. The indirect quotes are indicated in column 4 of Table 27-1. The direct quotes are the dollar/foreign currency rate, and the indirect quotes are the foreign currency/dollar rate similar to the spot exchange quotes.

The thirty-day forward quote for pounds is $1.5609 per pound. This means that if one purchases the contract for forward pounds on July 18, 1994, the bank will deliver a pound against the payment of $1.5609 on August 17,1994. The bank is contractually bound to deliver the pound at this price, and the buyer of the contract is legally obligated to buy it at this price on August 17, 1994. Therefore, this is the price the customer must pay regardless of the actual spot rate prevailing on August 17, 1994. If the spot price of the pound is less than $1.5609, then the customer pays *more* than the spot price. If the spot price is greater than $1.5609, then the customer pays *less* than the spot price.

The forward rate is often quoted at a premium to or discount from the existing spot rate. For example, the 30-day pound forward rate may be quoted as .0006 discount (1.5609 forward rate – 1.5615 spot rate). If the forward contract is selling for more dollars than the spot—that is, a larger direct quote—the pound is said to be selling at a premium. Note that the dollar is expected to strengthen against the pound. The market expects that in the future fewer dollars will be required to buy a pound. Conversely, the pound is expected to be worth fewer dollars in the future. When the forward contract sells for fewer dollars than the spot—a smaller direct quote—the pound is said to be at a discount from the dollar. Notice in column 2 of Table 27-1 that the forward contracts are selling at a discount for pounds and French francs. This premium or discount is also called the *forward-spot differential.*

Notationally, the relationship may be written

$$F - S = \textbf{premium (F > S) or discount (S > F)} \qquad \textbf{(27-1)}$$

where F = the forward rate, direct quote
S = the spot rate, direct quote

The premium or discount can also be expressed as an annual percentage rate, computed as follows:

$$\frac{F - S}{S} \times \frac{12}{n} \times 100 = \textbf{annualized percentage premium (F > S) or discount (S > F)} \qquad \textbf{(27-2)}$$

where n = the number of months of the forward contract

EXAMPLE

Compute the percent-per-annum premium on the 30-day forward pound.

Step 1: Identify F, S, and n.

$$F = 1.5609,\ S = 1.5615,\ n = 1 \text{ month}$$

Step 2: Because S is greater than F, we compute the annualized percentage discount:

$$D = 1.5609 - \frac{1.5615}{1.5615} \times \frac{12 \text{ months}}{1 \text{ month}} \times 100$$
$$= -0.46\%$$

The percent-per-annum discount on the 30-day pound is –0.46 percent. The percent-per-annum discount on the 30-day and 90-day pound and franc contracts are computed similarly. The results are given in Table 27-2.

Examples of Exchange Rate Risk

The concept of exchange rate risk applies to all types of international businesses. The measurement of these risks, and the type of risk, may differ among businesses. Let us see how exchange risk affects international trade contracts, international portfolio investments, and direct foreign investments.

Exchange Rate Risk in International Trade Contracts. The idea of exchange rate risk in trade contracts is illustrated in the following situations.

Case I. An American automobile distributor agrees to buy a car from the manufacturer in Detroit. The distributor agrees to pay $6,500 on delivery of the car, which is

TABLE 27-2 Percent-per-Annum (Discount)

	30-Day	90-Day
British pound	−0.46%	−0.26%
French franc	−1.21%	−0.83%

expected to be thirty days from today. The car is delivered on the thirtieth day and the distributor pays $6,500. Notice that, from the day this contract was written until the day the car was delivered, the buyer knew the *exact dollar amount* of the liability. There was, in other words, *no uncertainty* about the value of the contract.

Case II. An American automobile distributor enters into a contract with a British supplier to buy a car from the United Kingdom for 3,500 pounds. The amount is payable on the delivery of the car, thirty days from today. From Figure 27-2, we see the range of spot rates that we believe can occur on the date the contract is consummated. On the thirtieth day, the American importer will pay some amount in the range of $4,765.25 (3,500 × 1.3615) to $6,165.25 (3,500 × 1.7615) for the car. Today, the American firm is not certain what its future dollar outflow will be thirty days hence. That is, the *dollar value of the contract is uncertain.*

These two examples help illustrate the idea of foreign exchange risk in international trade contracts. In the domestic trade contract (Case I), the exact dollar amount of the future dollar payment is known today with certainty. In the case of the international trade contract (Case II), where the *contract is written in the foreign currency,* the exact dollar amount of the contract is not known. The variability of the exchange rate induces variability in the future cash flow.

Exchange rate risk exists when the contract is written in terms of the foreign currency or *denominated* in foreign currency. There is no direct exchange risk if the international trade contract is written in terms of the domestic currency. That is, in Case II, if the contract were written in dollars, the American importer would face *no* direct exchange risk. With the contract written in dollars, the British exporter would bear *all* the exchange risk because the British exporter's future pound receipts would be uncertain. That is, the British exporter would receive payment in dollars, which would have to be converted into pounds at an unknown (as of today) pound-dollar exchange rate. In international trade contracts of the type discussed here, at least one of the two parties to the contract *always* bears the exchange risk.

Certain types of international trade contracts are denominated in a third currency, different from either the importer's or the exporter's domestic currency. In Case II, the contract might have been denominated in, say, the Deutsche mark. With a mark contract, both importer and exporter would be subject to exchange rate risk.

Exchange risk is not limited to the two-party trade contracts; it exists also in foreign portfolio investments and direct foreign investments.

Exchange Risk in Foreign Portfolio Investments. Let us look at an example of exchange risk in the context of portfolio investments. An American investor buys a German security. The exact return on the investment in the security is unknown. Thus the security is a risky investment. The investment return in the holding period of, say, three months stated in marks could be anything from −2 to +8 percent. In

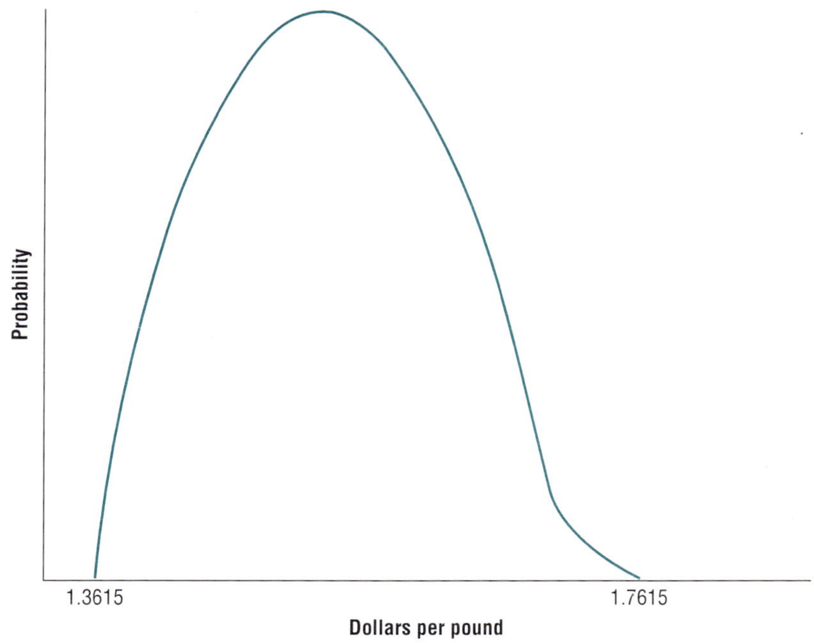

FIGURE 27-2
A subjective probability distribution of the pound exchange rate, thirty days in the future

addition, the mark-dollar exchange rate may depreciate by 4 percent or appreciate by 6 percent in the three-month period during which the investment is held. The return to the American investor, in dollars, will therefore be in the range of –6 to +14 percent.[3] Notice that the return to a German investor, in marks, is in the range of –2 to +8 percent. Clearly, for the American investor, the exchange factor induces a greater variability in the dollar rate of return. Hence, the *exchange rate fluctuations may increase the riskiness* of the investments.

Exchange Risk in Direct Foreign Investment. The exchange risk of a direct foreign investment (DFI) is more complicated. In a DFI, the parent company invests in assets denominated in a foreign currency. That is, the balance sheet and the income statement of the subsidiary are written in terms of the foreign currency. The parent company receives the repatriated profit stream in dollars. Thus the exchange risk concept applies to fluctuations in the dollar value of the *assets* located abroad as well as to the fluctuations in the home-currency-denominated *profit stream.* Exchange risk not only affects immediate profits, it may affect the future profit stream as well.

Although exchange rate risk can be a serious complication in international business activity, remember the principle of the risk-return tradeoff: Traders and corporations find numerous reasons that the returns from international transactions outweigh the risks.

[3]Example: Assume the spot exchange rate is .50 dollars per mark. In three months, the exchange rate would be .50 × (1 – .04) = .48 to .50 × (1 + .06) = .53. A $50 investment today is equivalent to a 100-mark investment. The 100-mark investment would return 98 to 108 marks in three months. The return, in the worst case, is 98 marks × .48 = $47.04. The return, in the best case, is 108 marks × .53 = $57.24. The holding-period return, on the $50 investment, will be between –6 percent ($47.04 – $50)/$50) and +14 percent ($57.24 – $50)/$50).

INTEREST RATE PARITY THEORY

Forward rates generally entail a premium or a discount relative to current spot rates. However, these forward premiums and discounts differ between currencies and maturities (see Table 27-2). These differences depend solely on the difference in the level of interest rates between two countries, called the *interest rate differential.* The value of the premium or discount can be theoretically computed from the **interest rate parity (IRP)** theory. This theory states that (except for the effects of small transactions costs) the forward premium or discount should be equal to the difference in the national interest rates for securities of the same maturity.

Interest rate parity (IRP) States that (except for the effect of small transaction costs) the forward premium or discount should be equal and opposite in size to the differences in the national interest rates for securities of the same maturity.

Stated very simply, what does all this mean? It means that because of arbitrage, the interest rate differential between two countries must be equal to the difference between the forward and spot exchange rates. If this were not true, arbitragers would buy in the forward market and sell in the spot market (or vice versa) until prices were back in line and there were no profits left to be made. For example, if prices in the forward market were too low, arbitragers would enter the market, increase the demand for the forward foreign currency, and drive up the prices in the forward market until those prices obeyed the interest rate parity theory.

PURCHASING POWER PARITY

Long-run changes in exchange rates are influenced by international differences in inflation rates and the purchasing power of each nation's currency. Exchange rates of countries with high rates of inflation will tend to decline. According to the **purchasing power parity (PPP) theory,** exchange rates will tend to adjust in such a way that each currency will have the same purchasing power (especially in terms of internationally traded goods). Thus, if the United Kingdom experiences a 10 percent rate of inflation in a year that Germany experiences only a 6 percent rate, the U.K. currency (the pound) will be expected to decline in value approximately by 3.77 percent (1.10/1.06) against the German currency (the Deutsche mark). More accurately, according to the PPP

Purchasing power parity (PPP) theory In the long run, exchange rates adjust so that the purchasing power of each currency tends to remain the same. Thus exchange rate changes tend to reflect international differences in inflation rates. Countries with high rates of inflation tend to experience declines in the value of their currency.

expected spot rate = current spot rate × expected difference in inflation rate

$$\textbf{expected spot rate (domestic currency per unit of foreign currency)} = \textbf{current spot rate (domestic currency per unit of foreign currency)} \times \frac{\textbf{(1 + expected domestic inflation rate)}}{\textbf{(1 + expected foreign inflation rate)}}$$

Thus, if the beginning value of the mark was £0.40, with a 6 percent inflation rate in Germany and a 10 percent inflation rate in the United Kingdom, according to the PPP, the expected value of the Deutsche mark at the end of that year will be £.40 × [1.10/1 06], or £.4151.

Stated very simply, what does this mean? It means that a dollar should have the same purchasing power anywhere in the world—well at least on average. Obviously, this is not quite true. However, what the purchasing power theory tells us that we should expect, on average, that differences in inflation rates between two countries should be reflected in changes in the exchange rates. In effect, the best forecast of the difference in inflation rates between two countries should also be the best forecast of the change in the spot rate of exchange.

Financial Management in Practice

TRADERS SAY DOLLAR MAY HAVE HIT BOTTOM

LONDON—The dollar's latest ten-day rally, following its stunning declines earlier this year, has foreign-exchange experts struggling to determine whether the U.S. currency has finally hit bottom.

A sustained dollar recovery isn't considered likely until other ingredients are present. Besides investor confidence that the Clinton administration wants a stable dollar, a broad rally would require higher U.S. interest rates, lower German rates, and settlement of the U.S. trade dispute with Japan, analysts say.

The interest rate outlook, at least, does seem to promise some relief for the dollar. Short-term German rates are currently higher than their U.S. equivalents, a difference that contributes to the mark's strength. But Hermann Remsperger, chief economist at Berliner Handles & Frankfurter Bank in Frankfurt, expects that to be reversed by year end as the Fed raises rates to damp U.S. inflation and lower German inflation possibly allows the Bundesbank to cut rates. **(A)**

Economists add that further Fed tightening could stabilize the U.S. bond market, which would further draw back investors, lending further support to the dollar. "For the dollar to strengthen in the long run, there must be the expectation that capital gains in the U.S. are in the offing—especially for foreign investors" says Remsperger. **(B)**

The U.S.-Japan trade front is more problematic. While many economists and traders are skeptical that U.S.-Japanese tensions will ease sufficiently enough to allow a resolution soon, "Sentiment can't turn fully positive for the dollar until the Clinton administration achieves satisfaction from the Japanese government on measures to stimulate domestic demand in Japan and to afford greater access to U.S. exports." **(C)**

Meanwhile, a strong yen is hurting the competitiveness of Japan's exports, and weighing down the country's already weak economy. "The very strong yen is a burden for the Japanese economy," says Mr. Remsperger. "If you look at the trade account in yen terms, you see that this burden has ready been shown in the figures—in other words they are exporting less." **(D)** But the weak Japanese economy is also cutting Japanese demand for U.S. imports.

Source: Excerpted from Michael R. Sesit, "Traders Say Dollar May Have Hit Bottom," *The Wall Street Journal*, July 25, 1994, Cl, 15.

The Law of One Price

Underlying the PPP relationship is the Law of One Price. This law is actually a proposition that in competitive markets where there are no transportation costs or barriers to trade, the same good sold in different countries sells for the same price if all the different prices are expressed in terms of the same currency. The idea is that the worth, in terms of marginal utility, of a good does not depend on where it is bought or sold. Because inflation will erode the purchasing power of any currency, its exchange rate must adhere to the PPP relationship if the Law of One Price is to hold over time.

Financial Management in Practice

ANALYSIS AND IMPLICATIONS. . .

A. As you recall, the interest rate parity theory states that the forward premium or discount should be equal to the difference in national interest rates for securities of the same maturity. As a result, if U.S. interest rates increase while German interest rates fall, the dollar should increase in value relative to the German mark.

B. In order for the dollar to strengthen, there must be increased demand for dollars. Perhaps the largest draw of money into any economy deals with investors' expectations regarding possible capital gains. As investors' expectations increase regarding capital gains in the U.S., more dollars will be purchased, thus strengthening the dollar.

C. Over the past four years, the dollar has dropped 35 percent versus the Japanese yen. The key here is the persistent and massive trade deficit with Japan, now at around $60 billion per year, which has pushed the dollar down versus the yen. Before the dollar can strengthen against the yen, the trade gap must be controlled. For this to happen, U.S. firms must gain access to Japanese markets.

D. As the dollar drops in value against the yen, Japanese goods become more expensive and less attractive to Americans. Likewise, U.S. goods sold in Japan become less expensive, increasing their desirability—although this is somewhat tempered by the weakness in the Japanese economy.

There are enough obvious exceptions to the concept of purchasing power parity that it may, at first glance, seem difficult to accept. For example, in the Spring of 1995 a Big Mac cost $1.80 in the United States and, given the then existing exchange rates, it cost an equivalent of $1.42 in Mexico, $2.91 in Japan and $3.09 in Germany. On the surface this might appear to violate the purchasing power parity theory and the Law of One Price; however, we must remember that this theory is based upon the concept of arbitrage. In the case of a Big Mac, it's pretty hard to imagine buying Big Macs in Mexico for $1.42, shipping them to Germany, and reselling them for $3.09. But for commodities like gold and other items that are relatively inexpensive to ship and do not have to be consumed immediately, the Law of One Price holds much better.

International Fisher Effect. According to the domestic Fisher Effect (FE), nominal interest rates reflect the expected inflation rate and a real rate of return. In other words,

$$\begin{array}{c}\textbf{nominal}\\ \textbf{interest rate}\end{array} = \begin{array}{c}\textbf{expected}\\ \textbf{inflation rate}\end{array} + \begin{array}{c}\textbf{real rate}\\ \textbf{of interest}\end{array}$$

While there is mixed empirical support for the FE internationally, it is widely thought that, for the major industrial countries the real rate of interest is about 3 percent when a long-term period is considered. In such a case, with the previous assumption regarding inflation rates, interest rates in the United Kingdom and Germany would be (.10 + .03 + .003) or 13.3 percent and (.06 + .03 + .0018) or 9.18 percent, respectively.

In effect, the International Fisher Effect (IFE) states that the real interest rate should be the same all over the world, with the difference in nominal or stated interest rates simply resulting from the difference in expected inflation rates. As we look at interest rates around the world, this tells use that we should not necessarily send our money to a bank account in the country with the highest interest rates. That course of action might only result in us sending our money to a bank in the country with the highest expected level of inflation.

EXPOSURE TO EXCHANGE RATE RISK

An asset denominated or valued in terms of foreign currency cash flows will lose value if that foreign currency declines in value. It can be said that such an asset is exposed to exchange rate risk. However, this possible decline in asset value may be offset by the decline in value of any liability that is also denominated or valued in terms of that foreign currency. Thus a firm would normally be interested in its net exposed position (exposed assets – exposed liabilities) for each period in each currency.

While expected changes in exchange rates can often be included in the cost-benefit analysis relating to such transactions, in most cases there is an unexpected component in exchange rate changes and often the cost-benefit analysis for such transactions does not fully capture even the expected change in the exchange rate. For example, price increases for the foreign operations of many MNCs often have to be less than those necessary to fully offset exchange rate changes, owing to the competitive pressures generated by local businesses, as the Japanese car makers found in 1988 for their U.S. sales.

Three measures of foreign exchange exposure are translation exposure, transactions exposure, and economic exposure. Translation exposure arises because the foreign operations of MNCs have accounting statements denominated in the local currency of the country in which the operation is located. For U.S. MNCs, the *reporting currency* for its consolidated financial statements is the dollar, so the assets, liabilities, revenues, and expenses of the foreign operations must be translated into dollars. International transactions often require a payment to be made or received in a foreign currency in the future, so these transactions are exposed to exchange rate risk. Economic exposure exists over the long term because the value of future cash flows in the reporting currency (that is, the dollar) from foreign operations are exposed to exchange rate risk. Indeed, the whole stream of future cash flows is exposed. The Japanese automaker situation highlights the effect of economic exposure on an MNC's revenue stream. The three measures of exposure now are examined more closely.

Translation Exposure

Foreign currency assets and liabilities are considered exposed if their foreign currency value for accounting purposes is to be translated into the domestic currency using the current exchange rate—the exchange rate in effect on the balance sheet date. Other assets and liabilities and equity amounts that are translated at the historic exchange rate—the rate in effect when these items were first recognized in the company's accounts—are not considered to be exposed. The rate (current or historic) used to translate various accounts depends on the translation procedure used.

While transaction exposure can result in exchange rate change-related losses and gains that are realized and have an impact on both reported and taxable income, translation exposure results in exchange rate losses and gains that are reflected in the company's accounting books, but are unrealized and have little or no impact on taxable income. Thus, if financial markets are efficient and managerial goals are consistent with owner wealth maximization, a firm should not have to waste real resources hedging against possible paper losses caused by translation exposure. However, if there are significant agency or information costs or if markets are not efficient, a firm may indeed find it economical to hedge against translation losses or gains.

Transactions Exposure

Receivables, payables, and fixed-price sales or purchase contracts are examples of foreign currency transactions whose monetary value was fixed at a time different from the time when these transactions are actually completed. *Transactions exposure* is a term that describes the net contracted foreign currency transactions for which the settlement amounts are subject to changing exchange rates. A company normally must set up an additional reporting system to track transactions exposure, because several of these amounts are not recognized in the accounting books of the firm.

Exchange risk may be neutralized or hedged by a change in the asset and liability position in the foreign currency. An exposed asset position (such as an account receivable) can be *hedged or covered* by creating a liability of the same amount and maturity denominated in the foreign currency (such as a forward contract to *sell* the foreign currency). An exposed liability position (such as an account payable) can be covered by acquiring assets of the same amount and maturity in the foreign currency (such as a forward contract to *buy* the foreign currency). The objective is to have a zero net asset position in the foreign currency. This eliminates exchange risk, since the loss (gain) in the liability (asset) is exactly offset by the gain (loss) in the value of the asset (liability) when the foreign currency appreciates (depreciates). Two popular forms of hedge are the money market hedge and the exchange market or forward market hedge. In both types of hedge the *amount* and the *duration* of the asset (liability) positions are *matched*. Note as you read the next two subsections how IRP theory assures that each hedge provides the same cover.

Money-Market Hedge. In a money-market hedge, the exposed position in a foreign currency is offset by borrowing or lending in the money market. Consider the case of the American firm with a net liability position (that is the, amount it owes) of £3,000. The firm knows the exact amount of its pound liability in thirty days, but it does not know the liability in dollars. Assume that the thirty-day money market rates in both the United States and United Kingdom are, respectively, 1 percent for lending and 1.5 percent for borrowing. The American business can take the following steps:

Step 1: Calculate the present value of the foreign currency liability (£3000) that is due in thirty days. Use the money market rate applicable for the foreign country (1 percent in the United Kingdom). The present value of £3,000 is £2,970.30 computed as follows: 3000/(1 + .01).

Step 2: Exchange dollars on today's spot market to obtain the 2,970.30 pounds. The dollar amount needed today is \$4,638.12 (2970.30 × 1.5615).

Step 3: Invest 2,970.30 pounds in a United Kingdom one-month money market instrument. This investment will compound to exactly £3,000 in one month. The future liability of £3,000 is covered by the £2,970.30 investment.[4]

Note: if the American business does not own this amount today, it can borrow \$4638.12 from the United States money market at the going rate of 1.5 percent. In thirty days the American business will need to repay \$4,707.69 [\$4,638.12 × (1 + .015)].

Assuming that the American business borrows the money, its management may base its calculations on the knowledge that the British goods, on delivery in thirty days, will cost it \$4,707.69. The British business will receive 3,000 pounds. The American business need not wait for the future spot exchange rate to be revealed. On today's date, the future dollar payment of the contract is known with certainty. This certainty helps the American business in making its pricing and financing decisions.

Many businesses hedge in the money market. The firm needs to borrow (creating a liability) in one market, lend or invest in the other money market, and use the spot exchange market on today's date. The mechanics of *covering a net asset position* in the foreign currency are the exact *reverse* of the mechanics of covering the *liability position.* With a net asset position in pounds: Borrow in the United Kingdom money market in pounds, convert to dollars on the spot exchange market, invest in the United States money market. When the net assets converted into pounds (i.e., when the firm receives what it is owed), pay off the loan and the interest. The cost of hedging in the money market is the cost of doing business in three different markets. Information about the three markets is needed, and analytical calculations of the type indicated here must be made.

Many small and infrequent traders find the cost of the money market hedge prohibitive, owing especially to the need for information about the market. These traders use the exchange or the forward market hedge, which has very similar hedging benefits.

The Forward Market Hedge. The forward market provides a second possible hedging mechanism. It works as follows: A net asset (liability) position is covered by a liability (asset) in the forward market. Consider again the case of the American firm with a liability of £3000 that must be paid in thirty days. The firm may take the following steps to cover its liability position:

Step 1: Buy a forward contract today to purchase £3,000 in thirty days. The thirty-day forward rate is, \$1.5609 per pound.

Step 2: On the thirtieth day pay the banker \$4,682.70 (3000 × \$1.5609) and collect £3,000. Pay these pounds to the British supplier.

[4]Observe that 2970.30 pounds × (1 + .01) = 3,000 pounds.

By the use of the forward contract the American business knows the exact worth of the future payment in dollars ($4,682.70). The exchange risk in pounds is totally eliminated by the net asset position in the forward pounds. In the case of a net asset exposure, the steps open to the American firm are the exact opposite: Sell the pounds forward, and on the future day receive and deliver the pounds to collect the agreed-on dollar amount.

The use of the forward market as a hedge against exchange risk is simple and direct. That is, match the liability or asset position against an offsetting position in the forward market. The forward market hedge is relatively easy to implement. The firm directs its banker that it needs to buy or sell a foreign currency on a future date, and the banker gives a quote.

The forward hedge and the money market hedge give an identical future dollar payment (or receipt) if the forward contracts are priced according to the interest rate parity theory. The alert student may have noticed that the dollar payments in the money market hedge and the forward market hedge examples were, respectively, $4707.69 and $4682.70. Recall from our previous discussions that in efficient markets, the forward contracts do indeed conform to IRP theory. However, the numbers in our example are not identical because the forward rate used in the forward hedge is not exactly equal to the interest rates in the money market hedge.

Currency Future and Option Contracts. The forward market hedge is not adequate for some types of exposure. If the foreign currency asset or liability position occurs on a date for which forward quotes are not available, the forward hedge cannot be accomplished. In certain cases the forward hedge may cost more than the money market hedge. In these cases a corporation with a large amount of exposure may prefer the money market hedge. In addition to forward and money market hedges, a company can also hedge its exposure by buying (or selling) some relatively new instruments—foreign currency futures contracts and foreign currency options. Although futures contracts are similar to forward contracts in that they provide fixed prices for the *required* delivery of foreign currency at maturity, options *permit* fixed (strike) price foreign currency transactions anytime before maturity. Futures contracts and options differ from forward contracts in that, unlike forward contracts, which are customized regarding amount and maturity date, futures and options are traded in standard amounts with standard maturity dates. In addition, although forward contracts are written by banks, futures and options are traded on organized exchanges, and individual traders deal with the exchange-based clearing organization rather than with each other. The purchase of futures requires the fulfillment of margin requirements (about 5 to 10 percent of the face amount), whereas the purchase of forward contracts requires only good credit standing with a bank. The purchase of options requires an immediate outlay that reflects a premium above the strike price and an outlay equal to the strike price when and if the option is exercised.

Economic Exposure

The economic value of a company can vary in response to exchange rate changes. This change in value may be caused by a rate-change-induced decline in the level of expected cash flows and/or by an increase in the riskiness of these cash flows. *Eco-*

nomic exposure refers to the overall impact of exchange rate changes on the value of the firm and includes not only the strategic impact of changes in competitive relationships that arise from exchange rate changes, but also the economic impact of transactions exposure and, if any, of translation exposure.

Economic exposure to exchange rate changes depends on the competitive structure of the markets for a firm's inputs and its outputs and how these markets are influenced by changes in exchange rates. This influence, in turn, depends on several economic factors, including price elasticities of the products, the degree of competition from foreign markets and direct (through prices) and indirect (through incomes) impact of exchange rate changes on these markets. Assessing the economic exposure faced by a particular firm thus depends on the ability to understand and model the structure of the markets for its major inputs (purchases) and outputs (sales).

A company need not engage in any cross-border business activity to be exposed to exchange rate changes, because product and financial markets in most countries are related and influenced to a large extent by the same global forces. The output of a company engaged in business activity only within one country may be competing with imported products, or it may be competing for its inputs with other domestic and foreign purchasers. For example, a Canadian chemical company that did no cross-border business nevertheless found that its profit margins depended directly on the United States dollar-Japanese yen exchange rate. The company used coal as an input in its production process, and the Canadian price of coal was heavily influenced by the extent to which the Japanese bought United States coal, which in turn depended on the dollar-yen exchange rate.

Although translation exposure need not be managed, it might be useful for a firm to manage its transaction and economic exposures because they affect firm value directly. In most companies, transaction exposure is generally tracked and managed by the office of the corporate treasurer. Economic exposure is difficult to define in operating terms, and very few companies manage it actively. In most companies, economic exposure is generally considered part of the strategic planning process, rather than as a treasurer's or finance function.

MULTINATIONAL WORKING-CAPITAL MANAGEMENT

The basic principles of working-capital management for a multinational corporation are similar to those for a domestic firm. However, tax and exchange rate factors are additional considerations for the MNC. For an MNC with subsidiaries in many countries, the optimal decisions in the management of working capital are made by considering the company as a whole. The global or centralized financial decision for an MNC is superior to the set of independent optimal decisions for the subsidiaries. This is the *control* problem of the MNC. If the individual subsidiaries make decisions that are best for them individually, the consolidation of such decisions may not be best for the MNC as a whole. To effect *global* management, sophisticated computerized models—incorporating many variables for each subsidiary—are solved to provide the best overall decision for the MNC.

Before considering the components of working-capital management, we examine two techniques that are useful in the management of a wide variety of working-capital components.

Leading and Lagging

Two important risk-reduction techniques for many working-capital problems are called *leading* and *lagging*. Often forward and money market hedges are not available to eliminate exchange risk. Under such circumstances, leading and lagging may be used to *reduce* exchange risk.

Recall that a net asset (long) position is not desirable in a weak or potentially depreciating currency. If a firm has a net asset position in such a currency, it should expedite the disposal of the asset. The firm should get rid of the asset earlier than it otherwise would have, or *lead,* and convert the funds into assets in a relatively stronger currency. By the same reasoning, the firm should *lag,* or delay the collection against a net asset position in a strong currency. If the firm has a net liability (short) position in the weak currency, then it should delay the payment against the liability, or lag, until the currency depreciates. In the case of an appreciating or strong foreign currency and a net liability position, the firm should lead the payments—that is, reduce the liabilities earlier than it would otherwise have.

These principles are useful in the management of working capital of an MNC. They cannot, however, eliminate the foreign exchange risk. When exchange rates change continuously, it is almost impossible to guess whether or when the currency will depreciate or appreciate. This is why the risk of exchange rate changes cannot be eliminated. Nevertheless, the reduction of risk, or the increased gain from exchange rate changes, via the lead and lag is useful for cash management, accounts receivable management, and short-term liability management.

Cash Management and Positioning of Funds

Positioning of funds takes on an added importance in the international context. Funds may be transferred from a subsidiary of the MNC in country A to another subsidiary in country B such that the foreign exchange exposure and the tax liability of the MNC as a whole are minimized. It bears repeating that, owing to the *global strategy* of the MNC, the tax liability of the subsidiary in country A may be greater than it would otherwise have been, but the overall tax payment for all units of the MNC is minimized.

The transfer of funds among subsidiaries and the parent company is done by royalties, fees, and transfer pricing. A *transfer price* is the price a subsidiary or a parent company charges other companies that are part of the MNC for its goods or services. A parent that wishes to transfer funds from a subsidiary in a depreciating-currency country may charge a higher price on the goods and services sold to this subsidiary by the parent or by subsidiaries from strong-currency countries.

INTERNATIONAL FINANCING AND CAPITAL STRUCTURE DECISIONS

An MNC has access to many more financing sources than a domestic firm. It can tap not only the financing sources in its home country that are available to its domestic counterparts, but also sources in the foreign countries in which it operates. Host countries often provide access to low-cost subsidized financing to attract foreign investment. In addition, the MNC may enjoy preferential credit standards because of its size and investor preference for its home currency. An MNC may be able to access third-country capital markets—countries in which it does not operate but which may have large, well-functioning capital markets. Finally, an MNC can also access external currency markets: Eurodollar, Eurocurrency, or Asiandollar markets. These external markets are unregulated, and because of their lower spread, can offer very attractive rates for financing *and* for investments. With the increasing availability of interest rate and currency swaps, a firm can raise funds in the lowest-cost maturities and currencies and swap them into funds with the maturity and currency denomination it requires. Because of its ability to tap a larger number of financial markets, the MNC may have a lower cost of capital; and because it may better be able to avoid the problems or limitations of any one financial market, it may have a more continuous access to external finance compared to a domestic company.

Access to national financial markets is regulated by governments. For example, in the United States, access to capital markets is governed by SEC regulations. Access to Japanese capital markets is governed by regulations issued by the Ministry of Finance. Some countries have extensive regulations; other countries have relatively open markets. These regulations may differ depending on the legal residency terms of the company raising funds. A company that cannot use its local subsidiary to raise funds in a given market will be treated as foreign. In order to increase their visibility in a foreign capital market, a number of MNCs are now listing their equities on the stock exchanges of many of these countries.

The external currency markets are predominantly centered in Europe, and about 80 percent of their value is denominated in terms of the U.S. dollar. Thus most external currency markets can be characterized as Eurodollar markets. Such markets consist of an active short-term money market and an intermediate-term capital market with maturities ranging up to fifteen years and averaging about seven to nine years. The intermediate-term market consists of the Eurobond and the Syndicated Eurocredit markets. Eurobonds are usually issued as unregistered bearer bonds and generally tend to have higher flotation costs but lower coupon rates compared to similar bonds issued in the United States. A Syndicated Eurocredit loan is simply a large term loan that involves contributions by a number of lending banks.

In arriving at its capital-structure decisions, an MNC has to consider a number of factors. First, the capital structure of its local affiliates is influenced by local norms regarding capital structure in that industry and in that country. Local norms for companies in the same industry can differ considerably from country to country. Second, the local affiliate capital structure must also reflect corporate attitudes toward exchange rate and political risk in that country, which would normally lead to higher levels of local debt and other local capital. Third, local affiliate capital structure must reflect home country requirements with regard to the company's consolidated capital structure. Finally, the optimal MNC capital structure should reflect its wider access to financial markets, its ability to diversify economic and political risks, and its other advantages over domestic companies.

DIRECT FOREIGN INVESTMENT

An MNC often makes direct foreign investments abroad in the form of plants and equipment. The decision process for this type of investment is very similar to the capital-budgeting decision in the domestic context—with some additional twists.

Most real-world capital-budgeting decisions are made with uncertain future outcomes. Recall that a capital-budgeting decision has three major components: the estimation of the future cash flows (including the initial cost of the proposed investment), the estimation of the risk in these cash flows, and the choice of the proper discount rate. We will assume that the NPV criterion is appropriate as we examine (1) the risks associated with direct foreign investment, and (2) factors to be considered in making the investment decision that may be unique to the international scene.

Risks in Direct Foreign Investments

Risks in domestic capital budgeting arise from two sources: business risk and financial risk. The international capital-budgeting problem incorporates these risks as well as political risk and exchange risk.

Business Risk and Financial Risk. International business risk is due to the response of business to economic conditions in the foreign country. Thus the U.S. MNC needs to be aware of the business climate in both the United States and the foreign country. Additional business risk is due to competition from other MNCs, local businesses, and imported goods. Financial risk refers to the risks introduced in the profit stream by the firm's financial structure. The financial risks of foreign operations are not very different from those of domestic operations.

Political Risk. *Political risk* arises because the foreign subsidiary conducts its business in a political system different from that of the home country. Many foreign governments, especially those in the Third World, are less stable than the U.S. government. A change in a country's political setup frequently brings a change in policies with respect to businesses—and especially with respect to foreign businesses. An extreme change in policy might involve nationalization or even outright expropriation of certain businesses. These are the political risks of conducting business abroad. A business with no investment in plants and equipment is less susceptible to these risks. Some examples of political risk are listed below:

1. Expropriation of plants and equipment without compensation.
2. Expropriation with minimal compensation that is below actual market value.
3. Nonconvertibility of the subsidiary's foreign earnings into the parent's currency—the problem of *blocked funds.*
4. Substantial changes in the laws governing taxation.
5. Governmental controls in the foreign country regarding the sale price of the products, wages, and compensation to personnel, hiring of personnel, making of transfer payments to the parent, and local borrowing.
6. Some governments require certain amounts of local equity participation in the business. Some require that the majority of the equity participation belong to their country.

All these controls and governmental actions introduce risks in the cash flows of the investment to the parent company. These risks must be considered before making the foreign investment decision. The MNC may decide against investing in countries with risks of types 1 and 2. Other risks can be borne—provided that

Financial Management in Practice

UKRAINE: NOT FOR THE FAINTHEARTED

KIEV, UKRAINE—S.C. Johnson & Son Inc., the $3 billion family-owned company that makes clothes, floor wax, furniture cleaners, bug killers, and air fresheners, has traditionally been challenged by new frontiers.

When the company opened a plant in Britain 80 years ago, it was one of the first American corporations to go abroad. At the end of the cold war, it trailblazed again this time into the uncertain precincts of the Ukraine.

Johnson Wax's experience since 1990—when the company started to make and bottle detergents and furniture polish in a renovated corner of a ramshackle factory on the outskirts of Kiev—helps explain the reluctance of other consumer-products companies to jump in.

A few months after Ukraine joined Russia and Belarus in leaving the crumbling Soviet Union, it introduced a coupon currency to replace the ruble. In relatively short order, the coupons became all but worthless. By late last year, inflation had reached about 100 percent a month, from almost zero two years before. A fierce credit squeeze by the government left wholesalers little money to buy Johnson's products. **(A)** And a government that had initially promised to create a friendly environment for Western investors became encrusted with old style—many say corrupt—former Communists.

Last year, Johnson Wax halved its production from that of 1992. And almost half of 1993's 10 million bottles that came off the assembly line had to be sold in Russia, where the economy, however turbulent, is far stronger than Ukraine's.

A major attraction for Western manufacturers here is low wages. Johnson would like to raise the pay of some workers above the monthly $150 that the best get, but a 92 percent tax rate on earned income above $150 makes it impossible to do so. **(B)**

Some improvements in everyday life make the difficulty of doing business here a little easier. To make an overseas telephone call took two days several years ago. Now they can be made on the spot. And there are more flights in and out of the country.

But unpredictability prevails. In the last six months, the Ukrainian government has raised or lowered the value-added tax rate three times. Now there are worries that the government might impose an excise tax on supplies coming across the border from Russia. And still another currency is expected, prompting further headaches. **(C)**

Source: Excerpted from Jane Perex "Ukraine: Not for the Fainthearted," *New York Times*, June 1, 1994, D1, 5.

the returns from the foreign investments are high enough to compensate for them. Insurance against some types of political risks may be purchased from private insurance companies or from the U.S. government Overseas Private Investment Corporation. It should be noted that although an MNC cannot protect itself against all foreign political risks, political risks are also present in domestic business.

Financial Management in Practice

ANALYSIS AND IMPLICATIONS. . .

A. Pricing, along with almost every other aspect of business, becomes increasingly complicated when inflation rates become both unpredictable and high. In the year ending in June 1993, inflation in Russia was running at 839 percent per year.

B. Unforeseen dilemmas seem to pop up with some regularity when dealing in the international arena. For example, the notion of a government-dictated upper end on wages, in this case imposed by a 92 percent tax rate, is hard to imagine beforehand.

C. From **The Risk-Return Tradeoff**—we learned that investors demand a return for delaying consumption as well as an additional return for taking on added risk. The discount rate that we use to move money through time should reflect anticipated inflation along with the level of risk. In Russia, the difficulty in determining the appropriate discount rate is compounded by the fact that risk abounds, taking the form of instability in terms of taxes, unchecked corruption, and difficulties in obtaining raw materials.

Exchange Risk. The exposure of the fixed assets is best measured by the effects of the exchange rate changes on the firm's future earnings stream: that being *economic* exposure rather than *translation* exposure. For instance, changes in the exchange rate may adversely affect sales by making competing imported goods cheaper. Changes in the cost of goods sold may result if some components are imported and their price in the foreign currency changes because of exchange rate fluctuations. The thrust of these examples is that the effect of exchange rate changes on income statement items should be properly measured to evaluate exchange risk. Finally, exchange risk affects the dollar-denominated profit stream of the parent company, whether or not it affects the foreign-currency profits.

SUMMARY

The growth of our global economy, the increasing number of multinational corporations, and the increase in foreign trade itself underscore the importance of the study of international finance.

- Exchange-rate mechanics are discussed in the context of the prevailing floating rates. Under this system, exchange rates between currencies vary in an apparently random fashion in accordance with the supply and demand conditions in the exchange market. Important economic factors affecting the level of exchange rates include the relative economic strengths of the countries involved, the balance-of-payments mechanism, and the countries' monetary policies. Several important exchange-rate terms are introduced. These include the asked and the bid rates, which represent the selling and buying rates of currencies. The direct quote is the units of home currency per unit of foreign currency, and the indirect quote is the reciprocal of the direct quote. Cross-rate computations reflect the exchange rate between two foreign currencies.

- The forward exchange market provides a valuable service by quoting rates for the delivery of foreign currencies in the future. The foreign currency is said to sell at a premium (discount) forward from the spot rate when the forward rate is greater (less) than the spot rate, in direct quotation. In addition, the influences of purchasing power parity (PPP) and the International Fisher Effect (IFE) in determining the exchange rate are discussed. In rational and efficient markets, forward rates are unbiased forecasts of future spot rates that are consistent with the PPP.
- Exchange risk exists because the exact spot rate that prevails on a future date is not known with certainty today. The concept of exchange risk is applicable to a wide variety of businesses including export-import firms and firms involved in making direct foreign investments or international investments in securities. Exchange exposure is a measure of exchange risk. There are different ways of measuring the foreign exposure including the net asset (net liability) measurement. Different strategies are open to businesses to counter the exposure to this risk including the money market hedge, the forward market hedge, futures contracts, and options. Each involves different costs.
- In discussing working-capital management in an international environment, we find leading and lagging techniques useful in minimizing exchange risks and increasing profitability. In addition, funds positioning is a useful tool for reducing exchange risk exposure. The MNC may have a lower cost of capital because it has access to a larger set of financial markets than a domestic company. In addition to the home, host, and third-country financial markets, the MNC can tap the rapidly growing external currency markets. In making capital-structure decisions, the MNC must consider political and exchange risks and host and home country capital-structure norms.
- The complexities encountered in the direct foreign investment decision include the usual sources of risk—business and financial—and additional risks associated with fluctuating exchange rates and political factors. Political risk due to differences in political climates, institutions, and processes between the home country and abroad. Under these conditions, the estimation of future cash flows and the choice of the proper discount rates are more complicated than for the domestic investment situation.

QUESTIONS

1. What additional factors are encountered in international as compared with domestic financial management? Discuss each briefly.
2. What different types of businesses operate in the international environment? Why are the techniques and strategies available to these firms different?
3. What is meant by *arbitrage profits?*
4. What are the markets and mechanics involved in generating (a) simple arbitrage profits, (b) triangular arbitrage profits?

5. How do the purchasing power parity, interest rate parity, and the Fisher effect explain the relationships between the current spot rate, the future spot rate, and the forward rate?
6. What is meant by (a) exchange risk, (b) political risk?
7. How can exchange risk be measured?
8. What are the differences between transaction, translation, and economic exposures? Should all of them be ideally reduced to zero?
9. What steps can a firm take to reduce exchange risk? Indicate at least two different techniques.
10. How are the forward market and the money market hedges affected? What are the major differences between these two types of hedges?
11. In the New York exchange market, the forward rate for the Indian currency, the rupee, is not quoted. If you were exposed to exchange risk in rupees, how could you cover your position?
12. Compare and contrast the use of forward contracts, futures contracts, and options to reduce foreign exchange exposure. When is each instrument most appropriate?
13. Indicate two working-capital management techniques that are useful for international businesses to reduce exchange risk and potentially increase profits.
14. How do the financing sources available to an MNC differ from those available to a domestic firm? What do these differences mean for the company's cost of capital?
15. What risks are associated with direct foreign investment? How do these risks differ from those encountered in domestic investment?
16. How is the direct foreign investment decision made? What are the inputs to this decision process? Are the inputs more complicated than those to the domestic investment problem? If so, why?
17. A corporation desires to enter a particular foreign market. The DFI analysis indicates that a direct investment in the plant in the foreign country is not profitable. What other course of action can the company take to enter the foreign market? What are the important considerations?
18. What are the reasons for the acceptance of a sales office or licensing arrangement when the DFI itself is not profitable?

SELF-CORRECTION PROBLEM

Selling Quotes for the German Mark in New York

Country	Contract	$/Foreign Currency
Germany—mark	Spot	.3893
	30-day	.3910
	90-day	.3958

You own $10,000. The dollar rate on the German mark is $2.5823/DM. The German mark rate is given in the table above. Are arbitrage profits possible? Set up an arbitrage scheme with your capital. What is the gain (loss) in dollars?

PROBLEMS

The data for Problems 1 through 7 are given in the following table:

Selling Quotes for Foreign Currencies in New York

Country	Contract	$/Foreign Currency
Canada—dollar	Spot	.8437
	30-day	.8417
	90-day	.8395
Japan—yen	Spot	.004684
	30-day	.004717
	90-day	.004781
Switzerland—franc	Spot	.5139
	30-day	.5169
	90-day	.5315

1. An American business needs to pay (a) 10,000 Canadian dollars, (b) 2 million yen, and (c) 50,000 Swiss francs to businesses abroad. What are the dollar payments to the respective countries?
2. An American business pays $10,000, $15,000, and $20,000 to suppliers, in, respectively, Japan, Switzerland, and Canada. How much, in local currencies, do the suppliers receive?
3. Compute the indirect quote for the spot and forward Canadian dollar, yen, and Swiss franc contracts.
4. The spreads on the contracts as a percent of the asked rates are 2 percent for yen, 3 percent for Canadian dollars, and 5 percent for Swiss francs. Show, in a table similar to the one above, the bid rates for the different spot and forward rates.
5. You own $10,000. The dollar rate in Tokyo is 216.6743. The yen rate in New York is given in the previous table. Are arbitrage profits possible? Set up an arbitrage scheme with your capital. What is the gain (loss) in dollars?
6. Compute the Canadian dollar/yen and the yen/Swiss franc spot rate from the data in the table above.
7. Compute the simple premium (discount) on the thirty-day and ninety-day yen, Swiss franc, and Canadian dollar quotes. Tabulate the percent-per-annum deviations as in Table 27-2.

INTEGRATIVE PROBLEM

For your job as the business reporter for a local newspaper, you are given the assignment of putting together a series of articles on the multinational finance and the international currency markets for your readers. Much recent local press coverage has been given to losses in the foreign exchange markets by JGAR, a local firm that is the subsidiary of Daedlufetarg, a large German manufacturing firm. Your editor would like you to address several specific questions dealing with multinational finance. Prepare a response to the following memorandum from your editor:

TO: Business Reporter
FROM: Perry White, Editor, *Daily Planet*
RE: Upcoming Series on Multinational Finance

In your upcoming series on multinational finance, I would like to make sure you cover several specific points. In addition, before you begin this assignment, I want to make sure we are all reading from the same script, as accuracy has always been the cornerstone of the *Daily Planet*. I'd like a response to the following questions before we proceed:

a. What new problems and factors are encountered in international as opposed to domestic financial management?
b. What does the term *arbitrage* profits mean?
c. What can a firm do to reduce exchange risk?
d. What are the differences between a forward contract, a futures contract, and options?

Use the following data in your response to the remaining questions:

Selling Quotes for Foreign Currencies in New York

Country-Currency	Contract	$/Foreign
Canada-dollar	Spot	.8450
	30-day	.8415
	90-day	.8390
Japan-yen	Spot	.004700
	30-day	.004750
	90-day	.004820
Switzerland-franc	Spot	.5150
	30-day	.5182
	90-day	.5328

e. An American business needs to pay (a) 15,000 Canadian dollars, (b) 1.5 million yen, and (c) 55,000 Swiss francs to businesses abroad. What are the dollar payments to the respective countries?
f. An American business pays $20,000, $5,000, and $15,000 to suppliers in, respectively, Japan, Switzerland, and Canada. How much, in local currencies, do the suppliers receive?
g. Compute the indirect quote for the spot and forward Canadian dollar contract.
h. You own $10,000. The dollar rate in Tokyo is 216.6752. The yen rate in New York is given in the table above. Are arbitrage profits possible? Set up an arbitrage scheme with your capital. What is the gain (loss) in dollars?
i. Compute the Canadian dollar/yen spot rate from the data in the table above.

SOLUTION TO SELF-CORRECTION PROBLEM

The German rate is 2.5823 marks/$1, while the (indirect) New York rate is 1/.3893 = 2.5687 marks/$.

Assuming no transaction costs, the rates between German and New York are out of line. Thus arbitrage profits are possible.

Step 1: Because the mark is cheaper in Germany, buy $10,000 worth of marks in Germany. The number of marks purchased would be $10,000 × 2.5823 = 25,823 marks

Step 2: Simultaneously sell the marks in New York at the prevailing rate. The amount received upon the sale of the marks would be:

$$25{,}823 \text{ marks} \times \$.3893/\text{mark} = \$10{,}052.89$$

$$\text{net gain is } \$10{,}052.89 - \$10{,}000 = \underline{\underline{\$52.89}}$$

Glossary

Accelerated Cost Recovery System. A means of accelerated depreciation for assets acquired after 1981, whereby assets are assigned to specific property classifications and depreciated accordingly.

Accelerated Depreciation Techniques. Techniques that allow the owner of the asset to take greater amounts of depreciation during the early years of its life, thereby deferring some of the taxes until later years.

Accrual Method. A method of accounting whereby income is recorded when earned, whether or not the money has been received at that time, and expenses are recorded when incurred, whether or not any money has actually been paid out.

Accumulated Earnings Credit. The greater of (1) the profits for the year retained for reasonable business needs, and (2) $150,000 less the retained earnings shown in the balance sheet.

Accumulated Taxable Income. The firm's taxable income less dividends paid and accrued during the year, and less an accumulated earnings credit.

Acid Test Ratio. (Current assets–inventories) ÷ current liabilities. This ratio is a more stringent measure of liquidity than the current ratio in that it subtracts inventories (the least liquid current asset) from current assets.

Acquisition. A combination of two or more businesses into a single operational entity.

ACRS. Accelerated Cost Recovery System.

Affiliated Group. A group of firms related by affiliation, expressed in terms of one firm's owning, either directly or indirectly, 80 percent of the firm paying the dividend.

Agency Costs. The costs, such as a reduced stock price, associated with potential conflict between managers and investors when these two groups are not the same.

Amortized Loans. Loans that are paid off in equal periodic payments.

Annuity. A series of equal dollar payments for a specified number of years.

Appraisal Value. The value of a company as stated by an independent appraisal firm.

Arbitrage-Pricing Model. A theory that relates stock returns and risk. The theory maintains that security returns vary from their expected amounts when there are unanticipated changes in basic economic forces. Such forces would include unexpected changes in industrial production, inflation rates, term structure of interest rates, and the difference between interest rates of high-and-low risk bonds.

Arbitrageur. A person involved in the process of buying and selling in more than one market to make a riskless profit.

Arrangement. A reorganizational plan involving a petition to the court requesting that the firm be required to make only partial or a delayed payment to its creditors.

Arrearage. An overdue payment, generally referring to omitted preferred stock dividends.

Assignee. The third party responsible for disposal of the debtor firm's assets and distribution of the proceeds to the creditors in an assignment.

Assignment. A method of liquidating a business that has been declared insolvent. To minimize court involvement (and therefore costs), a third party receives title for the firm's assets and is responsible for the disposal of the assets and distribution of the proceeds. Creditors have the right to refuse such a settlement, and if they so choose, to force the debtor into a court-administered liquidation.

Automated Depository Transfer System. A system that moves funds from local bank accounts to concentration accounts electronically. This eliminates the mail float from the local banks to the concentration banks.

Average Collection Period. Accounts receivable/(annual credit sales/365). A ratio that expresses how rapidly the firm is collecting its credit accounts.

Average Tax Rate. The rate calculated by dividing the total tax liability by the entity's taxable income.

Balance Sheet. A basic accounting statement that represents the financial position of a firm on a given date.

Balance Sheet Leverage Ratios. Financial ratios used to measure the extent of a firm's use of borrowed funds calculated using information found in the firm's balance sheet.

Bankers' Acceptances. A draft (order to pay) drawn on a specific bank by a seller of goods in order to obtain payment for goods that have been shipped (sold) to a customer. The customer maintains an account with that specific bank.

Bank Wire. A private wire service used and supported by approximately 250 banks in the United States for transferring funds, exchanging credit information, or effecting securities transactions.

Beta. The relationship between an investment's returns and the market returns. This is a measure of the investment's nondiversifiable risk.

Bird-in-the-Hand Dividend Theory. The belief that dividend income has a higher value to the investor than does capital gains income, since dividends are more certain than capital gains.

Bond. A long-term (ten-year or more) promissory note issued by the borrower, promising to pay the owner of the security a predetermined and fixed amount of interest each year.

Bond Par Value. The face value appearing on the bond, which is to be returned to the bondholder at maturity.

Book Value. The depreciated value of a company's assets (original cost less accumulated depreciation) less the outstanding liabilities.

Book-Value Weights. The percentage of financing provided by different capital sources as measured by their book values from the company's balance sheet.

Break Even Analysis. An analytical technique used to determine the quantity of output or sales that results in a zero level of earnings before interest and taxes (EBIT). Relationships among the firm's cost structure, volume of output, and EBIT are studied.

Business Risk. The relative dispersion or variability in the firm's expected earnings before interest and taxes (EBIT). The nature of the firm's operations causes its business risk. This type of risk is affected by the firm's cost structure, product demand characteristics, and intra-industry competitive position. In capital-structure theory, business risk is distinguished from financial risk. See Financial Risk.

Call Option. A call option gives its owner the right to purchase a given number of shares of stock or some other asset at a specified price over a given time period.

Call Premium. The difference between the call price and the security's par value.

Call Provision. A provision that entitles the corporation to repurchase its bonds or preferred stock from their holders at stated prices over specified periods.

Capital Asset. All property used in conducting a business other than assets held primarily for sale in the ordinary course of business or depreciable and real property used in conducting a business.

Capital Asset Pricing Model. An equation stating that the expected rate of return on a project is a function of (1) the risk-free rate, (2) the investment's systematic risk, and (3) the expected risk premium in the market.

Capital Budgeting. The decision-making process with respect to investment in fixed assets. Specifically it involves measuring the incremental cash flows associated with investment proposals and evaluating those proposed investments.

Capital Gain or Loss. As defined by the revenue code, a gain or loss resulting from the sale or exchange of a capital asset.

Capital Market. All institutions and procedures that facilitate transactions in long-term financial instruments.

Capital Rationing. The placing of a limit by the firm on the dollar size of the capital budget.

Capital Structure. The mix of long-term sources of funds used by the firm. This is also called the firm's capitalization. The relative total (percentage) of each type of fund is emphasized.

Cash Breakeven Analysis. Another version of breakeven analysis that includes only the cash costs of production within the cost components. This means noncash expenses, like depreciation, are omitted in the analysis.

Cash Budget. A detailed plan of future cash flows. This budget is composed of four elements: cash receipts, cash disbursements, net change in cash for the period, and new financing needed.

Cash Flow Process. The process of cash generation and disposition in a typical business setting.

Certainty Equivalents. The amount of cash a person would require with certainty to make him indifferent between this certain sum and a particular risky or uncertain sum.

Characteristic Line. The line of "best fit" through a series of returns for a firm's stock relative to the market returns. The slope of the line, frequently called beta, represents the average movement of the firm's stock returns in response to a movement in the market's returns.

Chattel Mortgage Agreement. A loan agreement in which the lender can increase his security interest by having specific items of inventory identified in the loan agreement. The borrower retains title to the inventory but cannot sell the items without the lender's consent.

Chop-Shop Value. A valuation approach that values a firm based on its various business segments. It is an attempt to identify multi-industry companies that are undervalued and would be worth more if separated into their parts.

Clientele Effect. The belief that individuals and institutions that need current income will invest in companies that have high dividend payouts. Other investors prefer to avoid taxes by holding securities that offer only small dividend income, but large capital gains. Thus, we have a "clientele" of investors.

Commercial Paper. Short-term unsecured promissory notes sold by large businesses in order to raise cash. Unlike most other money market instruments, commercial paper has no developed secondary market.

Common Size Financial Statements. Financial statements that have been converted to a percent of either sales in the case of the income statement or total assets in the case of the balance sheet. The information within the common size statements is standardized and consequently can be used to compare firms of very different sizes.

Compensating Balance. A balance of a given amount that the firm maintains in its demand deposit account. It may be required by either a formal or informal agreement with the firm's commercial bank. Such balances are usually required by the bank (1) on the unused portion of a loan commitment, (2) on the unpaid portion of an outstanding loan, or (3) in exchange for certain services provided by the bank, such as check-clearing or credit information. These balances raise the effective rate of interest paid on borrowed funds.

Composition. A voluntary remedy to insolvency in which the creditors receive a portion of the amounts originally owed to them. This may be preferable to forcing bankruptcy due to the high costs of bankruptcy courts and the possibility that the insolvent firm's resources may be further depleted by the bankruptcy proceedings.

Compounding. The process of determining the future value of a payment or series of payments when applying the concept of compound interest.

Compound Interest. The situation in which interest paid on the investment during the first period is added to the principal and, during the second period, interest is earned on the original principal plus the interest earned during the first period.

Concentration Bank. A bank where the firm maintains a major disbursing account.

Conglomerate. A multifaceted corporation involved in a variety of products and services.

Constant Dividend Payout Ratio. A dividend payment policy in which the percentage of earnings paid out in dividends is held constant. The dollar amount fluctuates from year to year as profits vary.

Contractual Interest Rate. The interest rate to be paid on a bond expressed as a percent of par value.

Contribution Margin. The difference between a product's selling price and its unit variable costs. It is usually measured on a per unit basis.

Conversion Ratio. The number of shares of common stock for which a convertible security can be exchanged.

Convertibles. Preferred stock or debentures that can be exchanged for a specified number of shares of common stock at the will of the owner.

Corporate Bylaws. Regulations that govern the internal affairs of the corporation, designating such items as the time and place of the shareholders' meetings, voting rights, the election process for selecting members of the board of directors, the procedures for issuing and transferring stock certificates, and the policies relating to the corporate records.

Corporation. An entity that legally functions separate and apart from its owners.

Cost Budgets. Budgets prepared for every major expense category of the firm, such as production cost, selling cost, administrative cost, financing cost, and research and development cost.

Cost of Capital. The rate that must be earned in order to satisfy the required rate of return of the firm's investors. It may also be defined as the rate of return on investments at which the price of the firm's common stock will remain unchanged. The cost of capital is based on the opportunity cost of funds as determined in the capital markets.

Cost of Common Stock. The rate of return the firm must earn in order for the common stockholders to receive their required rate of return. The rate is based on the opportunity cost of funds for the common stockholders in the capital markets.

Cost of Debt. The rate that has to be received from an investment in order to achieve the required rate of return for the creditors. The cost is based on the debtholders' opportunity cost of debt in the capital markets.

Cost of Preferred Stock. The rate of return that must be earned on the preferred stockholders' investment to satisfy their required rate of return. The cost is based on the preferred stockholders' opportunity cost of preferred stock in the capital markets.

Cost-Volume-Profit Analysis. Another way of referring to ordinary breakeven analysis.

Coupon Interest Rate. The interest to be paid annually on a bond as a percent of par value, which is specified in the contractual agreement.

Coverage Ratios. A group of ratios that measure a firm's ability to meet its recurring fixed charge obligations, such as interest on long-term debt, lease payments, and/or preferred stock dividends.

Credit Scoring. The numerical evaluation of credit applicants where the score is evaluated relative to a predetermined standard.

Cross Rates. The indirect computation of the exchange rate of one currency from the exchange rates of two other currencies.

Cumulative Feature. A requirement that all past unpaid preferred stock dividends must be paid before any common stock dividends are declared.

Current Ratio. Current assets/current liabilities. A ratio that indicates a firm's degree of liquidity by comparing its current assets to its current liabilities.

Date of Record. Date at which the stock transfer books are to be closed for determining the investor to receive the next dividend payments. See Ex-Dividend Date.

Debenture. Any unsecured long-term debt.

Debt Capacity. The maximum proportion of debt that the firm can include in its capital structure and still maintain its lowest composite cost of capital.

Debt Ratio. Total liabilities/total assets. A ratio that measures the extent to which a firm has been financed with debt.

Declaration Date. The date upon which a dividend is formally declared by the board of directors.

Default Risk. The uncertainty of expected returns from a security attributable to possible changes in the financial capacity of the security issuer to make future payments to the security owner. Treasury securities are considered to be default-free. Default risk is also referred to as "financial risk" in the context of marketable securities management.

Degree of Combined Leverage. The percentage change in earnings per share caused by a percentage change in sales. It is the product of the degree of operating leverage and the degree of financial leverage.

Depository Transfer Checks. A means for moving funds from local bank accounts to concentration accounts. The depository transfer check itself is an unsigned, nonnegotiable instrument. It is payable only to the bank of deposit for credit to the firm's specific account.

Depreciation. The means by which an asset's value is expensed over its useful life for federal income tax purposes.

Direct Quotes. The exchange rate that indicates the number of units of the home currency required to buy one unit of foreign currency.

Disbursing Float. Funds available in the company's bank account until its payment check has cleared through the banking system.

Discount Bond. A bond that sells at a discount below par value.

Discounting. The inverse of compounding. This process is used to determine the present value of a cash flow.

Discount Rate. The interest rate used in the discounting process.

Diversifiable Risk. See Unsystematic Risk.

Divestitures. The removal of a division or subsidiary from the company. Typically, the part of the firm being separated is viewed as not contributing to the company's basic purposes.

Dividend Payout Ratio. The amount of dividends relative to the company's net income or earnings per share.

Dividend Yield. The dividend per share divided by the price of the security.

Double-Declining Balance Depreciation. A method for computing declining balance depreciation expense in which the constant percentage is equal to 2/N, where N represents the depreciable life of the asset.

Dunning Letters. Past-due letters sent out to delinquent accounts.

Duration. A measure of responsiveness of the bond price to a change in interest rates.

EBIT. Common financial notation for earnings before interest and taxes.

EBIT-EPS Indifference Point. The level of earnings before interest and taxes (EBIT) that will equate earnings per share (EPS) between two different financing plans.

Economic Failure. Situation in which the company's costs exceed its revenues. Stated differently, the internal rates of return on investments are less than the firm's cost of capital.

Efficient Market. A market in which the values of all assets and securities at any instant in time fully reflect all available information.

EPS. Typical financial notation for earnings per (common) share.

Equivalent Annual Annuity (EAA). An annuity cash flow that yields the same present value as the project's NPV. It is calculated by dividing the project's NPV by the appropriate $PVIFA_{1\%,n,yr}$.

Eurodollar Market. This is a banking market in U.S. dollars outside the U.S. Large sums of U.S. dollars can be borrowed or invested in this unregulated financial market. Similar external markets exist in Europe and Asia and for other major currencies.

Exchange Risk. The variability in future cash flows caused by variations in the exchange rates.

Ex-Dividend Date. The date upon which stock brokerage companies have uniformly decided to terminate the right of ownership to the dividend, which is four days prior to the record date.

Exercise Price. The price at which a warrant allows its holder to purchase the firm's common stock.

Exercise Ratio. The number of shares of stock that can be obtained at the exercise price with one warrant.

Expected Rate of Return. The arithmetic mean or average of all possible outcomes where those outcomes are weighted by the probability that each will occur.

Extension. An arrangement requiring that the debtor pay the amount owed in full, but providing an extension in time.

Ex-Rights Date. The date on or after which the stock sells without rights.

External Common Equity. A new issue of common stock.

Factor. A firm that acquires the receivables of other firms. A commercial finance company that engages solely in the factoring of receivables is known as an old-line factor.

Factoring of Accounts Receivable. The outright sale of a firm's accounts to another party (the factor) without recourse. The factor, in turn, bears the risk of collection.

Fair Value. The present value of an asset's expected future cash flows.

Federal Agency Securities. Debt obligations of corporations and agencies created to carry out the lending programs of the U.S. government.

Federal Reserve System. The U.S. central banking system.

Field Warehouse Financing Agreement. A security agreement in which inventories are used as collateral, physically separated from the firm's other inventories, and placed under the control of a third-party field warehousing firm.

Financial Analysis. The assessment of a firm's financial condition or well-being. Its objectives are to determine the firm's financial strengths and to identify its weaknesses. The primary tool of financial analysis is the financial ratio.

Financial Assets. Claims for future payment by one economic unit upon another.

Financial Intermediaries. Major financial institutions, such as commercial banks, savings and loan associations, credit unions, life insurance companies, and mutual funds, that assist the transfer of savings from economic units with excess savings to those with a shortage of savings.

Financial Lease. A noncancellable contractual commitment on the part of the firm leasing the asset (the lessee) to make a series of payments to the firm that actually owns the asset (the lessor) for the use of the asset.

Financial Leverage. The use of securities bearing a fixed (limited) rate of return to finance a portion of the firm's assets. Financial leverage can arise from the use of either debt or preferred stock financing. The use of financial leverage exposes the firm to financial risk.

Financial Markets. Institutions and procedures that facilitate transactions in all types of financial claims (securities).

Financial Risk. The added variability in earnings available to the firm's common shareholders, and the added chance of insolvency caused by the use of securities bearing a limited rate of return in the firm's financial structure. The use of financial leverage gives rise to financial risk.

Financial Structure Design. The activity of seeking the proper mixture of a firm's short-term, long-term, and permanent financing components to minimize the cost of raising a given amount of funds.

Financial Structure. The mix of all funds sources that appear on the right-hand side of the balance sheet.

Fixed Asset Turnover. Sales/fixed assets. A ratio indicating how effectively a firm is using its fixed assets to generate sales.

Fixed Costs. Charges that do not vary in total amount as sales volume or the quantity of output changes over some relevant range of output.

Flotation Costs. The underwriter's spread and issuing costs associated with the issuance and marketing of new securities.

Foreign Direct Investment. Physical assets, such as plant and equipment, acquired outside a corporation's home country but operated and controlled by that corporation.

Formal Control. Control vested in the stockholders having the majority of the voting common shares.

Forward Exchange Contract. A contract which requires delivery of one currency at a specified future date for a specified amount of another currency.

Free Cash Flow Value. The value of a firm based on the cash flows available for distributing to any investors, both debt and equity. The free cash flows equal operating cash flows less any incremental investments made to support a firm's future growth. The value of these flows is equal to their present value.

Functional Control. Control executed by the corporate officers in conducting the daily operations.

Futures Contract. A futures contract is a contract to buy or sell a stated commodity (such as soybeans or corn) or financial claim (such as U.S. Treasury bonds) at a specified price at some future, specified time.

General Partnership. A partnership in which all partners are fully liable for the indebtedness incurred by the partnership.

Golden Parachute. A target management's attempt to ensure its own future in the event of an acquisition; stipulations regarding severance pay, extension of benefits, and other "extras" to be provided to outgoing management by the acquirer.

Gross Income. The firm's dollar sales from its product or services less the cost of producing or acquiring the product or service.

Gross Profit Margin. Gross profit/net sales. A ratio denoting the gross profit of the firm as a percentage of net sales.

Hedge. A means to neutralize exchange risk on an exposed asset position, whereby a liability of the same amount and maturity is created in a foreign currency.

Hedging Principle. A working capital management policy which states that the cash flow generating characteristics of a firm's investments should be matched with the cash flow requirements of the firm's sources of financing. Very simply, short-lived assets should be financed with short-term sources of financing while long-lived assets should be financed with long-term sources of financing.

Holding-Period Return. The return an investor would receive from holding a security for a designated period of time. For example, a monthly holding-period return would be the return for holding a security during a particular month.

Hostile Takeover. A merger or acquisition in which management resists the group initiating the transaction.

Hurdle Rate. The required rate of return used in capital budgeting.

Income Bond. A bond that requires interest payments only if earned. Failure to meet these interest payments will not result in bankruptcy.

Income Statement. A basic accounting statement that measures the results of a firm's operations over a specified period, commonly one year. Also known as the profit and loss statement. The bottom line of the income statement shows the firm's profit or loss for the period.

Increasing-Stream Hypothesis of Dividend Policy. A smoothing of the dividend stream in order to minimize the effect of company reversals. Corporate managers make every effort to avoid a dividend cut, attempting instead to develop a gradually increasing dividend series over the long-term future.

Incremental Cash Flows. The cash flows that result from the acceptance of a capital-budgeting project.

Indenture. The legal agreement between the firm issuing the bonds and the bond trustee who represents the bondholders, providing the specific terms of the loan agreement.

Indirect Quote. The exchange rate that expresses the required number of units of foreign currency to buy one unit of home currency.

Information Asymmetry. The difference in accessibility to information between managers and investors, which may result in a lower stock price than would be true if we had conditions of certainty.

Insolvency. The inability to meet interest payments or to repay debt at maturity.

Interest-Rate Parity Theory. States that (except for the effect of small transaction costs) the forward premium or discount should be equal and opposite in size to the difference in the national interest rates for securities of the same maturity.

Interest-Rate Risk. The uncertainty that envelops the expected returns from a security caused by changes in interest rates. Price changes induced by interest-rate changes are greater for long-term than for short-term financial instruments.

Internal Common Equity. Profits retained within the business for investment purposes.

Internal Growth. A firm's growth rate in earnings resulting from reinvesting company profits rather than distributing the earnings in the form of dividends. The growth rate is a function of the amount retained and the return earned on the retained funds.

Internal Rate of Return (IRR). A capital-budgeting technique that reflects the rate of return a project earns. Mathematically it is the discount rate that equates the present value of the inflows with the present value of the outflows.

Intrinsic Value. The present value of the investment's expected future cash flows, discounted at the investor's required rate of return.

Inventory Loans. Loans secured by inventories. Examples include floating or blanket lien agreements, chattel mortgage agreements, field warehouse receipt loans, and terminal warehouse receipt loans.

Inventory Turnover Ratio. Cost of goods sold/inventory. A ratio that measures the number of times a firm's inventories are sold and replaced during the year. This ratio reflects the relative liquidity of inventories.

Investment Banker. A financial specialist who underwrites and distributes new securities and advises corporate clients about raising new funds.

Investor's Required Rate of Return. The minimum rate of return necessary to attract an investor to purchase or hold a security.

Junk Bonds. Any bond rated BB or below.

Just-in-Time Inventory Control. A production and management system in which inventory is cut down to a minimum through adjustments to the time and physical distance between the various production operations. Under this system the firm keeps a minimum level of inventory on hand relying upon suppliers to furnish parts "just-in-time" for them to be assembled.

Lead and Lag Strategies. Techniques used to reduce exchange risk where the firm maximizes its asset position in the stronger currency and its liability position in the weaker currency.

Least-Squares Regression. A procedure for "fitting" a line through a scatter of observed data points in a way that minimizes the sum of the squared deviations of the points from the fitted line.

Leveraged Buyout. A corporate restructuring where the existing shareholders sell their shares to a small group of investors. The purchasers of the stock use the firm's unused debt capacity to borrow the funds to pay for the stock.

Leveraged Leasing. A leasing arrangement in which the lessor will generally supply equity funds of 20 to 30 percent of the purchase price and borrow the remainder from a third-party lender.

Limited Partnership. A partnership in which one or more of the partners has limited liability, restricted to the amount of capital he invests in the partnership.

Line of Credit. Generally an informal agreement or understanding between the borrower and the bank as to the maximum amount of credit the bank will provide the borrower at any one time. Under this type of agreement there is no "legal" commitment on the part of the bank to provide the stated credit. See Revolving Credit Agreement.

Liquidation by Assignment. A proceeding in which the debtor transfers title of the firm's assets to a third party, who has been appointed either by the creditors or by the court. This individual, known as an assignee or trustee, administers the liquidation process and sees that an appropriate distribution is made of the proceeds.

Liquidation Value. The dollar sum that could be realized if an asset were sold independently of the going concern.

Liquidity. A firm's ability to pay its bills on time. Liquidity is related to the ease and quickness with which a firm can convert its noncash assets into cash, as well as the size of the firm's investment in noncash assets vis-à-vis its short-term liabilities.

Liquidity Preference Theory. The shape of the term structure of interest rates is determined by an investor's additional required interest rate in compensation of additional risks.

Liquidity Ratios. Financial ratios used to assess the ability of a firm to pay its bills on time. Examples of liquidity ratios include the current ratio and the acid test ratio.

Loan Amortization Schedule. A breakdown of the interest and principle payments on an amortized loan.

Long-Term Residual Dividend Policy. A dividend plan by which the residual capital is distributed smoothly to the investors over the planning period.

Mail Float. Funds tied up during the time that elapses from the moment a customer mails his remittance check until the firm begins to process it.

Marginal Cost of Capital. The cost of capital that represents the weighted cost of each additional dollar of financing from all sources, debt, preferred stock, and common stock.

Marginal Tax Rate. The tax rate that would be applied to the next dollar of income.

Market Equilibrium. The situation in which expected returns equal required returns.

Market Risk. See **Systematic Risk.**

Market Segmentation Theory. The shape of the term structure of interest rates implies that the rate of interest for a particular maturity is determined solely by demand and supply for a given maturity. This demand is independent of the demand and supply for securities having different maturities.

Market Value. The value observed in the market place, where buyers and sellers negotiate a mutually acceptable price for the asset.

Market-Value Weights. The percentage of financing provided by different capital sources, measured by the current market prices of the firm's bonds and preferred and common stock.

Marketable Securities. Security investments that the firm can quickly convert into cash balances.

Maturity Date. The date upon which a borrower is to repay a loan.

Merger. A combination of two or more businesses into a single operational entity.

Money Market. All institutions and procedures that facilitate transactions in short-term instruments issued by borrowers with very high credit ratings.

Money Market Mutual Funds. Investment companies that purchase a diversified array of short-term, high-grade (money market) debt instruments.

Monitoring Costs. A form of agency costs. Typically these costs arise when bond investors take steps to ensure that protective covenants in the bond indenture are adhered to by management.

Mortgage Bonds. Bonds secured by a lien on real property.

Multinational Corporation. A corporation with holdings and/or operations in more than one country.

Mutually Exclusive Projects. A set of projects that perform essentially the same task, so that acceptance of one will necessarily mean rejection of the others.

Negotiable Certificates of Deposit. Marketable receipts for funds deposited in a bank for a fixed period. The deposited funds earn a fixed rate of interest. More commonly, these are called CDs.

Net Income. A figure representing the firm's profit or loss for the period. It also represents the earnings available to the firm's common and preferred stockholders.

Net Income Available to Common Equity (Also **Net Common Stock Earnings**). Net income after interest taxes and preferred dividends.

Net Operating Loss Carryback and Carryforward. A tax provision that permits the taxpayer first to apply the loss against the profits in the three prior years (carryback). If the loss has not been completely absorbed by the profits in these three years, it may be applied to taxable profits in each of the seven following years (carryforward).

Net Present Value (NPV). A capital-budgeting concept defined as the present value of the project's annual net cash flows after tax less the project's initial outlay.

Net Profit Margin. Net income/sales. A ratio that measures the net income of the firm as a percent of sales.

Net Working Capital. The difference between the firm's current assets and its current liabilities.

Non-Diversifiable Risk. See Systematic Risk.

Nominal Interest Rate. The interest rate paid on debt securities without an adjustment for any loss in purchasing power.

Normal Probability Distribution. A special class of bell-shaped distributions with symmetrically decreasing density, where the curve approaches but never reaches the X axis.

Operating Income Return on Investment. The ratio of net operating income divided by total assets.

Operating Lease. A contractual commitment on the part of the firm leasing the asset (the lessee) to make a series of payments to the firm that actually owns the asset (the lessor) for use of the asset. An operating lease differs from a financial lease in that it can be canceled at any time after proper notice has been given to the lessor.

Operating Leverage. The responsiveness to sales changes of the firm's earnings before interest and taxes. This responsiveness arises from the firm's use of fixed operating costs.

Operating Profit Margin. Net operating income/sales. A firm's earnings before interest and taxes. This ratio serves as an overall measure of operating effectiveness.

Opportunity Cost of Funds. The next best rate of return available to the investor for a given level of risk.

Opportunity Set. The return-risk relationship available for an investor interested in the purchase or sale of securities.

Optimal Capital Structure. The capital structure that minimizes the firm's composite cost of capital (maximizes the common stock price) for raising a given amount of funds.

Optimal Range of Financial Leverage. The range of various capital structure combinations that yield the lowest overall cost of capital for the firm.

Option Contract. An option contract gives its owner the right to buy or sell a fixed number of shares at a specified price over a limited time period.

Organized Security Exchanges. Formal organizations involved in the trading of securities. Such exchanges are tangible entities that conduct auction markets in listed securities.

Over-the-Counter Markets. All security markets except the organized exchanges. The money market is an over-the-counter market. Most corporate bonds also are traded in this market.

PacMan. A defensive tactic to a tender offer where the firm under attack becomes the attacker.

Partnership. An association of two or more individuals joining together as co-owners to operate a business for profit.

Par Value. On the face of a bond, the stated amount that the firm is to repay upon the maturity date.

Payable-Through Draft. A legal instrument that has the physical appearance of an ordinary check but is not drawn on a bank. A payable-through draft is drawn on and paid by the issuing firm. The bank serves as a collection point and passes the draft on to the firm.

Payback Period. A capital-budgeting criterion defined as the number of years required to recover the initial cash investment.

Payment Date. The date on which the company mails a dividend check to each investor.

Percent of Sales Method. A method of financial forecasting that involves estimating the level of an expense, asset, or liability for a future period as a percent of the sales forecast.

Perfect Markets. Hypothetical markets under the assumptions that (1) information is readily available to all investors at no cost, (2) there are no transaction costs, (3) investment opportunities are readily accessible to all prospective investors, and (4) financial distress and bankruptcy costs are nonexistent.

Permanent Investment. An investment that the firm expects to hold longer than one year. The firm makes permanent investments in fixed and current assets. Contrast with **Temporary Investments.**

Perpetuity. An annuity with an infinite life.

Physical Budgets. Budgets for unit sales, personnel or manpower, unit production, inventories, and physical facilities. These budgets are used as the basis for generating cost and profit budgets.

Pledging Accounts Receivable. A loan the firm obtains from a commercial bank or a finance company using its accounts receivable as collateral.

Poison Pill. A tactic used by the target of a hostile takeover; an unfavorable event, such as immediate repayment of all outstanding debt, triggered by an unfriendly party's acquisition of significant stock holdings.

Portfolio Beta. The relationship between a portfolio's returns and the market returns. It is a measure of the portfolio's nondiversifiable risk.

Portfolio Diversification Effect. The fact that variations of the returns from a portfolio or combination of assets may be less than the sum of the variation of the individual assets making up the portfolio.

Preauthorized Checks (PACs). A check that resembles the ordinary check but does not contain or require the signature of the person on whose account it is being drawn. A PAC is created only with the individual's legal authorization. The PAC system is advantageous when the firm regularly receives a large volume of payments of a fixed amount from the same customer over a long period.

Preemptive Right. The right entitling the common shareholder to maintain his proportionate share of ownership in the firm.

Present Value. The value in today's dollars of a future payment discounted back to present at the required rate of return.

Present Value of Dividend Growth (PVDG). The net present value of any dividend growth resulting from the reinvestment of future earnings.

Price/Earnings Ratio (P/E). The price the market places on $1 of a firm's earnings. For example, if a firm has an earnings per share of $2, and a stock price of $30, its price/earnings ratio is 15 ($30 ÷ $2).

Price Pegging. Buying orders placed by an underwriting syndicate manager for the security being marketed by his selling group. The objective is to stabilize the market price of the new issue.

Probability Tree. A schematic representation of a problem in which all possible outcomes are graphically displayed.

Processing Float. Funds tied up during the time required for the firm to process remittance checks before they can be deposited in the bank.

Profit Budget. A budget of forecasted profits based on information gleaned from the cost and sales budgets.

Profit Margins. Financial ratios (sometimes simply referred to as margins) that reflect the level of firm profits relative to sales. Examples include the gross profit margin (gross profit divided by sales), operating profit margin (operating earnings divided by sales), and the net profit margin (net profit divided by sales).

Profitability Index (PI). A capital-budgeting criterion defined as the ratio of the present value of the future net cash flows to the initial outlay.

Pro Forma Income Statement. A statement of planned profit or loss for a future period.

Prospectus. A condensed version of the full registration statement filed with the Securities and Exchange Commission that describes a new security issue.

Proxy. A means of voting in which a designated party is provided with the temporary power of attorney to vote for the signee at the corporation's annual meeting.

Purchasing Power Parity. In the long run, exchange rates adjust so that the purchasing power of each currency tends to remain the same and, thus, exchange rate changes tend to reflect international differences in inflation rates. Countries with high rates of inflation tend to experience declines in the value of their currency.

Put Option. A put option gives its owners the right to sell a given number of shares of common stock or some other asset at a specified price over a given time period.

Real Assets. Tangible assets like houses, equipment, and inventories; real assets are distinguished from financial assets.

Real Interest Rate. The nominal rate of interest less any loss in purchasing power of the dollar during the time of the investment.

Red Herring. Finance jargon for a preliminary prospectus, which outlines the important features of a new issue without specifying the selling price and offering date.

Refunding. The process of replacing an old debt issue with the sale of new debt.

Registration Statement. A lengthy document filed with the Securities and Exchange Commission containing pertinent facts about a firm planning to sell new securities.

Remote Disbursing. A cash management service specifically designed to extend disbursing float.

Reorganization. A procedure, administered by the courts, that attempts to revitalize a firm by changing its operating procedures and capital structure.

Repurchase Agreements. Legal contracts that involve the sale of short-term securities by a borrower to a lender of funds. The borrower commits to repurchase the securities at a later date at the contract price plus a stated interest charge.

Required Rate of Return. The minimum rate of return necessary to attract an investor to purchase or hold a security. It is also the discount rate that equates the present value of the cash flows with the value of the security.

Residual Dividend Theory. A theory asserting that the dividends to be paid should equal the equity capital left over after the financing of profitable investments.

Restrictive Covenants. Provisions in the loan agreement that place restrictions on the borrower and make the loan immediately payable and due when violated. These restrictive covenants are designed to maintain the borrower's financial condition on a par with that which existed at the time the loan was made.

Return on Common Equity. Net income available to the common stockholders/common equity. A ratio relating earned income to the common stockholder's investment.

Return on Total Assets. Net income/total assets. This ratio determines the yield on the firm's assets by relating net income to total assets.

Return-Risk Line. A specification of the appropriate required rates of return for investments having different amounts of risk.

Revolving Credit Agreement. An understanding between the borrower and the bank as to the amount of credit the bank will be legally obligated to provide the borrower. See **Line of Credit.**

Right. A certificate issued to common stockholders giving them an option to purchase a stated number of new shares at a specified price during a two- to ten-week period.

Risk. The possible variation associated with the expected return measured by the standard deviation or coefficient of variation.

Risk-Adjusted Discount Rate. A method for incorporating the project's level of risk into the capital budgeting process, in which the discount rate is adjusted upward to compensate for higher-than-normal risk or downward to compensate for lower-than-normal risk.

Riskless Rate of Return. The rate of return on risk-free investments, such as the interest rate on short-term U.S. government securities.

Risk Premium. The additional return expected for assuming risk.

Rule of Absolute Priority. Rule that the company must completely honor senior claims on assets before settling junior claims.

Sale and Leaseback Arrangement. An arrangement arising when a firm sells land, buildings, or equipment that it already owns and simultaneously enters into an agreement to lease the property back for a specified period, under specific terms.

Salvage Value. The value of an asset or investment project at the end of its usable life.

Scatter Diagram Method. A method of financial forecasting that involves visually "fitting" a line through a scatter of points so that the distance of points about the line is minimized.

Scenario Analysis. Simulation analysis that focuses on an examination of the range of possible outcomes.

Secondary Market. Transactions in currently outstanding securities. This is distinguished from the new issues or primary market.

Secured Credit. Sources of credit that require security in the form of pledged assets. In the event the borrower defaults in payment of principal or interest, the lender can seize the pledged assets and sell them to settle the debt.

Securities and Exchange Commission (SEC). The federal agency created by the Securities Exchange Act of 1934 to enforce federal securities laws.

Securities Exchange Act of 1933. A regulation that requires registration of certain new issues of public securities with the Securities and Exchange Commission (SEC). The registration statement should disclose all facts relevant to the new issue that will permit an investor to make an informed decision.

Securities Exchange Act of 1934. This act enables the SEC to enforce federal securities laws. The major aspects of the 1934 act include: (1) Major securities exchanges are required to register with the SEC; (2) insider-trading is regulated; (3) stock price manipulation by investors is prohibited; (4) the SEC has control over proxy procedures; (5) the Board of Governors of the Federal Reserve System is given the responsibility of setting margin requirements.

Security Market Line. The return line that reflects the attitudes of investors regarding the minimal acceptable return for a given level of systematic risk.

Sell-Off. The sale of a subsidiary, division, or product line by one company to another.

Selling Group. A collection of securities dealers that participates in the distribution of new issues to final investors. A selling group agreement links these dealers to the underwriting syndicate.

Semivariable Costs. Charges that behave as variable costs over certain ranges of output and as fixed costs over other ranges of output.

Shark Repellents. Any of a variety of legalistic means used to counteract a tender offer by the firm under attack.

Shelf Registration (SEC Rule 415). A procedure for issuing new securities where the firm gets a master registration statement approved by the SEC. For the next two years the firm can sell securities in a piecemeal fashion against this "blanket order."

Simulation. The process of imitating the performance of an investment project through repeated evaluations, usually using a computer. In the general case, experimentation upon a mathematical model that has been designed to capture the critical realities of the decision-making situation.

Sinking Fund. A required annual payment that allows for the periodic retirement of debt.

Skewed Distribution. A distribution that has a longer "tail" to the right or left.

Sole Proprietorship. A business owned by a single individual.

Spin-off. The separation of a subsidiary from its parent, with no change in the equity ownership. The management of the parent company gives up operating control over the subsidiary, but the shareholders maintain their same percentage ownership in both firms. New shares representing ownership in the averted company are issued to the original shareholders on a pro-rata basis.

Spontaneous Financing. The trade credit and other accounts payable that arise "spontaneously" in the firm's day-to-day operations.

Spot Transaction. A transaction made immediately in the market place at the market price.

Stable Dollar Dividend per Share. A dividend policy that maintains a relatively stable dollar dividend per share over time.

Standard Deviation. A statistical measure of the spread of a probability distribution calculated by squaring the difference between each outcome and its expected value, weighting each value by its probability, summing over all possible outcomes, and taking the square root of this sum.

Statement of Changes in Financial Position. A basic accounting statement, also known as a sources and uses of funds statement, identifying how the firm acquired its funds for the period and what it did with those funds.

Stock Dividend. A distribution of shares of up to 25 percent of the number of shares currently outstanding, issued on a pro-rata basis to the current stockholders.

Stock Market Value. See Market Value.

Stock Split. A stock dividend exceeding 25 percent of the number of shares currently outstanding.

Stock Repurchase. The repurchase of common stock by the issuing firm for any of a variety of reasons resulting in a reduction of shares outstanding.

Straight-Line Depreciation. A method for computing depreciation expenses in which the cost of the asset is divided by the asset's useful life.

Stretching on Trade Credit. Failing to pay within the prescribed credit period. For example, under credit terms of 2/10, net 30, a firm would be stretching its trade credit if it failed to pay by the 30th day and paid on the 60th day.

Subchapter S Corporation. A corporation that, because of specific qualifications, is taxed as though it were a partnership.

Subscription Price. The price for which the security may be purchased in a rights offering.

Synergistic Effect. An often-used reason for mergers; the benefit derived from the combination of the acquirer's operations (or financing capabilities) with the target's. Also referred to as "the sum of the parts equalling more than the whole."

Systematic Risk (Nondiversifiable Risk or Market Related Risk). The portion of variations in investment returns that cannot be eliminated through investor diversification. These variations result from factors that affect all stocks.

Target Debt Ratio. A desired proportion of long-term debt in the firm's capital structure. Alternatively, it may be the desired proportion of total debt in the firm's financial structure.

Taxable Income. Gross income from all sources, except for allowable exclusions, less any tax deductible expenses.

Tax Liability. The amount owed the federal, state, or local taxing authorities.

TBL Leases. Tax benefit transfer leases created under the Tax Act of 1981 and eliminated in 1982.

Technical Insolvency. Situation in which the firm can no longer honor its financial obligations. Although its assets may exceed its total liabilities, thereby indicating a positive net worth, the company simply does not have sufficient liquidity to pay its debts.

Temporary Financing. Financing (other than spontaneous sources) that will be repaid within a period of one year or less. Included among these sources of short-term debt are secured and unsecured bank loans, commercial paper, loans secured by accounts receivable, and loans secured by inventories.

Temporary Investments. These investments are comprised of the firm's investment in current assets that will be liquidated and not replaced within a period of one year or less. Examples include seasonal expansions in inventories and accounts receivable.

Tender Offer. A bid by an interested party, usually a corporation, for controlling interest in another corporation.

Terminal Warehouse Agreement. A security agreement in which the inventories pledged as collateral are transported to a public warehouse that is physically removed from the borrower's premises. This is the safest (and a costly) form of financing secured by inventory.

Term Loans. Loans that have maturities of one to ten years and are repaid in periodic installments over the life of the loan. Term loans are usually secured by a chattel mortgage on equipment or a mortgage on real property.

Term Structure of Interest Rates. The relationship between interest rates and the term to maturity, where the risk of default is held constant.

Times Interest Earned Ratio. Earnings before interest and taxes (EBIT)/interest expense. A ratio that measures the firm's ability to meet its interest payments from its annual operating earnings.

Total Asset Turnover. Sales/total tangible assets. An overall measure of the relation between the firm's tangible assets and the sales they generate.

Trade Credit. Credit made available by a firm's suppliers in conjunction with the acquisition of materials. Trade credit appears on the balance sheet as accounts payable.

Transaction Loan. A loan where the proceeds are designated for a specific purpose—for example, a bank loan used to finance the acquisition of a piece of equipment.

Transit Float. Funds tied up during the time necessary for a deposited check to clear through the commercial banking system and become usable funds to the company.

Treasury Bills. Direct debt obligations of the U.S. government sold on a regular basis by the U.S. Treasury.

Trend Analysis. An analysis of a firm's financial ratios over time.

Trustee. See Assignee.

Unbiased Expectations Theory. The shape of the term structure of interest rates is determined by an investor's expectations about future interest rates.

Uncommitted Earnings per Share. Earnings per share minus sinking-fund payments per share.

Underwriting. The purchase and subsequent resale of a new security issue. The risk of selling the new issue at a satisfactory (profitable) price is assumed by the investment banker.

Underwriting Syndicate. A temporary association of investment bankers formed to purchase a new security issue and quickly resell it at a profit. Formation of the syndicate spreads the risk of loss among several investment bankers, thereby minimizing the risk exposure of any single underwriter.

Undiversifiable Risk. The portion of the variation in investment returns that cannot be eliminated through investor diversification.

Unique Risk. See Unsystematic Risk.

Unlisted Securities. Securities that are not traded on an organized security exchange.

Unsecured Credit. All sources of credit that have as their security only the tender's faith in the borrower's ability to repay the funds when due.

Unsystematic Risk (Firm-Specific Risk or Unique Risk). The portion of the variation in investment returns that can be eliminated through investor diversification. These variations result from factors that are unique to the particular firm.

Value of a Bond. The present value of the interest payments, I_t in period t, plus the present value of the redemption of par value of the indebtedness, M, at the maturity date.

Value of a Security. The present value of all future cash inflows expected to be received by the investor owning the security.

Variable Costs. Charges that vary in total as output changes. Variable costs are fixed per unit of output.

Venture Capitalists. Investors interested in supplying capital to particularly high-risk situations, such as start-ups or firms denied conventional financing.

Voluntary Remedy. A voluntary reorganization that is acceptable to the creditors.

Warrant. An option to purchase a fixed number of shares of common stock at a predetermined price during a specified time period.

Weighted Cost of Capital. A composite of the individual costs of financing incurred by each capital source. A firm's weighted cost of capital is a function of (1) the individual costs of capital, (2) the capital structure mix, and (3) the level of financing necessary to make the investment.

Weighted Marginal Cost of Capital. The composite cost for each additional dollar of financing. The marginal cost of capital represents the appropriate criterion for making investment decisions.

White Knight. A defensive tactic to a tender offer whereby an able company comes to the rescue of the firm targeted for takeover.

Working Capital. A concept traditionally defined as a firm's investment in current assets. Net working capital refers to the difference between current assets and current liabilities.

Yield to Maturity. The rate of return the investor will earn if the bond is held to maturity.

Zero Balance Accounts. A cash management tool that permits centralized control over cash overflow while maintaining divisional disbursing authority. Objectives include: (1) Achieve better control over cash payments; (2) reduce excess cash balances held in regional banks for disbursing purposes; and (3) increase disbursing float.

APPENDIX A

Using a Calculator

As you prepare for a career in business, the ability to use a financial calculator is essential, whether you are in the finance division or the marketing department. For most positions, it will be assumed that you can use a calculator in making computations that at one time were simply not possible without extensive time and effort. The following examples let us see what is possible, but they represent only the beginning of using the calculator in finance.

With just a little time and effort, you will be surprised as how much you can do with the calculator, such as calculating a stock's beta, or determining the value of a bond on a specific day given the exact date of maturity, or finding net present values and internal rates of return, or calculating the standard deviation. The list is almost endless.

In demonstrating how calculators may make our work easier, we must first decide which calculator to use. The options are numerous and largely depend on personal preference. We have chosen the Texas Instruments BAII Plus.

We will limit our discussion to the following issues:

I. Introductory Comments
II. An Important Starting Point
III. Calculating Table Values for:
   A. Appendix B (Compound sum of $1)
   B. Appendix C (Present value of $1)
   C. Appendix D (Sum on an annuity of $1 for *n* periods)
   D. Appendix E (Present value of an annuity for $1 for *n* periods)
IV. Calculating Present Values
V. Calculating Future Values (Compound sum)
VI. Calculating the Number of Payments or Receipts

I. INTRODUCTORY COMMENTS

In the examples that follow, you are told (1) which keystrokes to use, (2) the resulting appearance of the calculator display, and (3) a supporting explanation.

The keystrokes column tells you which keys to press. The keystrokes shown in an unshaded box tell you to use one of the calculator's dedicated or "hard" keys. For example, if +/− is shown in the keystrokes instruction column, press that key on the keyboard of the calculator. To use a function printed in gray lettering above a dedicated key, always press the gray key 2nd first, then the function key.

II. An Important Starting Point

Example: You want to display four numbers to the right of the decimal.

Keystrokes	Display	Explanation
2nd		
FORMAT	DEC =	
4 [ENTER]	DEC = 4.0000	Sets display to show four numbers to the right of the decimal
[CE/C] [CE/C]	0.0000	Clears display

Example: You want to display two payments per year to be paid at the end of each period.

Keystrokes	Display	Explanation
2nd		
P/Y	P/Y =	
2 [ENTER]	P/Y = 2.0000	Sets number of payments per year at 2
2nd		
BGN	END	Sets timing of payment at the end of each period
[CE/C] [CE/C]	0.0000	Clears display

III. Calculating Table Values

A. The compound sum of $1 (Appendix B)

Example: What is the table value for the compound sum of $1 for 5 years at a 12 percent annual interest rate?

Keystrokes	Display	Explanation
2nd		
P/Y	P/Y =	
1 [ENTER]	P/Y = 1.0000	Sets number of payments per year at 1
2nd		
BGN	END	Sets timing of payment at the end of each period
[CE/C] [CE/C]	0.0000	Clears display
2nd		
CLR TVM	0.0000	Clears TVM variables
1 [+/–]	PV = –1.0000	Stores initial $1 as a negative present value
[PV]		Otherwise the answer will appear as a negative
5 [N]	N = 5.0000	Stores number of periods
12 [I/Y]	I/Y = 12.0000	Stores interest rate
[CPT] [FV]	FV = 1.7623	Table value

III. Calculating Table Values (continued)

B. The present value of $1 (Appendix C)

Example: What is the table value for the present value of $1 for 8 years at a 10 percent annual interest rate?

Keystrokes	Display	Explanation
2nd		
P/Y	P/V =	
1 [ENTER]	P/Y = 1.0000	Sets number of payments per year at 1
2nd		
BGN	END	Sets timing of payment at the end of each period
[CE/C] [CE/C]	0.0000	Clears display
2nd		
CLR TVM	0.0000	Clears TVM variables
1 [+/–] [FV]	FV = –1.0000	Stores future amount as negative value
8 [N]	N = 8.0000	Stores number of periods
10 [I/Y]	I/Y = 10.0000	Stores interest rate
[CPT] [PV]	PV = 0.4665	Table value

C. The sum of an annuity of $1 for *n* period (Appendix D)

Example: What is the table value for the compound sum of an annuity of $1 for 6 years at a 14 percent annual interest rate?

Keystrokes	Display	Explanation
2nd		
P/Y	P/Y =	
1 [ENTER]	P/Y = 1.0000	Sets number of payments per year at 1
2nd		
BGN	END	Sets timing of payment at the end of each period
[CE/C] [CE/C]	0.0000	Clears display
2nd		
CLR TVM	0.0000	Clears TVM variables
1 [+/–] [PMT]	PMT = –1.0000	Stores annual payment (annuity) as a negative number. Otherwise the answer will appear as a negative.
6 [N]	N = 6.0000	Stores number of periods
14 [I/Y]	I/Y = 14.0000	Stores interest rate
[CPT] [FV]	FV = 8.5355	Table value

III. Calculating Table Values (continued)

D. The present value of an annuity of $1 for *n* periods (Appendix E)

Example: What is the table value for the present value of an annuity of $1 for 12 years at 9 percent annual interest rate?

Keystrokes	Display	Explanation
2nd		
P/Y	P/Y =	
1 [ENTER]	P/Y = 1.0000	Sets number of payments per year at 1
2nd		
BGN	END	Sets timing of payment at the end of each period
[CE/C] [CE/C]	0.0000	Clears display
2nd		
CLR TVM	0.0000	Clears TVM variables
1 [+/–] [PMT]	PMT = –1.0000	Stores annual payment (annuity) as a negative number. Otherwise the answer will appear as a negative.
12 [N]	N = 12.0000	Stores number of periods
9 [I/Y]	I/Y = 9.0000	Stores interest rate
[CPT] [PV]	PV = 7.1607	Table value

IV. Calculating Present Values

Example: You are considering the purchase of a franchise of quick oil-change locations, which you believe will provide an annual cash flow of $50,000. At the end of ten years, you believe that you will be able to sell the franchise for an estimated $900,000. Calculate the maximum amount you should pay for the franchise (present value) in order to realize at least an 18 percent annual yield.

Keystrokes	Display	Explanation
2nd		
BGN	END	Sets timing of payment at the end of each period
[CE/C] [CE/C]	0.0000	Clears display
2nd		
CLR TVM	0.0000	Clears TVM variables
10 [N]	N = 10.0000	Stores *n*, the holding period
18 [I/Y]	I/Y = 18.0000	Stores *i*, the required rate of return

IV. Calculating Present Values (continued)

50,000 [PMT]	PMT = 50,000.0000	Stores PMT, the annual cash flow to be received
900,000 [FV]	FV = 900,000.0000	Stores FV, the cash flow to be received at the end of the project
[CPT] [PV]	PV = –396,662.3350	The present value, given a required rate of return of 18 percent. (Note: The present value is displayed with a minus sign since it represents cash paid out.)

V. Calculating Future Values (Compound Sum)

Example: If you deposit $300 a month (at the beginning of each month) into a new account that pays 6.25% annual interested compounded monthly, how much will you have in the account after 5 years?

Keystrokes	Display	Explanation
2nd		
BGN	END	Sets timing of payment at the end of each period
2nd		
SET	BGN	Sets timing of payments to beginning of each period
2nd		
P/Y	P/Y =	
12 [ENTER]	P/Y = 12.0000	Sets 12 payments per year
[CE/C] [CE/C]	0.0000	Clears display
2nd		
CLR TVM	0.0000	Clears TVM variables
60 [N]	N = 60.0000	Stores *n,* the number of months for the investment
6.25 [I/Y]	I/Y = 6.2500	Stores *i,* the annual rate
300 [+/–] [PMT]	PMT = –300.0000	Stores PMT, the monthly amount invested (with a minus sign for cash paid out)
[CPT] [FV]	FV = 21,066.0423	The future value after 5 years

VI. Calculating the Number of Payments or Receipts

Example: If you wish to retire with $500,000 saved, and can only afford payments of $500 each month, how long will you have to contribute toward your retirement if you can earn a 10 percent return on your contributions?

Keystrokes	Display	Explanation
2nd		
BGN	BGN	Verifies timing of payment at the beginning of each period

VI. Calculating the Number of Payments or Receipts (continued)

2nd P/Y 12 [ENTER]	 P/Y = 12.0000 P/Y = 12.0000	 Sets 12 payments per year
[CE/C] [CE/C]	0.0000	Clears display
2nd CLR TVM	 0.0000	 Clears TVM variables
10 [I/Y]	I/Y = 10.0000	Stores *i*, the interest rate
500 [+/−] [PMT]	PMT = −500.0000	Stores PMT, the monthly amount invested (with a minus sign for cash paid out)
500,000 [FV]	FV = 500,000.0000	The value we want to achieve
[CPT] [N]	N = 268.2539	Number of months (since we considered monthly payments) required to achieve our goal

VII. Calculating the Payment Amount

Example: Suppose your retirement needs were $750,000. If you are currently 25 years old and plan to retire at age 65, how much will you have to contribute each month for retirement if you can earn 12.5% on your savings?

Keystrokes	Display	Explanation
2nd BGN	 BGN	 Verifies timing of payment at the beginning of each period
2nd P/Y 12 [ENTER]	 P/Y = 12.0000 P/Y = 12.0000	 Sets 12 payments per year
[CE/C] [CE/C]	0.0000	Clears display
2nd CLR TVM	 0.0000	 Clears TVM variables
12.5 [I/Y]	I/Y = 12.5000	Stores *i*, the interest rate
480 [N]	N = 480.0000	Stores *n*, the number of periods until we stop contributing (40 years × 480 12 months/years = months)
750,000 [FV] [CPT] [PMT]	FV = 750,000.0000 PMT = −54.3955	The value we want to achieve Monthly contribution required to achieve our ultimate goal (shown as negative since it represents cash paid out)

VIII. Calculating the Interest Rate

Example: If you invest $300 at the end of each month for six years (72 months) for a promised $30,000 return at the end, what interest rate are you earning on your investment?

Keystrokes	Display	Explanation
2nd		
BGN	BGN	Sets timing of payments to beginning of each period
2nd		
SET	END	Sets timing of payments to end of each period
2nd		
P/Y	P/Y = 12.0000	
12 [ENTER]	P/Y = 12.0000	Sets 12 payments per year
[CE/C] [CE/C]	0.0000	Clears display
2nd		
CLR TVM	0.0000	Clears TVM variables
72 [N]	N = 72.0000	Stores N, the number of deposits (investments)
300 [+ / −]		Stores PMT, the monthly amount invested
[PMT]	PMT = −300.0000	(with a minus sign for cash paid out)
30,000 [FV]	FV = 30,000.0000	Stores the future value to be received in 6 years
[CPT] [I/Y]	I/Y = 10.5892	The annual interest rate earned on the investment

IX. Bond Value

A. Computing the value of a bond

Example: Assume the current date is January 1, 1993, and that you want to know the value of a bond that matures in 10 years and has a coupon rate of 9 percent (4.5% semiannually). Your required rate of return is 12 percent.

Keystrokes	Display	Explanation
2nd		
BGN	END	Verifies timing of payments to end of each period
2nd		
P/Y	P/Y = 12.0000	
2 [ENTER]	P/Y = 2.0000	Sets 2 payments per year; end mode (END) assumes cash flows are at the end of each 6-month period
[CE/C] [CE/C]	0.0000	Clears display
2nd		
CLR TVM	0.0000	Clears TVM variables

IX. Bond Value (continued)

Keystrokes	Display	Explanation
20 N	N = 20.0000	Stores the number of semiannual periods (10 years × 2)
12 I/Y	I/Y = 12.0000	Stores annual rate of return
45 PMT	PMT = 45.0000	Stores the semiannual interest payment
1,000 FV	FV = 1,000.0000	Stores the bond's maturity or par value
CPT PV	PV = −827.9512	Value of the bond, expressed as a negative number

Solution Using the Bond Feature:

Keystrokes	Display	Explanation
CE/C CE/C	0.0000	Clears display
2nd		
BOND	STD = 1-01-1970	(This will be the last date entered)
2nd		
CLR WORK	STD = 1-01-1970	Clears BOND variables
1.01.93 ENTER	STD = 1-01-1993	Stores the current date (month, day, year)
↓	CPN = 0.0000	
9 ENTER	CPN = 9.0000	Stores the coupon interest rate
↓	RDT = 12-31-1990	(This will be the last date entered)
1.01.03 ENTER	RDT = 1-01-2003	Stores the maturity date in 10 years
↓	RV = 100.0000	Verifies bonds maturity or par value
↓	ACT	
2nd		
SET	360	Sets calculations to be based on 360-day year
↓	2/Y	Verifies semiannual compounding rate
↓	YLD = 0.0000	
12 ENTER	YLD = 12.0000	Stores the investor's required rate of return
↓	PRI = 0.0000	
CPT	PRI = 82.7951	Value of bond as a % of par value; i.e., value of bond is $827.95

IX. Bond Value (continued)

B. Computing the yield to maturity on a bond

Example: Assume the current date is January 1, 1994, and that you want to know your yield to maturity on a bond that matures in 8 years and has a coupon rate of 12% (6% semiannually). The bond is selling for $1,100.

Keystrokes	Display	Explanation
2nd		
BGN	END	Verifies timing of payments to end of each period
2nd		
P/Y	P/Y = 12.0000	
2 [ENTER]	P/Y = 2.0000	Sets 2 payments per year; end mode (END) assumes cash flows are at the end of each 6-month period
[CE/C] [CE/C]	0.0000	Clears display
2nd		
CLR TVM	0.0000	Clears TVM variables
16 [N]	N = 16.0000	Stores the number of semiannual periods (8 years × 2)
1100 [+/−]		Value of the bond, expressed as a negative number
PV	PV = −1,100.0000	
60 [PMT]	PMT = 60.0000	Stores the semiannual interest payments
1,000 [FV]	FV = 1,000.0000	Stores the bond's maturity or par value
[CPT] [I/Y]	I/Y = 10.1451	The yield to maturity, expressed on an annual basis

Solution Using the Bond Feature:

Keystrokes	Display	Explanation
[CE/C] [CE/C]	0.0000	Clears display
2nd		
Bond	STD = 1-01-1993	(This will be the last date entered)
2nd		
CLR WORK	STD = 1-01-1993	Clears BOND variables
1.03.94 [ENTER]	STD = 1-03-1994	Stores the current date (month, day, year)
↓	CPN = 0.0000	
12 [ENTER]	CPN = 12.0000	Stores the coupon interest rate
↓	RDT = 1-01-2003	(This will be the last date entered)
1.03.02 [ENTER]	RDT = 1-03-2002	Stores the maturity date in 8 years

Solution using the bond feature: (continued)

Keystrokes	Display	Explanation
↓	RV = 100.0000	Verifies bonds maturity or par value
↓	ACT	
2nd		
SET	360	Sets calculations to be based on 360-day year
↓	2/Y	Verifies semiannual compounding rate
↓	YLD = 0.0000	
↓	PRI = 0.0000	
110 [ENTER]	PRI = 110.0000	Stores the bond value as a percentage of par value
↑	YLD = 0.0000	
[CPT]	YLD = 10.1451	Bond's yield to maturity

X. Computing the Net Present Value and Internal Rate of Return

A. Where future cash flows are equal amounts in each period (annuity)

Example: The firm is considering a capital project that would cost $80,000. The firm's cost of capital is 12 percent. The project life is 10 years, during which time the firm expects to receive $15,000 per year. Calculate the NPV and the IRR.

Keystrokes	Display	Explanation
2nd		
BGN	END	Verifies timing of payments to end of each period
2nd		
P/Y	P/Y = 12.0000	
1 [ENTER]	P/Y = 1.0000	Sets 1 payment per year; end mode (END) assumes cash flows are at the end of each year
[CE/C] [CE/C]	0.0000	Clears display
2nd		
CLR TVM	0.0000	Clears TVM variables
15,000 [PMT]	PMT = 15.0000	Stores the annual cash flows of $15,000
10 [N]	N = 10.0000	Stores the life of the project
12 [I/Y]	I/Y = 12.0000	Stores the cost of capital
[CPT] [PV]	PV = −84,753.3454	Calculates present value
[+/−]	PV = 84,753.3454	Changes PV to positive

X. Computing the Net Present Value and Internal Rate of Return (continued)

–80,000 =	4,753.3454	Calculates net present value by subtracting the cost of the project
80,000 [+/–]	–80,000.0000	
[PV]	PV = –80,000.0000	
[CPT] [I/Y]	I/Y = 13.4344	Calculates the IRR

B. Where future cash flows are unequal amounts in each period

Example: The firm is considering a capital project that would cost $110,000. The firm's cost of capital is 15 percent. The project life is 5 years, with the following expected cash flows: $–25,000, $50,000, $60,000, $60,000, and $70,000. In addition, you expect to receive $30,000 in the last year from the salvage value of the equipment.

Keystrokes	Display	Explanation
[CE/C] [CE/C]	0.0000	Clears display
[CF]	CF_0 = 0.0000	
2nd		
CLR WORK	CF_0 = 0.0000	Clears cash flow variables
110,000 [+/–] [ENTER]	CF_0 = –110,000.0000	Stores CF_0, the initial investment (with a minus sign for a negative cash flow)
↓	C01 = 0.0000	Stores CF_1, the first year's cash flow (with a minus sign for a negative cash flow)
25,000 [+/–] [ENTER]	C01 = –25,000.0000	
↓ [ENTER]	F01 = 1.0000	Stores the number of years CF_1 is repeated (in this case, one year only)
↓	C02 = 0.0000	
50,000 [ENTER]	C02 = 50,000.0000	Stores CF_2
↓	$F0_2$ = 1.0000	
[ENTER]	F02 = 1.0000	Stores the number of years CF_2 is repeated
↓	C03 = 0.0000	
60,000 [ENTER]	C03 = 60,000.0000	Stores CF_3
↓ 2 [ENTER]	F03 = 2.0000	Stores the number of years CF_3 is repeated (here, two years, so our response is 2 to the $F0_3$ prompt)
↓	C04 = 0.0000	
100,000 [ENTER]	C04 = 100,000.000	Stores CF_4, $70,000 plus expected $30,000

X. Computing the Net Present Value and Internal Rate of Return (continued)

↓ [ENTER]	F04 = 1.0000	Stores the number CF_4 is repeated
2nd QUIT	0.0000	Ends storage of individual cash flows
[NPV]	I = 0.0000	
15 [ENTER]	I = 15.0000	Stores interest rate
↓	NPV = 0.0000	
[CPT]	NPV = 29,541.8951	Calculates the project's NPV at the stated interest rate
[IRR]	IRR = 0.0000	
[CPT]	IRR = 22.0633	Calculates the project's IRR

APPENDIX B

Compound Sum of $1

n	1%	2%	3%	4%	5%	6%	7%	8%	9%	10%
1	1.010	1.020	1.030	1.040	1.050	1.060	1.070	1.080	1.090	1.100
2	1.020	1.040	1.061	1.082	1.102	1.124	1.145	1.166	1.188	1.210
3	1.030	1.061	1.093	1.125	1.158	1.191	1.225	1.260	1.295	1.331
4	1.041	1.082	1.126	1.170	1.216	1.262	1.311	1.360	1.412	1.464
5	1.051	1.104	1.159	1.217	1.276	1.338	1.403	1.469	1.539	1.611
6	1.062	1.126	1.194	1.265	1.340	1.419	1.501	1.587	1.677	1.772
7	1.072	1.149	1.230	1.316	1.407	1.504	1.606	1.714	1.828	1.949
8	1.083	1.172	1.267	1.369	1.477	1.594	1.718	1.851	1.993	2.144
9	1.094	1.195	1.305	1.423	1.551	1.689	1.838	1.999	2.172	2.358
10	1.105	1.219	1.344	1.480	1.629	1.791	1.967	2.159	2.367	2.594
11	1.116	1.243	1.384	1.539	1.710	1.898	2.105	2.332	2.580	2.853
12	1.127	1.268	1.426	1.601	1.796	2.012	2.252	2.518	2.813	3.138
13	1.138	1.294	1.469	1.665	1.886	2.133	2.410	2.720	3.066	3.452
14	1.149	1.319	1.513	1.732	1.980	2.261	2.579	2.937	3.342	3.797
15	1.161	1.346	1.558	1.801	2.079	2.397	2.759	3.172	3.642	4.177
16	1.173	1.373	1.605	1.873	2.183	2.540	2.952	3.426	3.970	4.595
17	1.184	1.400	1.653	1.948	2.292	2.693	3.159	3.700	4.328	5.054
18	1.196	1.428	1.702	2.026	2.407	2.854	3.380	3.996	4.717	5.560
19	1.208	1.457	1.753	2.107	2.527	3.026	3.616	4.316	5.142	6.116
20	1.220	1.486	1.806	2.191	2.653	3.207	3.870	4.661	5.604	6.727
21	1.232	1.516	1.860	2.279	2.786	3.399	4.140	5.034	6.109	7.400
22	1.245	1.546	1.916	2.370	2.925	3.603	4.430	5.436	6.658	8.140
23	1.257	1.577	1.974	2.465	3.071	3.820	4.740	5.871	7.258	8.954
24	1.270	1.608	2.033	2.563	3.225	4.049	5.072	6.341	7.911	9.850
25	1.282	1.641	2.094	2.666	3.386	4.292	5.427	6.848	8.623	10.834
30	1.348	1.811	2.427	3.243	4.322	5.743	7.612	10.062	13.267	17.449
40	1.489	2.208	3.262	4.801	7.040	10.285	14.974	21.724	31.408	45.258
50	1.645	2.691	4.384	7.106	11.467	18.419	29.456	46.900	74.354	117.386

n	11%	12%	13%	14%	15%	16%	17%	18%	19%	20%
1	1.110	1.120	1.130	1.140	1.150	1.160	1.170	1.180	1.190	1.200
2	1.232	1.254	1.277	1.300	1.322	1.346	1.369	1.392	1.416	1.440
3	1.368	1.405	1.443	1.482	1.521	1.561	1.602	1.643	1.685	1.728
4	1.518	1.574	1.630	1.689	1.749	1.811	1.874	1.939	2.005	2.074
5	1.685	1.762	1.842	1.925	2.011	2.100	2.192	2.288	2.386	2.488
6	1.870	1.974	2.082	2.195	2.313	2.436	2.565	2.700	2.840	2.986
7	2.076	2.211	2.353	2.502	2.660	2.826	3.001	3.185	3.379	3.583
8	2.305	2.476	2.658	2.853	3.059	3.278	3.511	3.759	4.021	4.300
9	2.558	2.773	3.004	3.252	3.518	3.803	4.108	4.435	4.785	5.160
10	2.839	3.106	3.395	3.707	4.046	4.411	4.807	5.234	5.695	6.192
11	3.152	3.479	3.836	4.226	4.652	5.117	5.624	6.176	6.777	7.430
12	3.498	3.896	4.334	4.818	5.350	5.936	6.580	7.288	8.064	8.916
13	3.883	4.363	4.898	5.492	6.153	6.886	7.699	8.599	9.596	10.699
14	4.310	4.887	5.535	6.261	7.076	7.987	9.007	10.147	11.420	12.839
15	4.785	5.474	6.254	7.138	8.137	9.265	10.539	11.974	13.589	15.407
16	5.311	6.130	7.067	8.137	9.358	10.748	12.330	14.129	16.171	18.488
17	5.895	6.866	7.986	9.276	10.761	12.468	14.426	16.672	19.244	22.186
18	6.543	7.690	9.024	10.575	12.375	14.462	16.879	19.673	22.900	26.623
19	7.263	8.613	10.197	12.055	14.232	16.776	19.748	23.214	27.251	31.948
20	8.062	9.646	11.523	13.743	16.366	19.461	23.105	27.393	32.429	38.337
21	8.949	10.804	13.021	15.667	18.821	22.574	27.033	32.323	38.591	46.005
22	9.933	12.100	14.713	17.861	21.644	26.186	31.629	38.141	45.923	55.205
23	11.026	13.552	16.626	20.361	24.891	30.376	37.005	45.007	54.648	66.247
24	12.239	15.178	18.788	23.212	28.625	35.236	43.296	53.108	65.031	79.496
25	13.585	17.000	21.230	26.461	32.918	40.874	50.656	62.667	77.387	95.395
30	22.892	29.960	39.115	50.949	66.210	85.849	111.061	143.367	184.672	237.373
40	64.999	93.049	132.776	188.876	267.856	378.715	533.846	750.353	1051.642	1469.740
50	184.559	288.996	450.711	700.197	1083.619	1670.669	2566.080	3927.189	5988.730	9100.191

n	21%	22%	23%	24%	25%	26%	27%	28%	29%	30%
1	1.210	1.220	1.230	1.240	1.250	1.260	1.270	1.280	1.290	1.300
2	1.464	1.488	1.513	1.538	1.562	1.588	1.613	1.638	1.664	1.690
3	1.772	1.816	1.861	1.907	1.953	2.000	2.048	2.097	2.147	2.197
4	2.144	2.215	2.289	2.364	2.441	2.520	2.601	2.684	2.769	2.856
5	2.594	2.703	2.815	2.932	3.052	3.176	3.304	3.436	3.572	3.713
6	3.138	3.297	3.463	3.635	3.815	4.001	4.196	4.398	4.608	4.827
7	3.797	4.023	4.259	4.508	4.768	5.042	5.329	5.629	5.945	6.275
8	4.595	4.908	5.239	5.589	5.960	6.353	6.767	7.206	7.669	8.157
9	5.560	5.987	6.444	6.931	7.451	8.004	8.595	9.223	9.893	10.604
10	6.727	7.305	7.926	8.594	9.313	10.086	10.915	11.806	12.761	13.786
11	8.140	8.912	9.749	10.657	11.642	12.708	13.862	15.112	16.462	17.921
12	9.850	10.872	11.991	13.215	14.552	16.012	17.605	19.343	21.236	23.298
13	11.918	13.264	14.749	16.386	18.190	20.175	22.359	24.759	27.395	30.287
14	14.421	16.182	18.141	20.319	22.737	25.420	28.395	31.691	35.339	39.373
15	17.449	19.742	22.314	25.195	28.422	32.030	36.062	40.565	45.587	51.185
16	21.113	24.085	27.446	31.242	35.527	40.357	45.799	51.923	58.808	66.541
17	25.547	29.384	33.758	38.740	44.409	50.850	58.165	66.461	75.862	86.503
18	30.912	35.848	41.523	48.038	55.511	64.071	73.869	85.070	97.862	112.454
19	37.404	43.735	51.073	59.567	69.389	80.730	93.813	108.890	126.242	146.190
20	45.258	53.357	62.820	73.863	86.736	101.720	119.143	139.379	162.852	190.047
21	54.762	65.095	77.268	91.591	108.420	128.167	151.312	178.405	210.079	247.061
22	66.262	79.416	95.040	113.572	135.525	161.490	192.165	228.358	271.002	321.178
23	80.178	96.887	116.899	140.829	169.407	203.477	244.050	292.298	349.592	417.531

24	97.015	118.203	143.786	174.628	211.758	256.381	309.943	374.141	450.974	542.791
25	117.388	144.207	176.857	216.539	264.698	323.040	393.628	478.901	581.756	705.627
30	304.471	389.748	497.904	634.810	807.793	1025.904	1300.477	1645.488	2078.208	2619.936
40	2048.309	2846.941	3946.340	5455.797	7523.156	10346.879	14195.051	19426.418	26520.723	36117.754
50	13779.844	20795.680	31278.301	46889.207	70064.812	104354.562	154942.687	229345.875	338440.000	497910.125

n	**31%**	**32%**	**33%**	**34%**	**35%**	**36%**	**37%**	**38%**	**39%**	**40%**
1	1.310	1.320	1.330	1.340	1.350	1.360	1.370	1.380	1.390	1.400
2	1.716	1.742	1.769	1.796	1.822	1.850	1.877	1.904	1.932	1.960
3	2.248	2.300	2.353	2.406	2.460	2.515	2.571	2.628	2.686	2.744
4	2.945	3.036	3.129	3.224	3.321	3.421	3.523	3.627	3.733	3.842
5	3.858	4.007	4.162	4.320	4.484	4.653	4.826	5.005	5.189	5.378
6	5.054	5.290	5.535	5.789	6.053	6.328	6.612	6.907	7.213	7.530
7	6.621	6.983	7.361	7.758	8.172	8.605	9.058	9.531	10.025	10.541
8	8.673	9.217	9.791	10.395	11.032	11.703	12.410	13.153	13.935	14.758
9	11.362	12.166	13.022	13.930	14.894	15.917	17.001	18.151	19.370	20.661
10	14.884	16.060	17.319	18.666	20.106	21.646	23.292	25.049	26.924	28.925
11	19.498	21.199	23.034	25.012	27.144	29.439	31.910	34.567	37.425	40.495
12	25.542	27.982	30.635	33.516	36.644	40.037	43.716	47.703	52.020	56.694
13	33.460	36.937	40.745	44.912	49.469	54.451	59.892	65.830	72.308	79.371
14	43.832	49.756	54.190	60.181	66.784	74.053	82.051	90.845	100.509	111.120
15	57.420	64.358	72.073	80.643	90.158	100.712	112.410	125.366	139.707	155.567
16	75.220	84.953	95.857	108.061	121.713	136.968	154.002	173.005	194.192	217.793
17	98.539	112.138	127.490	144.802	164.312	186.277	210.983	238.747	269.927	304.911
18	129.086	148.022	169.561	194.035	221.822	253.337	289.046	329.471	375.198	426.875
19	169.102	195.389	225.517	260.006	299.459	344.537	395.993	454.669	521.525	597.625
20	221.523	257.913	299.937	348.408	404.270	468.571	542.511	627.443	724.919	836.674
21	290.196	340.446	398.916	466.867	545.764	637.256	743.240	865.871	1007.637	1171.343
22	380.156	449.388	530.558	625.601	736.781	865.668	1018.238	1194.900	1400.615	1639.878
23	498.004	593.192	705.642	838.305	994.653	1178.668	1394.986	1648.961	1946.854	2295.829
24	652.385	783.013	938.504	1123.328	1342.781	1602.988	1911.129	2275.564	2706.125	3214.158
25	854.623	1033.577	1248.210	1505.258	1812.754	2180.063	2618.245	3140.275	3761.511	4499.816
30	3297.081	4142.008	5194.516	6503.285	8128.426	10142.914	12636.086	15716.703	19517.969	24201.043
40	49072.621	66519.313	89962.188	121388.437	163433.875	219558.625	294317.937	393684.687	525508.312	700022.688

APPENDIX C

Present Value of $1

n	1%	2%	3%	4%	5%	6%	7%	8%	9%	10%
1	.990	.980	.971	.962	.952	.943	.935	.926	.917	.909
2	.980	.961	.943	.925	.907	.890	.873	.857	.842	.826
3	.971	.942	.915	.889	.864	.840	.816	.794	.772	.751
4	.961	.924	.888	.855	.823	.792	.763	.735	.708	.683
5	.951	.906	.863	.822	.784	.747	.713	.681	.650	.621
6	.942	.888	.837	.790	.746	.705	.666	.630	.596	.564
7	.933	.871	.813	.760	.711	.665	.623	.583	.547	.513
8	.923	.853	.789	.731	.677	.627	.582	.540	.502	.467
9	.914	.837	.766	.703	.645	.592	.544	.500	.460	.424
10	.905	.820	.744	.676	.614	558	.508	.463	.422	.386
11	.896	.804	.722	.650	.585	.527	.475	.429	.388	.350
12	.887	.789	.701	.625	.557	.497	.444	.397	.356	.319
13	.879	.773	.681	.601	.530	.469	.415	.368	.326	.290
14	.870	.758	.661	.577	.505	.442	.388	.340	.299	.263
15	.861	.743	.642	.555	.481	.417	.362	.315	.275	.239
16	.853	.728	.623	.534	.458	.394	.339	.292	.252	.218
17	.844	.714	.605	.513	.436	.371	.317	.270	.231	.198
18	.836	.700	.587	.494	.416	.350	.296	.250	.212	.180
19	.828	.686	.570	.475	.396	.331	.277	.232	.194	.164
20	.820	.673	.554	.456	.377	.312	.258	.215	.178	.149
21	.811	.660	.538	.439	.359	.294	.242	.199	.164	.135
22	.803	.647	.522	.422	.342	.278	.226	.184	.150	.123
23	.795	.634	.507	.406	.326	.262	.211	.170	.138	.112
24	.788	.622	.492	.390	.310	.247	.197	.158	.126	.102
25	.780	.610	.478	.375	.295	.233	.184	.146	.116	.092
30	.742	.552	.412	.308	.231	.174	.131	.099	.075	.057
40	.672	.453	.307	.208	.142	.097	.067	.046	.032	.022
50	.608	.372	.228	.141	.087	.054	.034	.021	.013	.009

n	11%	12%	13%	14%	15%	16%	17%	18%	19%	20%
1	.901	.893	.885	.877	.870	.862	.855	.847	.840	.833
2	.812	.797	.783	.769	.756	.743	.713	.718	.706	.694
3	.731	.712	.693	.675	.658	.641	.624	.609	.593	.579
4	.659	.636	.613	.592	.572	.552	.534	.516	.499	.482
5	.593	.567	.543	.519	.497	.476	.456	.437	.419	.402
6	.535	.507	.480	.456	.432	.410	.390	.370	.352	.335
7	.482	.452	.425	.400	.376	.354	.333	.314	.296	.279
8	.434	.404	.376	.351	.327	.305	.285	.266	.249	.233
9	.391	.361	.333	.308	.284	.263	.243	.225	.209	.194
10	.352	.322	.295	.270	.247	.227	.208	.191	.176	.162
11	.317	.287	.261	.237	.215	.195	.178	.162	.148	.135
12	.286	.257	.231	.208	.187	.168	.152	.137	.124	.112
13	.258	.229	.204	.182	.163	.145	.130	.116	.104	.093
14	.232	.205	.181	.160	.141	.125	.111	.099	.088	.078
15	.209	.183	.160	.140	.123	.108	.095	.084	.074	.065
16	.188	.163	.141	.123	.107	.093	.081	.071	.062	.054
17	.170	.146	.125	.108	.093	.080	.069	.060	.052	.045
18	.153	.130	.111	.095	.081	.069	.059	.051	.044	.038
19	.138	.116	.098	.083	.070	.060	.051	.043	.037	.031
20	.124	.104	.087	.073	.061	.051	.043	.037	.031	.026
21	.112	.093	.077	.064	.053	.044	.037	.031	.026	.022
22	.101	.083	.068	.056	.046	.038	.032	.026	.022	.018
23	.091	.074	.060	.049	.040	.033	.027	.022	.018	.015
24	.082	.066	.053	.043	.035	.028	.023	.019	.015	.013
25	.074	.059	.047	.038	.030	.024	.020	.016	.013	.010
30	.044	.033	.026	.020	.015	.012	.009	.007	.005	.004
40	.015	.011	.008	.005	.004	.003	.002	.001	.001	.001
50	.005	.003	.002	.001	.001	.001	.000	.000	.000	.000

n	21%	22%	23%	24%	25%	26%	27%	28%	29%	30%
1	.826	.820	.813	.806	.800	.794	.787	.781	.775	.769
2	.683	.672	.661	.650	.640	.630	.620	.610	.601	.592
3	.564	.551	.537	.524	.512	.500	.488	.477	.466	.455
4	.467	.451	.437	.423	.410	.397	.384	.373	.361	.350
5	.386	.370	.355	.341	.328	.315	.303	.291	.280	.269
6	.319	.303	.289	.275	.262	.250	.238	.227	.217	.207
7	.263	.249	.235	.222	.210	.198	.188	.178	.168	.159
8	.218	.204	.191	.179	.168	.157	.148	.139	.130	.123
9	.180	.167	.155	.144	.134	.125	.116	.108	.101	.094
10	.149	.137	.126	.116	.107	.099	.092	.085	.078	.073
11	.123	.112	.103	.094	.086	.079	.072	.066	.061	.056
12	.102	.092	.083	.076	.069	.062	.057	.052	.047	.043
13	.084	.075	.068	.061	.055	.050	.045	.040	.037	.033
14	.069	.062	.055	.049	.044	.039	.035	.032	.028	.025
15	.057	.051	.045	.040	.035	.031	.028	.025	.022	.020
16	.047	.042	.036	.032	.028	.025	.022	.019	.017	.015
17	.039	.034	.030	.026	.023	.020	.017	.015	.013	.012
18	.032	.028	.024	.021	.018	.016	.014	.012	.010	.009
19	.027	.023	.020	.017	.014	.012	.011	.009	.008	.007
20	.022	.019	.016	.014	.012	.010	.008	.007	.006	.005
21	.018	.015	.013	.011	.009	.008	.007	.006	.005	.004
22	.015	.013	.011	.009	.007	.006	.005	.004	.004	.003
23	.012	.010	.009	.007	.006	.005	.004	.003	.003	.002

24	.010	.008	.007	.006	.005	.004	.003	.003	.002	.002
25	.009	.007	.006	.005	.004	.003	.003	.002	.002	.001
30	.003	.003	.002	.002	.001	.001	.001	.001	.000	.000
40	.000	.000	.000	.000	.000	.000	.000	.000	.000	.000
50	.000	.000	.000	.000	.000	.000	.000	.000	.000	.000

n	**31%**	**32%**	**33%**	**34%**	**35%**	**36%**	**37%**	**38%**	**39%**	**40%**
1	.763	.758	.752	.746	.741	.735	.730	.725	.719	.714
2	.583	.574	.565	.557	.549	.541	.533	.525	.518	.510
3	.445	.435	.425	.416	.406	.398	.389	.381	.372	.364
4	.340	.329	.320	.310	.301	.292	.284	.276	.268	.260
5	.259	.250	.240	.231	.223	.215	.207	.200	.193	.186
6	.198	.189	.181	.173	.165	.158	.151	.145	.139	.133
7	.151	.143	.136	.129	.122	.116	.110	.105	.100	.095
8	.115	.108	.102	.096	.091	.085	.081	.076	.072	.068
9	.088	.082	.077	.072	.067	.063	.059	.055	.052	.048
10	.067	.062	.058	.054	.050	.046	.043	.040	.037	.035
11	.051	.047	.043	.040	.037	.034	.031	.029	.027	.025
12	.039	.036	.033	.030	.027	.025	.023	.021	.019	.018
13	.030	.027	.025	.022	.020	.018	.017	.015	.014	.013
14	.023	.021	.018	.017	.015	.014	.012	.011	.010	.009
15	.017	.016	.014	.012	.011	.010	.009	.008	.007	.006
16	.013	.012	.010	.009	.008	.007	.006	.006	.005	.005
17	.010	.009	.008	.007	.006	.005	.005	.004	.004	.003
18	.008	.007	.006	.005	.005	.004	.003	.003	.003	.002
19	.006	.005	.004	.004	.003	.003	.003	.002	.002	.002
20	.005	.004	.003	.003	.002	.002	.002	.002	.001	.001
21	.003	.003	.003	.002	.002	.002	.001	.001	.001	.001
22	.003	.002	.002	.002	.001	.001	.001	.001	.001	.001
23	.002	.002	.001	.001	.001	.001	.001	.001	.001	.000
24	.002	.001	.001	.001	.001	.001	.001	.000	.000	.000
25	.001	.001	.001	.001	.001	.000	.000	.000	.000	.000
30	.000	.000	.000	.000	.000	.000	.000	.000	.000	.000
40	.000	.000	.000	.000	.000	.000	.000	.000	.000	.000

APPENDIX D

Sum of an Annuity of $1 for *n* Periods

n	1%	2%	3%	4%	5%	6%	7%	8%	9%	10%
1	1.000	1.000	1.000	1.000	1.000	1.000	1.000	1.000	1.000	1.000
2	2.020	2.020	2.030	2.040	2.050	2.060	2.070	2.080	2.090	2.100
3	3.030	3.060	3.091	3.122	3.152	3.184	3.215	3.246	3.278	3.310
4	4.060	4.122	4.184	4.246	4.310	4.375	4.440	4.506	4.573	4.641
5	5.101	5.204	5.309	5.416	5.526	5.637	5.751	5.867	5.985	6.105
6	6.152	6.308	6.468	6.633	6.802	6.975	7.153	7.336	7.523	7.716
7	7.214	7.434	7.662	7.898	8.142	8.394	8.654	8.923	9.200	9.487
8	8.286	8.583	8.892	9.214	9.549	9.897	10.260	10.637	11.028	11.436
9	9.368	9.755	10.159	10.583	11.027	11.491	11.978	12.488	13.021	13.579
10	10.462	10.950	11.464	12.006	12.578	13.181	13.816	14.487	15.193	15.937
11	11.567	12.169	12.808	13.486	14.207	14.972	15.784	16.645	17.560	18.531
12	12.682	13.412	14.192	15.026	15.917	16.870	17.888	18.977	20.141	21.384
13	13.809	14.680	15.618	16.627	17.713	18.882	20.141	21.495	22.953	24.523
14	14.947	15.974	17.086	18.292	19.598	21.015	22.550	24.215	26.019	27.975
15	16.097	17.293	18.599	20.023	21.578	23.276	25.129	27.152	29.361	31.772
16	17.258	18.639	20.157	21.824	23.657	25.672	27.888	30.324	33.003	35.949
17	18.430	20.012	21.761	23.697	25.840	28.213	30.840	33.750	36.973	40.544
18	19.614	21.412	23.414	25.645	28.132	30.905	33.999	37.450	41.301	45.599
19	20.811	22.840	25.117	27.671	30.539	33.760	37.379	41.446	46.018	51.158
20	22.019	24.297	26.870	29.778	33.066	36.785	40.995	45.762	51.159	57.274
21	23.239	25.783	28.676	31.969	35.719	39.992	44.865	50.422	56.764	64.002
22	24.471	27.299	30.536	34.248	38.505	43.392	49.005	55.456	62.872	71.402
23	25.716	28.845	32.452	36.618	41.430	46.995	53.435	60.893	69.531	79.542
24	26.973	30.421	34.426	39.082	44.501	50.815	58.176	66.764	76.789	88.496
25	28.243	32.030	36.459	41.645	47.726	54.864	63.248	73.105	84.699	98.346
30	34.784	40.567	47.575	56.084	66.438	79.057	94.459	113.282	136.305	164.491
40	48.885	60.401	75.400	95.024	120.797	154.758	199.630	295.052	337.872	442.580
50	64.461	84.577	112.794	152.664	209.341	290.325	406.516	573.756	815.051	1163.865

n	11%	12%	13%	14%	15%	16%	17%	18%	19%	20%
1	1.000	1.000	1.000	1.000	1.000	1.000	1.000	1.000	1.000	1.000
2	2.110	2.120	2.130	2.140	2.150	2.160	2.170	2.180	2.190	2.200
3	3.342	3.374	3.407	3.440	3.472	3.506	3.539	3.572	3.606	3.640
4	4.710	4.779	4.850	4.921	4.993	5.066	5.141	5.215	5.291	5.368
5	6.228	6.353	6.480	6.610	6.742	6.877	7.014	7.154	7.297	7.442
6	7.913	8.115	8.323	8.535	8.754	8.977	9.207	9.442	9.683	9.930
7	9.783	10.089	10.405	10.730	11.067	11.414	11.772	12.141	12.523	12.916
8	11.859	12.300	12.757	13.233	13.727	14.240	14.773	15.327	15.902	16.499
9	14.164	14.776	15.416	16.085	16.786	17.518	18.285	19.086	19.923	20.799
10	16.722	17.549	18.420	19.337	20.304	21.321	22.393	23.521	24.709	25.959
11	19.561	20.655	21.814	23.044	24.349	25.733	27.200	28.755	30.403	32.150
12	22.713	24.133	26.650	27.271	29.001	30.850	32.824	34.931	37.180	39.580
13	26.211	28.029	29.984	32.088	34.352	36.786	39.404	42.218	45.244	48.496
14	30.095	32.392	34.882	37.581	40.504	43.672	47.102	50.818	54.841	59.196
15	34.405	37.280	40.417	43.842	47.580	51.659	56.109	60.965	66.260	72.035
16	39.190	42.753	46.671	50.980	55.717	60.925	66.648	72.938	79.850	87.442
17	44.500	48.883	53.738	59.117	65.075	71.673	78.978	87.067	96.021	105.930
18	50.396	55.749	61.724	68.393	75.836	84.140	93.404	103.739	115.265	128.116
19	56.939	63.439	70.748	78.968	88.211	98.603	110.283	123.412	138.165	154.739
20	64.202	72.052	80.946	91.024	102.443	115.379	130.031	146.626	165.417	186.687
21	72.264	81.698	92.468	104.767	118.809	134.840	153.136	174.019	197.846	225.024
22	81.213	92.502	105.489	120.434	137.630	157.414	180.169	206.342	236.436	271.028
23	91.147	104.602	120.203	138.295	159.274	183.600	211.798	244.483	282.359	326.234
24	102.173	118.154	136.829	158.656	184.166	213.976	248.803	289.490	337.007	392.480
25	114.412	133.333	155.616	181.867	212.790	249.212	292.099	342.598	402.038	471.976
30	199.018	241.330	293.192	356.778	434.738	530.306	647.423	790.932	966.698	1181.865
40	581.812	767.080	1013.667	1341.979	1779.048	2360.724	3134.412	4163.094	5529.711	7343.715
50	1668.723	2399.975	3459.344	4994.301	7217.488	10435.449	15088.805	21812.273	31514.492	45496.094

n	21%	22%	23%	24%	25%	26%	27%	28%	29%	30%
1	1.000	1.000	1.000	1.000	1.000	1.000	1.000	1.000	1.000	1.000
2	2.210	2.220	2.230	2.240	2.250	2.260	2.270	2.280	2.290	2.300
3	3.674	3.708	3.743	3.778	3.813	3.848	3.883	3.918	3.954	3.990
4	5.446	5.524	5.604	5.684	5.766	5.848	5.931	6.016	6.101	6.187
5	7.589	7.740	7.893	8.048	8.207	8.368	8.533	8.700	8.970	9.043
6	10.183	10.442	10.708	10.980	11.259	11.544	11.837	12.136	12.442	12.756
7	13.321	13.740	14.171	14.615	15.073	15.546	16.032	16.534	17.051	17.583
8	17.119	17.762	18.430	19.123	19.842	20.588	21.361	22.163	22.995	23.858
9	21.714	22.670	23.669	24.712	25.802	26.940	28.129	29.369	30.664	32.015
10	27.274	28.657	20.113	31.643	33.253	34.945	36.723	38.592	40.556	42.619
11	34.001	35.962	38.039	40.238	42.566	45.030	47.639	50.398	53.318	56.405
12	42.141	44.873	47.787	50.895	54.208	57.738	61.501	65.510	69.780	74.326
13	51.991	55.745	59.778	64.109	68.760	73.750	79.106	84.853	91.016	97.624
14	63.909	69.009	74.528	80.496	86.949	93.925	101.465	109.611	118.411	127.912
15	78.330	85.191	92.669	100.815	109.687	119.346	129.860	141.302	153.750	167.285
16	95.779	104.933	114.983	126.010	138.109	151.375	165.922	181.867	199.337	218.470
17	116.892	129.019	142.428	157.252	173.636	191.733	211.721	233.790	258.145	285.011
18	142.439	158.403	176.187	195.993	218.045	242.583	269.885	300.250	334.006	371.514
19	173.351	194.251	217.710	244.031	273.556	306.654	343.754	385.321	431.868	483.968
20	210.755	237.986	268.783	303.598	342.945	387.384	437.568	494.210	558.110	630.157
21	256.013	291.343	331.603	377.461	429.681	489.104	556.710	633.589	720.962	820.204
22	310.775	356.438	408.871	469.052	538.101	617.270	708.022	811.993	931.040	1067.265
23	377.038	435.854	503.911	582.624	673.626	778.760	900.187	1040.351	1202.042	1388.443

n										
24	457.215	532.741	620.810	723.453	843.032	982.237	1144.237	1332.649	1551.634	1805.975
25	554.230	650.944	764.596	898.082	1054.791	1238.617	1454.180	1706.790	2002.608	2348.765
30	1445.111	1767.044	2160.459	2640.881	3227.172	3941.953	4812.891	5873.172	7162.785	8729.805
40	9749.141	12936.141	17153.691	22728.367	30088.621	39791.957	52570.707	69376.562	91447.375	120389.375

n	31%	32%	33%	34%	35%	36%	37%	38%	39%	40%
1	1.000	1.000	1.000	1.000	1.000	1.000	1.000	1.000	1.000	1.000
2	2.310	2.320	2.330	2.340	2.350	2.360	2.370	2.380	2.390	2.400
3	4.026	4.062	4.099	4.136	4.172	4.210	4.247	4.284	4.322	4.360
4	6.274	6.362	6.452	6.542	6.633	6.725	6.818	6.912	7.008	7.104
5	9.219	9.398	9.581	9.766	9.954	10.146	10.341	10.539	10.741	10.946
6	13.077	13.406	13.742	14.086	14.438	14.799	15.167	15.544	15.930	16.324
7	18.131	18.696	19.277	19.876	20.492	21.126	21.779	22.451	23.142	23.853
8	24.752	25.678	26.638	27.633	28.664	29.732	30.837	31.982	33.167	34.395
9	33.425	34.895	36.429	38.028	39.696	41.435	43.247	45.135	47.103	49.152
10	44.786	47.062	49.451	51.958	54.590	57.351	60.248	63.287	66.473	69.813
11	59.670	63.121	66.769	70.624	74.696	78.998	83.540	88.335	93.397	98.739
12	79.167	84.320	89.803	95.636	101.840	108.437	115.450	122.903	130.822	139.234
13	104.709	112.302	120.438	129.152	138.484	148.474	159.166	170.606	182.842	195.928
14	138.169	149.239	161.183	174.063	187.953	202.925	219.058	236.435	255.151	275.299
15	182.001	197.996	215.373	234.245	254.737	276.978	301.109	327.281	355.659	386.418
16	239.421	262.354	287.446	314.888	344.895	377.690	413.520	452.647	495.366	541.985
17	314.642	347.307	383.303	422.949	466.608	514.658	567.521	625.652	689.558	759.778
18	413.180	459.445	510.792	567.751	630.920	700.935	778.504	864.399	959.485	1064.689
19	542.266	607.467	680.354	761.786	852.741	954.271	1067.551	1193.870	1334.683	1491.563
20	711.368	802.856	905.870	1021.792	1152.200	1298.809	1463.544	1648.539	1856.208	2089.188
21	932.891	1060.769	1205.807	1370.201	1556.470	1767.380	2006.055	2275.982	2581.128	2925.862
22	1223.087	1401.215	1604.724	1837.068	2102.234	2404.636	2749.294	3141.852	3588.765	4097.203
23	1603.243	1850.603	2135.282	2462.669	2839.014	3271.304	3767.532	4336.750	4989.379	5737.078
24	2101.247	2443.795	2840.924	3300.974	3833.667	4449.969	5162.516	5985.711	6936.230	8032.906
25	2753.631	3226.808	3779.428	4424.301	5176.445	6052.957	7073.645	8261.273	9642.352	11247.062
30	10632.543	12940.672	15737.945	19124.434	23221.258	28172.016	34148.906	41357.227	50043.625	60500.207

APPENDIX E

Present Value of an Annuity of $1 for *n* Periods

n	1%	2%	3%	4%	5%	6%	7%	8%	9%	10%
1	990	.980	.971	.962	.952	.943	.935	.926	.917	.909
2	1.970	1.942	1.913	1.886	1.859	1.833	1.808	1.783	1.759	1.736
3	2.941	2.884	2.829	2.775	2.723	2.673	2.624	2.577	2.531	2.487
4	3.902	3.808	3.717	3.630	3.546	3.465	3.387	3.312	3.240	3.170
5	4.853	4.713	4.580	4.452	4.329	4.212	4.100	3.993	3.890	3.791
6	5.795	5.601	5.417	5.242	5.076	4.917	4.767	4.623	4.486	4.355
7	6.728	6.472	6.230	6.002	5.786	5.582	5.389	5.206	5.033	4.868
8	7.652	7.326	7.020	6.733	6.463	6.210	5.971	5.747	5.535	5.335
9	8.566	8.162	7.786	7.435	7.108	6.802	6.515	6.247	5.995	5.759
10	9.471	8.983	8.530	8.111	7.722	7.360	7.024	6.710	6.418	6.145
11	10.368	9.787	9.253	8.760	8.306	7.887	7.499	7.139	6.805	6.495
12	11.255	10.575	9.954	9.385	8.863	8.384	7.943	7.536	7.161	6.814
13	12.134	11.348	10.635	9.986	9.394	8.853	8.358	7.904	7.487	7.103
14	13.004	12.106	11.296	10.563	9.899	9.295	8.746	8.244	7.786	7.367
15	13.865	12.849	11.938	11.118	10.380	9.712	9.108	8.560	8.061	7.606
16	14.718	13.578	12.561	11.652	10.838	10.106	9.447	8.851	8.313	7.824
17	15.562	14.292	13.166	12.166	11.274	10.477	9.763	9.122	8.544	8.022
18	16.398	14.992	13.754	12.659	11.690	10.828	10.059	9.372	8.756	8.201
19	17.226	15.679	14.324	13.134	12.085	11.158	10.336	9.604	8.950	8.365
20	18.046	16.352	14.878	13.590	12.462	11.470	10.594	9.818	9.129	8.514
21	18.857	17.011	15.415	14.029	12.821	11.764	10.836	10.017	9.292	8.649
22	19.661	17.658	15.937	14.451	13.163	12.042	11.061	10.201	9.442	8.772
23	20.456	18.292	16.444	14.857	13.489	12.303	11.272	10.371	9.580	8.883
24	21.244	18.914	16.936	15.247	13.799	12.550	11.469	10.529	9.707	8.985
25	22.023	19.524	17.413	15.622	14.094	12.783	11.654	10.675	9.823	9.077
30	25.808	22.397	19.601	17.292	15.373	13.765	12.409	11.258	10.274	9.427
40	32.835	27.353	23.115	19.793	17.159	15.046	13.332	11.925	10.757	9.779
50	39.197	31.424	25.730	21.482	18.256	15.762	13.801	12.234	10.962	9.915

n	11%	12%	13%	14%	15%	16%	17%	18%	19%	20%
1	.901	.893	.885	.877	.870	.862	.855	.847	.840	.833
2	1.713	1.690	1.668	1.647	1.626	1.605	1.585	1.566	1.547	1.528
3	2.444	2.402	2.361	2.322	2.283	2.246	2.210	2.174	2.140	2.106
4	3.102	3.037	2.974	2.914	2.855	2.798	2.743	2.690	2.639	2.589
5	3.696	3.605	3.517	3.433	3.352	3.274	3.199	3.127	3.058	2.991
6	4.231	4.111	3.998	3.889	3.784	3.685	3.589	3.498	3.410	3.326
7	4.712	4.564	4.423	4.288	4.160	4.039	3.922	3.812	3.706	3.605
8	5.146	4.968	4.799	4.639	4.487	4.344	4.207	4.078	3.954	3.837
9	5.537	5.328	5.132	4.946	4.772	4.607	4.451	4.303	4.163	4.031
10	5.889	5.650	5.426	5.216	5.019	4.833	4.659	4.494	4.339	4.192
11	6.207	5.938	5.687	5.453	5.234	5.029	4.836	4.656	4.487	4.327
12	6.492	6.194	5.918	5.660	5.421	5.197	4.988	4.793	4.611	4.439
13	6.750	6.424	6.122	5.842	5.583	5.342	5.118	4.910	4.715	4.533
14	6.982	6.628	6.303	6.002	5.724	5.468	5.229	5.008	4.802	4.611
15	7.191	6.811	6.462	6.142	5.847	5.575	5.324	5.092	4.876	4.675
16	7.379	6.974	6.604	6.265	5.954	5.669	5.405	5.162	4.938	4.730
17	7.549	7.120	6.729	6.373	6.047	5.749	5.475	5.222	4.990	4.775
18	7.702	7.250	6.840	6.467	6.128	5.818	5.534	5.273	5.033	4.812
19	7.839	7.366	6.938	6.550	6.198	5.877	5.585	5.316	5.070	4.843
20	7.963	7.469	7.025	6.623	6.259	5.929	5.628	5.353	5.101	4.870
21	8.075	7.562	7.102	6.687	6.312	5.973	5.665	5.384	5.127	4.891
22	8.176	7.645	7.170	6.743	6.359	6.011	5.696	5.410	5.149	4.909
23	8.266	7.718	7.230	6.792	6.399	6.044	5.723	5.432	5.167	4.925
24	8.348	7.784	7.283	6.835	6.434	6.073	5.747	5.451	5.182	4.937
25	8.442	7.843	7.330	6.873	6.464	6.097	5.766	5.467	5.195	4.948
30	8.694	8.055	7.496	7.003	6.566	6.177	5.829	5.517	5.235	4.979
40	8.951	8.244	7.634	7.105	6.642	6.233	5.871	5.548	5.258	4.997
50	9.042	8.305	7.675	7.133	6.661	6.246	5.880	5.554	5.262	4.999

n	21%	22%	23%	24%	25%	26%	27%	28%	29%	30%
1	.826	.820	.813	.806	.800	.794	.787	.781	.775	.769
2	1.509	1.492	1.474	1.457	1.440	1.424	1.407	1.392	1.376	1.361
3	2.074	2.042	2.011	1.981	1.952	1.923	1.896	1.868	1.842	1.816
4	2.540	2.494	2.448	2.404	2.362	2.320	2.280	2.241	2.203	2.166
5	2.926	2.864	2.803	2.745	2.689	2.635	2.583	2.532	2.483	2.436
6	3.245	3.167	3.092	3.020	2.951	2.885	2.821	2.759	2.700	2.643
7	3.508	3.416	3.327	3.242	3.161	3.083	3.009	2.937	2.868	2.802
8	3.726	3.619	3.518	3.421	3.329	3.241	3.156	3.076	2.999	2.925
9	3.905	3.786	3.673	3.566	3.463	3.366	3.273	3.184	3.100	3.019
10	4.054	3.923	3.799	3.682	3.570	3.465	3.364	3.269	3.178	3.092
11	4.177	4.035	3.902	3.776	3.656	3.544	3.437	3.335	3.239	3.147
12	4.278	4.127	3.985	3.851	3.725	3.606	3.493	3.387	3.286	3.190
13	4.362	4.203	4.053	3.912	3.780	3.656	3.538	3.427	3.322	3.223
14	4.432	4.265	4.108	3.962	3.824	3.695	3.573	3.459	3.351	2.249
15	4.489	4.315	4.153	4.001	3.859	3.726	3.601	3.483	3.373	3.268
16	4.536	4.357	4.189	4.033	3.887	3.751	3.623	3.503	3.390	3.283
17	4.576	4.391	4.219	4.059	3.910	3.771	3.640	3.518	3.403	3.295
18	4.608	4.419	4.243	4.080	3.928	3.786	3.654	3.529	3.413	3.304
19	4.635	4.442	4.263	4.097	3.942	3.799	3.664	3.539	3.421	3.311
20	4.657	4.460	4.279	4.110	3.954	3.808	3.673	3.546	3.427	3.316
21	4.675	4.476	4.292	4.121	3.963	3.816	3.679	3.551	3.432	3.320
22	4.690	4.488	4.302	4.130	3.970	3.822	3.684	3.556	3.436	3.323
23	4.703	4.499	4.311	4.137	3.976	3.827	3.689	3.559	3.438	3.325

24	4.713	4.507	4.318	4.143	3.981	3.831	3.692	3.562	3.441	3.327
25	4.721	4.514	4.323	4.147	3.985	3.834	3.694	3.564	3.442	2.329
30	4.746	4.534	4.339	4.160	3.995	3.842	3.701	3.569	3.447	3.332
40	4.760	4.544	4.347	4.166	3.999	3.846	3.703	3.571	3.448	3.333
50	4.762	4.545	4.348	4.167	4.000	3.846	3.704	3.571	3.448	3.333

n	**31%**	**32%**	**33%**	**34%**	**35%**	**36%**	**37%**	**38%**	**39%**	**40%**
1	.763	.758	.752	.746	.741	.735	.730	.725	.719	.714
2	1.346	1.331	1.317	1.303	1.289	1.276	1.263	1.250	1.237	1.224
3	1.791	1.766	1.742	1.719	1.696	1.673	1.652	1.630	1.609	1.589
4	2.130	2.096	2.062	2.029	1.997	1.966	1.935	1.906	1.877	1.849
5	2.390	2.345	2.302	2.260	2.220	2.181	2.143	2.106	2.070	2.035
6	2.588	2.534	2.483	2.433	2.385	2.339	2.294	2.251	2.209	2.168
7	2.739	2.677	2.619	2.562	2.508	2.455	2.404	2.355	2.308	2.263
8	2.854	2.786	2.721	2.658	2.598	2.540	2.485	2.432	2.380	2.331
9	2.942	2.868	2.798	2.730	2.665	2.603	2.544	2.487	2.432	2.379
10	3.009	2.930	2.855	2.784	2.715	2.649	2.587	2.527	2.469	2.414
11	3.060	2.978	2.899	2.824	2.752	2.683	2.618	2.555	2.496	2.438
12	3.100	3.013	2.931	2.853	2.779	2.708	2.641	2.576	2.515	2.456
13	3.129	3.040	2.956	2.876	2.799	2.727	2.658	2.592	2.529	2.469
14	3.152	3.061	2.974	2.892	2.814	2.740	2.670	2.603	2.539	2.477
15	3.170	3.076	2.988	2.905	2.825	2.750	2.679	2.611	2.546	2.484
16	3.183	3.088	2.999	2.914	2.834	2.757	2.685	2.616	2.551	2.489
17	3.193	3.097	3.007	2.921	2.840	2.763	2.690	2.621	2.555	2.492
18	3.201	3.104	3.012	2.926	2.844	2.767	2.693	2.624	2.557	2.494
19	3.207	3.109	3.017	2.930	2.848	2.770	2.696	2.626	2.559	2.496
20	3.211	3.113	3.020	2.933	2.850	2.772	2.698	2.627	2.561	2.497
21	3.215	3.116	3.023	2.935	2.852	2.773	2.699	2.629	2.562	2.498
22	3.217	3.118	3.025	2.936	2.853	2.775	2.700	2.629	2.562	2.498
23	3.219	3.120	3.026	2.938	2.854	2.775	2.701	2.630	2.563	2.499
24	3.221	3.121	3.027	2.939	2.855	2.776	2.701	2.630	2.563	2.499
25	3.222	3.122	3.028	2.939	2.856	2.776	2.702	2.631	2.563	2.499
30	3.225	2.124	3.030	2.941	2.857	2.777	2.702	2.631	2.564	2.500
40	3.226	3.125	3.030	2.941	2.857	2.778	2.703	2.632	2.564	2.500
50	3.226	3.125	3.030	2.941	2.857	2.778	2.703	2.632	2.564	2.500

Index

E

F

R

S